AF718461

Competing Economic Theories

Providing a contemporary overview of the debate amongst theoretical stands in economics, this book brings together contributions from a number of eminent scholars. It covers important issues in methodology and the history of thought, as well as economic analysis.

- Part I focuses on the relevance of the history of economic ideas for current economic analysis.
- Part II centres around the role of the classical theory of value and distribution. In the light of Sraffa's unpublished papers, new suggestions as to Sraffa's interpretation of Ricardo are posited.
- Part III contrasts the equilibrium approach with an out-of-equilibrium perspective. Keynes's concept of equilibrium is reconsidered, problems in the existence of monopolistic general equilibrium are reviewed, and the role of demand in classical versus neoclassical theories of value is analysed.
- Part IV evaluates the legacy of Keynes in the light of the recent development of macroeconomics, and tries to answer the question of how much of Keynes's theory remains in current macroeconomic analysis.
- Part V is dedicated to the issue of how institutions ought to be embedded in current economic theorising.

Providing up-to-date, fresh and detailed perspectives on economic theory, this book will prove invaluable for students and academics in the fields of the history of economics and contemporary economic theory.

Sergio Nisticò is Professor of Economics at the University of Cassino, Italy. He graduated in Political Sciences at 'La Sapienza' University of Rome, where he also earned a PhD in Economics under the supervision of Giovanni Caravale. His research interests are mainly in the field of price theory.

Domenico Tosato is Professor of Economics at the University of Rome 'La Sapienza'. He has received degrees from the University L. Bocconi of Milan and Yale University. His current research interests are mainly in the field of general equilibrium theory and in the theory of money and growth.

Routledge Studies in the History of Economics

1 **Economics as Literature**
Willie Henderson

2 **Socialism and Marginalism in Economics 1870–1930**
Edited by Ian Steedman

3 **Hayek's Political Economy**
The socio-economics of order
Steve Fleetwood

4 **On the Origins of Classical Economics**
Distribution and value from William Petty to Adam Smith
Tony Aspromourgos

5 **The Economics of Joan Robinson**
Edited by Maria Cristina Marcuzzo, Luigi Pasinetti and Alesandro Roncaglia

6 **The Evolutionist Economics of Léon Walras**
Albert Jolink

7 **Keynes and the 'Classics'**
A study in language, epistemology and mistaken identities
Michel Verdon

8 **The History of Game Theory, Vol. 1**
From the beginnings to 1945
Robert W. Dimand and Mary Ann Dimand

9 **The Economics of W. S. Jevons**
Sandra Peart

10 **Gandhi's Economic Thought**
Ajit K. Dasgupta

11 Equilibrium and Economic Theory
Edited by Giovanni Caravale

12 Austrian Economics in Debate
Edited by Willem Keizer, Bert Tieben and Rudy van Zijp

13 Ancient Economic Thought
Edited by B. B. Price

14 The Political Economy of Social Credit and Guild Socialism
Frances Hutchinson and Brian Burkitt

15 Economic Careers
Economics and economists in Britain 1930–1970
Keith Tribe

16 Understanding 'Classical' Economics
Studies in the long-period theory
Heinz Kurz and Neri Salvadori

17 History of Environmental Economic Thought
E. Kula

18 Economic Thought in Communist and Post-Communist Europe
Edited by Hans-Jürgen Wagener

19 Studies in the History of French Political Economy
From Bodin to Walras
Edited by Gilbert Faccarello

20 The Economics of John Rae
Edited by O. F. Hamouda, C. Lee and D. Mair

21 Keynes and the Neoclassical Synthesis
Einsteinian versus Newtonian macroeconomics
Teodoro Dario Togati

22 Historical Perspectives on Macroeconomics
Sixty years after the 'General Theory'
Edited by Philippe Fontaine and Albert Jolink

23 The Founding of Institutional Economics
The leisure class and sovereignty
Edited by Warren J. Samuels

24 Evolution of Austrian Economics
From Menger to Lachmann
Sandye Gloria

25 Marx's Concept of Money: The God of Commodities
Anitra Nelson

26 The Economics of James Steuart
Edited by Ramón Tortajada

27 The Development of Economics in Europe since 1945
Edited by A. W. Bob Coats

28 The Canon in the History of Economics
Critical essays
Edited by Michalis Psalidopoulos

29 Money and Growth
Selected papers of Allyn Abbott Young
Edited by Perry G. Mehrling and Roger J. Sandilands

30 The Social Economics of Jean-Baptiste Say
Markets and virtue
Evelyn L. Forget

31 The Foundations of Laissez-Faire
The economics of Pierre de Boisguilbert
Gilbert Faccarello

32 John Ruskin's Political Economy
Willie Henderson

33 Contributions to the History of Economic Thought
Essays in honour of R. D. C. Black
Edited by Antoin E. Murphy and Renee Prendergast

34 Towards an Unknown Marx
A commentary on the manuscripts of 1861–63
Enrique Dussel

35 Economics and Interdisciplinary Exchange
Edited by Guido Erreygers

36 Economics as the Art of Thought
Essays in memory of G. L. S. Shackle
Edited by Stephen F. Frowen and Peter Earl

37 The Decline of Ricardian Economics
Politics and economics in post-Ricardian theory
Susan Pashkoff

38 Piero Sraffa
His life, thought and cultural heritage
Alessandro Roncaglia

39 Equilibrium and Disequilibrium in Economic Theory
The Marshall–Walras divide
Edited by Michel de Vroey

40 The German Historical School
The historical and ethical approach to economics
Edited by Yuichi Shionoya

41 Reflections on the Classical Canon in Economics
Essays in honour of Samuel Hollander
Edited by Sandra Peart and Evelyn Forget

42 Piero Sraffa's Political Economy
A centenary estimate
Edited by Terenzio Cozzi and Roberto Marchionatti

43 The Contribution of Joseph A. Schumpeter to Economics
Richard Arena and Cecile Dangel

44 On the Development of Long-Run Neo-Classical Theory
Tom Kompas

45 F. A. Hayek as a Political Economist
Economic analysis and values
Edited by Jack Birner, Pierre Garrouste and Thierry Aimar

46 Pareto, Economics and Society
The mechanical analogy
Michael McLure

47 Strategies and Programmes in Capital Theory
Jack Birner

48 Economics Broadly Considered
Essays in honour of Warren J. Samuels
Edited by Steven G. Medema, Jeff Biddle and John B. Davis

49 **Physicians and Political Economy**
Six studies of the work of doctor-economists
Edited by Peter Groenewegen

50 **The Spread of Political Economy and the Professionalisation of Economists**
Economic societies in Europe, America and Japan in the nineteenth century
Massimo Augello and Marco Guidi

51 **Historians of Economics and Economic Thought**
The construction of disciplinary memory
Steven G. Medema and Warren J. Samuels

52 **Competing Economic Theories**
Essays in memory of Giovanni Caravale
Edited by Sergio Nisticò and Domenico Tosato

53 **Economic Thought and Policy in Less Developed Europe**
The nineteenth century
Edited by Michalis Psalidopoulos and Maria Eugénia Mata

Competing Economic Theories

Essays in memory of Giovanni Caravale

Edited by
Sergio Nisticò and Domenico Tosato

London and New York

First published 2002
by Routledge
11 New Fetter Lane, London EC4P 4EE

Simultaneously published in the USA and Canada
by Routledge
29 West 35th Street, New York, NY 10001

Routledge is an imprint of the Taylor & Francis Group

© 2002 selection and editorial material, Sergio Nisticò and Domenico Tosato; individual chapters, the authors

Typeset in 10/12pt Monotype Baskerville by Graphicraft Limited, Hong Kong
Printed and bound in Great Britain by Biddles Ltd, Guildford and King's Lynn

All rights reserved. No part of this book may be reprinted or reproduced or utilised in any form or by any electronic, mechanical, or other means, now known or hereafter invented, including photocopying and recording, or in any information storage or retrieval system, without permission in writing from the publishers.

British Library Cataloguing in Publication Data
A catalogue record for this book is available from the British Library

Library of Congress Cataloging in Publication Data
Competing economic theories : essays in memory of Giovanni Caravale / [edited by] Sergio Nisticò and Domenico Tosato.
p. cm.
Includes bibliographical references and index.
1. Comparative economics. 2. Caravale, Giovanni. I. Caravale, Giovanni. II. Nisticò, Sergio, 1962– III. Tosato, Domenico A.
HB90 .C655 2002
330.1–dc21
2001048563

ISBN 0-415-24416-1

Contents

List of illustrations xiii
List of contributors xiv
Acknowledgements xv

Introduction 1
SERGIO NISTICÒ AND DOMENICO TOSATO

PART I
Economic theory and its history 13

1 **The relevance for present economic theory of economic theory written in the past** 15
DONALD A. WALKER

2 **The relevance of the economic ideas of the past** 33
AUGUSTO GRAZIANI

PART II
The classical school and the Ricardo debate 39

3 **The canonical classical growth model: content, adherence and priority** 41
SAMUEL HOLLANDER

4 **Sraffa: the theoretical world of the 'old classical economists'** 67
PIERANGELO GAREGNANI

5 **Misunderstanding classical economics: the Sraffian interpretation of the surplus approach** 80
MARK BLAUG

6 **Misunderstanding the Sraffian reading of the classical theory of value and distribution: a note** 97
CARLO PANICO

7 **Is it possible to define a canonical classical growth model?** 102
EUGENIO ZAGARI

8 **Garegnani's interpretation of the 'old classical economists'** 105
ENRICO ZAGHINI

9 **Different perspectives on distribution within classical political economy** 115
SERGIO NISTICÒ

10 **Sraffa's Ricardo after fifty years: a preliminary estimate** 130
PIER LUIGI PORTA

11 **Some reflections on Sraffa's Ricardo** 155
GARY MONGIOVI

PART III
Models of prices and allocations in equilibrium and out of equilibrium 165

12 **Reflections on Caravale's contributions relating to equilibrium and their relation to the interpretation of Keynes** 167
VICTORIA CHICK

13 **Sraffa's contributions to economics: some notes on his unpublished papers** 177
HEINZ D. KURZ

14 **Models of monopolistic competition and general equilibrium theory** 197
DOMENICO TOSATO

15 **Non-competitive general equilibrium in a dynamic perspective** 233
PIER CARLO NICOLA

16 Technology and employment in an out-of-equilibrium perspective 236
MARIO AMENDOLA

17 Strategic complementarity and near-rationality in New Keynesian models: a note 243
ANDREA BOITANI

PART IV
The legacy of Keynes 247

18 Keynes on probability, uncertainty and tragic choices 249
ANNA CARABELLI

19 Was Keynes a truly heretic economist? 280
MARCELLO DE CECCO

20 Keynes, disequilibrium theory and New Keynesian economics 284
BRUNO JOSSA

21 Keynesian economics from a non-price theoretic framework 300
ROY J. ROTHEIM

22 The controversies in contemporary macroeconomics 306
GIORGIO RODANO

23 On the relevance of the distinction between Keynesian and neoclassical macroeconomics 326
IGNAZIO MUSU

PART V
Economic theorising and institutions 329

24 Economic theory and institutions 331
LUIGI L. PASINETTI

25 Economic theory and institutions: an introductory note 340
GIOVANNI CARAVALE

26 Economics and institutions from a central bank perspective 348
PIERLUIGI CIOCCA

27 Economics and institutions: some reflections on Pasinetti and Caravale 354
LUIGI SPAVENTA

28 Economics and institutions: the constraints of history 357
PAOLO SYLOS LABINI

29 A summing up 361
LUIGI L. PASINETTI

References 364
Index 391

List of illustrations

4.1	Point E of 'effectual demand'	69
14.1	Negishi's subjective demand	208
14.2	Walras correspondence	213
14.3	Construction of the consumption feasible production set	215
14.4	Profit maximisation with different normalisation rules	220
14.5	The demand correspondence	225
14.6	Rationing at prices $p_j > \bar{p}_j$	227
16.1	What happens to the rate of growth, the rate of unemployment, productivity and real wages along the out-of-equilibrium path followed by the economy as the result of a shock represented by the adoption of a technology whose greater initial cost is more than compensated for by the reduction in costs during the utilisation phase	241

List of contributors

Mario Amendola University of Rome, 'La Sapienza', Italy
Mark Blaug University of Amsterdam, The Netherlands
Andrea Boitani Catholic University of Milan, Italy
Anna Carabelli University of Novara, Italy
Giovanni Caravale formerly University of Rome, 'La Sapienza', Italy
Victoria Chick University College London, England
Pierluigi Ciocca Bank of Italy
Marcello De Cecco University of Rome, 'La Sapienza', Italy
Pierangelo Garegnani University of Rome III, Italy
Augusto Graziani University of Rome, 'La Sapienza', Italy
Samuel Hollander Ben-Gurion University of the Negev, Israel
Bruno Jossa University of Naples, 'Federico II', Italy
Heinz D. Kurz University of Graz, Austria
Gary Mongiovi St John's University, Jamaica NY, USA
Ignazio Musu University of Venice, 'Ca' Foscari', Italy
Pier Carlo Nicola University of Milan, Italy
Sergio Nisticò University of Cassino, Italy
Carlo Panico University of Naples, 'Federico II', Italy
Luigi L. Pasinetti Catholic University of Milan, Italy
Pier Luigi Porta University of Milan–Bicocca, Italy
Giorgio Rodano University of Rome, 'La Sapienza', Italy
Roy J. Rotheim Skidmore College, Saratoga Springs NY, USA
Luigi Spaventa University of Rome, 'La Sapienza', Italy
Paolo Sylos Labini University of Rome, 'La Sapienza', Italy
Domenico Tosato University of Rome, 'La Sapienza', Italy
Donald A. Walker Indiana University of Pennsylvania, Indiana PA, USA
Eugenio Zagari University of Naples, 'Federico II', Italy
Enrico Zaghini University of Rome, 'La Sapienza', Italy

Acknowledgements

We wish to express our warmest thanks to Giovanni Caravale's wife, Lucia, his children, Giorgio and Benedetta, and his brother Mario for their generous encouragement and assistance in every phase of our endeavour. The Caravale Memorial Conference and this volume are not only a professional tribute to Gianni by friends and colleagues but also an expression of his family's unending love.

We are most grateful to Professor Ornello Vitali, who at the time of the conference was Chairman of the Department of Economic Theory and Quantitative Methods of the University of Rome 'La Sapienza'. The conference would not have been possible without his strong personal commitment to the project and the department's financial support.

Maria Teresa Duda patiently checked the typescripts for spelling, cross-references, formulae and bibliography. We know that a sincere esteem for her friend Gianni inspired her work throughout.

Finally, we thank the editors and publishers of *History of Political Economy* (© Duke University Press), *Cahiers d'économie politique*, *Rivista di politica economica*, *European Journal of the History of Economic Thought* (http://www.tandf.co.uk), *Journal of the History of Economic Thought* and the European Association for Evolutionary Political Economy for permission to reprint the following: M. Blaug (1999) 'Misunderstanding classical economics: the Sraffian interpretation of the surplus approach', *History of Political Economy* 31, 2: 213–26; A. Carabelli (1998) 'Keynes on probability, uncertainty and tragic choices', *Cahiers d'économie politique* 30–1: 187–226; G. Caravale (1996) 'Economic theory and institutions: an introductory note', *Rivista di politica economica* 86, 6: 125–35; P. Garegnani (1998) 'Sraffa: the theoretical world of the "old classical economists"', *European Journal of the History of Economic Thought* 5, 3: 415–29; S. Hollander (1998) 'The canonical classical growth model: content, adherence and priority', *Journal of the History of Economic Thought* 20, 3: 253–77; L. L. Pasinetti (1994) 'Economic theory and institutions', in R. Delorme and K. Dopfer (eds) *The Political Economy of Diversity. Evolutionary Perspectives on Economic Order and Disorder*, Aldershot: EAEPE and Elgar; D. A. Walker (1999) 'The relevance for present economic theory of economic theory written in the past', *Journal of the History of Economic Thought* 21, 1: 7–26. Chapter 10 is based on a chapter by Pier Luigi Porta previously published in *Reflections on the Classical Canon in Economics: Essays in Honour of Samuel Hollander*, edited by Evelyn L. Forget and Sandra Peart, London and New York: Routledge.

Introduction

Sergio Nisticò and Domenico Tosato

This volume originates from the conference held in memory of Giovanni Caravale at the University of Rome 'La Sapienza' on 4–5 June 1998, one year after his untimely death. For the occasion we invited eminent scholars, who had shared some of Caravale's scientific interests, to present papers on the themes that had characterised his research activity and that we thought could be arranged under the following five headings: Economic theory and its history; The classical school and the Ricardo debate; Models of prices and allocations in equilibrium and out of equilibrium; The legacy of Keynes; Economic theorising and institutions. The contributions included in this collection have, thus, been grouped into five parts which we have prefaced with significant passages from Caravale's own writings. The final part also includes the full text of Caravale's 1996 paper on the problem of economic theory and institutions. This paper, together with a contribution by Luigi Pasinetti (also reproduced in the volume), was the springboard for the round table discussion which, coordinated by Pasinetti himself, concluded the memorial conference.

The choice of title deserves some comment. If we look back at the development of economic theory, we find it is mainly characterised by intense and systematic debate between schools of thought as well as by strong rivalry over competing explanations of fundamental economic phenomena: in microeconomics, between the Sraffian and the marginalist theories of value and distribution; in macroeconomics, between the Keynesian and the monetarist theories of national income and employment.

Blanchard (2000) and Woodford (1999) have taken a different and possibly influential stand. They challenge the lack of communication that supposedly existed between schools of thought generally considered to be far apart. They detect, with specific reference to macroeconomics, the existence of objective scientific progress, to which various schools have, in different but significant ways, contributed. In brief, they seem to suggest that a widely accepted body of knowledge, which bears important policy implications, has finally emerged after the fierce debate which until recently characterised the evolution of economics, both on theoretical and empirical grounds.

The idea that in economic science we can perceive advances in the body of knowledge shared by a large part of the profession is, to our minds, an appealing intuition, which may be fruitfully used in the history of economic analysis as a second key of interpretation to be matched to that of opposition and debate. We believe, however, that Blanchard and Woodford's reading should not be mistakenly interpreted as supporting the view that theoretical homogenisation in economics should be looked on with favour. On the contrary, since 'debate' – bitter, tough and passionate debate – is the very source of those past achievements that Blanchard and Woodford bring to our attention, we should be wary of any possible drying up of the sources of discussion with regard to the new issues that continually arise from the observation of the real world, but also of the very 'fundamentals' of the discipline. Homogenisation would inevitably bring about a weakening of the urge to economic research and hence of the same source of scientific progress.

In line with this concern, right from its title this book emphasises the importance of open and transparent competition among different ideas and different schools. In particular, it aims to offer a new reading of some *old* controversial themes and to indicate *new* areas of potential debate among scholars. We are deeply convinced that this is the proper way to pay tribute to Giovanni Caravale, who firmly believed in the progressive nature of the economic debate and whose research activity in this connection will be briefly outlined below.

Part I focuses on the relevance of the history of economic ideas to current economic analysis. Walker warns against the damaging consequences of the widespread habit of separating the teaching of the history of economic thought from the teaching of current economic theory. The harmful effect of this mode of organising university curricula has been twofold: on the one hand, it has reduced the history of economic thought to a superficial review of a host of past theories and past economists, as such unsuitable to graduate programmes in economics; on the other hand, it has consequently impoverished the teaching of current economic theory, which risks missing the benefit of a rich background of ideas and past debates. Walker, however, 'without any hope that the state of affairs will change', conclusively argues that 'the part of past economic theory relevant to each specific modern theory should be taught in conjunction with that theory, in the regular macroeconomic or microeconomic course in current economic theory'. Graziani carries the argument a step further. He claims that 'there is no clear-cut distinction between current economic thought and the economic theorising of the past'. Thus, contrary to those who exclusively 'give weight to logical rigour and refined technicalities', Graziani believes that good theorising is possible only if we start by asking how the problems to be investigated ought to be selected and approached, so that the 'need will spontaneously emerge to know whether and in what manner similar problems were identified and solved in the past'.

Part II centres around the role of Ricardo's contribution to classical economics and economics *tout court*. Through the chapters by Hollander, Garegnani, Blaug, Panico, Zagari, Zaghini, Nisticò, Porta and Mongiovi a lively and wide-ranging debate emerges which touches upon old and new controversies. In their chapters, Hollander and Garegnani offer an up-to-date presentation of the two established and conflicting *rational* reconstructions of the classical theory of value, distribution and growth. Hollander proposes new textual evidence supporting the so-called canonical interpretation according to which a line of continuity exists between the neoclassical theory and the preceding theoretical formulations of Smith, Ricardo, John Stuart Mill and even of Marx. Garegnani, on the other hand, provides new arguments in favour of the Sraffian interpretation which identifies in the classical school the roots of a theory of value and distribution alternative to the marginalist explanation of goods and factor prices. Blaug criticises the historical accuracy of the neo-Ricardian interpretation and in particular the idea of a classical 'core' defined by a given real wage as well as by given techniques and sectoral outputs on the grounds that it inevitably leaves out some important, fruitful elements in the thinking of the classical authors. He casts serious doubts also on the legitimacy of *rational* as opposed to *historical* reconstructions, thus indirectly questioning the validity of both Garegnani's and Hollander's interpretations. The issue of rational versus historical reconstructions is taken up by Panico and Zagari. Panico rejects Blaug's criticism of Sraffa's interpretation of the classical school. To begin with, he questions the very existence of pure historical reconstructions – as any interpretation is inevitably 'rational' in as much as it is influenced by the historian's present knowledge – and thus argues that any evaluation ought to be based on different criteria. He then goes on to praise Sraffa's interpretation as the outcome of an outstanding example of editorial scholarship, pointing to the accuracy in collecting and presenting the textual evidence. Zagari critically discusses the alternative rational reconstruction of the classical theory of growth and distribution, namely the canonical growth model. He claims that precise constraints ought to be imposed on rational reconstructions, i.e. limits within which theories formulated in the past can be reinterpreted and re-elaborated with the help of today's analytical tools; and that such limits have been passed by the canonical model. Zaghini deals with the analytical problem of the convergence of market prices towards natural prices, a key issue for the explanatory validity of the classical long-period positions. In particular, he critically examines Garegnani's (1997) ambitious attempt to offer a coherent and general solution to this problem. Zaghini observes that the classical approach builds on the assumption that 'agents, outside of equilibrium, know the economic system's equilibrium configuration' (that is, natural prices and effectual demands) 'and are guided by it – a variant of the perfect knowledge or foresight hypothesis that plagues a good part of modern theory'. He grants that Garegnani tries to go beyond this unsatisfactory approach, but shows that Garegnani's refusal to use the concept of demand function, not necessarily to be anchored to the neoclassical paradigm of utility maximisation, also makes his approach unsatisfactory and flawed. Nisticò joins in the debate on the interpretation of the classical theory, addressing two issues. The first concerns the differences between Smith and the later classicists in the approach to price theory, from the viewpoint of the choice of the distributive variable to be considered as given from outside the model: the rate of profit, according to Smith, the real wage, according to the later classicists. A rationale is thus provided for Smith's theory of the component parts of price, later so heavily criticised by Marx and Sraffa under the label of the *adding up* theory. Nisticò's second concern regards Ricardo's notion of natural equilibrium, which he argues should be viewed as a temporary centre of gravity rather than a long-period position capable of persisting through time. In this perspective, he maintains that the Sraffian assumption according to which, in each given situation, one distributive variable is exogenously given is not necessarily incompatible with Hollander's thesis, that there is room in Ricardo for a declining real wage throughout the accumulation process. Finally, the chapters by Porta and Mongiovi tackle the issue of the role played by Sraffa's editorial work in the Ricardo debate. Porta argues, also on the basis of Sraffa's papers in the Wren Library at Trinity College, that Sraffa's *interpretation* is, on the one hand, heavily conditioned by his own theoretical research programme and, on the other, no more than a restatement of Marx's reading of Ricardo. Mongiovi rejects Porta's aim to belittle Sraffa's contribution to the reconstruction of Ricardo's theory. He argues that the well known circumstance that Sraffa's work on Ricardo 'was part of a larger project that culminated in *Production of Commodities by Means of Commodities* . . . has no bearing on the soundness of his interpretation'. Moreover, as far as the alleged Marxian connection is concerned, he denies the existence of any significant textual support for Porta's thesis and claims, on the contrary, that evidence indicates that Sraffa came to Ricardo not through Marx but via Marshall.

The role of the concept of equilibrium is the main issue touched upon in Part III. Chick provides a sympathetic assessment of Caravale's contribution to the study of the concept of equilibrium with special reference to its usefulness in interpreting the *General Theory*. Chick emphasises the importance of Caravale's proposal to modify the classical-type concept of long-period equilibrium to include the equality of expected rather than actual rates of return and then discusses the role of his notion from the viewpoint of the 'logical' as opposed to the historical nature of equilibrium. Chick does not appear to be fully convinced by Caravale's attempt to identify a line of continuity between the classics and Keynes on the role of long-period equilibrium in a logical sense. Instead, following Joan Robinson's notion of *history*, she believes that the short period cannot be dismissed in the interpretation of Keynes's theory and of the working of actual economic systems. Kurz provides a brief overview of Sraffa's unpublished papers and correspondence with the aim of clarifying the importance of Sraffa's contribution to economics and in particular to show that Sraffa succeeded in rescuing from oblivion a 'distinct' classical theory of value and distribution that cannot be revisited in terms of the neoclassical demand and supply determination of goods and factors prices. Tosato and Nicola address the issue of the existence of monopolistic general equilibrium. Tosato's analysis shows the results and potentialities of those works that aim to foster the general equilibrium theory with greater realism, while retaining the idea of interdependence typical of the benchmark model. Whereas the conjectural approach, with its *ad hoc* assumptions, may produce useful results on specific issues, it is inevitably to the objective approach, with its emphasis on analytical rigour, that we have to turn if the aim of the analysis is to establish a comparison between monopolistic and competitive general equilibrium. This comparison shows that the existence of equilibrium in a monopolistic market regime (1) requires further assumptions (uniqueness of the price or demand correspondence and quasi-concavity of the profit function) not needed in the standard Arrow–Debreu model; and (2) may depend on the choice of normalisation rule. After noting that most of the difficulties occur also at a partial equilibrium level, Tosato concludes that 'some of the problems that preclude the possibility of establishing existence results of the same degree of generality as under perfect competition are to be considered inherent in the situation of direct interaction between firms not mediated by the market'. Nicola's chapter emphasises the importance of abandoning the assumption of an auctioneer capable of instantaneously driving the whole system towards its equilibrium configuration. Nicola proposes the notion of imperfect general equilibrium that should place the out-of-equilibrium dynamics at the heart of the analysis of the price system. The out-of-equilibrium perspective is also central in Amendola's chapter, which discusses the limits of the equilibrium analysis from a technological viewpoint. In particular, Amendola addresses the relation between technology and unemployment using a neo-Austrian approach; in this context he analyses the *vertical* dimension of technology and the problems connected with the phases of construction and utilisation of productive capacity. The chapter shows how the attempts by economic agents 'at re-establishing the consistency over time of construction and utilisation disturbed by the original shock stir an out-of-equilibrium process that propagates the initial distortion over time'. Boitani finally evaluates the main conclusions reached by the New Keynesian literature on macroeconomic equilibrium, stressing the specific role of the assumption of near rationality to corroborate the findings of that literature about the soundness of the Keynesian notion of unemployment equilibrium. In particular, he emphasises the fact that even 'a small proportion of near rational agents, under strategic complementarity, has a disproportionately strong impact on the macroeconomy'.

Part IV offers an evaluation of the legacy of Keynes in the light of recent developments in macroeconomics. Carabelli traces back the Keynesian notion of radical uncertainty in Keynes's early interest in dilemmas and tragic choices, which characterise situations of indecision and of irreducible conflict. She argues that Keynes's refusal to assume comparability of magnitudes such as probability and real income or general price level may derive from his youthful studies in Greek tragedy. De Cecco proposes a different reading of Keynes's thought and argues against the thesis that Keynes renounced tradition. According to De Cecco, the sometimes ambiguous way in which Keynes expresses his revolutionary ideas on macroeconomics clearly shows his urge 'to be taken seriously by his fellow economists and to avoid being lumped with the heretics'. Jossa provides an up-to-date state of arts of the New Keynesian approach and raises the question of whether and how it can offer further arguments in favour of the Keynesian view of macroeconomics. He emphasises the importance of the New Keynesian microfoundation of fixed prices and wages in strengthening Keynes's crucial finding that equilibrium is reached through changes in output. Jossa grants that some of the New Keynesian models draw heavily from the neoclassical toolbox, thus justifying an attitude of rejection on the part of the more radical Keynesians. He argues, however, against the idea that New Keynesian and Post (orthodox) Keynesian economics should be viewed as incompatible and competing lines of analysis, as many in the Keynesian camp hold them to be. A quite different evaluation of the New Keynesian approach is contained in Rotheim's chapter. According to Rotheim, New Keynesians 'are treading on thinner and thinner ice' and will not be able to stay much longer between neoclassicism and Keynesianism. Some of them will go back to the safe neoclassical metaphor according to which unemployment equilibrium occurs because of the existence of various rigidities in the aggregate labour, goods and capital markets. But, for those other 'strong' New Keynesians who think in terms of spill-over effects and strategic complementarities, the neoclassical 'ice [will be] finally cracking'. They will be forced, therefore, to embrace Keynes's idea that the organic interdependence which characterises the capitalist economy is at the root of the 'fluctuations in output, spending, and therefore employment *as a whole*'. Rodano's chapter provides further arguments to Woodford and Blanchard's thesis mentioned above, according to which during the last century macroeconomics has witnessed a progressive accumulation of scientific knowledge. Rodano's reading of the macroeconomic debate emphasises the circumstance that each period of juxtaposition between schools of thought has generated an agreed synthesis and that 'eventually, these achievements will be brought into question by new debates and controversies, which sooner or later will converge to a richer synthesis, although a temporary one'. A different position on this issue is finally provided by Musu, who argues that the macroeconomic debate between conflicting schools of thought, far from having produced a shared body of knowledge, has actually yielded the relevant outcome of sharpening the reasons and the nature of the irreducible distinction between neoclassical and Keynesian macroeconomics. In fact, Musu concludes, 'modern Keynesian macroeconomics implies a complex vision of economic policy, which . . . cannot accept the minimalist approach to economic policy entailed by the New Classical macroeconomics and deriving from theoretical premises too distant from the features of market economies in the real world'.

Finally Part V is dedicated to the relationship between economic theorising and institutions. Pasinetti's and Caravale's chapters emphasise the limits of the neoclassical treatment of economic institutions, but express a different viewpoint as to how institutions ought to be embedded in current economic theorising. According to Pasinetti, the Keynesian and the classical-type formulations constitute a body of *pure* theory which might fruitfully be enriched, in a subsequent phase, with the findings of institutional economics. Caravale rejects this separation between a first phase of 'pure' theorising and a second phase in which institutions make their appearance on the stage. He thus praises the classical and Keynesian approaches precisely for their attempt to build theoretical models *starting from* realistic assumptions as to the institutional set-up: namely, the role of the social classes in explaining agents' behaviour as opposed to the assumption of atomistic utility and profit maximisation, the idea of exchange of commodities occurring at 'false' prices, the role of labour market institutions in determining unemployment equilibrium. Ciocca brings to the discussion the viewpoint of a central banker and deals with the role played by 'the *conventions* – what Keynes called changeable beliefs – of global finance' in constraining the economic policies of national governments and describes three possible ways out of this supremacy of finance over economic policy: the *enlightened* scenario, that envisages the introduction of a global currency; the *interventionist* scenario, based on the use of the Tobin tax to reduce speculative capital movements; and the *autarchic* scenario carrying with it the undesirable 'reaction by the [*local*] political sphere, claiming back its primacy over the economy'. Spaventa, on the one hand, accepts Pasinetti's and Caravale's starting point, according to which we should overcome the separation between 'a theory devoid of institutions and a prevalently descriptive analysis of institutions devoid of theory'. However, he is less pessimistic than Pasinetti and Caravale about the ability of recent mainstream economic research to deal with the problem of institutions, arguing that those who object to the mainstream treatment of institutions 'ought to propose and apply different tools of analysis' which are not yet available. Spaventa also expands on Caravale's criticism of Pasinetti's proposal of a two-phase economic theorising and points to 'the normative sterility that would result from the implicit suggestion that in an initial phase economic analysis should not be involved with studying institutions'. Sylos Labini provides three examples of the impact that historical and institutional changes may have on economic phenomena: the changing nature of the business cycle during the last two centuries; the relation between the structural changes both in the commodity markets and in the labour market on the growth rates of wages and prices; the effects of legislation on bankruptcy with regard to innovation and growth. The main upshot of the argument is that:

> the essence of economic analysis lies precisely in the harmonic integration between theory and history. The latter provides the factual premises which, when transformed into hypotheses, allow for the elaboration . . . of historically restricted theoretical models. It is not that their logical coherence is historically restricted; that coherence is on the contrary timeless. It is rather their interpretative capacity which is historically contingent.

In his conclusive remarks on the round table discussion on 'Economic theorising and institutions' Pasinetti, while minimising the differences between his stance and Caravale's, reiterates his criticism of mainstream economics as intrinsically unsuitable to accommodate realistic institutional features in the corpus of the theory.

As initially mentioned, this volume originated in a conference held in memory of Giovanni Caravale. We think it proper to conclude this introduction with a short profile of his career and with an evaluation of his scientific work which bears on the topics debated in this book and deserves the attention of those scholars who are actively engaged in the discussion of competing economic theories.

Giovanni Caravale was born on 18 August 1935. In 1953 he graduated from high school with highest marks, took up the study of law at the University of Rome 'La Sapienza' and began working in the research department of the Banca Nazionale del Lavoro, one of Italy's leading credit institutions. Work did not interfere with his studies, but it did influence his decision to write the thesis for his law degree in the field of economics. In 1958 he passed an extremely selective competitive examination and joined the technical staff of the Italian Senate, where, from 1965 to 1972, he served as Secretary to the Permanent Committee on Finance and Treasury Affairs, Industry and Foreign Trade. In 1960 and 1961, as a visiting student at Trinity College, Cambridge, he came in contact with Maurice Dobb, Piero Sraffa, Nicholas Kaldor and other great economists and began to accumulate notes on growth theory, particularly on the relationship between growth and cycles. In 1963 he qualified for university teaching and began lecturing on economics and fiscal policy at the University of Pescara while still holding his job at the Senate. From 1968 to 1971 he lectured on political economy at the University of Perugia. In 1972 he was awarded a full professorship at the University of Perugia and resigned from the staff of the Senate. He taught in Perugia until 1979, when he moved on to the University of Rome 'La Sapienza', in the Faculty of Political Sciences.

Among the prominent public positions that he held during his professional life, Giovanni was a member of Italy's Central Tax Commission, President of the Atlantic Economic Society, Minister of Transport in the Government of Prime Minister Lamberto Dini and a member of the board of directors of the *Italian Encyclopaedia.* Giovanni entered the government in January 1995, during one of the most delicate phases of post-war Italian history, the so-called 'fall of the first Republic'. The Dini government's mandate was to put Italy on track to financial stability. The difficulties that Giovanni faced at the Transport Ministry were compounded by the ending of public monopoly virtually throughout the transport sector, where previous governments had generally prized political consensus over technical and economic efficiency. The April 1996 general election brought the curtain down on Dini's 'government of technicians', but Giovanni's projects remained on the agenda of his successors at the Ministry. In June 1996 Giovanni returned to the University of Rome and his research work. He died unexpectedly on 29 May 1997.

Giovanni Caravale's scholarly contributions can be divided into groups corresponding to four phases in the development of his research work. Until the early 1970s he concentrated on formulating a comprehensive scheme for the joint interpretation of fluctuations and long-term growth in which oligopoly plays a major role. The principal results of this first research programme were *Cicli economici e trend* (1961), *Fluttuazioni e sviluppo nella dinamica di squilibrio di un sistema economico* (1967) and *Oligopolio differenziato e processo di sviluppo* (1973). The main threads running through all these publications are: (1) the role of structural unbalance, i.e. the divergence between the composition of demand and of output, in generating trade cycles; (2) the use of the 'equilibrium dynamic path' simply as a theoretical reference point to emphasise how non-fulfilment of the conditions defining that path may generate trade cycles with growth; (3) the study of possible disequilibrium dynamics, not constrained by the aim of proving convergence to the equilibrium path but rather as a theoretical tool with which to explore how systems evolve once they are displaced from the 'golden age' path.

The attempt to provide a historically accurate analytical reconstruction of Ricardo's theory of value and distribution occupied Caravale's intellectual energies in the second phase of his research, which roughly spanned the years from 1973 to 1980. The result was the influential Ricardian growth model that Caravale, together with Domenico Tosato, developed in those years. The essential elements of the model were first published in Italian in 1974 as *Un modello ricardiano di sviluppo economico*, and then in an expanded English version, published in 1980 as *Ricardo and the Theory of Value, Distribution and Growth.* The book provides an analytical solution of general validity – i.e. not subject to the limitations of the labour theory of value – of Ricardo's central problem: the relationship between diminishing agricultural returns and the general rate of profit. It also contains an analysis of the role that the 'standard commodity' played in the evolution of Ricardo's thought, an analysis that the authors had previously published in Italian in an article, 'Saggio di profitto e merce tipo nella teoria di Ricardo', which appeared in 1978 in *Rivista di politica economica.* Giovanni's reconstruction of Ricardo's theory rests on the following building blocks: (1) the identification of the natural, as opposed to the market, path of rent, profits and wages as the 'core' of Ricardo's scientific programme; (2) the key role consequently played by the natural wage, as defined by Ricardo in the *Essay on Profits,* in determining the natural equilibrium path; (3) the ensuing link, given the natural wage, between diminishing returns in agriculture and changes in distribution; in other words the inverse relation between the dynamics of rent, driven by the need to extend cultivation to less and less fertile land, and the rate of profit. The simultaneous inclusion of these three blocks within a unifying interpretative scheme marks the proposed reconstruction as substantially innovative with respect to the other main interpretations of Ricardo's theory. Caravale's emphasis on the role played by the natural wage constitutes a clear departure from the 'new view', which asserts the existence, within Ricardo's theory, of anticipation of the neoclassical determination of goods and factors prices on the basis of demand and supply functions. Yet his reconstruction markedly differs also from the neo-Ricardian interpretation in as much as it strongly rejects the idea of attributing to Ricardo a Sraffa-type inverse relationship between alternative levels of the real wage and the profit rate with given technological conditions.

From the early 1980s until 1990 Caravale took up the difficult task of providing a critical presentation of the most important interpretative strands of Ricardo's and Marx's thoughts. Prominent in this third phase was Caravale's efforts to counter, in a clear and constructive fashion, the various attempts to establish a direct link or line of descent from Ricardo to Marx primarily on the basis of a common appeal to the labour theory of value. *The Legacy of Ricardo* (1985) and *Marx and Modern Economic Analysis* (1991) offer the reader a comprehensive view of the positions held on this issue by distinguished contributors such as John Hicks, Samuel Hollander, Mark Blaug, Pierangelo Garegnani, Paul Samuelson, William Baumol and Caravale himself.

According to Caravale, the crucial divide between Ricardo and Marx regards the role played by the labour theory of value in their analytical constructions. In Marx's work, the labour theory of value is essential to proving the existence of exploitation in a capitalistic economic system; the transformation of labour values into prices of production is the analytical instrument through which such a result is allegedly achieved. The demonstration by Dmitriev, Bortkiewicz and Sraffa of the absence of a necessary causal relation going from labour values to production prices, which can be determined from the mere knowledge of the technical coefficients of production, deprives Marx's theory of exploitation of its claimed scientific basis. Nor, as Caravale repeatedly emphasised, is the argument acceptable that grounds the theory of exploitation in Sraffa's inverse relationship between wages and profits, since this relation is determined by the technology and has nothing to do with the gap between the value of labour power and the value of its product. In Ricardo, by contrast, the labour theory of value is an analytical tool that serves the role of eliminating the interdependence between prices and distribution and thus of showing the basic relation between rents and profits in a dynamic context in which the wage rate is supposed to be determined and to evolve independently. Notwithstanding the limitation of the labour theory of value, of which Ricardo was well aware, the attainment of his goal of determining the natural laws that govern the path of wages, profits and rents does not depend on the validity of that theory. In fact, that aim can be achieved on the basis of a theory of value not suffering from the limitation of Ricardo's tool, as Caravale and Tosato have shown, building on Sraffa's *Production of Commodities by Means of Commodities*.

In his last years Caravale was drawn to work on some unresolved Keynesian questions and on developing a novel research programme reflecting his long-standing view that economic analysis, economic policy and the history of economic thought were closely interconnected. To this end, Giovanni was forced to grapple with thorny methodological and analytical questions, beginning with the very possibility of adopting a new, more constructive, notion of equilibrium. His main contribution on this matter is included in the collection of essays he edited, *Equilibrio e teoria economica* (1994), subsequently translated into English as *Equilibrium and Economic Theory* (1997).

Caravale thought that the literature offered two opposing and equally unacceptable views: the apologetics of neoclassical theory, which holds that equilibrium is a desirable state of general market clearing spontaneously attained in decentralised market economies; and the critical Marxian view that equilibrium requires the fulfilment of such demanding conditions that its attainment is utterly unrealistic, so that the market system can produce only inefficiencies and conflict. Caravale proposed a notion of equilibrium of a classical and Keynesian flavour, capable of representing – naturally, in a stylised and simplified way – the potential centre of gravity of the economy (the classical component) and the not necessarily optimal outcome of the relevant and dominant forces (the Keynesian component).

However, it is not enough to prove the existence of equilibrium; it is at least as important to show that the economy tends to converge on it. But even proof of convergence may not be sufficient, according to Caravale, to settle the question of the relevance of the equilibrium position. A further issue must be faced: it concerns, from one point of view, the speed of convergence and, from another, the persistence of exogenous data. The Walrasian approach tends to promote the idea of rapid convergence of disequilibrium to equilibrium prices, so that one can argue as if markets were continuously in or close to equilibrium. The neo-Ricardian school addresses this issue from a different angle and looks at the relation between market and long-period prices by assuming that market forces continuously drive the former towards the latter; this is the classical notion of gravitation as distinct from that of stability typical of neoclassical theory. The gravitation of market prices towards the long-period prices is then considered as occurring in historical time, given the assumption of persistence of the data. In Garegnani's view, these data include the technology, the real wage rate and the level and composition of output (see Chapter 4 of this volume).

Caravale's notion of long-period positions tried to cope with the problem of the speed of convergence on equilibrium in the presence of ever changing exogenous data. He set himself the aim of avoiding both the Walrasian instantaneous way of conceiving the reaching of equilibrium and the neo-Ricardian hypothesis of data persistence. He resorted to a notion of equilibrium as a potential centre of gravity that can be defined only in logical rather than historical time. In his view, equilibrium is thus an analytical tool that one cannot do without in order to establish a logical correspondence between exogenous data and endogenous variables. This tool should be capable of offering a scientific explanation that can be applied in policy making. A typical example, frequently mentioned by Caravale, is Keynes's theory of effective demand, which sets a logical correspondence between a given amount of investment, substantially taken to be exogenous, and the equilibrium level of income. No one can deny that investment changes over time:

> However, this circumstance does not prevent each equilibrium position from exerting a strong attraction over the real variables in each period of time. The fact that the system will never be able to reach the equilibrium position (which is in continuous movement, through actual calendar time) does not deprive this position of its importance as a meaningful point of reference, as a centre of gravity for the system. On the contrary, it represents a mirror of the actual reality of contemporary economies, in their perennial unrest, in their continuous process of change – a reality which does not convey the image of a state of rest.
>
> (Caravale 1997b: 23)

Caravale's position thus appears to be close to Marshall's. From Marshall Caravale draws the basic idea that economic 'laws' and prescriptions are bound to the *ceteris paribus* clause; at the same time he differs from Marshall in thinking that the application of the *ceteris paribus* clause should not be confined to the historical short term, but could be used to tackle any logical problem independently of the time span involved. His approach breaks the classical and neoclassical connection between the long run and the notion of perfect adjustment of the economy to changing conditions. The equilibrium position may never be attained because conditions do in fact change in historical time, but it remains a fundamental benchmark of the analysis.

Caravale's most recent articles touched on the importance of uncertainty and expectations in the notion of Keynesian unemployment equilibrium ('Keynes, equilibrium and modern economic systems', in *Perspectives on the History of Economic Thought*, edited by R. F. Hébert, 1993), on the role of demand in the classical context ('Demand conditions and the interpretation of Ricardo', *Journal of the History of Economic Thought*, 1994; 'Prices and quantities: Walras, Sraffa and beyond', *Studi economici*, 1994), and on the issue of incomes policy ('On a recent change in the notion of incomes policy', in *New Keynesian Economics/Post-Keynesian Alternatives*, edited by R. J. Rotheim, 1998). All these papers express his conviction that the future of economics depends on the positive solution of a fundamental problem: the integration within the discipline of analytical rigour and relevance of the models. In line with this tenet, he addressed the general aspects of the relations between institutions and economic theorising ('Economic theory and institutions: an introductory note', *Rivista di politica economica*, 1996) and inaugurated a doctoral course on 'Political Economy and Institutional Reality' in his own Faculty of Political Science. This represented the final endeavour of a distinguished representative of the profession; one who was profoundly convinced that economics cannot escape the fascination of being technical and controversial at the same time, with the roots of controversy lying predominantly in the pre-analytical dimension. While he was aware that he himself was constrained by his own *Weltanschauung*, Caravale always sought to make analytical rigour and intellectual honesty prevail when tackling any economic issues. Faced with the main existing 'competing economic theories', he could not perfectly fit any of them. Though respectful of the neoclassical concern for analytical rigour, he felt that any convincing theoretical explanation of production, distribution and exchange had to abandon the assumption that human economic behaviour can be modelled exclusively by means of an objective function to be maximised under constraints. He was convinced that conventions and institutions are fundamental in shaping individuals' behaviour, and that the notion of social classes should have pride of place over that of self-interested individuals in economic theory. This is the main reason why he was in sympathy with Ricardo, Sraffa and Keynes, though always ready to recognise their ambiguities and logical inconsistencies.

Caravale felt that the debate among different schools of thought on what he considered the most fascinating and intricate phenomena to be explained – namely value, income distribution and unemployment – was marked by both apologetic attitudes and preconceived criticisms. He believed that the best way to help economic theory progress in understanding how actual economic systems work was to compare the competing theoretical strands in an open, transparent way. We thought it appropriate to apply his method to this memorial volume.

Competing Economic Theories is a tribute by friends and colleagues of different persuasion to a brilliant, open-minded economist and to an extraordinary teacher.

Part I

Economic theory and its history

the economist . . . cannot afford to ignore the existence of different lines of economic thought running parallel in the history of our discipline, often conflicting with one another, at times intersecting each other . . .

being a historian of economic thought and an economist (or political economist), are to a very large extent the complementary sides of the same coin. It is no accident that in the greatest economists of the past and of the present – from Ricardo to Marx, from Marshall to Pareto, from Schumpeter to Keynes, from Sraffa to Samuelson, to name but a few – the profound knowledge of the history of thought goes hand in hand with their capability to supply lasting contributions to economic analysis.

(Caravale 1992d: 206)

1 The relevance for present economic theory of economic theory written in the past

Donald A. Walker

Introduction

Terminology

In order that this chapter may be clear to the reader, some understandings about terminology must be established. First, if we speak of 'theories that were formulated in the past', ordinarily we mean to leave open the question of whether they are still valid, and if we speak of 'past theories', ordinarily we imply that they have been discarded and that implies that they were defective and were supplanted by current theories. Nevertheless, in this chapter the latter term, used for the sake of brevity, will have the same meaning as the former expression. If a past theory is considered to be invalid, that will be stated explicitly.

A second terminological consideration is the meaning of 'the past' and 'the present' in relation to economic theorising. There is no sharp line drawn between them in this study. There is a temporally spacious moving present which is not just the knife edge of the present instant. In the wide sense, 'the present' is today and a recent past period in which intellectual activity directly related to present concerns occurred. The view has been expressed in relation to J. A. Schumpeter's inclusion of the work of Paul Samuelson in his *History of Economic Analysis* (1954) that 'Samuelson was a contemporary and therefore not legitimate material for the history of economic thought in the sense that, because of the problem of inadequate perspective, one does not do current history of economic thought' (Samuels 1988: 25). That view is not shared in this chapter, nor, of course, was it shared by Schumpeter. One could argue that understanding anything, including the most recent economic theory, requires adequate perspective, and, in fact that is precisely the position taken here. The perspective in the latter case is given by a knowledge of the history of economic thought.

All writings on economics become part of the history of economics from the moment that they are produced. There is therefore no particular age that a theory must have for it to be considered a part of the history of economic thought. What distinguishes current theorising from the study of the history of economic thought is the approach taken by the investigator. The historian of economic thought, whether dealing with the work of Adam Smith or with an article published yesterday in the *Journal of Economic Theory*, is concerned with describing and viewing it in the light of other parts of the author's work, with finding the relationship of the material to the work of other past and contemporary writers, with interpreting it in the light of other doctrines, with revealing the methodology, preconceptions and biases of the author. The economic theorist, on the other hand, is concerned with rectifying a logical problem in a current theory, extending a theory or developing a new theory, arguing against another competing current view, or developing a new model of an empirical situation (Walker 1988: 99–100).

Third, this chapter does not refer to 'economic analysis' as something different from 'economic thought'. There is, of course, a distinction between rigorous analysis and opinions about appropriate policies and other distinctions that some writers mean to evoke when they use the two terms. In this chapter, however, those distinctions will be described directly, and 'economic analysis', 'economic thought', 'economic doctrine', 'economics' and similar terms will all be used to mean economic ideas and constructions.

Distinctions between theories, models, methods, tools

The differences among theoretical concepts or abstractions of a general nature, theories or theoretical models (the two terms are generally used interchangeably in this chapter), econometric theory, methods of theoretical and empirical economic investigation, analytical tools, and models of empirical situations are important for an understanding of the relation between past and present economics. Much of the confusion and controversy surrounding the question of the value of the study of the history of economic thought stems from a failure to discriminate between those different aspects in discussions of the topic. It has been argued, for example, that when a change in the tools used by economists occurs, past economic thought – that is, thought dealing with the displaced set of tools – becomes uninteresting for current theory (Cesarano 1983: 64). In fact, most tools, such as a formula for the elasticity of demand or the definition of the marginal rate of technical substitution, and many methods, such as the *ceteris paribus* technique, are not tied to a particular phase of economic history and are always useful in their proper domain of application. The same is true of economic concepts such as 'labour', 'capital', 'profits', 'entrepreneurship' and 'marginal product'.

There are theories or models that do not deal directly with a particular set of real economic variables and these may also be regarded as true at some time subsequent to the period when they were developed. Examples are the theories of the source of interest, of the nature and determinants of the rent of land, of the role of the entrepreneur, of choice, of the relation of the income generated by capital goods to their prices, of profit, and so forth. That type of theory becomes incorporated into one or another of the present-day theories dealing with that particular subject.

Interests for which past economic thought is relevant

There are as many respects in which past economic doctrine is relevant to present-day concerns as there are topics which involve it. It depends upon the sort of activity that is undertaken. For example, if the objective of a researcher is to discover how an economic theory developed into its present form, the study of the history of economic thought is not merely relevant but is the essence of the subject matter under consideration. It is relevant for people who desire a more complete picture of the past or richer understandings and modern interpretations of past intellectual endeavours achieved through contrasts and comparisons of the work of past writers, and so forth in endless variations. For the scholar who wishes to understand the rationale behind the economic policies followed by a past government, the economic theories that were accepted by the politicians of the time are relevant. Some obvious examples of policies related to economic doctrines are the repeal of the Corn Laws, Russian economic policy in the early 1920s, and the decisions of the US Federal Reserve system during the decade of the 1930s. For the scholar who derives satisfaction from learning about the intellectual life of George Bernard Shaw, the Fabian tracts of the 1920s are relevant. For the scholar who wants to write a history of modern Chile, the teachings of the Chicago school in the 1970s and 1980s are relevant.

Another motive at work in many instances of research into the history of economic thought is a desire to learn more about human behaviour:

> the highest claim that can be made for the history of any science or of science in general is that it teaches us much about the ways of the human mind. To be sure, the material it presents bears only upon a particular kind of intellectual activity. But within this field its evidence is almost ideally complete. It displays logic in the concrete, logic in action, logic wedded to vision and to purpose.
>
> (Schumpeter 1954: 5)

The work of Adam Smith, for example, has been used as a laboratory for enquiring into behaviour, morality and mores. We find research papers on Smith's treatment of the virtues which are really inquiries into the criteria that can be used to judge human actions and into the psychological make-up of humans as manifested in economic settings (see Pack 1997). A study of F. A. Hayek's thought on spontaneous socio-economic orders is an enquiry into how human societies form institutions, how cultural evolution occurs and transmits orderly behaviour, and whether humans do these things by rational economic calculation (Sabooglu 1996). The work of past economists may be used to study the use of metaphors and to learn about and evaluate techniques of persuasion (see McCloskey 1985).

There is, of course, no question about the relevance of current economic theories for the study of past economic theory. The activity of describing, interpreting and evaluating past theory is undertaken under the powerful influence of current economic thought. Indeed, it is the most important influence in the construction of our view of past economic thought. The ability of a historian of economic thought also influences his account of past economic theory. Historians of economic thought have different ideas about present-day economics and some are more capable than others. Since there is disagreement over which current ideas are worthwhile, there is no unanimous judgement on the value of the doctrines that were formulated in the past. For example, an economist of the modern Austrian school may believe that a particular past idea is worthwhile, but a modern neoclassical economist may believe it is not, as is the case in the evaluation of the ideas of F. A. Hayek on the efficiency of a socialist economy (Caldwell 1997: 1876–86). These considerations are of vital significance in understanding the work of any particular historian of economic thought. Knowledge about the historian helps us to understand why he develops the analysis that he does of a past doctrine, why he selects and emphasises some elements of a writer's work, why he interprets them as he does, and why he chooses particular criteria by which to evaluate it.

The supply of articles and books on the history of economic thought is forthcoming because individuals want to write them and educational institutions, foundations, government agencies, and publishers are willing to subsidise or reward their research directly or indirectly. Some universities believe that it adds to their lustre to have individuals in their departments of economics who publish research in the history of economic thought. In Europe and Japan, for example, some universities grant tenure and promotion as a reward for articles, books and conference activity on the subject. People are interested in the subject and are therefore willing to pay for journals and books on the topic. Students take courses in the history of economic thought in order to obtain a well rounded liberal education. Thus the history of economic thought is relevant to whoever is interested in the topic, for whatever reason the person finds it interesting. There are many such persons and reasons, so the supply of research will be forthcoming and the demand for research, if not for courses in the history of economic thought, will continue to flourish. The question at issue here, a question that has not been addressed in the foregoing remarks, is whether past economic theory is in fact relevant for current economic theory and, if so, in what ways, and this study now turns to those issues.

Two views of past economic theory

One opinion about the history of economic thought is that it is irrelevant for current economic theory and therefore that the study of the history of economic thought is unnecessary for someone who wishes to be a competent economist. Regarding economic theory, there is 'no necessity for including its history as a part of professional training' (Gordon 1965: 126). It is irrelevant, the argument goes, because in the process of the construction of economic theory, ideas that are worthwhile are incorporated into it, and ideas that are false or useless are discarded (see Schumpeter 1954: 4). The meaning of 'worthwhile' is usefulness in solving current economic problems or in understanding the behaviour of the modern economy. On this view, current economic theory incorporates all that is worthwhile that has been discovered in the past and what has been discarded is not worth studying for the purpose of attaining the best possible current theory. Additional worthwhile material would be useful new constructions.

It is true that economists do many things very competently that do not require a knowledge of the history of economic thought. Examples are studies of the standard of living of the population of California classed by ethnic origin, of the history of aluminium prices and production since World War II, of the savings rate of the Japanese, of the impact of the North American Free Trade Agreement on employment in the participating countries, of the costs and benefits of government policies and programmes, and the thousands of studies done by consulting firms and the economic research departments of banks and insurance companies. The history of economic thought is – up to a point – irrelevant for the new econometric field of simulation-based estimation. The great minds of the past never thought of methods of approximating high dimensional integrals to obtain unbiased estimators of economic variables and have nothing to add to the many empirical studies that use simulation methods (see Stern 1997). The same is true of many other new fields of economic studies.

Practitioners in empirical and technical fields like economic statistics and econometric theory have thought of the type of work that they themselves undertake when exhorted to recognise the current value of past doctrine and have therefore regarded the claims of historians of economic thought as being without merit. Economists are educated in graduate schools to perform studies like those mentioned above and to teach about them and the realisation of the irrelevance of the history of economic thought for such studies has contributed greatly to driving its study from lists of required graduate courses in the United States. Although a course in the subject might help a practitioner of applied economics to be a more interesting person and enrich his knowledge of human achievements, historians should recognise the irrelevance of discarded past doctrine for the empirical and technical aspects of current economics. They should base their argument in favour of its relevance upon a careful delimitation of the type of modern studies which do in fact benefit from it or can benefit from it.

Nevertheless, many things are wrong with the point of view expressed above. In the first place, although writers remote in time such as Sir William Petty, Adam Smith and David Ricardo are irrelevant for the development and understanding of new fields, especially highly technical ones such as simulation-based estimation, as time passes the new field of study accumulates its own very relevant history, a knowledge of which will be necessary in the ways discussed in the next section. Second, the point of view does not discriminate between the different types of economic thought. It does not recognise that empirical models and statistical studies are only a part of past economics, and that economic concepts, methods and theories or theoretical models are less time-bound and may therefore be useful in the present although they were produced many years ago. That matter will also be examined in the next section.

The next consideration is that there is no such thing as a generally accepted single body of doctrine or knowledge that can be called current economic theory. The diversity of theoretical views is reflected in the diversity of analyses of empirical problems (Swartz and Bonello 1997). Thus by 'current economic theory' in this chapter is meant simply one or another of the theories held today, with no implication that there is a single body of received doctrine. Economics is a vast discipline and is divided into fields of interest. To discuss the point of view that past economics is irrelevant today because current theory incorporates all worthwhile economic thought, therefore, it is first necessary to specify the part of economic theory that is under consideration.

For example, macroeconomic theory can be considered. That immediately leads to the observation that instead of presenting a unified body of generally accepted doctrine, economic theory in regard to macroeconomics has for many years been divided into a number of differing streams. The different and largely incompatible macroeconomic theories express different views of how the economy behaves. There are Keynesians, post-Keynesians, neo-Keynesians, New Keynesians, new classicals, monetarists, rational expectations theorists, real business cycle theorists, supply siders, and so forth. Given that situation, it is not an accurate reflection of the state of economic learning to say that there is a body of current theory which incorporates all good ideas into a generally accepted body of macroeconomic thought. Moreover, there have always been objections to macroeconomic theory itself on the part of some neoclassical economists (for example, Marget 1938–42; Knight 1937) and of others who do not believe that macroeconomic functions can represent economic reality because of the problem of aggregation.

Similarly, with respect to microeconomics, it is incorrect to say that there is a single accepted body of current economic theory into which all valid contributions have been gathered. It is often said that 'the' theory of general equilibrium is the core or centrepiece of microeconomic theory, but in fact there is no such thing. There are many different incompatible general equilibrium models, each portraying a different hypothetical economy, and none of them portraying the actual economy. There are models of perfectly competitive economies, and models in which the firms are imperfectly competitive. In some models, the economy is assumed to be always in equilibrium. In some models, there is disequilibrium but no disequilibrium transactions or disequilibrium production. In others, there are those disequilibrium phenomena. There are models in which there is no money, and models in which money is used. Some theorists believe there are no models which treat money and markets adequately (Clower and Howitt 1996). For each of those general types of models there are a wide variety of special models that differ in significant detailed respects (see Walker 1997).

The Italo-Cambridge school does not accept the validity of general equilibrium theory as a method, replaces it with sequence analysis, rejects marginalism, makes no use of supply and demand functions, and regards many of the modern neoclassical analyses as erroneous (Garegnani 1990). There is hardly any need to add that the theories of the behaviour of the economy held by heterodox economists (see Prychitko 1977), such as institutionalists, Marxists and modern Austrians, differ greatly from the microeconomic general equilibrium theories and have nothing in common with the macroeconomic dynamics that appear, for example, in the journal devoted to that subject (Barnett 1977). Mention of their ideas emphasises the diversity of views that exists about the behaviour of consumers, firms, markets, and the role of government. Moreover, for those types of economists, the influence of economics written in the past upon their present ideas about economic behaviour is abundantly evident.

The fact that there is no monolithic 'current economic theory', but rather 'current economic theories' about any given subject profoundly affects the terms of the discussion of the relevance of past economic theories to present economics. Since there is no generally accepted body of present doctrine, no general agreement on what ideas are worthwhile, it cannot accurately be said that a body of current economics, generally regarded as the received state of knowledge, incorporates all worthwhile economic ideas.

A second point of view is that the different economic theories that have been held at different times, including the present, are not intrinsically right or wrong. At some time in the past a problem was identified, either an aspect of the real economy for which an explanation was desired or a problem in the logical structure of an economic theory. Analysis of the problem led to a new or modified theory. It may be that the situation to which the theory was a response no longer exists, but the theory is not thereby invalidated. A theory may not be espoused by anyone currently, but that is simply because attention has shifted to subjects other than those with which it deals:

> what, in economics, to select for special attention partly depends on circumstances – on the world environment, factual knowledge and our particular interests at any time (Hicks 1976). From this it follows that an economic theory may be 'rejected' because it is inappropriate for the particular problems with which we are currently concerned, rather than because it is 'wrong'. It may often appear when there is a change in economic thought that one theory has displaced another because the first has somehow been proved, in some definitive sense, faulty, when nothing more than a change in 'concentration of attention' is involved.
>
> (Hollander 1987: 1)

According to this view, the past is a storehouse of different theories, each of which is potentially useful. It is a repository of the economic reasoning of many capable minds and some brilliant minds. Present-day economists can draw upon that rich heritage. The theory or model developed about a past situation is put aside until the time when it will be used as a source of inspiration or as the beginnings of a body of thought that will be constructed to deal with a similar sort of present situation.

One merit of the second point of view is that it does not postulate the existence of a single body of accepted economic theory. There are, however, some problems with the point of view if it is interpreted as maintaining that all past theories are potentially of some value. Is it true that those models are put on the shelf in the storehouse of economic theories awaiting a time when the situation with which they deal reoccurs and they once more become applicable? The answer depends partially on the type of model under consideration. Empirical models become outmoded when the economy changes in the respects that they model. A model which was directed at the understanding of a specific past empirical situation and correctly explains it does not become wrong in relation to that situation after it passes but it becomes largely irrelevant to explain new situations. Some of the elements of the model may be reused, but they cannot be applicable without changes in the overall model in which they appear because the economy does not recreate past situations. For example, the structure of the economy that existed during the 1929–36 depression in the United States and the events that took place will never occur again. If there were a correct model of that depression, it would never again be applicable because it would be a model of the structural features and economic behaviour of that particular time. W. S. Jevons's estimation of the periodicity of business cycles, for example, was strongly influenced by the data that he collected on prices and the way he analysed them. His data, it can now be shown, was inadequate as a representation of economic activity and his statistical techniques were comparatively primitive and will never be used again.

The further back in time that an empirical model was developed, the less relevant it is. An example is Léon Walras's model of the behaviour of a bimetallic monetary system (L. Walras 1881, 1889: 387–450). He used it to analyse a variety of monetary questions in an economy in which the circulating media were silver and gold. That may be a valid model of the monetary aspects of the economy of his time, but not of the modern economy. The successive monetary models that were constructed after Walras's time are increasingly relevant as explanations of the modern economy. That is not to say that one can identify a particular past monetary model which was the immediate progenitor of modern monetary modelling, because there are a number of different current theories of the role of money in the modern economy. Nevertheless, the most relevant empirical models are fairly recent. This is not only because they relate to an economy that is structurally and behaviourally substantially like the modern economy, but also because the modellers who have worked in recent years have been able to choose among a wider range of modelling techniques, economic concepts and tools. Moreover, they have been able to rely on better empirical information and to use computers to deal with large amounts of information and complex equation systems.

It may be argued that even though past situations are not exactly duplicated in the present, there are similarities between past and present empirical situations. Inflation has occurred many times in the past and may occur in the present. It may be argued, therefore, that a model that attempted to explain inflation in the United States in 1865 could be useful in explaining inflation in 1919, 1940–1, 1946–8, 1950–1, 1958–9, 1974–5, 1978–80 and in some subsequent period. The difficulty is, again, that for a theory to explain an empirical situation, the theory must contain structural and behavioural information drawn from the economy of the time. Otherwise, a general statement like '*ceteris paribus*, inflation is caused by increases in the quantity of money that are excessive in relation to increases in the quantity of commodities' is useless.

At any time in the past, there have been different theories about a given subject matter, just as at present. What is under discussion is not theories that differ because they have different subject matters, but theories about a particular aspect of economics. For example, the different theories of the source of interest that existed during the time of Eugen von Böhm-Bawerk and which were described and evaluated by him (Böhm-Bawerk 1884), and the theory that he proposed, were all different explanations of the same phenomenon. Thomas Malthus and David Ricardo held opposing theories on many topics. The controversy regarding the wage-fund doctrine in the third quarter of the nineteenth century is another example of conflicting views. In the 1920s and 1930s there were many incompatible theories of the depression that was occurring, among which were the theories that its cause was purely monetary, monetary over-investment, non-monetary over-investment, capital shortages, disproportionate investment, cost changes, horizontal maladjustments, over-indebtedness, under-consumption, psychological, and harvest variations (see Haberler 1937; Hutchison 1953: 334–408). Irving Fisher (1932, 1936) and J. M. Keynes (1936), for example, developed different theories about the great depression. To evaluate the competing theories, each represented by their supporters as being the exclusive explanation of one and the same set of economic events, the historian of thought has to study and evaluate the late 1920s and the 1930s in the United Kingdom and the 1930s in the United States – he has to study economic history or he has to leave that job to an economic historian.

Contradictory theories cannot all be true. In short, some past theories were erroneous. Some of the erroneous theories were stepping-stones to reach a better theory and some were stepping-stones to increased confusion. For example, the labour theory of value was wrong and led to confusion. Like many other past doctrines, it will never be adopted again and used to explain the pricing of commodities. W. S. Jevons's sunspot model of business fluctuations was wrong, and it will never become relevant for an explanation of them. The virtual perfectly competitive general equilibrium models and proofs of existence of the period 1936–71 had no relation to the real economy, were never useful for understanding or affecting it, and will never be used to explain its behaviour. In ardently supporting the study of the history of economic thought, one does not want to be thought to be arguing that the different incompatible theories were all equally valid regarding the same subject matter. The storehouse of the past contains many notions that will be left there.

Why the history of economic thought is relevant for the content of current economics

First, economists can learn useful information from a study of past doctrine. In the words of J. R. McCulloch (1845: vi–vii), 'whether a writer or a speaker undertakes to unfold principles, to set them in a novel and more striking light, or to recommend their application, he should know what has been already undertaken, what has been accomplished, and what remains for discovery and elucidation'. McCulloch went on to give 'sundry examples of the inconveniences resulting from the want of this information, by exhibiting able men engaged in the investigation of principles and the development of laws which had been previously established and traced, and putting forward speculations as original which had been long before the public' (ibid.). Edgeworth argued the point this way:

> I am unable to devote proportionate attention to the advantages of historical studies. But you will not expect me to expatiate upon advantages which are known to most of you from personal experience. I will only advert to a secondary and less obvious benefit attending historical researches. To trace the affiliation of ideas in the progress of science is calculated to correct our estimates of authority: to reduce in general the extravagant regard which the youthful student is apt to entertain for contemporary leaders, and to assign due weight to real originality.
>
> (Edgeworth 1891: 11)

J. A. Schumpeter emphasised some other kinds of useful information that are obtained by the study of the history of economics: 'We learn about both the futility and the fertility of controversies; about detours, wasted efforts, and blind alleys; about spells of arrested growth, about our dependence on chance, about how not to do things, about leeways to make up for. We learn to understand why we are as far as we actually are and also why we are not further. And we learn *what succeeds and how and why*' (Schumpeter 1954: 5).

Second, it has sometimes happened that ideas that were superior to the state of knowledge in the received doctrine were neglected. A failure to study the history of thought can cause

> oblivion of an older and a higher theory; so in political economy the theory which explains value by utility – utility in the sense defined by Galvanize – has so fascinated by no means the worst sort of economists, that they have almost forgotten, or at least degraded, the older, and in some respects more important theory which connects value with sacrifice and labour. There is ever a danger that, as we press on to seize new conceptions, we should lose the positions which have been already won. Hence the history of theory is particularly instructive in dialectics, and all that the Greeks comprehensively called *words*, seem the best corrective of the narrow prejudices and deceptive associations which are sure to be contracted by those who have been confined to a single school or system.
>
> (Edgeworth 1891: 6)

Theories of a general nature that have been neglected, as distinct from empirical models, may become useful again, inevitably with some modification:

> It is important, therefore, if this is so, to try to discover whether, how and why changes in concentration have occurred over time. Not to do so is to remain under the possibly false impression that what one has learned in basic theory courses is all there is to know; that earlier perspectives have been definitively disposed of as erroneous, when there is much that remains 'valid' albeit forgotten or neglected by the profession.

> There is good reason to support this view. A number of instances illustrate that theoretical constructs, lost from sight, have indeed proved to be of permanent usefulness as old problems re-emerge.
>
> (Hollander 1987: 1)

Economists who have some knowledge of its history do not accept the idea that the entire work of evaluation of a theory was done at the time of its original dissemination because the record shows that has not been true. The best theory is often not incorporated into the most recent theory. It may be that economists – either those who held professorships in prestigious universities or heterodox economists – wrongly rejected a theory, so that what was at that time the most recent doctrine received by one or another school of thought did not in fact contain all that was worthwhile. One type of neglected economist is 'the man whose ideas, no matter how original and brilliant judged by the standards of today, had little if any impact on the thought of his own day. Not time but his contemporaries neglected him' (Fetter 1965: 138). Of course, there were also economists who influenced their contemporaries and who were subsequently forgotten but their situation is not relevant for the present chapter. Of interest here are ideas that were neglected for a period of time but subsequently were used in the construction of economic theories. In fact, the record shows that it has been through studying the history of thought that neglected ideas have been uncovered, understood, and evaluated.

An example is the historical studies that led to an appreciation of the neglected ideas of Antoine Augustin Cournot in the book that he published in 1838. It was only many years after that date that his innovations in method and in regard to demand, pricing, and market structures were studied by Alfred Marshall (1890: x, 1920: ix–x) and Léon Walras (1900: VIII, 1905, 1988: 5, 1965, I: 5), recognised as being valuable, and used in their theoretical work. Similarly, after many years of virtually total neglect, Irving Fisher's macroeconomics and monetary ideas began to be studied and utilised by modern economists (Dimand 1998). The constant interplay between past and present economic studies becomes evident. Past ideas come to be used in the formulation of current theory and the understanding of past ideas requires the application of present economics to achieve a clear expression and satisfactory evaluation of them. The latter process occurred, for example, when J. M. Keynes reinterpreted and re-evaluated mercantilist doctrines (Keynes 1936: 333–50). It is a process that may be repeated many times with different results in reference to a particular set of past writings because current theories change and so our perception of the character of past theory and our judgements on it change. Thus Keynes's views on mercantilist doctrine have themselves in turn been recently scrutinised (Walker 1986: 15–29), and the doctrines have subsequently been interpreted and evaluated again (Magnusson 1993).

Neglect of valuable ideas is what Keynes argued was the case in the rejection of Thomas Malthus's theory that general over-production can occur and the acceptance of David Ricardo's contrary view (Keynes 1922/33, X: 98–102; see Walker 1986: 4–5). Another example is that today we do not believe that Keynes made an exhaustive and correct determination that classical and neoclassical economic theory was wrong in all the respects that he alleged. His followers thought he had done so and they therefore indiscriminately abandoned the older ideas and constructed a Keynesian model which they believed contained all the best latest theory (Lerner 1940: 575–6; Klein 1947). Their judgement was wrong. As one historian put it: 'Unfortunately Keynes had a totally distorted view of classical macroeconomics' (Hollander 1987: 3). Patient labours in the history of economic thought have either vindicated the worth of many of the pre-Keynesian ideas or revealed their inadequacy for reasons other than, or in addition to, the ones that Keynes gave. Thus the historian of thought analyses past doctrines and models to establish their true character and worth and those labours are valuable for the construction of current theory.

Third, economists use past theory in their construction of current theory and therefore that past theory should be studied. There is no point in simply asserting over and over that past economic theory is relevant for present economic theory, and no need to try to establish the value of studying the history of economic thought by that simple repetition because the hypothesis can be tested and has been tested with affirmative results many times. The work of economic theorists at any particular time can be studied to identify the ideas of their predecessors' upon which they drew in order to construct their theories. Past ideas are used as a basis for modern theory: 'our minds are apt to derive new inspiration from the study of the history of science' (Schumpeter 1954: 4–5). Current economic theory develops out of past economic theory and is largely composed of economic theories that were developed before the very recent past, often of theories written in the more or less distant past. That current theory uses past ideas has just been shown with respect to the resuscitation of valuable neglected ideas, but it is even more frequently the case that past ideas were not neglected but were incorporated into theory that has remained current for many years. That is a major reason why historians of economic thought are right to assert that the study of the past is relevant for current theory.

Assertions that the history of economic thought need not be studied in order to educate graduate students in economics imply that economics can be divided into current economics and the history of economic thought. That implies that everything that is part of current economics is not part of the history of economic thought and the reverse. In fact, that distinction cannot be made with respect to many economic subject matters. If it were to be said to a proponent of the view that the study of the history of economic thought is irrelevant for current theory that the analyses of product differentiation and of selling costs that Edward H. Chamberlin developed are relevant, he would have to reply that they are indeed valuable current theory, as can be seen by perusing the entries under those topics in each recent quarterly issue of the *Journal of Economic Literature*. By relevant is here meant that the real subject matter with which they deal exists today, so that the analyses are applicable to situations in the present. He would say the same regarding Joan Robinson's development of the falling marginal revenue function. But Chamberlin developed the indicated analyses about seventy years ago – before 1927 – and Robinson undertook her analysis sixty-five years ago, so they are certainly part of the history of economic thought (Chamberlin 1933; Robinson 1933). Similar remarks can be made about Chamberlin's analysis of the product as an economic variable, developed in 1935 (Chamberlin 1953: 105 n. 2). That proponent would therefore have to agree that parts of the past history of economics are not only relevant for current theory but are part of it.

Even further back in time – over 100 years ago – is the example of the construction of the ordinal indifference analysis by Vilfredo Pareto, his study of complements and substitutes, and his elaboration of the barter box (Pareto 1896–7, I: 10–11, 35, 1909: 168–70, 183–4, 249–84). A modern economist would have to say that those constructs are all currently worthwhile. The study of their construction, the assumptions underlying them, the uses to which Pareto put them are therefore all significant parts of both the history of thought and of modern theory. Still further back in time – about 120 years ago – Alfred Marshall developed the concepts of the elasticity of demand and of the short run and the long run for a competitive firm and industry. Once again, those ideas are accepted as a part of current theory.

There are many other examples of the inspiration provided by economic theory written in the past and therefore also of the impossibility of separating much of current theory from past theory. A modern concept of equilibrium is that it is a state in which the plans of economic agents are compatible and in which no one is either able or wishes to change prices, quantities or their type of economic activity. Giovanni Caravale, however, noted the classical concept of equilibrium as a centre of gravity (Caravale 1991a: 175, 179–81) and used that idea to construct his own view of the behaviour of the economy (Caravale 1997a). W. Hildenbrand and A. P. Kirman (1988: v) asserted that they drew their inspiration from two neoclassical economists, developing 'solutions or themes' that were 'due to Walras and Edgeworth'. 'Our fundamental debt intellectually', they believe, 'is still obviously to Edgeworth and Walras' (Hildenbrand and Kirman 1988: vii). It is true that J. R. Hicks did not think that the study of Ricardo and the other classicals was useful for the activity of constructing current economic theory and therefore 'made a practice of restraining [his] interest in the history of theory at 1870' (Hicks 1937a: 81), but his *Value and Capital* is permeated with a sense of the neoclassical foundations which were either incorporated into it or served as points of departure that he first had to understand (Hicks 1939: 2–4, *passim*). One hundred years after Knut Wicksell wrote *Geldzins und Güterpreise* (1889), Axel Leijonhufvud pointed out that 'modern monetary and macroeconomic theory starts *here*' (Leijonhufvud 1997: 1), so Wicksell's ideas are both part of the history of economic thought and of modern theory. Monetarism and rational expectations theory have thrust his themes into the background but there are good reasons to concentrate upon them again. 'After 100 years, the intellectual stimulus deriving from *Geldzins und Güterpreise* is not yet spent' (Leijonhufvud 1997: 9).

Thus to say that the history of economic thought is not sufficiently important to be a part of the required education and ongoing research effort of those who are interested in economic theory is a nonsensical statement. The study of that history merges into the study of current economics from a reflective and critical historical perspective, revealing the profound truth that, although there are differences between the work of a historian of economic thought and an economic theoretician, there is no absolute distinction between past and present theory. All economic theory was developed in the past, whether 120 years ago or yesterday, and many past theories are used today. The study of them is both the study of the history of economic thought and the study of current economics.

Fourth, another reason that the history of economics should be studied for the benefit of current economics is that a theory may have been invalid in reference to the situation about which it was constructed but nevertheless be valid in reference to the present. This is another reason for not making sweeping generalisations about the validity and fate of economic theories. For example, the model of a perfectly competitive securities market worked out by Léon Walras in 1874 was not a valid representation of the behaviour of the French securities market at the time that he constructed the theory, but it is a realistic and valid model of the establishment of the official price that rules for a trading session in the Brussels cash and account-settlement markets for securities (Spray 1964: 76–7).

Fifth, the history of economic thought is an aid to the understanding of modern theory, including an aid to understanding the problems that it faces. That view has been criticised by those who believe the history of economics is not sufficiently important to merit being a required field of study in economics curricula. Their argument goes as follows. The time available for studying is limited, so it should be used in the most productive manner. It is very important to know current economic theory and less important to know past economic theory. The study of the history of economic thought may help an economist to understand contemporary theory, but it does not do so as efficiently as a course in the latter so it should not be required (Gordon 1965: 121–2). That opinion has become widely accepted in graduate schools, and, in fact, the history of economic thought began to be displaced from graduate curricula shortly after 1930 because a great amount of the time of students and of professors came to be absorbed by the study of the emerging fields of monopolistic competition, Keynesian macroeconomics, and econometric inferential studies, and by the mathematisation of economic theory (Samuelson 1987a: 52). Many other introductions into the curriculum were made subsequently.

Donald Gordon's opinion has rightly been challenged with the argument that the study of the history of economic thought should be a part of professional training, because

> teachers or students who attempt to act upon the theory that the most recent treatise is all they need will soon discover that they are making things unnecessarily difficult for themselves. Unless that recent treatise itself presents a minimum of historical aspects, no amount of correctness, originality, rigor, or elegance will prevent a sense of *lacking direction and meaning* from spreading among the students or at least the majority of students. . . . Therefore, any

> treatise that attempts to render 'the present state of science' really renders methods, problems, and results that are historically conditioned and are meaningful only with reference to the historical background from which they spring. To put the same thing somewhat differently: the state of any science at any given time implies its past history and cannot be satisfactorily conveyed without making this implicit history explicit.
>
> (Schumpeter 1954: 4)

The sort of information yielded by a historical inquiry includes the questions that were considered and the lines of inquiry that were rejected; the errors that were discovered to have been made and the way in which those errors were rectified; the different ways that the problem was framed, and the choices that were made to follow one way rather than another.

A specific example of the value of a knowledge of the history of economics for understanding its present state is provided, according to one economist, by considering the means of solving 'today's methodological confusion' over whether microeconomic assumptions need to be psychologically realistic and whether economics can be independent of psychology:

> This confusion is difficult to resolve (I submit) partly because today's discussions occur in a temporal vacuum, and participants generally lack a good understanding of the historical roots of today's disagreements. This paper attempts to provide this much needed historical context by looking back to the birth of Sen's paradox. It studies a controversy very similar to today's debate, the crisis of hedonism, which occurred near the turn of the century. By studying this earlier historical episode, we learn that the debate over psychological assumptions is only a small piece of a much larger intellectual debate.
>
> (Lewin 1996: 1294)

For example, in a treatment of modern general equilibrium theory the teacher should start by studying work that had already been done on the subject in question, work that is part of the history of economic thought. A careful theorist would not only consult very recent writings, like (I hope) my book (1997) but also the forty-four-year-old model of Kenneth Arrow and Gerard Debreu (1954) and the 1971 models of Arrow and Frank H. Hahn. The theorist would be completely lost if he did not also examine the thirty-six-year-old non-virtual model constructed by Frank Hahn and Takashi Negishi (1962) and the fifteen-year-old work of Franklin M. Fisher (1983). The assumptions used in the construction of those models are in turn better understood by studying the work, about sixty-five years old, of Abraham Wald, John von Neumann, and J. R. Hicks. It is immediately apparent that the history of general equilibrium theory is relevant for understanding the present state of the perfect competition branch of that field of theoretical endeavour.

Yet another example of the value of studying past theory to understand the reasons for the form that present theory has taken is the indifference theory of demand. It would be impossible for someone to understand why that theory is constructed in the way that it is without some knowledge of the neoclassical theory of consumer demand. In the form developed by Alfred Marshall, that theory was based on the assumption that utility is cardinally measurable, could not deal with substitute and complementary commodities, and concluded that an increase in income would lead the consumer to consume more of every commodity. Without an understanding of these matters, a student of demand theory would not appreciate why the indifference analysis uses an ordinal measurement of utility, why the framers of the theory made an effort to develop a construction that would take account of relationships of substitutability and complementarity in the manner that is done with indifference curves, and why distinctions are made between inferior commodities, income-satiated commodities, and commodities that are normal with respect to income. The reasons for the directions taken by the developers of the indifference analysis are to be found in the inadequacies of the neoclassical construction.

As a final example, consider the modern macroeconomic theory of savings and investment. To give an exposition of it the teacher of a course in macroeconomics could dispense with a lecture on D. H. Robertson's interaction with J. M. Keynes when the former was writing *Banking Policy and the Price Level* (1926) and could neglect Keynes's *Treatise on Money* (1930). The teacher could even pass over Keynes's development of savings and investment theory in the *General Theory of Employment, Interest and Money* (1936), the contributions of Abba Lerner, and Keynes's pronouncements on savings and investment in his response to his critics in the *Quarterly Journal of Economics* in 1937. It would be essential, however, to examine the ex ante–ex post analysis either in the original source or as reported in historical surveys (Klein 1947: 110–17), J. R. Hicks's IS–LM analysis (Hicks 1937b), the contributions of Franco Modigliani (1944; and see Hynes 1998), and criticisms and modifications of IS–LM theory made over the last sixty years. In fact, that historical body of thought and analysis *is* a major current macroeconomic theory of savings and investment.

Conclusion

The study of the history of economic thought, it may be argued, does not need a pragmatic justification. It is valuable for its own sake; it should be part of a liberal education. Moreover, it deepens a student's comprehension of the scope and nature of economics. A survey course on the history of economic thought should therefore be included among undergraduate economics electives, and available to graduate students in economics. There are also the sorts of pragmatic justifications for the study of specific parts of past economic theorising that have been given in the introduction to this essay. This study is concerned, however, with a question that is independent of those issues, namely with the question of whether or not past economic theory is relevant for the study and development of current economic theory, and has concluded that, in several specific respects, it is. An understanding of past theories is therefore valuable, and consequently the work of the historian of economic thought is valuable. To be understood, they need to be studied and written down in intelligible terms, using modern terminology where possible. They need to be scrutinised to see if they are internally contradictory, to make clear their fundamental assumptions, to establish their lines of reasoning and conclusions, to interpret them correctly, and thus to present a clear picture of them. In evaluating the logical qualities of a theory, the questions that arise are whether its creators made correct deductions from their assumptions and whether it cleared up the logical difficulties that its creators were confronting. A further step is to evaluate the worth of the theory. That gives rise to questions as to whether it satisfactorily explained the economic subject matter with which it was concerned, whether its creators produced generalisations that covered the various phenomena relevant to the theory, whether it made accurate predictions, whether it was fruitful in terms of being useful for the formulation of policies to deal with the problems with which it was concerned, and whether policies that were framed on the basis of it were efficacious. Then it can be shown how the theory needs to be corrected or modified or amplified to deal with a past or present situation.

The question that may now be addressed is whether or not a survey course in the history of economic thought should be a required course in graduate economics curricula. Such a requirement is not an implication of the favourable judgements on the value of the study of the history of economic thought made in this study. It has been conceded in this chapter that a survey course on the history of economic thought would be of less value than courses in modern economics and quantitative methods to a student taking a Ph.D. in applied economics or in econometrics or in many narrowly technical fields. A knowledge of Nassau Senior's theory of interest is of no value to the officials who direct the US Treasury's funding operations. Karl Marx's theory of value is useless to an economist working in the human resources section of a corporation. David Ricardo's ideas about the course of the rate of profit are irrelevant for someone who wants to work in General Motors' profit accounts section. Furthermore, a general survey course, touching on the Greeks, William Petty, James Steuart, Ricardo, etc., is also of little value for those who wish to contribute to economic theory – although it would enrich their intellectual life in the ways mentioned earlier.

The history of economic thought has been taught in the wrong way at the graduate level. It has been sequestered in history of economic thought courses and has therefore been separated from the activity of teaching current economic theory. The effect has been twofold. First, it has caused the internment in those courses of subjects that would be useful to students who are trying to learn current economic theories, and that has resulted in expositions of the subjects that do not meet their needs. Survey courses in the history of economic thought are taught by someone who is not intimately conversant with all of the models and theories treated in courses in modern economic theory and who cannot possibly be a specialist in the work of every past major writer, nor even of writers active during a period of time of any length, such as 1936 to 1990. The courses therefore include a high proportion of material that is irrelevant for the pedagogical purposes under consideration and entail an unavoidable superficiality of the treatment of many theories, factors that have contributed to the neglect of those courses in graduate programmes. The second effect has been the impoverishment of courses on current economic theory. In losing the relevant historical material, they have lost some of the essential content of the subject matter with which they should be dealing.

The conclusion regarding this matter reached in this chapter, without any hope that the state of affairs will change, is that the part of past economic theory relevant to each specific modern theory should be taught in conjunction with that theory, in the regular macroeconomic or microeconomic course in current economic theory, as an integral part of the lecture in which a current economic theory is explained and analysed. That would enable a full and meaningful exposition of the theory and an adequate comprehension of the problems with which it deals, of the solutions it suggests, and of the strengths and weaknesses of competing theories. An intensive study of the special aspects of past writings that deal with the particular topics that concern a graduate student or a theorist would be of great value to him or her and are indeed indispensable for understanding modern theory and for good theorising. A statement stronger than Schumpeter's can be made about the history of economic thought and the understanding of current economics: the study of the former to a large extent literally is the study of the latter. To understand the history of a theory is to understand the form and content that it has at present. Current theory is evaluated in part by comparing it with comparatively recent past theory, and the high content of past theory in present theory means that judgements on the former are in many cases judgements on the latter also. Thus another reason why the work of the historian of economic thought is important is that it can furnish the teacher of current theory and the economist who is constructing current theory with information that is essential for them to do their job properly.

2 The relevance of the economic ideas of the past

Augusto Graziani

Giovanni Caravale's teaching supplies a basic starting point to anyone working in the field of the history of economic analysis. Caravale's research was largely devoted to exploring the economic ideas of the past. This was not the result of mere historical curiosity. It rather came out of a deeply felt need of understanding more thoroughly current economic theorising and the world in which we now live. Caravale taught us that if we want to contribute to the unending construction of present-day economic theory we cannot escape visiting again and again the thought of the past. His is a convinced and persuasive defence of the usefulness of studying the history of economic thought and a strong reaction against present-day tendencies to eliminate it altogether from university curricula.

1. The argument used by the opponents of the history of economic thought as a basic course is that, in the progress of research, what is valid of a theory never gets lost, since it is automatically embodied into newer, usually more rigorous, theoretical formulations. Conversely, according to the dominant view, what is not absorbed by new theories clearly no longer deserves attention. In this view, studying the theoretical formulations of the past is as good as useless for mastering the economics of today.

The main critical response to this attitude is that it is simply not true. Embodying or rejecting old theories is a continuous and unending process. Economists keep going to and fro between past and present in order to rescue from the past all that is worth rescuing. In the course of this process of continuous re-evaluation, new discoveries are often made and old theories, previously discarded, may be revised and belatedly incorporated into modern theory. Revision and inclusion are no once-and-for-all event but part and parcel of the economist's daily work. The theoretical body of the past, on this view, appears something like the remains of a ship, surrounded by busy divers going in and out just in case there may be something left to be rescued and reused.

2. Those who deny the usefulness of studying the history of economic ideas seem to start on the assumption that more modern theories are an improvement over the older ones.

Now, the very definition of theoretical progress is doubtful. In some limited cases the presence of an improvement is clear. If, for instance, we define speed as a quality, a modern car is better than a car of the 1920s, just because it can run faster. Something similar could be said of computing machines. However, such straightforward definition of an improvement is possible only because a well specified criterion has been selected and agreed upon: so long as speed is the agreed criterion, the reality of an improvement in the performance of cars or of computing machines is unquestionable. Parallel examples in economic theory are not hard to find: the introduction by Alfred Marshall of the coefficient of elasticity was clearly a technical improvement in the analysis of the demand function; the elaboration of linear programming techniques was an improvement in the calculation of optimum positions in the case of linear functions.

The trouble is that the range of validity of such simple criteria is severely limited even in the fields of knowledge where technical aspects seem to prevail over value judgements. A single isolated criterion is unable to generate a well defined judgement as to whether a new theory is better than an old one or whether an old theory is still meaningful and therefore applicable to present-day situations. Even new findings in mathematics should not be immediately regarded as final improvements: they may just be the consequence of a change in the general approach to the subject.

3. Let us now come to the positive side of the problem, namely: why do we think that studying the doctrines of the past is fruitful for present-day economic research? If asked a similar question, I would be inclined to give a very short answer, namely that there is no clear-cut distinction between current economic thought and the economic theorising of the past.

In general a theory, no matter whether ancient or brand-new, is accepted when it reflects our way of approaching a problem. An old theory can be cast in rudimentary technical terms and be inapplicable, at least in its original formulation, to present-day problems. And yet we may go back to it just because it shows us a problem we had not identified, or a way of approaching a problem that more modern theories have neglected. A possible example is supplied by Keynes's way of proceeding. When formulating his theory of aggregate demand, Keynes revived the Malthusian principle of unproductive consumption and the mercantilist theory of the balance of trade. Another example might be Sraffa's presentation. When elaborating his scheme of equilibrium prices and distribution Sraffa decided to neglect altogether the Marshallian theory of prices and go back to the Ricardian approach based on costs and labour inputs.

When judging the validity of theories inherited from the past a vital point is given by the general approach to economic theory. If, in evaluating a theory, we only give weight to logical rigour and refined technicalities, the study of history may well prove to be hardly relevant. If, on the contrary, our main interest is in how the problems to be investigated are selected and approached, a need will spontaneously emerge to know whether and in what manner similar problems were identified and solved in the past. In that case, the very analysis of present-day problems will urge a study of the theories formulated by our forerunners. If this is what pushes us to investigate the theoretical constructions of the past, the spirit in which we approach old theories will be different, in that we shall no longer be looking for analytical perfection but rather for the nature of the problems that were identified and analysed. In other words, the need of getting acquainted with old theories will not emerge as a mere obligation to pay a visit to the ruins of the past in order to ascertain the presence of anything useful. It will be part of current research.

4. A most illuminating example is contained in a basic indication that each of us gives to our first-year students when introducing the distinction between micro- and macroeconomics. The usual version is that microeconomics is the study of the rational behaviour of each agent, while macroeconomics is derived by aggregating the results of micro analysis so as to get a picture of the economic system in its entirety.

This general scheme allows of a number of different versions. The single agent may be assumed to be perfectly rational or moving within a range of imperfect knowledge and bounded rationality, his preferences may be assumed to be totally personal and independent or to be influenced by the social setting as well as by institutional constraints. The followers of each different version will maintain that theirs is a totally different construction of macroeconomics and that, far from being followers of the neoclassical tradition, they should be considered innovators, reformers and critics of the marginal school. In short, what the followers of the different schools do is to drop each time one of the basic assumptions of perfect competition. Just to mention a few patent cases: in the past, the usual simplification was to assume a perfectly transparent market, where any detail is known by every agent. Nowadays, information is commonly assumed to be imperfect and asymmetrical. Similarly, it used to be common to assume agents choose among given and certain alternatives, while it is now a must to assume uncertainty prevailing and to consider any value as being associated with a degree of probability. In the past, it was common to assume the agent to be endowed with the necessary knowledge and experience ever since his entry into the market; now agents are assumed to learn gradually and to acquire with effort the experience needed in order to take rational decisions. The traditional market was viewed as being populated by agents all alike and all enjoying the same rights and possibilities; nowadays, the fact is often stressed that, according to the prevailing institutional setting, different agents may meet different legal, political or social constraints and have access to different sets of goods (the teaching of A. K. Sen on this point is crucial). In the past, a theoretical analysis was considered adequate. Nowadays, no piece of work is considered really workmanlike unless it contains a mathematical model accompanied by the application of the more advanced quantitative techniques.

Still, in spite of modernisation taking place in so many different directions, the basic approach cannot be said to have changed a lot. The macro model, today as in the past, is built on the basis of micro foundations and derived from micro analysis by way of aggregation. This being the typical feature of neoclassical theory, a reasonable conclusion is that all the aforementioned versions are no more than variants of the traditional marginal approach.

The same conclusion is only reinforced if we consider the principles of economic policy implicitly contained in the theoretical approaches just mentioned. All those who emphasise the negative consequences of inadequate knowledge, asymmetrical information, poor working of the political institutions, can only reach one and the same policy recommendation: restore a transparent market, let information circulate freely, improve the working of institutions, and the drawbacks of the market will disappear. It seems clear that all those moving in such so-called critical streams are in fact modern followers of the Walrasian system of general economic equilibrium.

A totally different approach to macroeconomics can be detected only by going back to the founding fathers of economic theory. Neither Smith, Ricardo nor Malthus based their models on the analysis of individual behaviour. No doubt all of them here and there mentioned the behaviour of typical agents: the empirical remark made by Malthus that wage earners are too poor to create a market for luxuries, while entrepreneurs are too busy and have no time to enjoy the conveniences of life, is a clear example of the fact that none of them had forgotten the presence of single agents acting in the market. However, their starting point had little to do with individual behaviour. They rather started on a broad description of society, as made up of the three classes of landowners, wage earners and entrepreneurs, and their fundamental question was: under what conditions will a similar society be able to perpetuate itself in the future? Will the society be able to go on investing and growing or will it reach a final stationary state? These are already macroeconomic questions and the answers depend directly on the working of the whole system. In the Ricardian system, for instance, investments will be made provided profits are present, and profits will be present provided wages do not increase too much so that the marginal land allows a positive residual between average product and average real wage. In the Malthusian system, profits will be provided by the presence of some sort of autonomous expenditure on the maintenance of a number of unproductive wage earners.

The individualistic approach was to appear shortly after with such eminent scholars as Say and Senior. Their way of analysis was totally different, if compared with the classical approach, in that their starting point was the analysis of individual behaviour. The diffusion of marginal analysis after 1870 made the same tendency even stronger. Still, in spite of the triumph of marginal analysis in the late nineteenth century, a small number of divergent underground streams of thought survived, finally leading to the Keynesian revolution. The Keynesian system is based on questions not far from those raised by the classical authors. The first and foremost one is: what are the conditions for attaining full employment? The answer is that an adequate level of autonomous expenditure has to be reached, in the form of private investment, government expenditure or exports. The microeconomic requirements are inferred as a consequence of the macroeconomic equilibrium conditions: investors have to be adequately motivated, or the government has to come in with additional expenditure.

In all the aforementioned approaches, the requirements for the presence of a macroeconomic equilibrium are the first object of analysis. Individual behaviour is analysed in a second phase and deduced from the macro conditions as the behaviour that single agents should follow in order to make the perpetuation of the system possible. If a given society, having a given structure, is able to continue in existence, this means that the behaviour of agents, the institutional setting, the principles of the distribution of income, are all consistent with the same structure and therefore make it more and more solid.

The process of analysis is thus reversed. While in standard theory individual behaviour is reconstructed on the assumption of its being totally free and independent, in a true macroeconomic approach the behaviour of single agents is deduced as the only one being consistent with the whole that has been previously defined. In technical terms, while in traditional theory macroeconomics is deduced from microeconomic analysis, in a true macroeconomic approach the behaviour of individuals is deduced from the conditions of macroeconomic equilibrium. Similarly, while in the standard approach the role of an equilibrium position is of making individual choices mutually consistent, a true macroeconomic approach emphasises the presence of conflict among different social groups.

A true macro model can only be deduced from the initial definition of a macro equilibrium. If the starting point is the analysis of individual behaviour, the unavoidable result will be a neoclassical model or a close variant of it.

5. A conclusion to be drawn from the preceding remarks is that it is not enough to recommend the study of the history of economic thought. What we really need is to approach the theoretical body of the past with an eye to discovering the problems as they were seen by the authors of the time. The study of history is fruitful only when it opens new perspectives in the consideration of present-day economic and social problems. Paradoxically, I would say that what really matters is not whether the history of economic thought is studied or not, but *how* both current theory and the history of economic thought are studied. If current theory is well elaborated, the need of going back to the history of ideas will spontaneously emerge. If history is poorly studied, it will be of no help to theory.

This helps us to understand the reasons for the present-day neglect of the history of economic thought and for the often asserted aim of eliminating it altogether from the curriculum of an economist – two tendencies which raise well founded complaints. A similar attitude, as previously remarked, originates from the persuasion that theories of the past have been superseded by more modern and up-to-date formulations. But such persuasion is itself a consequence of the poor way of theorising that has become dominant nowadays.

It may appear, on a superficial observation of current economic theory, that teaching and research are divided into a number of differing and largely incompatible streams. This may be partly true. But a deeper inspection of the situation, especially if we consider the university teaching of economics, will reveal something different. In the past, economic theory was transmitted to the student as a multi-paradigm doctrine, resulting from a vast body of conflicting approaches, all having their own historical roots and a fully legitimate participation in the scientific debate. Nowadays, economics is taught as a one-paradigm doctrine, based on the implicit acceptance of the individualistic axioms and on the assumptions of maximisation and rational behaviour. The teaching of economics runs a high risk of becoming a kind of dogmatism, encouraging a passive attitude in students and suffocating any critical spirit.

The inevitable corollary of a similar approach to the teaching of economics is neglect of the history of economic thought or even open opposition to its inclusion in the basic curriculum of an economist. In addition the history of economic thought is considered to be a dangerous subject, in that it may reveal the existence of alternative heterodox approaches to economic problems, thus developing insane critical attitudes towards the standard dominant theory.

My conclusion is that if we want to restore the history of economic thought to the high standing it used to enjoy in the past, we should first revise the way in which economic theory is more and more largely taught nowadays.

Part II

The classical school and the Ricardo debate

> The building blocks of the unifying interpretative schema which is here suggested for the analysis of Ricardian theory . . . are, on the one hand, the concept of natural equilibrium, closely linked with the idea of a natural wage rate, which constitutes the pivot of the analysis both from the 'static' point of view (determination of prices and of the profit rate with a given technology) and from a 'dynamic' one (determination of the natural equilibrium growth path in the face of a changing agricultural 'technology'); and, on the other hand, the inseparable link between changes in technology . . . and changes in distribution.
>
> (Caravale 1985b: 129)

> 'the characteristic premise of surplus theories . . . [is, in Garegnani's words, that] the real wage and the social product are given *before* prices and the rate of profit are determined' (1981: 36). . . . Applying this interpretative schema to Ricardo's theory, Garegnani makes [the] relevant simplifying assumption . . . that 'fertile lands abound and that rent can therefore be ignored'. . . . This implies the impossibility of analysing the true essence of Ricardian theory, the inverse relation, that is, between the labour content of 'corn' and the general rate of profit – a relationship that expresses the basic class antagonism between *rentiers* and capitalists (with a given real commodity wage). The only possible antagonism remaining in Garegnani's interpretative context is that between *real* wages and profits.
>
> (Caravale 1985b: 168)

> [My approach] differs radically from that of the so-called 'New View' of the Ricardian theory . . . Hollander's interpretation of Ricardo depends on (1) practically eliminating Ricardo's identification of social categories, or classes, each disposing of its income in a specific fashion . . . and substituting for it the far less precise, and strict neoclassical, concept of a *consumer* with a given structure of preferences; and (2) attributing to Ricardo the idea that the wage is not a socio-historical datum, but a variable determined by the forces of supply and demand. Both of these hypotheses represent a profound alteration of Ricardo's thought.
>
> (Caravale 1985b: 178–80)

3 The canonical classical growth model

Content, adherence and priority

Samuel Hollander

> [Ricardo] and his chief followers . . . did not express their meaning with sufficient clearness, and they have been misunderstood by all but the most careful readers.
>
> (Marshall 1920: 84)

> Ricardo . . . has not been fortunate in finding careful students.
>
> (Cairnes 1874: 237)

Paul Samuelson, in his 'Canonical classical model of political economy' (1978), asserts that Adam Smith, David Ricardo, Thomas Malthus and J. S. Mill 'share in common essentially one dynamic model of equilibrium, growth and distribution', which 'agrees in behavioural essentials' with that understood by McCulloch, Senior, Bailey and various post-classical writers (Samuelson 1978: 1415, 1430). As I understand his paper, the term *canon* is used in the dictionary sense to mean a body of 'fundamental principles' excluding (as Samuelson puts it) 'misunderstandings' and 'semantics', 'negations and contradictions' – we are dealing with best-practice formulations; while *canonical*, also in the dictionary sense, implies 'authoritative, standard, accepted'. My investigation provides the textual evidence necessary to evaluate Professor Samuelson's assertions regarding the existence of a 'canon' relating to growth.

In the growth model in question, turning on the axiom of diminishing agricultural returns and a tacit belief that labour and capital are usually *complementary* inputs working the fixed land,[1] both the real wage rate and the profit rate tend downwards; the 'subsistence' wage rules in the stationary state alone and is reached simultaneously with that rate of profit corresponding to zero net capital accumulation. The downward wage path traces a 'dynamic equilibrium' path (the rates of growth of capital and labour proceeding in line), the precise breakdown between labour and capital of the incidence of diminishing returns depending on the particular elasticity properties of the factor-supply functions.[2]

Samuelson also attributes to the classics an approximation wherein the population supply 'adjusts so rapidly to any surplus of the real wage above subsistence that we can practically assume the truth of (what can be termed) Ricardo's 'short-circuited' approximation . . . the transient wage rate [being] insignificantly different from the long-run subsistence level' (ibid.: 1416). Certainly, with initial conditions representing a constant above-subsistence real wage, the more elastic the labour-growth function, the less will be the scope for any wage decline once diminishing returns are encountered. But this extreme elasticity is an empirical matter, not a matter of principle. Whether or not the wage decline is steep or shallow, rapid or slow, the essential feature of the canonical model[3] – to which, almost without exception, the writers we consider will be shown to have adhered – is *the necessarily simultaneous decline in wage and profit rates*. Several competent nineteenth-century (even modern) economists had trouble with this outcome, as we shall see, for it is not self-evident that the wage decline cannot insulate the profit rate from falling.

Much more is entailed by the alternative constant-wage version than a limiting case of shared incidence. The contrast has in fact become a matter of heated doctrinal debate: 'I am amazed to be told' – Stigler protested – 'that "all the evidence" points to Ricardo believing that the wage rate will fall secularly' (Stigler 1981: 101). Most significantly, the notion of a revolutionary break with classicism occurring in the 1870s turns partly on the rejection (as by W. S. Jevons) of the putative subsistence-wage model; whereas, to the contrary, 'Cambridge' or 'neo-Ricardian' writers applaud what, for them, is an archetypal form of sound analysis. Both reactions are to the same misconception – that classical growth theory either lacks (for the 'neo-classicists') or denies (for the 'neo-Ricardians') a *market-determined* solution for the secular wage rate. We are thus dealing with a major intellectual issue not the history of some technicality. But the significance of the issue extends beyond academic doctrinal history with its agendas; for the representation of 'classical' growth theory as a land-based model with population expanding at subsistence – a feature of the alleged 'Iron Law' doctrine – has filtered down to a broader public by way of sundry popularisers. Finally, the frequent inability of economists to comprehend one another in the present context may have wider implications regarding the profession.

I shall concentrate on the nineteenth-century British literature up until 1875. We should note that the Corn Law pamphleteers of February 1815 believed that Adam Smith lacked the diminishing-returns principle and its use in a land-based growth model (Malthus 1815: 39–40, 45–6; West 1815: 5–6, 39–40; Ricardo 1951–73 [1815], IV: 13 n., also Ricardo 1951–73 [1817], I: 374; Torrens 1820, IV: chapter I). There are certainly elements of the model in Smith's text. But the analysis is incomplete: while high wages and high profits are said to characterise early states not yet subject to land-scarcity constraints, the 'canonical' rationale for the downward course of wages in a deceleration of accumulation is not adequately spelled out (see Hollander 1995: chapters 19 and 20). And Smith did not ask why, given scope for a decline in the real wage, there should be a *necessary* reduction in the profit rate, and thus did not appreciate that the inverse wage–profit relation holds good in terms of proportionate shares, the falling secular wage entailing a necessary rise in labour's share in the declining 'marginal' product. There is also an uncoordinated 'increasing returns' component of Smith's economics which treats innovation as an endogenous variable.

The shared-incidence principle as it emerges in the formal writings of Malthus and Ricardo will be taken up in the next section. The exercise is extended in the following section to E. G. West, R. Torrens, James Mill, S. Bailey, J. R. McCulloch, T. Chalmers, N. Senior and J. E. Cairnes, a list including writers sometimes thought of as non- or even anti-Ricardian.[4] The evidence fully confirms Professor Samuelson's impressionistic judgement regarding a fundamental commonality of position. Two special cases are considered on pp. 51–3: that of J. S. Mill, who recognised the falling real wage but was ambiguous regarding the insulation of the profit rate; and that of Thomas De Quincey, a forceful Ricardian who yet adopted a constant-wage account – the only such case known to me.

These 'objective' sections are followed by two concerned with evaluation of Ricardo's position. Pages 53–5 concern Malthus's apparent failure to appreciate that Ricardo maintained the shared-incidence principle, though there are indications that he ultimately saw the light; and pp. 55–9 show that many other adherents to the canon – Senior, McCulloch and Cairnes are not guilty in this regard – also neglected Ricardo's true position. That our writers adhered to a 'canonical' or 'standard' position on shared incidence, yet in many instances failed to appreciate that Ricardo belonged to the club, is a major outcome of our investigation. Nearly all our authors did, however, pay tribute to Ricardo's inverse wage–profit relation as a *general* theorem regarding proportions. There was, in brief, wide recognition of Ricardo's inverse wage–profit relation *given* productivity (the wage–profit frontier), but wide neglect of his elucidations of inward displacements of the frontier with increasing land scarcity such as assure a contemporaneous decline in the returns to both variable factors.

Mountifort Longfield constitutes a unique case of an author who fully appreciated the falling wage and profit trends as a feature of 'orthodox' economics, but who rejected the canonical model on the (erroneous) grounds that the entire burden of diminishing returns might fall on labour. This case is considered on pp. 59–60.

Pages 60–62 consider matters of 'priority'. When account is taken of correspondence Ricardo emerges with precedence over Malthus. As for published texts, the Malthus and West contributions of February 1815 jointly take first prize (though subject to an 'error' of attributing the wage decline to *excess* population growth), for Ricardo's statement in his *Essay* of that month is defective and Torrens at that time maintained a subsistence-wage version. Evidently West arrived at his position before the publication date, but exactly when we cannot now say. On the other hand, it is very likely that Malthus learned much from Ricardo in early correspondence and personal contact.

Pages 62–3 touch briefly on the post-classicals, Walras and Jevons. Walras, strange as it may seem, adopted as his own a constant-wage growth model. But Jevons's case is equally fascinating, though in a different way, for Jevons attributed a subsistence-wage path to his predecessors and rejected their alleged position on the grounds that the burden of diminishing returns might 'chiefly' fall on labour. He had not the slightest notion that he was in effect proposing the *classical* 'shared incidence' principle.

Formal statements by Malthus and Ricardo

The essential proposition of Malthus's *Inquiry into Rent* of February 1815[5] is that, assuming ongoing growth of capital and labour, a fall in agricultural productivity depresses the profit rate, which – together with reductions in the corn-wage rate – ensures a payment for land services: 'But the accumulation of capital beyond the means of employing it on land of the greatest natural fertility, and the greatest advantage of situation, must necessarily lower profits; while the tendency of population to increase beyond the means of subsistence must, after a certain time, lower the wages of labour' (Malthus 1815: 17). This statement introduces *excessive* population growth into the picture, failing to emphasise that both profit and wage trends reflect precisely the same land-scarcity phenomenon. The weakness is absent in a brief reformulation: 'Rent . . . has been found to commence its separation from profits, as soon as profits and wages fall, owing to the comparative scarcity of fertile land in the natural progress of a country towards wealth and population' (ibid.: 20–1).[6]

There are splendid formulations of the principle of shared incidence in the fifth (1817) edition of the *Essay on Population*. The process entails deceleration of capital and population in consequence of the increasing exhaustion of 'cultivable land', and declining wage and profit rates until their respective minima are attained, at which point capital and population growth cease:

> long before [the] practical limit is attained in any country the rate of the increase of population will gradually diminish . . . [W]hen the capital of a country comes to a stop from the continued progress of accumulation and the exhaustion of the cultivable land, both the profits of stock and the wages of labour must have been gradually diminishing for a long period, till they are both ultimately so low as to afford no further encouragement to an increase of stock, and no further means for the support of an increasing population.
>
> (Malthus 1817, II: 433–4)[7]

In the *Principles*, constancy of the corn wage is represented as 'contrary to the actual state of things' and entailing a 'contradiction': for an initial real wage *above subsistence* to remain unchanged at that level implies constant population growth, despite the zero net capital accumulation characterising the ultimate stationary state; while an initial real wage *at subsistence* precludes population increase and 'the progressive cultivation of poorer land' (Malthus 1820: 297, 1836: 272–3). On the other hand, the fall in the real (corn) wage is constrained relative to that of the marginal product; accordingly, the effect of increasing land scarcity is to depress *both* the real wage and the profit rate until their respective minima, the profit rate varying inversely with labour's *proportionate share* in the marginal product, which necessarily rises despite the downward trend in the corn wage: 'if poorer land which required more labour were successively taken into cultivation, it would not be possible for the corn wages of each individual labourer to be diminished in proportion to the diminished product; a greater proportion [1836:

proportion] of the whole would necessarily go to labour [1836: to pay the wages of labour]; and the rate of profits would continue regularly falling till the accumulation of capital had ceased' (Malthus 1820: 298–9, 1836: 273–4). The precise incidence of diminishing returns is market determined: 'it would depend entirely upon the principles of demand and supply and competition, whether the increase in the price of corn would be such as to throw almost the whole of the increased difficulty of production upon labour, or such as to throw almost the whole of it upon profits, or finally such as to divide the loss more equally in various proportions between them [1836: . . . which is what generally happens]' (Malthus 1820: 336, 1836: 298). The message conveyed by all this, in a veiled criticism of Ricardo, is that 'no theory of profits . . . can approach towards correctness, which attempts to get rid of the principle of demand and supply and competition' (see also below, p. 54).

Ricardo's *Essay on Profits* turns on the assumptions 'that no improvements take place in agriculture, and that capital and population advance in the proper proportion, so that the real wages of labour, continue uniformly the same – that we may know what peculiar effects are to be ascribed to the growth of capital, the increase of population, and the extension of cultivation, to the more remote, and less fertile land' (Ricardo 1951–73, IV: 12). This justification of the working assumption of constant secular wages follows an allowance that profits would increase should population increase more rapidly than capital thus depressing wages, which neglects the fact that to remove wage fluctuations would not, on Ricardo's own terms before and after the *Essay* (see pp. 61–2), leave a constant wage path. At one juncture indeed Ricardo appears to deny a declining wage trend: 'The rise or fall of wages is common to all states of society, whether it be the stationary, the advancing, or the retrograde state. . . . As experience demonstrates that capital and population alternately take the lead, and wages in consequence are liberal or scanty, nothing can be positively laid down, respecting profits, as far as wages are concerned' (ibid.: 22–3). And on the basis of *constant* (though above-subsistence) real wages he constructed his famous agricultural model yielding a declining profit rate as capital and population are applied to increasingly disadvantageous plots of land (ibid.: 10, 13).[8]

All this is corrected in the *Principles*. There is first a statement that the 'market' wage may exceed the 'natural' or subsistence wage 'for an indefinite period':

> Notwithstanding the tendency of wages to conform to their natural [subsistence] rate, their market rate may, in an improving society, for an indefinite period, be constantly above it; for no sooner may the impulse, which an increased capital gives to a new demand for labour be obeyed, than another increase in capital may produce the same effect; and thus, if the increase in capital be gradual and constant, the demand for labour may give a continued stimulus to an increase of people.
>
> (Ricardo 1951–73, I: 94–5)

The growth rate of capital is *not*, however, constant; it accelerates in early periods 'when there is an abundance of fertile land', putting upward pressure on the real wage (ibid.: 98); and when ultimately diminishing returns set in, market pressures depress the real wage as the growth rate of labour demand decelerates. Notwithstanding Malthus's charge the formulation is explicitly expressed in demand–supply terms:

> In the natural advance of society, the wages of labour will have a tendency to fall, as far as they are regulated by supply and demand; for the supply of labourers will continue to increase at the same rate, whilst the demand for them will increase at a slower rate. If, for instance, wages were regulated by a yearly increase of capital, at the rate of 2 per cent, they would fall when it accumulated only at the rate of 1½ per cent. They would fall still lower when it increased only at the rate of 1, or ½ per cent, and would continue to do so until the capital became stationary, when wages also would become stationary, and be only sufficient to keep up the numbers of the actual population.
>
> (Ibid.: 101)

That the labour-supply growth rate (g_L) is constant – the 'supply of labour will continue to increase at the same rate' – implies a precipitous fall from some positive constant to zero when the wage actually reaches subsistence. But Ricardo seems to have allowed for some response of g_L to wage reductions from levels above but close to subsistence. This is suggested in the course of a translation into Ricardian 'money' terms, whereby commodity wages fall but the *money* wage (which 'measures' labour embodiment in the wage basket) rises, forcing down the return on capital:

> If . . . the money wages of labour should fall, whilst every commodity on which the wages of labour were expended rose, the labourer would be doubly affected, and would be soon totally deprived of subsistence. Instead, therefore, of the money wages of labour falling, they would rise; but they would not rise sufficiently to enable the labourer to purchase as many comforts and necessaries as he did before the rise in the price of those commodities.
>
> (Ibid.: 101–2)

It is precisely this rise in the money wage that causes the profit rate to fall despite the decline in the commodity wage. Ricardo's money wage also reflects *proportional* wages, the profit rate changing inversely with the share of wages in the constant value of the marginal product *per capita*.[9]

Other adherents to the shared-incidence principle

Edward West attempted to *prove* the phenomenon of diminishing agricultural productivity, presuming that the downward secular return on capital – taken to be an 'acknowledged fact' – is explicable solely by reference to that phenomenon (West 1815: 18, 25–6). The procedure contrasts with Ricardo's which perceives the 'principle' of diminishing returns as an *analytical* proposition holding good with technology given.

What now of the secular course of wages? West argued that movements of the real wage are governed by the *relative* growth rates of population and capital such that if 'the stock increases faster than the population, the demand increases faster than the supply, and wages must rise; if the stock and population increase equally, wages will remain stationary; and if population increase more rapidly than the stock, wages must fall' (ibid.: 23). Implicitly assuming a constant growth rate of population, he emphasised that the magnitude of any increase in real wage turns on the capital growth rate: 'Nor is it the greatness of the increase alone of stock which causes high wages, but it is the greatness of the ratio of the increase.' And the rate of increase in capital is in turn governed (*ceteris paribus*) by the profit rate: 'the greater . . . the profits of stock, if the country be equally parsimonious' – i.e. given the community's saving propensity – 'the greater the rate of the increase of stock' (ibid.: 24). West concluded that 'the greater the profits of stock the higher will be the wages of labour, and vice versa'. In brief, the profit and wage rates vary in the *same* direction such that the secular fall in the profit rate (assumed throughout) will be accompanied by a fall in the real wage rate. That the latter cannot compensate for the secular fall in agricultural productivity is taken for granted rather than proved: 'The powers of labour . . . in agriculture, becoming less productive, and the diminished expense [wage costs] of maintaining those powers not compensating such decreased productiveness . . . appears from the progressive fall of the profits of stock' (ibid.: 26). But the formulation starts out with the assertion that the real-wage movements turn on the *relative* growth rates of the factors which is technically erroneous – the 'dynamic equilibrium' wage path entails a falling trend notwithstanding a *common* decline.[10]

In his contribution of February 1815 Torrens recognised the depressing effects on profits flowing from reduced agricultural productivity: 'as a greater quantity of his labour, or (what is the same thing) of the produce of his labour, becomes necessary to the subsistence of the labouring manufacturer, and is consumed by him while at work, a smaller quantity of the productions of labour will remain with the employer' (Torrens 1815: 235). We recall also the contrast between Ricardo's *analytic* statement of the diminishing-returns principle and falling profit rate as holding good given technology and West's (and at times Malthus's) *empirical* formulations as holding good even when allowance is made for changing technology. Torrens too treated technical change somewhat as an 'exception' representing the war years as such (ibid.: 245). But nowhere did he recognise the simultaneous decline in the real wage and profit rates, for his argument proceeds on the strict assumption of a 'subsistence wage' in the technical sense of a real wage, assuring constant population (ibid.: xiv, 57–8, 62–6, 74, 92). In this respect, Torrens comes closest to 'textbook' Ricardianism.

In the 1826 and later versions of the *Essay* we do find the shared-incidence theorem:

> It is a principle capable of the most rigid and perfect demonstration, that increasing the productive cost and exchangeable value of food, and the materials of wrought necessaries, depresses the rate of profit. But when the rate of profit is depressed, the accumulation of capital is checked; and when

> the accumulation of capital is checked, the demand for labour and the real rate of wages are reduced.
>
> (Torrens 1826: 125–6, 127–8)

In an impressive appendix of 1829 Torrens clearly formulates the *balanced-growth* version of the canonical classical model and the limits to the wage path:

> When climate and custom have determined the point below which the reward of labour cannot fall, and when the quality of the soil, and the skill with which industry is applied, have fixed the maximum beyond which it cannot rise, then the ratio between population and capital . . . determines the intermediate point at which actual wages settle. But though labour and capital should go on increasing in the same proportion, and though they should constantly preserve the same ratio to each other, yet the necessity of resorting to inferior soils might gradually reduce the maximum of wages until it coincided with the extreme minimum, below which labour cannot be sustained. At this point the supply of labour could be no further increased.
>
> (Torrens 1829: 468–9; see also 1834: 21–2)

In his contribution 'Colony' (1818) for the *Encyclopaedia Britannica*, James Mill represents the 'habitual state of the population' as characterised by the subsistence wage. Apart from 'extraordinary cases . . . in which a country is but partially peopled, and in which part of the best land is still unemployed, the proposition of Mr. Ricardo is indisputable, that nothing can lower the wages of labour except a fall in the necessaries of the labourer' (quoted in Fenn 1991: 147). The *Elements* provides a fuller picture. Stigler, who considers Mill as subscribing to the constant-wage path such that 'the effects of diminishing returns in agriculture were to be borne only by profits' (Stigler 1990: 765), cites Mill from the chapter 'On profits':

> By the rise in the value of corn, the cost of maintaining labour is increased. A certain quantity of the necessaries of life must be consumed by the labourer, whether they cost little or much. When they cost more than they did before, his labour costs more than it did before; though the quantity of commodities which he consumes may remain precisely the same. His wages, therefore, must be considered as rising, though his real reward may not be increased.
>
> (J. Mill 1821: 61)[11]

But Stigler has erred. Mill's purpose here was to argue that the profit rate falls though the real wage rate should not *increase*. He did not maintain that a *declining* secular wage could insulate the profit rate from the effects of diminishing returns, as is clear from the chapter 'On wages': 'were [it] the natural tendency of population to increase faster than capital' – and this Mill purported to establish – '[t]here would be *a perpetual tendency in wages to fall*' until an equilibrium was achieved (ibid.: 29, emphasis added). Though Mill is technically in error – for the wage falls even if capital and population decelerate in tandem – he does describe a falling wage path.[12] He also emphasised the inverse wage–profit relation turning on a constant value of the marginal product (ibid.: 60). But he neglected to demonstrate that, in a system subject to increasing land scarcity, the proportionate share of labour necessarily rises as the real wage declines – for it is the *necessary* rise in labour's share of the marginal product, notwithstanding the decline of the wage in real terms, that depresses the profit rate. This weakness emerges also in the third edition:

> If a change in the quantity of commodities is meant, it will not be true, in that sense, that profits so depend upon wages, as to fall when wages rise, and rise when wages fall; *for both may fall, and both may rise together.* And this is a proposition that no political economist has called in question. If the powers of production are either increased or diminished, there will, in the one case, be more, in the other less, to divide. *The proportions remaining the same, both wages and profits will, in the one case, be raised, in the other depressed.*
>
> (J. Mill 1826: 72, emphasis added)

Bailey's *Inquiry* (1821)[13] presents elements of a dynamic-equilibrium version of the shared-incidence growth model:

> Supposing the degree of inclination to save and gain on the part of the capitalist, and to labour and to increase on the part of the labourer, to remain unaltered, or both to increase in equal proportions, the effect of increased cultivation in raising permanently the price of corn, would be borne partly by the labourer and partly by the employer: the labourer's [money] wages would not be raised in fully equal proportion with the price of corn, nor would they, on the other hand, remain quite stationary: profits would indeed fall, but the amount of the labourer's command of food would also be somewhat abridged.
>
> (Bailey 1821: 25)

He further clarifies that the profit rate varies with *proportionate* wages; simultaneously 'high' (low) profit and wage rates are quite consistent in conditions of high (low) productivity:

> Now where a little labour will produce a great deal, especially where it will produce a great deal of *food* in one country, compared to what it will in another, it is possible, that the *proportion* in which the produce is divided may be, in the former, more favourable to the employer than the latter, and, in the sense, profits may be said to be higher; and yet what the labourer gets may be more of absolute subsistence and enjoyment, in proportion to the quantity of trouble he takes, in the former than in the latter: and in *that* sense, *wages* may be said to be higher. This is, probably, the case in America.
>
> (Ibid.: 100)

The consistency of a simultaneous rise of wages and profits is also spelled out in the *Critical Dissertations* (Bailey 1825: 64 ff.).

In his exposition of Ricardian doctrine for the *Supplement to the Encyclopaedia Britannica* (1823), McCulloch spelled out the inverse wage–profit relation in the context of secular growth, indicating the joint incidence of diminishing returns:

> profits . . . do not depend on wages estimated in money, in corn, or any other commodity, but on PROPORTIONAL *wages, that is on the share of the commodities produced by the labourers, or of their value, which is given to him*. . . . In the advanced stages of society . . . proportional wages are high and profits low; but owing to the increased difficulty of production, these high proportional wages afford only a comparatively small supply of necessaries and conveniences.
>
> (McCulloch 1823: 56–7)[14]

Stigler (1990: 766) attributed to McCulloch a constant-wage model, citing an extract from the *Principles* which states that the burden of diminishing returns falls solely on capital. But the extract, which comes from the section on the profit rate (McCulloch 1825: 376–8), is obviously a first approximation, since in the previous section – devoted to the wage rate specifically – McCulloch had been crystal-clear regarding the secular fall in real wages:

> proportional wages may . . . be increased [and the profit rate thus fall] at the same time that wages, if estimated in silver, corn, or any other commodity, are reduced. . . . [W]hen cultivation is widely extended over lands of very inferior fertility, proportional wages are almost invariably high; but, owing to the increased difficulty that then obtains of producing supplies of food, these high proportional wages rarely afford a large supply of necessaries and conveniences.
>
> (Ibid.: 362–3)

Thomas Chalmers (like West) portrayed diminishing returns as an empirical rather than an analytical proposition; technical change or increased effort could not ultimately overcome the ‘absolute and impassable barrier’ imposed by land scarcity (Chalmers 1832: 17). In the absence of prudential population control the trend of both the wage and profit rates is inevitably downward until their respective minima (ibid.: 107, 110). Chalmers’s exposition is wanting in that each path is attributed to *excessive* expansion: ‘population through its excess, and the consequent lowering of wages, opens a way into inferior soils, which under higher wage, could not have been entered into . . . capital, through its excess, and the consequent lowering of profits, causes a similar descent, and so an extension of agriculture’ (ibid.: 108).[15]

The canonical model in its dynamic-equilibrium version is brilliantly formulated by Senior with attention to the downward trends of the factor returns to their respective minima under the market pressures generated by increasing land scarcity: ‘high wages and high profits have a tendency to produce their own diminution', for with both capital and labour 'increas[ing] in equal proportions' both wages and profits 'will have a tendency to fall, in consequence of the larger proportion which they will each bear to the power of the natural agents whose services they each require' (Senior 1836: 139). The declining wage rate, it is appreciated, reflects an increasing wage share in the marginal product: 'in general, the labourer is better paid, or, in other words, receives a larger amount of commodities, when profits are high, that is when he receives a small share, than when profits are low, that is when he receives a large share of the value of what he produces' (ibid.: 196–7).

An impressive formulation of the classical growth model is to be found in Cairnes's *Leading Principles*. J. S. Mill is cited to the effect that 'in all progressive countries, after a certain stage in their career is reached . . . the tendency of profits is to fall, and ultimately to approach the minimum which exists for each society' (Cairnes 1874: 216).[16] And there is reference also to a corresponding minimum wage rate, with the actual wage and profit rates lying somewhere above their respective minima and thus sharing the 'margin of return':

> To the share of the produce to be assigned to the labourer Nature has herself very obviously set a minimum limit in the requirements essential to his existence. . . . On the other hand, the capitalist's share also finds a minimum limit in his disposition and character. . . . But the produce may be indefinitely greater than this; and hence arises a margin of return over and above what the satisfaction of the minima of wages and of profits demands.
>
> (Ibid.: 273–4)

Full comprehension of the wage–profit relation is indicated by the fact that a general fall in the wage rate is shown to raise the profit rate specifically in the case of constant productivity: 'capitalists would gain what labourers had lost' (ibid.: 340, see also 205); whereas a fall of wages, 'on any other assumption' – one entailing also a fall in the profit rate – would inevitably imply diminished productiveness 'in some of the departments of productive industry'. The model is applied to explain the high real remuneration of American labour, in terms of 'low cost of production' due to 'the exceptional bounty of nature' (ibid.: 386); but with protection the prospect, indeed the actuality, was declining wage rates: 'the real remuneration of the United States labourer . . . has during the nine years ending 1868 positively fallen in a proportion not less than twenty per cent on his previous earnings' (ibid.: 392).[17]

The case of John Stuart Mill

J. S. Mill insisted on a regular functional relation between savings and the profit (interest) rate: 'The greater the profit that can be made from capital, the stronger is the motive to its accumulation' (J. S. Mill 1965 [1848], II: 161): 'it is . . . an almost infallible consequence of any reduction of profits, to retard the rate of accumulation' (ibid., III: 843). A minimum return on capital is also defined at which rate 'no further increase of capital can for the present take place' (ibid., III: 738).

A formal contrast is made between circumstances where land scarcity is not yet manifest such that an increase in population can proceed at its 'utmost rate' without pressure on the real wage rate, and situations where this possibility is ruled out because of impediments to the rate of accumulation: 'The increase of capital is checked because there is not fresh land to be resorted to, of as good quality as that already occupied' (ibid., II: 344). This particular formulation is wanting if intended to imply that the real wage would *not* decline in the event of population growth rate falling short of the maximum rate but corresponding with decelerating capital accumulation.

There is a related ambiguity turning on the possibility of ongoing factor expansion with the wage constrained to a constant level *exceeding subsistence*: 'We shall suppose [population and capital] . . . to increase with equal rapidity; the test of equality being, that each labourer obtains the same commodities as before, and the same quantity of those commodities' (ibid., III: 723). In this case:

> Population having increased, without any falling off of the labourer's condition, there is of course a demand for more food. The arts of production being supposed stationary, this food must be produced at an increased cost. To compensate for this greater cost of the additional food, the price of agricultural produce must rise . . . [and] wages, being supposed to be the same in quantity, will be greater in cost. The labourer obtaining the same amount of necessaries, money wages have risen; and as the rise is common to all branches of production, the capitalist cannot indemnify himself by changing his employment, and the loss must be borne by profits.
>
> (Ibid.)

Capital accumulation and population growth can thus proceed at the same rate with the return on capital *declining* – so that, considering the savings–interest relationship always insisted upon, the common factor growth rate must also be decelerating – and the wage rate *constant*. Now this outcome is formally consistent with the Malthusian 'prudential' version of the 'canonical' model (see above, notes 7, 15, 17). Yet according to the standard version the wage declines *notwithstanding* a simultaneous deceleration of factor growth. (All depends on whether the population growth curve is stable or not.) Unfortunately, one cannot be sure that Mill fully appreciated the point, for he intimated that a wage decline occurs only if the population growth rate *exceeds* the capital growth rate: 'Even in a progressive state of capital, in old countries, a conscientious or prudential restraint on population is indispensable, to prevent the increase of numbers from outstripping the increase of capital, and the condition of the classes who are at the bottom of society from being deteriorated' (ibid., III: 753).

There are further problems. Mill observed (in the standard case) that the 'margin' for a falling real wage is 'a very narrow one' if the 'avenues to an increased supply of food' – domestic technological change, easier food imports – be closed 'and population continued to increase, as it is said to do, at the rate of a thousand a day' (ibid., III: 740). In these circumstances 'the fall of profits would be retarded *if money wages did not rise*, or rose in a less degree [than the corn price]; but the margin which can be gained by a deterioration of the labourers' condition is a very narrow one: in general they *cannot* bear much reduction; when they can, they have also a higher standard of necessary requirements, and *will* not' (ibid., III: 740–1, emphasis added). This passage, though it confirms an initially above-subsistence wage and a downward trend, is problematic, first because the money wage rate *necessarily* rises, and secondly, because no matter what the 'margin which can be gained by a deterioration of the labourers' condition', the profit rate can never be entirely insulated.

Thomas De Quincey: a constant-wage theorist

Of self-confessed 'Ricardians' De Quincey is the only one known to me who himself adopted a subsistence-wage growth process. In the *Logic of Political Economy* the secular implications for the profit rate are illustrated entirely by reference to Ricardo's arithmetical example in the *Principles* (chapters 5 and 6) involving a constant mixed-wage basket (De Quincey 1897 [1844]: 224–5, 246, 253). Allusion is made to 'decaying' wages as well as to decaying profits (ibid.: 247), not in the canonical sense of a market process, but rather as an *arithmetic* outcome, again as in Ricardo's tables (ibid.: 256, 267). The elucidation of money wages as an index of labour's proportionate share is similarly rehearsed with no indication of a decline in the commodity wage and the consistency of such decline with a rising money wage (ibid.: 257). De Quincey conceded only that the constant-basket analysis is incomplete and requires allowance for 'the proportion which capital bears to labour' (ibid.: 292), as Malthus insisted. But this, so it seems, affects *market* wages only by way of fluctuations in the relative growth rates of capital and labour, a modification that Ricardo is said to have recognised.

Malthus on Ricardo

Malthus's representation of the shared incidence of diminishing returns as subject to the principles of 'demand and supply and competition' is directed against Ricardo. In the same vein, exception is taken to Ricardo's definition of the 'natural price of labour' as 'that price which is necessary to enable the labourers one with another to subsist, and to perpetuate their race, without either increase or diminution' (Malthus 1820: 247, 1836: 223). The objection is to the term 'natural', since that wage rate could only be expected to rule in the exceptional stationary state: 'This price I should really be disposed to call a most unnatural price. . . . But if this price be really rare, and, in an ordinary state of things, at so great a distance [1836: at a great distance] in point of time, it must evidently lead to great errors to consider the market prices of labour as only temporary deviations above and below that fixed price, to which they will very soon return'. Here we have the common error of reading Ricardo as positing a subsistence wage during the course of growth about which the market wage fluctuates without lengthy deviation. For Malthus, temporary fluctuations of the real wage occur about a secular path that tends towards the minimum, which is attained only in the far-distant stationary state (Malthus 1820: 247, 1836: 224). And in the second edition he expressly draws a parallel with the profit rate in line with this perspective: 'We might with almost as much propriety [as Ricardo's definition of the natural wage] define the natural rate of *profits* to be that rate which would just keep up the capital without increase or decrease. This is in fact the rate to which profits are constantly tending' (Malthus 1836: 224).

This same line is followed in a further analysis of the effect on profits of real-wage fluctuations, where Malthus complained that 'notwithstanding the utter inadequacy of this single cause [diminishing agricultural returns] to account for existing phenomena, Mr. Ricardo, in his very ingenious chapter "On Profits", has dwelt on no other' (Malthus 1820: 308). It was merely a truism to say that 'if the value of commodities be divided between labour and profits, the greater is the share taken by one, the less will be left for the other, or in other words that profits fall as labour rises, or rise as labour falls' (ibid.: 310);

> for [w]e can know little of the laws which determine profits, unless . . . we explain the causes which award a larger or a smaller share of . . . necessaries to each labourer. And here it is obvious that we must have recourse to the great principles of demand and supply, or to that very principle of competition brought forward by Adam Smith, which Mr. Ricardo expressly rejects, or at least considers as of so temporary a nature as not to require attention in a general theory of profits.
>
> (Ibid.: 310–11)

It may be added that Malthus drew a parallel between 'the laws which regulate the rate of profits and the progress of capital' and those which regulate the rate of wages and the progress of population', accepting but granting Ricardo priority for the falling profit rate with increasing land scarcity, and claiming for himself in the *Essay on Population* priority for the falling real wage owing to the same cause (ibid.: 370–1, 1836: 327). It is not clear from this whether he attributed the falling wage path to Ricardo. But in the chapter 'On rent', which spells out the principle of shared incidence, Malthus seems to concede that there are no differences other than linguistic ones between himself and Ricardo:

> When a given portion of labour and capital [1836: a given value of capital] yields smaller returns whether on new land or old, the loss is generally divided between the labourers and capitalists, and wages and profits fall at the same time. This is quite contrary to Mr. Ricardo's language. But the wages we refer to are totally different. He speaks of the cost [1836: mere labour cost] of producing the necessaries of the labourer; I speak of the necessaries themselves.
>
> (Malthus 1820: 154, 1836: 152)[18]

There is a further indication of a recognition of Ricardo's position regarding shared incidence. In late correspondence with William Whewell, Malthus maintained that Richard Jones in his *Rent* (1831) went too far in objecting to Ricardo:

> I am not sure . . . whether he has not gone beyond the truth in his unwillingness to admit the *tendency* of continued accumulation, and of the progress of population and cultivation to lower the rates of profits and corn wages on the land;. . . . If the progress of cultivation and population has no tendency to diminish corn wages, I do not see what cause should ever retard the rate at which population is known to increase in the new colonies.
>
> (28 February 1831; De Marchi and Sturges 1973: 386)

Moreover, despite Malthus's description of Ricardo's proportionality theorem – the inverse wage–profit relation – as a 'truism', his own analysis of the downward trend path of wage and profit rates proceeds in terms of proportions (Malthus 1820: 299, 1836: 274). And there is new support for the theorem in the second edition: 'whether the productive powers of labour are great or small, increasing, stationary, or diminishing . . . profits depend upon the proportion of the value of the whole produce, which goes to pay the wages of the labour employed to obtain it' (Malthus 1836: 267). That Malthus was warming to Ricardo's contribution is also confirmed in his *Measure of Value*, where he criticised Ricardo's (alleged) failure to deal satisfactorily with real wage-rate determination, but conceded frankly that Ricardo, by his proportionality theorem, had 'amply compensated for the errors into which he may have fallen, by furnishing us, at the same time, not only with the means of their refutation, but the means of improving the science of Political Economy' (Malthus 1823: 29).

Other evaluations of Ricardo

Several of his contemporaries and immediate successors – including West, Bailey, and J. S. Mill – neglected Ricardo's adherence to the shared-incidence principle.

In a charge by West against Ricardo of plagiarism – 'Most of the propositions enunciated in [West's 1815] essay were adopted by Mr. Ricardo in his Principles of Political Economy' (West 1826: v) – no explicit mention is made of the simultaneous secular decline in profit and real wage rates expounded in 1815 (see above, p. 47). But in his conclusion West explicitly claims that Ricardo was unaware of it: 'the diminution of the rate of reproduction will not fall upon profits alone, as Mr. Ricardo supposes, but it must inevitably fall in part upon the price or reward of labour' (ibid.: 135). This assertion is preceded by the proposition – again West is unaware that it was Ricardo's (see above, p. 46) – that '[t]he money price of labour would rise, but it could not rise in proportion to the enhanced price of food'. Moreover, West maintained that Ricardo had neglected the dependence of the wage rate on the rate of accumulation (ibid.: 64–5) – a criticism that flies in the face of Ricardo's explicit formulation of this relation.[19]

Bailey rejected Smithian 'competition of capitals' (Bailey 1821: 9 f., 13 f., 18), and adopted a land-scarcity explanation of profit-rate trends but ignored Ricardo's contribution to the 'canonical' model wherein the real wage is necessarily above the subsistence wage throughout the expansion process. Thus he cites first Ricardo's chapter 'On profits': 'There cannot be accumulated in a country any amount of capital which cannot be employed *productively* . . . until wages rise so high in *consequence* of the rise of necessaries, and so little consequently remains for the profits of stock, that the motive for accumulation ceases' (ibid.: 19), and allows only that Ricardo recognised 'temporary' increases in the wage, which reduce the profit rate, but have a tendency to restore themselves.

J. S. Mill neglected Ricardo's appreciation of above-subsistence wages subject to secular decline. This surprising fact emerges in an analysis of the effects of an increase in the corn price such that money wages rise to compensate, either by way of death-rate increase and positive population reduction assuming wages to be initially at *physiological* subsistence, or by way of birth-rate decrease assuming wages to be initially at *psychological* subsistence (J. S. Mill 1965 [1848], II: 340). Mill objected:

> Mr. Ricardo considers these two cases to comprehend all cases. He assumes, that there is everywhere a minimum rate of wages: either the lowest with which it is physically possible to keep up the population, or the lowest with which the people will choose to do so. To this minimum he assumes that the general rate of wages always tends; that they can never be lower, beyond the length of time required for a diminished rate of increase to make itself felt, and can never long continue higher. This assumption contains sufficient truth to render it admissible for the purposes of abstract science. . . . But in the application to practice it is necessary to consider that the minimum of which he speaks, especially when it is not a physical, but what may be termed a moral minimum, is itself liable to vary. If wages were previously so high that they could bear reduction, to which the obstacle was a high standard of comfort habitual among the labourers, a rise in the price of food . . . may operate in two ways: it may correct itself by a rise of wages brought about through a gradual effect on the prudential check to population; or it may permanently lower the standard of living of the class, in case their previous habits in respect of population prove stronger than their previous habits in respect of comfort. In that case the injury done to them will be permanent, and their deteriorated condition will become a new minimum, tending to perpetuate itself as the more ample minimum did before.
>
> (Ibid., II: 340–1)

It is noteworthy that Mill does *not* object to the assumption of a psychological 'subsistence' wage as such, but rather to ascribing firmness to it, on the grounds (very much like Marx's) that standards can degenerate. It none the less remains true that Mill gives no indication of Ricardo's insistence upon *above-subsistence* wages during the course of growth and on the contrary ascribes to him rapid responses such that wages 'can never long continue higher'. As for his own position in that regard, it will be recalled that even he perceived only a 'very narrow margin' for any wage decline (see above, pp. 52–3).

Mill did, however, pay tribute to Ricardo for the inverse relation as a theorem regarding proportions, the profit rate depending on the 'cost of labour' (labour embodied in wages) identified with labour's proportional share (ibid., II: 413). And, in the context of a money economy, he defined an inverse relation between the profit rate and the *money* wage rate in Ricardo's manner (ibid., III: 696).

Three of our contributors stand apart: McCulloch, Senior and Cairnes. McCulloch himself expounded the principle of shared incidence correctly (see above, p. 50). In this account, no formal attribution is made to Ricardo's *Principles*. But since his contribution to the *Encyclopaedia* represents an account of 'Ricardian' economics, and since on other crucial matters McCulloch did not always cite Ricardo, though evidently he had Ricardo's text before him,[20] there is a high likelihood that the principle of shared incidence was understood to be Ricardo's position. Moreover, had McCulloch laid claim to novelty, he would doubtless have said so.[21] The inverse wage–profit relation as a matter of proportionality – if not its use as rationale for shared incidence – is certainly derived from Ricardo (McCulloch 1823: 51).

In his methodological essays, Senior complained that Ricardo adopted 'arbitrarily assumed premises', including constant commodity wages in the analysis of growth and wage taxation (Senior 1852: 63–4). Yet he paid warm tribute to Ricardo for the inverse wage–profit relation as a proportionality theorem upon which he himself based the shared-incidence principle (Senior 1830: 99–100). And in the *Outline of the Science of Political Economy* there is an indication that he came to recognise Ricardo's falling wage trend:

> In ordinary language, Wages means the *amount of some commodity*, generally of silver, given to the labourer in return for a given exertion; and they rise or fall, as that amount is increased or diminished. In the language of Mr. Ricardo, they usually mean the labourer's *proportion of what is produced*, supposing that produce to be divided between him and the Capitalist. In this sense they generally rise as the whole [marginal] produce is diminished; though, if the word be used in the other sense, they generally fall.
>
> (Senior 1836: 238)

Admittedly, the fall in the real wage alluded to might be the perspective of Senior himself and not one attributed to Ricardo; but Senior also insisted that it is to misunderstand Ricardo to attribute to him the incompatibility of high wages and high profits or low wages and low profits using the terms in their normal sense:

> many of his followers and opponents have supposed the words high and low to be used by him as indicative of quantity, not proportion. The consequence has been that since the publication of his great Work, an opinion has prevailed that high wages and high profits are incompatible, and that whatever is taken from the one is added to the other.
>
> (Ibid.: 143)

Cairnes insisted on the Ricardian logic to the principle of shared incidence – that is, on the inverse wage–profit relation as a proposition regarding proportions such that both the wage and profit rates can move in the same direction under appropriate productivity conditions:

> Throughout the foregoing discussion it has been constantly assumed that an advance of wages involves as a consequence, *ceteris paribus*, a fall of profits. I beg to call the reader's attention to the condition here presupposed; for I observe, in some recent publications in which the relation of profits to wages is discussed, that there is an entire omission on the part of the writers to say whether, in challenging the doctrine just stated, they understand it as subject to, or irrespective of, this qualification.
>
> (Cairnes 1874: 235–6)

All depends on 'the efficiency of labour' presupposed; only in the case of constant productivity does a real wage change entail an inverse movement in the profit rate. That was precisely Ricardo's contribution:

> In truth, it is pretty clear that the entire controversy on this subject has arisen from some people not taking the trouble to understand what other people say. Ricardo, for example, has laid it down that profits are inversely as wages, but any tolerably careful student of Ricardo would see that by wages he meant 'proportional wages' – that is to say, the labourer's share of the product, or, if wages in the ordinary sense, then that the statement was to be received subject to the condition that the efficiency of labour remained the same. *Ricardo, however, has not been fortunate in finding careful students*; and scores of writers who have undertaken to refute his doctrine have in reality refuted only their own misconception of it.
>
> (Ibid.: 236–7, emphasis added)[22]

Two cases are a little ambiguous, those of Torrens and James Mill. Torrens paid warm tribute to Ricardo, whose 'great-work' had 'thrown new and important light upon almost every question connected with the distribution of wealth' (Torrens 1820: xviii); and he protested at Malthus's failure to recognise Ricardo's appreciation that the profit rate is affected by variations in the real wage as well as by the difficulty of production on the land (*The Traveller*, No. 6624, 26 April 1820).[23] None the less, there is no explicit indication that his own abandonment of a constant-wage for a declining-wage growth model in the 1826 *Essay* (see above, p. 47) owed anything to a rereading of the *Principles*.

As for James Mill, we have encountered his attribution to Ricardo in 1818 of a constant-wage axiom. In the early edition of the *Elements* we find the same attribution:

> If wages are already at the lowest point, to which they can be reduced; that is, just sufficient to keep up the number of labourers, and no more; the state of wages which seems to have been contemplated, by Mr. Ricardo,

> throughout his disquisitions on political economy, and which the tendency of population to increase faster than capital, undoubtedly leads us to regard as the natural state; no tax can fall upon the labourer.
>
> (J. Mill 1824: 253)

Yet there is also the observation in the 1826 edition that 'no political economist [had] called in question' the simultaneous decline in wage and profit rates in the event of diminishing productivity (see above, p. 49). Could Mill have been of two minds?

The case of Mountifort Longfield

Mountifort Longfield seems to be the only major British writer to *recognise but reject* the 'canonical' growth model. He appreciated that the model necessarily entails a wage exceeding subsistence (or else population growth could not occur), but objected to its 'unwarrantable' assumption that the burden of diminishing returns could not fall entirely on labour:

> The proof usually given of the theory to which I have alluded, may be thus briefly stated. When inferior lands are taken into cultivation to satisfy the increasing wants of the society, the same amount of labour and fixed capital produces a less return than before; but this diminution will not, and cannot, entirely fall upon the wages of labour, since the labourer could not support himself and family if it took place; some part of it must therefore fall upon the profits of agricultural capital.
>
> (Longfield 1834: 183)

This presumption Longfield disputed – the entire incidence might fall on labour:

> In the argument used to prove that the decreasing fertility of the soil is the great and necessary cause of a decline of profits, it is, I conceive, unwarrantably assumed, that the effect cannot be entirely borne by the labourer, and that therefore of necessity some part of it must fall upon capital. This necessity I cannot perceive. As population was advancing, the wages of labour must have been more than what would be necessary to the subsistence of the labourers, with such families as would keep up an unvarying population; they may sustain some reduction, and why not the entire amount of the reduction that has taken place in the returns made to labour and capital? It should be remembered that these diminutions in the returns to capital and labour proceed by imperceptibly small differences, and not by sudden steps, and that as long as population increases, the labourer may sustain some reduction in his wages.
>
> (Ibid.: 184–5)

The representation of the orthodox model is accurate, but the criticism is wholly misplaced, for the fall in the wage is limited relatively to the fall in the marginal product, so that proportionate wages *necessarily* rise, thereby depressing the profit rate.

Longfield also mistakenly believed that the orthodox model neglected the breakdown of the shared incidence of diminishing returns. He himself could see no way of allocating the burden, except in the stationary state:

> And even if the labourer cannot bear the entire reduction, and continue to support himself and his family as usual out of the diminished wages, what is it that determines how large a portion of the reduction shall be borne by *him*, and how much, from *his* inability to bear the whole, will be thrown upon the capitalist? . . . Even on the principle against which I am contending, I see no way of determining how much of the diminution the labourer can bear, except by leaving him such wages only as shall be sufficient for his subsistence, and that of such a family, on an average, as shall sustain a merely stationary population. This cause, therefore, of a reduction of profits, can only operate at the period when population ceases to increase.
>
> (Ibid.: 185)

In alluding to the orthodox position Longfield specified by name only West and McCulloch (ibid.: 182–3), not Ricardo. But he does refer more generally to 'supporters of this system' (ibid.: 184), and to the theory he opposed as one 'adopted by most of the English writers on Political-Economy' (ibid.: vii).

The question of priority

A. A. Brewer raises the question of 'priority' with respect to the dynamic equilibrium growth model involving the simultaneous determination of the wage and profit rates:

> Modern commentators have interpreted Ricardo's *Principles* (1817) in terms of a model of dynamic labour market equilibrium substantially identical to West's model . . . ; this is the 'new view' of Ricardo. . . . They have not, as far as I know, given West credit for it. Unlike West, Ricardo did not set the argument out explicitly. The main evidence cited to support the 'new view' is that the model is consistent both with Ricardo's assumptions and with his conclusions. . . . It is not surprising that this evidence can be found in Ricardo, since the assumptions are in essence those of Smith, while the conclusions are to be found in Smith as well, though admittedly intermixed with conflicting assertions. West's contribution was to set the argument out formally and clearly; he also has clear priority, at least over Ricardo's *Principles* (1817).
>
> (Brewer 1988: 512)

Brewer is correct to attribute the canonical model to West, though West focuses on *differential* factor growth rates in discussing the downward wage trend. But Brewer says nothing of Malthus, whose *Rent* appeared a week before West's

Essay. It would be more accurate to attribute priority in print to both Malthus and West, subject in Malthus's case too to the same qualification. 'Fool-proof' statements are provided by Malthus in 1817 and 1820. As for Ricardo, his *Essay* assumes wage constancy – though not at subsistence – and neglects entirely the shared-incidence principle. But that principle *is* explicitly formulated in the *Principles*, on which matter I part company with Brewer.

When one extends the canvas to include correspondence the picture changes radically. A letter from Ricardo to Malthus of 23 October 1814 contests a contention that Ricardo's land-based growth model could not account for the relatively low profit rate 'often' observed in low-density economies, and conversely in the case of high-density economies. This Ricardo rejected on the grounds that, in the first category, it would be found that real wages were 'enormously' high (constituting a major source of savings), and 'may be considered as part of the profits of stock'; and, in the second, that they were 'too low', apparently *artificially* depressed: 'too large a portion of the gross produce is retained by the owner of stock, and is reckoned as profit' (Ricardo 1951–73, VI: 147). This passage implies that with appropriate classification of 'profits' the declining profit trend would be apparent, notwithstanding the downward trend of wages. On 18 December he explicitly argued that the increasing incidence of diminishing returns is necessarily shared by both capitalists and labourers:

> A diminution of the proportion of produce, in consequence of the accumulation of capital, does not fall wholly on the owner of stock, but is shared with him by the labourers. *The whole amount of wages paid will be greater, but the portion paid to each man, will in all probability, be somewhat diminished.*
>
> (Ibid.: 162–3, emphasis added)

Ricardo's subscription to the joint-incidence principle also emerges in post-*Essay* correspondence: 'Observe that I do not question that each individual labourer might receive a less corn price of labour because I believe that would be the case' (ibid., 14 March 1815: 189). On 8 May he maintained that a rise in the real wage reflecting upward pressure in the labour market would be at the expense of profits, unless the upward movement were accompanied by technical progress: 'wages even if they should rise would not lessen profits, they will only keep them lower than they otherwise would be' (ibid.: 226–7). Now if *rising* real wages and profit rates are consistent, assuming increasing productivity, then presumably *falling* real wage and profit rates are consistent, assuming diminishing returns. And this is confirmed in a letter of 10 January 1816 insisting on the consistency of a rising money wage – which for Ricardo implies a falling profit rate – notwithstanding the real wage decline:

> I cannot think it inconsistent to suppose that the money price of labour may rise when it is necessary to cultivate poorer land, whilst the real price may at the same time fall. Two opposite causes are influencing the price of labour: one the enhanced price of some of the things on which wages are expended, – the other the fewer enjoyments which the labourer will have the power to

> command, – you think they may balance each other, or rather that the latter will prevail. I on the contrary think the former the more powerful in its effects. I must write a book to convince you.
>
> (Ricardo 1951–73, VII: 10)

The fall in productivity necessarily outweighs that of the real wage, forcing up the money wage and thus reducing the profit rate.

As for Malthus, he had positively denied on 6 July 1814 that reduced agricultural productivity lowers the profit rate, on the grounds that the incidence will fall on labour alone: 'The effects of a great difficulty in procuring corn would in my opinion be, a diminution of capital, a diminution of produce, and a diminution in the real wages of labour, or their price in corn; but not a diminution of profits' (Ricardo 1951–73, VI: 111). Malthus was, therefore, suggesting that profits would be completely insulated from diminishing returns. Only in autumn 1814, under pressure from Ricardo, did he concede a direct effect of land scarcity on the profit rate, though there remained hints that he had not completely abandoned the notion of 'insulation' (Hollander 1997: chapter 2).

An excursus on the post-classical

As a final matter I shall briefly address an aspect of Paul Samuelson's belief that the canonical classical model was subscribed to by late nineteenth-century 'neoclassicals' and moderns – that 'they all tell essentially the same classical story', for Samuelson denies (I believe correctly) that classical political economy offers an '*alternative paradigm* – in the sense of Thomas Kuhn . . . – to modern mainstream economics' (Samuelson 1978: 1430, 1415).

As for the 'post-classicals', it is worth noting a complexity. Part VII of Walras's *Elements* (The 'Conditions and consequences of economic progress') deals with the distributional implications of expanding labour and capital, given land: 'What does need to be discussed . . . in view of its extremely weighty consequences, is the fact . . . that the quantity of land cannot possibly increase though it is possible to increase the number of persons and the quantity of capital goods proper in an economy that saves and converts its savings into capital' (L. Walras 1954 [1874]: 382). Now his system of equations generates 'the *laws of the variation of prices in a progressive economy*', and include the proposition that '*In a progressive economy, the price of labour (wages) remaining substantially unchanged*' – an assumption – '*the price of land-services (rent) will rise appreciably and the price of capital-services (the interest charge) will fall appreciably*' (ibid.: 390–1). With his 'Ricardo-like' model Walras out-Ricardoes Ricardo.[24]

The position of W. S. Jevons is equally striking though in a different way. Jevons attributed to the British writers a constant wage and implied that he himself saw merit in shared-incidence: 'It is the accepted opinion of writers of the present day, that the rate of interest tends to fall because the soil does not yield proportionate returns as its cultivation is pushed. But I must hold that this decrease in the proportionate returns would chiefly fall upon the wages of the labourer' (Jevons 1862: 287). Again, in a lecture of 1875 he objected to the subsistence-wage growth concept (attributed to Ricardo and Malthus) on the grounds that 'every enlargement of our resources only tends to land us in a larger . . . but more straightened population' (Jevons 1977, VI: 60). As expressed by Peart:

> Jevons's argument, whereby (in the absence of technological innovation) there must be a tendency for the real wage to fall eventually as a result of resource scarcity, is contrasted here to the position mistakenly attributed to Malthus and Ricardo whereby the wage rests at a minimum in a growing economy with short-run increases that elicit labour supply responses.
>
> (Peart 1990: 39)

Jevons had no inkling that the position he was forwarding was precisely that of the orthodoxy from whose grip he sought to escape.[25]

Conclusion

This study has confirmed Paul Samuelson's position on the existence of a 'canonical' classical model of growth characterised by the shared incidence of diminishing agricultural returns between labour and capital. Nearly all the expert or properly qualified economists adopted the position, including – rather surprisingly – James Mill and McCulloch. J. S. Mill's formulations are, however, ambiguous in some respects; De Quincey proceeded formally with the fixed-wage assumption; and Longfield recognised but rejected (on untenable grounds) the canonical falling-wage version.

It has also emerged that adherence to the shared-incidence model turns more on the logic of the case than on appeal to authority. There is absent a leader equivalent to Quesnay in eighteenth-century France. While warm tribute was widely paid to Ricardo for the inverse wage–profit relation or the proportionality theorem, he was neglected by a considerable number – most conspicuously by J. S. Mill – as an adherent to the shared-incidence principle.[26] However, McCulloch, Senior, Cairnes and probably Longfield did appreciate his position. And there are even hints that Malthus, somewhat begrudgingly, may have realised his error.

Now, the difficulties impeding an unqualified attribution of the 'canonical' model to Adam Smith (including reconciliation of those features of the model that indubitably exist in the *Wealth of Nations* with the increasing-returns component of that work) are all absent in Ricardo's case. He clearly outlined the principle of joint incidence in informal contexts and in the *Principles*; indeed, he has precedence over Malthus for it, his constant-wage formulation in the *Essay on Profits* falling short of his own best practice. He insisted that relevant for profit-rate analysis is *proportionate* wages, to which end he sought an appropriate measuring device in terms of which a rise in wages, notwithstanding the secular fall in the *real* wage, implies a rise in the proportionate share of wages in the net product to be distributed between labourers and capitalist. That many readers neglected Ricardo's contribution to the shared-incidence principle, and failed to realise that the inverse wage–profit relation – which they acknowledged having learned from Ricardo – was applied by him to explain that very principle, constitutes a problem in itself.

Notes

I owe much to Paul Samuelson for his instructive and patient advice. Thanks are also due to Larry Moss, Brenda Spotton, André Lapidus, Elizabeth Huck, Ingrid Peters-Fransen and Tony Brewer. I alone, of course, bear responsibility for the final outcome.

1 In cases where a competitive relation pertains – as in Ricardo's analysis of machinery in his *Principles* of 1821 – additions to capital will depress the real wage while raising the return on produced inputs, so that the penultimate movements of the wage and interest rates are in opposite directions. Factor independence, a singular case, would permit non-shared incidence.

2 For accounts of the underlying technical concepts see also Baumol (1970: chapter 2), especially the qualifications, pp. 20–1; Hollander (1995: chapters 7–9).

3 By 'best practice' formulation I intend the standard imposed by the writers in question, not by present technical knowledge. This needs to be said, since George Stigler proposed the following interpretative rule whereby to 'maximize the value of a theory to the science': 'The man's central theoretical position is isolated *and stated in a strong form* capable of contradiction by the facts. The net scientific contribution, if any, of the man's work is thus identified, *amended if necessary*, and rendered capable of evaluation and possible acceptance' (Stigler 1982: 69, emphasis added). 'Scientific exegesis' is thus concerned not necessarily with what the subject 'really believed', but with the derivation of theoretical formulations in an intellectual vacuum. I intend to avoid Stigler's rule by staying with the *unamended* texts.

4 In selecting 'expert' economists, I have adopted a stricter classification than in Fetter (1980).

5 According to Brewer there is no purpose in debating which of the 1815 contributors (Ricardo, Malthus, Torrens or West) has priority, since Turgot (1767) 'anticipated the main points of the [classical growth] theory half a century earlier' (Brewer 1988: 512). But Turgot proceeds with the real-wage constant; there is no appreciation of the shared-incidence principle.

6 The intensive margin is also alluded to, though less conspicuously; see Malthus (1815: 35–6).

7 The argument for a 'regular' decline in the wage and profit rates assumes 'no agricultural improvements to save labour' (Malthus 1817: 435). (Malthus is not always clear whether he is formulating an *analytical* or an empirical proposition; see Hollander 1997.) It is further clarified that by the appropriate exercise of prudential population control the decline in the corn wage can be avoided (Malthus 1817, III: 12–13).

8 Ricardo referred also to an intensive margin (Ricardo 1951–73, IV: 14–15).

9 A nice summary is given in the *Notes on Malthus*: 'the loss of *quantity* is generally divided between the labourers and capitalists', but though the corn wage declines the 'value' of the wage increases (Ricardo 1951–73, II, *Note* 61: 124). And subsequently in *Note* 171 (ibid.: 266), 'I do not say that the labourer's earnings will always be the same, but whatever they may be, profits will depend on the proportion which their value bears, to the whole value produced on the last land.'

10 Brewer (1988), however, attributes to West a full-fledged model of dynamic equilibrium. Stigler's evaluation is vitiated by insistence that the 'Malthusian' population theory to which West appealed 'assumes constant real wages' (Stigler 1982: 177).

11 This passage appears also in the second edition (J. Mill 1824: 79), but not in the third (J. Mill 1826).

12 This is further confirmed by Mill's policy prescription – usually attributed only to the younger Mill – which is to assure a reduction in the birth rate while wages are still 'ample', thereby preventing any further decline and bringing growth to a halt prematurely: 'Were that accomplished, while the return to capital from the land was yet high, the reward of the labourer would be ample, and a large surplus would still remain' (J. Mill 1821: 52).

13 On the authorship of the anonymous pamphlet see O'Brien and Darnell (1982: chapter 5).

14 Improvements are said to be only 'temporary'; 'for, by stimulating population, they never fail, in the long run, to force recourse to poor soils; and whenever this is the case, *profits must unavoidably fall*' (McCulloch 1823: 57).

15 Prudential restraint, however, transforms the character of stationariness: 'high wages are not necessarily confined to the period when the wealth of society is in a state of progressive increase; . . . neither does it follow, that, when this wealth has attained its maximum, and become stationary, the wages of labour must be low' (Chalmers 1832: 555). That these alternatives were, as Chalmers claimed, 'generally admitted', is supported by the earlier accounts of Malthus and James Mill.

16 It is asserted that declining productivity 'on the whole prevails', though counteracted by invention and improvements.

17 There is, however, the usual qualification. That the returns to both capital and labour must fall to their respective minima supposes no population control; but in contrast to 'the tendency of profits to a minimum . . . no such tendency can happily be asserted of wages' because of the possibility of improved prudential behaviour (Cairnes 1874: 281).

18 Ricardo accepted this in his *Note* 61.

19 Brewer (1988: n. 9) takes West at his word.

20 For example, the critique of Smith's 'objectionable' position that 'In manufactures nature does nothing, man does all' rendering manufactures inferior to agriculture (McCulloch 1823: 35–6).

21 Elie Halévy, however, maintained that McCulloch 'either modified or failed to understand' Ricardo on wages: 'Ricardo's natural or necessary wage was for him no longer the central point around which occur oscillations in the price of labour, but only the lower limit below which the current price cannot fall' (Halévy 1955 [1928]: 367, citing McCulloch 1825: 335). This is, to my mind, precisely Ricardo's position.

22 The 'inductivist' William Whewell asserted that Ricardo's system incorporates a given (long-run) real wage – the postulate 'that the labourer's command of food and other necessaries is never permanently augmented or diminished' (Whewell 1831: 5). This alleged axiom hinged upon the Malthusian population mechanism, to which Whewell took strong exception. In his mathematical formulation of Ricardo's system the average wage rate is at subsistence but the general profit rate is on the decline, a classic case of the *short-circuited* growth model.

23 Torrens represented Malthus as 'appear[ing] as the ingenious opponent of the new theory of profit, which may be traced by a process of reasoning, self-evident in all its steps, from those discoveries respecting the nature and origin of rent which he himself has made' (Torrens 1821: xii–xiii). To read Malthus as positively *rejecting* the land scarcity-based growth model is, of course, unjustified.

24 Elizabeth Huck has directed me to Auguste Walras's earlier statement that in a progressive society entailing growth of 'capitaux artificiels' and of population, given land, 'le propriétaire foncier a le rare avantage de voir s'accroître la valeur échangeable du capital qu'il possède et le montant du revenu que lui assure cette possession', whereas 'la vie devient de plus en plus difficile pour le capitaliste' and 'pour le travailleur, elle ne devient ni plus facile ni plus difficile' (A. Walras 1849: 154, 155, 159).

25 As Peart notes, Jevons's version differs only in recognising additional pressures due to resource exhaustibility.

26 As for the authority of Malthus (a matter left in abeyance in the body of the paper), it is my impression that from their careless reading of his *Essay on Population* several of his contemporaries and successors derived the notion of *excess* population growth relative to accumulation in accounting for the falling wage path, although the canonical case – as formulated by Malthus himself – does not turn on such excess. Yet more striking, certain of Malthus's formulations, especially those directed against Ricardo in the aggregate demand context, were so strong as to suggest to Torrens that he actually rejected the land-based growth theory (see above, note 23).

4 Sraffa: the theoretical world of the 'old classical economists'

Pierangelo Garegnani

Production of Commodities: a difficult book

1. The contributions that established Sraffa's reputation in the 1920s concerning imperfect competition and the limitations of received partial equilibrium analysis (Sraffa 1925, 1926) have tended to overshadow the constructive project upon which he was already engaged. That project was to re-establish the supply-oriented, objective approach to price determination that Marshall had recognised in the classical economists – as opposed to the demand-oriented, subjective approach which Marshall himself had rendered dominant and in which Sraffa had already detected serious cracks. This overshadowing of his early constructive agenda has, I believe, made it more difficult to comprehend Sraffa's mature work, when it emerged in typically terse form in his introduction to Ricardo's *Principles* (1951) and in his *Production of Commodities by Means of Commodities* (1960).

2. In fact by the late 1920s that constructive project had already led Sraffa to find seriously wanting the Marshallian interpretation of the classical economists which he had accepted in his early articles. It had thus led him to what was in effect a rediscovery of the original approach of the 'old classical economists from Smith to Ricardo'[1] – an approach which, as Sraffa observes, had been 'submerged and forgotten since the advent of the marginal method' (Sraffa 1960: v). This evolution of his thought towards a 'submerged' approach was of course an obstacle to the understanding of *Production of Commodities* specially for those who had focused on his previous critique of the theory of the firm and of received partial equilibrium analysis. The obstacle was all the more serious because the approach, which had been evolving for over a century from Petty and the Physiocrats to Smith, Ricardo and Marx, reappeared in the book as an advanced product, without the account of its development which would have eased comprehension, by bringing out the forgotten or unrecognised traces it had left in the history of economic thought. Ironically enough, the difficulty of understanding *Production of Commodities* would have been less if the book had been a completely new departure (like, say, the works of Joan Robinson or Nicholas Kaldor in the 1950s) the germs of which would have necessarily lain in a literature generally known, and not in an approach 'forgotten' to which, therefore, the profession had little or no clues.[2]

3. Thus in approaching Sraffa's mature work the central difficulty is that of entering into, or at least establishing communication with, a theoretical world which is basically different from that which had progressively come to dominate economic thought starting from the second quarter of the nineteenth century and, thanks also to the 'submergence' of classical theory, has become so totally established that concepts highly specific to it, like those of demand and supply functions, have almost acquired the status of indisputable facts (see below, section 9). That different theoretical world may indeed require, in order to be entered into, some of Keynes's famous 'struggle to escape from habitual modes of thought and expression'. Even more than for the *General Theory* it is there true that 'the ideas . . . are extremely simple and should be obvious. The difficulty lies, not in the new ideas, but in escaping from the old ones, which ramify, for those brought up as most of us have been, into every corner of our minds' (Keynes 1936: xxiii), though here, paradoxically, the 'new ideas' are also the oldest ones.

The classical theoretical world: two key differences from modern theory

4. That classical world may be best brought into focus by starting from what are perhaps its two most striking differences from the theoretical world we are used to:

1 Normal prices of products are there determined without recourse to their demand and supply functions.
2 The division of the social product between wages and profits is determined by broad economic and social forces, and not by demand and supply functions founded on 'substitutability' between productive factors.

The first of these differences constitutes the feature of classical theory perhaps most surprising for the modern economist.[3] Indeed in classical theory, demand ('effectual demand') and supply ('quantity brought to market') were introduced only to explain the tendency of a commodity's actual price – or 'market price' as the classical economists called it – towards a normal or 'natural' level which was itself determined without reference to any such demand and supply. Thus 'effectual demand' was defined by Smith as 'the demand of those who are willing to pay the natural price of the commodity', with the 'natural' or normal price being therefore a datum for defining that 'demand' itself.

In fact Smith's 'effectual demand' could only be described as a *point*, and not a *schedule*, in the price–quantity space (see Figure 4.1): north-west of that point there lay an *area* in which the 'market price' – defined simply as larger than the natural price – was postulated to lie whenever the output fell short of the 'effectual demand'. It was that higher market price that caused the output to ultimately increase towards the effectual demand, with the 'market price' accordingly falling towards the natural price. A similar area existed at the south-east of the

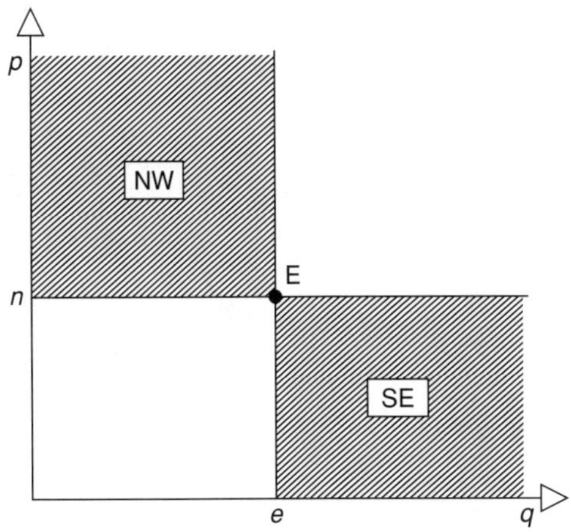

Figure 4.1 Point E of 'effectual demand': the quantity *e* is demanded at the 'natural' price *n*.

effectual-demand point, entailing conditions for a symmetrical tendency upwards to the normal price in the opposite case of excess supply.[4]

This character of classical demand and supply of being single quantities, and not functions, is what explains the word 'proportion' which Adam Smith (e.g. 1950 [1776], I: 49) and the other old classical economists applied to the relationship between the two – a word which would of course have made no sense had demand been there understood however vaguely as a schedule. And in fact that word was promptly found to be inappropriate when, soon after Ricardo, the idea of demand as a schedule began to take shape in economic theorising.[5]

5. The second above difference between the classical and the modern theoretical worlds concerns, we saw, distribution and not product prices. In classical theory the wage is determined by broad social forces (as expressed for example by the notion of a culturally determined 'subsistence') and not by demand and supply functions.[6]

Now the first, most immediately striking, of those two differences – the absence of demand and supply functions in the determination of product prices – is in fact but a result of the second, more basic difference, concerning distribution between wages and profits. As modern economic literature had to rediscover in the form of a 'non-substitution theorem', long-period competitive prices (prices implying, that is, a uniform rate of return on the supply prices of the capital goods) are fully determined, leaving no room for the operation of demand and supply once the real wage (or the interest rate) is given together with the technical conditions of production.[7] However, what in neoclassical theory is no more than a clarification of the logical structure of the theory (i.e. that demand conditions for products can influence their prices only to the extent in which they influence distribution) was *a*, or perhaps *the*, basic proposition in classical theory. It is there that, as we just saw, we find a real wage which – being determined *separately* from prices and the profit rate because of the kind of economic and broader social circumstances that are seen to influence it – has to be taken as given when determining those very profits and prices.

It is in fact this *given* real wage that entails the notion of 'surplus' characterising classical theory. Because of the given wage, and, we shall see, the associated given outputs, the shares of the product other than wages will logically emerge as a *difference* between the social product (net of the replacement of means of production) and the part of it going to the workers[8] – as the surplus, that is, of the former over the latter.[9]

Social product (net of replacement of means of production)
– Aggregate wages = Shares other than wages.

6. An important peculiarity of classical theory has come our way with that 'given' real wage, and we must note it before going a little deeper into the implications of those two differences between the classical and the neoclassical theoretical worlds. The given real wage constitutes in fact what we could call an *intermediate datum* of the theory, in the sense that it is not a datum for the theory as a whole, which has of course to explain it, but is such in that particular part of the theory where the shares of product other than wages, and therefore the prices, are determined by means of the competitive price equations.

This kind of 'intermediate datum' reflects the specific logical structure of a theory in which it is recognised that two fields of analysis have to be kept separate in economics. A first field is that where general quantitative relations of sufficiently definite form are seen to exist: it consists essentially of the competitive price equations. Alongside that field there lies a second, wider field of analysis where relations in the economy are seen to be generally too complex and variable according to circumstances to allow for a system of quantitative relations having a form definite and general enough to be useful in the *theory* as such, as distinct, that is, from particular examples or *models* within it. In that second field a more inductive kind of analysis, continually supported by what Marshall used to call 'specific experience' (Marshall 1961: 637), would be more often required. It was there that wages were dealt with: unlike in neoclassical theory, they were therefore determined separately from, and not simultaneously with, relative prices and the remaining distributive variables and had to appear as (intermediate) data when determining the latter variables.[10]

The real wage is *not* in fact the only such 'intermediate datum' of classical analysis. A similar separate determination, and consequent treatment as data, applies to normal outputs ('effectual demands'). In fact, as we shall presently see, the different theory of wages and distribution frees outputs from the postulate of functional relations with prices of sufficiently general and definite properties (the demand functions), and thus allows for their separate determination. And, finally, a similar logical role of 'intermediate datum' is attributed by the classical economists to a third set of circumstances: the technical conditions of production, which they generally regarded as endogenously determined (think e.g. of Smith's analysis of the division of labour) and therefore as something to be analysed in the theory with all their broad social and historical conditionings, and determined separately from prices, not unlike what is to be done for wages and the outputs.

7. A 'core' can thus be detected within classical theory, consisting essentially of the price equations, and concerned with quantitative relations which are both general and sufficiently definite in their properties: there the above three groups of 'intermediate data' play their role of provisional data in determining relative prices and the rate of profits.

The rest of the theory is instead viewed as essentially concerned with relations of a more inductive kind, like those governing changes in the real wage or in the outputs, or in the technical conditions of production – a part of the theory which also includes the interactions between such 'intermediate data', as well as any feedback on them of the prices and profits, the unknowns of the 'core'.[11]

Two questions which classical theory raises for neoclassical economists

8. The overturning of neoclassical demand and supply analysis which is thus implied in Sraffa's resumption of classical theory, raises two questions, to which it is essential to turn for an understanding of the work of the mature Sraffa and of the old classical economists:

1 The first question, familiar to all participants in the debates on Sraffa's work is whether constant returns – on whose basis, e.g., the non-substitution theorem of section 5 above is generally formulated[12] – are in fact required for the relevance of Sraffa's determination of prices and the rate of profits contrary to what he contends (1960: v).
2 The second, less familiar, but perhaps more basic question is how a normal real wage determined under conditions of free competition can be reconciled with the possibility of labour unemployment, entailed and in fact generally admitted in the work of the old classical economists.[13]

9. With respect to question 1, the belief in the necessity of the assumption of constant returns to scale for the significance of prices as determined by Sraffa seems a good example of the tendency to think of the concepts of demand and supply functions as immediate reflections of facts, rather than as the hypothetical propositions which they in fact are, founded on a specific theoretical structure, and which, therefore, may have no place in an alternative structure like that of the classical economists.

The reason underlying the claimed necessity of constant returns to scale appears in fact to be the following. It is *taken for granted* that, as prices change, outputs have to change according to functions predefinable within the system – the demand functions – and, thus, that prices can only be determined simultaneously with outputs, in one and the same system of equations. The exception would be when no feedback of outputs on prices is possible and this, in the circumstances of the case, is taken to require constant returns to scale – where it is not always made clear whether, as logic would dictate, that expression stands for constant supply prices, where changes in factor prices due to output changes have to be considered, or indicates instead the more general purely physical relation of a proportionate change in outputs when all factors were to vary in the same given proportion.[14] Only constant returns would thus legitimate Sraffa's separate determination of prices and he would therefore be incorrect in claiming the contrary: the possibility is not conceived, that is, that the effect of prices on outputs, and vice-versa, be considered *separately*, according to the circumstances which do not lend themselves to a useful and general formal treatment by means of equations to be included in a single system with the equations determining prices.

In fact, this allegation of the necessity of constant returns seems to forget, first of all, that the main cause of variable returns in received theory is absent in classical theory and the latter does not therefore need to assume them away. The cause concerns the first of the above meanings of constant returns and the way in which outputs can affect the relative scarcity of factors and, therefore, the wage and profit rates of Sraffa's long-period prices – an effect which is excluded in its functional expression by the different classical theory of the distribution between wages and profits.

But the ultimate reason of the irrelevance of constant returns for Sraffa's, and the classicals' determination of prices, goes deeper and it regards variable returns in the second, physical sense, no less than in the first sense above. It is the absence of demand functions for products. Thus the effects which quantities demanded could have on prices through increasing physical returns from the division of labour, or decreasing physical returns from scarce natural resources can be seen, and were seen by the classical economists, to fall largely outside the sphere of the determination of price (outside the 'core'), and in that of capital accumulation. And the classical theory of distribution further undercuts the potential relevance of demand functions by doing without the demand-and-supply equalities for factors determining the individual incomes which are at the basis of the demand functions for products. It is only natural, then, that the notion of a predefined functional relation between prices and quantities demanded of products should have remained foreign to Smith and Ricardo, where it would have had no clear general determining role on prices nor, even, a definite basis in individual incomes.

This is indeed what underlies the determination of outputs separately from prices and therefore the treatment of the former as data in that 'core' of the theory where prices are determined. But with outputs as data the question of returns cannot of course arise in that 'core' and for Sraffa's price equations. It can only arise *outside* the 'core', where the results reached in the 'core' are used, but they are used by the more inductive methods appropriate to the problem which is being studied, and in any case separately from the determination of prices. In other words, the results of the 'core' are no less 'intermediate' than its data are: they need completion outside the 'core' before being applied to explaining the phenomena of the economy considered.

Thus, no need arises of supposing constant returns to scale with respect to a first kind of output changes: those which are a *direct* effect – not mediated, that is, by prices – of changes in the 'intermediate data' and which we may call 'primary' to distinguish them from the 'secondary' ones which result from the same changes of data, but *via* prices. Clearly with respect to 'primary' changes of outputs we have no reason to bind our hands with a constant-returns assumption: we are free to assume the kind of returns to scale which better fit the circumstances of the case, and to allow for whichever changes in prices non-constant returns may then entail.

A difficulty in separating the determination of prices from that of outputs, and a corresponding need to assume constant returns, might however still seem to arise for the 'secondary' changes of outputs which would occur because of the price variations. Under non-constant returns to scale we would require knowing the effects on prices of also the 'secondary' output changes, which, however, would depend on those very changes in prices we have to ascertain. It appears however that – with respect to the 'secondary' output changes, and to their interactions with prices – the possibilities will essentially be two. The first will be when the effects of prices on the relevant outputs will be too comparatively small to render plausible, or necessary, any consideration of (long-period) non-constant returns. Then of course the problem, with respect to prices, can be solved by in fact assuming constant returns to scale. The second possibility is when the output changes resulting from the price change are of sufficient quantitative importance to give rise to, and compel consideration of, non-constant returns to scale. Those changes will then be generally part of the multiple interactions between prices, outputs and technical conditions of production that should provide the centre of a theory of accumulation. There, however, assumptions like those of 'given tastes', or of reversibility of price–quantity movements, needed for the use of demand functions would be generally admitted to be unjustified also by neoclassical authors. Demand functions, even if they were definable in a classical context, would therefore be of little use for the problem.[15]

10. As we turn then to question 2 above and to the compatibility between a positive wage and unemployed labour under competitive conditions, the key point – which for question 1 was the 'classical' absence of general and predefinable functional relations between product prices and outputs, is now, for question 2, the absence in classical theory of a wage-elastic labour demand function. That absence could not but prevent the classical economists up to Ricardo from having a conception of free competition in the labour market entailing indefinite flexibility of the wage in the presence of involuntary labour unemployment. Such a conception would in fact have led them to the absurd result of real wages tending to zero in situations of labour unemployment which they viewed as possible or even normal.[16]

In order to understand the alternative classical conception it is important to start from acknowledging the generally admitted fact that competition can be free only within an institutional framework, customary or legal, which will make that competition workable and safe for the community.[17] Now, the neoclassical conception of a wage-elastic demand function for labour has appeared to ensure a realistic full employment 'halt' to falls in wages which could threaten the economic and social order. This has in turn made it possible to think that there has been no need for the community to develop conventions or other institutions preventing any such threatening movements in wages. In this way it has made it possible to suppose that any really effective institutional framework within which free competition has to be defined could essentially be confined to *outside* the sphere of the strict wage bargain, leaving instead room in that bargain for the conception of an indefinite wage flexibility which is a keystone of the neoclassical competitive theory of distribution.

If that is so, it can be easily understood how, on the contrary, in the absence of that conception of a wage-elastic demand function for labour, the classical economists could not but take for granted the presence *within* the sphere of the wage bargain of an effective conventional or legal framework, preventing an indefinite flexibility of the wage and setting minimum and also, when necessary, maximum limits related to the past levels within which only could wage competition operate in any given situation. That was all the more natural in that it was simply a question of admitting as effective the conventions and institutions immediately observable in the labour market: it was indeed the task of neoclassical theorists to explain those phenomena as merely retarding frictions, or as subjective expressions of objective underlying demand-and-supply forces.

It is in this way that Smith can refer to a minimum wage 'below which it seems impossible to reduce, for any considerable time, the ordinary wages even of the lowest species of labour' (Smith 1950 [1776]: 60), or that he can refer to limits to a rise of wages.[18] These and similar passages by Smith and the other old classical economists have indeed long puzzled the more attentive modern interpreters of the classical economists, who – having taken for granted the modern notion of a competitive labour market, and overlooked how that notion rests on the presupposition of an elastic demand function, which is absent in the classical economists – find those passages difficult to reconcile with the free competition clearly assumed by the classical economists in other respects.[19] It may be submitted that once the wage-elastic demand function is recognised for what it is, a hypothetical proposition of post classical theory absent in the old classical economists, the meaning of those passages will begin to emerge, together with the different conception of free competition in the labour market which they express.

Sraffa's contribution

11. The above basic elements of classical theory provide the background for an understanding of Sraffa's mature work and its main contributions. It appears that these contributions can be summarised under three main headings.

1 *The rediscovery of the classical approach*, the essential structure of which was outlined by Sraffa in his introduction to Ricardo's *Principles*. That structure was in fact tersely brought to light in the interpretation of Ricardo's early principle of the determining role of agricultural profits (Sraffa 1951: xxxi–xxxiii). Sraffa pointed out there how the rationale of that doctrine lay in a determination of profits as the *difference* between corn output and corn capital, in accordance therefore, with the 'surplus' procedure we described in section 5 above. He further pointed out how labour values, often recognised as a main element in the development of classical theories, played essentially the same measuring role in Ricardo's later *Principles* (1817). And a further decisive element of classical theory was brought to light by Sraffa when in the preface to *Production of Commodities* (1960) he indicated the irrelevance of the assumption of constant returns to scale for the classical economists' determination of prices, thus pointing to the absence of demand functions in their theoretical system.[20]

2 *The development of the approach*. As just seen, the relation for which, given the real wage, the profit rate (interest rate) is determined had been dealt with by the early Ricardo on the assumption of an agricultural capital consisting of corn, and then, again, by Ricardo (and later by Marx) on the basis of the labour theory of value. Further steps forward were later taken by such writers as Bortkiewicz and Dmitriev and, more recently, by Seton (1957) and by others. No full solution bringing out the structure of the classical system and its differences from post-classical thought had, however, been available until Sraffa's *Production of Commodities* (1960). The properties of the relations between wages, profit rate and relative prices are there analysed also for the cases of scarce natural resources, of fixed capital and joint production – and, above all, those relations are mastered by such means as the 'standard commodity' and the reduction of prices to quantities of dated labour.

3 *The critique of the marginalist system*. The critique emerges from an investigation of the properties of that choice of alternative production processes which underlies the marginalist idea of factor substitution. The possibility which emerges from *Production of Commodities* (Sraffa 1960: 81) of the 'reswitching' of production processes, and of 'reverse capital deepening', as the wage (interest rate) changes monotonically, has in fact revealed radical deficiencies in the traditional marginalist treatment of such choices. These deficiencies, uncovered in the course of the capital controversies with respect to the long-period equilibrium of the traditional versions of marginal theory,[21] are now beginning to be seen as affecting equally the intertemporal general equilibrium versions in which, at high cost for the significance of the analysis, pure theorists have increasingly sought shelter in the belief they could find there a systematic statement of the theory, free of such difficulties.[22]

12. This is not the place to consider in any detail how the seminal work of the mature Sraffa has been followed up in the years after the publication of his

introduction to Ricardo's *Principles* (1951) and *Production of Commodities* (1960). The capital controversies just mentioned have been in the public eye, as have been, and still are, the controversies concerning the interpretation of the classical economists. Less in the public eye has been other work which, in our opinion, has been no less important, but has been more internal to the development of the classical approach, like that concerning the possibility of deficiencies of aggregate demand, or the analysis of the distribution of the surplus between wages and profits once it is recognised that in modern economies wages are not confined to subsistence. The same is true of more specific subjects, like the determination of individual outputs independently of demand and supply functions we touched on in section 9 above, or the deter-mination of prices in the presence of fixed capital and joint production, or the tendency of market prices towards natural prices (section 5 above). I would here like to confine myself to briefly noting two developments among those just listed.

The first is that which concerns the possibility of deficiencies of aggregate demand in the long-period context of a theory of growth no less than in the Keynesian short period. The criticism of the neoclassical theory of distribution, an essential element of which is the role of the interest rate in adjusting investment to savings, appears to reveal that deficiencies of aggregate demand should be admitted as a normal possibility in both short- and long-period analysis. And for the reasons we have already seen (section 10), no new problem is created there by a contrast between a competitive positive wage and labour unemployment. (This has of course some bearing on the kinds of problem modern New Keynesian macroeconomics is trying to solve in order to effect a reconciliation between neoclassical theory and facts. It may indeed appear that modern theory has been trying to reinvent a 'classical' wheel when attempting to explain why wages may not fall indefinitely in the presence of unemployment, or why the latter persists when wages do decline.)

As for the second question, concerning the distribution of the *surplus* between wages and profits[23] we have on the one hand the role which financial institutions can play in influencing the long-term trend of interest rates, thereby regulating the rate of profits and, hence, indirectly, wages. On the other, we have the economic, social and historical factors that may act directly on wages, confining long-term interest rates to a passive role. The price level may then appear to be as the rope which the two parties to the tug-of-war are pulling.

Notes

This chapter is a revised version of the text with the same title, which has appeared already in the *European Journal of the History of Economic Thought* (1998). Note 11 below has been added to take into account some comments which Professor Blaug has addressed to positions of mine recalled in this chapter.

1 The qualification of 'old' classical economists is Sraffa's who specifies 'from Adam Smith to Ricardo' (Sraffa 1960: 5). Cf. note 5 below on the different positions, for example, of J. S. Mill, generally listed among the classical economists.

2 Nor were those difficulties decreased by the apparent similarity with other works of the period which, though having some roots in that same past, had shown little awareness of it and, above all, had had altogether different purposes and import (cf. von Neumann 1945 [1937], or Leontief 1941: on the theoretical roots of the former work see Kurz and Salvadori 1995: 412).

3 Cf. e.g. Harrod (1961: 783).

4 Market clearing in a sufficiently unambiguous sense – as entailing, that is, constancy of prices under existing data – is thus ensured by the natural prices. The 'market price' can, however, be also seen to ensure a temporary market clearing, in which liquidation/accumulation of inventories, whether because of speculation or of reservation prices, play a role jointly with other temporary factors (cf. e.g. Garegnani 1997 [1990]: 167–70).

5 The phrase 'ratio, as between demand and supply' was infact criticised by J. S. Mill, the key figure in the post-classical transition to modern demand and supply analysis. (Cf. J. S. Mill 1961 [1871]: 448, quoted in Bharadwaj 1989: 138.)

6 This difference is witnessed e.g. by the labour unemployment freely admitted by classical authors, as exemplified in Ricardo's famous chapter XXXI 'On machinery' in his *Principles* (Samuelson's different interpretation in e.g. Samuelson 2000 is discussed by the present author in Garegnani 2000b). For Ricardo and the other classical economists, lower wages could favour the eventual absorption of unemployment by affecting the relative speeds of growth of capital and population – a process quite different, of course, from that of factor substitution assumed in the neoclassical demand function for labour.

7 For the assumption of constant returns to scale, often stated to be necessary for the theorem, cf. note 12 below.

8 'Shares other than wages' become profits on capital when, with Ricardo, and the treatment of outputs as 'intermediate data' (section 6 below), we can take as given the position of the margin of cultivation for 'corn', and can then deduct the corn rent from the output before determining the surplus in accordance with the equation above.

9 The original notion of surplus is linked to that of wages consisting of the subsistence of workers, so that the equation would indicate the part of the social product of which society can dispose without endangering the material conditions or its own continuance. When, however, wages are no longer seen to consist of necessaries only, the two meanings of the equation become separate. A problem regarding the sharing out of the surplus between wages and profits arises then. It can be solved by resorting to a 'surplus wage' which, according to circumstances, either constitutes an intermediate datum, controlled by the wage bargain, or becomes an unknown resulting from a profit rate taken then as the 'intermediate datum', determined by monetary conditions below the maximum level corresponding to the subsistence wage (Sraffa 1960: 9–10; cf. also section 12 below).

10 Marshall (1961, appendix C: 771–2). For the present distinction between two fields of analysis in classical theory cf. also Garegnani (1987: 561).

11 Some of the notions expounded in these pages are criticised by Professor Blaug in the next chapter. A comment on his position is forthcoming (Garegnani 2002). I shall here confine myself to pointing out a misreading which underlies his argument and leads to some paradoxes. The misreading concerns the role of 'data' which I would attribute to the wage, the outputs and the technical conditions of production in Smith's and Ricardo's theories. What I have argued at the time, and is recalled in the text above, is a different point. It is that the three sets of circumstances were taken as data by the classical economists *when determining the non-wage distributive variables and the relative prices* (e.g. Garegnani 1984: 293, 1987: 560) and not therefore as data for their theories as a whole, where such circumstances clearly had to be determined in turn. The misreading is favoured by some indefiniteness of the interpretation which Blaug

attributes to me, for which the classical economists would have addressed the question of 'how an economic surplus is generated, spent, and augmented from period to period' (p. 82 below). Since first advancing in a 1958 Cambridge Ph.D. thesis an interpretation of those economists in terms of 'social surplus' (see Garegnani 1958, 1960, chapters I and II; cf. also Garegnani 1970: 427–8, 1987: 560), I had qualified by that notion a particular theory of distribution and relative prices alternative to neoclassical demand-and-supply for 'factors of production'. That theory in which profits are obtained as the difference, or 'surplus' of the product over wages, entailed a treatment of the two magnitudes as 'data' in the calculation, i.e., as separately determined in another part of the theory.

The clarification of the above misreading should on the other hand make clear that when Sraffa writes (1960) that 'no changes in outputs' are considered within the standpoint of the 'old classical economists', he is referring to that 'core' of classical theory where the determination of prices and non-wage variables – the exclusive concern of his book – is carried out and not to classical theory as a whole, as Blaug paradoxically interprets, when attributing to him what would indeed be a 'grotesque' (p. 87) denial of any classical concern with capital accumulation. The misreading leads thus Blaug to the basic paradox in his chapter – that an interpretation tracing the roots of the historical richness of classical authors to the socio-institutional factors to which they referred the distribution between wages and profits and the accumulation of capital, is on the contrary seen as providing an 'amazingly narrow' interpretation ignoring that very richness.

12 In fact the demonstration of that theorem entails no output changes, thus rendering irrelevant any assumption of constant returns to scale (cf. note 14 below).

13 Cf. note 6 above.

14 That independence of prices from output levels requires in fact what Marshall and Sraffa called 'constant returns' (Sraffa 1926, 1960), i.e. constancy in the relative supply prices of the commodities as their outputs change. Constant returns to scale, in the physical meaning used when e.g. defining a production function, are of course not a *sufficient* condition for constant supply prices though they are in fact, if not in principle, a *necessary* condition for them.

15 Indeed, in neoclassical theory that kind of interdependence between prices and outputs would presumably have to be dealt with by a separate consideration of changes in 'tastes', in fact equivalent to the separate consideration of outputs of classical theory in that it would have to be determined outside the equations system determining prices. For a discussion of the question cf. Garegnani (1990: 128–32). It should perhaps be made clear that the argument in the text does not exclude that appropriately defined quantitative relations between prices and quantities demanded might not be of use in specific problems (e.g. in taxation): the 'demand functions' referred to in the text are of course those which underlie the neoclassical general explanation of prices and distribution.

16 Cf. note 6 above.

17 As Edwin Cannan, quoted by Pigou (1950 [1932]: 128), observed: 'The working of self-interest is generally beneficent, not because of some natural coincidence between the self-interest of each and the good of all, but because human institutions are arranged so as to compel self-interest to work in directions in which it will be beneficent.' And of course that applies in particular to that self-interest which is at play in free competition, where 'non-beneficent effects' are prevented by exactly such 'human institutions'. (It is enough to recall in that respect the multiple hardly dispensable regulations which affect the provision of, say, pharmaceuticals or airline passenger transport, or indeed almost any product.)

18 E.g. Smith (1950 [1776]: 59). On the question of these institutional limits to the wage cf. Garegnani (1990: 118–22).

19 Cf. Cannan (1967 [1897]: 185); Knight (1956 [1935]: 80–1); Hollander (1973a: 185–6).

20 Cf. note 11 above on 'no changes in outputs being considered' in Sraffa (1960).
21 For these versions cf. note 7 above.
22 Cf. Schefold (2000); Garegnani (2000a).
23 Cf. note 9 above.

5 Misunderstanding classical economics

The Sraffian interpretation of the surplus approach

Mark Blaug

I begin with a fundamental distinction between rational and historical reconstructions of past thinkers. By *rational reconstruction* I mean what Herbert Butterfield called the 'Whig interpretation of history': the tendency to view history as a relentless march of progress from past errors to present truths. Thus a rational reconstruction of, say, Adam Smith or David Ricardo treats their writings as if they were written now and had been submitted to the *American Economic Review* or the *Journal of Political Economy*; it appraises *their* ideas in *our* terms in order to confirm the belief that there has been progress in intellectual history. A historical reconstruction, on the other hand, attempts to recover the ideas of past thinkers in terms that they, and their contemporaries, would have recognised as a more or less faithful description of what they had set out to do; it tries to see the past as the past saw itself.

Unfortunately, rational reconstructions are invariably anachronistic, frequently involving almost incredible mathematical transformations of ideas originally expressed in now outdated terminology. On the other hand, faithful historical reconstructions are literally impossible if only because we cannot forget all the modern economics we know. What we have here is a standard Scylla and Charybdis problem. Rational reconstructions, for all their anachronism, may be illuminating, even startlingly so, but the more skilfully they are executed the more irrelevant they become: if we have finally attained knowledge of absolute truth in economics, what point is there in studying the history of economic thought except as a brand of morbid antiquarianism? That leaves us with the unenviable task of trying to come as close as possible to a genuine historical appreciation of the past without benefit of hindsight, impossible as it may be ever to achieve fully that goal. Therefore, and without denying a perfectly legitimate role for rational reconstructions, I vote for historical reconstructions as the only legitimate occupation of historians of economic thought.

When I first drew this distinction (Blaug 1990, 1997b: 7–8)[1] I noted that many interpretative exercises in the history of economic thought start out as rational reconstructions but end up as historical reconstructions, thus demonstrating the principle of having your cake and eating it too. I gave examples of how writers like Samuel Hollander and Michio Morishima begin by presenting Ricardo attired in modern garb but soon claim that they have grasped what Ricardo really meant to say had he not been held back by primitive technique; in short, they imply that a faithful historical reconstruction is an unexpected bonus of an ingenious rational reconstruction. This may actually be the case on occasion, but, in general, there is likely to be a difference between what a great economist of the past believed himself to be saying and what he would have said had he understood his own model as well as we do. Very few rational reconstructions are valid historical reconstructions, and so it is, I argued, with the Hollander–Morishima versions of Ricardo.

What I want to do in this chapter is to offer a new example of the same phenomenon: the Sraffian or neo-Ricardian interpretation of classical economics as a theory about the generation, disposal, and accumulation of the so-called economic surplus. I am not concerned with the validity of Sraffian economics as such, or even with the Sraffian interpretation of classical economics as an illuminating, rational reconstruction, capable of affording a springboard for a wholly new style of long-run equilibrium theorising, rooted in Ricardo but culminating in Sraffa's *Production of Commodities by Means of Commodities* (1960), as an alternative heritage to the mainstream lineage of neoclassical economics. My only topic is the historical accuracy of the Sraffian interpretation of classical economics, that is, the British tradition of classical political economy, starting more or less with Smith in the third quarter of the eighteenth century and ending more or less with John Stuart Mill and Karl Marx in the third quarter of the nineteenth century.

The distinction between a rational and a historical reconstruction of past thinkers is recognised and acknowledged even by Sraffian writers. Thus Heinz Kurz and Neri Salvadori (1998b: 1) assure us in a book on classical economics that their interest is 'not purely and even predominantly historical':

> What we have in mind [they say] is a particular rational reconstruction of 'classical' economics, which in our view, is useful for an understanding of certain important arguments found in several classical authors and for the developments of these arguments. Our concern with classical economics is therefore first and foremost a concern with its analytical particulars which in our view have not been fully explored.

However, approximately 200 out of the 600 pages of their book are devoted to matters of historical exegesis, demonstrating clearly that what may well have started out for the two authors as a useful rational reconstruction serves them at the same time as a penetrating historical reconstruction.

The question before us then is this: have Kurz and Salvadori, not to mention Maurice Dobb, Krishna Bharadwaj, Pierangelo Garegnani, Gary Mongiovi, Luigi Pasinetti, Alessandro Roncaglia, Giancarlo de Vivo and even Piero Sraffa himself – to cite only the most prominent advocates of the Sraffian interpretation of classical economics – given us a historically compelling reconstruction of the ideas of Smith, Ricardo, Mill, and Marx? My answer to that question is no. The Sraffian interpretation is just another 'Whig interpretation of history'. We assume that perfect truth is found in *Production of Commodities*, and then we read backward, finding Sraffa in much of Ricardo and Marx, although much less in

Smith and Mill, and forget about almost everything else in classical economics because it will not fit the Procrustean bed of the interpretation. I will not go so far as to say that the Sraffian reading is a historical travesty, but it certainly is an amazingly narrow interpretation that omits some of the most exciting and indeed fruitful elements in the thinking of the classical authors. No doubt, neo-classical economists like W. S. Jevons, Léon Walras, and Alfred Marshall created a history of classical economics which likewise operated selectively to confirm the ascendancy of post-1870 marginal utility economics. But that is hardly a reason for Sraffians to commit the same sin of literally manufacturing a historical pedigree for neo-Ricardian linear production theory.[2]

The exogenous variables

The Sraffian interpretation of classical economics comes in two versions – which we may call 'soft' and 'hard' – and both versions are found in Garegnani (1987), although the most persuasive account of the soft version is by Vivian Walsh and Harvey Gram (1980).[3] In the soft version, classical economics 'had its beginning with writers like William Petty and Richard Cantillon, found its first systematic expression in Quesnay's *Tableau Economique* of 1758, became dominant with the classical economists from Adam Smith to Ricardo, was then taken over and developed by Marx' (Garegnani 1987: 560; see also Aspromourgos 1996; Groenewegen 1997). According to this view, the classical economics addressed the question of how an 'economic surplus' is generated, spent, and augmented from period to period. The 'economic surplus' is the disposable part of total output that is left over after capital consumption has been made good and the workers fed; it is the net national product minus the wage bill, which must be maintained or added to if output is going to be reproduced year after year; in Quesnay it accrues to landowners as ground rent, but in Smith, Ricardo, Mill, and Marx it accrues both to landowners as rent and to capitalists as profits.

There is little doubt that this is as good a one-line characterisation of classical economics as we are ever likely to get. It captures the emphasis on thrift and capital accumulation as well as the crucial Smithian distinction between productive and unproductive labour – a distinction in terms of employment between the desirable disposition of the surplus in the form of investment and its undesirable disposition in the form of consumption which runs like a red thread though the writings of all the major and minor classical economists (with the exceptions of Jean-Baptiste Say and John McCulloch (O'Brien 1975: 233–4)). Likewise, it incorporates the classical vision of a future 'stationary state' in which the rate of profit on capital has fallen so low as to discourage further investment. On the other hand, it fails to reflect Smith's view that least government is best government, that rent-seeking 'merchants and manufacturers' are greater enemies of capital accumulation than landlords, not to mention his and Mill's top-heavy 'agenda' for government action to improve the workings of markets and the institutional structures in which markets are embedded. Nor does it account for the striking contrast between Smith's dynamic theory of international trade and Ricardo's static theory of the gains of trade. Finally, it leaves one wondering why both Ricardo and Marx were so obsessed with the labour theory of value, the 'invariable measure of value', the 'transformation problem', and all that, namely the analytical niceties of price theory.

This brings us to the 'hard version', which can at least address some of the issues left out of the soft version. What we need in order to determine the size of the economic surplus, Garegnani (1987: 560) asserts, is to take as given (1) real wages; (2) the 'social product: that is, the output of the commodities produced in the year'; and (3) 'the technical conditions of production'. 'The peculiar feature of those [classical] theories', Garegnani continues, 'has its logical basis in the consideration of real wage and social product as being determinable *prior to those shares*.' And again: 'the surplus theories have, so to speak, a core which is isolated from the rest of the analysis because the wage, the social product and the technical conditions of production appear there as already determined' (Garegnani 1987: 562). All the three exogenous variables may influence each other, and the relative prices and profits determined within the core may in turn influence the exogenous variables, but those influences, Garegnani insists, are always 'separate from and not simultaneous with the examination of the relationships characteristic of the core'. The relationships inside the core can be quantitatively established on the basis of competitively determined uniform rates of wages, profits, and rent, whereas outside the core only loose qualitative generalisations are possible. This is not to say, Garegnani adds, that these are less important; it is simply that 'the relationships studied in the core had been found to provide the necessary basis for dealing with just those questions', namely, questions of functional income distribution, capital accumulation, technical change, and the like (ibid.).

Exactly the same core–periphery formulation of the hard version is found in Kurz and Salvadori (1998b: 67–8) and indeed in the work of dozens of other Sraffian historians of economic thought (Blaug 1987: 220–1).[4] Over and over again, we are told that the classical writers analyse the determination of relative prices and the associated rate of profit by starting from a set of exogenous variables, which always include (1) the techniques of production of the various commodities, (2) the volume and composition of total output, and (3) one of the distributive variables, that is, either the ruling wage rate or the ruling rate of profit. These data are then contrasted with the very different variables taken as given by neoclassical writers, namely (1) the set of technical possibilities or blueprints from which producers can choose the cost-minimising alternative, (2) the tastes or preferences of consumers for particular goods, and (3) the initial endowments of individual agents and associated property rights in these endowments. The differences between classical and neoclassical economics are then attributed in large measure to the different data taken as exogenously determined in the two approaches and in particular to the third of these, namely one of the distributional variables in classical economics and the initial endowments of owners of productive services in neoclassical economics. It is this and not marginalism or utility theory or demand functions that is the source of contrasts between, say, Ricardo and Marshall.

This is clearly an ingenious rational reconstruction in which Sraffa's *Production of Commodities* says all that Ricardo would have said about the determination of relative prices in the core if he could have emancipated himself from the primitive level of analysis of his day, while at the same time making room for Ricardo's lengthy discussions of agricultural 'improvements', the 'machinery question', the savings of workers, the effect of foreign trade on the likely onset of the stationary state, and so on, as asides that belong to the periphery of his system. Likewise most of Volume I of *Capital*, wherein Marx deduces from a pure labour theory of value that profits are in the nature of 'surplus value' stolen from workers, belongs to the core of classical economics, while large parts of Volume II and the whole of Volume III, devoted to 'the laws of motion' of capitalism, are consigned to the periphery. In this way, we seem to gain a vital distinction between the still tenable elements in classical economics and the more controversial and possibly dated parts of classical thinking. It is indeed an ingenious and even striking rational reconstruction of classical economics. But is it an even remotely accurate historical reconstruction?

The technology of production

Let us consider in turn the three parameters taken as given in classical economics according to the strong version of the Sraffian interpretation. We begin with 'the technical conditions of production', meaning the physical input–output relations posited for the production of different commodities that are written down on the first page of Sraffa's book and whose fixed coefficients are in stark contrast to the variable coefficients of neoclassical economics.

It is perfectly true that the classical economists rarely addressed the problem of choice of technique, virtually implying that it was usually impossible to choose among a number of technical alternatives. But there are a number of glaring exceptions, including Ricardo's famous third edition chapter on machinery, which Mill reiterated at greater length (Blaug 1997c [1962]: 181–2); Sraffians are well aware of Ricardo's *volte-face* on machinery, which is for them a perfect example of a periphery question (Kurz and Salvadori 1998b: 38–9). However, they do not mention Ricardo's analysis of 'agricultural improvements' in chapter 2 of his *Principles of Political Economy*. Ricardo divides these farming innovations into two types – land-saving and capital- and labour-saving innovations – and he gives practical examples of each of these (Blaug 1997c [1962]: 104–5, 112–13). This was no idle matter for him because his theoretical system led to the conclusion that the action of diminishing returns in agriculture would cause the rental share of output to rise in the course of economic growth; this conclusion was subject to the proviso that diminishing returns would not be offset by technical progress in farming. He thus took pains to argue that the short-run effects of agricultural improvements of both types is to lower rents per acre as well as the rental share; hence landlords would have no incentive to introduce them. The striking feature of Ricardo's analysis of technical change in agriculture is his emphasis on the short run, while elsewhere, of course, he concentrates on long-run effects. This curious reversal in his standard method of analysis may be taken as presumptive evidence of his ideological bias against landlords. Be that as it may, to consign so much of his rent chapter to the periphery of his system, when the very nerve centre of the Ricardian system is the theory of differential rent, is a highly questionable procedure.

But all this is as nothing to the utter indifference of Sraffian interpreters to the opening three chapters of the *Wealth of Nations* on the division of labour, a subject they never discuss or even mention. It is well known that Smith blew up the age-old topic of the specialisation of tasks within a farm or enterprise into a veritable theory of technical progress (Schumpeter 1954: 187–8), and he seems to have attributed the pace of economic growth in a nation to (1) the length to which the division of labour is carried and (2) the ratio of productive to unproductive labour (Blaug 1997c [1962]: 35–6, 53–4; Eltis 1984: chapter 3). Of course, so much of the book is about the appropriate course of action by governments to ensure a maximum rate of economic growth, and we do well to remember that the whole of Book 3 of the *Wealth of Nations* is focused on 'the different Progress of Opulence in different Nations'.

Paul Samuelson and William Nordhaus (1992 [1981]: 376) once described the *Wealth of Nations* as 'a practical handbook that might be entitled *How to Make the GNP Grow*', and, while that is a slight exaggeration, it must be said that what Sraffians call the 'core' of classical economics does not occupy more than seven or eight chapters in Book 1 of the *Wealth of Nations*, that is, less than 10 per cent of the total.[5] In general, it is fair to say that the overwhelming emphasis in the *Wealth of Nations* is on the optimistic possibilities of economic growth in a country like Britain, in contrast to the pessimistic vision of growth in Ricardo's *Principles*, qualified no doubt by the repeal of the Corn Laws.[6] I am hardly the first to be struck by the extent to which Smith's insistence on dynamically increasing returns to both scale and scope conflicts with the emphasis on diminishing returns in his classical successions, which was one of the legacies of the 'Ricardian revolution' (Hicks 1990: 99; Winch 1997). By the time we reach Mill, a generation later, economic progress is essentially conceived as a race between technical change and diminishing returns in agriculture; *stalemate* is the best description of the ambiguous attitude to economic progress that Mill eventually adopted (Blaug 1997c [1962]: 182–3, 202, 204).

But Smith, Ricardo, and Mill aside, it is when we consider Marx that we come face to face with the historical misrepresentation of technology as an exogenous variable in classical economies. Marx was fundamentally concerned with the nature of profit as a source of income to capitalists, and he employed the labour theory of value to establish the proposition that profits are due to the fact that workers produce more than the cost of their own maintenance and replacement. But he had another explanation which had nothing whatever to do with the labour theory of value: it was the theory of 'the labour process', which runs alongside the explanation of profit as surplus value in the crucial chapters 6 and 7 of Volume I of *Capital* (1976 [1867]). Under capitalism labourers are ostensibly free but are actually forced to work by virtue of their utter dependence on employment and, being so dependent, they must subordinate their interests and desires to those of the capitalist. This would not matter were it not for the fact that the employment contract under capitalism is necessarily 'incomplete' in the sense that it stipulates a rate of pay for so many hours of work but fails to specify the intensity or quality of work that is to be performed, if only because these qualitative dimensions of work never can be written down. In consequence, capitalists succeed in maintaining the quality of labour only by constant monitoring of job performance, backed up by the 'carrot' of promised promotion and the 'stick' of threatened dismissal. In short, capitalism maintains what Marx called the 'despotism of the workplace', and profits accrue only to capitalists who are effective despots.

Many modern Marxists, inclined to abandon the labour theory of value as untenable by the standards of modern economics, find this analysis by Marx of 'the valorisation of the labour process' a more fruitful way of studying the exploitative nature of profits. Moreover, it is remarkable how Marx's insights into 'the labour process' foreshadow recent work in industrial organisation by neoclassical economists employing principal–agent theory to show how employers secure labour discipline on the factory floor in the face of an inherently incomplete employment contract (Blaug 1993, 1997c [1962]: 233–4, 257–8). From our point of view, however, what is even more remarkable is that Marx's analysis of the labour process is for some Marxists their very bone of contention with Sraffian economics. Far from technology being given to capitalists, the choice of technique is the very heart of the contested terrain between workers and capitalists. In the words of Bob Rowthorn:

> Provided our sole aim is to study the formal relationships between technology, real wages and the rate of profit, there is little to choose between the approaches of Marx and Ricardo. . . . If however, our aim is to understand capitalism as a mode of production and to 'reveal the economic law of motion of modern society' it is ridiculous to concentrate exclusively on quantities which appear in the equations of Sraffa and other Neo-Ricardians. . . . It is this emphasis on the labour-process which characterises Marx's analysis, and which, more than anything else, distinguishes him from all main schools of bourgeois economy.
>
> (Rowthorn 1974: 39–40, 41)

One can, of course, argue that Marx was not a typical classical economist and hence that he is an exception to almost every generalisation that we can advance about classical economics. But Marx looms large in the generalisations of Garegnani, Roncaglia, Bharadwaj, Kurz, and Salvadori about the 'surplus approach', and the fact of the matter is that Marx did not take as given the 'technical conditions of production'. One can also argue that Marx's analysis of the labour process is part of the periphery of Marxian economics, but enough has been said to show that what some regard as a peripheral topic in Marx, others regard as the very core of Marxism.

The volume and composition of output

It was Sraffa (1960: v) himself who invented the myth that the method of analysis based on the assumption of 'given quantities' is that of 'the old classical economists from Adam Smith to Ricardo'. This method of given quantities, he explained, presupposes 'no changes in output and no changes in the proportions in which different means of production are used by an industry'. As a description of what the *Wealth of Nations* is all about, even the chapters in Book 1 on the theory of value and distribution, this is simply grotesque. It might just do as an account of Ricardo's search for an 'invariable measure of value', but even then, as we have seen, there are too many awkward bits to fit in. As for Marx, Sraffa's description fits the first volume of *Capital* almost perfectly, but how surprised Marx would have been to learn that his extended investigation of the law of the falling rate of profit in volume III of *Capital*, the linchpin of all of Marx's economic predictions about the fate of capitalism, was somehow not proper classical economics because it violated the fundamental postulate of 'given quantities'.

Let us take the bull by the horns and ask whether Sraffa's characterisation is an accurate historical reconstruction even of Ricardo, the classical economist who must have been uppermost in his mind when he wrote that opening paragraph of *Production of Commodities* just quoted. In one sense it is of course true that Ricardo had no theory of how the level of output is determined, much less a theory of why output is made up of one set of goods rather than another. But then neither did any other pre-modern economist. However, can we really describe the economics of Ricardo, with its obsessive concern about the action of diminishing returns in both extensive and intensive cultivation, as presupposing 'no changes in the proportions in which different means of production are used by an industry'? Ricardo asked only one big question: why does the rate of profit tend to fall in the course of economic progress? To answer that question he had to show that the extra inputs required to produce one unit of output on marginal land did not simply raise the real price of 'corn', the predominant wage good of workers, but raised it relative to the price of 'cloth', that is, all non-wage goods; a physical relationship between marginal inputs and output in agriculture had to be shown to lead to a similar relationship between the value of marginal inputs and output in both agriculture and manufacturing. This explains his almost frantic insistence on the validity of the labour theory of value despite the many objections to the theory which he emphasised so strikingly that they served as a master puzzle to all those who came after him. (Of course, Marx believed that he had solved Ricardo's puzzle successfully.) But, for Ricardo, the qualified validity of the labour theory of value was never conceived as a solution to a static equilibrium problem along Sraffian lines according to which the prices of individual commodities are determined simultaneously with the rate of profit on capital.

There is ample evidence in Ricardo's *Principles* that he had in mind a moving equilibrium along which the increased marginal cost of growing corn alters the terms of trade between corn and cloth so as to depress the rate of profit on capital; the increased marginal cost of growing corn is the consequence of a constantly increasing ratio of extra doses of capital-and-labour to a fixed number of acres of land. If that is not a change in 'the proportions in which different means of production are used by an industry' I don't know what is! So there is factor substitution in Ricardo, and not just when he analyses technical change in agriculture or produces his afterthoughts on 'the machinery question'. Likewise, Sraffa tells us that there are 'no changes in output' in 'the old classical economists'. Come, come: the volume of output, alongside the size of the labour force, is constantly rising in Ricardo.

One of the reasons Ricardo insisted on the idea of a no-rent margin in agriculture, in fact and not just in theory, was that he thought it 'got rid of rent' and so reduced the 'natural price' of corn to the sum of wages and profits. But what determined the location of the margin? Why was cultivation extended only so far and no further? The obvious answer in any rational reconstruction of the system is the workers' level of demand for wheaten bread made out of corn (Samuelson 1991). But if this demand varied with the price of corn, the action of diminishing returns on the price of corn might be offset by intercommodity substitution in consumption away from corn. One way of closing this avenue of escape was to assume that the demand for corn was perfectly inelastic, being a strictly linear function of population size, and that is precisely what Ricardo seems to have assumed, although not, of course, in such stark modern terms.[7] In short, if we can assume that he took the size of the population as given, then we would be justified in assuming that he likewise took the volume of output as given. But, of course, he believed in the Malthusian theory of population, and if there was one thing he did not take to be exogenously determined outside the sphere of economics it was the growth of population.

The real wage rate

We come at long last to the most disputable of all the three variables that are said to be given in classical economics, namely the real wage rate. The first problem is: what wage rate? Labour is not homogeneous, and there is no such thing as *the* real wage rate. According to Kurz and Salvadori (1998b: 322–4), it is classical doctrine that the heterogeneity of labour is to be reduced to homogeneous labour via relative wage differentials, so that better rewarded skilled labour is just more units of unskilled raw labour. This is said to be Smith's, Ricardo's, Marx's, and even Sraffa's method *par excellence*: the different kinds of labour are to be aggregated via money wage rates.

Now, as is well known, there is a little problem with this solution to the 'labour reduction problem' (Blaug 1982), namely that wage rates are involved in what purports to be an explanation of how prices are determined by physical labour costs. So long as labour is differentiated only in terms of required skills, there is no problem; we can assume that skills are produced in a private 'training industry' at cost prices, in which case labour skills are simply peculiar 'machines' that are produced and reproduced at the going rate of profit. This argument fails, however, the moment we recognise that labour is also differentiated in terms of 'ability', regardless of whether those ability differences are innate or acquired as a result of family rearing. Such ability differences cannot be interpreted as given technical coefficients in a national industry called the 'family', producing workers in accordance with the principle of equal profitability. Moreover, wages in different occupations differ not just because some jobs require more manual or mental skills, but also because they require more endurance, more risk of injuries, more indifference to routine, more responsibility, and more risk of unemployment than others, as Smith argued persuasively in chapter 10 of Book 1 of the *Wealth of Nations*. In short, what Smith showed was that the labour market tends to equalise not the rate of wages for labour regarded as homogeneous by employers, but the 'net advantages' of different jobs to individual workers – and every classical economist was perfectly familiar with this striking chapter in Smith's book. Now, without pausing to consider the significance of this analysis for Smith's theory of competition (Blaug 1997c [1962]: 46–8), let us note that Ricardo tackled the labour reduction problem quite differently from the way Marx solved it.[8] Ricardo (1951–73, I: 21–2) simply asserted that relative wage differences altered little from year to year and therefore could be taken as given for accounting for *changes* in relative prices over time, and it was these changes to which his theory of value was mainly addressed.

On the very first page of his *Principles* Ricardo announced that all the language of value comparisons in his work referred to commodities located at different points of time and not in different places at the same time.[9] It is extraordinary how frequently this fundamental point is ignored by Ricardian commentators, particularly of the Sraffian inclination. In my first jejune publication, written before Sraffa's *Production of Commodities*, I noted that 'the peculiar feature of Ricardo's approach, which sets it apart from the common run of value theories, is its concern with . . . intertemporal rather than intratemporal comparisons of value' (Blaug 1958: 20; see also Blaug 1997c [1962]: 107–81), citing a paper by John Cassels (1935), who had made the same point twenty years earlier. Terry Peach, in his masterly exegetical study of Ricardo, comes to the same conclusion:

> For most nineteenth-century commentators, and the great majority of later ones, it has been common knowledge that Ricardo was particularly concerned to elaborate the dynamic course of wages, profits and rent under the influence of progressively diminishing agricultural returns, that he envisaged a declining general rate of profit in the absence of a free trade in corn and that the 'prediction' of a falling rate of profit was central to his case for agricultural protection.
>
> (Peach 1993: 6)

It is only in the aftermath of Sraffa's book, Peach adds, that emphasis has been placed instead on Ricardo's alleged concern with the purely notional division of a given social product between wages and profits so as to determine the pricing of commodities in static equilibrium.[10] Sraffian writers like Kurz and Salvadori (1995: 121, 128, 1998b: 161) admit as much when they distinguish between Sraffa's 'standard commodity' and Ricardo's 'invariable measure of value': Sraffa's *numéraire* was created solely to deal with the impact of changes in distribution on relative prices in the same technical environment, whereas Ricardo's 'invariable measure' was also addressed to the measurement of prices when technology has changed.[11]

However, we have strayed too far from the question before us: did the classical economists take the real wage as given? Now, there is no question that they regarded the minimum-level-of-existence wage rate – that wage bundle sufficient to rear a family with two children, such that the size of the labour force is reproduced year after year – as something that was determined by slowly changing historical traditions and which, therefore, could be taken as given in analysing a practical question, like a tax on wage goods. On the other hand, any excess of the current 'market price' of labour over that subsistence wage rate, the 'natural price' of labour according to Smith, would induce positive population growth, and vice versa for a market wage below the natural wage. This is the notorious wages–population mechanism, which, slowly but surely, acting over a generation or more, drives the market wage steadily toward the subsistence wage rate and at the same time drives the subsistence rate upward along a gently rising trend (Blaug 1997c [1962]: 43–4, 72–3).[12] The classical economists, and Malthus in particular, devoted much attention to the institutional setting that governed workers' attitudes to family size, and that is indeed why the abolition of the Poor Law was the one policy stance that they all held in common. This original Malthusian demand for total abolition eventually became the principle of reforming the old Poor Law so as to get rid of 'outdoor relief'. Nevertheless, the recognition that the long-run subsistence wage rate depends critically on the psychological motives that underlie the growth of population appears just as much in Mill, writing fifteen years after the death of Malthus, as in the young Malthus himself. In other words, to say that the classical economists treated the 'natural price' of labour as exogeneous, meaning as determined outside their theoretical system, is to impose on them the modern economist's conception of demography as a subject best left to sociologists.

Perhaps this explains why the Sraffian interpretation of classical economics typically does little more than allude to the central role of the Malthusian theory of population in the classical theory of growth and development and sometimes fails so much as to mention the Malthusian theory in accounts of what was classical economics (e.g. Garegnani 1983: 162, 1984: 295, 1987: 118–229; Bharadwaj 1985; but see Kurz and Salvadori 1998b: 70–1, which mentions it parenthetically). No doubt, they would argue, all that belongs to the periphery and not to the core of classical economics, concerned as it is with long-period pricing in accordance with a uniform rate of return on capital. But to present the essence of classical economics as having no room for the Malthusian theory of population is to present Hamlet without mentioning the Prince of Denmark.

Besides (and now we come to the crux of the matter) the idea that the classical economists must have taken the real wage as a datum because the logical consistency of their theory demanded it is a perfect example of a rational reconstruction of past theories: it reads Smith and Ricardo and Marx through Walrasian-tinted glasses. It is not always appreciated, least of all by Sraffians, how thoroughly Sraffa's *Production of Commodities* is steeped in Walrasian general equilibrium theory: by page 5 of his book Sraffa is already counting equations and unknowns to check that he has enough independent equations to determine his unknown prices uniquely, and the notion that long-run linear production equations have at least one degree of freedom, and therefore that at least one distributional variable must be taken as given to close the model, is pure Walras. It so happens that the problem of not-enough-equations would not even arise if Sraffa had allowed production coefficients to vary, but that is irrelevant. The real point is that this rigorous Walrasian counting of equations and unknowns to solve 'the existence problem' certainly tells us what determines prices in final end-state equilibrium – if that is what we really want to know – but in no way helps us to grasp how prices ever converge on an end-state equilibrium. Indeed, if the history of ideas tells us anything it is that theories like those of Walras or Kenneth Arrow and Gerard Debreu, which concentrate their attention on solving the existence problem rigorously, consistently fail to throw light on how markets adjust in disequilibrium to attain final end-state equilibrium. There really is a hiatus in thought between a Walrasian and an 'Austrian' notion of market adjustments, between what I call an 'end state' and a 'process' conception of competition (Blaug 1997b; Rosen 1997).

It is one thing to pay due attention to the interdependences between markets and the simultaneous determination of output and input prices to escape the logical traps of circular reasoning about critical economic variables, but, in general, to pursue ruthlessly the goal of a watertight, mathematically consistent theory of price determination is to fall into the type of sterile formalism that has characterised general equilibrium theory in its modern Arrow–Debreu form. In one way or the other, some Sraffians sense that danger and distinguish between general equilibrium modelling – a good thing – and general equilibrium theory *à la* Walras – a bad thing (Walsh and Gram 1980: 63, 148, 167; Mongiovi 1996). All too often, however, the counting of equations and unknowns to check how many variables we need to take as data is regarded as a sacrosanct first step in rigorous analysis. I suggest that Marshall knew better: he kept his general equilibrium theory in an appendix and employed the *ceteris paribus* method of partial equilibrium to practise substantive economics.

Competition

We are not yet done with the misunderstanding of classical economics conveyed by Sraffian historians of economic thought. The classical economists were renowned in their own day for their celebration of the market mechanism, and, while they qualified their endorsement of the 'invisible hand' of competition, their constant disparagement of government action left little doubt that they believed in *laissez-faire*, that is, the doctrine that least government is best government. We read Dobb, Garegnani, Kurz, Salvadori, John Eatwell, Roncaglia, Bertram Schefold, de Vivo, and Bharadwaj in vain looking for so much as a reference to the classical conception of competition. That conception was a far cry from the modern conception of perfect competition, which was virtually invented *de novo* by A. A. Cournot in 1839 (Backhouse 1990). The classical idea of competition was a process-conception or 'Austrian' view of competition as a form of rivalry between producers involving price and non-price dimensions, implying not the impotence of price takers in perfect competition but the potent adversarial struggle of price makers to gain profits by almost any means that would attract customers. We think of it as 'imperfect competition', but it is of course ironic that the only competition that is ever observed in a capitalist economy is labelled *imperfect* (Blaug 1997c [1962]: 579–80, 592–4, 1997a: 60–1).

Let us call this type of competition, perceived as a dynamic process taking place in real time, *free competition*, which, by the way, is what Marshall, who of course shared the classical process conception of competition, called it. Both Garegnani (1990: 113) and Kurz and Salvadori (1998b: 16, 53) refer to 'free or perfect competition' as if it were the same thing and seem oblivious of the fact that the gulf between the classical notion of competition and that of Cournot, Walras, Ysidro Edgeworth, and Vilfredo Pareto is greater than the gulf between those of Marx and Frederic Bastiat. And why this lacuna in such otherwise acute economists? Because there is no competition of any kind in Sraffa, not even of the perfect-competition variety. Competitive prices are just competitive prices in Sraffa, and not a word is wasted on telling us how we got there and how we would get back to them in case of a demand or supply shock.

Some years ago, Ian Steedman (1984) considered the stability of classical long-period equilibrium, characterised as it is, among other things, by the equality of the market price and the natural price of a commodity. Steedman raised the question of what would happen if a commodity's market price exceeded its natural price; would this also imply that the industry's profit rate would always exceed its natural rate, with subsequent adjustments restoring the long-period equilibrium with a uniform rate of profit in all industries? He showed that this was not necessarily the case; in short, a classical long-period equilibrium may be unstable. Others soon reasserted the stability of a classical long-period equilibrium, but to this day Sraffians do not agree among themselves that the 'cross-dual dynamics' involved in classical adjustment processes are in fact stabilising (Semmler 1987; Flaschel and Semmler 1987; Duménil and Lévy 1987, 1998; Boggio 1998; Cesaratto 1996; Roncaglia 1996a; Garegnani 1997 [1990]). Be that as it may, what is striking about this mini-debate within the Sraffian camp is the extent to which the stability of competitive adjustments is discussed entirely in terms of price and quantity adjustments in response to the existence of positive new excess demand. It is as if Marshall had never written, so that economic dynamics can be considered only in general equilibrium terms *à la* Walras.

Conclusion

In the words of Garegnani, 'The fact that, as Harcourt puts it, "there is no history in Sraffa" has to do with *Production of Commodities* being exclusively concerned with the relations in what I have here called the "core" of classical theory and is not due to the theoretical approach he is reviving here' (Garegnani 1990: 139). This core–periphery distinction allows Garegnani to kill two birds with one stone: Ricardo and bits of Marx for the core, and the whole of Smith, Mill, and most of Marx for the periphery. To his credit, he, alone among all Sraffian interpreters, denies that the core is somehow superior to or more significant than the periphery (Garegnani 1990: 151–2), but that is merely a fail-safe rhetorical device; he pays little or no attention to the periphery and clearly suggests that the choice between classical and neoclassical economics is a choice between two cores.

The core–periphery distinction is perfectly defensible for a rational reconstruction of classical economics, although even here one has to say that it works perfectly for Marx only when he tackles the 'transformation problem' in Volume III of *Capital*. Contrary to a widespread belief, Sraffa's concern in *Production of Commodities* is not the same as Ricardo's in *Principles*: Ricardo was innocent of the Walrasian problem of how one can simultaneously determine relative prices and the rate of profit, which is the underlying question that Sraffa addresses. Ricardo's question was: how do relative prices change when income distribution varies and, in particular, when technology causes the rate of profit to decline in real time?

The core–periphery distinction will stand as a rational reconstruction of classical economics, but it is an inaccurate and positively misleading historical reconstruction. It squeezes classical economics down into a Walrasian box and leaves out all the interesting elements that have proved fruitful down the years and are still bearing fruit in institutional, evolutionary, and radical economics.

I admit that faithful historical reconstructions are literally impossible and that, of course, every new departure in modern economics leads to an inevitable tendency to construct a historical pedigree, tracing the newly found truths back to earlier sources of inspiration, the more so in this case because Sraffians believe themselves to be confronted with a hostile neoclassical world. But one must either totally forgo historical reconstructions, in the manner of Morishima's (1996) readings of Ricardo and Marx, or aim to make historical reconstructions as descriptively accurate as possible, leaning heavily on what contemporaries made of these ideas. This is an aim of which Sraffians have totally lost sight. Compared with their tendentious accounts of Smith and Ricardo – they actually say relatively little about Marx and ignore poor Mill altogether – even Hollander's Ricardo is a model of anti-Whig historical interpretation.

So is there a 'core' of classical economics? Obviously yes, if by *core* we mean a central strand by which we recognise a work as belonging to 'classical economics', the strand that unites Smith in 1776, Mill in 1848, and Marx in 1867. It is made up, all commentators agree, of a particular theory of value and distribution. First, classical value theory focuses on long-period equilibrium prices characterised by a uniform rate of profit on capital, uniform rates of pay for every different type of labour, and uniform rents per acre for every qualitatively different type of land; in short, what Smith called 'natural prices' in contrast to 'market prices', subject to the vagaries of demand and supply. These natural prices were determined by competitive jockeying between buyers and sellers in the context of a technology of production characterised in physical terms and expressed for practical purposes in hours of labour. Natural prices evolved through time in response both to changes in technology and to changes in the supply of the augmentable inputs into the productive process, that is, capital and labour. In other words, the 'core' of classical economics always involved some version of the labour theory of value, a more or less detailed analysis of the forces making for capital accumulation and, of course, a thin or thick version of the Malthusian theory of population. Indeed, theories of capital accumulation and population growth are more characteristic of the 'core' of classical economics than a theory of value grounded in a linear production technology. That still leaves a huge periphery of concerns regarding monetary policy, banking control, labour relations, industrial organisation and reform, education policies, health and safety regulation, and so on, where considerable disagreement prevailed even among contemporary classical economists, such as Say and James Mill or Nassau Senior and John Stuart Mill, not to mention early eighteenth-century and late nineteenth-century classical economists. But even then the 'core' of classical economics, the moving equilibrium theory of value and distribution, is always discernible. It is, however, a larger and rather different core from the one that Sraffians claim to have delineated.[13]

I give the last word to Stefano Zamagni, who is more sympathetic to the 'classical revival', as Sraffa's followers would have it, than I am: 'Because the classical theory is a theory of an evolutionary process rather than a theory of rational choice between known alternatives, one is not doing the classical vision a service if one continues to look at it through the lenses of the linear production model' (Zamagni 1990: 217). That expresses my basic criticism of the Sraffian interpretation of classical economics more succinctly than ever I could.

Notes

I wish to thank my discussant at the commemorative symposium for Giovanni Caravale held at the University of Rome 'La Sapienza' in June 1998, and Roger Backhouse, D. P. O'Brien, and Terry Peach for helpful comments on an earlier version of this chapter.

1 The distinction itself derives from Richard Rorty. It is similar to the distinction between what Quentin Skinner calls 'intellectual history' and Joseph Schumpeter calls 'history of economic analysis' (Waterman 1998: 303–4).

2 By the way, everything in this chapter I have said before (Blaug 1987) but apparently to no purpose, because Sraffian writers have simply ignored my objections. Hopefully, the present version of my arguments is better expressed than before and *may* receive a hearing.

3 The first 'strong' version of the surplus approach appears in Dobb (1973: 33–5, 169, 257, 261) and even earlier in Meek (1967: 161), which draws on his Ph.D. dissertation, 'The Development of the Concept of Surplus in Economic Thought from Mun to Mill', supervised by Dobb and Sraffa.

4 A handbook to classical economics, edited by Kurz and Salvadori (1998a), adds more than 100 names to the list of those who endorse the Sraffian 'understanding' of classical economics. But among these see Steedman for a welcome note of caution (Kurz and Salvadori 1998a: 117–22).

5 As Nicholas Kaldor once said: 'to pinpoint the critical area where economic theory went astray . . . when the theory of value took over the centre of the stage – which meant focusing attention on the *allocative* functions of markets to the exclusion of their *creative* functions – as an instrument for transmitting impulses to economic change. To locate the source of error with more precision, I would put it in the middle of the fourth chapter of Vol. I of *The Wealth of Nations* [when Smith turns from the division of labour to the distinction between money price and real price]' (Kaldor 1972: 1240).

6 Whether Ricardo's pessimism was merely a rhetorical ploy to frighten the friends of agricultural protection or a genuine expression of doubt about Britain's long-term growth prospects is, of course, an old question in the history of economic thought (see Blaug 1958: 32–3).

7 It was Marshall who first underlined this assumption of zero price elasticity of demand for corn, but it must be granted that Ricardo sometimes denied it outright. In the *Protection of Agriculture* pamphlet, he said: 'The demand for corn, with a given population, must necessarily be limited, and although it may be, and undoubtedly is, true, that when it is abundant and cheap, the quantity consumed will be increased, yet it is equally certain that its aggregate value will be diminished' (Ricardo 1951–73, IV: 219–20; see also Blaug 1958: 11, 1997c [1962]: 110, 131; Barkai 1965, which disagrees with Marshall; Barkai 1967; Peach 1993: 250–6). Garegnani (1983) denies that Smith and Ricardo had any inkling of negatively inclined demand functions, and he is quite right in respect of Smith but not in respect of Ricardo, who had at least a glimpse of the concept, as witnessed by the above quotation.

8 Marx did not, of course, solve it, but he did advance the novel, vaguely articulated thesis that a historical process of 'deskilling' under capitalism would soon render all labour homogeneous and thereby solve the labour reduction problem in reality.

9 Ricardo made the same point in a famous letter to Malthus, quoted in Peach (1993: 208).

10 Along identical lines, Denis O'Brien in his classic survey *The Classical Economists* commented: 'It is true that the method of comparative statics . . . is . . . to be found in the Classicists, above all in Ricardo: but the comparative-statics method was principally employed at a macro-economic level. . . . Although it certainly makes its appearance, it was far from exclusively used by the Classical economists who were in general at least as much interested in the dynamic problem of the path between successive equilibria as in the equilibria themselves. . . . They were concerned in particular with situations in which technology, tastes and incomes were *not* fixed, and with problems framed against a background of those variables rather than with static maximisation' (O'Brien 1975: 54). We do well to remember each time we claim to have grasped what Ricardo really meant that, with the exception of Marx and Keynes, Ricardo has attracted more conflicting exegeses than any other great economist (Aksoy 1991). Incidentally, E. G. Aksoy's valuable but neglected book just missed the boat in being *the* book on Ricardo interpretations, but, appearing in 1991, it takes no account of Morishima and Peach. However, it includes a careful review of such famous interpreters as Samuel Bailey, Marx, Marshall, Wesley Clair Mitchell, Joseph Schumpeter, Frank Knight, George Stigler, Sraffa, and Hollander.

11 I said exactly that in 1987 (Blaug 1987: 157). Giovanni Caravale and Domenico Tosato (1980: chapter 3) said it long before that in the 1974 Italian version of their book. Kurz and Salvadori (1998b: 144–5) criticise me, quite rightly, for suggesting that Sraffa's standard commodity makes prices independent of distribution, which is logically impossible, since the standard commodity is only a particular *numéraire.*

12 Did Ricardo assume a constant real wage, and hence a steadily rising money wage in response to the rising price of corn, or a variable money wage that might sometimes fall, alongside the falling profit rate, if the supply of labour were to outrun the demand for labour? This is a much debated question in the Ricardo industry, with no clear decision either way, because Ricardo was simply inconsistent on this issue, most of all in his muddled fifth chapter on wages in the *Principles* (Blaug 1985, 1997c [1962]: 139–40). Of course, it is always dangerous to attribute inconsistency to an author, because then we have no way of knowing whether the inconsistency is the fault of the text or of our understanding of it; this is the so-called hermeneutic circle of Frederick David Schleiermacher, the German theologian who invented hermeneutics at just the time that Ricardo was writing. Let's escape from the circle by saying that Ricardo was usually consistent, amazingly so compared with Smith, but on wages he was simply driven into inconsistencies by Malthus's relentless criticisms.

13 Kurz and Salvadori's (1998a, I: 159–65) entry 'Classical political economy' in their handbook on classical economics emphasises that the classical economists 'were concerned with an economic system in motion' but adds that static, long-period analysis 'was the best available to them' because they lacked the analytical tools to allow a rigorous 'dynamic analysis of the highly complex system'. If this is not reading backward I don't know what it is: they simply cannot conceive of analytical rigour except in modern terms.

6 Misunderstanding the Sraffian reading of the classical theory of value and distribution

A note

Carlo Panico

1. In 1985 Giovanni Caravale published a book entitled *The Legacy of Ricardo* in which he made an important contribution to one of the most controversial themes in political economy: the interpretation of the classical theory of value and distribution. The controversy is of long standing. Different interpretations of this theory had already been presented at the end of the nineteenth century by those who contributed to the elaboration of the neoclassical theory of value and distribution. Jevons (1879), for instance, argued that the classical approach had little in common with the neoclassical one. Marshall, however, argued that there was continuity between the two approaches. His interpretation was prevailing in the literature when Sraffa started to publish his *Works and Correspondence of David Ricardo*. The quality of Sraffa's editorial work was soon appreciated by the most outstanding figures of the economic profession, like Robbins, who defined it 'a truly monumental work of scholarship'.[1] It brought a broad consensus to the idea, opposite to that proposed by Marshall, that the classical point of view was substantially different from that of the neoclassical tradition. The controversy, however, was not settled. A few years later Hollander (1973b, 1979) rekindled it. More recently Peach (1993, 1998) and Blaug (Chapter 5 in this volume) have challenged the neutrality of the interpretation of classical economics proposed by both Sraffa and his followers. According to Blaug, Sraffian authors, but 'even Piero Sraffa himself', do not give us 'an historically compelling reconstruction of the ideas of Smith, Ricardo, Mill, and Marx' (p. 81 above). They provide us rather with a 'rational reconstruction', which means, for Blaug, with an 'inaccurate' description of the ideas held by contemporaries. For him, 'Sraffians have totally lost sight' of the need 'to make historical reconstructions as descriptively accurate as possible, leaning heavily on what contemporaries made of these ideas'. Indeed – he concludes – their accounts of the classical authors are 'tendentious'.

In this chapter I will try to argue that Blaug's critique is ill founded and misrepresents the analyses of the Sraffian tradition. Without this misrepresentation, the differences between Blaug's position and those of Sraffian authors on classical economics would be easily appreciated by both parties and would be reduced to a minimum.

2. Let us start with the distinction between 'rational' and 'historical' reconstructions, which is the main argument used to criticise the Sraffian interpretation. This distinction may seem, at a first reading, appealing. Yet, on closer consideration, it proves elusive and even misleading, if it is used to evaluate the interpretations proposed by other historians of economic thought.

Like all other scientists, the historian always presents a model of what the historical reality was; the model abstracts, simplifies, looks for those elements which are of interest for him, either for rational or ideological reasons. Thus the attempts to formulate historical reconstructions are necessarily influenced by what we now know and feel. These attempts may lead to alternative hypotheses as to how to interpret the piece of historical reality under consideration and the hypotheses are better formulated by those who have already some knowledge of the particular elements investigated. It is not difficult to think of instances in which a person acquainted with the elements under investigation stands a better chance of achieving a satisfactory historical reconstruction than somebody who knows nothing about them, even if the former runs a greater risk of using present knowledge in performing this work than the latter.

What is thus important in evaluating the quality of a reconstruction is not whether it moves from present knowledge but whether it provides an accurate and complete collection and presentation of the relevant evidence related to the interpretation proposed. It is on these grounds (i.e. on the grounds of the evidence presented) that the scholarship of the analysis must be judged: it is the accurate collection and presentation of the evidence that must therefore be seen as the only legitimate occupation of historians of economic thought.

3. Now the question is: 'Is the Sraffian reconstruction accurate in the treatment of the relevant evidence related to the classical economists?' Let us move from Sraffa's 1951 introduction to Ricardo's *Principles*, which led to the widespread acceptance of a new interpretation of Ricardo's position. Before then, the work of Ricardo had been interpreted as that of a pre-marginalist. The focus of both these interpretations was on the theory of value and distribution, which Ricardo (1951–73, I: 6) considered 'the principal problem in Political Economy'. For the neoclassical school too this theory was the major element of the foundations of economics.[2]

As Kurz and Salvadori (1995: 7–11) recall, according to Sraffa's (1951: xxxi–xxxiii) new interpretation, the development of Ricardo's thinking on the matter can be divided in four steps.[3] Kurz and Salvadori (1995: 88) also point out that Sraffa clearly stated that 'it was only when the Standard system and the distinction between basics and non-basics had emerged in the course of the present investigation that the above interpretation of Ricardo's theory suggested itself as a natural consequence' (Sraffa 1960: 93). So his interpretation was a consequence of the analytical development of his own work on value and distribution. In Blaug's words, it was a rational reconstruction.

But can we say that this interpretation is not based on an accurate collection and presentation of historical evidence? Sraffa's edition of Ricardo's *Works and Correspondence* has always been unanimously considered 'a work of rare scholarship'

(Stigler 1953). For its accuracy it was honoured by the Swedish Royal Academy in 1961 with the Söderström gold medal.

This strong commitment to accuracy led Sraffa to stress carefully that the corn model was never stated by Ricardo in his extant letters and papers. Yet Sraffa referred to indirect evidence in support of the claim that Ricardo 'must have formulated it either in his lost "papers on the profits of Capital" of March 1814 or in conversation' (Sraffa 1951: xxxi).[4] Kurz and Salvadori (1995: 88, 382) also argue that Sraffa's interpretation is further supported by what Torrens (1820: 361) wrote on the subject and still appears 'to hold the ground as the best available' even after consideration of alternative interpretations, like that proposed by Peach (1993).

4. Of course, Sraffa's reconstruction of Ricardo's theory of value and distribution does not exhaust the analysis of Ricardo's writings. In opposition to Blaug's statement that 'even Piero Sraffa himself . . . omits some of the most exciting and indeed fruitful elements in the thinking of the classical authors' (pp. 81–2 above), one can observe that Sraffa's edition of Ricardo's *Works and Correspondence* is not limited to the problem of value and distribution. The accuracy of his editorial work, as is widely recognised, covers all the problems examined by Ricardo, a view which is further confirmed by the analysis of what is contained in the Sraffa papers, now available at the Wren Library of Trinity College in Cambridge.

Thus the evidence does not confirm that Sraffa considered the theory of value and distribution more significant than other aspects dealt with by classical economists. Nor can one argue that since in some publications an author concentrates his attention on one problem, as Sraffa did in *Production of Commodities*, it implies that he considers the other problems irrelevant. From this point of view one can add that if one wants to draw a distinction between the theories of value and distribution of the different schools of thought (i.e. between the aspect of economics which is contained, according to the dominant school, in the foundations of the discipline), the reference to static long-period equilibrium and to the three groups of data generally recalled by Sraffian authors is correct. After all, as Kurz and Salvadori (1995: 385) recall, already in 1906–7 Bortkiewicz had pointed out 'that the *data* from which the classical approach to the theory of value and distribution starts are sufficient to determine the rate of profit and relative prices; no additional data are needed to determine these variables'. Thus, *on this subject* a distinction between these two great traditions in the history of economic thought, based on the elements just mentioned, appears correct.

5. Of course, the analysis of Ricardo's writings does not exhaust that of all classical economics, which is composed of several elements, sometimes even alternative to each other. This is not denied by Sraffian authors. According to them, the tradition developing from Sraffa's work is part of that more general tradition, known as Post-Keynesian, which attributes great relevance to elements like Smith's, Young's and Kaldor's theories of increasing returns and cumulative processes; to the evolutionary processes affecting economic variables; to the actions of the monetary authorities and to the organisation of financial markets in the analysis of the rates of interest; to the historical and institutional elements affecting the real wage; and so on. From this point of view, Sraffian authors

agree with Marshall's view that the function of analysis and deduction is to forge rightly many short chains of reasoning. They consider this notion a useful way of organising thoughts on a complex subject like the working of the economic system. The structure of their theory of value and distribution makes it possible to achieve this goal. It focuses on the *relationships* between relative prices and distributive variables, leaving the study of the *level* of those variables, as well as the study of the level of output and of the dynamic process of technological change, open to further investigation, in which historical and institutional elements can play a role. For them, it is thus possible to combine the analytical relationship linking the rate of wages, the rate of profit and relative prices with other analytical structures dealing with technology, labour markets, financial markets, and so on, structures which belong to the Post-Keynesian tradition and which can also come from the writings of different classical economists.

This view may appear obvious to Sraffian authors, who do not reject or consider irrelevant whatever is not static long-period analysis of value and distribution.

6. To sum up, the criticisms advanced by Blaug against the Sraffian interpretation of classical economics do not seem convincing. They fail to take account of the scholarship of Sraffa's editorial work on Ricardo's writings and misrepresent the analyses of the Sraffian tradition.

None the less, his essay may stimulate some reflections on which are to be considered the main features of classical economics. Blaug objects to the use of the expression 'core', adopted by some Sraffians in relation to the theory of value and distribution. He claims that Smith's analysis of the division of labour and technical progress and the institutional and demographical analyses proposed by Smith, Malthus and Ricardo to determine the level of the real wage rate are to be considered among the main features of classical economics in the same way as the theory of value and distribution.

In my view, Sraffians would agree that a satisfactory theoretical approach *must* deal with the problems recalled by Blaug. They would only add that, from an analytical point of view, since the data from which the classical approach to the theory of value and distribution starts are sufficient to determine the rate of profit and relative prices, the analyses of technical change and of the other elements, however important, do not need to be included within the essential analytical structure of the theory of value and distribution. This makes it possible to combine the results of this theory with several alternative analyses of the other equally important elements, in order to achieve an articulated view of the complex working of the economic system.

If the expression 'core' is the source of the problems, there can be something to gain in abandoning it: by avoiding the misrepresentations it seems to cause, it is possible to appreciate clearly and reduce to a minimum the differences between Blaug's position and that of Sraffian authors on classical economics.

Notes

The author gratefully acknowledges the financial support received from the Italian MURST and CNR to the research projects on which the content of this chapter draws.

1 See Rosselli (2001: 192).
2 To justify this claim it is sufficient to recall the content of Marshall's *Principles of Economics* or that of Volume I of Wicksell's *Lectures on Political Economy*.
3 In the first step, he got rid of the problem of rent. In the second, he tried to solve the problem of value by assuming in 1815 the 'corn model', in which the composition of the product is exactly the same as that of the capital advanced. In the third step, in the *Principles*, he presented the labour theory of value 'in order to overcome the analytical difficulty encountered in his attempt to explain profits in terms of the surplus product left after making allowance for the cost of production, including the wages of productive workers' (Kurz and Salvadori 1995: 10). The fourth step was his subsequent search for a measure of value which did not change when distribution changes.
4 For more details on the evidence presented by Sraffa in 1951 see Kurz and Salvadori (1995: 88–9).

7 Is it possible to define a canonical classical growth model?

Eugenio Zagari

This brief chapter addresses the historiographical problem raised by the attempt of two eminent scholars, Paul Samuelson and Samuel Hollander, to single out a 'canonical classical growth model'. Samuelson (1978) elaborated the analytical structure of such a model. Hollander (Chapter 3 in this volume) provides instead the textual references which support, on the one hand, Samuelson's work and, on the other, the existence of a single informatory principle, beginning with Smith, then on to Ricardo, Malthus, McCulloch and, to some extent, Marx. This one principle is capable of placing the opinions of many scholars on economic growth into one unique formulation.

The informatory principle, according to the two scholars, is characterised by the following three circumstances:

1 reduction in agricultural yields,
2 complementation of labour and capital,
3 tendency of the profit rate to fall.

The advantages of this approach are immediately evident: it brings classical scholars into a unitary formulation, thus creating common ground for debate instead of the scission which, in the years to come, will be worked on by scholars facing the same arguments. It also allows the identification of the roots of modern theoretical formulas which have brought up again the inverse relationship between the growth rates of wages and profits in order to explain the laws of distribution.

Furthermore, it gives an opportunity to experience the formal strictness of propositions at times formulated in an approximative way and to accept completely new implications with the help of modern techniques of economic analysis. However, we must acknowledge that an underlying problem exists, and one which we believe has been underestimated by the two scholars. The problem has two aspects which can be summarised as:

1 To what extent is it possible to individualise, select and utilise single parts of a complex argument with the purpose of formulating theoretical propositions which become explicit only in the theses of the scholars who formulate them?

2 What is the limit up to which it is possible to reinterpret and re-elaborate theories created in a specific historical and cultural context, with methodologies and techniques of analysis evolved in different cultural contexts?

We all know that these two question marks are represented in every historian of thought's work and that perhaps the historian's work is justified and has substance in so far as it individualises streams of research with homogeneous characteristics or as it rediscovers the validity of theses elaborated in the past. The question of the limitations for the historian of thought remains open in any case. How far can we push ourselves in these two directions?

If we listen to the suggestions coming from the supporters of a methodological approach different from Samuelson's or Hollander's, we can use the following guide for the solution:

1 Economic theories – it is said – are the fruit of wide-ranging thought which are heavily linked with defined historical and cultural contexts; therefore, it is possible to epitomise parts of theories, as long as it is done out of the context being referred to, and is read as an enunciation of paradigms which have recognisable historical coordinates.
2 It is possible to demonstrate, with the aid of modern methodologies, the analytical developments of the past as long as these methodologies are neutral.

These are commonsense suggestions which tend to maintain a link between the history of ideas and the history of facts, and moreover, to connect analytical results with the complex significance of the theories.

Getting back to Hollander, it is important to verify whether the two limits indicated above have become outdated and then to formulate the first question: is it feasible to presuppose that the individualisation of a unique model of development in the classics is not in contradiction with the work of each scholar? In Smith's philosophy, undeniably, the theoretical mechanism which characterises development is the utilisation of surplus in order to enlarge the productive work base and so to offset decreasing land profits with manufacturing innovations. Malthus instead thought that the condition for development is the creation of demand effective enough to be able to absorb surplus products produced by workers. Ricardo believed economic development is linked with the accumulation of capital and with safeguarding profits through the reduction of the cost of wage goods.

Through the comparison of these theories, it is clear that the main scholars of the 'classical' period in the theory of development attributed different roles to innovations, to the market, to the distribution of profit and wages, and that only incidentally, except for Ricardo, did they consider the inverse relationship between wages and profits.

The next question regards the possibility of utilising the outlines of relationships which today's economic theory uses to represent past theories. On this subject we would recall the recommendation that Samuel Hollander made on another occasion: 'the use of modern analytical tools, concepts and procedures may be of considerable aid in an analysis of the work of an early writer, *provided that he was operating within the general frame of reference for which these devices are appropriate*' (Hollander 1973a: 13).

The diversity of the referral framework would make the representation techniques of economic phenomena non-neutral. A question then arises for Hollander: is it possible to have doubts on the diversity of the general referral framework of classical and modern theorists on economic development? Was it not the classical scholar's theory which was dominated by the law of population and by the conviction that a natural order exists in economic relationships?

Therefore we can conclude that the attempt to formalise a 'canonical model of development' with modern analytical techniques is bound to be criticised for reasons which should not be neglected, as in substance those techniques dress the classical theory up in a new outfit and, what is more, in new modern fabric unsuited to characters which had much different attributes.

8 Garegnani's interpretation of the 'old classical economists'

Enrico Zaghini

This chapter proposes an initial, synthetic assessment of Garegnani's interpretation of the position of the classical economists emerging from Sraffa's mature work – essentially the introduction to Ricardo's *Principles* (1951) and *Production of Commodities by Means of Commodities* (1960). In particular, I shall focus upon the two essays 'On some supposed obstacles to the tendency of market prices towards natural prices' (1997 [1990]) and 'Sraffa: the theoretical world of the "old classical economists"' (Chapter 4 of this volume).

Before taking issue with Garegnani's interpretation, I should like to highlight a major point of agreement. Judging from the two essays in question, I think we share the conviction that a theory that identifies a specific position of a given phenomenon can be considered empirically significant only if the theory also demonstrates that the phenomenon will over time conform with the configuration identified by the theory. This implies the existence of a dynamic process describing the behaviour over time of the variables representing the phenomenon, with the values of these variables tending to converge towards the position predicted by the theory and to remain there in the absence of shocks, and with that position consequently constituting a resting point in the dynamic process.[1] In the discussion below, the expressions 'long-run position' and 'equilibrium' will always mean a persistent position of rest of a dynamic, real-time process.

The space available here does not allow systematic examination of Garegnani's interpretation of classical theory. I shall therefore concentrate on several points concerning the adjustment process, which should be sufficient to elucidate my position.

According to Garegnani, the classic dynamic process that should 'explain the tendency of a commodity's actual price – or "market price" as the classical economists called it – towards a normal or "natural" level'[2] satisfies the following hypotheses:

1 The real wage, being determined by economic and social forces independent of labour demand and supply functions, remains at its normal level throughout the process and is thus a datum with respect to it.
2 The adjustment of each commodity's market price to its normal value is based on the relation between market supply (quantity brought to the market) and effectual demand, defined by Smith as 'the demand of those

who are willing to pay the natural price of the commodity' and hence representing the normal level of demand. In particular, the following rules apply: (a) if supply exceeds (falls short of) effectual demand, the market price will be lower (higher) than the normal level;[3] (b) if the market price is higher (lower) than the natural price, the quantity supplied will increase (decrease); (c) as supply increases but remains below effectual demand, market prices will decrease but remain above the normal level.[4]

The main general criticism that I have to raise concerning this depiction of the adjustment process is the following. On the one hand, the mechanism in question is supposed to represent the operation, outside the long-term position, of a decentralised economy in which decisions are made by individual agents. On the other, these decisions are supposed to be guided by the observation of unobservable variables, such as effectual demand and natural prices. In other words, the description is vitiated by the assumption that agents, outside of equilibrium, know the economic system's equilibrium configuration and are guided by it – a variant of the perfect knowledge or foresight hypothesis that plagues a good part of modern theory.[5]

I am firmly convinced that a realistic description must, in principle, recognise that agents' decisions are directly or indirectly based on actual, observable variables, allowing a common capacity for knowledge on their part. In our case, for example, the effective market price should be compared not with the natural price, an unobservable variable, but with the cost of production expressed in terms of the effective market prices of the inputs. By the same token, the term of comparison of market output should be current demand and not the effectual demand corresponding to the economy's normal position.

In truth, reading the classical economists may give one the impression that Garegnani's interpretation is correct, since there are frequent comparisons between current variables, prices or quantities, and the corresponding normal or natural levels. However, the impression is misleading and arises because in treating problems of disequilibrium the classical economists, for the sake of simplicity, nearly always start out from an equilibrium condition, so that the term of the first (and often the only) comparison is quite naturally the normal, long-term value.

In the event, Garegnani himself appears to admit the weakness of the previous description of the classical adjustment process: in fact, in Garegnani (1997 [1990]), where he addresses a specific analytical problem relating to the adjustment of market prices towards natural prices, he moves away from the schema presented above, with the motivation of employing a more realistic description of adjustment than the one he attributes to the classical economists but one that is none the less entirely consistent with the latter. In particular, he introduces the concept of *market effectual demand*, i.e. the 'quantity . . . which would be demanded for use in the current "market" position of the economy' and which will therefore 'be referred to the actual prices and outputs of that position'. Garegnani views this notion as a generalisation of Smith's concept of (normal) effectual demand to positions of the economy other than the natural position and justifies it as follows: 'The usefulness of this concept of market effectual demand lies in the fact that the current behaviour of market prices will depend on the "proportion" which the current output bears on it, rather than on the proportion it bears to normal effectual demand' (Garegnani 1997 [1990]: 146).

With this concept Garegnani takes a major step towards acknowledging that any realistic description of the process whereby prices and quantities are determined must be based on observable quantities. Even so, his model still does not completely satisfy this criterion, since the concept of the market effectual demand for a commodity is also based on an unobservable variable, i.e. its *reference price*, defined as the price that 'would yield the natural rate of profit r^* on the wages and the prices of the means of production estimated at their *market levels*' (Garegnani 1997 [1990]: 145).

Even if the concept of market effectual demand is incomplete for the reasons just stated, it none the less allows us to discuss the problem of whether or not demand functions are present in classical theory. What does it mean that market effectual demand is that which is referred, except for its reference price, to the actual prices and outputs of the economy's current position? It means that, corresponding to actual prices and actual incomes, which derive from those prices and from the actual levels of output, the total quantity demanded of every commodity is defined. And this can be done for every subsequent position of the system during the adjustment. But *this potentially infinite possibility of determining market effectual demand in relation to the potentially infinite actual market positions of prices and quantities necessarily implies that it is possible to express the quantities demanded in terms of prices and incomes – that is, to formulate demand 'functions'*.

Actually, Garegnani avoids using the word 'function' in connection with his definition of the market effectual demand for commodity i and simply indicates it with D_i^m. But having referred it to its *reference price* m_i^*, to the current prices m_j of other commodities and to current outputs O_j, he could easily (and indeed, by the current standards of economic theory, should) have written it as:

$$D_i^m(m_1, \ldots, m_{i-1}, m_i^*, m_{i+1}, \ldots, m_n, O_1, \ldots, O_n)$$

i.e. as a function of prices and output levels, rendering explicit its dependence on these variables.

Once the market effectual demand function has been defined, a market demand function can be derived from it by replacing the reference price with the corresponding market price m_i, thus obtaining a demand function that depends on all the current market values and whose use in the framework of the price adjustment mechanism is not subject to the above criticism for violating the reality principle.

Naturally, one can avoid calling a function by its name and resort to circumlocution to express its dependence on the variables on which it effectively depends. But if one does recognise this dependence, which obviously implies defining a function, there is no reason for such a course: the use of the concept of function considerably simplifies exposition, and one can hardly deny that one is actually using that concept.

If instead the motive is to avoid using neoclassical demand functions, it is appropriate to point out two things. First, the demand functions that emerge from analysis of the classical economics can be considered as original data; there is no need to follow the subsequent neoclassical tradition and consider them as being derived from constrained maximisations of utility functions. Second, they differ from the traditional ones in an important respect: they lack the notional nature of the latter, which derive from the incomes that agents presume they will obtain in the event that they are able to realise their plans, but are based instead on actual incomes arising from current levels of output. In other words, they are *effective* demand functions, according to the terminology of Clower (1965), and are thus also compatible with the existence of equilibria in the presence of excesses of supply. This constitutes an appreciable difference with respect to traditional theory and is an important link with the Keynesian school.

We can now clarify just what normal effectual demand is. The normal effectual demand for a commodity, i.e. 'the quantity . . . of the commodity which would be demanded when the prices and outputs of *all* commodities were at their normal levels' (Garegnani 1997 [1990]: 141), is simply the *value* of that commodity's demand function when prices and outputs are at their normal levels. That value, together with the value of the natural price, constitutes a *point* in the price–quantity space. The existence of demand functions, which operate in the adjustment process, is therefore not incompatible with demands being represented in the long-term position by individual values that constitute 'points' when coupled with the corresponding natural prices. This conclusion shows that Garegnani's statement that 'Smith's "effectual demand" could be described only as a *point*, and not a *schedule*, in the price–quantity space' (p. 69 above), while obviously true, is quite irrelevant to the question of the existence of demand functions in the classical competitive mechanism.[6]

We come now to what is perhaps the fundamental question, which has three closely interrelated aspects: (1) the identification of the data in the classical competitive mechanism; (2) the possibility of distinguishing between two separate parts in the classical theory; (3) whether the economy is in a stationary state.

Garegnani is rather evasive on the first two points: he includes normal effectual demands along with the real wage rate and technical conditions of production among the data of the natural price determination process[7] but also states that natural prices are necessary data for defining effectual demands.[8] Moreover, when Garegnani (pp. 70–1) distinguishes between a part of the classical theory where profits and prices 'are determined by means of the competitive price equations', deemed to be the theory's core, and a part 'concerned with relations of a more inductive kind like those underlying changes in the real wage or in the outputs, or in the technical conditions of production', deemed to play the role of 'intermediate data' with respect to the 'core', he tells us that this second 'part of the theory . . . also includes the interactions between such "intermediate data", *as well as any feedback on them of the prices and profits, the unknown of the "core"*' (italics added), thus denying the possibility of keeping the two parts separate.

Now, how can some variables be data for determining others and the latter in turn be data for determining the former? In reality, the existence of such strong links makes it legitimate to doubt that these are true data, all the more so bearing in mind that prices and outputs are precisely the variables involved in the adjustment process. I think the explanation for this unhappy situation lies in the logical impossibility of Garegnani's interpretation of the classical economic theory. To grasp this, it is necessary to consider the nature of the competitive process governing the determination of prices and outputs according to the classical economists.

Apart from qualifications that have no material impact on the conclusions to be reached below, it is universally acknowledged that the classical competitive mechanism is based on the idea that disequilibria in quantities – represented by differences (however defined) between outputs and demands for commodities[9] – stimulate variations in prices, whereas disequilibria in prices – expressed by differences in expected profit rates, equal to current rates, or, equivalently, by differences in the ratios between prices and production costs – stimulate variations in outputs. In this mechanism one cannot speak of a price adjustment process that is independent of the adjustment of outputs; the dynamics of the first group of variables depends on the position of the second group, and vice versa. In other words, the two processes are part of a single competitive process that operates inseparably and simultaneously on current market prices and quantities.

It follows that the first group of variables can assume a position of rest if *and only if* the second group is also at rest. In other words, the equalisation of all the rates of profit, implying that market prices are equal to their natural level, can persist in time if and only if outputs are equal to the demands generated on the basis of those same outputs and the natural levels of prices. If all prices were at their natural levels but the output of one commodity were, say, lower than the demand corresponding to those prices, there would be a stimulus to increase the price of that commodity, and its actual increase would make prices diverge from their natural values. Symmetrically, if outputs were equal to the quantities demanded at market prices not coinciding with their natural levels, there would be a diversity of profit rates and a consequent stimulus to modify outputs and thus to break the temporary market-clearing situation.

Accordingly, in the long-term position the equalisation of profit rates, i.e. the realisation of natural prices, and market clearing in all goods markets necessarily go hand in hand.

As already noted, in the long-term position outputs are equal to the demands generated by those same outputs and by the natural levels of prices. That is, they are equal, commodity by commodity, to what Garegnani (1997 [1990]: 141) calls normal effectual demand: 'the quantity . . . of the commodity which would be demanded when the prices and outputs of *all* commodities were at their normal levels'. With prices remaining at the natural levels implying a uniform profit rate, these outputs receive no stimulus to change and thus remain equal to the values of normal effectual demands, so that in the long-term position all quantities (i.e. the levels of both output and demand) remain constant. Recalling that natural prices are constant, this implies that *the long-term position of the classical competitive mechanism is stationary with respect to all variables, prices and quantities.*[10]

In conclusion, these two properties – market clearing and stationarity of the long-term position – are necessary implications of the classical competitive model.

Let us now return to the statements by Garegnani that were our starting point. Taken together, they imply that in the classical competitive process the real wage, technical conditions of production, normal effectual demands and natural prices are given, as are normal levels of output, since the latter are equal to effectual demands.

In the light of the above analysis, the literal import of these statements is that among the data of the classical competitive process is the whole long-term configuration of the variables of the process, i.e. its equilibrium. But equilibrium – its existence and its stability – is precisely what the theory ought to explain. The equilibrium position is a property of the process that can be derived only after the process has been completely defined from the point of view of both the relations of change of the variables and its data; by its very nature it cannot belong to the category of data. Garegnani's choice of data and variables thus appears to contain an irremediable contradiction.[11]

I think there is no escaping this conclusion, but I also think it is useful to understand the origin of the contradiction. This can best be done by taking as a point of departure the following succinct summary by Garegnani of his position:

> In the course of our argument we shall follow in the footsteps of Adam Smith and the old classical economists and take as *given*, and therefore as *constant* during the process of adjustment, the normal effectual demand of each commodity – the quantity, that is, of the commodity which would be demanded when the prices and outputs of *all* commodities were at their normal levels. It should be immediately noted that this classical postulate does not imply any assumption of stationarity of the economy. It only rests on the view that the forces of competition, which may bring market prices towards the natural prices, will be acting in a way which is broadly independent of what the normal outputs (effectual demands) happen to be or of how they happen to evolve over time. It follows that market prices are best studied *separately* from the circumstances determining the normal quantities produced and the latter may be taken as given when studying the former.
>
> (Garegnani 1997 [1990]: 141)

The above passage contains all the elements we have mentioned: normal effectual demands and normal outputs among the data, the values of these demands referred to natural prices, non-stationarity of the economy and the consequent possibility of splitting the classical analysis into two parts. Underpinning Garegnani's position is the idea that demand conditions play no role in determining prices: not only in defining their equilibrium position, which would be a consequence of the theorem of non-substitution and of the hypothesis of given real wages, but also in the dynamic process explaining the tendency of effective prices towards that position, with the result that the classical competitive mechanism can be reduced to the part that determines prices, isolating it from the part that determines quantities and giving it a privileged position in the framework of the classical theory. This procedure alone would support distinguishing two fields of analysis in classical theory and giving priority to the determination of natural prices as the 'core' of the classical theory and the object of the first, more theoretical field, relegating the determination of quantities to a second, more empirical field of analysis (p. 70, this volume) and thus, even more sharply, distinguishing classical theory from neoclassical theory, in which prices and quantities are assumed to be strictly interdependent and hence studied together.

In Garegnani's view, the clearest sign that the two fields of analysis can be kept separate in classical theory lies in the fact that in the long-term position natural prices can go together with values of normal outputs (effectual demands) that are arbitrary and that can even vary over time. As the above quotation shows, Garegnani expressly denies that the long-term position must be stationary (or, in particular cases, in balanced growth), whereas the foregoing analysis has shown that the long-term position of the classical competitive mechanism is necessarily stationary in its levels or at least its structure.

If Garegnani's interpretation did not in fact imply stationarity, we would have to acknowledge the success of his attempt to reduce the classical competitive mechanism to the part that determines prices, and this would blunt the criticism set out above. The crucial importance of the stationarity or non-stationarity of the long-term position is therefore evident. As will be demonstrated below, Garegnani's attempt is not successful. Even in his two formulations (Garegnani 1997 [1990] and Chapter 4 of this volume) we find not only the property of market clearing, which he appears to admit,[12] but also that of stationarity, which he instead explicitly denies.

For example, in his most completely articulated formulation of the classical competitive process, presented in Garegnani (1997 [1990]), stationarity follows from assumption (7.8):

$$\text{if } O_i \gtreqless D_i^m, \text{ then } m_i \lesseqgtr m_i^* \ (i = 1, 2, \ldots, n)$$

$$\text{and } \frac{d(m_i/m_i^*)}{dt} \gtreqless 0 \text{ according as } \frac{d(O_i/D_i^m)}{dt} \lesseqgtr 0,$$

where all symbols have already been defined.[13] In fact, from the first part of (7.8) it follows that only $O_i = D_i^m$ (market clearing) for all commodities is compatible with $m_i = m_i^*$ for all commodities and hence, as can be readily understood, with market prices equal to the natural levels. Furthermore, from the second part and from what has just been said it follows that the persistence of natural prices in time is compatible only with

$$\frac{d(O_i/D_i^m)}{dt} = 0$$

i.e. taking into account that if prices are at their normal levels market effectual demands become normal effectual demands, only with

$$\frac{d(O_i/D_i^n)}{dt} = 0$$

i.e. with a situation in which outputs are continually equal to normal effectual demands D_i^n, which in general implies a stationary state. If the market effectual demand functions satisfy the particular hypotheses referred to in note 11, continual equality between outputs and normal effectual demands is compatible with proportional growth of the economy and hence of these variables, since the ratios O_i/D_i^n remain constant and the condition

$$\frac{d(O_i/D_i^n)}{dt} = 0$$

continues to hold.[14]

The above shows that, in addition to market clearing, stationarity (or, in particular cases, balanced growth) is a property that follows mathematically from Garegnani's interpretations of the classical competitive process. In other words, this property is a theorem that derives directly from the hypotheses he formulates on the competitive process.

This result is a consequence of the inseparability of the classical competitive process and derives from the logical impossibility of isolating the determination of commodities' prices from the determination of quantities without betraying classical economic thought. Although Garegnani's formulations emphasise price determination, they none the less recognise the classical link between prices and quantities to a degree that is sufficient to impose stationarity on quantities as well. Consequently, if there is convergence, there is convergence towards a well defined set of prices, natural prices, *and* a well defined set of quantities, normal effectual demands (linked with natural prices), which are a result of the process and cannot be considered as data of that process, arbitrarily imposed from outside.[15]

Although the above analysis demonstrates that the idea that normal effectual demands are data in the classical competitive process is unfounded and refutes the thesis of the two distinct fields of analysis, it does not affect what I think is the crucial point for Garegnani: that the classical competitive process is such that its long-term position can be defined, as far as prices are concerned, in terms of technology alone, once the hypothesis is adopted that the real wage is given. It is important that this result is a direct consequence of the hypothesis of a given real wage, for, if I interpret Garegnani correctly, it is precisely this hypothesis that in his view distinguishes the theory of the classical economists from the neoclassical strand of Marshall, Wicksell and Schumpeter, who share with the former the definition of dynamic equilibrium in real time and the principal features of the adjustment process. In fact, with respect to distribution, whereas for the neoclassical economists the real wage is determined by labour demand and supply functions, for the classical economists it is determined by social and economic forces *different* from those governing the adjustment of commodities' market prices towards their corresponding natural prices.

Two distinct problems emerge on this point. The first concerns the correctness of the above interpretation and constitutes a question of the history of economic thought that cannot be discussed in the present context. The second is an analytical problem and consists in ascertaining whether the hypothesis of a given real wage can help economic theory to advance, particularly in the difficult problem of the stability of equilibrium. The analysis of convergence contained in Garegnani (1997 [1990]) transcends the limits of the present remarks. If validated, it should be considered a major contribution to the dynamic problem of stability. In this field – now completely abandoned by traditional theory, with its singleminded concentration on the concept of instantaneous equilibrium, whose justification requires a non-existent 'logical' time – there is ample scope for a common analytical effort aimed at exploring the problems in rigorous fashion and settling at least some of the open questions.

Notes

Financial support from the University 'La Sapienza' of Rome and MURST is gratefully acknowledged.

1 My position is presented in Zaghini (1990, 1993), where I focus on the preliminary task of defining (and demonstrating the existence of) an equilibrium as a resting point of a dynamic process. As for Garegnani, I offer the following quotation: 'a problem as central as the tendency to the positions of the economy determined by the theory, on which tendency the validation of classical theory, as of any conceivable alternative theory, does ultimately depend' (Garegnani 1997 [1990]: 161).

2 Natural prices are those prices that imply a uniform rate of profit in relation to production costs.

3 Indicating point E, identified by effectual demand and the natural price, in the quantity–price space, '[n]orthwest of that point there lay an *area* in which the "market price" . . . was postulated to lie, whenever the output fell short of the "effectual demand"' (p. 69, this volume). This rule implies that if an equilibrium obtains in which output is equal to effectual demand and the price is equal to its natural level, and if a shock occurs that makes output fall short of effectual demand, the price will rise.

4 In other terms, if $q_1 > q_0$, then $p_1 < p_0$, where the meaning of the symbols is self-evident. Rules b and c render explicit what Garegnani states: 'It was the higher market price that caused the output to ultimately increase towards the effectual demand [rule b], with the "market price" accordingly falling towards the natural price [rule c]' (ibid.).

5 For a similar argument see Caravale (1994a: 237–8).

6 It also allows us to understand that Garegnani is incorrect where he states: 'This character of the classical demand of being single quantities and not functions is what explains the word "proportion" which Adam Smith . . . and the other classical economists applied to the relationship between "demand and supply", i.e. "the quantity brought to market" – a word which would of course have made no sense, had demand been there understood however vaguely as a schedule' (page 69, this volume). On the contrary, the ratio (proportion) between a variable (the quantity brought to market) and a function (the demand function) simply means the ratio between the value of that variable and the *value* assumed by the function (the demand function) in correspondence to the values of the variables on which it depends (market prices and current outputs). Garegnani himself admits as much (1997 [1990]: 146) when he considers the ratio O_i/D_i^m between market effectual output and demand for commodity i, which, as was seen above, is a function dependent on (referred to) market prices and outputs as well as dependent on (referred to) its reference price.

7 In Garegnani (see p. 70, this volume) (normal) effectual demands are included as data along with the real wage and technical conditions. As regards Garegnani (1997 [1990]) see the first sentence of the quotation reported below in the text.

8 'Thus "effectual demand" was defined by Smith as "the demand of those who are willing to pay the natural price of that commodity", with the "natural" or normal

price being therefore a necessary datum for defining that "demand" itself' (Garegnani, pp. 68–9, this volume).

9 For example, it is irrelevant whether the imbalance between quantities is represented by the algebraic differences between demands and outputs or by those between outputs and demands or by their ratios.

10 Adopting particular hypotheses on demand and saving, the property of the stationarity of the 'levels' of quantities is transformed into that of balanced growth, with stationarity of the structure, i.e. the set of 'ratios' between levels, and growth in the levels at a constant rate over time. However, those hypotheses which imply that the structure of consumption and the propensity to save are independent of the level of income are so restrictive as to make this special case of balanced growth – the only one addressed in the recent literature – practically irrelevant. On this point see Zaghini (1993), the only study I know of that considers the general case of stationarity.

11 The only way I see to make sense of the hypothesis that the equilibrium configuration is a given is to interpret it as meaning that agents, during the adjustment process and hence under disequilibrium conditions, *know* the equilibrium configuration and are accordingly endowed with perfect foresight. But, as argued at the outset, this would render the description of the adjustment process wholly unrealistic. In any event, I am convinced this is not the meaning that Garegnani attributes to the hypothesis.

12 This follows from note 4 in Garegnani's contribution to this volume and from the numerous points in Garegnani (1997 [1990]), where the expression 'effectual demands' or 'normal effectual demands' appears in brackets alongside the expression 'normal outputs'.

13 In other words, 'when O_i exceeds the *market* effectual demand D_i^m, then m_i falls short of m_i^* (and *vice-versa*). Morever, . . . as the proportion O_i/D_i^m rises, the ratio m_i/m_i^* falls (and *vice-versa*)' (Garegnani 1997 [1990]: 146).

14 With regard to the first formulation, presented at the beginning of this chapter, it will be seen that in the long-term position, according to rule 2(a), output cannot be lower (higher) than effectual demand; otherwise, the price could not remain at its normal level, but would have to be higher (lower). Therefore, for prices to remain at their natural levels, there must be market clearing, i.e. equality between output and effective demand in the Smithian sense. In addition, the constancy of natural prices allows the common level of demand and supply to remain unchanged. In this formulation too, if the demand functions satisfy the hypotheses referred to in note 11, stationarity of the levels is transformed into stationarity of the ratios (balanced growth).

15 When Garegnani, after stating that the normal levels of demand constitute data in the determination of natural prices, recognises that those levels depend on natural prices (see note 8), he denies *de facto* that those levels are given. If they were true data, they could assume arbitrary values – perhaps within certain sets guaranteeing their technical and/or economic significance – and not values linked with particular sets of prices, constituting a property of the process.

9 Different perspectives on distribution within classical political economy

Sergio Nisticò

According to Sraffa, the source of a logically consistent non-marginalist theory of prices and distribution can be found in Ricardo and the classical authors in general. Opposed to that of Sraffa is Hollander's interpretation (e.g. Hollander 1987) of the classical authors which essentially aims at demonstrating the affinity and the continuity between the neoclassical orthodoxy and the preceding theoretical formulations of Smith, Ricardo, John Stuart Mill and even of Marx. Hollander's reconstruction plays down any classification by 'schools' and represents the history of economic thought as a progressive refinement of common analytical tools employed for the solution of one fundamental theoretical problem: the optimum allocation of given resources.

Along the furrow cut by Sraffa, Garegnani (e.g. 1984) considers the exogenous determination of the real wage and the demonstration of the existence, with a given technology, of an inverse relationship between the real wage and the resulting rate of profit, as the distinguishing features of the classical theory of prices and distribution.

While leaving aside both the important question whether the classical theory actually represents 'a bold attempt to determine values independent of demand considerations' (Arrow 1991: 75) and the recently reiterated objection (Blaug in Chapter 5 of this volume) to 'rational' as opposed to 'historical reconstructions', the aim of this chapter is to emphasise the limits of the above interpretations and to assess the differences, within the classical school, between Smith's position on the one hand and that of the other main classicists on the other.

Hollander's 'continuity thesis' is critically discussed in the next section, particularly the idea that – unlike Sraffa – both the classicists and the neoclassicists founded their analysis on the notion of interdependence between prices and distribution. The section proposes an alternative interpretation of the role played by the notions of 'sequence analysis' and 'interdependence' within the theoretical models of the classical economists and of Sraffa.

The function of the labour theory of value within the classical theory of prices and distribution is briefly discussed in the following section (pp. 118–20), with reference to Garegnani's interpretation. It is here argued that Smith's shift from the labour theory of value to the 'theory of the component parts' should not be considered a drawback of his theory.

Pages 120–4 deal with the relationship between the determination of relative prices and distribution with given productive conditions, and the analysis of growth. It is there argued that: (1) the classical natural equilibrium solutions for relative prices and distribution should be considered as temporary centres of gravity within which one of the distributive variables is exogenously given, rather than as persistent through time; (2) the question of the change of the exogenously given distributive variable should be analysed within a methodological framework where the growth process is conceived in terms of a sequence of (temporary) natural equilibrium positions. Once the classical theory is portrayed in terms of a sequence of temporary natural equilibrium positions, the conclusion stemming from the 'canonical growth model' (see Hollander in Chapter 3 of this volume) reveals itself to be compatible with the natural equilibrium interpretation of Ricardo's theory.

Pages 124–8 deal with the peculiarities of Smith's position. It is maintained that: (1) the conclusions stemming from the 'canon interpretation' do not fit the Smithian theory; (2) while some classical authors surely tended to consider the real wage as exogenously given, Smith treated the rate of profit as exogenous when determining relative prices. The section contains also an attempt at representing the two classical approaches – that of Smith, on one side, and that of Ricardo, J. S. Mill (and Marx) on the other – through a very simple model of temporary natural prices. It is also argued that the difference in these two ways of approaching the determination of relative prices and distribution could depend on the circumstance that Smith faced an institutional context different from the competitive one which Ricardo, J. S. Mill and Marx referred to in their analyses. This circumstance can also explain why Smith held a different position, with respect to the other classical economists, as to the effect on prices of an increase in the wage rate.

The 'continuity thesis' and the interdependence problem

The thesis according to which there is no difference between the classical and the marginalist approaches to the theory of prices and distribution has been recapitulated by Hollander (1987: 1–14). Hollander's argument is based on the contrast between the neoclassical orthodoxy and what he defines as the 'Italo-Cambridge' tradition generated by the publication of Piero Sraffa's *Production of Commodities by Means of Commodities*. What discriminates the two paradigms is, according to Hollander, the fact that while the neoclassical school has founded its analysis on the notion of interdependence between commodity and factor prices, the Italo-Cambridge tradition has on the contrary built a sort of 'sequence analysis', determining distribution prior to and independently of relative prices:

> In sharp contrast [with the neoclassical tradition], the Italo-Cambridge school rejects general equilibrium analysis in favour of a kind of sequence analysis. . . . *On this view there is no relationship of mutuality between final prices and distribution.*
>
> (Hollander 1987: 5, emphasis added)

The theoretical formulations of the classical economists have erroneously been associated, Hollander proceeds, to the Sraffian paradigm:

> Piero Sraffa . . . did more than anyone to define the Cambridge notions of sequence analysis. . . . Indeed for Cambridge historians such as Maurice Dobb (1973), Ricardo stands at the head of the line of thought . . . wherein distribution is prior to pricing, rather than on the general equilibrium line.
>
> (Ibid.: 6)

An interpretative error which, according to Hollander, also Schumpeter incurred by presuming that both these alternative paradigms were already present in the nineteenth century's theoretical models:

> The Dobb and Schumpeter perspectives have much in common, since both envisage the development of economics from the eighteenth century in terms of a dual process reflecting two paradigms. . . . The present text envisages matters very differently. It will be my major theme that the notion of alternative 'paradigms' does not adequately describe the development of nineteenth century economics. . . . There was no Kuhnian 'revolution' or paradigmatic change in 1817 from this perspective.
>
> (Ibid.)

Hollander's reading clearly conflicts with Sraffa's claim that '[the] standpoint . . . of the old classical economists from Adam Smith to Ricardo, has been submerged and forgotten since the advent of the "marginal" method' (Sraffa 1960: v).

According to Hollander, the demonstration that both the classical and the neoclassical economists shared a theory of allocation of given resources based on the demand and supply functions within a general equilibrium setting turns on the classicists' determination of the real wage. Contrary to what the 'Italo-Cambridge' historians of thought maintain, classical economists did not take the real wage as exogenously given. The reward for labour was rather determined within an interdependence model, together with all the other variables of the system:

> there is no justification for attributing to Ricardo (or Marx) the assumption of a wage rate given exogenously from outside the economic system. Like Smith (and J. S. Mill) Ricardo and Marx were not 'fix-wage' theorists. With wages variable it is legitimate to introduce into the model one of the key relationships of general equilibrium economics – that between commodity and factor markets; that is a mutual relationship between pricing and distribution. . . . They [classical and neoclassical economists] shared a common 'core' – the theory of allocation.
>
> (Hollander 1987: 7)

A discussion of Hollander's argument on the issue of the real wage is postponed to p. 122. Here it should be noticed that, contrary to what Hollander maintains, the determination of relative prices and distribution which is contained in the works of Dmitriev (1974 [1904]), Bortkiewicz (1906–7) and Sraffa (1960) is founded on the unequivocal interdependence of prices and the distributive set-up. And the assumption that *one* of the distributive variables is given – while distinguishing Sraffa-type solutions from the neoclassical general equilibrium models – does not imply a determination of the whole distributive set-up as prior to prices. Within Sraffa's theory, the endogenous distributive variable depends on prices to the same extent that prices depend on it. Neither distribution nor prices are logically prior to one another. And, as Kurz recalls, the standard commodity should not be interpreted as a device with the power of neutralising the interdependence of relative prices and distribution, since 'Sraffa has made it abundantly clear that a particular standard of value cannot change the "mathematical properties" of a given system of production' (Chapter 13 in this volume). In turn, the classical economists, though recognising the interdependence of relative prices and distribution, tried in various ways to escape from it. And the scientific outlook favoured by Smith and Ricardo, grounded as it was on the notion of causality, would have probably led them to consider a simultaneous solution as deficient in heuristic value.[1] The assumption of the validity of the labour theory of value, the search for an invariable measure of value, Smith's determination of money prices starting from the levels of wages, profits and rents given prior to and independently of commodity prices, the Marxian transformation of values into prices, all these may be interpreted as separate attempts to escape from the interdependence problem.

A simultaneous determination of relative prices and distribution becomes part of the classical-type theory only with the works of Dmitriev, Bortkiewicz and Sraffa. Only these latter works, therefore – and not those of the classical economists – could in principle be assimilated, from a methodological viewpoint, to the neoclassical general equilibrium approach.

Garegnani on the wage–profit rate frontier as the distinguishing feature of the classical theory

Garegnani's interpretation is founded on the idea that the classical theory of prices and distribution is characterised by the residual determination of the non-wage shares starting from two magnitudes taken as given: the real wage and the quantities produced.

On the basis of this premise, Garegnani criticises Smith's theory of value and in particular Smith's idea that prices can be determined by adding up[2] wages, profits and rents and that they should be measured in terms of 'labour commanded'. According to Garegnani, Smith's approach is incompatible with the classical theory, since the 'adding up doctrine' and the use of labour commanded as the unit of measure imply the dependence of the value of the product on the value of its components, thus making it impossible to determine the non-wage share as a difference between the value of the given social product and the given wage share. The determination of prices as a sum of wages, profits and rents, given prior to and independently of the commodity prices (and thus of the value of the product) gives, according to Garegnani, a 'harmonious' representation of the distributive mechanisms. An increase in one of the components will tend to determine a proportional increase in prices without affecting the level of the others. In Garegnani's words:

> Smith had defined the natural price as the sum of the wages and profits (we are ignoring rents) which must be paid in order to produce the commodity, reckoned at their 'natural' or 'average' rates. As for the unit in which these natural prices should be expressed, Smith had suggested . . . the quantity of labour which a commodity can 'command', that is, in modern terms, the wage unit. If, however, we use Smith's measure . . . the *value* of the *physically given* social product will not be known before the rate of profit is known. . . . This dependence of the value of the product upon distribution means that, when we look at the Social product and the necessary consumption in value terms, the constraint by which one class cannot have more without the other class having less – so evident if we could look at the product in physical terms – is no longer apparent: might not the real wage rise without affecting the rate of profit, or vice versa? Indeed, Smith often lost sight of the constraint and envisaged the rate of profit and the wage as determined *independently of each other.*
>
> (Garegnani 1984: 301–2)

To the Smithian theory of prices Garegnani opposes the labour theory of value, the theory that Smith had put aside and that Ricardo, quite correctly, brought back to light:

> Ricardo's great merit was in fact that he saw through these 'appearances' and brought consistency back into economic theory. This achievement of Ricardo's *Principles* was rendered possible by relating the exchange value of the commodities to the quantity of labour necessary to produce them.
>
> (Ibid.: 302)

> The ratio between the values of any two aggregates of commodities – or between sums or differences of such values – would accordingly be equal to the ratios between the respective quantities of labour embodied. . . . Thus . . . [t]he constraint binding changes in wages and changes in the rate of profit becomes self evident and no space is left for the illusion, generated by the appearance of price as a sum of wages and profits.
>
> (Ibid.: 303)

Garegnani's position will be taken up again at p. 121. But it is here worth noticing that his idea, whereby the determination of relative prices on the basis of the labour theory of value reflects 'Ricardo's great merit' in that it 'brought consistency back into economic theory', neglects some important aspects of Ricardo's own evaluation of the matter. In particular, it neglects the circumstance that Ricardo was perfectly aware of the limits of the labour theory[3] and that he had criticised Smith, not for abandoning the labour theory of value, but for not having clarified the reasons that make it impossible to determine relative prices on the basis of the relative quantities of labour outside the 'early and rude state of society'.

Equally questionable is Garegnani's evaluation of Smith's theory of price. It is true that Smith's 'adding up' determination of prices and the use of labour commanded as the unit of measurement imply the dependence of the value of the product upon the money wage rate and upon the rate of profit. However, this dependence should definitely be accepted by contemporary classical-type theorists precisely because it emerges from the (correct) Sraffian solution. Therefore the impossibility of determining profits as a difference between a given product – whose value is independent of the way it is distributed – and a given wage bill cannot be said to constitute an obstacle to an elaboration, along the lines indicated by Smith, of a theory of prices and distribution based on the role played by the relative bargaining power of the various social classes.[4]

As it will be made clearer below, Smith's theory, far from being an expression of a harmonious view of the capitalistic economic system, is based on the idea that in *each period* the profit rate should be treated as the exogenous distributive variable depending on the bargaining power of the capitalists with respect to the workers.

A possible reconstruction of the classical method: a sequence of temporary natural positions

In one of his last contributions on the classical school Caravale drew a distinction between 'the determination of one single position of equilibrium, identified on the basis of some fundamental features of the economic system' and the 'specification of a systematic change in one of the basic conditions circumscribing the identification of a single position of equilibrium' (Caravale 1994a: 241–3). The importance of this distinction, which, in my view, has been overlooked by most of the scholars in the field, is connected with the circumstance that the classical theory is a fascinating mixture of equilibrium analysis and analysis of change; of laws of motion derived from comparative static propositions and counteracting tendencies. And the richness of all these theoretical materials cannot be captured by restricting the whole classical theory either within the narrow boundaries of the 'given technology hypothesis' or within the analysis of how the relevant variables react on one another when the system moves through time. On the contrary, the richness of the classical theory can be captured by a method of analysis wherein each natural equilibrium position, identified on the basis of a given set of data, including one of the distributive variables, is sooner or later destined to be replaced by a different one defined on the basis of the *new* values of the *same* set of data. The classical natural equilibrium positions are, therefore, temporary in nature though dominant with respect to market phenomena.

In the light of this methodological distinction between 'statics' and 'dynamics' (ibid.), the limits of both Garegnani's and Hollander's positions can be discussed.

The main characteristic of Garegnani's interpretation (see Garegnani 1976) is that of conceiving the classical natural equilibrium as a persistent long-period position,[5] an interpretation that forces Garegnani to consider any change in one of the distributive variables as taking place within the static side of the classical method described above. However, Ricardo's natural prices are not at all persistent through time.[6] They are bounded to the type of land cultivated and are therefore 'temporary' though guaranteeing a uniform rate of profit. Moreover the existence of an inverse relationship between alternative levels of the real wage and the rate of profit, with a given technology, cannot be considered a characteristic of Ricardo's model. While the worsening of production conditions in the wage goods sector is always associated with a reduction in the general rate of profit, this progressive reduction in profitability occurs, in Ricardo's theory, with a real wage which can be taken as either exogenously given at its natural level (see Caravale and Tosato 1980: chapter 2 and appendix) or, as it is in the 'canon' interpretation, continuously decreasing throughout the accumulation process.

It should also be noticed that one important aspect of Garegnani's interpretation, namely the core–periphery distinction,[7] can easily be fitted into the 'temporary (natural) positions framework' here proposed. The determination, on the basis of the Sraffa-type set of data, of the natural relative prices and of the distributive set-up corresponding to it, can accordingly be labelled as the 'core' analysis aiming at identifying 'defined quantitative relations between the real wage (the independent variable) and the remaining rates of remuneration and the relative prices' (Garegnani 1990: 124). Moreover, since the ways in which the system abandons its old temporary natural position and starts to be (still temporarily) attracted by the new one have to be studied 'on the basis of special hypotheses . . . in their multiplicity and diversity according to circumstances' (ibid.), it could be legitimate to say that 'the multiplicity of these dependencies . . . made it necessary to study them separately from the relations of the core and not simultaneously with them' (ibid.: 125). If, however, Garegnani's core–periphery distinction is perfectly in line with the thesis here proposed that the classical natural positions are temporary in nature, it remains true that it can hardly be fitted within a 'static' framework wherein all the data of the system are at the same time persistent and compatible with the resulting endogenous variables.[8] In other words, the circumstance that Garegnani relegates the identification of those important relations between the endogenous variables and the data of the theory to a separate logical phase compels him to *arbitrarily assume* that those data are 'the right ones', an assumption which clearly contradicts the very nature of the data.[9] If, on the contrary, the data are not arbitrarily supposed to be compatible with the endogenous variables, the absence of any definite relations imposing the compatibility between the endogenous variables and the data (for instance, between relative prices, sectoral effective demands and the given sectoral outputs or between the rate of accumulation and the given real wage), does not allow one to consider the system's solution as persisting through time.[10]

On the other hand, Hollander's rejection of the natural equilibrium interpretation is founded on a reading of the classical theory which is almost exclusively centred on the relative change of the distributive variables through time. Hollander's canonical interpretation puts aside the marked theoretical interest of the classical economists in the determination of relative prices and distribution in a 'static' context, that is, for a given point of the dynamic path followed by the system.

On the contrary, it can be maintained that the classical authors aimed at providing a theoretical explanation of relative prices and distribution for a given technique precisely as a prerequisite for analysing the evolution through time of those variables. Smith apart, the determination of the rate of profit for a given point of the accumulation process was the cornerstone of their theory of the falling rate of profit. And the theoretical explanation they have provided, be it good or bad, clearly assumes the real wage as given. Here is some textual evidence.

According to Marx:

> the foundation of modern political economy . . . is the conception of the value of the labour power as something fixed, as a given magnitude.
>
> (Marx 1969 [1862–63], I: 45)

Even clearer is J. S. Mill:

> It thus appears that the two elements on which, and which alone, the gains of the capitalists depend, are, first, the magnitude of the produce, in other words, the productive power of labour; and secondly, the proportion of that produce obtained by the labourers themselves; the ratio, which the remuneration of the labourers bears to the amount they produce. *These two things form the data for determining the gross amount divided as profit among all the capitalists of the country.*
>
> (J. S. Mill 1965 [1848], III: 413, emphasis added)

And finally Ricardo:

> In all countries, and all times, profits depend on the quantity of labour requisite to provide necessaries for the labourer, on that land or with that capital which yields no rent.
>
> (Ricardo 1951–73, I: 126)

Let us stay with Ricardo. There is no way to deny his strong concern (perhaps of a pre-analytical nature) with providing an analytical proof of the tendency of the profit rate to fall. The strong assumption of decreasing returns in the wage goods sector did the job, once it was clear that the general rate of profit could be determined on the no-rent land as a residual magnitude, given the real wage. However, the possible retroaction of a decreasing rate of capital accumulation on the real wage could obscure the effects of decreasing returns in agriculture on the rate of profit. And this is why Ricardo was inclined to assume (but also to admit the opposite) that the real wage is given not only for a given point in time (for a given extension of corn cultivation) in order to determine the profit rate, but also during the dynamic sequence through time, or across land of decreasing fertility:

> I think it may be most satisfactorily proved, that in every society advancing in wealth and population, *independently of the effect produced by liberal or scanty wages*, general profits must fall, unless there be improvements in agriculture, or corn can be imported at a cheaper price.
>
> (Ricardo 1951–73, IV: 22–3, emphasis added)

> It may be said that I have taken it for granted, that money wages would rise with a rise in the price of raw produce, but that this is by no means a necessary consequence, as the labourer may be contented with fewer enjoyments. It is true that the wages of labour may previously have been at a high level, and that may bear some reduction. If so, the fall of profits will be checked; but it is impossible to conceive that the money price of wages should fall, or remain stationary with a gradually increasing price of necessaries; and therefore *it may be taken for granted that, under ordinary circumstances, no permanent rise takes place in the price of necessaries, without occasioning, or having been preceded by a rise in wages.*
>
> (Ibid., I: 118)

It is, however, undeniable that the principle of the 'shared incidence' (see Hollander in Chapter 3 of this volume) is sometimes admitted by Ricardo, though it cannot be conceived as a contradiction of Ricardo's theory of the determination of the profit rate (for a given point of the accumulation process) on the basis of an exogenously real wage. Both the treatment of the real wage as exogenous for the determination of the profit rate and the admission of its decline throughout the accumulation process are admissible when the growth process is conceived as a sequence of temporary natural equilibrium positions.[11] In other words, once the classical natural equilibrium positions are not considered as being persistent through time, it becomes evident that Hollander's convincing thesis, according to which there is room, in Ricardo, for a declining real wage throughout the accumulation process, cannot be seen as a proof of the homogeneity between the classical and neoclassical theories of value and distribution. The natural wage still plays a fundamental role in Ricardo's theory. When labour productivity in the wage sector falls, and with it the general rate of profit, the system enters a new natural equilibrium phase in which the 'old' natural real wage becomes a market wage, since it generates a yearly increase of labour supply above that of labour demand (now lower). However, the market mechanisms will drive the market (previously natural) wage towards its 'new' lower natural level in correspondence with which the growth rate of labour supply equals the growth rate of labour demand.[12]

Moreover, the idea that the natural wage can decrease throughout the accumulation process is consistent with Ricardo's recantation of the definition of the natural wage that he had given in the *Principles*. In the *Notes on Malthus* Ricardo writes:

> I am however very little solicitous to retain my definition of the natural price of labour. Mr Malthus's will do as well for my purpose.
>
> (Ricardo 1951–73, II: 228)[13]

Here is Malthus's passage referred to by Ricardo:

> Mr Ricardo has defined the natural price of labour to be 'that price which is necessary to enable the labourers one with another to subsist, and to perpetuate their race, without either increase or diminution'. This price I should really be disposed to call a most unnatural price; because in a natural state of things, that is, without great impediments to the progress of wealth and population, such a price could not generally occur for hundreds of years. But if this price be really rare, and, in an ordinary state of things, at so great a distance in point of time, it must evidently lead to great errors to consider the market-prices of labour as only temporary deviations above and below that fixed price to which they will very soon return.
>
> The natural or necessary price of labour in any country I should define to be 'that price which, in the actual circumstances of the society, is necessary to occasion an average supply of labourers, sufficient to meet the average demand'. And the market-price I should define to be, the actual price in the market, which from temporary causes is sometimes above, and sometimes below, what is necessary to supply this average demand.
>
> (Ibid.: 227–8, emphasis added)

Some peculiarities of Smith's position

Some important differences between Smith and the other classical economists should now be emphasised both as regards the 'static' and the 'dynamic' aspects of the theory. As far as statics is concerned, I have tried to show elsewhere (Nisticò 1991a, b) that Smith's theory of the component parts is logically compatible with an endogenous determination of the real wage once the rate of profit is, in turn, assumed to be exogenously given. The rationale for such a different type of solution, which by the way is perfectly consistent with Sraffa's own formulation,[14] is that the 'Smithian capitalists' are not passive victims of their mutual competition. They 'seldom meet together, even for merriment and diversion, but the conversation ends in a conspiracy against the public or in some contrivance to raise prices' (Smith 1976 [1776], I: 144); moreover, they are protected by corporations and by 'the policy of Europe'. The Smithian institutional context is therefore incompatible with the later classicists' idea that profits should be considered as the residual distributive share. For a given point of the accumulation process, the rate of profit should be considered as exogenously given:

> The revenue or profit arising from stock naturally divides itself into two parts; that which pays the interest, and which belongs to the owner of the stock; and that surplus part which is over and above what is necessary for

> paying the interest. This latter part of profit is evidently a subject not taxable directly. . . . The employer must have this compensation, otherwise he cannot, consistently with his own interest, continue the employment. If he was taxed directly, therefore, in proportion to the whole profit, he would be obliged either to raise the rate of his profit or to charge the tax upon the interest of money; that is to pay less interest. If he raised the rate of his profit in proportion to the tax, the whole tax, though it may be advanced by him, would be finally paid by one or other of two different sets of people.
>
> (Smith 1976 [1776], V: 373–4)

On the other hand, Smith did not assume the real wage as exogenously given. On the contrary:

> In Great Britain the wages of labour seem, in the present times, to be evidently more than what is precisely necessary to enable the labourer to bring up a family. . . . There are many plain symptoms that the wages of labour are nowhere in this country regulated by this lowest rate which is consistent with common humanity . . . the wages of labour do not in Great Britain fluctuate with the price of provisions. These vary everywhere from year to year, frequently from month to month. But in many places the money price of labour remains uniformly the same sometimes for half a century together.
>
> (Ibid.: 82–3)

Interestingly enough, in Smith the class antagonism between workers and capitalists plays a fundamental role in the course of capital accumulation and the principle of 'shared incidence' cannot anyhow fit within the picture. In *The Wealth of Nations*, where all types of returns are admitted, the autonomous movements through time of the rate of capital accumulation drive the evolution of the real wage, which goes always in the opposite direction to that taken by the rate of profit.

In a country which is undergoing neither continuous progress nor a marked decline, masters combine 'not to raise the wages of labour above their actual state' (ibid.: 75) and the question of the relative movements of wages and profits is not at stake. The question of the relation between wages and profits becomes relevant, in Smith, for instance, for a country which is experiencing a rising rate of capital accumulation:

> When in a country the demand for those who live by wages; labourers, journeymen, servants of every kind, is continually increasing . . . the workmen have no occasion to combine in order to raise their wages.
>
> (Ibid.: 77)

Smith considers the rise in the wage rate as the consequence of a general reduction in the degree of industrial concentration and hence of the worsening of capitalists' bargaining position:

> The rise and fall in the profits depend upon the same causes with the rise and fall in the wages of labour, the increasing or declining state of the wealth of the society; but those causes affect the one and the other very differently. The increase of stock, which raises wages, tends to lower profit.
>
> (Smith 1976 [1776], I: 98)

Let us now go back to the 'static' side of the Smithian theory. With regard to what has been said above, while an increase in the wage rate is accompanied by a fall in the rate of profit,[15] the former should be considered the consequence rather than the cause of the latter. This consideration implies that, even as regards the determination of prices and distribution within any given temporary position of the system, two different 'classical' solutions can be identified.

Though all the classicists (and Marx) tried to determine relative prices and distribution by starting from an exogenous value of *one* of the distributive variables, given the different institutional context they had to analyse, they made different choices as to which variables should be treated as exogenous: the real wage by Ricardo, J. S. Mill and Marx, the rate of profit in Smith.[16]

A very simple model can express these two classical approaches. Let us suppose that two commodities are produced only with circulating capital and that only commodity 1 enters the wage basket so that prices and distribution can be determined as a solution of the following system of equations:

$$
\begin{aligned}
p_1 &= (a_{11}p_1 + a_{21}p_2 + l_1\bar{w}) \cdot (1 + r) \\
p_2 &= (a_{12}p_1 + a_{22}p_2 + l_2\bar{w}) \cdot (1 + r) \\
x &= \frac{\bar{w}}{p_1}
\end{aligned}
\tag{1}
$$

where the a_{ij} and the l_i represent, respectively, the technical and the labour coefficients, x the real wage, r is the rate of profit and $\bar{w}$ the money wage. The assumption can be made that the latter is given in both Smith's and the later classicists' approaches, and that it plays the role of the *numéraire* (prices are measured in terms of 'labour commanded').

Given the money wage ($\bar{w}$), system (1) contains three equations and four unknowns p_1, p_2, x and r thus requiring, within the natural equilibrium interpretation, that one of the two (real) distributive variables, x or r, be given from outside the model. It is with reference to this choice that the difference between the two classical approaches emerges. Within the *Smithian* solution the uniform profit rate – depending on the degree of concentration for the economy as a whole – is exogenously given[17] while the real wage is endogenously determined simultaneously with the money prices and will be equal to the ratio $\bar{w}/p_1$.

Although endogenously determined, in the Smithian model the real wage encounters a lower floor corresponding to the subsistence level:

> But though in disputes with their workmen, masters must generally have the advantage, *there is however a certain rate below which it seems impossible to reduce*, for any considerable time, the ordinary wages even of the lowest species of labour.
>
> (Smith 1976 [1776], I: 76, emphasis added)

To the three equations of the model the constraint $\bar{w}/p_1 \geq \bar{x}$ should be added, where $\bar{x}$ represents the subsistence real wage. This constraint, by setting a lower floor for the real wage, sets also an upper limit for the profit rate.

Within what may be termed the *competitive* approach – that can be associated with Ricardo, J. S. Mill and Marx – it is on the contrary the real wage that is assumed as given from outside the model. The third equation of the system becomes $\bar{w}/p_1 = \bar{x}$ and it determines the money price (p_1) of the wage commodity.[18]

It is important to emphasise that, for the case in which the wage commodity requires only itself and unassisted labour as means of production ($a_{21} = 0$), the constraint exerted on p_1 by the third equation holds indirectly also as a constraint on the rate of profit, which would be unambiguously determined by the first equation of system (1). This circumstance is evidently consistent with Ricardo's idea that the uniform profit rate is determined in the wage commodity sector. Any change in the productive conditions obtaining in the 'luxury' sector would modify the relative price p_1/p_2 but not the general rate of profit:

> suppose the price of silks, velvets, furniture, and any other commodities, not required by the labourer, to rise in consequence of more labour being expended on them, would not that affect profits? Certainly not: for nothing can affect profits but a rise in [money] wages.
>
> (Ricardo 1951–73, I: 118)

It should be clear that the 'competitive' solution reflects the circumstance that capitalists cannot control the profit rate, which is dependent exclusively on the technical conditions of production and on the real wage.

This different treatment of the rate of profit – exogenously given in Smith, endogenously determined in the later classical economists – provides also a rationale for the different opinions that Smith, on the one hand, and Ricardo, Marx and Mill, on the other, held with respect to the effect on prices of an increase in wages. Since he was assuming the rate of profit to be given, Smith was inclined to think that an increase in money wages would be transferred by capitalists to prices, leaving therefore the distributive set-up unaltered giving rise to a sort of cost-push inflation:

> Our merchants and master-manufacturers complain much of the bad effects of high wages in raising the price, and thereby lessening the sale of their goods both at home and abroad. They say nothing concerning the bad effects of high profits. They are silent with regard to the pernicious effects of their own gains. They complain only of those of other people.
>
> (Smith 1976 [1776], I: 110)

Conclusion

The main upshot of the argument here proposed is that the classical theory is based on the recognition that, for a given 'point' of the accumulation process, the distributive antagonism among social classes plays an essential role in the mechanisms governing prices and distribution. From an analytical viewpoint, this singularity brings with it the assumption that one of the distributive variables must be taken as exogenously given. Two classical determinations of prices and distribution have been identified, each linked with a different perspective as to the market structure. The differences in perspective have been translated, in modern terms, into differences relating to the choice as to which of the distributive variables should be taken as given.

It has also been argued that, contrary to what Garegnani maintains, the classical-type natural equilibrium positions, identified on the basis of the exogenous level of one of the distributive variables, should be interpreted as temporary and not persistent centres of gravity. On the basis of this methodological proposal, the limits of Hollander's interpretation of the classical school have been discussed. In particular, it has been maintained that (1) the 'shared incidence principle' does not fit Smith's treatment of the dynamics of a capitalist economy; (2) the circumstance that Ricardo admitted the 'shared incidence principle' does not contradict Ricardo's unequivocal endorsement of the real wage as the exogenous distributive variable for the determination of the profit rate within any given natural temporary position.

It should be emphasised finally that the ability to identify different models within the same theoretical approach allows the classical-type theory to establish an important link between the historical-institutional features of the real world and the economic theory. This openness is perfectly consistent with the classical economists' conception of Political Economy: a conception wherein 'the usefulness of theoretical propositions . . . hinged critically upon the empirical validity of the axiomatic foundation . . . [and the] postulates were always intended to reflect a specific time- and space-bound reality' (Hollander 1987: 12).

Notes

I am grateful to Samuel Hollander, Gary Mongiovi, Neri Salvadori and Donald Walker for their constructive comments on a previous version of this chapter.

1 In his *Lectures on Rhetoric and Belles Lettres* Smith declares, for instance, in favour of the Newtonian method characterised by the attempt to explain the phenomena in recursive terms, that is, by starting from given, original principles, 'proved in the beginning, from whence we account for the severall Phenomena, connecting all together by the same Chain' (Smith 1983 [1762–63]: 146).

2 Garegnani's position on this point echoes that expressed by Sraffa in his introduction to Ricardo's *Works*. See Sraffa (1951: xxxv).

3 'Strictly speaking then the relative quantities of labour bestowed on commodities regulate their relative value, when nothing but labour is bestowed upon them, and that for equal times' (Ricardo 1951–73, VIII: 193).

4 It is obviously true that, given the circumstance that he lacked the tools for identifying an analytically sound solution, Ricardo made good use of the labour theory of value, as an approximation, when trying to explain his theory of the profit rate.

5 According to Roncaglia, the idea of the persistence of the *classical*-type natural positions should be rejected also because 'we must admit that available productive capacity is constantly changing, however short the period to which we refer, because of investment decisions taken in the past' (Roncaglia 1990: 147).

6 On this point see D'Orlando and Nisticò (2000).

7 See Garegnani (1984) and (1990). For a critique of the Garegnani proposal see also Blaug's Chapter 5 in this volume.

8 For the logical inconsistency between the assumption of given sectoral outputs and the adoption of the long-period method within a classical-type solution see D'Orlando and Nisticò (2000).

9 For an attempt to fit both prices and outputs determination within a classical-type model see Caravale (1994b).

10 Interestingly enough, in Chapter 4 of this volume Garegnani does not mention the 'persistence of the data' as a characteristic of the classical long-period method.

11 On the confusion between 'fix' and 'natural' (i.e. exogenous) wage within Hollander's interpretation see Caravale (1985b: 133).

12 A discussion of a Ricardian 'step model' of growth characterised by a sequence of static equilibria is contained in Casarosa (1985: 53–5) and Hicks (1985: 307, 311, 317). However, neither Casarosa nor Hicks discusses the implications of the step model in favour of the natural equilibrium interpretations of Ricardo's theory.

13 The quoted sentence has been replaced by Ricardo with a shorter but similar one.

14 See Sraffa (1960: 33).

15 Smith was fully aware that an increase in labour productivity plays the role of a counteracting tendency: 'The same cause, however, which raises the wages of labour, the increase of stock, tends to increase its productive powers, and to make a smaller quantity of labour produce a greater quantity of work. . . . There are many commodities, therefore, which, in consequence of these improvements, come to be produced by so much less labour than before, that the increase of its price is more than compensated by the diminution of its quantity' (Smith 1976 [1776], I: 96–7).

16 A different interpretation has been proposed by O'Donnell (1990).

17 With a low degree of intersectoral competition, the system would be characterised by different profit rates throughout the economy, and the entire vector of sectoral profit rates should be taken as given for the determination of relative prices and distribution.

18 Although this circumstance could give the impression that the price of the wage commodity is determined independently of the technical conditions of production ($p_1 = \bar{w}/\bar{x}$) the relative price p_1/p_2 is still dependent on technology.

10 Sraffa's Ricardo after fifty years

A preliminary estimate

Pier Luigi Porta

One of the sessions of the Caravale memorial conference was rightly occupied by papers on classical economics: it was in that session that a first draft of this chapter was read. Nobody will deny, I think, that a major contribution to the critical reappraisal of *classical economics* during the twentieth century has come from the scientific and intellectual work of Piero Sraffa. Sraffa's own conception of the nature and the development of classical economics was once very popular and still remains an issue to be faced by economists and historians of economics. The Sraffian notion of classical economics is closely connected with Sraffa's interpretation of Ricardo. It is proper to recall here Giovanni Caravale's early work in the field and particularly his book, co-authored by Domenico Tosato, published in Italian in 1974 and translated into English in 1980. The book went against the stream at the time and has subsequently been quite influential on the course of classical studies and as a critical discussion of Sraffa's own conception.

Thus Sraffa's work as David Ricardo's editor has a special place in this book and rightly so. Not only was the Ricardo edition almost Piero's Sraffa lifelong work (1930–73),[1] but a special character associated with Sraffa's contribution lies precisely in a peculiar interaction between theory and interpretation on one hand and interpretation and text on the other. Although it is a difficult philosophical problem to establish which comes first, theory or text, within the limits of our subject and in the case under investigation it will be a contention of this chapter that *theory* comes first: Sraffa, indeed, provides a strong case in point. It is evident that, from this perspective, the editorial work on Ricardo becomes the clue to understanding Sraffa.[2]

The same idea seems to be conveyed by the obituary of Sraffa in the *Economic Journal*, by Bertram Schefold. It was – Schefold writes, as he summarises Piero Sraffa's scientific curriculum – 'above all, his magnificent edition of the works of David Ricardo which was recognised in the whole world as a landmark of scholarship and which, on account of the editorial introduction, provided a link between classical economic theory and the post-war discussions on growth and distribution' (Schefold 1996: 1314).

It is the aim of this chapter to put Sraffa's Ricardo in a historical perspective. After fifty years this appears to be timely on two grounds. First, as we shall have occasion to recall below, Sraffa had been singularly enshrined and made into a bloodless entity for a considerable time; only today has it become possible to revive his image in flesh and blood, and it seems proper to do so. Second, the Sraffa archives at Trinity College have been made accessible and permission may be granted to make use of the extant documents for the purpose.

Sraffa's Ricardo: from the definitive edition to the 'definitive interpretation'

While the half-centenary of Piero Sraffa's work on the introduction to Ricardo's *Principles* is rapidly approaching, a curious reflection comes to the mind. This particular work of Sraffa's, though celebrated in many ways, has surprisingly *never* been read *in itself*, at least to the extent to which such an exercise is legitimately conceivable. Its fate has been the singular one of being read, in time, following two opposed extreme canons, as is in fact hinted in Schefold's statement, namely the 'landmark of scholarship' on one side and the link with past and present theory on the other – call them respectively pure transparency and pure theory – neither of which is entirely satisfactory and fully suited to do justice to the work itself. Especially to scholars who are well acquainted with Sraffa's personality and work, and with the wealth of Sraffian literature which mushroomed for a considerable while, this opening statement may seem purely provocative. That it is not so will be the purpose of this chapter to argue.

Let me recall that a few years ago I ventured to face a similar problem, in a paper entitled 'Piero Sraffa, "superb editor"', presented at the Lausanne conference on editing economists and economists as editors (Porta 1992). That paper of mine has certainly profited from being included in an otherwise very attractive volume. Further to that my 1992 paper has gained some reputation within the inner circle through the good offices of Giancarlo de Vivo. In a comment (de Vivo 1996; my rejoinder) de Vivo has taken issue with me on the title of the paper; he points the finger at the fact that the words 'superb editor' are in inverted commas. Those inverted commas appear to him a form of mockery or at least irony. Of course, it is not so in the least, and this in fact turns out to be a case where a sensitive reader can be driven to a complete misunderstanding. My inverted commas simply contain a quotation from an article by Kenneth Arrow on 'Ricardo's work as viewed by later economists' in the spring 1991 issue of the *Journal of the History of Economic Thought.* I had chosen to quote Arrow because he was providing one of the then latest and clearest instances of an unending series of appreciations of a similar kind concerning Sraffa. What is interesting and makes it worth here going back to that paper by Arrow is that Arrow, much as other authors – although he certainly does not rule out other perspectives – evidently appears to imply that his judgement of excellence must be understood mainly on *philological* grounds. Sraffa was, Arrow wrote, the 'diligent and very slow' editor of Ricardo. Of course, he noted, both Sraffa and his sponsor Keynes had each his own intellectual agenda, where (as Arrow was probably right to take for granted) the points of difference greatly outnumber those of contact. It is, however, to Keynes's credit that he 'did not confuse an antiquarian interest in seeing Sraffa produce a good edition of Ricardo with any excessive respect for an obstacle to what he saw as correct thinking'. Thereby he 'correctly foresaw that Piero Sraffa would be a superb editor' (Arrow 1991: 72–3). The task is one that requires, Arrow observed, 'leisure', with which of course Sraffa was abundantly provided, having given up lecturing in 1930 precisely in coincidence with the assignment of the Ricardo enterprise in February of that year. This observation about leisure is evidently designed to describe an ideal condition for work of an editorial kind and it would certainly not be made in the same fashion in the case of analytical work in any branch of economic research. Arrow aptly summarised the ingredients of the legendary figure of the 'superb editor' besides recalling how that characteristic image of Piero Sraffa came to take shape with its aureola of academic laziness.

One of the best pictures we have of Piero Sraffa was sketched by his professor and mentor Luigi Einaudi, who had known the young Sraffa as a student and as a scholar and had been otherwise involved with his familial and social milieu since the turn of the century. In a famous review article on the Ricardo volumes, in the *Giornale degli economisti* for 1951, under the title 'From the legend to the monument', Luigi Einaudi praised the edition unreservedly. Comparing Sraffa's achievement with Cannan's enterprise on Adam Smith, Einaudi concluded that 'Sraffa emulates Cannan and surpasses him'. Einaudi's celebration of the edition focuses on its philological and aesthetic qualities. He had himself in a paper published sixteen years earlier, in 1935, prompted by the then recent edition of Francesco Ferrara's *Lectures*, established and discussed at some considerable length a few fundamental canons for the editing of economic classics. Among other things Einaudi had emphasised that editorial introductions and notes should never intrude. Their function – Einaudi explained – is to supply missing references or soberly illustrate a view; 'never to correct, integrate or criticise'. And he added: 'An editor does not give evidence of sound taste when he seizes the occasion and prefaces the texts with an exposition of his own.' The examples of Cannan, Ashley and Hollander were then mentioned approvingly. Sixteen years later, in 1951, Sraffa appears to Einaudi to have fully and satisfactorily fulfilled all the requirements of the model editor. Unspoilt crystal transparency appears to be the substance of which Sraffa's 'monument' is made.

Perhaps the clearest comment on the Sraffa edition at the time of its first appearance came from Austin Robinson. It is interesting that Sir Austin's comments, in his review of the edition for the *Economic Journal*, were directly concerned with the now famous introduction to Volume I, although of course the remarks of the reviewer did extend to the style and character of the edition as a whole.

> Mr. Sraffa's preface [Sir Austin wrote] is a model of what such a preface should be. He is concerned wholly and exclusively with Ricardo, with Ricardo's own controversies with his contemporaries, and with anything in Ricardo's own letters and writings which can contribute to our ability to understand what Ricardo was trying to say. He is *not* concerned to provide us with ready-made judgements as to whether it was Ricardo, or Jevons, or neither, who 'shunted the car of Economic Science on to a wrong line'. He

> does *not* provide us with a 'Ricardo in modern dress', with Ricardo's ideas translated into the terminology in which most of us can more readily think today. But just so far as he can help Ricardo to speak to us for himself, and in his own language, he gives us every possible assistance. That I believe is as it should be. We are given all help in going back to Ricardo himself. But Mr. Sraffa firmly refuses to stand between Ricardo and his reader as an intermediary and interpreter, creating, as such interpreters so often do, a host of new misconceptions and misunderstandings.
>
> (Robinson 1951: 850)

Particularly after Keynes's death, Austin Robinson had experienced very directly the effects of the labours of a superb editor. It is not improper to conjecture that he must have written the above words with that sense of liberation and satisfaction which accompanies a great achievement. But, perhaps more significant, these plain unequivocal words are, in a sense, the tip of an iceberg; they express at best a very common sentiment towards the Ricardo edition at the time of publication and a sentiment that would then be dominant throughout the 1950s. That is a very simple common opinion: for any question that may arise on Ricardo, it will be enough to turn to Sraffa. That is the service the edition has rendered. In the same vein Mark Blaug – setting out in 1958 to 'ask, once again, what Ricardo really meant' – wrote that nothing could justify another forced march over such well worn terrain were it not that the recent edition of the complete *Works and Correspondence of David Ricardo* had thrown new light on almost every aspect of Ricardo's writings.

Let us now turn to the latter half of the title of this section. The 'monument' of the superb editor is, in actual reality, a powerful rhetorical construct deserving of wonder and admiration. It was, in fact, Sraffa's supreme ability to replace the foundations of the edifice of Ricardian economics without any of the onlookers taking the slightest notice of what was going on for a considerable time.[3] *After* the publication of *Production of Commodities by Means of Commodities* in 1960 the introduction to Ricardo's *Principles* came to be seen in a different light. In the heyday of Sraffian economics in Cambridge I remember a number of jokes about neoclassical economics. One such joke depicted the representative neoclassical economist as a rather dull person totally unable to understand the message of Sraffa's introduction. Sraffa felt then obliged to deliver his book, to the benefit of the neoclassicals. Of course the story gained currency as the benefit had turned into scorn. However that may be, there is a grain of truth in Paul Samuelson's 1987 dictum that no scholar had so great an impact on economic science as Piero Sraffa did; further, the impact increased with Sraffa's age and also, in his view, with the passage of time.[4]

Now I should venture to put my readers to the test. Take the following statement:

> Sraffa's edition of the *Works and Correspondence of David Ricardo* proved to be more than a great scholarly achievement. For in his Introduction to the *Principles of Political Economy and Taxation* Sraffa presented an entirely new

> interpretation of Ricardo's theory of value and distribution. Sraffa's interpretation established a new, theoretically consistent version of the surplus approach to the analysis of distribution in the Essay on Profits. Further, he demonstrated that this approach was sustained in the *Principles* by Ricardo's use of the labour theory of value.

Suppose now you are in a kind of wine-tasting contest and are asked to guess which vintage (pre- or post-1960) this particular wine belongs to. I do not want to anticipate your answer at this stage, as I am pretty sure that any careful reader will have no difficulty in coming up with the right response.[5]

In spite of the grain of truth in Samuelson's dictum (just quoted), it is a fact of life that some may well prefer the young wine to the old in many cases. In our present instance the meaning and impact of Sraffa's work *seem*, indeed, to have turned stronger and clearer as time goes on (i.e. after 1960), but what *actually* happened was that the reception and the image of Sraffa's work on Ricardo *changed in nature*. As a consequence of inertia, however, little wonder that the *new* image did show a marked tendency to get squeezed, as it were, into the old one, giving rise to the 'definitive interpretation' of Ricardo. The *definitive edition*, almost inadvertently and automatically, became the *definitive interpretation*. For a number of years nobody noticed the curious transformation; more particularly, the circumstance that, while the former phrase makes perfect sense, the latter is an insult to science went completely unnoticed.

An echo of that transformation seems to surface even today in the opening sentences of the *Economic Journal* obituary.

> But it was, above all, his magnificent edition of the works of David Ricardo which was recognised in the whole world as a landmark of scholarship and which, on account of the editorial introduction, provided a link between classical economic theory and the post-war discussions on growth and distribution. His *definitive* work, *Production of Commodities by Means of Commodities*, a slender volume, caused two controversies, one on the validity of neoclassical theory, the other on the revival of classical thought.
>
> (Schefold 1996: 1314, emphasis added)

In what sense can *Production of Commodities* be described as a 'definitive work'? This is far from clear, unless perhaps it is thought to be the work which renders definitive the 'link between classical economic theory and the post-war discussions on growth and distribution' provided by the introduction to Ricardo. That this means travelling long distances in some logical dimension *still* seems to remain totally unremarked.

Back to the text: philology and interpretation in the work of the greatest economist-editor

The curious deplorable fate met by Sraffa's introduction to Ricardo's *Principles* seems to create a moral obligation on the part of any scholar who has acquired full conscience of the facts to go back humbly to the text itself. Some may find the idea awkward to start from scratch and *read* Sraffa's introduction, simply and directly, 'for the first time' as it were. Years ago, as one participant in a colloquium appeared to offer rather naive remarks and commonplace quotes, a friend, sitting by me, somewhat disparagingly observed, 'You cannot just *read* Ricardo and Sraffa.' 'Be careful!' I whispered back. 'You *may* end up *very* close to saying that it is not necessary at all, even *dangerous*, to read!' And such things do indeed happen.

After fifty years we can, at last perhaps, be confident that we can actually *read*, unintruded upon and probably unobserved.

To be fair, back in the 1950s, at least one of the top commentators, George Stigler, in his review of the Ricardo edition in the *American Economic Review* (1953), had made some qualification in his appreciation of the 'pure transparency' qualities of the edition. '*Aside from the introduction to vol. 1,*' Stigler wrote, 'Sraffa's editorial prefaces and notes serve an informative, rather than an interpretative, function. This severe self-abnegation was wise; the facts are relatively timeless but even the best analysis of a predecessor will change with the interests and knowledge of the science' (Stigler 1953, emphasis added, 1965 reprint: 304).

In what follows we shall propose a reading of Sraffa's introduction, by focusing upon those elements which appear to go beyond pure philology and discuss the links of those elements with Ricardo's own texts and with the Ricardian literature. Next we propose to discuss Sraffa's sources and trace whatever evidence exists on the construction of Sraffa's interpretation of Ricardo.[6] Finally we shall draw some conclusions on Sraffa's Ricardo in historical perspective.

The 'corn model'

The passage on the 'rational foundation' in Sraffa's introduction to the *Principles* is too famous. Even the humble readers that we are here and now can dispense with the quotation. Precisely on this issue Samuel Hollander started to challenge the consensus on the 'definitive interpretation' in his *Economica* paper (1973b). The effectiveness of Sraffa's exposition here takes advantage from the beauty, simplicity and robustness of the corn-ratio principle and from the suggestion that the principle itself must have been formulated by him in his (as Sraffa wrote) 'lost "papers on the profits of Capital" of March 1814 or in conversation, since Malthus opposes him in . . . terms which are no doubt an echo of Ricardo's own formulation' (Sraffa 1951: xxxi). The charisma of the economist-editor, whose expert eye has evidently acquired an unparalleled knowledge of the original documents as well as of the primary literature, is indeed very great; thanks to that charisma, that the principle was 'never explicitly stated by Ricardo' becomes an advantage. Wouldn't it be flatly obvious, were the principle to be found in plain words just stated by Ricardo? It would be disappointing indeed. The way the principle is actually carved out of Ricardo's frame of mind makes it a precious discovery.

All the above, in turn, makes it just plain sailing for Sraffa to proceed like this:

> The advantage of *Ricardo's method of approach* is that, at the cost of considerable simplification, it makes possible an understanding of how the rate of profit is determined without the need of a method for reducing to a common standard a heterogeneous collection of commodities.
>
> (Sraffa 1951: xxxii, emphasis added)

The result is that a number of treatments of Ricardian economics deal with *Ricardo's* corn-ratio theory of profits.[7] Of course this is *not* the desirable outcome of the work and influence of an editor, who is *necessarily* at the same time an interpreter; this is, rather, the product of a peculiar conflation of philology and interpretation, the product of which is the monster of the 'definitive interpretation'.

'Adding-up' theory of price

The phrase has become the common expression to designate Smith's theory of price. Here too the belief is widespread among scholars that the phrase itself belongs to Adam Smith.[8] This is hardly the case. The adding-up theory of price, in fact, is an original contribution of Piero Sraffa, who appears to have been the first to coin the English term and who made use of it in his introduction to Ricardo's *Principles*.

Sraffa's introduction calls attention to the fact that the development of Ricardo's thought on income distribution were bound to call into question 'the generally accepted view that a rise in corn prices, through its effects upon wages, would be followed by a rise of all other prices', thus leading Ricardo to establish the proposition 'that a rise of wages does not raise prices' (Sraffa 1951: xxxiii). Ricardo soon discovered the important principle – which would later occupy the first section heading in the chapter 'On value' of his *Principles* – that (in Sraffa's words) 'the value of a thing was regulated by the quantity of labour required for its production, and not by the remuneration of that labour' (ibid.: xxxv). These two statements should be read carefully: although they appear almost side by side in Sraffa's text, they are *not* equivalent, the latter statement including, as it does, Ricardo's value theory, on which the former says nothing. More important here, there is another difference between the two statements, and that is that the former implies that wages and prices move in the same direction, while the latter only criticises the existence of a relationship between wages and prices, whatever its sign may be. For example, in the *Principles*, chapter XXII ('Bounties on exportation and prohibitions of importation') Ricardo resorts to the former of the two arguments and criticises Smith for considering (Ricardo's words) 'a rise in the price of commodities as a necessary consequence of a rise in the price of corn';[9] but in the opening section of chapter I ('On value') Smith is criticised for adopting the labour command standard of value, which coincides with the latter of the two above arguments. The implication of Ricardo's text in this case actually concerns an *inverse* relationship between wages and prices, because higher wages imply a lower command of labour and therefore a lower value of commodities. This is the same criticism Ricardo will level against Malthus: 'What we want is a standard measure of value which shall be itself invariable. . . . And on what does Mr Malthus fix as an approximation to this standard? The value of labour' (Ricardo 1992: *Note* 11). Pages of sharp controversy follow in the *Notes on Malthus* at this point, as this is precisely the greatest conceivable mistake to Ricardo's eye, namely to make the measure of value depend on a value: a vicious circle and therefore vitiated reasoning.

On this point Sraffa intervenes with an interpretation of his own. Sraffa's interpretation reads *any* proposition on the relation of wages to prices in the additive sense, which is in fact only *one* of two possibilities *both* utilised by Ricardo. That Ricardo thus appears to be a *critic* of the wage–price relationship in the additive sense only paves the way for his being turned into the critic of the adding-up theory as a perfectly natural consequence of 'Ricardo's approach'. Let us read Sraffa:

> The importance which Ricardo came to attach to the principle that the value of a thing was regulated by the quantity of labour required for its production, and not by the remuneration of that labour, reflected his recognition that what his new theory was opposed to was not merely the popular view of the effect of wages on prices but another and more general theory of Adam Smith (of which that effect came to appear as a particular case) – what Ricardo referred to Mill as Adam Smith's 'original error respecting value'. This latter theory, in brief, was that 'as soon as stock has accumulated in the hands of particular persons' and 'as soon as the land of any country has all become private property', the price of commodities is arrived at by a process of *adding up* the wages, profit and rent: 'in every improved society, all the three enter more or less, as component parts, into the price of the far greater part of commodities'. In other words, 'wages, profit, and rent, are the three original sources . . . of all exchangeable value'. Adam Smith speaks also of the natural price varying 'with the natural rate of each of its component parts, of wages, profit, and rent'.
>
> (Sraffa 1951: xxxv–xxxvi)[10]

This is the passage which has created the ongoing misperception of the nature of Adam Smith's theory. Again: Sraffa's procedure is perfectly legitimate once you realise that it is *one* interpretation.[11] The question then becomes a matter not so much of seeing through the 'true' Ricardo as of understanding what *Sraffa* is doing. Let me offer, as a consolation to the reader, Cannan's opinion on the point. Speaking of Smith's Book 1, chapter VI, Edwin Cannan wrote:

> It is not very clear what exactly is supposed to happen – whether products acquire an *addition* to their labour-value for profit and rent or not; [at any rate] the equality of the wages, profits and rents with the price is no proof that the price is caused by the wages, profits and rents: it may be the other way round.
>
> (Cannan 1929: 168, 171, emphasis added)

The standard of value

In his analysis of the standard of value Ricardo was concerned with the requirement of invariability of the standard itself. The standard, in fact, must be invariable with respect to difficulty of production *and* with respect to changes in the distribution of income. These two aspects are naturally linked together in Ricardo's system, where diminishing returns in agriculture and the labour theory of value are the building blocks of the theory of production and distribution. In the course of his investigation of the problem of the standard of value Ricardo became gradually convinced that a satisfactory standard, i.e. one possessing invariability, could *not* be found. He therefore discussed a number of cases in order to reach the conclusion that a perfect standard was unattainable. In so doing, Ricardo discussed in detail the effects of changes in the distribution of income on the relative value of commodities produced under different circumstances, without extending the analysis to include the fact that the conditions of production themselves are subject to change with changes in the income distribution. Typical is his discussion of Malthus's position. Malthus had argued in favour of a labour-commanded principle and had introduced the example of a commodity obtained by labour alone, 'without any advances above the food of a day', a standard in terms of which 'no rise in the price of labour could take place' (Malthus 1820: 111; in Ricardo 1951–73, II: 81). Ricardo, who had initially addressed to Malthus the same criticism of arbitrariness and lack of invariability already levelled against Smith, was later led to argue that Malthus's case provided yet another special case of conditions of production of a standard – indeed, an extreme case – which made it no more liable to objection than any other standard that can be imagined. That fact is – he concluded in one of his very last letters to Mill – that 'there is not in nature any correct measure of value nor can any ingenuity suggest one, for what constitutes a correct measure for some things is a reason why it cannot be a correct one for others' (Ricardo 1951–73, IX: 387).

All these Ricardian discussions on the standard of value are dominated by the *negative* purpose of a proof of impossibility; as a matter of fact, only going through a number of examples (and indeed *counter-examples*), Ricardo was able to reach the general negative conclusion just reported from his last letter to James Mill.

It is against that background that we are left to read the interpretation given by Sraffa on Ricardo's continuing preoccupation with the effects of changes in wages.

> This preoccupation with the effect of a change in wages arose from his approach to the problem of value, which, as we have seen, was dominated by his theory of profits. . . . Thus the problem of value which interested Ricardo was how to find a measure of value which would be invariant to changes in the division of the product; for, if a rise or fall of wages by itself brought about a change in the magnitude of the social product, it would be hard to determine accurately the effect on profits. (This was, of course, the same problem as has been mentioned earlier in connection with Ricardo's corn-ratio theory of profits.)
>
> (Sraffa 1951: xlviii–xlix)

The sources of Sraffa's analysis

In a series of papers of mine, over the last twenty-odd years (see, for example, Porta 1982, 1985, 1986, 1988, 1990, 1991, 1992), I have argued that Sraffa's analysis of Ricardo's *Principles* is largely inspired, on the constructive side, by Marx's *Theorien über den Mehrwert*, together with a pervasive need – on the negative and destructive side – to counter the Marshallian synthesis in economics.[12] For a considerable time, as hinted above in this chapter, any attempt to put Sraffa in a historical perspective was generally found unacceptable and sometimes publicly condemned. The absurdity of turning Sraffa into an absolute was, however, bound to finish, although it is only at present that it is giving way to the buds of a new Sraffian historiography.[13] The core of the new historiography, in my view, can be developed through simple-minded exercises in going back to the actual reading of Sraffa's own text (as exemplified in the above), undoubtedly supplemented with what has not been done in the above, i.e. to bring in the relevant texts by Ricardo and Marx for proper comparison.

The above, in a sense, puts together the upshot of past research and tries to show how they can be improved upon and the case made richer with new subtleties and other arguments, such as I propose to develop in my forthcoming book, in order to reach, through Sraffa's analysis, a consistent image of his own conception of the nature and importance of classical economics. This corresponds roughly to the former of the two grounds (see the opening of this chapter) for the present enquiry. It is contended that only this approach can possibly do justice to Piero Sraffa as one of the great scholars of the twentieth century.

There remains the latter ground to be dealt with. It is necessary, in other words, to trace the actual development of Sraffa's thought and consider whatever evidence exists on the sources of his analysis also in the light of the archival materials and literary remains of Piero Sraffa around the world. It is the purpose of the present section to introduce a first discussion of the extant documents and evidence with particular reference to the papers left, in Sraffa's own will, to Trinity College, Cambridge, and kept there at the Wren Library. Here we shall actually confine ourselves to a few documents dating from the late 1920s, i.e. drafted during the period when Sraffa's thought indeed appeared to pass from the criticisms of the Marshallian system to the reconstruction of the classical approach to economic theory. We shall see presently that our conjecture on the Marxian inspiration of Sraffa as an interpreter of the classical economists is entirely brought out by the documents, which prove essential to adding a number of original aspects and perspectives.

Early attempts at a catalogue, during Sraffa's own lifetime, were made by John Eatwell and Alessandro Roncaglia; work was resumed after Sraffa's death by the late Krishna Bharadwaj and by Pierangelo Garegnani, Sraffa's literary executor. Piero Sraffa's papers in the Wren Library have now been catalogued by Jonathan Smith, archivist and manuscript cataloguer at Trinity. In what follows we shall discuss sundry items among Sraffa's literary remains of the late 1920s.

Notes and jottings from the Sraffa papers

Sraffa's legacy at Trinity includes a number of items, such as, for example, Sraffa's own magnificent library. As far as Piero Sraffa's papers are concerned, they have been classified under ten headings, including, for example, career, family, diaries, correspondence, notes and lectures. The section heading of interest in the present context is section D ('Notes, lectures and publications'), from which we shall quote below.

A folder marked 'Notes/London, summer 1927/(Physical Real Costs etc.)' in Piero Sraffa's hand, plus other less legible indications for personal use, makes up a rather nice set, now catalogue item D3/12/3 on Physical Real Costs, of seventy-one (as numbered by Piero Sraffa) ruled exercise-book sheets mostly written on one side in ink in Piero Sraffa's hand. This is in fact a set of coherent notes, sometimes in the form of quickly sketched sentences, sometimes written down in more expository style. They come under the title (cf. p. 1) of 'General Scheme/The adventures of the T.V. The problems which were prominent in the mind of the older economists' etc.

We find here a telling sketch for a possible history of economic analysis centred upon 'T.V.' (which in those days, of course, meant 'Theory of Value').

> It is with Ricardo that T.V. becomes the central doctrine of P.E., and from him that schools and controversies originate. . . . But then taken up by Marx, and used as weapon for workers. . . . Immediate (?) simultaneous success of utility with Jevons, Menger, Walras. It always happens with discoveries: and, as always, it is later found that unsuccessful predecessors had already discovered the whole thing. Reason to be found in anti-socialism. . . . It should not be thought that theories devised (or accepted generally) for partisan purposes have no scientific value: they contain element of truth, which is of scientific value, and is added to knowledge and seldom is lost again. How thus theory goes on improving. Work of Marshall is combining results of two schools: 'causes' of value, notion of equilibrium, fundamental, whatever we think of Marshall's particular applications. Curious misunderstanding as to Marshall and Ricardo's relation to Marx's surplus value: acceptance of Marshall due to belief that it combined classical with orthodox school, and did not lend itself, like the former did, to Socialistic interpretation. Nonsense: Marx's surplus value does not depend upon labour being the only cause, or even one cause of value, but to its being proportional to value: explain in detail difference of the two notions. Ludicrous belief that Marx says 'labour is the only cause of value, therefore all value must go to labour'.
>
> (D3/12/3)

Two ideas should be singled out from this passage which are very important to illustrate Sraffa's intellectual development: (1) the ideological sources of the success of utility and (2) the tendency of value theory, with the ideological reaction based on utility, to focus on causes rather than measures of value. These points are hinted in the pages quoted above and we have to turn to other documents to reconstruct the two ideas more fully.

Let us now consider a set of notes dated, from a pencil annotation in Piero Sraffa's hand, end of November 1927. These are classified D3/12/4 and can be considered as preparations for the lectures 1928–31: the latter are the best and most interesting manuscript in this section of his papers.[14] Here Sraffa presents a summary sketch of the historical enquiry he has in mind. In the fourth set of sheets, item 10, we read:

> *Classical Political Economy* (the age of Ricardo) . . . (A. Smith had strong 'vulgar' tendencies: he can truly be said to be the 'founder of modern economics'!) / *Vulgar Political Economy* (the age of Mill). . . . Period dominated by Mill: Marx stands here towering as the last of the classical amongst the vulgar, just as Smith stood isolated among the classicals, being the first of the vulgars / *Economics* (the age of Marshall). . . . Highly refined technique, rotten conceptions and fundam. assumptions. . . . *Note* that at the end of the classics developed primitive socialism (Owen, Hodgskin) and *caused* Vulgar P.E. At the end of vulgar period came Marx and *caused* economics.
>
> (D3/12/4)

Sraffa clarifies what this historical progression entails: (1) *Classical political economy*: 'Right conception, fundamental assumptions primitive rudimentary technique.' (2) *Vulgar political economy*: 'All wrong here: *they* have the wrong conceptions of modern economics and the rudimentary technique of the classical.' (3) *Economics*: 'Highly refined technique, rotten conceptions and fundam. assumptions.' (Ibid.)

We dwell on the issues and examine first the full force of the ideological element in Sraffa's image of the historical progression from political economy to economics. A premiss of all this is given by the importance Sraffa attributes to the historico-analytical approach. In a set of papers (D3/12/11) again dated November 1927 he speaks of the approach to be adopted in a prospective book. The only way – he notes in writing (cf. the original text in the footnote) – is in going through history in reverse, i.e. from the present state of economics; how that came to be reached, showing the difference and the superiority of the old theories. Then expound the theory. If a chronological order is followed: Petty, the Physiocrats, Ricardo, Marx, Jevons, Marshall – Sraffa continues – then it is necessary to give as a premiss to all that a statement of my own theory in order to explain where we drive at; which means expounding first *all* of the theory. And then there is the danger to end up like Marx, who started publishing his *Capital* and later was unable to complete the *History of Doctrines*. And what is worse he has been unable to make himself understood without the historical explanation. My plan is: first, treat the history, which is what is really essential; second, make myself understood, which requires me to proceed from the known to the unknown, from Marshall to Marx, from disutility to material cost.[15]

Sraffa's ambitions are very clear. The lectures he has been appointed to deliver at Cambridge are to be made the occasion of a book in which the historico-analytical method is adopted for an eminently theoretical purpose. Marx, but *not*

Marx in general, Marx the historian of analysis *manqué*, must provide the guide both in method and in content, as also the list of past authors indicates. Marshall, of course, i.e. the present, is the starting point.

I propose now a rather lengthy quotation from the same period. It is not my purpose here to be exhaustive, as the amount of notes and documents is very large indeed and, at any rate in the present context, it would be impossible to follow all nuances and variations on the themes proposed. Therefore, let me turn to what looks like a lucid typical statement of that stage in the development of Piero Sraffa's thought. In a note entitled 'Metaphisics', again in November 1927, Sraffa further wrote:

> In this theory it will be thought that the important part is the analytical and constructive. The significance of the historical side will be missed. And yet, this is truly important, that which gives us a real insight into the mystery of human mind and understanding, into the deep unknown relations of individuals between themselves and between individual and society (the social, or rather the class mind).
>
> It is terrific to contemplate the abysmal gulf of incomprehension that has opened itself between us and the classical economists. Only one century separates us from them: how can we imagine to understand the Greeks and the Romans? The classical economists said things which were perfectly true, even according to our standards of truth: they expressed them very clearly, in terse and unambiguous language, as is proved by the fact that they perfectly understood each other. We don't understand a word of what they said: has their language been lost? Obviously not, as the English of Adam Smith is what people talk today in this country. What happened then?
>
> I foresee that the ultimate result will be a restatement of Marx, by substituting to his Hegelian metaphysics and terminology our own modern metaphysics and terminology: by metaphysics here I mean, I suppose, the emotions that are associated with our terminology and frames (*schemi mentali*) – that is, what is absolutely necessary to make the theory living (*lebendig*), capable of assimilation and at all intelligible. If this is true, it is an exceptional example of how far a difference in metaphysics can make to us absolutely unintelligible an otherwise perfectly sound theory. This would be simply a translation of Marx into English, from the forms of Hegelian metaphysics to the forms of Hume's metaphysics. (Keynes today, 26.XI.27, has clearly outlined the divorce between English and Continental thought: the first descending from Descartes and Hobbes, two original geniuses, to Locke, Hutcheson and ultimately Hume; the second from Spinoza (did he say that of S.?) from Kant to Hegel: they always remained foreign to one another.)
>
> If this is true it also shows (or is it an exceptional case? in Physics it doesn't seem to be indifferent) how little our metaphysics affects the truth of our conclusions, and how the same truths can be expressed in two widely divergent forms. Our metaphysics is in fact embodied in our technique; the danger lies in this, that when we have succeeded in thoroughly mastering a technique, we are very liable to be mastered *by* her.

The typical case of Marx's metaphysics is his statement that 'only human labour produces (causes) values', 'values are embodied human energy (crystallised)': there is no doubt that he attached to it some metaphysical meaning.

The extraordinary thing is that the same metaphysical notion is held by such an anti-Marxian as Cannan (*Theories*, p. 380).

The metaphysics of the modern economist is that 'a commodity . . . is the embodiment of measurable efforts and sacrifices' (Marshall, *Memorials*, 126); on the same plane as Marx's 'crystallised labour'. And much more Clark's notion that marginal distribution being equal to product of each is 'just'. *V. Retro.* Clark's metaphysics is much more *grossolana* than Marx's: it is equal to Proudhon's, Hodgskin etc. who believed (*against* Marx) that since labour produces the whole it must get the whole.

All the enquiry about value has always been (and still is and probably always will be) a purely metaphysical quest. When the old economists asked for the 'causes' or the 'measure' of value, they really were looking – as in fact we are, under the illusion of our equations 'determining' value – for the 'nature' of value (it is not by accident, as Cannan, elsewhere, says that the word is in A. Smith's title) in the same metaphysical sense in which we look for the nature of 'matter' or of 'mind'. In fact, we want to 'explain' in terms of familiar words, or notions (i.e. to which we are used) the 'new' thing that we meet: but when we have got used to them (as now economists have with prices) we take them for granted and require no further explanation. The explanation has simply to be 'satisfactory' that is to provide the accommodation suited for our mental habits, and prove restful to the mind – cool down the fever of quest and satiate the thirst for explanation.

Still more terrific. In the middle of the 19th century a man succeeds, either by accident of by superhuman effort, in getting again hold of the classical theory: he improves it, and draws its practical consequences from it. (D3/12/4)

The manuscript, unfortunately, breaks off at this point. Who could that man be remains to be guessed, although it does not seem too difficult.

History, to Sraffa, means a sort of entropy of the theory of value. We are in the presence of a degenerating ('rotten conceptions') research programme. The great fears aroused by the advent of socialism have made economic theory respond on the same degenerate theoretical plane on which the vulgar had argued: in that way the entire body of economic theory is affected by the illness, and the soundness of the classical approach is lost. This is a crude reconstruction of what is in Sraffa's mind at the time and it seems particularly useful to the understanding of Sraffa-editor-of-Ricardo and his sources. The basic point is that Marx himself is at risk of being confused with the vulgar, while in truth it is the contrary ('stands towering'). It becomes imperative to go back to the classical approach to value theory, which to Sraffa must be the right approach to cost and value to be highlighted in the lectures. But before turning to the lectures, let us see another example (again November 1927) of the description of the process of degeneration itself.

> *Degeneration of cost and value*
>
> A. Smith, Ricardo and Marx indeed began to corrupt the old idea of cost – from food to labour. But their notion was still near enough to be in many cases equivalent.
>
> The decomposition went on at a terrific speed from 1820 to 1870: Senior's abstinence and Mill's mess of the whole thing. Cairnes brought it to the final stage 'sacrifice' (did Marshall take it from Cairnes? see his *Princ.* note p. 339; seems not). Simultaneously a much bigger step was taken in the process of shifting the basis of value from physical to psychical processes: Jevons, Menger, Walras.
>
> This was an enormous breach with the tradition of Pol. E.; in fact, this has meant the destruction of the classical P.E. and the substitution for it, under the old name, of the Calculus of Pleasure and Pain (Hedonistic). *V. Retro.*
>
> When the Jevonsians turned back to write their own history, they found with pride (it ought to have been with dismaly) that they had no forerunners amongst P.E.; their forerunners were mainly two or three cranks, an engineer Dupuit, a mathem. Cournot, a prussian Civil Servant Gossen, who had only cultivated P.E. as a Hobby. *V. Retro.* They had not the slightest knowledge of the works of the Classical economists. They drew out of their fancy. In fact, no competent P.Emist, with a conscience of his tradition, would have degnato to entertain those views.
>
> (D3/12/4: item 2)

The two *Retros* read:

> I do not mean by this that cranks can never find new theories: on the contrary, when a big breach with tradition is required, their intervention is usually necessary. What I meant to prove is that *there has actually* been a breach with tradition, and the intervention of the cranks is an element of the evidence; and that Marshall's attempt to bridge over the cleavage and establish a continuity in the tradition is futile and misguided.
>
> It is unfortunate that so much time has been taken to change the name of P.E. into Economics: but it is appropriate: it marks the cleavage, or rather the abyss, between the two.
>
> (Ibid.)

The main text of these notes continues thus (on a new sheet numbered '2' by Piero Sraffa):

> What had happened in the meantime, to change so much the mind of the economists, and induce them to scrap all that had been done up to that time? (It was in fact scrapping the whole: Jevons, Preface, & Cannan, *Theories*, 379–383, 'must be visited with almost unqualified condemnation' are right from the point of view of *Economics.*)

> Socialism has been the cause of all this. In fact, classical P.E., with its surplus to be arbitrarily divided, leads straight to Socialism. When after the death of Ricardo the first timid attempts of using socialistically his theory of value were made (Hodgskin, Thompson: they were misguided if (?) they used the moral argument that labour produces everything as Proudhon, but not Marx did), Senior and Mill and Cairnes rallied to the defence by making cost psychological.
>
> But when the mass attack of Marx, and the threat of the rampant International and the Paris Commune came, a much more drastic defence was called for: not only sacrifice, but utility, – and simultaneously J. M. W. and their success. The classical economy was becoming too dangerous as a whole, it had to be scrapped bodily. It was a burning house which threatened to set to fire the whole structure and foundations of the capitalist society – it was forthwith removed.
>
> (Ibid.)

A pencilled remark is added at the bottom of the page and completes it: 'Mention Rae, Ferrara, Carey?, Schuling cost of reproduction as a link between disutility and utility, to justify the passing from one to the other.'

Here significantly comes a sheet with the most famous quote from Petty ('The Method I take . . . Angles of Incidence and Reflection', from the preface to *Political Arithmethick*). Carefully written down, this shows the significance the passage has for Sraffa, to whom it epitomises the *correct classical* conception of cost of production. Compare with the following vivid highlight from the following sheet:

> Evolution of concept of cost.
>
> It was only Petty and the Physiocrats who had the right notion of cost as 'the loaf of bread'. Then somebody started measuring in labour, as every day's labour requires the same amount of food.
>
> Then they proceeded to regard cost as actually an amount of labour. Then A. Smith interpreted labour as 'the toil and trouble' which is the 'real cost' (Ricardo, p. 10, 15 n) and the 'hardship'.
>
> Then this was by Ricardo brought back to labour, but not far back enough, and Marx went only as back as Ricardo.
>
> Then Senior invented Abstinence. And Cairnes unified all the costs (work, abstinence and risk) as sacrifice.
>
> Now Davenport, Cassell, Henderson, have carried it a step further, the last step in the wrong direction.
>
> (Ibid.: item 4)

Also in his published articles of the mid-1920s, as is well known, Sraffa had chosen to criticise 'the wrong direction', though approaching the subject from a different starting point. But behind the scenes the ambition was much larger. The lectures, and *a fortiori* the notes and documents, are indeed behind the scenes. We are now in a position to appreciate that the Ricardo edition is probably the place where Sraffa (helped by Dobb) comes closest to committing his entire ambitions to the printed page. Marx, of course, is the pivot of the 'new' theory born from the resurrection of classicism, suitably dressed this time in the impeccable positivist–empiricist 'metaphysics'. If Smith continues to play the herald of the vulgar, Ricardo must be defended: only by misinterpreting him can we put him among the degenerate, as we shall see below. For example, when he reads Hollander in that sense, that makes him literally furious. In a leaflet, dated November 1927, he wrote:

> Hollander, Ricardo,/p. 126 'Perversions of R. by Marx' / '. . . Ricardo regarded embodied labour as merely one of a series of possible units of value measurement but he was very far from asserting its unique efficacy, and indeed ultimately arrived at . . . agnosticism. . . . He wrote to McCulloch . . . we have a choice only among imperfect measures . . .' / Idiot! It is sufficient to see Ricardo's Works, p. 11 / Cp. p. 68 n. 3. R. 'unwilling to concede' that command over labour instead of labour embodied is the foundation of value!!!
>
> (D3/12/11: 105)

Here are the remote sources of Sraffa's pervasive harshness on Hollander throughout the Ricardo edition.

Sraffa's lectures on value, 1928–31

We have now to turn to Sraffa's notion of cost, developed at that time. Here, again, our analysis is not intended to be exhaustive, but it is limited to the essential points. It is proper to turn to the lectures, mentioned above and listed under D2/4, with D3/12/4, discussed above, in mind.

Although we do not mean here to discuss the whole development of Sraffa's argument in the lectures, it is worth going back through that particular text to the theory of value: that issue not only was in fact the main subject of the lectures, but logically does provide the necessary background to the classical notion of cost, which is among Sraffa's main objects to emphasise.

The theory of value – Sraffa argues – is no purely logical exercise. It is influenced by 'practical problems', which makes room for history. Sraffa's compelling reasons are for a historico-analytic approach.

> There is also another reason for the necessity of the knowledge of the history of their origin in order to understand economic theories. Every economist finds that the public to whom he addresses himself has already found for himself an explanation, whether right or wrong, of economic phenomena; and therefore a large part of his work is directed to correct popular opinions and to dispel widespread prejudices. Thus every economist tends to frame his theories in such a way that certain elements acquire in them an importance which is entirely out of proportion of the part they play in real life, but reflects the necessity in which the economist has been of opposing obsolete theories or popular prejudices. And when the theory has crystallised and

> we have forgotten the way in which it has grown, we are often inclined to over-estimate the importance of certain elements simply because for long forgotten historical reasons they play a very large part in accepted economic theory.
>
> A further disturbing element is that in the background of every theory of value there is a theory of distribution. The real problem to be solved by a theory of value, that is 'Why is a commodity exchanged with another in a given ratio?' is constantly transformed into the entirely different one: 'How is the price received for the product distributed between the factors of production?'
>
> (D2/4: 3–4)

Thus 'Ricardo's theory of value, whatever may have been in the back of his mind, or in his footnotes and in his private letters to Malthus and McCulloch, was understood by everybody in his time to mean that quantity of labour was the only cause of value, and this is what in practice mattered' (ibid.: 11). Now, as the social conflict from one between landlords and manufacturers turns historically into one between labour and capital, Ricardo's theory of value 'obviously becomes a strong argument in favour of labour. / A Socialist school arose in the twenties and thirties of last century which seized this opportunity.' That 'caused a good deal of confusion amongst the orthodox Ricardian economists, who saw their doctrines used in such an unexpected way' (ibid.); the Ricardians in this country (Torrens, McCulloch, Malthus) were still at work to understand Ricardo's exceptions to the labour value rule. But the turning point is the early 1870s with the publication of *Das Kapital* by Marx, 'in which his critique of capitalism is entirely based upon Ricardo's theory of value, although of course he interpreted it in an entirely different way from the early Utopian socialists' (ibid.: 14) on one side and the rise of marginalism on the other. Concerning the latter point, after a brief discussion of the issue, 'I rather prefer – Sraffa wrote – to accept Prof. Fetter's and Sir W. Ashley's view, that there is a close relation between the emerging of Marxism and the extraordinarily ready acceptance of the theory of marginal utility amongst orthodox economists' (ibid.: 16–17).

At this point Sraffa first makes clear the main purpose of the historical reconstruction, which leads to the central role of the notion of cost and to the imperative of a return to the classical conception of it.

> The point I wish to make is the independence in the development of the two opposite conceptions of cost and of utility. In Marshall's theory they appear as closely connected, in fact they are for him two quantities of the same nature, one positive and the other negative; they can be added or subtracted and balanced against one another. But this unification, and therefore the statement of the symmetry between cost and utility, and through them of supply and demand, has been to a large extent the result of Marshall's work – not the historical development of the theory of value. Their origin has to be traced to entirely distinct sources, and their development has been quite independent of one another. Then Marshall has brought them together and

> has made an attempt to conciliate the two opposite views, which I shall refer to as of Ricardo and of Jevons, each of whom thought that it was possible to group all causes of value under one single notion at the exclusion of the other. / What is important to realise however is that the notion of cost of production, as understood by the classical economists, would not have allowed such a unification; to make this possible it had itself to pass through a series of small changes which gradually brought it to its present position.
>
> (D2/4: 17–18)

We come now to the classical conception of cost:

> Marshall regards the 'real cost of production' of a commodity as the sum of 'efforts and sacrifices' involved in the abstinences or waitings and in the labour of all kinds that is directly or indirectly required for the production of a commodity. Real cost therefore is an aggregate of the unpleasant feelings of various sorts felt by the individuals connected with production. / For Petty and the Physiocrats cost i.e. what in their theory plays the role of cost is nothing so subjective; on the contrary, it is a stock of material, that is required for the production of a commodity; this material being of course mainly food for the workers. But Petty wants to make it quite clear that his notion of cost has nothing to do with the pleasant or unpleasant feelings of men, and he defines 'the common measure of value' as 'the days food of an adult Man, at a Medium, and not the days labour'. / This cost is therefore something concrete, tangible, and visible, that can be measured in tons or gallons. It stands therefore at the opposite extreme of Marshall's cost, which is absolutely private to each individual, and can only be measured (if at all) by means of the monetary inducement required to call forth the exertion.
>
> (Ibid.: 20–1)

In Chapter 13 of this volume Kurz maintains that there is no evidence (see also Kurz 1998a, especially section 4: 447) that Sraffa aimed at re-establishing the labour theory of value. While this is no doubt true, it would be unwarranted to infer that Sraffa had little contact with, even little knowledge of, Marx's thought at an early stage and that his starting point was Marshall's theory. If we connect the published articles with the lectures and finally with his personal notes, the emerging picture of Sraffa is one of an ambitious reconstruction of economic theory centred upon Marx. Marx, in other words, is to Sraffa far from being a synonym for the labour theory of value. In this way he undoubtedly also relied on the lesser known parts of Marx's analysis and he did not even need to mention Marx too often, although his intellectual background comes out quite clearly from the personal notes. Sraffa's quotations from Petty, for example, had been, without significant exception, accurately sieved by Marx himself.

Similar remarks on the classical conception of cost[16] do apply to the view Sraffa conveys to his students on the Physiocratic system, which, he argues,

> turns upon the conception of cost which I have outlined. . . . Measuring both the product and the cost in physical amount it is obvious that in agriculture, say in a corn farm, the amount of corn produced is greater than the amount used for seed and for the subsistence of the workers. . . . [N]o doubt . . . in agriculture, owing to the identity in the quality of the product and the materials used up in production, the comparison for the calculation of the surplus is possible to some extent without introducing the disturbing element of price for measuring the quantities.
>
> (D2/4: 25–6)

All this also heeds Marx's *Mehrwert* analysis quite closely.[17] This is far from being the end of the analysis that can be done on Sraffa's sources but, at least, is it not clear enough where the 'corn model' comes from? It may be useful to learn, as it is natural to conclude, that the surplus approach together with the notion of fixed capital (the latter not discussed here) both originate from that period during the 1920s.

Another unmistakable Marxian element is the attribution to Smith of the usual ambiguous role. 'It is A. Smith,' Sraffa noted in 1927, 'that shunted the car on the wrong track. In fact we have ceased to understand value from the moment the economic science was found.'[18] In his lectures Sraffa wrote:

> A. Smith adopted this notion of surplus and with it the idea of cost of the Physiocrats. But he has also a different idea of cost – and it is in a sense true that the *Wealth of N.* as a whole represents the connecting link between eighteenth century economics and the modern one. Thus he conceives of labour as an amount of 'toil and trouble': although he uses this expression only incidentally, Marshall has thought it so important and significant as to say that 'the point of view . . . from which a commodity is regarded as the embodiment of measurable efforts and sacrifices' 'was conquered for us by A. Smith' (Memoirs, 126).
>
> (D2/4: 27)

Of course this sets in the transformation or degeneration of the conception of cost, eventually leading him to conceive, with Marshall, of 'wages, interest and profits . . . simply [as] shares in the product; they are co-ordinate quantities, that can be regarded as acting upon the value of the product in the same way' (ibid.: 22). Is it not clear, much as it is for Marx's *Zusammenaddierung*, that Sraffa's adding-up conception belongs to the 'degenerative' process? Ricardo was different: of course he had his own doubts; he 'reduces cost to a single element, labour with some doubts as to whether to include the services of capital in addition' (ibid.: 36). A passage from a letter to McCulloch on the 'by two causes instead of by one' is given here on p. 39; that is the letter of June 1820, very well known to Ricardian scholars, which appears in the 1951 introduction, pp. xxxix–xl, and of which the introduction itself changed totally the interpretation.

In sum, the causal degeneration of the theory of value starts with Ricardian socialism and continues with marginalism, which is fully fledged 'vulgar' political economy. Sraffa's reaction is to rectify the historico-analytical interpretation of Ricardo and Marx by eliminating the metaphysics on value via the return to the classical conception of cost.

The above, as already hinted, is of course meant only to offer a few highlights of the work that needs to be done on Sraffa's sources. That work is necessary for an adequate discussion of the classical school in economics and allows the proper historical perspective on the interpretation of Ricardo on which Sraffa is likely to emerge as an extreme case.

Sraffa's Ricardo in historical perspective

Piero Sraffa's interpretation of Ricardo largely occupies the centre of the stage in the literature on Ricardo and on the classical economists down to the present day. Sraffa produced the most fascinating bold endeavour to implement the Marxian programme whereby the surplus perspective becomes the unifying element of a number of systems constituting 'Classical Political Economy' in Marx's sense. The Sraffian reading of Ricardo – too often misrepresented either as a 'definitive' reading (as if that could be thought of) or as a preferred target of criticism – needs to be reconsidered in a comparative perspective with respect to its own sources of inspiration as well as with regard to parallel or different readings.

With the necessary critical reconsideration completed, the following problems emerge. In the first place Sraffa's interpretation shares with the neoclassical interpretations the strong tendency to involve Ricardian analysis with disputes on the origin of the distributive rates and thereby with problems on which Ricardo had little to say. In the second place each party claims Ricardo as a predecessor. While a number of neoclassical authors focus on Ricardo in a continuistic perspective, Sraffa's interest lies in making room for the dichotomy of a classical versus a neoclassical school in a fashion which resembles the contribution by Jevons or, more directly, Marx's analysis on the dissolution of the Ricardian school and the advent of the *Vulgärökonomie*. This Marxian factor is also a force pushing Ricardo in the same unwarranted direction. Thirdly Sraffa's perspective should also be judged within the context of the post-war revival of Marxian economics and of Marxian studies more generally. The criticisms levelled against Sraffa from the Marxian camp have now ended up in silence but were far from unfounded. In particular giving up the labour theory of value implies that the core concept of exploitation becomes problematic.

The analysis developed in this chapter has demonstrated, under the conditions discussed and with the proviso that no definitive judgement is possible in economics, that the editorial work of Piero Sraffa has shown conclusively that the implementation of the Marxian programme on classical economics has failed to establish the new orthodoxy or mainstream interpretation. Canon ambitions are at present probably to some extent misplaced, which incidentally, besides being a historical fact, also provides a methodological guideline worth considering. The notion of a classical school in economics no longer appears centred on Ricardo to the same extent. Although it remains true that economics is based upon *different* paradigms, Ricardo plays a lesser role in the distinction.

Samuel Hollander (1998; see also Hollander 2000), who is well known to have made significant and extensive contributions on the classical economists, and on Ricardo more particularly, disputes, at least in part, the present historical perspective on Sraffa's work more generally. It is now proper to end this chapter with a discussion of Hollander's views, which is indeed a convenient opportunity to clarify a number of points.

'In what follows,' Hollander writes (Hollander 1998: 431–2; cf. Hollander 2000: 195–6), 'I approach the general position of Bronfenbrenner and Porta as a hypothesis: can the "Sraffian" reading of Ricardo be rationalised only in "post-Marxian" terms?' He goes on to argue that an investigation must be undertaken, which is in fact one object of the paper, of 'how *in actuality* did Sraffa arrive at his reading'. In brief, the upshot of the exercise is a demonstration that 'to take the "Sraffian" view requires that one constrains the reading of Ricardo those parts of select chapters in the *Principles* – specifically chapters one and six – involving highly simplified illustrative exercises'. Therefore, Hollander concludes, as 'an appropriately "truncated" view of Ricardo yields the Sraffian attributions, Porta's objections to the Sraffa reading prove too severe. Nonetheless, the hypothesis that this perspective might reflect a reading through Marx's spectacles cannot be dismissed out of hand.' However, in spite of a number of concessions, in the final instance Hollander's assumption seems to be one of selective reading. Hollander's approach on this point is indeed parallel to the approach adopted by Heinz Kurz and Neri Salvadori (1993a). Limiting themselves to the search for the invariable measure of value, Kurz and Salvadori observe that Sraffa's 1951 introduction 'focussed attention on those aspects of Ricardo's search for an invariable measure of value which concerned the theory of value and distribution with a given technological environment, whereas the intertemporal and interspatial aspect of Ricardo's problem is neglected' (Kurz and Salvadori 1993a: 107).

In the light of the evidence examined in the present chapter it is maintained that the Marxian perspective provides the most powerful and convincing assumption on the development of Sraffa's thought and particularly on the formative process of his interpretation of Ricardo. To take the contrary view leads to Hollander's conclusion – in my own view an unsatisfactory one – which is the following: we cannot 'exclude the possibility that Sraffa was inclined towards the "narrow" view of Ricardo for independent reasons'. Which reasons, we may ask? One suggestion, advanced by Hollander, is his 'hostility towards subjectivist economics including the Marshallian synthesis'. I refer the reader back to my analysis above to show that this is *not* in fact an 'independent reason' and that, in the present state of knowledge, the Marxian connection must be retained as the only viable hypothesis in the reconstruction of the development of Sraffa's thought and particularly in the reconstruction of his interpretation of Ricardo.[19]

Notes

This chapter reproduces, with slight modifications, the text published in *Reflections on the Classical Canon in Economics: Essays in Honour of Samuel Hollander*, ed. by E. L. Forget and

S. Peart, London and New York: Routledge. I am grateful to Ross Emmett, Augusto Graziani, Gary Mongiovi, Samuel Hollander, Nerio Naldi, Luigi Pasinetti and Paul Samuelson for appreciations, discussions and criticisms through the formative stages of this chapter. The usual disclaimer applies. I have certainly not been able to take full advantage of their valuable suggestions in the present version. A special obligation must be recorded to Pierangelo Garegnani for permission to quote from Piero Sraffa's unpublished writings. Acknowledgement is also due to the Master and Fellows of Trinity College, Cambridge, for granting access to their collection. I have a special obligation to the staff of the Wren Library, and particularly to Jonathan Smith and Diana Chardin, for help and assistance on a number of occasions.

1 The reader should be reminded that the publication of David Ricardo's *Notes on Mr. Malthus's 'Measure of Value'* (Ricardo 1992) was virtually due to Sraffa's work.

2 Sraffa was himself sympathetic to a kind of an *ante-litteram* Schumpeterian approach. Theories, he wrote in his yet unpublished lectures, 1928–9 (pp. 2–3), arise from practical problems; 'once they have arisen in this way, theories transform and develop in a way which to some extent is independent from the practical interests from which they have originated.' But, Sraffa added, 'this is not the end of the story.' For it is precisely 'by reason of this independence and of the prestige [theory] derives from it, [that] its effectiveness for supporting or opposing a particular policy is again increased, and thus inevitably the theory again becomes the object of controversies of a practical character.' This is an essential qualification of the Schumpeterian view, implying that the historico-analytical perspectives are *never* definitive, as we shall argue in the course of this chapter.

3 That was of course the very same indictment Sraffa had issued against Marshall in the 1920s. This instance is an example of an important psychological mechanism: we are never so able to expose a behavioural or mental process in our fellows as is the case when we are pursuing the very same process to a much higher degree. The following well known passage in Luke's Gospel provides a striking illustration of the mechanism: 'And why beholdest thou the mote that is in thy brother's eye, but considerest not the beam that is in thine own eye? Or canst thou say to thy brother, Brother, let me cast out the mote that is in thine eye, when thou thyself beholdest not the beam that is in thine own eye? Thou hypocrite, cast out first the beam out of thine own eye, and then shalt thou see clearly to cast out the mote that is in thy brother's eye' (Luke, VI: 41–2). Parenthetic overtones aside, the above is an admirable description of a psychological process of which Sraffa may well have been entirely unconscious.

4 See the close of the entry on 'Sraffian economics' by Paul A. Samuelson in *The New Palgrave*. 'Piero Sraffa', Samuelson concludes, 'was much respected and much loved. With each passing year, economists perceive new grounds for admiring his genius' (Samuelson 1987b).

5 You are welcome to check the details of the source of the passage in note 19 below.

6 The present work is incomplete as far as these extensions of the analysis are concerned.

7 Schefold (1998) affirms that the entry 'Corn-ratio theory of profits' in Sraffa's index to the Ricardo edition 'is almost unique in taking up an economic concept used not by Ricardo but by his editor'. On the other hand, he goes on to observe, 'Ricardo was not very good at naming concepts which he had created,' whereas, he adds, Sraffa was equally good at naming new concepts and at creating them. Whose creation the corn-ratio idea actually was remains mysterious (see, however, p. 149). In my essay on Ricardo (Porta 1990: 113) I put forward the view that the corn model, if it ever entered Ricardo's head at all, did so as a 'strong case', i.e. a counter-example to refute Malthus's theory of profits. I surmise I did argue that way in the same logic, leading Sam Hollander to write: 'Ricardo's emphasis upon corn in the wage basket has its source in . . . the very strong objection Ricardo took to Malthus's view that the profit rate is affected by events which do not work their way through changes in the cost of producing wage goods at all' (Hollander 1979: 146). Curiously enough (but this is a

special by-product of their friendship) *if* the idea of a corn model ever was at all present in Ricardo's mind, that came through Malthus himself, who on the other hand was keen to point out that perfect homogeneity of inputs and outputs ought to be excluded. Cf. also Hollander (1997: 455 ff.); Porta (1985).

8 No less an authority than Sam Hollander (1973a) lists Adam Smith's adding-up theory of price in the index to his volume on Smith.

9 This is what Ricardo had called, in a letter to Mill a few months before, Smith's 'original error respecting value'. See Ricardo (1951–73, VII: 100) and cf. ibid.: 105.

10 Sraffa's footnotes in this passage refer the reader to the *Wealth of Nations* (Book 1, chapter VI; Cannan edn, vol. I: 50, 51, 52, 54, 65).

11 It may be usefully added that the term 'adding up' is the English translation of Marx's *Zusammenaddierung* and *Zusammensetzung*, used in his *Theorien über den Mehrwert* in the context of a discussion of Smith's concept of natural price (see Marx, *Marx–Engels Werke* XXVI. I. 3. 7: 'Seine Ansicht vom "natürlichen Preis" als Summe von Arbeitslohn, Profit und Rente'). According to Marx, Smith had initially (and correctly) established that the value of a commodity regulates wages, profit and rent. However, he later came to adopt the opposite procedure (closer to empirical appearance and current opinion), whereby natural price comes to be determined through the adding up (*Zusammenaddierung*, *Zusammensetzung*) of the natural prices of wages, profit and rent. It is Ricardo's main merit, Marx goes on to observe, to have put an end to such confusion.

12 To a lesser extent, but probably no less important to Sraffa, is the need to retort on Jacob Hollander's centenary estimate of Ricardo's work. Luigi Pasinetti, in a contribution read at the Sraffa conference at the Fondazione Einaudi, Turin, October 1998, on continuity and change in Sraffa's thought (Pasinetti 1998b), argues that it is possible to discern a fundamental continuity in Sraffa's transition from the criticism of Marshall's theory to the reconstruction of the classical approach on cost and value. He appeared to differ from Pierangelo Garegnani (who presented a paper at the same conference on Sraffa's interpretation of the classical economists through the late 1920s) on several points. I look forward to reading both contributions in written form. In particular I found Pasinetti's continuity argument extremely robust and appealing. As far as the late 1920s are concerned, Sraffa's lectures, 1928–9, seem to me to provide compelling evidence on continuity. May I mention on the issue, in passing, a significant addition to the Sraffian literature: the English translation of Sraffa's 1925 article 'Sulle relazioni fra costo e quantità prodotta', in Pasinetti (1998a: 323–63).

13 Hollander (1998, 2000); Kurz (1998a). I had been pleading for a new historiography in the above sense since 1979, when I circulated a first draft of my introduction to the Italian edition of Ricardo. At the time I was able to call in support of my argument, by Sraffa's own permission, a few passages from his unpublished lectures on the 'Advanced Theory of Value' (cf. below, note 17). I am pleased to recall that precisely from 1979 I became acquainted with Giovanni Caravale. As a member, at the time, of a national committee on full professorships he noticed my early draft. Subsequently I was fortunate enough to meet him on innumerable occasions and discuss Ricardian issues with him. At least fifteen papers of mine have since developed the subject over the years, a story I summarise in my forthcoming book. I am now relieved that the buds of the new historiography have at last started to develop and bear the names of two outstanding scholars of Sraffa.

14 Sraffa's lectures are a beautiful manuscript of well over a hundred foolscap sheets, largely in Sraffa's hand. I was deeply impressed when I first had the privilege of studying the manuscripts during Sraffa's own lifetime. It bears the inscription in Piero Sraffa's hand '16 Lectures in Michaelmas Term 1928–29 "Advanced Theory of Value" e 1929–30 e Lent 1931'. It is now classified D2/4.

15 Here is the full wording of what is paraphrased in English in this page of the present text: 'Impostazione del libro/L'unico sistema è di far la storia a ritroso, e cioè: stato attuale dell'ec.; come vi si è giunti, mostrando le differenze e la superiorità delle vecchie teorie. Poi, esporre la teoria./Se si va in ordine cronol., Petty, Fisiocr., Ric.,

Marx, Jevons, Marsh., bisogna farlo precedere da uno statement della mia teoria per spiegare dove si "drive at": il che significa esporre prima *tutta* la teoria. E allora c'è il pericolo di finire come Marx, che ha pubbl. prima il Cap., e poi non è riuscito a finire l'Hist. des Doct. E il peggio si è che non è riuscito a farsi capire, senza la spiegaz. storica./Il mio scopo è: I esporre la storia, che è veramente l'essenziale II farmi capire: per il che si richiede che io vada dal noto all'ignoto, da Marshall a Marx, dalla disutilità al costo materiale' (D3/12/11: item 55).

16 The flavour of Sraffa's classicism as far as cost theory is concerned can be captured in the following (fully Ricardian) explanatory note among his November 1927 slips: 'When I say that the value of a product is "determined" by the physical volume of commodities used up in its production, it should *not* be understood that it is determined by the value of those commodities. This would be a vicious circle, because – by what then is determined their value? Besides it would be wrong because the value of the product is equal to the value of the factors *plus* the surplus produced.

What I say is simply that the numerical proportions between amount of factors and amount of product *is*, by definition, the absolute value of the product.' (D3/12/11: item 101.)

17 In a note from his reading of Marx's *Histoire des doctrines économiques*, Sraffa wrote: 'Marx, Hist, I, 44–45 / Physiocrats, why they saw surplus value in agriculture and not in industry: because in agriculture the labour produces and consumes the same thing (seed & food) and the difference between outlay & produce is easily perceived, it requires only a subtraction. In industry the process is more intricate,' etc. Cf. D3/12/11: item 100, November 1927. Let us mention further that the point, among a few others, is the object of a pencilled annotation in Sraffa's hand ('Physiocrates: pourquoi ils ont vu la plus value en agriculture et non en industrie 44–45') on the inside back cover of his own copy of the Molitor translation of the Kautsky edition of Marx's *Theorien*, published in Paris in 1924.

18 See Sraffa papers, D3/12/11: item 64. This is a slip on 'History of cost'.

19 The passage quoted on pp. 133–4 (cf. note 5) is from the entry 'Sraffa Piero' by J. Eatwell and C. Panico in the *The New Palgrave. A Dictionary of Economics* IV.

11 Some reflections on Sraffa's Ricardo

Gary Mongiovi

Few problems in the history of economic thought are as contentious as those surrounding the interpretation of Ricardo. Controversy over Ricardo is of relatively recent vintage, however. Prior to the publication of Samuel Hollander's *Economica* paper 'Ricardo's analysis of the profit rate' (1973b), discussions of Ricardo's work were, by and large, dry, dispassionate affairs. If they did not cast much light, nor did they generate noticeable heat. Jevons of course had seen Ricardo as an 'able but wrongheaded man [who] shunted the car of economic science on to a wrong line' (1879: lvii); and Marshall (1920: appendix I), partly in reaction to Jevons, had defended Ricardo's economics as an embryonic version of the marginalist theory of supply and demand. Marshall's disagreement with Jevons concerning Ricardo was a minor skirmish that received, and probably warranted, little notice at the time. But viewed in retrospect it anticipates the very issues that have driven Ricardo scholarship since the publication of Sraffa's edition of the *Works and Correspondence* (Ricardo 1951–73).

There are two main points of contention. The first concerns whether the theory Ricardo sought to articulate was in some essential sense the same as the marginalist theory that rose to dominance after 1870. The second is whether he had in fact shunted economic science onto the wrong track, as Jevons charged. These issues are closely interconnected, and they account for the enduring interest of Ricardo studies. Scholars such as Hollander (1979) and Morishima (1989) maintain, as did Marshall, that Ricardo's economics should be interpreted as a primitive form of a fundamentally sound orthodoxy. The interpretative tradition established by Sraffa views Ricardo as one of the founders of a distinct classical surplus approach which had been 'submerged and forgotten' in the wake of marginalism's ascendance (Sraffa 1951, 1960; Dobb 1973). On this reading, Jevons was at least perceptive enough to recognise that Ricardo's economics was not an imperfectly developed version of marginalism, but an altogether different theoretical system.

But the question of Ricardo's relation to marginalism would be of interest mainly to antiquarians had Sraffa not reopened the second issue raised by Jevons. Sraffa's *Production of Commodities by Means of Commodities* (1960) exposed a serious defect in the marginalist explanation of distribution, and demonstrated moreover that the classical surplus theory could be given a rigorous formulation. Ricardo had been on the right track: it was Marshall, Walras and Menger – and Jevons – who had pushed economic science off the rails.

A central element of the modern revival of the classical theory is the effort to clarify its logical structure. The spectacular rise of marginalism after 1890 so thoroughly eclipsed classical political economy that its distinctive features had become nearly lost. Marshall's characterisation of Ricardo's theory as an unsophisticated precursor of the theory of supply and demand, that is, as a special case in which costs were assumed to be constant and demand therefore played a subordinate role, further obscured the features of classical economics. Before the classical approach could be restored to prominence, its logical structure needed not merely to be clarified and distinguished from marginalist theory: it needed first of all to be rediscovered.

This then is what is at stake in the Ricardo debates, and what accounts for their undiminished intensity after nearly three decades. The underlying issue concerns not just what a long-dead nineteenth-century economist 'really meant', but whether the analytical framework associated with Ricardo, and with Marx, constitutes a coherent and scientifically robust alternative to modern orthodoxy.

Pier Luigi Porta reflects this tension in the previous chapter. His aim is to encourage us to revisit Sraffa's interpretation of Ricardo with a critical eye. Classic works – and Sraffa's introduction (1951) to *The Works and Correspondence of David Ricardo* certainly qualifies as one – should of course be subject to ongoing scrutiny, not only because they have much to teach us, but also because their authoritative status is no guarantee that their arguments are sound. But Professor Porta here takes a curious line of approach. He does not offer any direct refutation of Sraffa's interpretation of Ricardo, but instead suggests that the main justification for thinking there is something suspect about that interpretation lies in what is already well known: that this interpretation was part of a larger project that culminated in *Production of Commodities by Means of Commodities*. If I have read Professor Porta correctly, the idea is that Sraffa's interpretation of Ricardo was somehow moulded – and perhaps, Porta implies, tainted – by his theoretical views.

The gist of Sraffa's interpretation is that Ricardo conceived of the profit rate and relative prices as regulated by the technical conditions of production and the real wage, with the latter determined not by the forces of supply and demand but by social and institutional factors. This describes as well the theoretical framework of *Production of Commodities*. At the start of Chapter 10 Professor Porta remarks that Sraffa's introduction 'has never been read in itself', by which he means that the substance of Sraffa's interpretation has not been evaluated independently of the issues raised in his 1960 book. But of course the introduction appeared a decade before *Production of Commodities*, and therefore could be, and indeed was, read 'in itself' for at least ten years.

Sraffa's book brought to light a serious defect at the heart of the neoclassical theory of distribution. The properties of this defect, and its damaging consequences for the orthodox theory, were fully exposed in subsequent contributions (see, for example, Garegnani 1970). By the early 1970s the connection between the capital critique and Sraffa's interpretation of Ricardo had no doubt begun to register on historians of economic thought. The traditional version of the marginalist theory of distribution is irremediably flawed, owing to difficulties relating to the specification of capital; and a robust alternative to the marginalist approach was near to hand – the classical theory as outlined in Sraffa's introduction and in *Production of Commodities*.

The classical approach explains income distribution not in terms of substitution mechanisms that impute the value of the social product to factor owners according to the contributions those factors make to output, but in terms of the institutional and historical setting within which workers, capitalists and landlords pursue their separate, and generally conflicting, material interests. Furthermore, Sraffa's work suggests that progress in economics requires us to look *backwards*, to the classicals and Marx. That is to say, it suggests that a hundred years' worth of marginalist economics ought to be scuttled in favour of a recovered theoretical tradition that was abandoned in error during the nineteenth century.[1] In light of all this, we should not be surprised to note that the first shot in the modern Ricardo debates – Hollander's *Economica* essay (1973b) – was fired while economists were licking the still fresh wounds inflicted in the capital controversy.

There can be no doubt that Sraffa's thinking on theoretical questions influenced his reading of Ricardo. But this unremarkable fact has no bearing on the soundness of his interpretation. Sraffa's interest in Ricardo and the classicals dates from before *Production of Commodities* began to take shape in the late 1920s. Indeed, as early as 1925, in his critique of the Marshallian theory of supply, Sraffa gives an indication of being aware of the classical method of logical separation of the analysis of outputs, prices and distribution. His recognition of the need for an approach to the analysis of value that could accommodate non-constant returns may have directed his attention to the classicals, and in particular to Ricardo, in whose explanation of the profit rate diminishing returns played a central role (see below).

It seems most reasonable to suppose that there was a relation of mutual determination between Sraffa's analytical work and his interpretation of Ricardo. This, I imagine, is the way it is with most of us who appreciate the relevance of intellectual history to theoretical work. At the start of his scientific career Sraffa had an intuitive awareness that neoclassical theory is defective in some important respects; initially the focus of his attention was on the treatment of supply in conditions of non-constant returns. He suspected that a return to the approach of the classicals (which prior to 1927 he understood imperfectly) might put the theory of value and distribution on a sounder footing. His reflections on Ricardo and the classicals informed his theoretical work; that much is clear from his manuscripts. As his theoretical framework developed and took shape, so too did his understanding of the classicals come into sharper focus.

There is nothing exceptional in this. So I do not quite understand Professor Porta's remark that the introduction is 'in reality a powerful rhetorical construct' – as though Sraffa had some hidden agenda other than to make clear what Ricardo was getting at. If there is another thing we learn from Sraffa's manuscripts it is that he was painstakingly self-critical; he repeatedly subjected his ideas to counter-arguments, discarding lines of thinking that did not withstand his own severe scrutiny.

Ironically, Professor Porta offers a 'rhetorical construct' of his own, one that is highly questionable: that is, his transformation of Sraffa's definitive edition into a 'definitive interpretation'. Porta asserts that such a transformation has been undertaken by adherents of Sraffa's interpretation, but the transformation is in fact entirely of Professor Porta's making. I know of no one who has claimed that Sraffa's interpretation is definitive in any monolithic sense. The claim has been made that it is a correct interpretation, and evidence has been put forth in support of it; it has been defended against criticisms that began to appear in the 1970s; and it has been fleshed out and extended, especially with regard to other classical writers and to the classical treatment of wages. But to conclude that an interpretation is correct, after weighing the evidence and considering the counter-arguments, is not the same as accepting the interpretation solely on the basis of Sraffa's 'charisma' (Professor Porta's word) or authority, without reflection on the evidence. No major participant in the Ricardo debates has followed the latter path.

Midway through his piece, Professor Porta begins to place quotation marks around the term 'definitive interpretation' – a clever rhetorical strategy, if I may say so, intended no doubt to convey the impression that this label has been used by defenders of Sraffa's reading. But the only passage that Professor Porta can find to support his accusation, from Bertram Schefold's *Economic Journal* (1996) obituary of Sraffa, refers not to the introduction but to *Production of Commodities*, as Sraffa's 'definitive work'. As the context of the remark makes plain, Schefold meant that *Production of Commodities* is definitive in the sense of being the culmination of a lifetime's work. There is nothing in the passage, or elsewhere in the obituary, to suggest that Schefold meant to apply the term 'definitive' to Sraffa's interpretation of Ricardo.[2]

I might add that the very fact that I can refer to the Ricardo debates with the expectation that every reader will know what I mean indicates how far from true it is to say that Sraffa's interpretation has acquired the status of an unassailable fortress. That's unfortunate, I suppose, since it is the interpretation that aligns most closely with the available textual evidence. But this is not the occasion to rehearse that polemic.

Professor Porta offers little in the way of concrete arguments against Sraffa's interpretation of Ricardo, perhaps because that ground has been well trod. The focus is instead on what Porta calls 'the sources of Sraffa's analysis'. My own remarks will mainly stick to the same issue, though I will also touch a bit upon what Porta has to say about the corn-ratio model and the invariable standard of value.

The central thrust of Professor Porta's argument is that *Production of Commodities* and the introduction were crucial elements of a larger project aimed at rehabilitating Marx's theory of value and distribution. 'Marx,' Porta writes, 'is the pivot of the "new" theory born from the resurrection of classicism, suitably dressed this time in the impeccable positivist-empiricist "metaphysics".' Porta rightly notes that Sraffa's manuscripts are voluminous, and that it is impossible in a single paper to explore all of the nuances of his thinking on so large a theme as the connection between economic theory and the history of economics. Some nuances are important, however, and are ignored only at great cost to one's argument. The manuscript passages reproduced by Professor Porta, aside from giving evidence of the richness and acuity of Sraffa's approach to intellectual history, reflect what is already well known and uncontroversial – that Sraffa's understanding of the classicals was informed by his reading of Marx and by the analytical problems with which he was grappling in the composition of *Production of Commodities*. No one would deny this. Professor Porta's claim, though, is that Sraffa's interpretation was driven by his commitment to the resurrection of Marx's theory. The textual record falls far short of supporting this claim.

On the contrary, the evidence indicates that Sraffa came to Ricardo, in the first instance, not through Marx but via Marshall.[3] Sraffa first turned his attention to theoretical economics in 1923, when he obtained a position at the University of Perugia and was required to lecture on the theory of value. His careful study of Marshall's *Principles* during this period led to his first important publications, his two papers on the Marshallian theory of supply (1925, 1926). In these papers, Sraffa showed that Marshall's theory could accommodate increasing returns only under highly special circumstances, i.e. if the industry under consideration is the sole user of a particular factor of production, or when falling costs arise from economies that are external to the firm but internal to the industry.

In the 1925 paper Sraffa concluded that unless we are prepared to confine our attention to cases where these special circumstances hold, we must suppose, as a first approximation, that industries operate under conditions of constant costs. But the practical importance of increasing returns apparently nagged at him, and he was reluctant to leave the discussion in an unsettled state. Hence in the 1926 sequel he suggested that value theory might proceed beyond the constant cost case by replacing the competitive framework with the conventional theory of monopoly.

At this stage in his intellectual development Sraffa held a Marshallian interpretation of Ricardo's value theory. That is, he attributed to the classicals a horizontal unit cost curve and argued that this construction enabled them to de-emphasise the role of demand in determining prices (see Marshall 1920: 814). Sraffa appears to have had an intuitive appreciation of the classical method of logical separation several years before he started his editorial work on Ricardo's writings and correspondence (see Sraffa 1925: 279, 1926: 536–7). The classical discussion of diminishing returns in agriculture was developed in connection with the theory of distribution, in particular to explain rents. Increasing returns due to induced technical progress or to the division of labour were an important element of the classical analysis of *production and accumulation*; but the classicals placed consideration of the effects of increasing returns outside the scope of the static theory of normal value. To the classicals, then, there was nothing inappropriate about assuming constant costs in their explanation of price. But the Marshallian flavour of his early reading of the classicals is evident in his inference that it is the invariability of costs that destroys the symmetry between demand and supply.

However, at some point between the publication of the 1926 *Economic Journal* paper and the autumn of 1927, when he showed Keynes an early draft of the main propositions of *Production of Commodities*, Sraffa's understanding of the classicals came into sharper focus. The process by which he moved from the critique of 1925–6 to the argument of his 1960 book was no doubt highly complex, and we should resist the temptation to explain that process in terms of a single analytical preoccupation. Nevertheless, we can reasonably surmise that his interest in Ricardo was motivated in part by his interest in how non-constant returns might be incorporated into the theory of value. As we have just seen, Sraffa was aware as early as 1925 that the classicals dealt with diminishing and increasing returns not within the static theory of value, but as phenomena that belong properly to the separate analyses of distribution and accumulation. It was the development of this insight, I suspect, that led Sraffa to recognise the classical theory as an analytical framework that is radically distinct from the marginalist theory of Marshall.

It is clear of course that Sraffa drew inspiration from Ricardo and Marx in his own theoretical work, as he acknowledges in the preface and appendix D to *Production of Commodities*. Nor can we doubt that, as Sraffa refined his own theoretical views, his understanding of Ricardo underwent a process of evolution and refinement. But a number of critics, including Porta, in Chapter 10 of this volume and in an earlier paper (1986), as well as Martin Bronfenbrenner (1989) and Samuel Hollander (2000), have suggested that Sraffa's interpretation represents an inappropriate projection of Marx's analytical system on to Ricardo.

Porta's chapter in the present volume elaborates a theme he has explored before (1986). He has made much of Sraffa's remark 'that it was only when the standard system and the distinction between basics and non-basics had emerged in the course of the [composition of *Production of Commodities*] that the [corn-ratio interpretation of Ricardo's early theory of profits] suggested itself as a natural consequence' (Sraffa 1960: appendix D). According to Porta (1986), this remark reveals Sraffa's interpretation to be 'contingent' not on Ricardo's own analytical concerns, but on 'the conception of the standard commodity'; that is, 'the . . . corn model [is] in fact a by-product of [Sraffa's] study of the standard system' (1986: 444).

The matter is not so simple, though. Sraffa's statement provides some insight into the long intellectual process that culminated in *Production of Commodities*; it suggests, in particular, that his project was almost from the very start comprised of three tightly intertwined elements – interpretation, critique, and reconstruction. Though Sraffa developed the standard system in the 1940s, his manuscripts, including his lecture notes from the late 1920s, indicate that he had come to recognise classical political economy as an analytical framework distinct from and incompatible with marginalist theory very shortly after the publication of his 1926 article. Furthermore, as noted above, the seeds of that recognition were already present in his 1925 paper – that is, *well before he had noticed the connection between his project and Marx's*.

Porta rejects the analogy between Sraffa's standard commodity and Ricardo's invariable standard of value, and contends instead that 'the standard commodity [was] designed to solve a Marxian problem', that is, the transformation problem. The evidence offered for this claim consists mainly of the observation, which is not in dispute, that Ricardo was primarily concerned with the consequences for the profit rate of diminishing returns in agriculture. The complications raised for this project by the interdependence of distribution and prices was, according to Porta, a subordinate issue that 'had no interest [for Ricardo] . . . in itself'; unable to resolve the problem, Ricardo 'went on to treat the actual problem of distribution at the center of his analysis' (1986: 444).[4]

The criticism is seriously off-target, however. Neither Sraffa nor anyone working in the surplus tradition has ever suggested that Ricardo's exclusive, or even his principal, focus was the effect on the profit rate of notional changes in the real wage. His direct concern was indeed to show how a deterioration of technical conditions of production in agriculture would affect the profit rate. But in investigating this problem Ricardo soon found himself 'stopped by the word price' (Ricardo to Mill, 30 December 1815, in Ricardo 1951–73, VI: 348), and so was forced to confront the question of how distribution and relative prices are connected. This is the aspect of his work that has enduring relevance for the analysis of capitalist reality, and that had been least understood by interpreters prior to the publication of *The Works and Correspondence*. There is nothing surprising or misleading, therefore, in Sraffa's emphasis on what was for Ricardo a vexing side issue; the problem was disturbing precisely because Ricardo understood its solution to be essential not only to the case he wanted to make about the effects of diminishing returns on the profit rate, but also to a more fundamental understanding of the laws that regulate distribution. Moreover, contrary to what Porta suggests, the textual record indicates that Ricardo was deeply troubled by the complexities of the theory of value; indeed, he was working on this problem almost up to the moment of his death (see Ricardo 1823).[5]

Porta argues that though Marx's transformation problem and Ricardo's search for an invariable standard of value are 'quite different problems in their *economic* interpretation', the fact that they 'are different sides of the same mathematical problem' – i.e. the problem posed by the interdependence of prices and distribution – has led many interpreters inappropriately 'to dress Marx in a Ricardian garb' (and presumably also to dress Ricardo in Marxian garb). What Porta doesn't grasp is that the transformation problem and Ricardo's search for an invariable standard manifest themselves as different aspects of the same mathematical problem precisely because the interdependence of prices and distribution posed a problem of economic theory that both Ricardo and Marx needed to solve. Moreover, both of them had the same reason for wanting to solve it: to render their explanations of the profit rate coherent.

Sraffa was by no means unique in noticing that Marx and Ricardo were working in the same theoretical tradition. Schumpeter thought it an 'obvious truth'

> that, as far as pure theory is concerned, Marx must be considered a 'classic' economist and more specifically a member of the Ricardian group. Ricardo is the only economist whom Marx treated as a master. I suspect that he learned his theory from Ricardo. . . . Marx used the Ricardian apparatus: he adopted Ricardo's conceptual layout and his problems presented themselves to him in the forms that Ricardo had given to him. No doubt, he

> transformed these forms and he arrived in the end at widely different conclusions. But he always did so by way of starting from, and criticizing, Ricardo – *criticism of Ricardo was his method in his purely theoretical work.*
>
> (Schumpeter 1954: 390)

There is nothing new or controversial in the observation that Sraffa's understanding of Ricardo was influenced by his reading of Marx. One finds in Marx numerous statements that depict classical political economy as a theory concerned with explaining how a capitalist economy generates and allocates a surplus to consumption and accumulation, and among social classes. And in his 1873 afterword to the second German edition of *Capital*, Volume I, Marx refers approvingly to the assessment of a Russian professor, Nikolai Sieber, 'of my theory of value, money and capital, as in its fundamentals a necessary sequel to the teaching of Smith and Ricardo'. Marx also cites with approval Sieber's judgement that '[i]n so far as it deals with actual theory, the method of Marx is the deductive method of the whole English school whose failings and virtues are common to the best theoretic economists' (Marx 1967 [1867]: 17).

Theories of Surplus Value contains an intriguing passage on the Physiocrats (to which Porta alludes), which is strikingly evocative of the corn-ratio theory of profits that Sraffa attributes to Ricardo:

> The difference between the *value* of labour-power and *the value created* by it – that is, the surplus-value which the purchase of labour-power secures for the user of labour-power – appears most palpably, most incontrovertibly, of all *branches of production*, in *agriculture*, the primary branch of production. The sum total of the means of subsistence which the labourer consumes from one year to another, or the mass of material substance which he consumes, is smaller than the sum total of the means of subsistence which he produces. In manufacture the workman is not generally seen directly producing either his means of subsistence or the surplus in excess of his means of subsistence. The process is mediated through purchase and sale, . . . and the analysis of value is necessary for it to be understood. In agriculture it shows itself directly in the surplus of use-values produced over use-values consumed by the labourer, and can therefore be grasped without an analysis of value in general.
>
> (Marx 1963 [1862–63]: 46)[6]

As it happens, Sraffa refers to this passage himself, in his appendix D to *Production of Commodities*, and connects it to Ricardo's theory of profit. Professor Porta asks (rhetorically, of course), 'Is it not clear enough where the "corn model" comes from?' Well, yes, it *is* clear – because Sraffa tells us. But what relevance this has for how we are to evaluate the soundness of the corn-ratio interpretation is *not* apparent. That Sraffa may have been led to the corn-ratio interpretation through his reading of Marx has no bearing in itself on whether that interpretation is sound. Nor does it constitute evidence that the 'Marxian perspective' was the 'most powerful [influence] on the development of Sraffa's thought', as Professor Porta contends. It does constitute evidence that Sraffa believed Marx had succeeded 'in getting hold again of the classical theory' that had been lost and obscured in the years after Ricardo's death.

What seems to be missing from the arguments put forth by Porta, and others who take this line, is a convincing demonstration that Marx's interpretation of classical political economy is wrong. The question of whether Ricardo ever articulated a corn-ratio argument is in fact less important than what appears to be beyond doubt: that at some point during 1813 he began to distance himself from the competition of capitals theory of the profit rate, and began moving toward a theory that explains the profit rate in material terms – that is, in terms of the real wages of labour and the technical conditions of production.[7] The difficulties Ricardo encountered in composing the *Principles* – in particular his efforts to reconcile the labour-time theory of price with his recognition that intersectoral differences in capital structure cause prices to deviate from ratios of embodied labour, and his related search for an invariable standard of value – these arose in the course of his attempt to extend the essential logic of the corn-ratio theory to more general conditions.

The manuscript passages reproduced by Professor Porta show that Sraffa had highly sophisticated views about how intellectual history is shaped and about the link between economic analysis and the history of economic ideas. They reveal also that he regarded Marx's understanding of Ricardo and classical political economy as perceptive and accurate. Scholars may disagree about whether Sraffa's interpretation of Ricardo (which, though one would not know it from Professor Porta's account, was not identical to Marx's) is correct. But one cannot offer as evidence against his interpretation the mere fact – unexceptional in itself – that Sraffa took Marx seriously.

Notes

This chapter originated as a comment on an early version of Pier Luigi Porta's chapter in the present volume. I have benefited from the discussion that followed the presentation of these remarks in June 1998 at the conference in memory of Giovanni Caravale. The introductory paragraphs are adapted from remarks that have been published in Italian in the proceedings of another conference, which took place in Rome in October 1998 to commemorate the centenary of Piero Sraffa's birth (see Mongiovi 2000).

1 Sraffa's choice of words – 'submerged and forgotten' (1960: v) – to describe what happened to the classical theory was not haphazard. That theory, he believed, had not been confronted, critiqued and replaced by a better theory; rather, it had been set aside, largely on ideological grounds, for a theory that has proved to be unable to explain how capitalism functions. Several of the passages from Sraffa's manuscripts quoted by Professor Porta in the previous chapter offer some insights into Sraffa's views on this point.

2 One cannot help but agree with Professor Porta about 'the absurdity of turning Sraffa into an absolute'. But this 'curious transformation' has been perpetrated by Porta alone, as in his misrepresentation of Schefold's remarks. Porta likewise distorts the significance of the title ('From the legend to the monument') of Luigi Einaudi's review essay on *The Works and Correspondence*. Einaudi's 'monument' refers to the scholarly achievement represented by the entire eleven-volume edition, in particular, to the discovery of hitherto unknown documents of enormous importance, and to the meticulous

arrangement and presentation of the material. Within two paragraphs of first mentioning this review essay, however, Porta misleadingly applies the term 'monument', in quotation marks, to Sraffa's introduction – 'The "monument" of the superb editor is . . . a powerful rhetorical construct . . .' – though this is not at all what Einaudi meant.

3 Some of what follows is drawn from Mongiovi (1996); see also Kurz (1998a) for a careful account, based upon the manuscript record, of the evolution of Sraffa's thinking on the classicals, Marx and marginal theory.

4 Terry Peach (1993), Giovanni Caravale (1985b) and Mark Blaug (Chapter 5 of this volume) have questioned Sraffa's interpretation on similar grounds.

5 Porta writes, toward the end of Chapter 10 in the present volume, that Sraffa's interpretation involves Ricardo in disputes on distribution about which he – Ricardo – 'had little to say'. This is an astonishing statement to make, when one considers that in the preface to the *Principles* Ricardo (1821: 5) identifies the determination of 'the laws which regulate . . . distribution' as 'the principal problem in Political Economy'.

6 In Volume III of *Capital* Marx (1967 [1894]: 114) comes close to attributing this sort of argument to Ricardo (though not with specific reference to Ricardo's pre-1816 writings): 'It leaps to the eye, particularly in the case of agriculture, that the causes which raise or lower the price of a product, also raise or lower the value or capital, since the latter consists to a large degree of this product, whether as grain, cattle, etc. (Ricardo).'

7 In August 1813 Ricardo suggested to Malthus that improvements in agricultural methods might offset the depressive effects of capital accumulation on the profit rate (Ricardo 1951–73, VI: 94–5). A few months later Ricardo made his famous assertion that 'the profits of the farmer . . . regulate the profits of all other trades' (Ricardo to Trower, 8 March 1814, in Ricardo 1951–73, VI: 104). Ricardo eventually abandoned the claim that agriculture regulates the general rate of profit, but he never retreated from the view that the profit rate is regulated by the real wage and the technical conditions of production; that is, he came to recognise that agriculture was not the only basic sector.

Part III

Models of prices and allocations in equilibrium and out of equilibrium

> The problem of the correct identification of the prices and quantities corresponding to a situation of equilibrium is a vital one for economic theory. . . . The neoclassical approach is unacceptable because, among other things, the adjustment mechanism on which the theory pivots does not refer to the real economic systems that should represent the object of our investigations – the Walrasian auctioneer does not exist, *non-renegotiable* transactions take place at all time at 'disequilibrium' prices and so on. . . . The classical and classical type approach, which is based on the idea that the 'right' quantities are *given* at the outset is no better equipped to supply a satisfactory answer to our problem. In fact, not only some kind of explanation of how the quantities are determined is highly desirable, but also – and primarily – there is in general no certainty that the prices corresponding to the technological coefficients appropriate to a set of quantities taken *au hasard* are compatible with the demands expressed by the system at those prices.
>
> (Caravale 1994b: 44–5)

> The classical theoretical construction is . . . centred on the Smithian idea of point of effectual demand which is taken to represent the centre of gravity for the whole system. This perspective raises however a crucial question. . . . How can this centre of gravity represent the logical presupposition of the whole sequence if the natural prices, the quantities corresponding to the various effectual demands, and the equilibrium rate of profit can be determined only within the model as part of its solution? Unfortunately an adequate answer to this problem cannot be found in Smith's or Ricardo's theory. Their approach must then be strengthened and a step forward in the direction implicitly indicated by them must be taken.
>
> (Caravale 1998b: 437)

12 Reflections on Caravale's contributions relating to equilibrium and their relation to the interpretation of Keynes

Victoria Chick

I am interested in dynamic systems, and Giovanni Caravale was himself a dynamic system. The area of his thought which I observed closely was one of his most dynamic: his work on the concept of equilibrium. If an autobiographical note may be excused in an academic paper by the nature of the present occasion, I first gave a seminar on the character of equilibrium appropriate to different 'periods', in Perugia over twenty years ago when Gianni was professor there; then he asked me first to give a seminar in the University of Rome 'La Sapienza' in 1994, when again I spoke about equilibrium, and later to join in a session on the topic at the Eastern Economic Association meeting in Washington in 1997. The ideas of the Perugia paper were eventually incorporated in a paper I wrote with Maurizio Caserta (1997), and the Rome seminar generated comments, by Gianni, Claudio Sardoni and others, which were fundamental in shaping my thinking on equilibrium in open systems (Chick 1996), in particular as used by Keynes in the *General Theory* (Chick 1998 [1996]).

The EEA meeting was the last time I saw Gianni, full of health and vigour and intellectual vitality, and it was there that the striking originality of the ideas which he had been developing (Caravale 1992a, b, 1993, 1997b, c) finally got through to me, though I had sensed a convergence of our thinking also at the Rome seminar. I want in this chapter to consider the three main contributions he made to the study of the concept of equilibrium and assess their usefulness in interpreting the *General Theory*. Gianni also related his work to the interpretation of Keynes, but my interpretation will be somewhat different from his own. The chief reason for this difference, which may be more semantic than substantive, relates to our starting points: as is well known, Gianni was a Ricardo scholar, steeped in classical thought and its central concepts of 'natural' or normal prices, 'dominant' or 'fundamental' forces and long-period equilibrium. These he was not willing to relinquish, and I shall argue that in interpreting Keynes these ideas are a hindrance, not a help. Within what I shall have to argue is the limitation of those classical concepts, Gianni developed three points which I believe are extremely helpful in interpreting the system devised by Keynes and therefore also helpful in the general project of open-system theorising. My aim therefore is to analyse his arguments in the context of the concerns I have spelt out in my own papers (Caserta and Chick 1997; Chick 1985, 1996, 1998 [1996]) to attempt to realise the convergence of thinking which I sensed emerging. To accomplish this I shall first set out Gianni's contributions and then my own perspective in brief, then attempt to demonstrate how the ideas can be fitted together.

Caravale's contributions to the methodology of equilibrium

Gianni's first contribution in this field was to distinguish concepts of equilibrium from the point of view of their place in economic analysis. He defined four categories: neutral equilibrium, 'apologetic' equilibrium, the 'heretical' approach and 'analytical' equilibrium. The first, neutral equilibrium, refers to statements about the conditions which would need to hold if certain other conditions were to be sustained – steady growth, for example. This concept is 'neutral' because there are no statements about whether or not the conditions are likely to be found in the real world. Another name for this class of concepts might be 'hypothetical equilibrium'. 'Apologetic' equilibrium refers to the neoclassical concept in which equilibrium carries with it the implication of optimality and absence of unexploited opportunities. 'Heretical' equilibrium 'consists of the (purposely unrealistic) definition of the conditions that should be verified for the "reproduction" of the economic system . . . specified for the purpose of showing that the economic system will *not*, except by a fluke, be able to comply with those conditions' (Caravale 1992b: 83). Finally he calls his own concept, which will be outlined below, 'analytical' equilibrium.

The second contribution related to the character of the only equilibrium Caravale was prepared to entertain as reflecting 'dominant', 'systematic' forces: equality of profit rates. The breakthrough lies not in this criterion for equilibrium, which I shall later argue is far too restrictive, but in the simple substitution he proposes: namely altering the traditional concept of equal rates of return to incorporate expectations. This suggestion has many advantages, and it provides a bridge between the neo-Ricardian and Post-Keynesian systems which can be warmly welcomed. As a corollary of this suggestion he recast the theory of investment to reflect equal expected profits in all industries, by combining different marginal efficiency profiles expected for different projects with declining expected marginal efficiencies by scale of project (Caravale 1993). This is clever and potentially fruitful, but not, I believe, as important or as central as the introduction of expectations to the equi-profit criterion.

It is, however, his concept of equilibrium existing in logical time, and convergence to equilibrium also taking place in logical time, which is the most fundamental contribution of the three. The Washington paper (Caravale 1997c) is perhaps the clearest exposition of this idea. The idea is that equilibrium must be a position to which the economic system, as portrayed by the theorist's analytical scheme, must converge. But no analytical scheme can mirror the behaviour of an actual economy, for in real life economies are continually subject to exogenous shocks. Thus we cannot expect to find actual economies converging to some analytical position we call equilibrium. Those who say that equilibrium is not a realistic concept would also appeal to this point, but to Gianni the issue was not 'realism'. He took the view that all theory was abstraction and therefore not 'realistic' (surely correct), and then went further, to argue that historical time was a 'confused notion' which has no place in theorising. He equated working in historical time with description, though he acknowledged the place of history in determining the values of variables to be taken as given in the theoretical structures of Marshall and Keynes, in sharp distinction from neoclassical timelessness.

He pointed to the many attempts, all failures, to demonstrate the convergence to long-period equilibrium through chronological time, even in pure theory, and concluded that the attempt itself was misguided: what was needed instead, he argued, was to demonstrate the convergence of the system to its equilibrium in *logical* time. Only in logical time could the appropriate thought experiment be performed, namely to determine how the system would behave if the initial conditions were fixed and the system was protected from further exogenous shocks while the implications of the initial situation work their way through the system.

The central idea is that equilibrium need never be attained in practice. The concept of equilibrium refers to a circumstance which would obtain if the preconditions for it were sustained long enough for equilibrium to manifest itself, without any requirement for actual observations – subject as they are to continual perturbations – even to tend toward the equilibrium position, let alone arrive at it. Equilibrium in this conception exists in logical time, precisely to insulate the system. Another name for it could be virtual equilibrium.

This concept closely corresponds to Keynes's notion of long-period employment in the *General Theory*, as Caravale has pointed out. Long-period employment is defined as follows:

> If we suppose a state of expectation to continue for a sufficient length of time for the effect on employment to have worked itself out so completely that there is, broadly speaking, no piece of employment going on which would not have taken place if the new state of expectation had always existed, the steady level of employment thus attained may be called the long-period employment corresponding to that state of expectation.
>
> (Keynes 1936: 48)

Path dependence and equilibrium

By contrast to Caravale's idea of historical time as description, I have, in the papers cited above, tried to show that there is more to theorising in historical time than the determination of the values of 'given' variables. Thus while, in terms of Joan Robinson's famous dichotomy history versus equilibrium, Gianni is firmly on the latter side, I have argued against the dichotomy itself (the subtitle of Chick 1985 is 'History and equilibrium'). I see the *General Theory* as squaring the circle: the process which is the subject of theory, and the character of theory itself, is dynamic, and yet the dynamic process has an equilibrium, expressed in static terms though actually referring to something like the classical stationary state. This combination could be regarded as a paradox, or at any rate a problem, and many have taken this view or seen only one side (hence the debate over whether the *General Theory* is static or dynamic when I would argue it is both). The combination of static and dynamic theorising is the most ingenious aspect of Keynes's system: he has, I believe, created a path-dependent system which in general has no equilibrium and therefore tells us nothing in general, and contrived to make it tell us something in general by deriving from it an equilibrium.

I also believe that this is precisely what Vercelli (1991, 1997) is asking for in his various calls for 'semantic equilibria', that is, equilibria which mean something, as opposed to being nothing more than solutions of mathematical problems or puzzles, where values outside the solution set create logical contradictions. He argues forcefully that equilibrium outside a dynamic framework is vacuous.

Let us fix ideas by looking at the simplest model in the *General Theory*. Take one production period as typical. We are in the short period: the capital stock and state of technology are given by history; the problem is to decide the scale of production. We follow chapter 3 of the *General Theory* and take the determination of the rate of interest also as given, i.e. we abstract from monetary factors. The system is recursive: a wage bargain is struck at the beginning of the period; this bargain begins with last period's wage, and wages may rise if, last period, entrepreneurs failed to get the workers they required; otherwise last period's wage may be sustained. Once the wage is settled, firms will know their cost function for any level of output and be able, on the basis of their expectation of demand, to decide the optimum price and output strategy. They decide a strategy despite the fact that Keynes uses the small firm as typical; these firms are uncertain of their market, which is in the future; thus although they are small they are not price takers (see Kahn 1989; Chick 1992; Tamborini 1995). Given their expectations, they determine optimum output, which will then determine the level of employment. Workers produce output during the 'period'. In chapter 3 the assumption is made that expectations are correct. Thus output is sold, at the end of the period, at the prices which the firms anticipated. Expectations of sales and profits are met[1] and the decisions made last period will be repeated next period. This is equilibrium.

Straight away let us refer back to Caravale's idea of heretical equilibrium, for that is what we have – a result which appears by fluke (entrepreneurs are assumed to, or happened to, form correct expectations). There is no convergence procedure, but if the appropriate values are chosen the system will reproduce itself. Far from being 'impossible', and thus destroying the value of the concept of equilibrium, Keynes's method has shown the usefulness of the concept, for without equilibrium the system would take a dynamic path which was particular to the expectations and adaptive strategies of every entrepreneur. The system also partakes of the character of 'neutral equilibrium', since it sets up the preconditions for an equilibrium in the sense of a steady state to emerge from the dynamic construction. And it exists in logical time though the theory itself is couched in historical time.

In chapter 5 the possibility of incorrect expectations is admitted. In general we would not learn much from such a dynamic system because of the wealth of possibilities which are opened up; the equilibrium result is one result among too many and the paths of adjustment which could be followed are too numerous: in adjusting to incorrect expectations, firms will be generating income above or below what would have been the equilibrium level, and these deviations will have effects which may divert the process of adjustment. The problem is analogous to the generation of 'income effects' when 'false trading' is allowed in general equilibrium systems. By specifying the equilibrium properties we learn something specific about the functioning of the system: this is the configuration which would replicate. It is not necessarily the dominant outcome in terms of frequency, but, because the system can get stuck in it, it may be the most important.

The same kind of assertions can be made of the 'model' expanded to take interest rate determination into account. This is the model which has been represented to generations of students by IS–LM but which we know to be, like the last model, recursive (summarised in Chick 1983a, figure 13.1: 244). The model begins by determining the rate of interest by liquidity preference and the supply of money. Of the three famous motives to liquidity, transactions, precaution and speculation, the shortest time horizon relates to speculation. The other two motives are assumed to react in a stable fashion to changes in aggregate income, which by definition changes rather slowly (because production and sale are time-consuming processes). Two conclusions follow: first, the expectations of speculators at any given time dominate the determination of the rate of interest; we can take the level of income as given. Second, the rate of interest so determined will inevitably alter as investment reacts to the rate of interest, but such changes affect future investment plans, not the current ones. Investment previously decided on will not be altered; it is the earlier interest rate which governs the cost of borrowing. This is a timeful model, in which contracts are made and decisions cannot be revoked, just as in the short-period model the employment contracts are not 'recontracted' after prices come to be known.

Once investment is determined, actual aggregate demand will be determined by the expectations of entrepreneurs, through their decision to hire and produce, and the marginal propensity to consume. The story goes through as for the truncated model, with one troublesome exception: we must revisit the money market. (Messori 1991: 138 applies the term 'monetary retroaction' to this process.) While in the dynamic story the rate of interest was determined by speculators, the level of income having been taken as given at 'yesterday's' level, now, to establish equilibrium, either we must return to yesterday's level of income or a change in transactions and precautionary demand must be compensated for by a change in the rate of interest.

From the dynamic point of view this procedure is impossible, as it goes back in time. *It is possible to undertake this 'retroaction' only in logical time.* The conditions required sound impossible, but they are not: the rate of interest has already done its work in determining the level of investment, and all we are interested in here is the existence of an equilibrium, not the approach to it. The rate of interest is free to take whatever value is now necessary to give us that equilibrium, and the one-off investment multiplier would indeed take us back to the original level of income – eventually.

I hope that with these examples I have made the case that in the *General Theory* we have a theory which embodies history in more than its given variables: it also establishes a sequence of irrevocable events. This system, once started off, could take any number of paths. What equilibrium shows us is the conditions which would be required if the system were to replicate itself, but in contrast to the agenda of 'heretical equilibrium' we have a positive statement: that should the expectations formed by entrepreneurs give rise to unemployment, the very effects of unemployment on aggregate demand could be such as to confirm those expectations, and the system would then not 'climb out of' its unemployment state – because it is an equilibrium state – without an exogenous shock.

Equilibrium and dynamics

Keynes was very aware of the need to embed the concept of equilibrium in a dynamic model:

> My object has been to find a method which is useful in describing, not merely the characteristics of static equilibrium, but also those of disequilibrium, and to discover the dynamical laws governing the passage of a monetary system from one position of equilibrium to another.
>
> (Author's preface, *A Treatise on Money*, Keynes 1971–89, V: xvii)

And also he was aware of the unusual nature of the system he was constructing:

> I should, I think, be prepared to argue that, in a world ruled by uncertainty, with an uncertain future linked to an actual present, a final position of equilibrium, such as one deals with in static economics, does not properly exist.
>
> (Letter to H. D. Henderson, Keynes 1971–89, XXIX: 222)

As we have, I think, demonstrated, the combination Keynes put together blended a path-dependent, recursive system which in principle could go anywhere, with a derivation of one combination of factors which would leave the system replicating itself. It is, therefore, at a position of rest, in the sense that the variables do not change, and we call that an equilibrium. The fact that this equilibrium may entail unemployment is incompatible with a market-clearing notion of equilibrium but is acceptable here, because the workers, though not able to work as much as they, collectively, would like at the going wage, are powerless to change their situation:

> whilst labour is always in a position to refuse to work on a scale involving a real wage which is less than the marginal disutility of that amount of employment, it is not in a position to insist on being offered work on a scale involving a real wage which is not greater than the marginal disutility of that amount of employment.
>
> (Keynes 1936: 291)

Back to Caravale's contributions

We have shown that the concepts of equilibrium in logical time and a theory which is recursive and thus historical or path-dependent in its character are not incompatible. We have perhaps also given an illustration of the kind of theorising which takes account of history without being mere description. Ironically, we have also shown that there is a compatibility between Gianni's concepts of analytical and neutral equilibrium and the replication criterion of the 'heretics' – now not using the criteria of equilibrium to show that crisis is inevitable, but that self-righting mechanisms are not necessarily available.

I have generated these results in the context of Keynes's short-period models. I remarked at the beginning that, for Gianni, the long period was the only kind of equilibrium which involved systematic, dominant forces. In Chick (1998 [1996]) I expressed a puzzlement which anyone who has not drunk deep of the classical well must feel, for these terms are never explained. I understand the classical idea that the systematic, dominant forces were assumed to be 'productivity and thrift' and the transitory forces monetary. But economics – at least, some economics – has also moved on to reflect the pervasive character of money in the modern economy: in Keynes, money is important in every 'market' and there is no separation of the monetary from the 'real'. Yet the rhetoric continues, while no satisfactory explanation of what is now meant by these powerful terms is ever offered. Worse, it is simply assumed that 'everybody knows' that the systematic, dominant forces concern the distribution of investment to more profitable sectors until rates of profit are equalised. Thus in this framework the idea that the short period is not really worthy of serious consideration is perpetuated, yet there is no doubt that production always takes place with the capital which is already in place and that unemployment is a serious issue for economists. Let me try to put another interpretation on this notion of systematic, dominant forces and on the concept of a position of rest which will give the short period its due.

As Gianni emphasised on many occasions, theory involves abstraction. The question, always, is what governs the criteria for abstraction. It often seems to be the case that among neoclassical economists the only criterion is mathematical tractability; otherwise the choice is arbitrary, provided only that the rationality axioms are maintained. Other schools of economics offer 'realism' as one of their criteria, but realism must, by the definition of what theory is, stop short of description. This is true whether or not historical time is allowed to have an influence within the theory. What criteria for abstraction are there? How do we choose between one abstraction and another? The answer, surely, is that one tries to construct a theory to capture the systematic, dominant forces in the economy. In other words, it seems to me that the role of identifying systematic, dominant forces is in theory construction, not in the choice of concept of equilibrium.

The second place where I would part company with Gianni is the assumption that the long period is somehow the only arena in which dominant forces will be manifest. I take issue with all those who look to a circumstance in which absolutely nothing more can happen as the only acceptable definition of equilibrium, that is, with all those who equate the short period with a transitory state, or who point out that, since investment is taking place, the short period cannot be considered an equilibrium, etc. I would argue – and have argued (in the unpublished Perugia paper and in Caserta and Chick 1997) – that equilibrium can be defined only with respect to the constraints which the theorist imposes. My metaphor here is the familiar one of balls in a bowl. The equilibrium attained by the balls depends on the dimensions of the bowl (the assumptions or constraints under which the theory was constructed). The balls (economic agents) cannot dictate those dimensions: the theorist does that and s/he is free to change the dimensions to suit the purpose at hand. The 'dimension' of the short period is determined by the existing capital stock and technology. The long period releases that constraint. As the dimensions (constraints) change, so will the character of the equilibrium, and that is all.

The search for an equilibrium in which *no* further changes take place is a teleological concept. In Caserta and Chick we compare such 'final equilibria' to the physicists' conception of the end of the thermodynamic process, when all the world is cold. To accept only the final 'state of rest' is to deny the legitimacy of equilibria which are contingent on the constraints imposed by other frameworks. The balls at rest in a small bowl are just as much at rest as they would be in a larger one, though their positions will be different in the two cases. The invalidation of the short period on the grounds that its equilibrium is not 'final' is common; it is then only a short step to regard the short period as 'transitory' and of no real interest. I would suggest that it was to avoid this misinterpretation that Keynes felt it necessary to devise his concept of long-period employment.

Long-period equilibrium

It follows from the position taken in the last section that there is nothing special about the end-point of capital accumulation as assumed in classical theory and its modern descendants. Having said that, however, let us not lose sight of the immensely valuable suggestion made by Gianni to substitute equality of *expected* profits for equality of actual profits as the criterion for long-period equilibrium. This proposal recommends itself on two grounds: it avoids the implication, drawn for example by Potestio (1986, 1989), that chapter 17 of the *General Theory* is not compatible with the rest of the book because long-run equilibrium cannot encompass the uncertainty which characterises the short-period theory, or the objection of for example Tonveronachi (1992), that Keynes's long-period equilibrium is unacceptable because it involves subjectivity. With Caravale's suggestion these objections disappear, and in my view rightly so. The other advantage of this suggestion is that there is no requirement for the expectations relating to investment to be confirmed in order to qualify for equilibrium: Gianni's long-period equilibrium is an equilibrium of action. This conforms to Keynes's characterisation of the long period, where the issue of validation of expectations does not arise.

Confirmation of expectations is the key feature of short-period equilibrium but does not figure in long-period equilibrium at all. There is, however, no paradox: it is a matter of time and what is assumed to happen in time. The reason why confirmation of long-period expectations is not important is that it gives no useful information: by the time the original expectations come to be confronted with the facts, the context of investment will have changed too much for the information to be useful. One could, of course, construct the relevant experiment in logical time, but there really is no point.

Caravale (1992b) made a point which provides another possible area of convergence, once some semantic problems are cleared up. He appealed to the distinction, always a seminar and teaching preoccupation of Geoff Harcourt but brought to print by Carvalho (1990), between the long period and the long run. Caravale stressed the atemporal, logical nature of the long period and the similarity of this concept, which is defined by what is allowed to stay constant and what to change, to his own concept of natural equilibrium. So far, no news. But he goes on to remark that the way of handling history within this concept gives it 'both a classical and a Keynesian flavour; it relates in fact to a short-period situation (in the Marshallian sense) in which a number of variables are given . . . as a consequence of past history' (Caravale 1992b: 80). He contrasts the concept of history both with the neoclassical version of atemporalism and the historical approach he understood Robinson was advocating. What he does not do – and this offers an exciting opportunity – is to make something of the point that is just barely discernible in what I have quoted: that the concept of the long period, from the point of view of defining an equilibrium, may be applied in the short-period context.

Of course the criterion/a for equilibrium must be different, for capital is fixed and the criterion of equal profits cannot hold: the short period works with the existing capital stock and accepts both differences in capacity utilisation and the existence of, and variation across firms in, quasi-rents. The opportunity lies in uncoupling the concept of 'long period' as an atemporal logical thought experiment devoted to characterising equilibrium and convergence to it from the long period in Marshall's sense of the period in which capital is allowed to fluctuate; the latter, as said before, is an assumption, a property of the theory's construction. To stress both the logical character of Caravale's idea without prejudice as to Marshallian assumptions, and also to stress its role, I propose the term 'virtual equilibrium'.

Now we are in a position to use Caravale's concept for both short-period and long-period analysis; the labels which narrowed the application of his idea to 'final', equi-profit equilibrium have been set aside.[2] The important part of the idea of convergence in logical time can, I argue, be used with equal effect in the context of any of Marshall's 'periods' – indeed, in the section summarising my own work, that is exactly what I had done, without the benefit of Caravale's insight.

Convergence

Almost everything I have said up to now concerns the existence of equilibrium rather than convergence, which was central to Gianni's concerns. In my earlier paper on the dynamic model of the *General Theory* and its equilibria I argued that convergence was a minor matter. I was happy enough with equilibrium as a fluke but did suggest that the multiplier provided the necessary adjustment mechanism in the short period. It is also the case that Keynes suggested that the producers of consumer goods would have quite frequent observations of a repetitive nature and would therefore be able to locate the demand for their products easily. The same is not true, however, for the producers of capital goods. Nor is the ability to locate the level of demand sufficient to demonstrate the convergence to equilibrium – because of the income effects alluded to earlier.

Running the multiplier through chronological time has posed problems: it is obvious that the interest rate will change along the way and would have effects on investment, etc. (see Chick 1983a: chapter 14, 1997, and Davidson's work on the demand for 'placements', e.g. 1972). The question Gianni's work raises is whether it is appropriate to 'run' the multiplier in chronological time at all, or whether its action should be restricted to logical time. Keynes himself was ambivalent on the matter (see Chick 1983a: appendix to chapter 14). On these extremely important matters the serious work, even after all this time, remains to be done.

Conclusion

Giovanni Caravale produced three important contributions to the methodology of equilibrium. I have tried to unbundle them from his classical preoccupations in order to broaden their applicability to encompass the short period as well as indicating why they are so important for the long period. I believe, and hope I have demonstrated, that they are helpful in that seemingly endless process, the understanding of the structure and method of Keynes's economics; and since I believe that Keynes's method is the best ever devised, that improved understanding is part of a forward-looking research programme.

Notes

1 Naturally we cannot suppose that *everyone's* expectations are *exactly* met. See Keynes (1937) 'Ex post and ex ante', notes for 1937 lectures, 1971–89, XIV: 179–83.

2 I once made a seemingly confusing though I think correct proposition (Chick 1983b), that since the rate of investment had been very low throughout the inter-war years, the (Marshallian) short period existed, in those years, for a long *time*.

13 Sraffa's contributions to economics

Some notes on his unpublished papers

Heinz D. Kurz

The year 1998 was the centenary of Piero Sraffa's birth. Sraffa was born on 5 August 1898 in Turin; he passed away on 3 September 1983 in Cambridge.[1] He became known essentially for the following contributions to economics: first, his discussion of the bank crisis in Italy and the involvement of the Fascists in it (Sraffa 1922); second, his analysis of the foundations of decreasing, constant and increasing returns in Marshall's theory and his critique of partial equilibrium analysis (Sraffa 1925, 1926); third, his critique of Friedrich August von Hayek's monetary overinvestment theory of the business cycle (Sraffa 1932a, b); fourth, his edition, with the collaboration of Maurice H. Dobb, of *The Works and Correspondence of David Ricardo* (Ricardo 1951–73); and, fifth, his book *Production of Commodities by Means of Commodities*, which laid the ground for a critique of marginalist theory in the so-called Cambridge controversies in the theory of capital and distribution in the 1960s and 1970s (Sraffa 1960). He published a few other short papers and comments, an obituary of Maffeo Pantaleoni, and edited, together with John Maynard Keynes, *An Abstract of a Treatise on Human Nature*, whose author he identified as David Hume (see Hume 1938). In 1961 Sraffa was awarded the Söderström gold medal by the Swedish Royal Academy for the Ricardo edition.[2]

All the major works Sraffa was prepared to have put in print had a deep and lasting impact on the profession. His criticism of Marshallian partial equilibrium analysis triggered a rich literature on market forms which flowered during the 1930s. Apart from a contribution to the 1930 *Economic Journal* symposium on increasing returns (Sraffa 1930), Sraffa did not publicly participate further in the debate on the Marshallian theory of value. He rather focused attention on an analysis of 'the process of diffusion of profits throughout the various stages of production and of the process of forming a normal level of profits throughout all the industries of a country' (Sraffa 1926: 550), a problem beyond the scope of his early work. This problem constituted the main topic of his *magnum opus*, his 1960 book. His criticism of Hayek's *Prices and Production* dealt a serious blow to the Austrian's reputation as an economic theorist and helped Keynes, who was unable to effectively ward off Hayek's attack on the *Treatise on Money*, out of an impasse; in chapter 17 of the *General Theory* Keynes tried to use the concept of the 'commodity rate of interest' introduced by Sraffa in his critique of Hayek – with little success, however, as Sraffa argued in one of his unpublished papers (see below).

Sraffa's highly praised Ricardo edition and his introduction to Volume I (cf. Sraffa 1951) changed fundamentally the received view of classical economics, as it was handed down by Alfred Marshall, and clarified important elements of the classical theory of value and distribution. Sraffa succeeded in showing that there was a distinct classical theory which could not be considered a special case of marginalist, that is, demand and supply, theory, with the demand side still in its infancy. In the late 1920s Sraffa had started to work on the coherent reformulation of the classical approach to the theory of value and distribution, a project he had to interrupt from the early 1930s to the early 1940s and from the mid-1940s to the mid-1950s, partly because the Ricardo edition absorbed most of his attention and energy. He could accomplish the project only towards the end of the 1950s: the year 1960 brought the publication of *Production of Commodities by Means of Commodities*, a slim book of just under a hundred pages, which, however, had a remarkable impact on the profession: it inspired many economists and provided the starting point of various non-neoclassical developments in economic theory.[3]

With the twentieth century behind us we can safely say that Sraffa was one of its major intellectuals. The people who knew him were deeply impressed by the breadth and depth of his knowledge, his quick understanding and sharpness, his capacity to see through complex arguments and swiftly detect weaknesses in them, his pronounced concern with realism. It was essentially Sraffa's impact that prompted Ludwig Wittgenstein to abandon the view put forward in the *Tractatus logico-philosophicus* and move on to the *Philosophical Investigations*. In economics, Sraffa insisted that theoretical concepts had to be grounded in, or derived from, phenomena that had a real existence. He abhorred abstraction-mongering and despised concepts that were idealistic. He would not accept reasoning by authority.

The twentieth century saw two major challenges to marginalist economics: one came from Keynes, the other from Sraffa. The latter refuted effectively the conventional interpretation of the history of economic thought as a one-way avenue leading from primitive conceptualisations of the demand and supply approach to ever more sophisticated ones, merely leaving behind errors of reasoning and unnecessarily restrictive assumptions. Sraffa's interpretative and reconstructive work will remain essential reading for the profession, just like the works of the old classical economists from Smith's *Wealth of Nations* to Ricardo's *Principles*.

The purpose of this chapter is to commemorate the centenary of Sraffa's birth in terms of some observations on his unpublished papers. Sraffa donated these papers and correspondence and his huge and precious library to Trinity College, Cambridge. The donations are kept in the Wren Library of Trinity College and are open to the public. Sraffa appointed Professor Pierangelo Garegnani, Rome, his literary executor. The latter asked me in 1997 to serve as the general editor of the papers and correspondence of Piero Sraffa. Soon it is planned to publish a selection from the material. To this effect a group of scholars has been invited to accomplish the task.

The composition of the chapter is the following. The next section provides a brief overview of Sraffa's unpublished papers. The following one illustrates in terms of a few examples Sraffa's remarkable contribution to economics. The final section contains some concluding remarks. It goes without saying that the following account is of necessity incomplete and highly selective. Sraffa's ideas can only be touched upon, no thorough discussion of his arguments can be provided here. However, the handful of examples may suffice to accomplish the purpose of this chapter: to excite an interest in Sraffa's work by providing some evidence of the fecundity and originality of his thinking.

Sraffa's unpublished papers

'Sraffa finds it immoral to write more than one page per month.' Thus wrote Amartya K. Sen, a former student of Piero Sraffa's and since early 1998 the Master of Trinity College, Cambridge, the college in which Sraffa spent most of his life (see Sen 1974: 331). Had Sen been right, the task of the editor of Sraffa's manuscripts and correspondence would be a trifle. To the benefit of the scientific community at large Sraffa was somewhat immoral. In an interview in December 1985 Sen spoke also about his time as a student in Cambridge and his teacher Sraffa. He called Sraffa 'one of the cleverest persons I have ever met, with tremendous originality and an enormous range of interests'. He added:

> For reasons that are not altogether clear, he confined his economic writings to rather narrow and mechanical subjects. He had wonderful ideas on such subjects as rationality, human behaviour, the role of society in value formation, the part that politics plays in the genesis of economic theory, and so on. I don't think that he wrote any of these down.
>
> (See Klamer 1989: 138)

Sraffa did write some of his respective ideas down. His unpublished manuscripts and notes comprise several thousand pages, slips of paper and a couple of notebooks.[4]

General remarks

Sraffa's manuscripts and correspondence document the intellectual fascinations, social passion and scholarly achievements of one of the most brilliant intellectuals of his century. In addition they reflect important aspects of the intellectual history of the twentieth century with Cambridge as a focal point of scientific, philosophical and political discourse and people like Keynes, Wittgenstein and Russell as important players. Large parts of the material are directly relevant to economic theory and to the history of economic thought. The papers and correspondence are a treasure trove of original and important insights into a variety of economic problems and into the history of economic doctrines. They also reflect Sraffa's wider interests and his contacts with leading scholars of his time.

The material Sraffa bequeathed to Trinity College is not only enormous, it is also very complex. Sraffa generally wrote for himself and obviously had no plans to publish the manuscripts. Many of the ideas he wrote down are bound to look cryptic to the reader, at least at first sight, because of lack of knowledge on the reader's part of the implicit premises underlying Sraffa's reasoning. And Sraffa is rightly known as someone who did not waste words. His style is terse; his texts cannot be accused of being prolix. A considerable part of the material consists of notes, pointed observations on particular themes, occasionally of an aphoristic character. But there are also longer manuscripts, consecutive attempts to solve a problem, several versions of a particular argument, etc.

As regards the present location, organisation and arrangement of the material the following should be pointed out. The papers are kept in the Wren Library, Trinity College, Cambridge. During Sraffa's lifetime John (now Lord) Eatwell and Alessandro Roncaglia made a first rough attempt to take stock of the papers. After Sraffa's death Pierangelo Garegnani and Krishna Bharadwaj prepared a detailed inventory of the material; they took care not to destroy the order of the papers as Sraffa had left them in 1982. Partly on the basis of the previous work Jonathan Smith, archivist of Wren Library, prepared a catalogue, which is the one currently in use. In the following all references to Sraffa's papers refer to this catalogue, first giving the signature of the file under consideration and, after a colon, the number of the sheet.[5]

The papers are arranged in the following series: (A) Personal and family papers; (B) Academic career; (C) Correspondence; (D) Notes, lectures and publications; (E) Diaries; (F) Memoirs of colleagues; (G) Publications by others; (H) Bibliographical material; (I) Items removed from printed books; and (J) Miscellaneous material. To the scholar interested in Sraffa's contributions to economics, series (D) is the most interesting; in addition there is Sraffa's correspondence (C) including his exchange of letters with major economists. Series (D) is subdivided into: (D1) Notes; (D2) Lectures; and (D3) Publications.

Most of the manuscripts and notes are in Sraffa's hand. Fortunately, his handwriting is easy to read. Most of the material is in English, some is in Italian and only a few pieces are in French or German. From an early time onward Sraffa used to date his manuscripts and notes, which is tremendously helpful: we know in many cases exactly when he was concerned with which problem, which difficulties he encountered in solving it and which solution he arrived at, if any. It is fascinating to see in particular that he anticipated several results of others by several years, some even by decades. Given this evidence it is all the more regrettable that Sraffa was so reluctant to put the fruits of his work into print. His fastidiousness and perfectionism made him hold back arguments as long as he had the faintest doubt about their correctness. He wanted to be absolutely sure that he had completely thought through the problem under consideration, taking into account each and every aspect relevant to its understanding, following through all its ramifications and thereby anticipating every objection that could possibly be levelled at it. In a letter to a colleague he stressed that one must not be afraid to rewrite a paper again and again, because that is the only way to get the argument right. Sraffa himself took that maxim seriously. It is one of the reasons why he published so little.

Notes

There is a huge number of notes on various problems, ideas, concepts and doctrines. Here I can draw the reader's attention only to some of the themes dealt with. There are a couple of notes and short manuscripts dealing with epistemological and methodological problems in economics. For example, there are notes on 'Interdependence and causality', on 'Explanation and causality' and on 'Long and short periods'. At the beginning of his career Sraffa was interested in probability theory, which is reflected in several papers written before 1928. Then there are discussions of particular concepts and problems. Several notes deal with the concept of 'Consumer surplus'; there is a very large number of papers dedicated to the 'Laws of return' and Marshall's analysis. We encounter all the problems Sraffa was concerned with in his constructive and critical work, including, for example, the problem of the 'Standard and cause of value' and of the concept of 'Utility' and marginal utility and marginal productivity theory. Marshall's illustration of marginal productivity theory in terms of an argument referring to the 'marginal shepherd' figures prominently in the papers. A set of notes deal with the 'Necessity of interest', another one with Senior's concept of 'Abstinence'. Then there are Sraffa's comments on the *Treatise on Money*, his discussion of contributions by Wicksteed, Edgeworth and many others, etc. In short, there is very rich material waiting to be explored in detail and prepared for publication.

Lectures

As is well known, Sraffa, who was appointed to a lectureship in Cambridge, lectured only for the short period from 1928 to 1931 on 'Advanced theory of value' to students undertaking the economics tripos. In 1930 he assumed the position of librarian of the Marshall Library; in addition he was placed in charge of the Cambridge programme of graduate studies in economics. There is some discussion as to why he gave up lecturing. An important reason appears often to be overlooked: in the late 1920s Sraffa became convinced that the Marshallian theory of value and distribution could not be remedied, but he was not yet able to offer something in its stead. In that case the only possibility was to stop lecturing.

'Advanced theory of value'

When Sraffa began to lecture on advanced value theory he drafted lecture notes, not least because he felt that his spoken English was not yet good enough to allow him to speak freely. Therefore we are in the possession of a full manuscript containing a detailed account of the content of the lectures and for the greater part also fully worked out arguments in regard to the themes dealt with. It is planned to publish these lectures plus some related notes as the first volume of the edition of Sraffa's papers and correspondence mentioned above.

In the lectures Sraffa analyses the development of the theory of value from its beginnings to his own time: he starts with Petty and the Physiocrats and ends with Marshall. In a note written in August 1931 Sraffa states: 'The study of the "surplus product" is the true object of economics' (D3/12/7: 161.1). The concept of surplus presupposes a concept of 'cost'. According to Sraffa one way to look at the history of economic thought is in terms of changes in these two concepts over time. The lectures on value theory are in fact concerned with the history of the gradual 'transformation of the notion of cost from the original one of a stock of material goods, to the conception of an amount of human sacrifice – that is to say, the gradual transformation from an objective to a subjective point of view' (D2/4: 36). This transformation of the concept of cost (and value) was accompanied by the gradual evaporation of the concept of surplus.

Here we cannot enter into a detailed discussion of Sraffa's complex views on the matter, which changed considerably over time, especially after he had begun to grasp the analytical structure of the classical theory of value and distribution. As a consequence his understanding of the marginalist theory, and its deficiencies, also underwent a change. Whilst originally Sraffa was above all opposed to the subjectivist part of that theory – he even contemplated the possibility of having Marshall's theory of value purged of all subjectivist elements (see D3/12/7: 114) – later the target of his criticism became the explanation of profits in terms of the marginal product of a factor called 'capital'. It was in the late 1920s that Sraffa all of a sudden saw a glimpse of the alternative point of view which fundamentally changed his outlook – a change that is also reflected in his lectures on advanced theory of value. In one place Sraffa notes that contrary to his earlier opinion even with constant returns to scale value cannot be assumed as given and constant, because it does not depend only on real physical costs, but also on the distribution of income between wages and profits. A change in that distribution will generally change relative values. This insight derived from the systems of production equations he began to study in 1927.

Sraffa's lectures on value theory contain a host of insights and pointed remarks on the literature, on Senior's concept of 'abstinence' as well as on the 'Austrian' theory of value and the problem of imputation into which Menger, Böhm-Bawerk and Wieser ran and which they could not resolve satisfactorily, on Pareto's theory of general equilibrium and, first and foremost, on Marshall's theory of value. In his critical discussion of these authors Sraffa anticipates, *en passant*, several of the implications of the long-period version of marginalist theory that were brought out only later. His perspective is that of general equilibrium theory, because, as Sraffa made clear, the correctness or otherwise of any results obtained in a partial framework is decided in a general framework. For example, he stated very clearly (within the context of a discussion of marginalist theory) that relative prices and relative factor rewards depend on consumer tastes and thus demand compositions. With regard to a model with homogeneous land and homogeneous labour, the familiar workhorse of later general equilibrium models of the Heckscher–Ohlin–Samuelson trade theory variety, he stressed:

> Note that: 1) If the change in demand is from one product to another, which employs [labour and land] in the same proportions as the first product, all values will remain unchanged. – 2) If the proportions are different, the values of the article the demand for which increases will *always rise* in terms of the article the demand for which falls.
>
> (D2/4: 107–8)

The reason for the change in relative prices is that income distribution, that is, the wage–rent ratio, changes. It is made clear that demand has an impact on relative prices only to the extent to which it has an impact on income distribution. Hence, as Sraffa was to emphasise later, alternative theories of value differ essentially in terms of their respective explanations of income distribution.

Other lectures

The lectures on advanced theory of value were not the only ones Sraffa gave. In 1929 he gave lectures on Continental banking and from 1941 to 1943 lectures on industry to students undertaking the economics tripos. As is well known, as a student Sraffa worked on problems of monetary economics: he wrote a Laurea thesis on the problem of inflation in Italy during and after the First World War. His papers reflect his continuing interest in the field of monetary economics. In this context it is also worth mentioning that Sraffa, Richard Kahn and Keynes were active players in the stock market and that Sraffa's profound knowledge of that institution and his well informed judgement about the trend of the market earned him the respect of his colleagues. In his lectures on industry Sraffa deals with what nowadays would be called problems of industrial organisation. He is particularly concerned with the development of economic institutions over time in American capitalism, showing a concern with important structural changes and their probable long-term economic impact.

Then there are a couple of single lectures Sraffa delivered on various occasions, dealing with various topics. I should like to mention his lecture on 'The corporative state' which he gave in 1927 to the 'Keynes Club'. The lecture notes contain a profound analysis of the institutions created under Italian Fascism in order to balance the conflict between production and distribution goals.

Publications

In the folders assembled under this heading we find the preparatory notes and manuscripts leading to Sraffa's published works. There is a substantial amount of material related to Sraffa's critique of Hayek. Then there are numerous documents reflecting Sraffa's work on the Ricardo edition, how he managed to trace the locations of hitherto unknown letters exchanged between Ricardo and the people he corresponded with, the difficulties Sraffa encountered and the way he dealt with them, etc. Yet the most important and by far the largest part of the papers is related to the making of *Production of Commodities by Means of Commodities*. The following observations concern exclusively that part. It goes without saying that only a small number of aspects of the enormous material can be touched upon.

It is perhaps interesting to note that originally Sraffa intended to elaborate a theory of accumulation (see, for example, D3/12/36: 6). He was overwhelmed, however, by the difficulties encountered in providing a general theory of value and distribution that would include the treatment of joint production, fixed capital, scarce natural resources, and the problem of the choice of technique. In several documents he expresses his interest in the problem of capital accumulation and discusses the views of major economists on the matter. We find, for example, critical disquisitions on Ricardo's treatment of the machinery problem in the third edition of the *Principles* and on Marx's explanation of the tendency of the rate of profits to fall.

It is also interesting to note that originally Sraffa sought to deal with industrial production differently from agricultural production. For a fairly long time he intended to deal with the former in terms of an approach with continuous time, reflecting the fact that in industry production can in principle be organised steadily. Production in agriculture, however, was best dealt with in terms of an approach with discrete time, reflecting the natural periods of production from seed to harvest. The possibility of subdividing an actual process of production into an arbitrary number of fictitious processes, with some kind of work in progress or intermediate products obtaining at the end of each of these fictitious processes, made him eventually drop the idea of the coexistence of a time-continuous and a time-discrete perspective and adopt the one we encounter in his book.

The material available in the Wren Library is an impressive document of the questions Sraffa raised and the ways he attempted to tackle them, the dead ends into which he got, his self-criticism and the gradual elaboration of the propositions which eventually were published in his 1960 book. Over the many years that elapsed from the beginning of Sraffa's work on the problems under consideration to its very completion he frequently removed items written at an earlier time to other files, as he was preparing the manuscript for publication. Therefore, it is very helpful that he had started to date the manuscripts from early on. This allows us to form a clear opinion about when certain ideas were born and arguments developed by him. In his papers we find also mathematical notes by Frank Ramsey and A. S. Besicovitch, the two eminent Cambridge mathematicians with whom Sraffa discussed the problem of the solutions of the systems of equations he elaborated. It is a remarkable fact that in the preface to his book Sraffa thanked Ramsey, Besicovitch and a further mathematician, Alister Watson, but no economist. Watson was of help especially in the final phase when Sraffa put together his notes and prepared the final typescript and then when the galley proofs of the book had to be corrected (see Kurz and Salvadori 2000a).

In the interpretative literature one encounters contradicting views on certain aspects of Sraffa's book and several myths. The unpublished papers provide an opportunity to scrutinise the available interpretations. In what follows I shall attempt to dispel a few widespread but untenable opinions. They concern the relationship between the labour theory of value and Sraffa's work and the role of the standard commodity in it, and the role of given quantities.[6]

It is frequently contended that the starting point of Sraffa's analysis was Marx and the labour theory of value, and that he was concerned with solving the problem of the so-called 'transformation' of labour values in prices of production. It should be emphasised that there is no evidence in support of this interpretation. While the young Sraffa clearly had socialist leanings and shared elements of Marx's materialist point of view, in terms of economic theory his starting point was first Marshallian and then classical analysis. He despised the subjectivist part of the former and contemplated, as we have heard, the possibility of doing away with it. But at the same time he was also critical of the labour theory of value. That theory involved, he stressed, a 'corruption' of the theory of value based on the concept of 'physical real cost', which he traced back to Petty and the Physiocrats and considered the right starting point (cf. D3/4: 2; see also D3/11: 79–80). In another note also dating from the beginnings of his constructive work, Sraffa stressed that there is no 'objective difference' between the labour of a wage earner and that of a slave, of a slave and of a horse, of a horse and of a machine, and added: 'It is a purely mystical conception that attributes to labour a special gift of determining value' (D3/9: 89). However, Sraffa quickly understood that in the special case of zero profits the labour theory of value gave the same answer as his own systems of equations: in the special case under consideration he suggested speaking of the 'Value Theory of Labour' (rather than the labour theory of value).[7]

Sraffa developed his systems of equations apparently from scratch. At the end of November 1927 he put down equations representing two industries, without and with a surplus (see D3/2: 32–5). If there is no surplus, exchange ratios between commodities are fully determined by the physical scheme of production and reflect physical real costs. If there is a surplus things are more difficult. One of the systems with a surplus discussed by Sraffa is given by:

$$11A = 3A + 9B$$

$$13B = 7A + 3B$$

$$S = 1A + 1B$$

where A and B indicate the prices of the two commodities and S the value of the surplus product of the system as a whole. Sraffa observed that these equations are 'contradictory' (ibid.); in another document he added that 'the problem is overdetermined' (D/3/11: 17). In the case with a surplus a rule is needed according to which the surplus is distributed. It is only after this rule has been fixed that relative prices can be ascertained. In conditions of free competition, and setting aside the problem of scarce natural resources, such as land, the surplus is distributed according to a uniform rate of return on the capital advanced in each sector of production.

In Sraffa's argument labour values at first played no role whatsoever. There was indeed no analytical scope for them, because, as Sraffa demonstrated, the problem of value and distribution is fully settled in terms of the two data contemplated: (1) the system of production (and productive consumption) in use;

and (2) the rule governing the distribution of the surplus. The argument could be elaborated without ever referring to labour values. However, Sraffa saw clearly that in exceedingly special circumstances, that is, essentially those that had already been pointed out by Ricardo, the exchange ratios are proportional to the relative quantities of labour embodied in the different commodities. The special circumstances are: first, the case in which the rate of profits is equal to zero, and, second, the case in which the proportions of direct labour to means of production are identical in all industries. Neither of these cases was in itself very interesting.

The standard system and *Standard commodity* in Sraffa's book has occasionally been the object of wild speculation and is occasionally considered a kind of surrogate for the labour theory of value. According to Mark Blaug, the standard commodity is a device with exceptional power, because employing it as *numéraire* allows one to do away with the dependence of relative prices on income distribution, given the system of production in use. A change in distribution, Mark Blaug (1987: 436) contended, 'has no effect on relative prices measured in terms of the Standard commodity for the simple reason that the change alters the measuring rod in the same way as it alters the pattern of prices being measured'. This is of course not true.[8] In his book Sraffa made it abundantly clear that a particular standard of value cannot change the 'mathematical properties' of a given system of production; it may, however, help to 'give transparency' to these properties (Sraffa 1960: 23). Before having had access to Sraffa's papers, Neri Salvadori and I had argued that the standard commodity is essentially a tool of analysis which allowed Sraffa to see through the intricacies of the movements of relative prices as income distribution changes, given the technique in use (see Kurz and Salvadori 1993a). In the light of Sraffa's unpublished papers we do not feel obliged to withdraw this interpretation.

Finally, it would be incorrect to contend that Sraffa attempted to determine relative prices and income distribution independently of the levels of output, or 'demand' in that sense. The idea that quantities (or 'demand', in that sense) play a role in determining prices and the distribution of the product was present right from the beginning of Sraffa's work on production equations to its very completion. In 1927 he commented that the values resulting from his equations 'equally show the use, or disposal, of each product' (D3/12/2: 31). And in a note written in 1955 he stressed that the equations 'contain an element of the "demand side" as well as the "supply side"' (D3/12/49: 9). The 'element' of the demand side referred to consists of given quantities. What Sraffa rejected was the marginalist theory of demand, derived from marginal utility theory (or its modern equivalent). More important, he was able to conclusively show that the critics of the classical theory of value and distribution were wrong in assuming that that theory was in need of a 'closure' in terms of 'demand functions' for commodities and factors of production.

Important themes in Sraffa's papers

In this section I shall exemplify the interest of Sraffa's papers in terms of some important themes dealt with and the results obtained by him. The examples throw some light on the method of analysis Sraffa adopted, the genesis of his theory and his views about other theoretical conceptualisations. I shall deal with Sraffa's analysis of the dependence of relative prices on income distribution; elements of his criticism of marginal theory; his treatment of joint production and its relationship with the von Neumann model; and Sraffa's criticism of Keynes's liquidity preference theory.

Relative prices and income distribution

Reconstructing the classical theory of value and distribution obliged Sraffa to go back to square one, that is, the beginnings of systematic economic analysis, and to work out the implications of adhering consistently to the concept of physical real cost. The method of Sraffa's reconstruction bears a close resemblance to what he called the '"physician's" outlook of Petty'. He quoted approvingly from Petty's *Works*, in which Petty says that he has chosen to take

> the course (as a Specimen of the Political Arithmetick I have long aimed at) to express my self in Terms of *Number*, *Weight* or *Measure*; to use only Arguments of Sense, and to consider only such Cases, as have visible foundations in Nature; leaving those that depend upon the mutable Mind, Opinions, Appetites and Passions of particular Men, to the Consideration of others.
> (D3/12/4: 3; see also 13: 2–5 and 14)

In another document he referred to a paper on 'Goethe's view of nature', whose authors stressed that Goethe called his own way of thinking *gegenständliches Denken* (thinking in objects); they added: 'Any idealistic argument that obscured this objective reference is disliked' (D3/12/9: 46). Sraffa was apparently in sympathy with this point of view.

Values, he surmised, are essentially to be explained in terms of the 'true absolute costs of commodities' (D3/12/6: 11), that is, those costs that cannot be avoided if the respective commodities are to be procured. These costs can be directly seen in systems without a surplus: the physical real costs necessarily incurred consist of the necessary means of production used up and the necessary means of subsistence in support of the workers. Any real economic system normally generates a surplus. Therefore, in order to render the costs or 'absolute values' in the system under consideration visible, one first has to hypothetically cut down the product, which is 'obviously identical with the shortening of the working day', until the surplus vanishes (D3/12/40: 175). Seen from this perspective, chapter I of Sraffa's 1960 book, which deals with 'Production for subsistence', is nothing but the actual system with the surplus chopped off: it is a hypothetical economic system designed to clear the ground for a distinction between cost and income.

In the simplest case possible, that is, assuming single production and setting aside scarce natural resources, the equations show: 'how the factors produce the commodities (one equation per commodity), so the commodities produce the factors (one equation per factor)' (D3/12/13: 14; my translation from Italian).

The interesting result that emerges from the equations without surplus is that values are rigidly fixed: they 'spring directly' from the methods of production and productive consumption, as Sraffa was later to stress (1960: 3). The resulting 'absolute ratios of value are the only ones that restore the initial distribution of resources' – in Sraffa's view 'a sufficient necessity to justify the conception' (D3/12/6: 7).

Next Sraffa returned to the original system with a surplus and assumed that the latter would be distributed according to the rule of 'equal percentage surplus', that is, a uniform rate of profits. He justified this premiss in terms of the entrepreneurs' 'self-interest': 'If they did not get equal percentages, they would move to other industries' (D3/12/6: 10); competitive conditions are taken to prevail (D3/12/27: 2). It is then shown that relative prices and the rate of profits are fully determined, given the physical scheme. Sraffa emphasised: 'Distribution determines values, & values justify that distribution' (D3/12/44: 7). By assuming wages to be at the subsistence level, the resulting rate of profits is the maximum one supported by the system.

These findings showed that Sraffa's intuition had been correct: a consistent solution to the problem of value and distribution could be found, using exclusively the data encountered in the approach of the Physiocrats and the classical economists: (1) the system of production in use; and (2) the real wage rate(s). Only after this step had successfully been taken could Sraffa begin systematically to study the problem that had bothered Ricardo until the end of his life: the impact of a rise (or fall) of the real wage on the rate of profits and relative prices.

That problem turned out to be much more intricate than economists generally were (and still seem to be) aware of. Sraffa stressed: 'In such a world, where everything moves in every direction . . . one sympathises with Ricardo in his search for an "invariable measure of value". In a universe where everything moves we need a rock to which to cling, a horizon to reassure us when we see a brick falling that it is not we who are going up – nor that we are falling when we see a balloon rising' (D3/12/52: 17). As Ricardo had already maintained, the fact that 'profits [are] increasing at a compound rate . . . makes a great part of the difficulty' (Ricardo 1951–73, IX: 387).

To facilitate the study of the change of prices as distribution changes, Sraffa, in a series of steps, groped his way to the concept of the 'Standard commodity', which proved to be a powerful tool of analysis and a useful pedagogical device. As Sraffa stressed, while it 'cannot alter the system's mathematical properties', it is explicitly designed to 'give transparency to a system and render visible what was hidden' (1960: 23). The first important mathematical property of a given system is its maximum rate of profits, the determination of which had already concerned Sraffa at an earlier stage of his investigation. The standard system allows one to ascertain that rate in a straightforward manner. It also provides 'tangible evidence of the rate of profits as a non-price phenomenon' (D3/12/43: 4), an observation which echoes Ricardo's contention that 'the great questions of Rent, Wages and Profits . . . are not essentially connected with the doctrine of value' (Ricardo 1951–73, VIII: 194). It should be noted that Sraffa related his concept explicitly only to that aspect of Ricardo's problem of an 'invariable measure of value' connected with the impact of changes in distribution on relative prices within a *given* technical environment, that is, a given technique. The other aspect that concerned Ricardo, interspatial and intertemporal comparisons, which refer to *different* technical environments, plays no role whatsoever; in fact, Sraffa accused Ricardo of confounding the two (see D3/12/43: 3).

Sraffa's (re)constructive work culminated in his 1960 book. He demonstrated that the theory of classical derivation was capable of dealing with a wide range of phenomena, including joint production, fixed capital and scarce natural resources, such as land, and the choice of technique. The characteristic features of the theory emerge with great clarity. Production is conceived as a circular flow. The means of production are divided into scarce and reproducible: scarce means of production yield their owners a rent, whereas reproducible means of production, that is, capital goods, yield their owners profits which in conditions of free competition tend to be proportional to the value of the capital invested.

The elaborate version of the classical theory typically starts from the following data, or independent variables:

1 The set of technical alternatives from which cost-minimising producers can choose.
2 The size and composition of the social (gross) product, reflecting the needs and wants of the members of the different classes of society and the requirements of reproduction and capital accumulation.
3 The ruling real wage rate(s) (or, alternatively, the rate of profits).
4 The quantities of the different qualities of land available.

The treatment of the wage rate (or the rate of profits) as an independent variable and of the other distributive variables as dependent residuals exhibits a fundamental *asymmetry* in the classical approach. Prices are considered the means of distributing the social surplus; they reflect both technical and social causes.

It deserves to be emphasised that these data are sufficient to determine the unknowns, or dependent variables: the rate of profits (the wage rate), the rent rates, and the set of relative prices supporting the cost-minimising system of producing the given levels of output. No other data, such as, for example, demand functions for commodities and factors of production, are needed or could indeed be utilised. The classical approach allows the consistent determination of the variables under consideration. It does so by separating the determination of income distribution and prices from that of quantities, which are taken as given or independently variable. Quantities were considered as determined in another part of the theory, that is, the analysis of capital accumulation, structural change and socio-economic development.

Marginalist theory and the problem of capital

Sraffa was convinced that the marginalist theory of value and distribution was fundamentally flawed. In his view its main flaw was the concept of capital. From an early time onwards we see him develop criticisms of the different variants in which the marginalist doctrine was put forward. He arrived at important insights many years before the controversies in the theory of capital triggered by an article of Joan Robinson in the early 1950s.

Marginalist theory and the labour theory of value

As early as in a note dated 19 June 1943 Sraffa put forward an observation which at first sight is perplexing. He maintained that the marginalist authors are precluded from raising objections to the labour theory of value: 'For the Marginal Product theory of capital *presupposes, implicitly*, that Hypothesis' (D3/12/34: 33). And in a note written at the beginning of 1946 he pointed out:

> The Irony of it is, that if the '*Labour Theory of Value*' applied exactly throughout, *then, and only then*, would the '*marginal product of capital*' theory work!
>
> It would require that all products had the same org.[anic] comp.[osition]; and that at each value of *r* [rate of profits], *each* commod.[ity] had an 'alternative method', and that the relations within each pair should be the same . . . ; so that, even when the System is switched, and another Org. Comp. came into being, it should be the same for all products.
>
> Obviously, this would be equivalent to having only one means-product (wheat).
>
> Then, commodities would *always* be exchanged at their Values; and their relative Values would not change, even when productivity of labo[u]r increased.
>
> (D3/12/16: 34)

Sraffa was thus clear at an early stage of his investigation that the 'parable' of neoclassical theory presupposes the 'realism' of the labour theory of value.[9]

'Quantity' of capital

As early as summer 1929 Sraffa pointed out: 'In order to have a marginal theory of distribution . . . we must have a physical measure of the quantity of each factor, independent . . . of its share of distribution' (D3/12/13: 17.5). And on 29 August 1946 he wrote:

> The idea of capital as a 'quantity' is so deeply ingrained in anyone who has been brought up as an economist, that it requires some effort to get rid of it. One feels that there is 'some sense' in speaking of 'more' or 'less' capital and that there must be a way to make this more precise so as to be able to speak of 'how much more' & 'how much less'.
>
> (D3/12/44: 1)

The 'rational basis' of this belief is said 'to lie in the fact that if capital were of uniform quality, then one could speak of its quantity – and measure it in tons, etc. as well as in price, *all with consistent results*' (ibid.; emphasis added; similarly

D3/12/16: 27). Yet when the capital consists of different objects, there is only a singularly special case in which one can unambiguously say whether the quantity of capital has increased or decreased, and by how much: this is the case in which all objects vary in the same proportion. Otherwise this is not possible. The worst possible case is the one in which the amounts of some objects increase, whereas those of others decrease. Here the concept of 'quantity of capital' totally fails us – or leads us into 'nonsense' (D3/12/44: 2). This case, however, is said to be the normal one.

Some authors, including Böhm-Bawerk and the early Wicksell, believed they had found in the concept of the 'average period of production' a measure of 'the quantity of capital' that is independent of distribution and thus prices. Yet Sraffa observed on 15 December 1942, with reference to Wicksell's 'candid' admission that, if compound interest and fixed capital are allowed for, the concept is no longer independent of the rate of interest:

> The tautology is even more obvious than in the preceding case: to determine the rate of profit we must first know the q.[uantity] of capital; to measure the q. of cap. we must first know the period of production; and to find the period of prod. we must first know the rate of profit. But economists are so well adapted to the interdependence of economic quantities that they accept even the dependence of the constants of the problem upon its variables.
>
> (D3/12/29: 3)

In a footnote he added:

> There is of course no sense in using simple interest, which means that the longer a period of investment is, the lower its effective return: which is impossible under competition. The point of using it is that it introduces an error in the result, which is sufficient to conceal the tautological character of the whole procedure.
>
> (Ibid.)

The unavoidable implication of this was that the marginalist theorists had to conceive of the 'quantity of capital' as a sum of *value*. However, they failed to find a measure that is invariable with respect to changes in the rate of profits (see D3/12/16: 14). Sraffa concluded: 'It seems clear that it will never be possible *a priori* to speak, in general, of an increase in the quantity of capital in the way required by the marg. prod. theory – i.e. before solving the equations & knowing the rate of interest' (D3/12/16: 42). Or, as he stressed elsewhere, representing the stock of social capital '*as one of the fundamental quantities* [as given] . . . is the source of many fallacies' (D3/12/21: 54).

Ordering of techniques

In his paper 'Capital Intensity and the Trade Cycle', published in 1939, Kaldor had argued that the indices giving the capital–labour ratios of different methods of production or techniques might be brought into an 'ordinal' ranking. Sraffa, in a note of 1942, observed:

> There is no assurance that, owing simply to a change in the rate of interest, the order is not reversed. Suppose two commodities produced by similar proportions of capital & labour (i.e. which are similarly divided between profits & wages): but one contains more capital in the 'early' stages & less in the later ones – i.e. although the total quantity of interest is equal in the two commodities, in this one it is made up to a larger extent of compound interest: it is clear that if the rate of profits rises, the composition of this commodity will come to contain more profits (i.e. capital) than the other.
>
> (D3/12/15: 10–11)

He added: 'But if interest changes, wages must change, & thereby the stock of capital required (i.e. the real structure) also must have changed', and 'the indices may register variations in the *opposite* direction to changes occurring in the structure of capital' (ibid.). Therefore, it generally makes no sense to say that one industry is more 'capital-intensive' than another unless the level of the rate of profits is specified at which the ranking of industries in terms of 'capital intensity' is meant to apply.

On 13 November 1942 Sraffa pointed out, and illustrated graphically, that in systems using (scarce) land the 'order of fertility' into which the different plots of land can be brought generally depends on income distribution, that is, the level of the real wage rate. A change in that level may involve a change in the order according to which lands will be cultivated by cost-minimising producers.

Joint production and negative labour values

One may be inclined to speculate whether Sraffa began to work on the problem of joint production only after he had seen the English version of John von Neumann's paper on equi-proportionate growth (cf. von Neumann 1945 [1937]). Nicholas Kaldor, then the managing editor of the *Review of Economic Studies*, had arranged a translation of the paper of his friend and fellow countryman from German into English and had asked David Champernowne to write a commentary in which the economics underlying von Neumann's terse mathematical argument was to be explained to the 'semi-numerates'. Champernowne consulted Sraffa, who assisted him with understanding and interpreting von Neumann's paper. As we know from Champernowne, he would have been unable to accomplish this task without Sraffa's advice. In the commentary the von Neumann model emerges as one characterised essentially by classical features (see Champernowne 1945). In particular, the rate of interest is not determined in a marginalist way via the relative scarcity of a factor called 'capital' (see also Kurz and Salvadori 1993b).

At that time Sraffa's own thought on the matter was already quite advanced. As his unpublished papers show, Sraffa had been working on the problems of fixed capital and joint production for some time before he got to know von

Neumann's paper.[10] There are also no indications that reading von Neumann's paper had a noticeable impact on his own ideas. It seems that he was in sympathy with the general thrust of the paper but did not approve of some of its simplifying assumptions. He did not retain, for example, the rule of free goods, which was employed by von Neumann in dealing with overproduced joint products. In his mature work he rather assumed that whenever consequent upon a hypothetical change in the rate of profits the price of a joint product tends to turn negative there will always be one or several processes of production which, if adopted, will make the phenomenon of negative price disappear. This assumption, peculiar as it may seem at first sight, is no more *ad hoc* than the assumption of free disposal. In fact the latter is equivalent to the assumption that for each process producing a given product there is another process which is exactly identical to the first except that the product under consideration is *not* produced.[11]

It also deserves to be mentioned that as early as around the turn of 1942–43 Sraffa mentioned the possibility of negative labour costs or values in joint production systems (cf. D3/12/28). And in February 1946 he stated that in such systems, 'when we change *r* [the rate of profits] from its actual value, and make it, say, = 0, we may obtain negative Values' (D3/12/16: 35). With his finding that strictly positive prices need not involve strictly positive labour values, Sraffa anticipated the debate about negative labour values in the 1970s.

Critique of Keynes's liquidity preference theory

As is well known, Sraffa participated in the discussion of Keynes's *Treatise on Money* and then his *General Theory* in the 'Circus'. Sraffa admired Keynes as a person and intellectual and the two were on friendly terms, but Sraffa, the perfectionist, could have hardly been happy with the way Keynes worked. The latter's journalistic style, his lack of precision and the publication of ideas not fully worked out must have irritated the fastidious younger colleague, who over the time appears to have reduced his participation in the 'Circus'. This did not mean that Sraffa would no longer form an opinion on the ideas Keynes put forward; it meant only that he would not necessarily communicate them to Keynes. One such case seems to have been Sraffa's criticism of Keynes's liquidity preference theory. In Sraffa's personal copy of the *General Theory* there were placed two manuscript fragments dealing with that part of Keynes's analysis (see I100). The documents are undated but it seems safe to assume that they were written shortly after the publication of the *General Theory* in 1936. In addition to the two papers Sraffa's annotations in his copy of Keynes's book are of interest.

The theory of liquidity preference occupies a central place in Keynes's *General Theory*. The liquidity preference of the wealth owners is said to prevent the money rate of interest from falling to a level at which a volume of investment would be forthcoming that is equal to that of full employment savings. The liquidity preference is taken to make itself felt at any given moment of time and therefore also in the long run. Hence it is the ultimate cause of depressions and stagnative tendencies in advanced capitalist economies. The theory of liquidity preference has therefore been interpreted as a core element of Keynes's analysis.

Sraffa in one place stresses that it is indeed 'Keynes's system'. The question is whether that theory can bear the brunt. As is well known, in chapter 17 of the *General Theory*, 'The essential properties of interest and money', Keynes had recourse to a concept employed by Piero Sraffa in his critique of Hayek's *Prices and Production*. Against Hayek's idea that in a disequilibrium the actual rate of interest deviates from the 'equilibrium rate of interest' Sraffa had put forward the notion of multiple 'commodity rates of interest' (Sraffa 1932b). In chapter 17 Keynes developed the liquidity preference theory against the background of that concept. In the light of the importance Keynes attributed to the concept it is perhaps of some interest to know what its originator thought of the use Keynes had made of it.

Sraffa's observations in the papers and on the margin of his copy are highly critical of Keynes's argument and can essentially be grouped in two. First, there are those questioning the inner coherence and consistency of Keynes's reasoning. The criticism put forward is purely immanent. Are the concepts Keynes used well defined and did he develop his argument in a conclusive manner, or did he contradict himself? Sraffa's assessment is largely in the negative. Secondly, there are remarks concerned with the realism of Keynes's analysis. Are the economic agents referred to in the argument faithful representations of their real-world counterparts, do they adequately reflect the latter's motives and actions, or does the view provided distort reality in important ways? Sraffa finds fault with some of Keynes's main agents. He does not assess Keynes's approach in terms of an alternative one. He rather scrutinises each single building block of Keynes's analysis and whether those blocks can carry the weight of the edifice as a whole. He does not argue by authority – he does not confront Keynes with the views of other major economists. He simply asks whether Keynes's argument makes sense or not.

Sraffa's annotations and papers disclose several blunders and contradictions in Keynes's argument. As regards the latter's notion of liquidity Sraffa criticises the fact that various meanings are lumped together under that heading. In addition Keynes is criticised for not having fully grasped the concept of 'own rates of interest'. While, as Sraffa observes, Keynes first distinguishes strictly between the rate of interest on the one hand and the marginal efficiencies of capital goods on the other, he then appears to think that the distinction is perhaps superfluous and treats them all as own rates. The latter, however, are 'important *only* in the short period . . . till production is adjusted to demand'. Yet Keynes erroneously uses them in a long-period context. In addition he commits the following blunder. If a capital good exhibits a higher marginal efficiency, equilibrium can be restored in either of the following ways: through an increase in the value of the object or through an increase in its production. Keynes now assumes that these two possibilities are available with regard to all assets – *except* money. Neither the quantity nor the value of money can rise. It is around this untenable premise that Keynes is said to develop his analysis. In 'normal' conditions, that is, in a long-period equilibrium of the economic system, all own rates are uniform. Only in the short period, characterised by disequilibrium, do the own rates differ from one another, where the differences depend *exclusively* on the *expected price changes* and are thus defined with regard to the forward prices of the commodities. In a depression, in which prices can be expected to fall, the value of money can be expected to rise. Yet an expected rise in the value of money implies a *lower* own rate of interest of money: 'therefore the money rate will be *lower* than other rates & not higher'. As Sraffa notes, this is 'Fisher's effect, which K.[eynes] admits for all commodities except money'.

Sraffa then turns to Keynes's 'confusion' of the rate of interest and the marginal product of capital in section II of chapter 17. There Keynes tries to build up the (own) rate of interest of each commodity 'by adding up the advantages & disadvantages of *holding* that potential article'. Understandably, he gets different results for different articles. He is then forced to assume that for each commodity or asset 'there is such an expectation of appreciation or deprec., in terms of an arbitrary standard, as will equalize their rates of interest'. The upshot of this reasoning is Keynes's concept of the 'own rate of money interest'. The latter Sraffa calls 'hybrid' and remarks that it is never used again by Keynes, '& indeed has no other use than to patch up the confusion created'.

The main criticism of Keynes's procedure comes immediately afterwards: 'Now it is necessary to emphasize that the advantages involved in *holding* a commodity have no relation to its particular "own rate of interest"', and that no properties of that commodity with the exception of the expected change of its price 'have any relations to the difference between its rate & other rates.' A person who borrows money or something else typically does not borrow in order to keep the proceeds. Normally the person will rather use them to buy things needed in production. It is thus irrelevant to the person whether the payment is in money or wheat, and the commodities purchased will typically be consumed productively, that is, they will not just be held. Therefore, it is of no concern to the person whether these things have carrying costs, etc., or not. From Keynes's whole treatment of the subject it may be concluded 'that K.[eynes] has in the back of his mind two wrong notions, which have entirely misled him': (1) commodities are borrowed in order to be held until the end of the loan; (2) therefore only durable objects can be borrowed. Sraffa comments on this: 'But in fact it is as convenient to make a loan of fresh fish for 100 years, as it is to make it of gold.' The properties mentioned are, however, typically 'properties of investments in fixed capital'; therefore Keynes's argument ought to have referred to the marginal productivities of different capital goods.

Concluding remarks

Sraffa variously stressed that it would be naive to assume that there are no broader philosophical concerns behind the theories of value and that politics plays no role in the genesis of economic theory. In 1927 he wrote about the theory he intended to develop:

> In this theory it will be thought that the important part is the analytical and constructive. The significance of the historical side will be missed. And yet, this is the truly important [*sic*], that which gives us a real insight into the

> mystery of human mind and understanding, into the deep unknown relations of individuals between themselves and between the individual & society.
> (D3/12/4: 14)

While Sraffa's anti-fascist and socialist orientation inspired his intellectual work, they did not overshadow it. He would not allow ideological commitments to blur his logic. His unpublished papers document his honesty, self-criticism and love of truth. They show a meticulous scholar, possessed of a mind as independent as a human mind can possibly be. His questioning and critical bent did not come to a halt when his own ideas were under scrutiny. The judgement Hicks passed on Ricardo applies also to Sraffa: 'Ricardo had candour and courage; he followed his reasoning where it led him, not just where he (or his friends) wanted it to go' (Hicks 1969: 151).

Sraffa was a remarkable intellectual, an original and profound thinker. His contributions to economic theory and to the history of economic thought stand out for their excellence in the twentieth century.

Notes

I should like to thank Jonathan Smith, archivist at the Wren Library, Trinity College, Cambridge, for his assistance. Useful comments on an earlier version of this chapter were received from Giancarlo De Vivo and Neri Salvadori. In addition I should like to thank Pierangelo Garegnani, literary executor of Sraffa's papers and correspondence, for granting me permission to quote from them. The chapter draws freely on Kurz (1998a, b).

1 For Sraffa's life and career see Potier (1991).
2 The award is commonly considered equivalent to the Nobel prize in economics when the latter had not yet been established.
3 See, for example, the collections of essays in Steedman (1988), Schefold (1989), Bharadwaj and Schefold (1990), Kurz (2000) and the summary accounts of the literature in Bidard (1991) and Kurz and Salvadori (1995).
4 A microfilm that has been produced of the material is said to have well above 30,000 shots.
5 Unless otherwise stated, all emphases are in the original.
6 On pp. 186–90 we shall return to these aspects in less general terms.
7 The evidence suggests that with the exception of *Theories of Surplus Value*, which he first read in French, it was only much after the development of his first systems of equations in the second half of 1927 that Sraffa started to study Marx's contributions systematically. A close scrutiny of Marx's theory of value and the 'transformation problem' dates from the early 1940s when Sraffa came across Ladislaus von Bortkiewicz's criticism and 'rectification' of Marx's argument. Sraffa studied and carefully excerpted Bortkiewicz's papers and put down numerous critical comments.
8 After these lines had been written I had the opportunity to see the paper Mark Blaug presented at the conference in memory of Giovanni Caravale in which he admitted that his above statement is wrong. See Chapter 5 above.
9 As regards the argument about parable and realism see Samuelson (1962); see also the critique by Garegnani (1970).
10 The first document I do remember in which he deals with joint production and even assumes free disposal, that is, a joint product that if overproduced fetches a zero price, dates from November 1927 (cf. D3/12/11: 25).
11 For this interpretation see Kurz and Salvadori (1995: 424–6, 2000b).

14 Models of monopolistic competition and general equilibrium theory

Domenico Tosato

Opening, in October 1991, the session of the thirty-second annual meeting of the Italian Economic Society on 'Equilibrium Theories: Recent Developments and New Critiques', Giovanni Caravale forcefully stated the case for a new approach to the notion of equilibrium, which should be capable of constituting 'the focal reference point of the attempt to interpret [economic] reality'. To this end, he maintained that 'equilibrium should simultaneously represent: (1) a "significant" position; (2) a position that expresses the "rational" choices and behaviour of the "active" economic agents also in the presence of uncertainty; (3) a "long period position in the logical sense"' (Caravale 1997b: 18).

The condition that equilibrium should represent a 'significant' position of the economy meant to him, in particular, that one should 'avoid the construction of theories which, explicitly or implicitly, presuppose institutional frameworks or hypotheses of behaviour of economic agents so far removed from reality as to render the theoretical model a difficult tool to use for the interpretation of the working of actual economic systems' (Caravale 1997b: 19).

This idea led Caravale to assume a critical position towards general equilibrium theory. He pointed out that the basic assumptions on which the theory is built – perfect competition, full and symmetrical information, completeness of markets, price flexibility, absence of out-of-equilibrium transactions, and so on – are so abstract and unrealistic as to make it 'increasingly difficult to believe that the equilibrium position defined by neoclassical theory can represent a logical coherent expression of the fundamental forces at work in real economic systems' (ibid.: 14).

I do not intend to go into the merits of Caravale's position here.[1] I share his view that the limitations of the theory of general equilibrium deriving from its basic assumptions should in no way be minimised; I am far less convinced of the thesis that we should abandon the general equilibrium approach altogether. The idea of an overall interdependence that links all markets seems to me to remain a fundamental intuition hard to relinquish, without incurring the cost of missing one of the most important aspects of the working of a decentralised market economy. Progress towards greater realism rather lies in removing some of the assumptions of the benchmark model, while retaining the idea of interdependence.

In line with this conviction, and with Caravale's constant concern for the construction of relevant economic theories,[2] I intend in this chapter to reflect on the consequences for general equilibrium theory of substituting the assumption of perfect competition with that of monopolistic competition in the theoretical framework of a non-cooperative approach to the problems of strategic interdependence among firms. This may be considered only a little step towards greater realism, but it is none the less a step, as modern economies are all characterised by the more or less extensive presence of large firms with market power linked among themselves by relations of competition as well as cooperation, unions with monopoly power over the labour supply, cartels of countries and firms that control the supply of natural resources and energy. But the model of general equilibrium with imperfect competition[3] is of considerable interest on its own, in as much as it raises new and unexpected problems with respect to the traditional partial equilibrium approach to the theory of monopoly, oligopoly and monopolistic competition. Moreover the analysis of an economic system in which agents, or some of them, have the power to set prices would appear essential also for a better understanding of the theory of perfect competition itself (Arrow 1959).

The focus of this chapter is not on the technical issues involved in demonstrating the existence of equilibrium, but on comprehension of the basic problems posed by the assumption of monopolistic competition in a general equilibrium framework. This objective leads me to concentrate on simpler models that better typify the various relevant strands of the theory. I make no claim to originality or exhaustiveness but rely heavily on the excellent surveys of Hart (1985), Gary-Bobo (1988) and Bonanno (1990), which I have tried to integrate with specific consideration of the further contributions to the subject that have subsequently appeared in the literature, especially on the issue of price normalisation.

I begin in the next section by comparing perfect and imperfect competition as they bear on two preliminary matters: the decisions of individual producers and the resulting consequences for the appropriate notion of equilibrium. I then take up on p. 204 the key analytical issue that the theory of monopolistic competition has to face when one passes from partial to general equilibrium analysis, namely the problem of determining the general equilibrium or objective (direct and inverse) demand functions, which are required for the definition of producers' optimal choices. I move on at this point to examine the main theoretical constructs found in the literature, bringing out the essential features of their descriptions of the economy, the definitions of equilibrium, the critical points in the construction, and the development of each theory in response to criticism. The criterion for classification used here, as in other surveys, distinguishes first of all between theories that take the quantity of output and those that take price as the firms' strategic decision variable; reference respectively to the names of Cournot and Bertrand for these alternative approaches is immediate. Within the quantity-setting approach, a further distinction is made between *conjectural theories*, that assume that firms can do no more than conjecture the inverse market demand (p. 207), and *objective theories* that assume, on the contrary, that quantity decisions are based on the objective market demand, with all the problems connected with its determination (p. 211). The problems raised by the choice of normalisation rule are separately examined at pp. 218–21. The price-setting approach is considered at pp. 222–8. After a presentation of Nikaido's *objective approach* to the determination of the equilibrium position, attention is concentrated on the implications of the different ways of dealing with the 'feedback' effect of profits on market demand. A further recent strand of analysis, that takes a position somewhat intermediate between the above mentioned two and is based on the consideration of a pricing scheme as a coordination device, is briefly examined in the same section. Some conclusions are drawn in the final section.

The specific problems posed by the assumption of monopolistic competition

A convenient way of bringing out the problems posed by introducing the hypothesis of monopolistic competition is to set the new situation against the perfect competition benchmark. Accordingly we take the number of goods, consumers and firms as given. We suppose in line with the standard description, as for instance in Debreu (1959), that consumers aim at the maximisation of preferences under the relevant budget constraint, defined by the initial endowments of commodities plus the share of the profits of the various firms received by each consumer. Aggregate consumers' behaviour can therefore be represented by market demand (supply) functions (correspondences) with the appropriate continuity properties.

We must be more specific in the description of producers' behaviour, so as to be in a position to clearly contrast the consequences for the structure of the theory ensuing from different hypotheses about the market regime.[4] Under perfect competition, producers' behaviour is characterised by three elements: (1) the hypothesis of price-taking for all outputs and inputs; (2) profit maximisation; and (3) an optimal choice expressed as a supply function (correspondence) of outputs and a demand function (correspondence) for inputs which depend exclusively on the set of relevant prices for the individual firm.

The assumption that prices are given, independently of the decisions of any single producer, is of course the analytical formulation of the perfect competition hypothesis. On this hypothesis the Marshallian demand curve for the outputs of the firm, and in parallel the supply curve for its inputs, is horizontal and clearly distinct from the market demand and supply curves.

As Arrow (1986) remarked, not without a tinge of irony, in the language of economists the profit maximisation hypothesis is synonymous with rational behaviour. And this is the specific role attributed to this assumption in the theory of the firm. In reality, at least in ordinary language, the common understanding of the notion of rationality is broader, comprising, in Arrow's words, 'the complete exploitation of information, sound reasoning, and so forth'. Considering the matter from this broader point of view, we can say that the information requirement of perfect competition is that all producers know all prices and be thus in a position to take sound decisions, which clearly obtain only if the chosen production plans are in the best interest of the owners of the firms. Profit maximisation then appears as the criterion on which the various shareholders unanimously agree, because it is consistent with the maximisation of preferences by each one of them.

Profit maximisation together with price taking leads to the definition of optimal behaviour in terms of output supply and input demand functions (correspondences) that are continuous (upper semicontinuous) provided that the production set of each firm is convex. As is well known, non-convexity could result in the non-existence, discontinuity or non-convexity of the supply correspondence. While the input demands of the various firms naturally aggregate into an overall market demand for input services, the concept of industry, as the subset of firms producing a given homogenous product, becomes relevant for the purpose of aggregating the supply functions of the different firms.

At this point the problem of equilibrium consists in solving, for prices, a system of equations or weak inequalities expressing the condition that demand should not exceed supply on any market. It is thus possible to construct a mapping of the set of prices on to itself, or of a broader space constituted by prices and excess demands still on to itself. It can be shown that under appropriate conditions – in substance, the continuity conditions mentioned above in describing agents' behaviour – such a mapping satisfies the requirements for applicability of some fixed-point theorem, and that the fixed points of the mapping are the economy's equilibrium positions.

When we replace perfect with imperfect competition, the first question to consider concerns the causes that may determine a situation of market imperfection. There may be several: the presence of agents with market power, i.e. regimes of monopoly, bilateral monopoly or homogenous oligopoly; product differentiation, leading to regimes of monopolistic competition in Chamberlin's sense or differentiated oligopoly; incomplete information, giving rise to a large variety of possible situations; absence, *tout court*, of specific markets due to transaction costs.

Leaving altogether aside all consideration of the issues raised by the third and fourth cause, it would seem that the case of product differentiation could be likened to a situation characterised by a number of connected monopolies with differing degrees of output substitutability or to the analogous case of a number of differentiated oligopolies. This is the approach followed by Gabszewicz and Michel (1997) in the context of a pure exchange economy, in which some traders realise that by supplying to the market only a restricted share of their initial holdings they may influence the price and thereby obtain a higher utility level. Actually, the assimilation of product differentiation to a situation of as many monopolies as there are product varieties is not truly satisfactory, especially if we consider a production economy. As Chamberlin (1933) has observed, product differentiation introduces a new dimension to firms' decision problem, which now becomes that of price determination as well as of quality choice. And if the number of products is taken as given, this second aspect ends up by being eliminated (Negishi 1972: 104). This suggests that the type of market imperfection stemming from product differentiation should be dealt with separately and differently from that stemming from the presence of sheer market power; it undoubtedly requires appropriate tools to come to grips with the more complex questions raised. For the present, therefore, I shall consider only the hypothesis of agents possessing market power and hence the problems of general equilibrium in a system of markets that are interrelated by means of consumer demand. We may think, for simplicity, that in each of these markets there is a single producer, but this hypothesis is not necessary. In traditional partial equilibrium analysis this would correspond to the canonical case of monopoly. It is perhaps surprising to discover that in a general equilibrium approach this case generates a situation of strategic interdependence as in the partial equilibrium analysis of homogenous oligopoly. Following the prevalent usage in the literature, this situation will be generically called monopolistic or imperfect competition.

In this new context, let us take the number of products, of consumers and of firms as given. Suppose that consumers are price takers and that their behaviour coincides with that described for the case of perfect competition. Suppose, instead, that each firm is a price maker in its own product market and a perfect competitor in the market for inputs. Assume, further, that there are no pure intermediate goods, which would generate states of bilateral monopoly. This final assumption is undoubtedly restrictive; it can be justified in the present context by the consideration that the analysis of situations of bilateral monopoly would require the use of solution concepts derived from cooperative rather than from non-cooperative game theory, which is the main analytical tool involved in the definition of equilibrium in the models to be examined.

Market power carries significant implications for each one of the three aspects of producers' behaviour examined above with reference to the model of perfect competition, namely the information requirement, the criterion of profit maximisation as an expression of rational decision-making, and the analytical form of the firm's maximising choices.

In partial equilibrium analysis, we assume that the monopolist knows the whole demand curve for his output; this is obviously a much more consistent information requirement than just knowing the market price. But when we move on from partial to general equilibrium, the problems grow enormously more complex. To cite Arrow:

> From a general equilibrium point of view, the difficulties are compounded. The demand curve relevant to the monopolist must be understood *mutatis mutandis*, not *ceteris paribus*. A change in the monopolist's price will in general cause a shift in the purchaser's demands for other goods and therefore in the prices of those commodities. These price changes will in turn by more than one channel affect the demand for the monopolist's produce and possibly also the factor prices that the monopolist pays. The monopolist, even in the simple case where there is just one in the entire economy, has to understand all these repercussions. In short, the monopolist has to have a full general equilibrium model of the economy.
>
> (Arrow 1986: 207)

Arrow notes that these information and computational requirements are further heightened and take on a new dimension when a regime of oligopoly is hypothesised or when – as we consider here – there are several monopolists in the economy, since every agent assumes rational behaviour on the part of the others. The rationality of all agents must therefore be part of *common knowledge*, which implies that the principle of rationality and the knowledge of rationality is not just an individual phenomenon but becomes a social one. As we see, in an economy where agents have market power the information requirement takes on features and dimensions that are not just broader than under perfect competition, but completely new.

As we turn to the firm's criterion for decision making, the traditional hypothesis that also under monopolistic competition rational behaviour should be identified with profit maximisation has been vigorously challenged. As mentioned above, the rationale for profit maximisation in perfect competition comes from its being instrumental to the maximisation of the utility of the owners of the firm. But when firms can affect prices, the production plan that maximises profits, i.e. the owners' wealth, need not yield the highest utility level for the shareholders, who might prefer choices leading to lower profits in order to obtain even lower product prices. This shows that the separation of the production decision of the firm from the consumption decision of its owners, typical of perfect competition, does not carry over to the situation of imperfect competition.

Correct reasoning would thus require replacing profit maximisation with shareholders' utility maximisation as the firms' decision criterion. This is an analytically easy step to take when there is a single owner of each firm,[5] but a practically impossible task to solve when there are several shareholders to each firm, who may have – and generally do have – different preferences. Aggregation of preferences according to the legal framework of majority voting leads to Arrow's well known paradox (Arrow 1950). It follows that whereas under perfect competition we have unanimous consensus from the shareholders of every firm on the objective of profit maximisation, under imperfect competition it is not clear how the objective of the firm should be formulated. Note, incidentally, that the problems posed by the objective of the imperfectly competitive firm are not peculiar to the general equilibrium approach. The same problems arise in a partial equilibrium framework, as Gabszewicz and Vial (1972) rightly point out.

Actually, no satisfactory alternative to profit maximising has been suggested,[6] so that notwithstanding valid logical criticism it remains the sole practicable decision criterion. Marschak and Selten (1974) are quite explicit about this. Anticipating the criticism of those who argue that consumers are the ultimate agents of the economy, that firms are consequently coalitions of consumers and that the action of firms should be choices with which the members of these coalitions are satisfied, they take the view that in observed economies firms are typically owned by many consumers who effectively relinquish control to an autonomous management. Marschak and Selten proceed, therefore, with the assumption of profit maximisation without further discussion as to the status of this criterion among the objectives of the management. It is not in the scope of this chapter to pursue the matter further, but a final remark in line with the theme of the introductory section may be here appropriate. There is no doubt that profit maximisation is hard to defend on logical grounds; logically weak is the idea that it offers a good approximation, as long as we don't know what profit maximisation should approximate and how it would do it (Cornwall 1977), and equally unconvincing is the approach taken by Arrow and Hahn (1971), who omit all reference to firms' objectives and directly posit the existence of decision rules (supply functions) having particular properties. Yet, all this having been said and acknowledged, it is difficult to escape the conclusion that 'it is not realistic to assume that firms actually recognise that their production choices influence the consumption possibilities which are feasible for the firms' owners and that the firms consequently choose non-profit-maximising plans' (Cornwall 1977: 69). If we agree to give credit to Caravale's plea for relevance of the theory and to Malinvaud's diagnosis that price theory must pay increasing attention to its operational purposes, we could take sides with Marschak and Selten and justify the assumption of profit maximisation simply on grounds of empirical relevance.

A further issue is linked to the assumption of profit maximisation; it concerns the fact that profits are not independent of the choice of the normalisation rule. We will dedicate specific attention to this question in connection with the problems of indeterminacy of the equilibrium in an imperfectly competitive economy.

As regards finally the question of the nature of the firm's maximising choice, it is well known that in a regime of monopoly there is no analogue of the supply function of a firm operating under perfect competition. Given that the maximisation problem has solution, and that this is unique, the monopolist sets his price or product quantity on the basis of a given market demand function. Hence there is no supply schedule, defined as a functional relation between hypothetical product price and output levels that the monopolist finds it profitable to put on the market, distinct from the demand schedule. Naturally, the monopolist's choices can be described in relation to changes in variables other than the price – e.g. the prices of substitute goods, quantities produced by other producers in adjoining markets, and so on – but these relations are clearly conceptually different from the supply function of a perfectly competitive economy.

This has important consequences for the very formulation of the equilibrium conditions of the economy. It is no longer possible, or convenient, to use the concept of industry, or its homologue in Chamberlin, the 'large group'. More fundamentally, it is impossible to define equilibrium in terms of the condition of zero excess demand in all markets. The point is formulated with extreme clarity by Lange:

> The nature of economic equilibrium, as well as of disequilibrium, in a monopolistic or monopsonistic market differs from that in a perfectly competitive market. In the latter, disequilibrium consists in excess demand or excess supply. Monopolistic supply, however, is always equal to the demand for the good in question and monopsonistic demand is always equal to supply. A monopolistic or monopsonistic market is in equilibrium when the quantity sold and bought is such that it maximizes the profit of the monopolist or monopsonist.
>
> (Lange 1944: 35)

An imperfectly competitive economy is, then, in equilibrium only if the monopolistic firms realise consistently and simultaneously maximum profits (Nikaido 1975: 9).[7]

This leads to the necessity to model equilibrium in an imperfectly competitive economy as a two-stage process. In the first stage, the price-making firms choose their strategic variable – quantity in the Cournotian approach, price in the Bertrandian approach – anticipating, correctly or imperfectly according to the different models, the effect of their choices on the conditions of the market. In the subsequent stage, market-clearing prices (or market-clearing quantities of output) are determined in a Walrasian fashion. This two-stage process can be looked at as a sequential game, in which firms decide first, and the markets are then cleared. From the analytical point of view, the solution is reached in reversed order, through a process of backward induction in which the effects of firms' decisions on the rest of the economy are first determined and profit-maximising choices of quantities or prices are then considered. The outcome of the market stage of the process is a general equilibrium, direct or inverse, demand function of the monopolistic firms; the outcome of the strategic stage of the process is a Nash equilibrium in which quantities or prices are the strategic variables and profits the pay-off functions.

Partial and general equilibrium demand functions

The partial equilibrium approach to the maximising choices of a monopolistic firm takes into account only the dependence of the quantity demanded on the own price of the product. The effects on demand of other variables, such as the prices of substitutes and complements in consumption and the wealth of consumers, are ignored on the presumption they may be considered invariant with respect to the decision of the firm. But these variables cannot be properly taken as given. On the one hand, the prices of other outputs depend on the simultaneous decisions of other monopolistic producers, who react to the optimal choices of the firm being considered; input prices are influenced, in turn, by the chain reaction of adjustments just hinted at. On the other hand, consumers' wealth depends on the value of initial endowments and on the distribution of profits, including those of the firm under consideration. It is clear that in a general equilibrium approach these induced effects cannot be *a priori* ignored.

The nature of the problems raised by the induced effects of the interdependent choices of the monopolistic firms are, from an anlytical point of view, similar in the quantity-setting and in the price-setting approach to the study of non-cooperative equilibria. It is, therefore, convenient to give preliminary attention to the common nature of these problems before turning to a separate presentation of the different approaches.

Let us consider an economy with L goods ($l = 1, \ldots, L$), divided into two subsets respectively of K ($k = 1, \ldots, K$) productive inputs and J ($j = 1, \ldots, J$) final consumption goods. There are I ($i = 1, \ldots, I$) consumers who behave as price takers both in input and output markets; x_i denotes the column vector of L components which expresses, for the first K components, consumer i's own use of productive factors and for the next J components his demand of final goods. There are J firms, each producing as a monopolist a single good in quantity q_j and acting as a perfect competitor in the input market, where the K-component input vector z_j is obtained. The production plan $y_j = (q_j; -z_j)$ is constrained to belong to the production set Y_j. Input and output prices are indicated by the partitioned row vector $p = (p_k, p_j)$. Price-taking consumer i maximises his utility function under his budget set:

$$B_i(p, m_i) = \{x_i \in X_i \mid px_i \leq m_i \equiv p\bar{x}_i + \Sigma_j \theta_{ij} \Pi_j\}$$

where m_i stands for consumer i's wealth, the sum of the market value of the initial endowments of commodities $\bar{x}_i$, including factors of production, and of the profit income received by consumer i according to his share θ_{ij} of the profits Π_j of firm j. Indicating with p_{-j} the vector of prices of all outputs different from j, the resulting individual demand function for commodity j can be written as $x_{ij} = x_{ij}(p_j, p_{-j}, p_k, m_i)$; by aggregation, the market demand function $x_j = x_j(p_j, p_{-j}, p_k, m)$ for the output of firm j is obtained; m is an I-component vector of consumers' wealth.

The partial equilibrium approach to the maximising choices of firm j takes as given p_{-j}, p_k and m and concentrates on the relationship between quantity demanded and its own price. Let us first suppose that the firm's strategic variable is, *à la* Cournot, the quantity of output. The analytical formulation of the optimisation problem requires to make use of the inverse demand function which, in a partial equilibrium context we are considering and on the usual assumption that the monopolist satisfies the market demand, can be simply written as $p_j = p_j(q_j, p_{-j}, p_k, m)$. The optimum production plan is then determined as the solution of the profit maximisation problem:

$$\max_{q_j \geq 0} \Pi_j = p_j(q_j; p_{-j}, p_k, m) \cdot q_j - C_j(q_j, p_k) \tag{1}$$

where $C_j(q_j, p_k)$ is the cost of production, in the derivation of which the technological constraint represented by the production set Y_j is taken into account.

In moving from partial to general equilibrium, the assumption of given prices and wealth can no longer be maintained. Using again the standard notation q_{-j} to denote the vector of outputs of the firms different from j, the *general equilibrium* or *objective inverse demand function*,[8] if it exists, takes the form:

$$P_j(q_j; q_{-j}) = p_j(q_j; \ldots, p_h(q_h; p_{-h}, p_k, m), \ldots; p_k(q_j; q_{-j}), m(q_j, q_{-j}; p_k)) \tag{2}$$

where the feedback effects of the output decisions of the monopolistic firms on input prices and consumers' wealth are fully recognised. On account of these effects the price obtained by each monopolist depends not only on his own production decision, but also on the decisions currently made by all the other monopolists.[9]

The thought experiment that must be performed to determine the vector of general equilibrium inverse demand functions $P_j(q_j; q_{-j})$ consists substantially in taking an arbitrarily given set of output decisions of the J firms and studying the conditions under which there exists a market-clearing set of commodity prices. The resulting mapping from the given quantities $(q_1, \ldots, q_J)$ to the corresponding prices $(p_1(q), \ldots, p_J(q))$, where $q = (q_j, q_{-j})$ is the J-component vector of outputs of all firms, represents precisely the general equilibrium inverse demand functions.

Let us now turn to the case that firms are price setters *à la* Bertrand. The profit maximising problem can be written as:

$$\max_{p_j \geq 0} \Pi_j = p_j q_j - C_j(q_j, p_k) \tag{3}$$

such that

$$q_j = x_j(p_j, p_{-j}, p_k, m)$$

where the constraint reflects the assumption that firms satisfy the market demand. Consideration of the induced effects of each firm's price decision on the price and output decisions of all the other monopolists, on input prices and on consumers' wealth makes it possible to write the constraint as:

$$q_j = x_j(p_j, p_{-j}, p_k(p, q), m(p, q)) = X_j(p, q) \tag{4}$$

The *general equilibrium* or *objective direct demand functions* are then determined as the solution, if it exists, of the J equations (4) and takes the form of the explicit functions $q_j = Q_j(p_j, p_{-j})$ that verify the condition $q_j = X_j(p, Q_j(p_j, p_{-j}))$.

The thought experiment we are now called on to perform, in order to define the general equilibrium direct demand functions, consists in taking arbitrarily given price decisions of the J monopolists and determining the levels of output which are compatible with market demands being met by the producers. The resulting mapping from the given prices $(p_1, \ldots, p_J)$ to the corresponding quantities $(q_1(p), \ldots, q_J(p))$ represents the general equilibrium demand functions.

The nature of the dependence of direct and inverse general equilibrium demand functions on commodity prices, in one case, and on commodity outputs, in the other, is quite complex; as Nikaido (1975: 56) writes, the general equilibrium demand function 'need not be downward sloping even with respect to the price of the good in question'.

Given the intrinsic difficulty of determining the true demand functions, theory can take one of two paths. The first is to avoid the problem, assuming that firms make a simple conjecture concerning the form of their own demand functions, which somehow sidesteps the general equilibrium issue. The second is to meet the problem head-on, with the advantage that we can make firms' maximising choices depend on objective factors (true general equilibrium demand) rather than subjective ones (conjectured partial equilibrium demand), but with the disadvantage of requiring firms to be able to solve a general equilibrium problem. Both paths – the *conjectural* one and the *objective* one – have been explored with regard to both approaches to non-cooperative general equilibrium. We begin by considering models in Cournot's quantity-setting tradition.

The quantity-setting approach

The conjectural equilibrium

The model developed by Negishi (1961), which represents the first full study of the problems posed by monopolistic competition in the general equilibrium framework, makes use of the subjective approach to demand. Negishi assumes that each firm chooses its production plan on the basis of a conjecture on its inverse demand function of the form:

$$p_j^e = p_j(q_j; \hat{p}, \hat{\omega}) \tag{5}$$

where $\hat{p}$ and $\hat{\omega}$ denote a given state of the market, or *status quo* of the economy, formulated with reference to the price system and to the consumption–production allocation $\hat{\omega} = (\hat{x}_1, \ldots, \hat{x}_I; \hat{z}_1, \ldots, \hat{z}_J; \hat{q}_1, \ldots, \hat{q}_J)$.[10] The subjective demand function, which is assumed to be continuous in the arguments, thus expresses firm j's conjecture on the price it can get when it produces the quantity q_j, given the state of the market. In terms of change rather than level, the subjective demand expresses firm j's conjecture on the price it can get when it varies the quantity of output from its current level, while all other prices and quantities remain unchanged. A weak consistency requirement is imposed, namely that the anticipated price coincides with *status quo* price when the level of output is equal to the initial level, i.e. when no change from the current level of production is envisaged:

$$\hat{p}_j = p_j(\hat{q}_j; \hat{p}, \hat{\omega}) \tag{6}$$

Negishi further assumes that perceived demand belongs to the set of affine functions and can thus be expressed in the linear form:

$$p_j^e = a(\hat{p}, \hat{\omega}) - b(\hat{p}, \hat{\omega})q_j \tag{7}$$

A diagram helps to clarify the approach. For any given *status quo*, e.g. point A in Figure 14.1, Negishi's hypothesis requires of the firm's subjective demand curve only that it pass through that point, with no constraint concerning slope. Given the true demand D, perceived demand could thus equally well be D^e or D'^e. Any change in the *status quo* of the economy would, in general, lead to a change in the position and slope of firm j's perceived demand.

A *monopolistic competition conjectural equilibrium* (a Negishi equilibrium) can now be defined as a market state (p^*, ω^*) such that:

1 For every consumer i, x_i^* maximises consumer i's utility function over his budget set:

$$B_i = \{x_i \in X_i | p^* x_i \leq p^* \bar{x}_i + \Sigma_j \bar{\theta}_{ij} \Pi_j^*\} \tag{8}$$

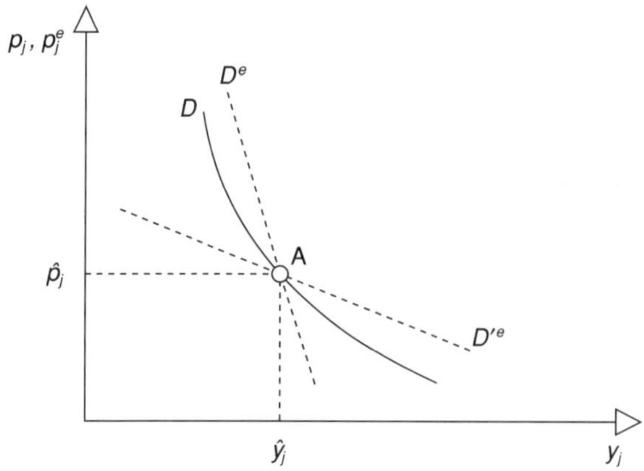

Figure 14.1 Negishi's subjective demand.

2 For every firm j, the production plan $y_j^* = (q_j^*; -z_j^*)$ maximises profits:

$$\Pi_j = p_j^e(q_j; p^*, \omega^*)q_j + p_k(-z_j^*) \tag{9}$$

in the production set Y_j and with the subjective demand $p_j^e(q_j; p^*, \omega^*)$ satisfying the consistency condition (6),[11]

3 There are no excess demands either of inputs:

$$\Sigma_i x_{ik}^* - \Sigma_i \bar{x}_{ik} + \Sigma_j z_{jk}^* = 0 \quad \text{for all} \quad k = 1, \ldots, K \tag{10}$$

or of outputs:

$$\Sigma_i x_{ij}^* - \Sigma_i \bar{x}_{ij} - q_j^* = 0 \quad \text{for all} \quad j = 1, \ldots, J \tag{11}$$

As we can see, the definition of the equilibrium in Negishi's model is exactly analogous to that in the competitive model. The demonstration of its existence follows the same lines. The role of perceived demand and of the related assumption of continuity with respect to the state of the economy is crucial.

There are a number of critical points in the model, well worth careful attention.

1. Comparison of equation (5) with (2) shows that Negishi's formulation of the inverse demand function does not bear any strict relation to the theoretical model and is more in the nature of an *ad hoc* procedure than of a simplifying assumption. With specific reference to the consistency condition (6), Nicola (1994: 15) further observes that also this requirement is hard to interpret when applied outside an appropriate dynamic context, in so far as it would seem to imply a process of adaptation and learning which is not specified and is difficult to conceive of in the framework of a static model.

2. Even considering the more general formulation of the subjective demand adopted by Hart, who makes the parameter of the function depend on the *status quo* of the entire economy rather than of the single market of firm j, Negishi's approach remains essentially one of partial equilibrium, owing to the way in

which the problem of strategic interdependence between firms is posed. Interdependence, which becomes relevant only through each firm's conjectures concerning the values of the parameters of its subjective demand function, is hidden in the variables defining the *status quo* of the economy, which includes not only the production plan of all other firms, but also irrelevant variables such as the prices of all commodities and the consumption plans of all consumers. It is thus hard to detect in the state of the market which constitutes a monopolistic general equilibrium a situation of optimal response of each firm to the optimal strategy of all others. Notwithstanding the reference to the state of the market, the optimal production plan of each firm thus maintains the nature of a partial equilibrium optimisation. These considerations lead one into questioning the opportunity of indicating, as Nikaido (1975) and Bonanno (1990) have done, Negishi's framework as a 'conjectural Cournot–Nash–Walras equilibrium', because the definition of equilibrium, though formally fulfilling the requirement for a Nash equilibrium, in no way makes use of the crucial notion of a best response to other producers' decisions.

3. As noted, the property that is essential to demonstrating the existence of equilibrium – namely, that the optimal choice of each firm consists of a single element or, if it is a correspondence, of a convex set – follows from the assumption of a concave profit function, which in Negishi's model is obtained from the combination of the linearity of subjective demand and the convexity of the production set. The latter restrictive assumption was relaxed by Arrow (1971), by Arrow and Hahn (1971) and by Silvestre (1977), who admit the possibility of increasing returns provided, intuitively, that the marginal revenue curve intersects the marginal cost curve from above. The question of the concavity of the profit function will receive further attention when dealing with the objective demand approach.

4. Maximising profits with respect to the subjective demand could have an unexpected consequence. Owing to the substantially arbitrary nature of the subjective demand curve, it could happen in fact that, while satisfying the conditions for an optimum, firms find themselves at a point of minimisation, rather than maximisation, with respect to objective demand, if the latter were known. The question is somewhat technical; a good exposition is to be found in the works of Bonanno (1988, 1990), who has produced a convincing diagrammatic approach to make the issue readily comprehensible. I shall return to the point shortly in the course of a brief account of recent developments along this line of enquiry.

5. Repeating the observations of Hart (1985) and Gary-Bobo (1988, 1989), the great generality of the subjective demand functions gives Neghishi's model very little predictive power. One can show that nearly all the production choices admitted by the technology and yielding non-negative profits can be supported as Negishi equilibria by making appropriate conjectures. Hart (1985: 107) says: 'To an outside observer who is asked to predict the market outcome but who does not know what these conjectures are, almost anything could be an equilibrium.' To clarify the point, and following again Hart's suggestion, let us refer to Figure 14.1. Two possible perceived demand curves are drawn: the curve D^e,

relatively rigid, and the curve D'^e, relatively elastic. Intuitively, an economy with rigid conjectures should have a highly monopolistic equilibrium position compared with that of an economy with elastic conjectures.

6. The poverty of the objective elements on which firms' demand conjectures rest in Negishi – let us recall that the sole requirement considered is consistency with the *status quo* – can be relaxed following a line of research begun by Silvestre (1977), actually in the framework of a price-setting rather than a quantity-setting approach, and further developed by Gary-Bobo (1987, 1989), Bonanno and Zeeman (1985) and Bonanno (1988). Silvestre's idea is that firms can engage in experiments around the *status quo*, and that these enable them to make demand conjectures that are consistent not just with a given state of the economy, but also with the price change resulting from a small variation, *ceteris paribus*, in the quantity produced. This means imposing upon the subjective demand not only condition (6) but also the additional condition:

$$\frac{\partial p_j^e(q_j; \hat{p}, \hat{\omega})}{\partial q_j} = \frac{\partial P_j(q_j, q_{-j})}{\partial q_j} \tag{12}$$

where $P_j(q_j, q_{-j})$ denotes the true general equilibrium or objective inverse demand which, as indicated above, depends not only on the output of firm j but also on the quantities produced by all the other firms.

With this further condition perceived demand is nothing other than a first-order Taylor series approximation of objective demand. So it is clear that there is nothing to keep us from considering higher-order approximations and therefore defining, in Negishi's spirit, as many corresponding equilibria, called in the literature *locally consistent equilibria*, of the order determined by the degree of approximation of Taylor's polynomial.

Gary-Bobo (1988) finds support for this type of procedure in a little-known passage of Joan Robinson's *The Economics of Imperfect Competition* in which, after determining the monopoly optimum at the point of intersection between marginal revenue and marginal cost, she writes:

> Of what use, the reader may ask, to discuss fine points of analysis which depend on the shapes of demand curves when no everyday monopolist has any such ideas in his mind, and when even the most up-to-date businesses have only the vaguest notion of what kind of demand curves they have to deal with? . . . But if the conditions of demand and supply remain constant over a fairly long period of time, the monopolist will be able to hit upon the exact monopoly output merely by balancing marginal receipts against marginal cost. We need not imagine that he is able to plot the demand and cost curves throughout their length, but merely that he can see whether selling a little more of his product than he does at present increases or decreases his net gains.
>
> (Robinson 1933: 56–7)

Developing Negishi's approach in the direction of locally consistent equilibria also enables us to overcome the risk of decisions that actually minimise rather than maximise profits: it is sufficient to consider locally consistent equilibria of at least the second order. It is, furthermore, clear that as we increase the order of approximation the subjective demand comes nearer and nearer to the objective demand and more and more independent of the *status quo* around which the approximation is made; consequently, the set of equilibria that can be supported in the class of conjectures considered decreases. From this standpoint, locally consistent conjectural equilibria represent an intermediate state between the subjective equilibria of Negishi and the objective ones of the Cournot–Nash–Walras approach to which we now turn.

The Cournot–Nash–Walras equilibrium

In contrast to the subjective demand approach – proposed by Negishi and substantially followed by Arrow (1971), Arrow and Hahn (1971) and the authors that have investigated the idea of locally consistent monopolistic equilibria – Gabszewicz and Vial (1972) examine the problem of general equilibrium under monopolistic competition from a new and different angle, that has revealed itself rich in as yet unresolved implications. Their innovation consists in supposing that firms know – or, better, are capable of determining – the 'true' general equilibrium demand for their product and that they base their decisions on it. Arbitrary conjectures are thus replaced by objective elements; the approach to monopolistic general equilibrium accordingly turns from *conjectural* to *objective*. With output still considered as the strategic variable of the firms, the central problem of the analysis then becomes that of establishing the existence of the inverse demand function and of determining its properties, with the ensuing implications for the equilibrium of the economy.

Gabszewicz and Vial conceive of the economy as being institutionally organised in the following way. Consumers supply labour and other primary resources to firms. Firms set their production plans with a view to maximising profits, taking the other firms' plans as given. The exchange of input for output between households and firms is supposed to take place in real terms: firms compensate households for the labour and other services provided with quantities of final output; inputs and outputs are exchanged in proportion to the ownership share of each household in every firm. At the end of this process each consumer has a new endowment of goods, consisting of his original endowment less the quantity of inputs provided to firms plus the quantity of outputs obtained in exchange. Once the initial endowments have been thus modified, the economy enters a phase of pure exchange, governed by price competition. The resulting market-clearing prices act as information signals that each firm uses to recalculate its optimal production plan.

Formally, given an arbitrary production plan $y_j \in Y_j$ for each firm j, the modified endowments $\bar{\bar{x}}_i(y)$ are defined by:

$$\bar{\bar{x}}_{il}(y) = \bar{x}_{il} + \sum_1^J \theta_{ij} y_{jl} \quad \text{for all} \quad l = 1, \ldots, L \tag{13}$$

where $\bar{x}_{il}$ is the initial endowment of commodity l of consumer i. Let $x_i = x_i(p, y)$ be the demand (supply) functions of consumer i obtained as a result of the maximisation of preferences over the budget constraint:

$$B_i = \{x_i \in X_i | px_i \leq p\bar{\bar{x}}_i(y)\} \tag{14}$$

We are now in a position to study the equilibrium solution of the pure exchange economy with initial endowments $\bar{\bar{x}}_i(y)$. Let $x = x(p, y)$ and $\bar{\bar{x}}(y)$ be respectively the market demands and the total endowments. The market-clearing conditions:

$$x(p, y) - \bar{\bar{x}}(y) = 0 \tag{15}$$

may have one, many or no solution at all in the price vector p, given the vector of production plans y; in other words, the pure exchange economy with endowments $\bar{\bar{x}}(y)$ could have one equilibrium, many or none. Absence of equilibrium could occur if some components of the modified endowments fell outside the consumption set or were negative. We rule out this possibility by constraining admissible production plans to be such that the exchange economy has an equilibrium. This is not a significant limitation, because production plans resulting in no equilibrium for the pure exchange economy could not be equilibrium plans for the overall production and exchange economy. For the subset of admissible production plans we can, then, construct the map $W(y)$ which associates to each element in this subset the price system:

$$W(y) = \{p \in \Delta | x(p, y) - \bar{\bar{x}}(y) = 0; \forall i \in I, \bar{\bar{x}}_i(y) \in X_i\} \tag{16}$$

where Δ is the unit simplex in R^L.

This mapping, represented in Figure 14.2, is known to the literature as the *Walras correspondence* (Debreu 1970; Balasko 1988); the alternative term *price correspondence* will also be used here. Note that, in order to focus on the problem under consideration, consumers' modified endowments have been replaced in the diagram by firms' production plans.

The Walras correspondence defined in (16) represents just the set of general equilibrium or objective inverse demand functions we were looking for.

As already remarked, the form of these demand functions may be far from usual. Figure 14.2 immediately spotlights the basic problem, namely that the equilibrium may not be unique. It is demonstrated that for a smooth economy – essentially, an economy with differentiable demand functions – all equilibria are isolated and therefore locally, but not globally, unique (Debreu 1970). Translated into the terms of inverse demand functions, this means that we cannot exclude that different prices may be associated with the same set of production plans of the firms. If we want each firm's profit function to be well defined, i.e. uniquely defined, we must therefore make a selection among the possible equilibria $W(y)$.

Taking as given a selection function $p(y) \in W(y)$, we can define a *Cournot–Nash–Walras equilibrium* as a system of non-negative prices p^* and an allocation $(x_1^*, \ldots, x_I^*; y_1^*, \ldots, y_J^*)$ such that:

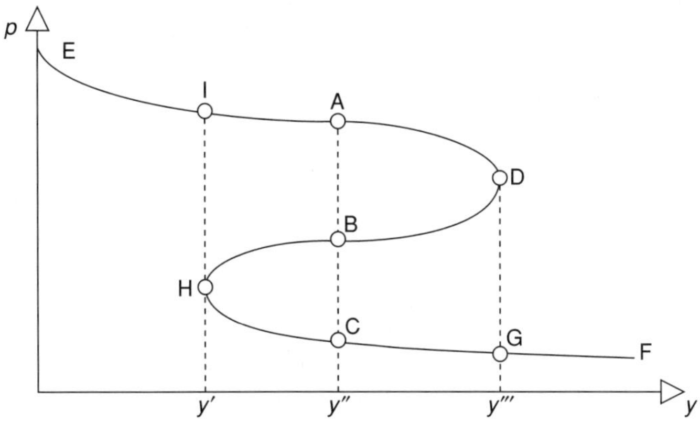

Figure 14.2 Walras correspondence.

1 For every consumer i, x_i^* maximises consumer i's utility under the budget constraint (14).
2 All markets are in equilibrium, thus satisfying condition (15).
3 $p(y^*) = p^*$ and $p(y_j^*, y_{-j}^*)y_j^* \geq p(y_j, y_{-j}^*)y_j$ for every firm j and every admissible production plan.

Several clarifying comments, as well as some critical remarks, are in order with regard to the Cournot–Nash–Walras equilibrium.

1. Comparing this definition of equilibrium with that of competitive equilibrium, one important difference is immediately apparent: the profit-maximising condition now identifies a Nash equilibrium, since it is required that in equilibrium each firm's decision must be an optimal response to the optimal choices of all the others. This circumstance, which marks a clear difference with respect to Negishi's equilibrium, explains the denomination of the new equilibrium as Cournot–Nash–Walras. On the one hand, the determination of the inverse demand functions requires us to find the equilibrium solution of a pure exchange perfectly competitive economy. This is, then, the Walras component of the definition. On the other hand, the maximising choices of the monopolistic firms emerge as a Nash equilibrium of a situation of strategic interdependence under Cournot's hypothesis that firms take as given the production plans of all competitors. This is, obviously, the Cournot–Nash component of the definition.

2. The use of game theory to study the equilibrium of a social system is not new: the existence of a competitive equilibrium has been proved in the framework of a game theory approach, in which in addition to the traditional agents of the economy – consumers and producers – a third, fictitious agent – the market – is introduced, each agent behaving so as to maximise respectively utility, profits and the value of excess demands (Arrow and Debreu 1954; Debreu 1982). The novelty of the situation generated by the presence of monopolistic competition lies in the transformation of the framework of the analysis from that of a simultaneous

to that of a sequential game, in which the agents with market power (the producers, in our simplified description) assume a position of leadership with respect to the rest of the social system. The solution of such a game by backward induction corresponds precisely to the institutional organisation described by Gabszewicz and Vial.

3. The perfectly competitive equilibrium of a production economy can be thought of not only in the traditional way of a simultaneous balancing of consumers' net demands and producers' net supplies, but also as the sequential equilibrium of a pure exchange economy in which endowments have been modified by given production plans and the latter are subsequently chosen so as to maximise profits in a Cournotian framework.[12] The equivalence between these two approaches is easily established through the definition of consumers' wealth, in terms of modified endowments in the one case, of initial endowments plus profit income in the other:

$$p\bar{\bar{x}}_i = p(\bar{x}_i + \Sigma_j \theta_{ij} y_j) = p\bar{x}_i + \Sigma_j \theta_{ij} p y_j = p\bar{x}_i + \Sigma_j \theta_{ij} \Pi_j \tag{17}$$

where Π_j are the profits associated with the production plan y_j when the price vector is p. If p^* is a Walrasian equilibrium, the budget set associated with the endowments modified by the production plan y^* coincides with that associated with the initial endowments and the profit income $\Sigma_j \theta_{ih} \Pi_j^*$. This means that the monopolistic general equilibrium model can do without the phase of barter exchange between consumers and producers described by Gabszewicz and Vial and can, therefore, be cast in the usual value terms.

4. A point underlined by Gabszewicz and Vial's approach none the less remains, namely that attention must be restricted to production plans that are consumption-feasible, i.e. plans for which the set of equilibrium prices for the exchange economy resulting from the profit income generated by the arbitrarily given production plans is non-empty (Mas-Colell 1982). We have already remarked that constraining the production set to the subset of plans such that the exchange economy has an equilibrium does not appear to impose a significant limitation. The exclusion of a production plan such as $\hat{y}$ in Figure 14.3, taken from Arrow (1971: 88) and Arrow and Hahn (1971: 155), is indeed of little relevance. Equally irrelevant would be the case of an economy in which the consumption-feasible production set is empty: hardly an interesting case to consider. A real difficulty could, on the contrary, come from the non-convexity of the production set and the ensuing possibility that the consumption-feasible production set may break up into two disjointed parts.[13] Equilibrium may not exist in that case. This possibility must, therefore, be ruled out, either supposing *tout court* the convexity of the production set or introducing the 'visibility' hypothesis adopted by Arrow and Hahn: in both instances a strong assumption is required to avoid the difficulty.

5. As we have seen, the determination of the inverse demand function calls for a selection $p(y)$ to be made out of the set $W(y)$ of equilibrium prices for the modified exchange economy. Let us note two issues that arise in this connection: it is not clear who should make the selection or according to which criteria it should be made. Gabszewicz and Vial shun both problems, simply assuming

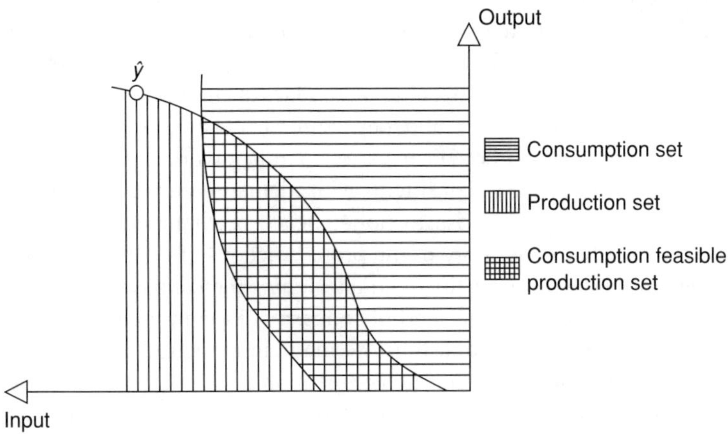

Figure 14.3 Construction of the consumption feasible production set.

that the price correspondence is single-valued, but this is hardly a satisfactory answer. A different answer to the first issue could be that the selection should be considered external to the system and trusted to an imaginary auctioneer, who is anyhow in charge of determining the equilibrium prices of the modified exchange economy. Consideration of the second issue shows that this solution is not without shortcomings, even were we willing to disregard its unrealistic nature. The graphical representation of the price correspondence in Figure 14.2 shows that in the range of the double fold of the curve, i.e. between points I and G, there is an infinite number of potential selection functions. Even taking into consideration only those that minimise the discontinuities and may therefore appear more reasonable than others, there are two alternative possibilities represented by the curves EDGF and EIHF. If we have confidence that the economy is reasonably close to equilibrium, we may think that price selection is the outcome of past history. This is a more appealing hypothesis than that of the auctioneer, which, given the selection, would none the less remain the unchallenged *deus ex machina* for the determination of the general equilibrium inverse demand functions.

6. Demonstrating the existence of a Cournot–Nash–Walras equilibrium requires two strong assumptions, namely the continuity of the price selection function and the quasi-concavity of the profit function of the firms in their own output. As Figure 14.2 shows, at the critical points D and H the selection function $p(y)$ is unavoidably discontinuous, and so therefore are firms' optimal choices. A Cournot–Nash equilibrium may thus fail to exist. But even assuming that the selection function is continuous, the profit function need not be quasi-concave. The firms' reaction functions may, as a consequence, present discontinuities and the possibility of demonstrating the existence of a Cournot–Nash equilibrium would be jeopardised. Here we come again upon a point raised above: the quasi-concavity of the profit function is an assumption that practically all imperfect competition models cannot do without, whether they are partial or general

equilibrium, use objective or subjective demand, take quantity or price as strategic variable. The point is that quasi-concavity cannot be taken for granted. Roberts and Sonnenschein (1977) have shown that the quasi-concavity of the profit function cannot be deduced from the standard assumptions on preferences, endowments and technology, and departures from quasi-concavity are in no way to be viewed as pathological cases; in other words, the standard assumptions on preferences are consistent with demand curves presenting convex regions, which could give rise to non-concave profit functions even if technology is convex. Quasi-concavity of the profit functions of the firms, which in models of general perfectly competitive equilibrium is the consequence of the assumptions of price-taking behaviour and of convexity of the production sets, is then a further specific assumption that must be made in models of general (but also partial) equilibrium with monopolistic competition.

7. Several lines of research have been explored in the attempt to find an answer of general validity to the question of the existence of a Cournot–Nash–Walras equilibrium. One way is to adopt a broader concept of equilibrium, namely a mixed-strategy Nash equilibrium. Dasgupta and Maskin (1986) have shown that an equilibrium in mixed strategies exists even if the profit function is not quasi-concave and, in some cases, even if it is not continuous. Many people are critical of this notion of equilibrium on methodological grounds: they argue that the mixed strategy approach presupposes that agents are, on the one hand, capable of assigning a probability measure on the space of strategies and are led, on the other, to decide on the basis of a probabilistic combination of their pure strategies, i.e. to delegate their choice of action to the outcome of the metaphorical toss of a coin. Various lines of defence of mixed strategy equilibrium have, none the less, been proposed; they have a special appeal in the context of monopolistic competition, where conjectures, subjective beliefs and private information are essential aspects of a situation of strategic interdependence. Harsanyi (1973) suggests interpreting a mixed-strategy Nash equilibrium as a pure-strategy Bayesian Nash equilibrium in a closely related game with a bit of incomplete information. In the same vein, Aumann (1987) argues that the probabilities assigned to the different strategies should be viewed not as the individual's probabilities of selecting one pure strategy or another, but rather as the subjective beliefs that competitors hold about what each agent will do. Independently of the methodological status of the mixed strategies approach, there is nevertheless a negative analytical result to report. The use of mixed strategies cannot guarantee the existence of equilibrium if the price selection function is discontinuous (Dierker and Grodal 1986).

A second approach belongs to the line of research that investigates the Cournotian foundations of perfectly competitive equilibria and actually applies to situations of oligopoly rather than monopoly. The asymptotic behaviour of oligopoly equilibria when the number of producers increases indefinitely is considered, with the idea that if the sequence of these equilibria converges to a regular competitive equilibrium, one may find an oligopoly equilibrium in the neighbourhood of this competitive equilibrium. Difficulties, again related to the presence of multiple equilibria, emerge also with this line of investigation (Roberts

1980; Mas-Colell 1982). If the limit point of the sequence of equilibria of the exchange economy modified by arbitrarily fixed production levels of the oligopolistic firms does not occur at one of the critical points of the Walras correspondence, such as points D and H in Figure 14.2, the sequence of oligopolistic equilibria converges to a perfectly competitive equilibrium. If, on the contrary, the limit point occurs at a critical point of the Walras correspondence, no such inference can be drawn. Looking now at the problem in the opposite direction, it can be shown that if a competitive equilibrium occurs at a regular point, it will be a limit point of monopolistic competition. Since under mild assumptions we can state that competitive equilibria are generically regular (Debreu 1970), we can conclude that oligopolistic equilibria must exist at most stages of replication of the economy. This final result is, however, less than fully comforting. The relevant propositions for the theory of monopolistic general equilibrium are those concerning the limit points of an oligopolistic regime, rather than the properties of regular perfectly competitive equilibria, and on that account research has yet to produce 'reasonable' conditions under which one can say that monopolistic competition always approximates perfect competition when the economy becomes large.

More promising appears to be a third line of research related to the heterogeneity of preferences. Grandmont (1992) has proved that increasing demand heterogeneity has relevant consequences for the prevalence, in the aggregate, of the weak axiom of revealed preferences and of gross substitutability and, consequently, on uniqueness and stability of the perfectly competitive exchange equilibrium. Grandmont (1993) has subsequently proved the conjecture that demand heterogeneity may generate concave revenue functions in the context of a partial equilibrium model in which firms compete in quantities. The extension of this approach to a general equilibrium framework could produce new and interesting conditions for the existence of monopolistic general equilibrium.

If one takes a pessimistic view as to the possibility of demonstrating the existence of monopolistic general equilibrium under sufficiently general conditions, one might be led to reject the model of monopolistic competition altogether. Roberts and Sonnenschein (1977) thus envisage the possibility of abandoning the assumption of non-cooperative behaviour and replacing it with that of implicit cooperation as observed in the repeated play of prisoners' dilemma-type games. Gabszewicz (1999) goes further and suggests that the absence of non-cooperative equilibrium should be interpreted as a situation in which firms prefer coordination of their decisions to competition. That the study of cooperative monopolistic general equilibrium, for instance along the lines of a Nash bargaining solution, should be worth undertaking on its own is beyond doubt. That it should be undertaken because it represents a more realistic description of the behaviour of firms with market power may well be, though this is a point far from being established and certainly at odds with a constant legislative drive on the part of the governments of most industrialised countries to curb collusive practices. But that we should draw the inference that the non-cooperative monopolistic competition regime should be dismissed as a relevant object of analysis because of the difficulty of proving the existence of the Cournot–Nash–Walras equilibrium under general conditions is entrusting to economic theory a role which, to my mind, goes beyond what theory can achieve.

Profit maximisation and the choice of normalisation rule

The Cournot–Nash–Walras equilibrium carries an implication that is surprising to those familiar with the properties of competitive equilibrium: the equilibrium solution is not invariant with respect to the choice of price normalisation, as Gabszewicz and Vial first noticed working out a numerical example. While equilibrium prices determined by the market-clearing conditions of the modified exchange economy are relative prices, absolute prices are involved in the definition of the profit function of the firms. When perfect competition obtains, the choice of *numéraire* – more generally, the choice of a normalisation rule – does not have any real effect; when, on the contrary, conditions of monopolistic competition are envisaged, the profit-maximising decisions of the firms – and, consequently, the equilibrium allocation of the economy – depend on the way prices are normalised. This is an unexpected circumstance, which deserves separate attention also on account of the further implications it carries for the proper specification of the objectives of the firm.

To illustrate the problem we take into consideration a simple partial equilibrium situation in which we model only the production decisions. We refer, accordingly, to an economy with a single firm which produces the output q using a single input z with a technology described by the input requirement function $z = g(q)$. Alternative assumptions will be made as to the market regime in which the output of the firm is traded, whereas the input market is supposed to be perfectly competitive. There is a third non-produced commodity in the economy, say money; the prices of money, of the produced commodity and of the production input are respectively π_0, π_1 and π_2. Results of general validity can be found in Böhm (1994) and Grodal (1996).

Let $P = \{\pi \in R^3_+\}$. We can define a normalisation rule as a continuous mapping $p : P \to R^3_+\backslash\{0\}$ such that:

$$p(\pi) = \frac{\pi}{f(\pi_0, \pi_1, \pi_2)} \tag{18}$$

Let us take as our reference benchmark the normalisation rule implicit in standard partial equilibrium analysis of production decisions, in which money is assumed to be the *numéraire*. We have accordingly $f(\pi_0, \pi_1, \pi_2) = \pi_0$ and

$$p(\pi) = \left\{1, \frac{\pi_1}{\pi_0}, \frac{\pi_2}{\pi_0}\right\} = \{1, p_1, p_2\}$$

so that p_1 and p_2 are now the money prices of the output q and of the input z. We will alternatively consider the normalisation rule typically adopted in general equilibrium theory, namely that the sum of prices is equal to 1; this implies, on the one hand, $f(\pi_0, \pi_1, \pi_2) = \sum \pi_l$ $(l = 0, 1, 2)$ and, on the other:

$$p(\pi) = \left\{ \frac{\pi_0}{\sum \pi_l}, \frac{\pi_1}{\sum \pi_l}, \frac{\pi_2}{\sum \pi_l} \right\} = \{\tilde{p}_0, \tilde{p}_1, \tilde{p}_2\}$$

Consider now the profit-maximising choices of a firm operating in a perfectly competitive market. When money is taken to be the *numéraire*, profits are

$$\Pi = p_1 q - p_2 g(q) = \frac{1}{\pi_0} [\pi_1 q - \pi_2 g(q)] \tag{19}$$

Assuming the existence of an interior maximum, the optimal production plan is determined by the condition $p_1 = p_2 g'(q)$ or, equivalently, $\pi_1 = \pi_2 g'(q)$. Suppose, instead, that the alternative normalisation rule is adopted, profits are defined as:

$$\tilde{\Pi} = \tilde{p}_1 q - \tilde{p}_2 g(q) = \frac{1}{\sum \pi_l} [\pi_1 q - \pi_2 g(q)] \tag{20}$$

The first-order condition for a maximum is now $\tilde{p}_1 = \tilde{p}_2 g'(q)$ or, equivalently, again $\pi_1 = \pi_2 g'(q)$. It follows that a change in the normalisation rule does not alter the optimal production plan but influences only the level of profits.

As we pass from perfect to imperfect competition, the definitions of profits are formally the same, but in the determination of the optimal production plan account must be taken of the dependence of the output price on the quantity produced by the monopolist, $p_1 = p_1(q)$. If money is the *numéraire*, the profit-maximising condition corresponding to the definition (14) is the standard equality of marginal revenue and marginal cost:

$$p_1'(q) \cdot q + p_1(q) - p_2 g'(q) = 0 \tag{21}$$

and the optimal production plan is thus $(q_M, -g(q_M))$. Note that an increase in the quantity produced by the monopolist leads to a negative effect only on the price of the output and not on the price of the input, since the latter is independent of the quantity produced, barring the general equilibrium effects working through the consumption sector, which are, however, excluded from consideration by assumption.

If, on the contrary, the *numéraire* is the value of a composite commodity made up of one unit of each good, a change in output determines an effect not only on its own price but also on the price of the input, since $\tilde{p}_2 = 1 - \tilde{p}_0 - \tilde{p}_1$ depends as well on the quantity of output. Specifically, an increase in the quantity produced by the monopolist has a double negative effect on marginal profits: marginal revenue falls and marginal cost rises. The optimal production plan $(\tilde{q}_M, -g(\tilde{q}_M))$ is now defined by the first-order condition:

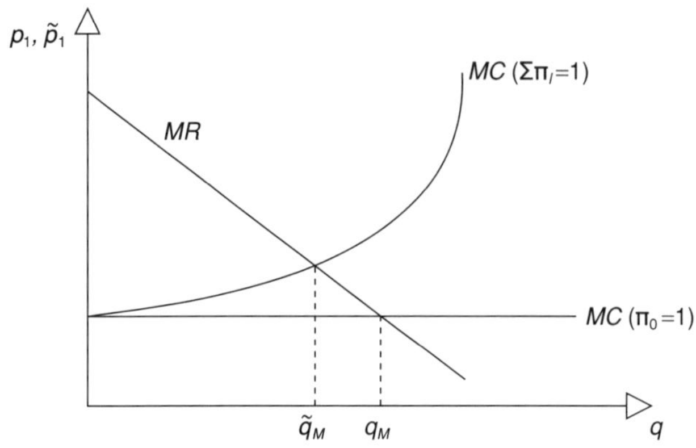

Figure 14.4 Profit maximisation with different normalisation rules.

$$p_1'(q) \cdot q + p_1(q) - [(1 - \tilde{p}_0 - \tilde{p}_1(q)) \cdot g'(q) - \tilde{p}_1'(q) \cdot g(q)] = 0 \tag{22}$$

Comparison of (21) with (22) shows that $\tilde{q}_M < q_M$ if the demand function is downward-sloping. Figure 14.4 illustrates the two different situations. The same linear marginal revenue function is assumed, while marginal cost, which is supposed to be constant in the first instance, becomes increasing in the second.

This illustration clearly shows that the equilibrium allocation is not independent of the choice of normalisation rule. Generalisations in two directions have been offered. The first concerns the indeterminacy of the equilibrium allocation: given an arbitrary price selection from the Walras correspondence and arbitrary production plans $(y_1, \ldots, y_J)$ for all firms not dominated at those prices, there exists a normalisation rule $p(\pi)$ such that $(y_1, \ldots, y_J)$ is a Cournot–Nash–Walras equilibrium production associated with those prices and with that normalisation rule. The second, which somehow represents the opposite side of the same coin, regards the non-existence of equilibrium: the existence of a Cournot–Nash–Walras equilibrium associated with a fixed normalisation rule depends crucially on the choice of that rule (Cornwall 1977; Grodal 1996). We have already commented on this result in the previous section; the study of the problems connected with the choice of *numéraire* makes it now possible to establish a connection between the non-existence of equilibrium and the choice of normalisation rule.

Let us at this point return to the question of why normalisation matters. At the beginning of this section we took it for granted, following Gabszewicz and Vial and many others, that normalisation matters because profits depend on absolute prices, the definition of which requires the choice of a *numéraire* commodity, single or composite. In Dierker and Grodal's (1999: 258) words: 'The reason why equilibrium allocations depend on the normalization rule is, of course, that profit functions based on different price normalizations are objectives that are generally not related to each other by monotone transformations.' Dierker and Grodal (1986) present, however, a numerical example in which equilibrium does not exist even though the criterion of profit maximisation is replaced by that of maximisation of the utility function of the (single) owner of the firm. They conclude that the cause of the absence of equilibrium lies in the discontinuity of the price selection function when the Walras correspondence presents a double fold. Böhm (1994), considering the same model as Roberts and Sonnenschein in which production is costless, concludes that different normalisation rules imply different general equilibrium (objective) demand functions against which firms maximise. Normalisation would then matter not because profits are defined in terms of absolute prices, but rather because the choice of *numéraire* changes the constraint against which the monopolists optimise.

The illustrative exercise carried out above is too simple and partial equilibrium to offer an adequate basis to evaluate Böhm's point. It does show, however, that Böhm's suggestion would apply only to models in which production is costless. When the cost of production depends on the level of output – and this is certainly the most realistic case – the price normalisation rule may influence the very definition of profits and thereby the optimal choices of the firms. The exercise shows, furthermore, that this effect occurs only if the normalisation rule includes the prices of monopolised commodities. This explains the reason for the choice often made, especially in models of monopolistic pure exchange economies, to express prices in terms of money, which is supposed to be a non-produced commodity.

The status of a firm's profit as opposed to shareholders' utility maximisation comes into question again from the specific angle of the indeterminacy of the equilibrium solution or the possible absence of it. If we stick to the pragmatic position that profit maximisation is the realistic objective of the firm, one line of defence against the specific criticism originating from the dependence of profits on the choice of the normalisation rule may consist in investigating the existence of equilibrium for the modified pure exchange economy, when the normalisation rule is confined to the subset of prices of the commodities traded in perfectly competitive markets only. 'Reasonable' conditions, on economic grounds, may indeed be found for such a restricted choice of *numéraire*. If we insist, instead, on rejecting profit maximisation in favour of shareholders' utility maximisation, it may be worth while to look into a different line of approach that has been explored by Dierker and Grodal (1998, 1999). They suggest that the problem of aggregation of individual preferences into a 'social' preference ordering can be 'solved' if we assign to the firm the objective of maximising the aggregate wealth of the shareholders, as it results from an appropriate definition of their aggregate budget set. Dierker and Grodal's idea is that in order to overcome the problem of price normalisation one must take simultaneously into consideration both the way that profits are earned by the firms and the way they are spent by their shareholders. The essential feature of their approach is that an endogenously determined, rather than arbitrarily imposed, commodity bundle comes into play which is used to measure profits somehow objectively, thereby overcoming the problem raised by the choice of normalisation rule. Both lines of research, as well as others mentioned at the end of the previous section, seem to be well worth further investigation.

The price-setting approach: the Bertrand–Nash–Walras equilibrium

We turn now to considering the price-setting approach to monopolistic general equilibrium. To avoid substantial repetition, we will not deal here with the analogue of Negishi's subjective inverse demand approach, which can be found in d'Aspremont *et al.* (1999); we will directly examine the problem posed by the existence of equilibrium in the framework of the objective demand approach and consider subsequently a typical simplifying assumption made in this context. In the presentation reference will be made particularly to Nikaido's model, which has the advantage of exhibiting in a simple way, thanks to appropriately chosen assumptions, the problems connected with determining the general equilibrium demand functions discussed on pp. 204–6. A similar approach can be found in one of the models studied by Marschak and Selten (1974) and in Stahn (1996).

With respect to the economy described at pp. 204–6, Nikaido makes the following further assumptions.

1. There is only one non-produced input, namely labour, which is taken to be the *numéraire* of the economic system; its price p_L is set equal to 1; all commodity prices p_j are then expressed in terms of labour.
2. Each monopolist has a linear production technology, that specifies the unit input requirements of labour and other produced commodities; the technology of the economy is thus represented by a Leontief input–output matrix $A = (a_{kj})$ and a $\mathcal{J}$-component row vector l of labour inputs.
3. Classically, the model distinguishes between workers' and capitalists' behaviour. There are I workers, who do not share in the property of firms and derive their income, totally spent on consumption, from the supply of labour. Workers' behaviour, resulting from utility maximisation under the budget constraint, is expressed by the aggregate supply of labour $\bar{x}_L - x_L(p, 1)$ and the vector-valued aggregate demand function $x^W(p, 1)$.
4. There are I' capitalists, whose wealth is represented by the profit income received in proportion to their shareholdings in the different firms. Capitalists are supposed to be price setters as producers and to exhibit, on the contrary, as consumers price-taking behaviour. Their aggregate demand, again resulting from utility maximisation under constraint, is expressed by the vector-valued function $x^C(p, 1, \Pi)$, where Π is the $\mathcal{J}$-component vector $\Pi = (\Pi_1, \ldots, \Pi_{\mathcal{J}})$ of sectoral (firms') profits.

Remembering the two-stage approach to monopolistic general equilibrium and the need to proceed by backward induction, we examine first the market-clearing aspect which leads to the determination of the objective direct demand functions and turn subsequently to the Bertrand-type price-setting game. Consider a price vector $p \in P = \{p \in R^{\mathcal{J}}_{+}\}$. Given the assumption that workers do not receive any profit income, their supply of labour and demand of commodities is at once determined. Owing to the assumption of constant returns to scale, unit profits of all firms are determined as well:

$$\tilde{\Pi}_j(p, 1) = p_j - \Sigma_k p_k a_{kj} - l_j \tag{23}$$

For profits to be non-negative – a condition that must be fulfilled, since firms can always, at no cost, stop producing – prices must be chosen in an appropriate subset of P, namely the subset $P' = \{p \in P \mid p(I - A) - l \geq 0\}$, where I is an identity matrix. The set of admissible prices P' is certainly not empty, if the Leontief technology refers to a viable economy. Total profits of firm j can then be written as $\Pi_j(p, 1, q_j) = \tilde{\Pi}(p, 1)q_j$. Let accordingly $\Pi(p, 1, q)$ stand for the vector of sectoral profits.

The market-clearing conditions for the economy just described are:

$$lq = \bar{x}_L - x_L(p, 1) \tag{24}$$

$$x^W(p, 1) + x^C(p, 1, \Pi(p, 1, q)) + Aq = q \tag{25}$$

the first concerning the labour market and the second the output markets, where total demand is the sum of workers' and capitalists' consumption plus intermediate uses in production Aq.

It can be shown that under standard assumptions there exists a vector q satisfying the equilibrium conditions (24) and (25) for all admissible price vectors p in P'.[14] We can therefore establish a vector-valued relation $q(p)$, which we can call, by analogy with the price or Walras correspondence encountered in the quantity-setting approach, the *demand correspondence*. As remarked on p. 206, this relation need not be single-valued, nor well behaved. If single-valued, this correspondence represents the general equilibrium direct demand functions of the firms; if multi-valued, one must resort to a selection from such a correspondence in order to identify the general equilibrium direct demand functions. This completes the first part of the backward induction process.

With knowledge of well behaved objective demand functions the second part of the process can be achieved.[15] Assuming that the profit function of each firm is quasi-concave in its own price and exhibits an appropriate boundary behaviour, there exists a Nash equilibrium in which the choice of an optimal price strategy of each firm is the best response to the optimal price strategies of all others.

We can now define, in Bonanno's well chosen terminology, a *Bertrand–Nash–Walras equilibrium* as a system of non-negative admissible prices $\hat{p}$ and an allocation $(\hat{x}_i^W, \hat{x}_{Li}; \hat{x}_{i'}^C; \hat{q}_j, a_{kj}\hat{q}_j, l_j\hat{q}_j)$ such that:

1 For every worker i, the vector $(\hat{x}_i^W, \hat{x}_{Li})$ maximises utility under the budget set $B_i^W = \{(x_i^W, x_{Li}) \in X_i^W \mid px_i^W \leq \bar{x}_{Li} - x_{Li}\}$.
2 For every capitalist i', the vector $\hat{x}_{i'}^C$ maximises utility under the budget set $B_{i'}^C = \{x_{i'}^C \in X_{i'}^C \mid p\hat{x}_{i'}^C \leq \Sigma_j \theta_{i'j}\Pi_j\}$.

3 $\hat{q} = q(\hat{p})$ verifies the market-clearing conditions (24) and (25).

4 $\hat{p}$ is a Nash equilibrium of the price-setting game between monopolistic firms defined by the condition:

$$\hat{\Pi}_j(\hat{p}_j, \hat{p}_{-j}, 1, q_j(\hat{p}_j, \hat{p}_{-j}))q_j(\hat{p}_j, \hat{p}_{-j}) \geq \tilde{\Pi}_j(p_j, \hat{p}_{-j}, 1, q_j(p_j, \hat{p}_{-j}))q_j(p_j, \hat{p}_{-j}) \qquad (26)$$

where $\hat{\Pi}_j$ is the unit profit of firm *j* when its price is set optimally given the price choice $\hat{p}_{-j}$ of the other producers.

5 $a_{kj}\hat{q}_j$ and $l_j\hat{q}_j$ are the optimal intermediate and labour inputs of firm *j*.

Many of the comments previously made with respect to the Cournot–Nash–Walras approach could be repeated here with little if any change. This applies in particular to the remarks concerning profit maximisation as the objective of the firm, the quasi-concavity of the profit function and the implications of the choice of *numéraire*. It is therefore convenient to fix the attention on aspects that are peculiar to the price-setting approach and to the attempts to generalise Nikaido's model.

As mentioned, the existence of a Nash equilibrium for the price-setting game requires not only the quasi-concavity of the pay-off function, but also an appropriate behaviour of the profit function for large values of p, since the space of strategies is now unbounded. In Nikaido's context, where there is only one primary input the price of which is set equal to 1, it is sufficient to assume that the supply of labour tends to zero as the price of labour in terms of commodities goes to zero as well. The market-clearing vector of outputs solving the conditions (24) and (25) would in consequence also tend to zero, thus establishing the required boundary behaviour of the profit functions. In Stahn's (1996) model, in which a more general technology than Nikaido's Leontief input–output matrix is envisaged, it becomes necessary to formulate the explicit assumption that as the price of any output progressively increases a point is reached at which profits begin to fall.

Little attention has been devoted to the study of the properties of the general equilibrium direct demand functions $q(p)$, as opposed to the analysis of the properties of the inverse demand functions $p(y)$ and of the problems of price selection that derive from the presence of two or more folds in the graph of the price correspondence. Strong assumptions have been made to ensure that the demand correspondence is actually a uni-valued function, so that the questions posed by the need to consider a quantity selection from the demand correspondence have been substantially ignored. Nikaido assumes that capitalists' aggregate demands are differentiable and non-decreasing with respect to each of the sectoral profits. Analogous assumptions are formulated by Stahn in the context of a generalised model, to be briefly examined below. In substance the problems for the existence of a Bertrand–Nash–Walras equilibrium arising out of the possible multiplicity of solutions of the market-clearing demand correspondence $q(p)$ have not been adequately analysed. Hart (1985: 121–2) remarks that there is an asymmetry between the quantity-setting model and the price-setting model, in the sense that the multi-valuedness of the price correspondence would not occur with the demand correspondence. On this basis he argues in favour of the price-setting as opposed to the quantity-setting approach. His claim does not seem, however,

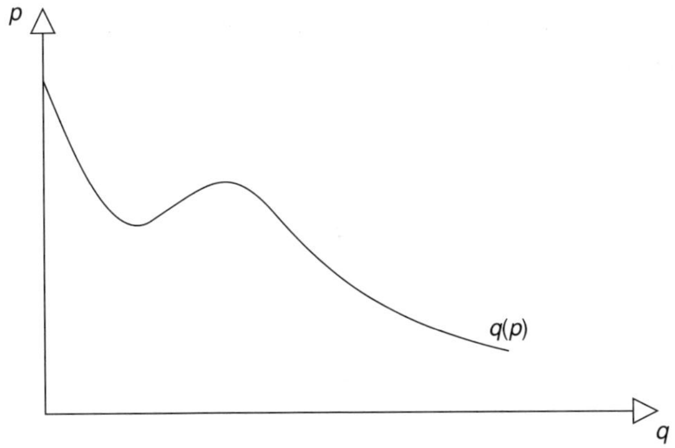

Figure 14.5 The demand correspondence.

to be of general validity or to carry over to models that take full account of the feedback effect of price decisions on market-clearing quantities of output through their impact on consumers' wealth. In conclusion, the need of a quantity selection in order to determine the profits of the firms cannot be avoided in general, as Figure 14.5, which shows a double fold in the demand correspondence $q(p)$, suggests.

Nikaido's neat results are based, as we have remarked, on very stringent assumptions, particularly that of a Leontief production technology. In fact, this assumption makes it possible to easily solve, by matrix inversion, the feedback problem arising out of the presence of intermediate goods. No conceptual difficulty is met in order to remove this specific limitation. Assume that the technology requires the use of labour and intermediate inputs, but is not of a Leontief type. Labour and intermediate inputs would have then to be defined as conditional factor demands and would depend, therefore, on output levels and the given commodity prices, while maintaining the price of labour equal to 1. Existence of a solution to equations (24) and (25), modified as just indicated, would now require the assumption that the conditional demand of inputs of the firm j increases with its level of output; the linear technology clearly fulfils this requirement.

It has been observed that there would be a further and more basic analytical asymmetry between quantity-setting and price-setting equilibria, so that the two concepts could not be considered dual of each other. Let us look again at the two-stage sequential process consisting of a strategic decision first and a market-clearing moment subsequently. In the Bertrand–Nash–Walras approach, given the first-stage price choice of strategic agents, second-stage quantities to clear the markets (together with perfectly competitive prices) are determined. These quantities need not coincide, however, with the optimal choices of strategic agents, 'meaning either that some rationing must occur or else that the voluntary exchange principle is violated' (d'Aspremont *et al.* 1999). This circumstance would motivate a different approach to the second stage of the process in terms of a fixprice non-Walrasian equilibrium (Benassy 1988), so that the market outcome may emerge compatible with the arbitrarily given prices of the produced commodities.

The claim that the general equilibrium notions of Cournotian and Bertrandian derivation are not dual to each other is correct, but the construction of the price-setting model in dual terms to the quantity-setting one need not compel us to abandon Nikaido's Walrasian market-clearing approach to the second stage of the procedure.

The thought experiments carried out in the two sequential games are not exactly opposite to each other. In the Cournotian case, the question that strategic agents ask is: given arbitrary quantity decisions, at what prices would these levels of output be absorbed by the market? Obviously there could be none, so that the question is reformulated as: given arbitrary consumption-feasible quantity decisions, at what prices would they be absorbed by the market? In the Bertrandian case, the question that strategic agents ask is now: given arbitrary price decisions, what levels of output are compatible with consumers' demand for final outputs and market-clearing prices for perfectly competitive inputs? Clearly there may be none that is profitable. If one insists, therefore, on taking prices arbitrarily in the whole price domain, the Walrasian market-clearing approach may indeed give rise to a contradictory situation and the price-setting model would have to be formulated differently from the quantity-setting one. If, on the contrary, the arbitrarily given prices are *a priori* constrained to the subset P' of prices compatible with non-negative profits, as we have done above, the construction of the price-setting approach becomes truly dual to that of the quantity-setting model.

Though in somewhat different ways, Benassy (1988) and Stahn (1996) follow the fixprice non-Walrasian approach to the study of monopolistic general equilibrium with price-setting agents and thus abandon the assumption that monopolistic firms serve whatever demand is addressed to them by the market at given prices.

Benassy constructs a model that takes account of all spill-over effects of quantity rationing (Benassy 1982) and claims two advantages for this approach: the existence of equilibrium for all strictly positive prices and all individually non-manipulable rationing schemes; the global uniqueness of the fixprice equilibrium under the assumption that changes in quantity constraints spill over on to the other markets by less than 100 per cent in value terms (Schulz 1983).[16] This assumption is not sufficient, however, to guarantee the uniqueness of equilibrium in a production economy, since the feedback effects originating in the distribution of profits are left out of account (Stahn 1993).

If uniqueness of the demand functions cannot be established, the Bertrand–Nash fixprice equilibrium faces the same sort of problems as the more traditional Bertrand–Nash–Walras approach. Moreover, the argument that in the fixprice approach the general equilibrium demand functions exist on the whole domain of strictly positive prices rather than just in the subset meeting the requirement that profits are non-negative does not seem to be so cogent as to justify the

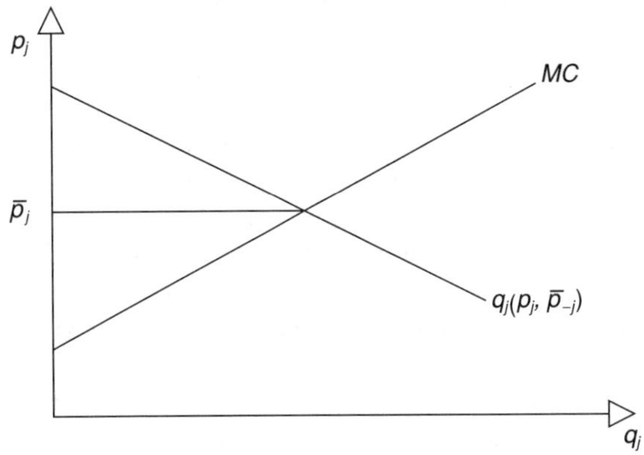

Figure 14.6 Rationing at prices $p_j > \bar{p}_j$.

choice of the quantity rationing approach, since in any case equilibrium could not occur if this condition were not fulfilled.

An idea somewhere in between Nikaido's and Benassy's approaches has been explored by Stahn. He observes that it makes sense for a monopolistic firm to serve the market demand only if such a strategy is more profitable than that resulting from adopting price-taking behaviour. The situation is illustrated in Figure 14.6, where the marginal cost function coincides with the perfectly competitive supply function. It is apparent that, given $p_{-j} = \bar{p}_{-j}$, firm j finds it profitable to satisfy market demand only if $p_j \geq \bar{p}_j$. Rationing is, on the contrary, convenient if $p_j < \bar{p}_j$. The consequences of the rationing of consumers can either be carried to the extreme position taken by the fixprice approach, in which spill-over effects are fully taken into account, or stopped at the very first stage of the process, as Stahn supposes. In this latter case, spill-over effects are disregarded and the assumption is made that it is common knowledge that when $p_j < \bar{p}_j$ every firm j will produce a level of output corresponding to its Walrasian supply. This type of assumption leads to a reformulation of the above equation system (4); as indicated by Figure 14.6, continuity of the relation describing the quantity of output put on the market as a function of its price is preserved, but differentiability is lost. An extension of the implicit function theorem to continuous Lipschitzian functions, in addition to specific assumptions about the demand behaviour of agents,[17] is then required to establish the existence of the general equilibrium demand functions $q(p)$ and to prove that monopolistic equilibrium can occur only when consumers are not rationed.

Marschak and Selten's (1974) subsidies model and Hart's (1985) islands model move in the opposite direction with respect to Nikaido's, Benassy's and Stahn's efforts to take full account of the feedback effects operating through the distribution of profits and represent 'a retreat from "true" equilibrium' (Marschak and Selten 1974: 65). In these models the idea of considering the general equilibrium effect of each firm's price and quantity decisions on all other firms' demand is completely abandoned.

Marschak and Selten consider an institutional arrangement in which profits are taxed away by the government and paid out to consumers. The link between the profit income distributed to consumers (dividends in Marschak and Selten's terminology) and the amount of profits realised by the firms is thus severed. The authors show that under appropriate conditions an equilibrium exists for any pre-selected vector of percentage shares in the total subsidy payment.

In the framework of substantially the same basic approach, Hart's major aim is to offer a justification for the assumption that each firm takes the distribution of wealth as given. He resorts to the Phelps–Lucas model of an economy made up of different islands. While consuming only the commodities produced on their island (only money is traded between islands), consumers are supposed to have initial shareholdings in firms operating in all the different islands, so that demand in each island actually depends on the profits realised in all other islands. But if there is a large number of consumers in each island and the number of islands is equally large, a change in profits of any firm j in island t affects only the subset of consumers holding shares in that type of firm on that island. As a consequence changes in the profits of that type of firm will have only a negligible effect on the market demand of firms producing in any given island.

Though intellectually appealing, both constructions appear to be quite artificial and have a strong partial equilibrium flavour, as their authors openly recognise.

Let us finally consider a 'third' way, elaborated in several papers by d'Aspremont *et al.* (1991, 1997, 1999), that draws inspiration from those theories that view the whole economy as a 'market game', where all agents behave strategically and send both quantity and price signals to the markets. D'Aspremont *et al.* move from the observation that quantity decisions of Cournot oligopolists (monopolists in our general equilibrium approach) are coordinated by the inverse market demand function, which determines the price at which the total output produced by the different firms (the quantity produced by each monopolist) is absorbed by the market. The inverse demand function can, therefore, be looked at as a *pricing scheme*, or a *price outcome function* in the language of strategic market games, i.e. as a particular rule that associates with the quantity signals sent by the agents a market price.[18] Other pricing schemes, that depart from the inverse demand function, may, however, be conceived of. They may be assimilated to so-called 'facilitating practices' (Salop 1985), namely to more or less explicit customs established in some trades to allow price coordination. In the model proposed by d'Aspremont *et al.* strategic agents send both quantity and price signals. Their price signals are coordinated by a pricing scheme that replaces the inverse demand function of Cournot's approach. According to the degree of unilateral manipulability attributed to the pricing scheme different equilibria, indicated as P equilibria, are obtained. D'Aspremont and collegues have so far developed the theory of P equilibria mainly in the direction of exploring the connections with other forms of market coordination. Actually the principle interest of P equilibria could lie in the possibility of analysing pricing schemes capable of capturing important features of the industrial organisation of the economy, particularly situations of restricted differentiated oligopoly.

Conclusion

An impressive research effort has been devoted to the study of the theory of monopolistic general equilibrium. The seminal papers of Negishi and Gabszewicz–Vial have paved the way to many contributions that have sharpened the analytical results and extended them to more general cases, shown the nature of problems intrinsic to the model of imperfect competition and investigated possible avenues of solution. An overall evaluation is clearly far from easy. If success is measured by the capacity to explore new issues, to stimulate awareness of new questions and to identify more exacting conditions for the existence of equilibrium solutions, then monopolistic general equilibrium can rank high on such a scale. If, on the contrary, success is determined by the ability to produce existence theorems of very general validity, then monopolistic general equilibrium models achieve a lower score.

Caught between the risk of *ad hoc* conjectures, on one side, and unrealistic abstraction as to the degree of rationality of agents, on the other, research has moved along two lines that run parallel to each other both in the quantity-setting and in the price-setting approach to monopolistic general equilibrium theory. They have opposite strengths and weaknesses.

The first – called here the objective approach, for short – is based on the abstract presumption that agents share a common view of how markets react to their own decisions and consequently act thereupon. To this line of research belong the models that make use of the notion of general equilibrium (direct or inverse) demand and develop the concepts of Cournot–Nash–Walras and Bertrand–Nash–Walras equilibrium.

The second line of research – named the conjectural approach, for short – is sceptical of the capacity of agents to solve the infinite regress problem implicit in the determination of general equilibrium demand functions and takes the more realistic view that agents proceed on the basis of subjective elements and that markets are characterised by an unclearly specified mixture of tentative co-ordination, trial and error, and temporary disequilibrium. This approach can be found in the subjective inverse (or direct) demand *à la* Negishi, in the disregard of feedback effects *à la* Marschak–Selten and Hart, and in the assumption *à la* Laffont–Laroque (1976) and Hart (1982) that strategic agents behave competitively in the markets where their power is negligible.

The first strand of analysis, with its rigorous and abstract nature, offers the basis of a direct and telling comparison with the perfectly competitive model of resource allocation and thus plays an unreplaceable role in the study of the functioning of the price mechanism. Profit maximisation comes to be challenged as the right objective of the firm; new strong assumptions are required to prove the existence of equilibrium: first, the uniqueness of the price correspondence, in the quantity-setting model, and of the demand correspondence, in the price-setting approach; and, second, the quasi-concavity of the firm's profit function in the relevant strategic variable. The need for these two additional assumptions arises out of the consideration that market clearing is but one stage of the process that describes monopolistic general equilibrium, the other being the stage concerning strategic decisions, and that the dependence of the demand function of the firm on its own price destroys the neat properties of the supply correspondence of competitive producers, when increasing returns to scale are supposed to be absent. It turns out, furthermore, that the choice of normalisation rule may not only influence the equilibrium allocation, but also cause its non-existence. As a consequence, some of the positive achievements of the objective approach to the theory of monopolistic general equilibrium are not robust to the change of assumptions, while some of the negative results have succeeded in producing valuable new insights.

The objective approach has, in particular, the merit of having revealed that most of the problems that are met at the general equilibrium level occur also, in much the same form and with the same consequences, at a partial equilibrium level of analysis, where they had previously been ignored. So it is at the simplest level of elaboration that the fundamental issues of the theory of imperfect competition manifest themselves: from the hypothesis of profit maximisation to that of the existence of optimal strategies in conditions of sufficient generality. It is likely that further research will succeed in producing convincing solutions to some of these problems, but it is hard to imagine that the present difficulties may be fully resolved. The core message of the analysis is that some of the problems that preclude the possibility of establishing existence results of the same degree of generality as under perfect competition are to be considered inherent in the situation of direct interaction between firms not mediated by the market, i.e. by prices. If account is taken of this situation, the possible non-existence of equilibrium under very general conditions ought to appear less surprising than one may at first sight imagine and free from any pathological connotation.

This carries a number of implications. It means that perfect competition, though it is certainly an irreplaceable benchmark, must be viewed as a unique case. It means that theorems designed to demonstrate the existence of perfectly competitive outcomes as the limit of monopolistic competition given a sufficient number of replicas, while surely valid on the analytical plane, could result in a leap in logic when it is asserted that strategic interaction becomes negligible in the limit. It suggests that the study of monopolistic competition may derive advantage from the use of more refined instruments of game theory, capable of modelling repeated games with incomplete information instead of once-only situations, and from considering the possibility of outcomes that are not necessarily competitive but could also be collusive.

The second line of research is hardly satisfactory from the point of view of the analytical rigour, the motivation of the simplifying assumptions adopted, the description of the process of strategic interdependence among agents and of the interaction among agents and markets. And yet the exploration of specific assumptions – for instance, demand conjectures leading to the definition of locally consistent Negishi equilibria and pricing schemes as tentative coordination devices much less demanding, in terms of information and computation capacity, than a full general equilibrium demand function – has produced interesting results. Progress on this line of research would seem to depend on the ability to produce simple assumptions capable of capturing ever more significant features of the actual decision-making process in the framework of strategic interdependence.

As stated at the beginning of this tentative summing up, it is hard to take sides between the rigour of the objective approach and the potential relevance of the conjectural one; even harder to strike the right balance between them. I think that Giovanni Caravale might have sided with relevance, but I am not sure of it. It is a great pity he is no longer with us to further the argument.

Notes

1 See Victoria Chick's Chapter 12 in this volume for a sympathetic discussion of Caravale's notion of equilibrium.

2 In a recent contribution to an evaluation of how the theory of prices and resource allocation may evolve in the next ten years Malinvaud (1999) seems to share Caravale's concern. He argues that the theory is now facing the obligation to pay increasing attention to its operational purposes, in the sense that theoreticians are forced to come closer to practitioners and better understand their need to explain, predict and decide. This may lead to abandoning the more general assumptions of the theory in favour of more particular properties suggested by empirical evidence, in order to establish specific propositions. He states, by way of conclusion, in a vein close to Caravale's frame of thought, that 'aiming at relevance is an important aspect of scientific rigour' (Malinvaud 1999: 29).

3 The terms 'monopolistic' and 'imperfect' competition will be used interchangeably in the course of this chapter and will generically refer to market regimes different from perfect competition. For simplicity, the reference model taken into consideration is one that assumes that every output is produced by a monopolist, while all inputs are traded in perfectly competitive markets.

4 Arrow (1971) offers a comprehensive and illuminating analysis of the theory of the firm in general equilibrium.

5 Two analytical formulations have been actually proposed. Grodal (1996) suggests formulating the utility-maximising criterion in the sense that the firm should choose a production plan such that the utility of the owner, when he trades at the market-clearing price, is maximised. In different words, following Nikaido's idea (see below), Grodal sharply distinguishes the behaviour of the owner of the firm in his double role of being at the same time a producer and a consumer: price setting as producer, while price taking as consumer. This means, in analytical terms, that the firm should choose a production plan that maximises the indirect utility function of the owner. Codognato and Gabszewicz (1991) and Gabszewicz and Michel (1997), on the contrary, consider the question of utility maximisation as a matter of deciding not only the production plan of the firm, but also the quantity of its output to be delivered directly to the owner for his own consumption. In this approach, the owner's direct consumption does not pass through the market. The two models clearly lead to different equilibria, so that, even in this apparently uncontroversial case as to the criterion to be adopted, there is room for ambiguity. Grodal aptly observes that in this second approach the firm, and thereby the owner, knowing the price that clears the market as a function of the quantity of output sold, may have a further choice of strategic behaviour connected with the possible non-existence of a continuous price selection. It appears, however, that the notion that the owner may prefer a low price of the product to high profits is better captured by the idea that part of the output of the firm is directly delivered to its owner.

6 Dierker and Grodal (1998, 1999) have suggested a solution to the problem of aggregation of shareholders' preferences in the sense that firms should maximise the aggregate real wealth of their shareholders. The proposed criterion suffers, however, from a severe limitation in as much as it does not generalise to the case of simultaneous

ownership in several firms. We will return to this question subsequently when the issue of the normalisation rule is discussed.

7 In contrast with Lange's position, Benassy (1976, 1988) has adopted a disequilibrium approach, which will be considered at p. 226, when the models that take prices as the strategic variables of the firms are examined.

8 The terms 'general equilibrium demand function' and 'objective demand function' will be used with the same meaning, though our preference is for the first, which has the advantage of clearly referring to its analytical derivation. The literature, however, almost exclusively uses the second.

9 A rigorous construction of the general equilibrium inverse demand functions is presented in the next section.

10 The analytical formulation (5) of the subjective demand is taken from Hart's (1985) presentation of the model. Actually, Negishi (1961, 1989) adopts a partial equilibrium approach in as much as the *status quo* is expressed only in terms of firm j's price and quantity demanded.

11 Definition (9) of profits is preferable in this context to the definition (1) that was used in the previous section to show the dependence of the general equilibrium inverse demand on the quantities produced by all firms.

12 The point is noted by Grodal (1996).

13 See again Arrow (1971: 87–9) and Arrow and Hahn (1971: 155–6).

14 To give a hint of a proof, let $Q = \{q \in R^J_+ | lq = \bar{x}_L - x_L(p, 1), p \in P'\}$; the set Q is a simplex in R^J which performs in the present context the same role as the price unit simplex Δ, defined above, in the standard proofs of the existence of a perfectly competitive equilibrium. The left-hand side of (25) defines a mapping $\varphi : Q \rightarrow Q$. If we assume, as is customarily done, that workers' demand and capitalists' demand are continuous (or upper semi-continuous correspondences) in their arguments, φ is a continuous function (or an upper semi-continuous correspondence) that satisfies the conditions for the existence of a fixed point.

15 The assumption of product differentiation and of a single producer in each market is essential to avoid the discontinuity of the demand function of the individual firm, typical of Bertrand's homogenous oligopoly model.

16 This requirement is akin to Nikaido's condition, formulated in the context of a model with saving and investment, that the capitalists' marginal propensity to consume is less than 1 (Nikaido 1975: 47).

17 These assumptions are that all produced commodities are non-inferior in consumption and that demand for non-produced commodities is strictly increasing in wealth.

18 Analytically, a pricing scheme is a function P_j that associates to the individual price signals ψ_j a market price $p_j = P_j(\psi_1, \ldots, \psi_J)$. A substantial difference needs to be remarked between the inverse demand of equation (2) and a generic pricing scheme: while the market price depends on quantity signals in the inverse demand approach, it depends instead on firms' price signals in d'Aspremont *et al.*'s approach.

15 Non-competitive general equilibrium in a dynamic perspective

Pier Carlo Nicola

A constant feature of Caravale's scientific work was the continuous and critical discussion of the various equilibrium notions and his dissatisfaction with (all) the existing ones. A good testimony of Caravale's position is the paper (1997b) he contributed to the volume he himself edited (1997a) and for which he chose the meaningful title *Equilibrium and Economic Theory*.

Competitive general equilibrium *à la* Walras, as formalised by modern writers such as Arrow, Debreu and McKenzie, seems to be, for good or for ill, the universal paradigm which every economic theory, static or dynamic, must confront. It is actually admitted that it is a pity for the Walrasian theory to have to rely so heavily on a tacit assumption, namely the existence of an auctioneer whose only task is to compute centrally a vector of equilibrium prices.

An equilibrium price vector, it is generally agreed, is a price vector such that all markets simultaneously clear; hence all individual optimal decisions can be fully implemented. In a competitive general equilibrium state every agent is thus satisfied, so that no economic force is working to change the equilibrium state.

But such a paradigm is far from offering a realistic description of how actual economic systems operate. Real-world economies abundantly show that in many branches of activity perfect competition does not prevail and, more important, there is no universal auctioneer (maybe she/he could be the model builder!) to steer prices towards an equilibrium state.

Modern real economies never seem to operate at an equilibrium position, but at best are converging to such a state (if some strong stability conditions are introduced). This implies that, in a more or less satisfactory way, consumers and firms are well aware that their preferred actions may not be realisable if actual prices diverge from equilibrium prices, and that in consequence not all individual decisions can be fully implemented at present: some must be deferred to a later date. All this implies that money, or some other monetary tool, must be present in the economy to help agents to transfer purchasing power across dates.

Why should an economy not be in a permanent equilibrium? The immediate and obvious answer is: because its fundamentals (i.e. consumers' preferences and endowments, firms' technologies, and also subjective beliefs when there are some missing markets) change continuously and in unpredictable ways; but even if one assumes stationarity in all fundamentals, the absence of an auctioneer is enough to explain the persistence of out-of-equilibrium states. Indeed, due to this absence, individual agents must find by trial and error what prices they can charge, generally under the knowledge of only a small part of the economy in which they live.

Long ago Cournot (1838) developed his oligopoly models, where firms directly choose their quantities (or prices) and progressively adjust them so that their decisions may become mutually compatible; hence, maybe without being fully aware of it, he presented models in which equilibrium is reached without the need of an auctioneer and in which dynamics is a crucial aspect of the theory. He was able to define firms' subjective reaction functions, a notion which is essential in order to understand why a full equilibrium state can be reached in general only in calendar time (of course when some stability conditions are verified). The crux of Cournot's models is that they are only partial equilibrium models, since demand functions are not derived inside his models by individual behaviours and no explanation is given of the destination of firms' profits.

A model able to overcome these shortcomings is the monopolistic competition system proposed by Negishi (1961) and discussed by Tosato in the previous chapter. However, an *ad hoc* assumption had to be introduced by Negishi with reference to the individual subjective functions in order to prove the existence of a general equilibrium. Another non-competitive model, also discussed by Tosato, was proposed by Nikaido (1975), who considered objective demand functions, but in a system in which production is of the simple constant returns single output Leontief type. Both models are at any rate one-period models and, as such, unable to cope with dynamic elements.

Similar shortcomings are to be found in other interesting non-competitive general equilibrium models. At present, all these models seem to build on very specific assumptions, which render them unsuited to offer a basis for a truly non-competitive general (dis-)equilibrium theory. Hart's (1985) critical remarks on these models are still valid, together with the observations contained in the comments on his paper by Gabszewicz (1985) and Sonnenschein (1985).

In my opinion, the major drawback of all this literature on non-competitive general equilibrium theory is the absence of any consideration of the dynamic aspects of the theory. When the assumption is made that agents have market power, the analysis of the process by means of which the equilibrium position is reached is just as important as the determination of the equilibrium itself; and it cannot be viewed in terms of the traditional stability analysis of the equilibrium solution.

An attempt to move a step forward in this direction is contained in the approach called *imperfect general equilibrium*, which I have developed elsewhere (Nicola 1994). One of the aims of the model that I have there analysed is to prove that even outside a general equilibrium state an economy can behave in an orderly way. The essential characteristics of the model, which is truly dynamic, are that current prices and outputs are chosen directly, period after period, by the producing firms under some perceived (hence subjective) demand functions. But since the model is a dynamic one, individual firms can learn (under stationary fundamentals), by adding new market information as time unfolds, their true (objective) demand functions, or at least they can approximate the objective demand functions in some satisfactory manner. Naturally enough, at the current prices quoted by firms very likely there is no general equilibrium (namely no market clearing of Walrasian demands and supplies), but only a general compatibility among transactions, obtained by random rationing directly implemented by the selling firms.

What the numerous computer simulations of the model show is that current prices and quantities can fluctuate in time in very complex ways, mimicking the true behaviour observable in the time series of economic variables, and that different goods can manifest very different time paths, so that any possible aggregation of quantities, such as those adopted to measure GDP and employed in applied work, can be quite misleading if used for economic policy purposes.

16 Technology and employment in an out-of-equilibrium perspective

Mario Amendola

1. There is a strict relation between the definition of technology, the determinants of unemployment and the analytical perspective from which we look at the phenomenon of production, a perspective upon which the above relation essentially depends.

The usual definition of technology in terms of technical coefficients reflects an equilibrium perspective. However, the equilibrium context behind the standard theory is likely to obscure the essential aspects of the phenomenon of production. We are all accustomed to repeat the consideration that, in equilibrium, production is looked at from the vantage point of trade and exchange, without, however, daring to go the whole hog and draw the analytical implications of this consideration.

Let us look at these implications. The first point to be stressed is that, by definition, only in equilibrium can we count on an established relation between the basic magnitudes (output, employment, capital) of the production process. The existence of this established relation, on the other hand, draws the attention to the functioning of a *given* productive capacity – defined in terms of given production coefficients – that brings about a regular behaviour of the economy. In equilibrium, then, the 'utilisation' moment of productive capacity comes into light, while the 'definition' moment of this capacity, that is, the process through which it actually comes about, remains in the background. This process appears in fact as an analytically instantaneous assembling of resources, since once productive capacity is defined in terms of a given combination of inputs we are already dealing with the capacity itself from the analytical viewpoint the very moment the required inputs are available in the right proportions.

Summing up: only in equilibrium can we reasonably define a technique as we usually define it, that is, in terms of given production coefficients. Only in equilibrium, in fact, we can rely on the relations expressed by these coefficients. This, we repeat, depends on the *ex-post* perspective under which we look at production in equilibrium, that is, on the fact that we focus on the result of the functioning of an already established productive capacity. But this also means that the coefficients which we assume to stand for the technique do not define the process of production in general terms, but only do so when the economic condition which characterises an equilibrium state is established. When this is so, each technique has its own productivity level, and the relation between technology and employment becomes one between productivity and employment.

This has an important bearing not only on theory but also on policy. Let us see how, starting from the consideration of the relation between technology and employment within an equilibrium context.

2. The equilibrium hypothesis implies an analysis carried out by means of a comparison of alternative equilibrium states.

Competitive behaviour of markets and flexible prices assure full employment of resources, whatever the prevailing technology, in the equilibrium state associated with the latter. In this context unemployment can only appear as a transitory phenomenon, due to the time needed for the adjustment mechanism set in motion by a change in technology to work out its effects. The idea that time is required for the adjustment that necessarily assures the transition from one to another equilibrium position, defined by intrinsic characteristics of the technology, to take place, is already present in the analysis of economists at the beginning of this century, who look on equilibrium as a state towards which the economy gravitates.

An instantaneous determination of the equilibrium positions associated with the different technological states to be compared, and imperfections in the working of the adjustment mechanisms set in motion by technological advances rather than the time required for these adjustments to take place, are stressed instead in the modern versions of the theory of technical progress, usually sketched out within a comparative dynamics analytical framework.

The characteristics of a change in technology – its being neutral, capital-saving or labour-saving – together with the value of the elasticity of substitution which reflects the conditions prevailing in the market for productive factors, determine the changes in the demand for labour due to 'substitution' between factors, while the changes in productivity and the conditions prevailing in the market for final output determine the changes in the demand for labour triggered by changes in output. Numerous studies and papers have explored the effects on employment of all possible cases of adjustments associated with different values of production coefficients and elasticities. This analysis shows the possibility of incomplete reabsorption of the labour force displaced by a change in technology, mainly owing to the existence of imperfectly competitive conditions in markets and of price rigidities which hinder the full working of adjustment mechanisms.

A vicious circle clearly looks through this analysis. The technical coefficients and elasticities on which it stands are not intrinsic characteristics of technology, as already stressed, but can be defined only in equilibrium, where by definition all adjustments have already been realised. But the analysis itself consists in dealing with alternative adjustment processes, although instantaneous ones, which depend exactly on the above coefficients and elasticities.

3. Unemployment appears no longer as a transient phenomenon, but as a 'natural' state of the economy due to structural factors – in particular stable features of the labour market – in the equilibrium interpretation which has gradually become dominant today.

This leads to the definition of an equilibrium rate of unemployment called the 'natural rate', determined together with the real wage rate on the labour market, whether under competitive or non-competitive conditions. This rate depends on real things: not only the traditional 'fundamentals' (technology and preferences) but also on other structural factors like the institutions and, above all, the factors affecting wage bargaining. Different interpretations – focusing on job search, hiring and quitting rates, shirking, efficiency wages, and the like – have pointed to various factors, concerning mainly the quality and the motivation of the work force, which in the different models determine the shape and position in the quadrant of the supply/demand curves that determine the equilibrium conditions of the labour market and hence the equilibrium rate of unemployment itself. This rate is invariant not only to monetary disturbances (which can only bring about mounting inflation) but to all sort of changes in demand, whether real or nominal, and in some cases, due to particular *ad hoc* assumptions, even to technical progress.

The comparative analysis of equilibrium positions and of the associated levels of unemployment made possible by the above analytical framework fully confirms the structural interpretation of unemployment and the associated policy requirements. In particular, the accent is put on the inertia of real wages in adjusting to shocks affecting the supply or the demand of labour. The belief that perfect wage flexibility would assure the quick reabsorption of those unemployed owing to these shocks – a belief that comes from postulating the existence of an inverse relation between employment and the real wage rate – suggests policy interventions in the labour market aimed at modifying wage-fixing institutions so as to remove the obstacles to this flexibility.

Curiously enough, the conclusions reached by the economists following an evolutionary analytical approach – the main antagonist of the standard approach – come surprisingly close to the conclusions of standard theory as regards the focus on structural factors. In this case it is technology and its specific character, rather than the particular features of the labour market, that determine unemployment levels. Learning, a structural adjustment aimed at rendering the labour force consistent with the particular requirements of technology, appears then as the way out of unemployment, which mainly arises from the skill mismatches brought about by changes in technology. The requirements of technology, on the other hand, reflect features of the latter which are independent of the process through which this is established in the economy. The economy is again required to adjust to benchmarks which can be defined only on the assumption that it has already adjusted to them. The economic process through which the economy has to go in order to transform a target into an actual state recedes into the background as it is once again looked at as a predetermined trajectory rather than as a thorough process itself determining its point of arrival.

4. There is a fact that we should keep in mind when considering the problem of the relation between technology and employment, a fact that standard theory does not, and cannot, take into account. The fact that the immediate result of whatever shock, and in particular of a technological shock, is to throw the economy out of equilibrium, that is, to disrupt the working of the productive capacity which brings about the regular behaviour that defines an equilibrium state. In other words a technological shock, whether a change in the technique or a technological advance, implies a structural modification.

To see this point more clearly it is convenient to think of a production process in Austrian or, better, in neo-Austrian terms; that is, to portray it as a fully vertically integrated process taking place through a sequence of periods which make up a phase of construction and, following it, a phase of utilisation of productive capacity. In such a process production costs are reckoned in terms of requirements of the only primary input contemplated, that is, in terms of labour. In this context an equilibrium structure of productive capacity is represented by an array of production processes in the (different periods of the) phase of construction and of the phase of utilisation which are consistent with each other, in the sense of supporting a steady state of the economy. This age structure of productive capacity implies not only a *horizontal* dimension, the number and age structure of production processes at each given moment of time, but also a *vertical* dimension, the time pattern of production consistent with the former. Then, together with construction and utilisation, also the economic activities behind these phases, investment and consumption and the supply of and demand for final output, are consistent with each other, at each moment of time and over time. The complementarity over time of the production process (that is, the complementarity between construction and utilisation) implies the coordination over time of the decision (and allocation) process. When this is so, as already stressed, we can focus on the utilisation moment of productive capacity, the time dimension of production recedes in the background, and production itself can be looked at as a synchronous process.

Consider now an economy in the equilibrium state associated with a given technique. This state is supported by a productive capacity characterised by a given equilibrium structure as just defined, and, given the labour requirements of the latter, by a given level of employment.

A technological shock, whether a change in the technique or a technological advance, implies a change in the balance of production processes, that is, a distortion of the structure of productive capacity with respect to its previous equilibrium configuration. There is then a break in the intertemporal complementarity of the production process which brings back to light its time dimension. The appearance of complementarity problems in the production process, on the other hand, also implies the appearance of problems of coordination over time of the economic activity. As we have just seen, when construction and utilisation are no longer consistent over time, the same is true of investment and consumption and of supply and demand.

The sequential articulation of the production process, in the neo-Austrian representation, makes possible the appearance at the analytical level of the problems of intertemporal complementarity which result from the breaking of an equilibrium state. For the associated coordination problems to emerge at the analytical level as well we must count on a sequential articulation not only of the production process but also of the decision process. This can be obtained by considering a sequence of decision periods and letting all decisions concerning quantities and prices change only at the junction of one period with the next, not within each given period. This implies a lag in response which makes the market disequilibria which we have seen to originate in the production side come to the surface rather than be immediately reabsorbed, as would be the case if we assumed instantaneous responses.

Reaction to these disequilibria, if we assume adaptive behaviour on the part of economic agents, and the adjustments of productive capacity aimed at re-establishing the consistency over time of construction and utilisation disturbed by the original shock, stir an out-of-equilibrium process that propagates the initial distortion over time without needing any further shock. What happens to the economy then must be looked at as a process sketched out step by step by sequentially interacting disequilibria which engender a complex dynamics, rather than as a series of snapshots each reflecting a different equilibrium state of the economy. The backbone of this process is the accumulation through which adjustments to new technologies, which necessarily imply a restructuring of productive capacity, take place in time.

To re-establish the consistency over time between the construction of productive capacity and its utilisation, and hence the coordination over time of investment and consumption, and of supply and final demand, depend on establishing the right complementarity relation between productive resources (resulting from saving behaviour, monetary policy, learning processes . . .) and the adequate working of the coordination mechanisms involved, in particular price and wage changes that determine the extent to which productive resources are devoted either to the construction or to the utilisation of productive capacity.

5. In this different perspective unemployment appears as a disequilibrium phenomenon owing to the breaking of the complementarity relation between productive resources following a structural shock which affects the economy. Unemployment will then be the result of the distortions in the structure of productive capacity resulting from this shock, and its reabsorption will no longer appear as a problem of matching the existing supply of and demand for labour but rather as that of creating jobs through the process of accumulation required to re-establish the consistency of the structure of productive capacity of which labour is an essential element.

In this context real wages and employment both become endogenous variables; and, out of equilibrium, there is sequential rather than simultaneous determination of prices and quantities. The sequential order of events, which is completely absent from standard comparative analysis, acquires a crucial role. Thus, for example, falling wages, the standard treatment for taking care of unemployment, may result in further distortions of productive capacity rather than in re-establishing coordination and hence reabsorbing unemployment.

More generally, the impact of changes in technology on employment cannot be reduced to technological factors, whose characteristics and effects, we have seen, cannot themselves be verified out of equilibrium, but reflects rather the complexity of the interaction of decisions (as to current production, investment, prices, wages, etc.) and existing constraints which determines the evolution of the economy in a sequential process.

This implies in the first place that, whatever the character of the change in technology under consideration, the resulting distortion of productive capacity always implies the appearance of temporary unemployment (the well known Ricardo's 'machinery effect'). The latter is the result of dissociation between investment at cost and investment of capacity: which, in the words of Hicks, emblematically describes the breaking of the synchronic character of the production process out of equilibrium. In particular, the increase in construction costs implied by the introduction of a new technology – if it is not fully matched by a corresponding increase in available financial resources, and even then if this comes with a delay or if there is some constraint on complementary productive resources (e.g. on labour supply) – will necessarily bring about a fall in the gross product when a smaller productive capacity (with respect to the previous equilibrium state of the economy) reaches the phase of utilisation. This implies a fall in employment which can be a temporary phenomenon if the economy behaves in such a way as to overcome the coordination problems encountered on the way and to reach a new steady state associated with a productive capacity fully shaped according to the new technology. But it may be – and such is usually the case – that the sequence of disequilibria stimulated by a change in technology leads the economy to a state where unemployment and lower productivity become permanent features (see Figure 16.1).

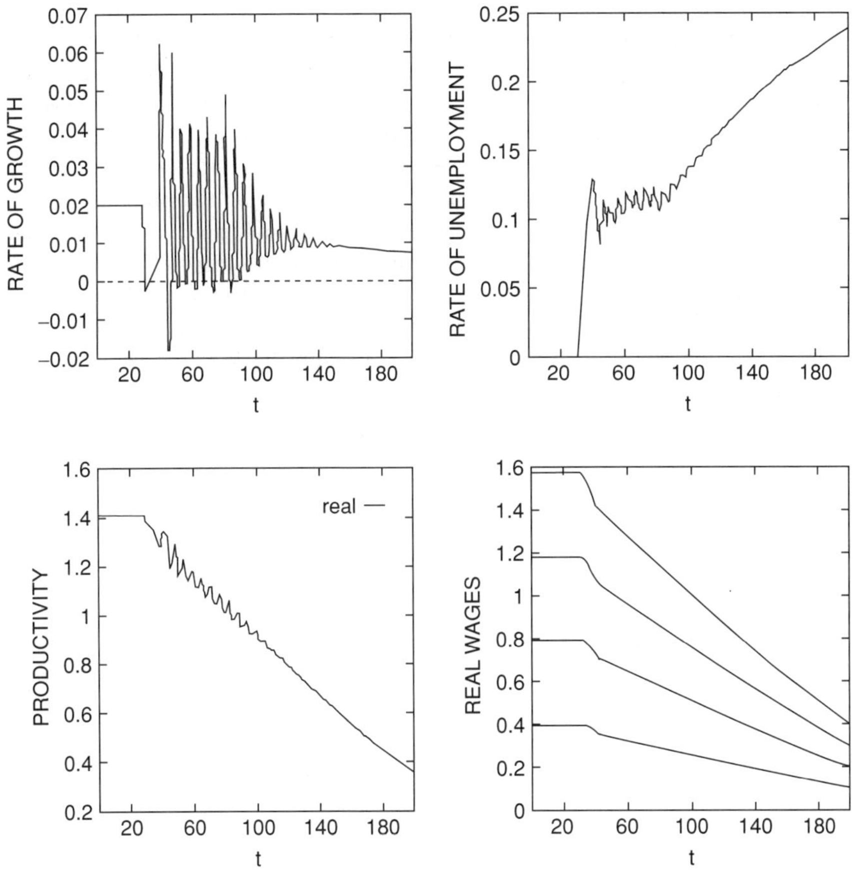

Figure 16.1 What happens to the rate of growth, the rate of unemployment, productivity and real wages (four different types of labour are taken into consideration) along the out-of-equilibrium path followed by the economy as the result of a shock represented by the adoption of a technology whose greater initial cost is more than compensated for by the reduction in costs during the utilisation phase. The different evolution paths have been obtained by means of simulations using a sequential model whose main features are mentioned in section 4 above and which is presented and analysed in Amendola and Gaffard (1998).

This proves not only a dissociation from technology, as usually interpreted, and employment, but also the productivity paradox – looked at as the result of a divorce between the productivity of any given technology, as it can be verified only in the equilibrium state of an economy whose productive capacity is already fully shaped by that technology, and the effective productivity of the economy as determined by what actually takes place during the out-of-equilibrium process stimulated by a technological change. (In the case portrayed in Figure 16.1 the adoption of a technique defined as more productive actually results in a fall in productivity.)

Productivity and employment, rather than the expression of specific technical conditions, appear then as the outcome of the way in which the economy is able to deal with the problems of complementarity and coordination over time which appear as a result of structural shocks, and which shape the evolution of the economy itself. More specifically, they are the outcome of a process of transformation of the productive structure which involves the functioning of the whole economy, and of the ability to organise and carry out this process.

If the heart of the matter is this process of accumulation, technology, as well as institutional aspects (and more generally, the 'fundamentals' of dominant theory), has little to do with employment. Whatever the prevailing technology we can carry out a process of accumulation of capital which assures full employment, provided that the growth of complementary resources keeps pace and the adjusting mechanisms make this possible. The economic process, and how to manage it, not the supposed fundamentals, must be brought back to the centre of the stage.

17 Strategic complementarity and near-rationality in New Keynesian models

A note

Andrea Boitani

A common structural feature of New Keynesian models is the presence of positive externalities among (at least some) economic agents (Drazen 1987) and the presence of strategic complementarity, i.e. 'the interaction between agents at the level of strategies' (Cooper and John 1988). With strategic complementarity and positive externalities, economic agents would prefer high activity (and employment) levels to low activity (and employment) levels. However, either the preferred situation cannot be achieved as a Nash equilibrium – hence there is a *cooperation failure* – or this situation is one in a range of multiple Nash equilibria. If the Pareto dominant equilibrium in the range is not attained there is a *coordination failure*.[1]

Real and nominal rigidity models are often associated with cooperation failures, mirrored in macroeconomic or aggregate demand externalities and money non-neutralities (Mankiw 1985; Akerlof and Yellen 1985a, b; Blanchard and Kiyotaki 1987; Dixon 1990) whilst strategic complementarity – at least since Cooper and John (1988) – is associated with coordination failure models, which are entirely real and hence do not allow for money non-neutralities (Romer 1996: chapter 6.14). The aim of this chapter is to suggest that the basic analytical 'ingredients' are shared by both approaches, although the role played by any single 'ingredient' may differ according to the purpose of the model employed.

It is by now well known that non-responder behaviour on the part of even a small number of near-rational firms may cause nominal frictions and hence may be at the origin of real effects of nominal shocks (Akerlof and Yellen 1985a, b). In a sequence of papers Haltiwanger and Waldman (1985, 1989, 1991) examined the relations between near-rationality and strategic complementarity, showing that strategic complementarity causes near-rational agents to be disproportionately important for macroeconomic outcomes, whilst under strategic substitutability the macroeconomic consequences of near-rationality are of minor importance. Not only is strategic complementarity essential to the above result but it is also possible to show (Boitani and Damiani 2000) that for any proportion of near-rational agents in the population there is a multiplicity of post-shock reactions on the part of maximising firms, ranging from near-full adjustment (under low strategic complementarity and low real rigidity) to almost complete non-adjustment (when strategic complementarity and real rigidity are high).

It is interesting to note that policy actions aimed at neutralising the effects due to the presence of near-rational agents may be very difficult to implement, as the environment in which rational agents and the government act is significantly altered by heterogeneity (Boitani and Damiani 1999). The presence of near-rational agents greatly increases the information requirements for the policy action to be successful: full knowledge of all structural parameters of the economy is actually needed. In such a context, rule-of-thumb behaviour on the part of the government may lead to outcomes preferable to those attainable by (frustrating) attempts at overcoming near-rationality. The government commitment to a simple policy rule then turns out to be more effective, since it reduces the interdependence of private agents' actions and government's actions, thus reducing the strategical uncertainty and favouring coordination (Boitani and Damiani 1999).

The interplay of nominal rigidities, real rigidities and strategic complementarity began to be explored in the early 1990s (Alvi 1993). As for the relation between nominal and real rigidities, it can be shown that the impact of nominal rigidities is strengthened by the presence of real rigidities. Without real rigidities, nominal frictions – due to small menu costs, near-rationality or imperfect indexation – may cause only marginal impacts on real variables. In other words, when only nominal shocks of minor magnitude are plausible, the presence of real rigidities become a necessary condition in order to justify large macroeconomic fluctuations. As Ball and Romer (1990: 64) aptly write:

> nominal rigidity is an equilibrium if an agent does not adjust his real price when demand shifts. An increase in real rigidities means that an agent desires a smaller change in his real price after a given change in demand. When the desired change is smaller, the cost of foregoing it is smaller.

Thus a small nominal friction is sufficient to prevent adjustment for a wider range of shocks.[2]

Strategic complementarity has a direct relation to real rigidities (whatever the source of such rigidities). The higher the degree of strategic complementarity the more rigid is the relative price desired by maximising imperfectly competitive firms, hence the lower is the individual price change induced by a change in the quantity of money. In turn real rigidity and strategic complementarity are lower the higher is the degree of monopoly power. Thus the degree of monopoly power has a negative influence on the desired rigidity of relative prices through strategic complementarity. In a highly monopolised market firms' constraints to price changes are lower than in more competitive markets. As there is a positive relation between real rigidities and nominal rigidities, it follows that high strategic complementarity and low market power entail high nominal rigidity, whatever the source of such rigidity.

A further step to link the strategic complementarity approach with the nominal rigidity analysis is provided by Ball and Romer (1991). They argue that models based on coordination failures and those featuring nominal rigidities are not to be considered as alternative, competing approaches but as two complementary explanations of inefficient macroeconomic fluctuations. Indeed, even though strategic complementary models are real ones and attribute no role to monetary policies, they may be seen 'at the root of inefficient non-neutralities of money' (Ball and Romer 1991: 539).

Coordination failure models are capable of delivering many Keynesian results in a very natural way (Boitani and Delli Gatti 2001). However, such models have sometimes been criticised by those who maintain that the Pareto-dominant Nash equilibrium within the range should be regarded as a 'natural' focal point (Harsanyi and Selten 1988). If this is the case, 'then understanding the macroeconomic implications of coordination failures would be somewhat less interesting' (Cooper 1999: chapter 1). This is why a good deal of attention has been devoted to experimental evidence on coordination failures (Cooper *et al.* 1994) and to the complementary subject of equilibrium selection in coordination games (Cooper 1999; Sacco 1996). This research shows that coordination failures are frequently observed in experimental games and that selection criteria rigorously based on individual rationality, such as risk dominance, sometimes fail to explain observed behaviour (Van Huyck *et al.* 1990).

However, the presence of a small proportion of near-rational agents, thanks to strategic complementarity, may help in selecting an equilibrium, albeit not necessarily the payoff-dominant one (Haltiwanger and Waldman 1989; Bhaskar 1990).[3] It can actually be shown that the presence of some near-rational agents can also justify an equilibrium selection criterion according to which the (equilibrium) outcome observed is determined by the (equilibrium) outcome observed in the previous period (Cooper 1994). Such an equilibrium selection criterion may be justified if there is a small proportion of near-rational agents who behave adaptively and use 'history' as a guideline for their actions. Under strategic complementarity this behaviour may create a focal point and allow an equilibrium selection, as it reduces the risk associated with playing the 'adaptive' strategy also on the part of fully rational agents. Thus the existence of near-rational agents helps the working of the economy but precludes the attainment of Pareto-superior outcomes.

A two-faceted conclusion may be suggested. On one hand near-rationality may be helpful in equilibrium selection, by providing a (not necessarily optimal) focal point to rational agents in economies with multiple equilibria. On the other hand even the small degree of heterogeneity introduced by near-rationality may make some Pareto-improving economic policy both difficult and ineffective. The two conclusions are not necessarily contradictory, as both point to the fact that a small proportion of near-rational agents, under strategic complementarity, has a disproportionately strong impact on the macroeconomy.

Notes

1 Such a clear-cut distinction between *cooperation* and *coordination* failures is due to Silvestre (1993). Note that the kind of coordination failures stressed by Clower (1965) and Leijonhufvud (1968) do not correspond to *cooperation* or *coordination* failures as defined by Silvestre. The reason is of course that both Clower's and Leijonhufvud's contributions refer to a Walrasian economy with no strategic interaction. The coordination failure arises there because, without an auctioneer, economic agents may trade at false prices (Garretsen 1992).

2 The source of nominal rigidity in Ball and Romer (1990) is the existence of small menu costs. But the point these authors make in the quotation above applies to other sources of nominal rigidity. A remarkable attempt to test the validity of the many theories of nominal rigidities can be found in Blinder *et al.* (1998).

3 Adding noise to information and/or to processing capabilities of some economic players has been proved to be a helpful equilibrium selection device by Carlsson and Ganslandt (1998).

Part IV

The legacy of Keynes

[F]or Keynes . . . contrary to what was maintained by orthodox theory, there exists – to use Joan Robinson's words – 'no automatic self-righting mechanism to establish full employment in an unplanned private-enterprise economy' (Robinson 1966: 134). Recognition of this, of course, leaves open the question of what it is that prevents full employment from prevailing – 'imperfections' in the functioning of the system that by itself would be capable of attaining that goal; or rather something more fundamental, such as a spontaneous tendency to reach an equilibrium with less than full employment. . . . Keynes's methodological tools were essentially those he had learned from Marshall; consequently his analysis – developed in that methodological territory – oscillated between the Scylla of the short period and the Charybdis of the long period in a Marshallian sense. . . . Clearly oscillations and ambiguities apparently legitimise different readings of Keynes. The dilemma may be solved . . . through a 'rational reconstruction' . . . Keynes's analysis is viewed as referring to a short period in the Marshallian sense where a number of important variables are assumed to be given as a result of the past 'history' of the system, and where there is a certain state of expectations which influences present decisions and therefore the amount of effective demand, and of employment, that the economy generates. The position *corresponding* to these data exerts its attraction on the actual variables and represents the system's natural equilibrium (or long-period equilibrium in the logical sense).

(Caravale 1992b: 85–6, 88)

The cultural climate that has come into being in the past two decades has produced . . . the legitimization of the increasingly common decision, of considering as an essential pillar of economic analysis the assumption of an inverse relation between the real wages and employment – the very relation whose denial represents the theoretical core of Keynes's analysis.

(Caravale 1998a: 334)

18 Keynes on probability, uncertainty and tragic choices

Anna Carabelli

Right from the beginning (that is, in the period 1904–6) Keynes was interested in moral dilemmas which are typical of ancient Greek tragedy and classical drama. In the first section I will examine the evidence of the early influences of tragedy upon Keynes and the main themes of tragedy in which he was interested; Keynes's tragic view of ethics and aesthetics will be investigated in the next four sections; finally, Keynes's situations of moral and rational conflicts and dilemmas will be considered in the last four sections.

In this chapter I try to show how Keynes's constant attention to the incommensurability and non-comparability of magnitudes (probability and economic magnitudes such as real income, real capital and the general level of prices) may derive from his early interest in dilemmas and how his concept of uncertainty is to be linked with tragic dilemmas and choices. Dilemmas characterise situations of indecision, of irreducible conflict where moral claims or reasons (*some* reasons to be precise) cannot be weighed one against the other on a common scale and using a common and homogeneous unit of measure. These situations are the domain of radical uncertainty, a concept which is dominant in Keynes's mature economic writings and in the *General Theory* in particular.

Tragedy

The main influences

References to Greek tragedy are recurrent in Keynes's early writings. In his 1904 essay on Burke, Keynes refers to Agamemnon's behaviour and his tragic choice:

> Agamemnon's behaviour to his daughter would not have met with approval in Burke's eyes, whether it were certainly conducive to general utility or not.
> (Keynes MSS, *The Political Doctrines of Edmund Burke*: 12)

In his 1905 paper *Virtue and Happiness* he refers to Euripides' *Troads* with its depiction of Hecuba's heroism and Agamemnon's tragic dilemma:

> For instance, persons, in such situations as we call tragic, may I think be at the same happy in the sense I am suggesting. When at the end of the *Troads*,

> despite and through the overwhelming horror of her situation Hecuba suddenly realises the splendour of her own tragedy, she is happy. There is an element of happiness in most heroic states of mind. Occasions, felt intensely to be good, are happy. A man, who feels securely that he has a grip on something really worth having is happy.
>
> (Keynes MSS, *Virtue and Happiness*: 8)

In his paper *Modern Civilisation* of 28 October 1905 a reference to tragedy is also present.[1] In his August 1906 civil service exams Keynes wrote for English Composition, 'Drama Melodrama and Opera'. Skidelsky (1983: 174) mentions that he had also already written a paper for the Apostles.

In addition to the ancient Greek authors of tragedy, another main influence upon Keynes was his interest in Elizabethan theatre: in particular, Shakespeare's and Ben Jonson's tragedies. References to the 'tragedy of Lear' and Macbeth are common throughout Keynes's writings (see Keynes MSS, *Beauty*: 30; 1971–89, XVII: 300, 302, XXVIII: 100).

Another important source of Keynes's interest in tragedy was his early interest in Burke's politics. As we have seen, Keynes wrote an essay on Burke's politics in 1904. As we know, Greek tragedy and the eighteenth-century revival of the Elizabethan theatre influenced Burke and his view of politics considerably. Hindson and Gray (1988: 6–7) note that, in Burke's day, the Elizabethan theatre was the great focus of social attention. The language of the stage and the leading characters in the drama were so familiar to the public imagination that the drama provided a lead to the minds of the people. For Burke the stage was a mirror of the ethics of contemporary society; he saw the stage not only as a reflection of real life, but indeed as a performance of real life – it had an impact upon the world beyond the stage door. Burke felt that the organisers of society, politicians and statesmen, should be aware of the theatre. He held that drama was an education for statesmen: politicians should analyse and test men in much the same way as a dramatist does. Eighteenth-century politics was, in Burke's eyes, a theatrical as well as a dramatic arena (see Hindson and Gray 1988: 9). For Burke, human behaviour has a dramatic expression: each individual is required to perform heroically before an audience of willing observers. He saw life and the world as a stage. Burke considered human life and history as a tragedy. In his *Hints for an Essay on Drama*, Burke claimed that tragedy is always about dead men, and is necessarily respectful, while comedy is always a satire on the living. In Burke, tragedy and drama also emphasise submission to fate and acceptance of the natural order of human life. In his eyes the European system of politics of the time was based upon a recognised process of cooperation (and antagonism) between independent states which established 'the arena of the theatre of Europe'. The European arena was an 'aggregate of nations': the 'commonwealth'.

As we shall see, Keynes was clearly aware of Burke's tragic elements in his reading of Burke's writings. And more; while the role Burke attributed to tragedy was certainly one of the early stimuli of the young Keynes, the mature Keynes carried this Burkean influence further. Tragic elements hover in Keynes's *The Economic Consequences of the Peace* (1919): he sees Europe in a very Burkean tragic manner.[2]

Keynes's attention to tragedy and dramatic theatre also emerges in his use of metaphors and antinomies. In his 1906 essay *Egoism*, when comparing the Greek and Christian attitudes to ethics, he notices that in Christian ethics 'the world' is no more seen as 'a stage' but has become 'a police court':

> [in Christian ethics] . . . the Universe is so constructed, causal laws are such that, as a matter of fact, no conflict can arise. The same acts which tend to increase the individual goodness also tend to increase general goodness. In other words the Universe is governed in accordance with the principle of Justice: a man can obtain goodness, only in so far as his actions are directed towards general goodness. General goodness is Man's Duty, personal goodness is his reward. The world is no longer a stage, as in the earlier view; it has become a police court.
>
> (Keynes MSS, *Egoism*: 7)

It should be noted that the metaphor of the play has been used by political theorists for centuries. In *The Laws* Plato describes the relationship between man and the gods in theatrical terminology. Dramatic metaphors are also used by Shakespeare, who is most famous for likening the world to a stage and for describing men and women as merely players. Like other Elizabethans, Shakespeare often used drama to signify despair or anxiety at the events of the human world.

Tragedy: the main themes

Tragedy plays a central role in Greek poetry. The common features of tragedy are well known. Most tragedies concentrated greatly on the theme of aristocratic suffering. The downfall of human greatness was felt to have greater emotional weight. Aeschylus' motto is that 'we learn by suffering'. The suffering of majesty, of the noble hero, is more affecting to watch than the misery of lesser mortals because the extent of their fall is so much greater: 'the greatest of kings and the unhappiest of mankind' (Hindson and Gray 1988: 156).

History is replete with stories of heroic failure. Poetic justice required that the tragic hero should suffer an ignominious death in keeping with the tragic theme of the flawed character of human greatness. History is a story of the fragility of human civilisation. Tragedy considers the inevitable downfall of human pride, the humiliation following the peak of human greatness. Anxiety and fear were also important in the tragic outlook, which put man constantly in a dilemma as to the necessary course of human action. Indecision and vacillation of judgement are a common human condition.

By offering a complex experience and demanding a complex response the Greek theatre – tragedy and drama in particular – was uniquely placed to voice more relative ways of thinking and feeling. By conveying the complexity of human life and experience, tragic theatre and drama help men take decisions and face dilemmas, helping men in the process of forming their decisions in situations of tragic choices, what we would now call radical uncertainty in economics.

In this chapter I will concentrate on just a few of these features of tragedy, those relevant to Keynes: the myth of the tragic hero; the existence of a plurality of heterogeneous moral claims; the problem of conflict between opposite moral claims; tragic dilemmas due to incommensurability and non-comparability of conflicting moral claims.

The tragic hero

The tragic hero is a recurrent theme in tragedy. Keynes, too, devoted particular attention to this subject in his early papers. What in his eyes are the characteristics of the hero, and of the tragic hero in particular? Keynes wants his heroes to have a 'true combination of passion and intellect': what he calls 'passionate contemplation' in his 1905 letter to his friend Swithinbank. There he writes that it is difficult for him to find this combination in reality and that he finds increasing comfort in Plato and Shakespeare:

> I find my chief comfort more and more in Messrs Plato and Shakespeare. Why is it so difficult to find a true combination of passion and intellect? My heroes must feel and feel passionately – but they must see too, everything and more than everything. What is there worth anything except passionate contemplation?
>
> (Keynes MSS, *General Correspondence*; letter to B. W. Swithinbank, 18 April 1905)

The requirement for the 'true combination' of passion and intellect (or reason) that Keynes desires for his heroes matches a general requirement for a rich human personality that will mix the characteristics of artists with those of scientists. The mixing of reason or intellect with sentiment, feeling and passion that Keynes requires of his heroes is actually a general request to men: they should have a rich personality, complex attitudes towards life and knowledge. In brief, Keynes asks men to be like his heroes.

In his paper *On Beauty and Art. On Art Criticism and the Appreciation of Beauty* (n.d.), Keynes asks another combination and collaboration: that of reason and intuition. In his view, the analytical characteristics of the scientist and the intuitive characteristics of the artist should collaborate. There are two types of perception: the piecemeal perception of the scientist-analyst and the synthetic perception of the artist. He wishes the

> collaboration of the analytic and intuitive powers . . . knowledge and creation will advance together. Nothing can be more fatal for the existence of the truly good, than the supposed antagonism between the precise and verbal notions of philosophy and the organic, indivisible perceptions of beauty and feeling between those things which we perceive piecemeal and those which we perceive as wholes . . . reconciling the operation of knowledge and of feeling.
>
> (Keynes MSS, *On Beauty and Art. On Art Criticism and the Appreciation of Beauty*: 2)

In his 1909 essay *Science and Art* the point is stressed again. He believes that scientists, like artists, manifest a creative attitude in their research: the intuitive process of seeing through the obscurity of a scientific argument is similar to the artist's 'sudden insight' (Keynes MSS, *Science and Art*).[3]

In his early essays Keynes also hopes for a mixing of reason and will: a combination also typical of heroes. But, in an ancient Greek way – Aristotelian in particular, as we shall see – he also admits *akrasia*, the human weakness of the will: we ought but we can't. In his 1906 paper *Egoism* Keynes clearly distinguishes between rational motive as a ground of action and psychological motive as an efficient cause of action: 'Rationally we ought, psychologically we can't.'

> There may be some confusion between rational motive as a ground of action and psychological motive as an efficient cause of action. . . . We ought, but we can't. Rationally we ought, psychologically we can't. Universal good is supreme – in heaven. Private good is supreme – on earth.
>
> (Keynes MSS, *Egoism*: 11–12)

In his theory of probability we again find his requirement for the 'heroic' mixings of reason and passion or of reason and intuition. In probability what he requires is the mixture of *limited reason* and intuition, that is, the mixture of non-demonstrative logic, on the one hand, and intuition and direct judgements, on the other. In *A Treatise on Probability* (Keynes 1971–89, VIII) he stresses that 'In all knowledge . . . there is some direct element, and logic can never be made purely mechanical' (ibid.: 15). Probability cannot do 'without any assistance whatever from intuition or direct judgement (ibid.: 56). He underlines that 'the appeal to intuition is not as explicit as it should be' (ibid.: 57). He aims to bring out 'the hidden element of direct judgement or intuition' (ibid.: 69). Again, while logic is analytic and 'piecemeal', intuition is synthetic and creative.[4]

In his view of economics, also, the richness and 'heroic' mixture of attitudes is a must. In his economics Keynes did not forget Burke's famous passage on the end of the age of chivalry as a reminder – to economists – of a lost past:

> But the age of chivalry is gone. That of sophisters, economists, and calculators, has succeeded; and the glory of Europe is extinguished for ever.
>
> (Burke 1969: 170)

Economists, like his heroes, should manifest a broad range of attitudes. In 1910, and in his 1924 essay on Marshall, his early point on the necessity of a mixture of logic and intuition is revived to deal with the specific material of economics.[5] Economic facts are not precisely determinable and are imperfectly known, so reason alone is powerless without intuition:

> a salient example of the application of a needlessly complex mathematical apparatus to initial data, of which the true character is insufficiently explained, and which are in fact unsuited to the problem in hand.
>
> (Keynes 1971–89, XI: 195)

> [mathematical economics] . . . but the amalgam of logic and intuition, and the wide knowledge of facts, most of which are not precise, which is required for economic interpretation in its highest form is, quite truly, overwhelmingly difficult for those whose gift mainly consists in power to imagine and pursue to their furthest points the implications and prior conditions of comparatively simple facts which are known with a high degree of precision.
>
> (Keynes 1971–89, XI: 186 n. 2)

Keynes's attention to the imprecise nature of the economic material may be seen as a reminder of the contrast placed by Aristotle in his *Ethics* between exactness and precision. If things are indefinite, imprecise and vague, one runs the risk of being 'precisely wrong'. In his ethics Aristotle distinguishes between precision and exactness. Precision is appropriate for mathematical objects, while exactness is for indefinite, not fixed, things; that is, exactness is appropriate for human action:

> Our treatment [of ethical and political matters] will be adequate, if it achieves that amount of precision that belongs to its subject matter. The same exactness must not be sought on all accounts, as it is not in all products of art.
>
> (Aristotle, *Nicomachean Ethics* 1094b 13)

> The noble and just things, which political science studies, exhibit much difference and fluctuation . . . for it is the mark of the educated man to seek that amount of precision in each class of things which the nature of the subject matter admits: it is evidently foolish to accept probable reasoning from a mathematician and to demand demonstrations from the rhetorician.
>
> (Ibid.: 15–27)[6]

Aristotle's exactness stands for adequateness, appropriateness and correctness as to the situations and the objects considered; his idea is that differences in the nature of the subject matter correspond to differences in types of cognition.[7] This explains why the application of mathematical methods to social and moral sciences was problematic for Keynes. It also explains his early distrust of mathematical probability in guiding human decisions:

> As soon as mathematical probability ceases to be the merest algebra or pretends to guide our decisions, it immediately meets with problems against which its own weapons are quite powerless.
>
> (Keynes 1971–89, VIII: 6)

The tragic hero: states of mind and states of affairs

We have so far seen the main characteristics of Keynes's hero: the 'true combination' of emotional, intuitive and cognitive attitudes. But in Keynes's *tragic* hero these attitudes are associated with tragedy, disaster and dilemmas.

In ethics, Keynes distinguishes between 'speculative ethics' and 'practical ethics' (or 'morals'). 'Speculative ethics' concerns ultimate ends and values which are intrinsically good: what in his 1938 paper *My Early Beliefs* he called his 'religion', a religion which he got from Moore. And in line with Moore, Keynes includes love, friendship, beauty, truth and knowledge among these ultimate intrinsic values. But, in his *Miscellanea Ethica* of 31 July 1905, Keynes also explicitly includes tragedy among these values:

> Speculative ethics. . . . The nature of beauty and tragedy and love and the attitude a man should have towards truth would prove of interest in the discussion.
>
> (Keynes MSS, *Miscellanea Ethica*, 31 July 1905)

In his paper *On the Principle of Organic Unity* (undated but read again on 22 January 1921) also, Keynes maintains that noble and heroic states of mind may be associated with tragedy and in particular with tragic states of affairs. Here Keynes criticised Moore for having considered 'good' states of mind in isolation. In his view, on the contrary, one should also consider the states of affairs associated with those states of mind. In this paper he again explicitly includes tragedy among the attributes of the states of affairs to be desirable ('beauty, harmony, justice, *tragedy*, virtue, consistency, truth'). Thus heroic and noble states of mind and feelings may be associated with tragic, bad or unjust states of affairs. Consequently, before judging a situation as good, the situation should be analysed as a whole. States of mind and states of affairs are organically interconnected. They are relational goods: to show pity, there must be something to be pitied. This is the reason why even a good life may be associated with dilemmas and disasters. Keynes describes the attributes of these tragic states of affairs:

> The attributes which belong to states of affairs and not, in every case, to states of mind in isolation are those which are suggested by the words – Beauty, harmony, Justice, tragedy, Virtue, Consistency, truth – or by their opposite. . . . In a similar way, a state of affairs may be tragic and, therefore, not to be desired, although the feelings of the actors in it may be all noble and heroic. But I am not certain that all tragic states of affairs are bad on the whole, when everything has been taken into account, or that the goodness of the states of mind, if it is very great, may not outweigh the badness of the state of affairs, – because in our final judgement we must take into account both the states of mind and the state of affairs. It is possible, I think, to imagine two states of affairs, one of which is tragic or unjust and the other not, such that the states of mind in each are of exactly equal value, and to believe that the tragic state of affairs is less desirable than the other.
>
> (Keynes MSS, *On the Principle of Organic Unity*: 5–6)

In considering virtue and the virtuous man, Keynes similarly believed that one should consider not single acts or single virtuous actions but a 'complex' or 'an organic unity'. Similarly to ancient Greek ethics – again with Aristotle in particular – he thought one should consider the whole life, the whole conduct and character of man:

> The complex to which the attribute of virtue can be given is of a different kind. Only persons can be virtuous. But it is not on account of single states of consciousness that they are virtuous. It is an attribute of their conduct as a whole, of the organic unity composed of their successive states of consciousness. . . . It is, in fact, to these things rather than to states of mind regarded in isolation that our emotions of approval and disapproval instinctively refer. I do not think that these feelings would be as direct as they appear to be, if they were based in reality on a calculation of the effects on states of mind of the states of affairs in question, and were only hated in the way in which we hate the rain that wets us.
>
> (Ibid.: 8)

In contrast to modern ethics, Keynes's ethics takes as its main subject matter not simply a narrow domain of specifically moral duties and obligations, but the whole conduct of human life. Its starting point is the question 'How should one live?' So it is not single acts that are important but a whole life. Not only the agent's acts, but also the whole texture of the character from which the acts flow, asking about motives and intentions, as does Kantian ethics, but asking, as well, about reactive feelings and emotions – insisting that an action is not really virtuous unless it is chosen without painful and tragic struggle, and manifests a stable disposition to choose actions of this sort. The whole of character is taken to be available for ethical cultivation; and human goodness requires not just obeying certain external rules, but also forming choice, desire, passion, and attention, in a comprehensive and exacting way over the course of an entire life which may comprehend tragic situations.

As Keynes points out in the same paper, the evaluation of the connection between states of mind and states of affairs raises the problem of the existence of other people's states of mind and of our belief in their existence.[8] While recognising the difficulty of knowing the content of other minds, Keynes reaffirms that some conception of other people's states is necessary for any ethical judgement:

> It is very seldom that we have any clear or definite conception of states of mind other than our own. Some conception of other people's states is necessary for any ethical judgement. . . . Systems of metaphysical ethics always refer to organic unities; and most other systems ostensibly deal with them.
>
> (Ibid.: 10–11)

In this regard it should also be noted that, in contrast to Moore, Keynes thought that not only states of mind but also some states of affairs may have intrinsic value. For him, goodness is different from usefulness; thus some states of affairs can be judged on their intrinsic value, that is, totally apart from their influences on experience. This again raises the problem of evaluating tragic states as a whole:

> If a good state of affairs is only useful, it is useful in the way that a poem or a picture is, not in the way that a pen or a brush is useful; and we can judge its value absolutely, apart from its actual usefulness, just as we can judge absolutely the value of a poem or a picture. But I think that I go further than this and hold that the intrinsic value is ethical. Some state of affairs ought to exist rather than others apart from their influence on experience.
>
> (Ibid.: 11)

Keynes's ethics: pluralism of ends and values

In ethics Keynes believes in the existence of a plurality of heterogeneous ends and values. As we shall see (p. 267), this is also true of his view on aesthetics. He sees 'many different kinds of beauty as of virtue' (Keynes MSS, *On Beauty and Art. On Art Criticism and the Appreciation of Beauty*: 5).

The end has a plurality of parts, each qualitatively distinct from every other, and each essential to the fullness or completeness of the life. This means that it is inappropriate to conceive the job of choice in a utilitarian or consequentialist way, as that of maximising the quantity of some *single* end or good, and quite unreasonable to think that one may advance towards the good by trading in one end component for another. Each and every one is necessary, and they are not commensurable or comparable one with another. This is at the root of the difficulties of the *intra*-subjective comparison of values stressed by Keynes.[9]

Irreducibility of heterogeneous plural ends and values: Keynes's pleasure, goodness and happiness

On pluralism Keynes follows Aristotle rather than Plato. Aristotle stresses the plurality and variety of goodness and the fact that good is not reducible to a univocal scale. On the contrary, Platonic tradition – as does utilitarianism – accepts the idea of a uniqueness of ends and values: it reduces goodness to one dimension alone (Nussbaum 1984). Keynes, like Aristotle, disagrees with this tradition. It should be noted, however, that in his mature dialogues Plato himself criticises his early position. Thus we could say, more precisely, that Keynes's position on ethics is in line with Plato's *mature* dialogues and with Aristotle's ethical writings.

In his 1905 paper *Virtue and Happiness* Keynes identifies three ultimate ends of life: pleasure, goodness and happiness. First, he distinguishes pleasure from goodness; secondly, goodness from happiness. For him, pleasures are:

> The gratification of bodily desires, both legitimate and illegitimate; the excitement of expectation, such as gambling or daydreaming; the excitement of novelty; the pleasures of gratification – of pride, or vanity, or ambition, or enmity; all kinds of pleasures of success.
>
> (Keynes MSS, *Virtue and Happiness*: 10–11)

In his view, it is often difficult to distinguish between pleasure and goodness in human actual experience. But the two ends are quite different. This position is in line with Moore's:

> Good and pleasure are not always readily distinguished; this other confusion, if confusion it be, is even easier.
>
> (Ibid.: 10)

He then distinguishes happiness from goodness and pleasure:

> I am aware the hedonist would claim these as instances of pleasure. But I am maintaining that the state of mind that accompanies such occasions as these is really specifically different from what is usually meant by pleasure. The confusion is naturally made because both pleasure and happiness are of the ultimate, satisfactory self explanatory nature which I have described.
>
> (Ibid.)

To clarify his conception of happiness Keynes refers to Plato's dialogues, especially the *Symposium*. The then current interpretation of it appears to him unsatisfactory or, better, 'cause of complete delusion'. Keynes criticises the praise of Platonic love and abstinence.

Keynes's own conception of happiness is based in particular on a reinterpretation of the passage of Plato's *Symposium* (203b, c, d) on the birth of Love by Poros and Penia. In his view Love, who takes on both the father's and the mother's characteristics, lies in a middle position between good and pleasure and between wisdom and ignorance. In this middle position lies Keynes's notion of happiness:

> There may however be yet another way out, rather different in its procedure from any of those that I have described; and I fancy it may have been the way of Socrates and Plato. . . . This method is, in brief as follows: – I have been dealing with a class, whose characteristics I have indicated, and which I have supposed to consist of two members – pleasure and good. Imagine a third member standing midway between the two, and bearing a family likeness to both. It will be convenient to call it happiness, but it will be necessary to dissociate ourselves from some but not all of the usual associations of the word. This state can be distinguished on introspection from a state of pleasure; but the two are so closely cognate that they are easily classed together and confused. It is, of its nature, as satisfactory a composition of tendencies of our desires, as pleasure itself, and it has this additional advantage – it has an intimate connection with the good. One day as the good lay asleep, pleasure, who is, of course, of a very lustful nature, came and lay beside him and conceived this child happiness. Now despite the circumstances that attended his birth, his father has never forsaken him and he has succeeded in inheriting the characteristics of both his parents. Now the most obvious criticism of this is to point out that all I mean by happiness is the enjoyment of that class of pleasurable things which

> happen at the same time to be good. But I do not think I am making this mistake. I admit the relationship but I deny the identity.
>
> (Keynes MSS, *Virtue and Happiness*: 6–7)

Keynes denies that happiness is reducible to pleasure: 'The happy state which I am thinking of is specifically different from the pleasurable state; and I must try and make clearer what it is precisely that I mean' (ibid.: 8). While pleasure implies the absence of pain, happiness does not: 'In the first place I would say – and this is, to some extent, an answer to the criticism I have suggested – that it does not imply the absence of pain.' Happiness can exist together with pain and also 'with depression'. Sometimes it may be difficult to distinguish pleasure and happiness; but, he notes, while happiness may be associated with pain and even with depression, pleasure is not:

> Pain and happiness can easily exist together: but pain and pleasure can scarcely be supported to coexist – save in the sense that a state involving elements of pain can still contain a balance of pleasure on the whole.
>
> (Ibid.: 8)

Keynes avoids reducing happiness either to pleasure or to goodness. Happiness is a synthesis, a composition (not a sum) of heterogeneous values, desires and virtues. First, it is a mixture of body pleasure and goodness. Secondly, as seen, happiness may coexist with pain.

Keynes's happiness is not a unidimensional or uni-scalar attribute of man's states of mind. His happiness is the result of the composition of the tendencies of our desires, where desires are considered by him heterogeneous and incommensurable. This is why, as we will see on p. 268, different desires may give rise to moral conflicts and eventually to weakness of the will (*akrasia*).

Keynes's concept of happiness is also associated with virtue: a virtuous man is a happy man. His desires are balanced with his possibilities:

> When we are told that the virtuous and consequently happy man is he who is in harmony with his environment, who modifies his desires to match his opportunities, who puts himself beyond the reach of disappointment, something of this kind seems to be suggested.
>
> (Ibid.: 12)

This means that his happiness is also 'contentment': a satisfaction with one's environment; a state beyond disappointment:

> Some of these overlap with happiness; just as good and pleasure can overlap. States can exist which are both pleasurable and happy; not only, however, can happiness coexist with pain but even, I think, with depression. In the ordinary use afterward, if we eliminate those occasions in which it is not at all to be distinguished from pleasure, its most obvious equivalent seems to be contentment. An almost perpetual temperamental satisfaction

> with one's environment – the cat-on-the-matting attitude – is known as happiness.
>
> (Ibid.: 11–12)

This notion of happiness as contentment seems to rule utopian ideals and desires out of Keynes's realm of practical possibilities. Should we desire more than we can actually attain? In his early writings Keynes answers positively while, for example, Burke – in his view – answers negatively. In fact, Burke held that 'all virtue which is impracticable is spurious'. In his early essay on Burke, Keynes disagreed with Burke precisely on the fact that without ideals we have nothing to aim for. Thus, for Keynes, disappointment may, in general, be better than contentment. But it should be noted that Keynes's justification of pursuing happiness, 'the truly good', is only probabilistic ('more likely'). This is in line with his whole methodological approach:

> But it is, surely, sufficiently obvious that it may be sometimes right to desire something more supreme than one can ever get, and to hate and despise the environment, if be bad. Disappointment may be better than contentment. But if the preacher of contentment were to be cross-questioned, it might be found that he only meant that he who pursues the truly good is more likely than another to find satisfaction in attainment. Perhaps.
>
> (Ibid.: 12)

Many are the authors who may have influenced Keynes on the theme of the plurality and irreducibility of ends and values. First of all, Moore himself. In his *Principia Ethica* Moore too recognised the plurality of values (Moore 1903: sections 47–8). Thus Keynes's disagreement with Moore does not concern the existence of a plurality of values or claims but – as we shall see (p. 272) – his method of solution of the possible conflict between them.[10] In Keynes's view, in the end Moore reduces goodness to one dimension alone, by denying pleasure any role: goodness without lust and bodily pleasures. Keynes criticises him for having reduced love to platonic love only and having praised Plato's abstinence. In contrast, Keynes's notion of happiness, as seen, is a mixture of goodness and pleasure–lust and may also be associated with pain and depression. This may explain Keynes's early choice of a life of action versus Moore's choice of a life of contemplation. In his view, Moore's method of reducing the plurality of ends and values also implied reducing the number of virtues to private virtues only and the activities of life to contemplation only. In *My Early Beliefs* (1938) Keynes noted that Moore reached neither Plato's *Republic* nor the *Laws*, thus implicitly stressing the difference between Plato's early and mature dialogues.[11] Plato's mature dialogues, as we know, are closer to Aristotle's interest in the multidimensional character of goodness and in the possible conflict between individual and public values. In contrast with his early dialogues, in the *Republic* and in the *Laws* Plato presses for intervention by philosophers in public life to change the 'politeia'. He wants the philosopher not to limit himself to moulding his own character but to become a demiurge of wisdom, justice and of all public virtues towards other men (*Republic* 500d 6). He urges intervention in public life to modify men and their way of organising themselves. In his mature dialogues Plato also wishes for tranquillity and quietness (*hesychia*) (*Republic* 496d 6): a concept which seems close to Keynes's happiness in the sense of 'contentment'.

Another author who may have influenced Keynes on the plurality of ends and values is Franz Brentano. During the long vacation 1905 Keynes read Brentano's *The Origin of our Knowledge of Right and Wrong* (precisely on 6 July 1905). At para. 32 of his book Brentano deals with the plurality and mutual irreducibility of goodness. Finally, Keynes may have been influenced by his reading of Aristotle himself. During the same period (1905–6) Keynes read Aristotle's writings on ethics repeatedly.[12]

Happiness and tragedy

As we have seen, Keynes's concept of happiness is in contrast with pleasure and may be associated with pain. It is now clear that Keynes's notion of happiness is connected with tragedy. In his 1905 *Virtue and Happiness* Keynes considers Hecuba in Euripides' *Troads* as *happy*. For him, heroic states of mind are happy. The tragic hero is happy. In fact, heroic states of mind are the manifestation of intense feelings and passions; but heroic and noble states of mind are often associated with tragic states of affairs. Thus happiness is connected with tragedy and pain, that is, with tragic and bad states:

> For instance, persons, in such situations as we call tragic, may I think be at the same happy in the sense I am suggesting. When at the end of the *Troads*, despite and through the overwhelming horror of her situation, Hecuba suddenly realises the splendour of her own tragedy, she is happy. There is an element of happiness in most heroic states of mind. Occasions, felt intensely to be good, are happy. A man, who feels securely that he has a grip on something really worth having, is happy. A man who sees ill lead suddenly to good, is happy.
>
> (Keynes MSS, *Virtue and Happiness*: 8)

Keynes's early attitude towards tragic happiness is recurrent in his thought. It was taken up by him again in 1928. In a letter to his friend F. L. Lucas on 19 April 1928 he reaffirms that noble states are associated with 'troubles, misfortunes, and disasters':

> In actual life many of the feelings which we deem noblest and most worth having are apt to be associated with troubles, misfortunes, and disasters. In itself we generally judge the state of mind of the hero going into battle as good – but it is a pity that he should be killed. Similarly, feelings of sympathy are good in themselves. In fact, the worst of real life is that feelings good in themselves are too often stimulated or occasioned or provoked by evil happening.
>
> (Keynes MSS, *General Correspondence*, letter to F. L. Lucas, 19 April 1928)

Ethics of virtue

Keynes's ethics is an ethics of virtues in the way ancient Greeks – and Aristotle in particular – understood it. It emphasises the importance of friendship, moral emotions and pays precise attention to the contextual particularity of right action: Keynes's notion of changing circumstances in *A Treatise on Probability*.[13] A good life is a life worth being lived, that is, a moral life: in *Egoism* Keynes maintains that to be good is more important than to do good (Keynes MSS, *Egoism*).

The good and happy life

Keynes accepted the Aristotelian notion of the good and happy life. The Aristotelian influence on his ethics is clearly recognised by him. In a letter to Strachey of 23 January 1906: 'Have you read the Ethics of that superb Aristotle? . . . There never was such good sense talked – before or since.' And in a letter on 7 February 1906: 'I have been deep in Greek philosophy . . . I don't wonder Aristotle put this intellectual activity first. Still I don't agree with him. Love first, philosophy second, Poetics third, and Politics fourth' (quoted in Skidelsky 1983: 167). In his *Miscellanea Ethica* of 31 July 1905 he writes that speculative ethics should deal with the nature of beauty and tragedy and love and the attitude a man should have towards truth. There is also an explicit reference to Aristotle here and to his conclusions considered wise and unsurpassable. In a passage we have already seen, he points out that in the end the conclusions will appear no wiser than Aristotle's:

> Speculative ethics. . . . The nature of beauty and tragedy and love and the attitude a man should have towards truth would prove of interest in the discussion, though the conclusions appear in the result no wiser than Aristotle's.
>
> (Keynes MSS, *Miscellanea Ethic*, 31 July 1905)

The good and happy life implies friendship and affiliation. The emphasis is on forms of friendship and affiliation, which enter into the structure of the good life not only as aids to the development and exercise of the virtues, not only as constituent parts of the good life, having intrinsic worth – but also as elements in all the ends of life. For, as Aristotle stresses, every form of virtuous action is action for and to others; it is in this sense that distributive justice (*dikaiosune*) can be correctly regarded as the whole of virtue. In his ethics Keynes too draws a distinction between good as instrument and good in itself.

In none of his good choices does the virtuous agent stand alone; and yet one must insist, as well, that the good life of each single separate person is of separate worth and importance. Aristotle, unlike Plato, refuses to endorse the idea of a corporate good life in which individuals depend on one another in the way that parts of the body do. Like Kant and unlike most Utilitarians, then, Aristotelian ethics, while emphasising affiliation, still sees the separateness of persons as a fundamental ethical fact, and will seek social solutions that make it possible for 'each and every one' to achieve *eudaimonia*, in each separate life. Here it appears that Aristotelian ethics offers a valuable alternative both to utilitarianism, with its emphasis on the interchangeability of satisfactions across lives, and to Kantian ethics, which in some versions seems unduly neglectful of the depth of love and affiliation. In a similar way, in the *General Theory* Keynes defends what he calls the 'traditional advantages of individualism': 'personal liberty', 'personal choice' and 'the variety of life'. He abhors the 'homogeneous or totalitarian state' while he insists on the necessity of macro intervention (Keynes 1971–89, VII: 380). Keynes's attention to the agent's special concern with his or her own 'projects' is also Aristotelian. In his early paper *Egoism* Keynes defends egoism and, similarly, in his later paper *The Economic Possibilities for our Great-grandchildren* does not care much for future generations. His interest is in the present generation and this may be connected with his non-conventional attitude and immoralism.

Happiness

Keynes's notion of happiness also recalls Aristotle's happiness (*eudaimonia*). Keynes himself points out its connection with Aristotle's notion in his *Virtue and Happiness*: 'Sometime, perhaps always, the Greeks, and especially mr. Aristotle, came nearer to meaning this' (Keynes MSS, *Virtue and Happiness*: 11). Aristotle's happiness is the state of one's life having a point or meaning. A meaningful life is just a sum of activities worthwhile in themselves (*Nicomachean Ethics* 1097b 17). *Eudaimonia* is the activity of soul in accordance with virtue. One deliberates about what kind of life one wants to lead. Virtuous persons are contrasted with persons dominated by *techne*: the latter are persons whose reason has nothing to do with the real ends of human life.

In the ancient theories of good life, the goal of human choice is *eudaimonia*, happiness or 'human flourishing', the good (complete) life for a human being. Aristotle claims that the goods that make up human good are not unitary: 'But of honour, wisdom and pleasure, just in respect of their goodness, the accounts are distinct and diverse' (*Nicomachean Ethics* 1097a 24). For Aristotle, *eudaimonia* is conceived as an interlocking whole made up of a number of related yet distinct parts, each of which is chosen and valued for its own sake.

Usually these parts are forms of activity, for example activity in accordance with each of the virtues, reflective and contemplative activity, activity with and towards friends. Ancient Greek ethical theory offers a distinct alternative to the common types of both deontological and consequentialist theories. It resembles deontological theories in that virtuous actions are chosen for their own sake, and an action will not count as virtuous if it is chosen simply as a means to a further end. On the other hand, an agent is to think about the ends and interrelated goals of his own life as a whole to a degree rarely imagined in deontological theories, and the emphasis on rightness of desire and passion would be regarded with suspicion by many Kantians. Ancient Greek ethics resembles a consequentialist theory in the sense that an agent will properly see that his action was aimed at some end, and the rightness of an act depends on its relation to the end. But, notice, the end is constituted by forms of virtuous action; so, in choosing a right action, one is not simply choosing an instrumental means to some further end. Deliberation can concern the concrete specification of a more general end; and choice can be of the constituent parts of the end, as well as of the instrumental means.

In line with Aristotle, Keynes believes that the good life has necessary material and institutional necessary conditions. Unlike most forms of Kantian ethics, ancient ethics insists on the necessity of material resources for the exercise of virtue. The good life requires material prerequisites for human flourishing. For Keynes, the task of political economy as a moral science is precisely to supply these material conditions for the good and happy life: they are necessary preconditions for it. Aristotelian political thought focuses on the job of making citizens capable of choosing to function in the ways characteristic of *eudaimonia.* This is in contrast with the moral philosophy both of utilitarianism and Kantianism but not with Keynes's own view on economic intervention (see Carabelli and De Vecchi 1999).

Nobleness and heroism: the 'fragility of goodness'

As we have seen, Keynes believed that states of mind should not be evaluated in isolation, that is, apart from the state of affairs associated with them: pity requires somebody or some situation to be pitied. Keynes's notion of happiness means that human goodness is *fragile* and happiness is *tragic*. In the ancient Greek view of ethics, noble and heroic states of mind were constantly associated with tragedy, disasters and dilemmas. In her book on Greek tragedy Martha Nussbaum (1986) calls these situations 'the fragility of goodness'. It means that the good and virtuous life is normally associated with disasters and dilemmas. In these situations, whatever we do will cause pain to somebody else. It will cause something we will regret. This brings to indecision and vacillation in human judgement and action.

Tragedy, theatre and education

Keynes not only accepted Aristotle's view of happiness but also accepted Aristotle's view of the importance of education in forming good states of mind (Burnyeat 1980). We have seen that Keynes urged his heroes to have the 'true' mix of passion, emotions or intuition, on the one hand, and reason or intellect, on the other. There is not a strict separation between the two groups of faculties: just recall his request for a 'passionate contemplation' or perception. He was contrary to the separation of passions and intuition from reason required by Kantian and Humean ethics.

In the ancient Greek conception there is no tension between virtuous passion and rational enlightenment – because virtuous passion is a form of rational enlightenment. The light of reason is imagined not as a detached, cold ray. It combines the emphasis on character and passion with the case for reflection.

The Greek ideas of virtue and character are connected with the classical idea of the cognitive complexity of passion. If one grafts the norm of virtue on to a Humean or even a Kantian conception of the passions, one finds that the virtues will have to be seen as somewhat impervious to reflection and systematic ethical argument.

In ancient Greek ethics, virtues are indeed traits of character formed by a long process of habituation. Thus they do indeed involve the formation of desire and passion as well as belief. But the process of formation of character is not a mindless process. For Aristotle it requires cultivation of the ability to make discrimination and more complex cognitive activities. Above all, the passions that virtues incorporate are themselves not mindless surges of affect. These passions rest upon beliefs or judgements, which can be modified by reasoning in a way that entails the modification of the passion itself.

Not only are passions to be associated with reason, but reason itself should and can influence passions. This is again in line with the ancient Greek view and is in contrast with Hume's view on passions. Passions can be modified by reasoning. It is possible for reflection to modify passions – anger, for example. This is why the 'unexamined life' seems so unfortunate to Aristotle and reflection so beautiful. It is critical reflection that forces the agent out of local habits towards the commonly human.

In ancient Greek ethics, reason can modify passions and desires through education. Precisely because passions and desires are multiple, heterogeneous and incommensurable, one way of solving any conflict between them is to modify one of them. While Burke stresses that 'because in events like these our passions instruct our reason' (Burke 1969: 175), Keynes attributes the task of education to 'practical ethics'.[14]

Keynes's view is also in line with Aristotle's view of art. In the Greek view, tragedy and drama are ultimately a medium through which man can learn from the visual performance of the perennial tragedies of life and politics. Dramatic lessons teach men how to cope with the never-ending temptations of evil, and how to put up with the rigours of misfortune and tragedy which are the continuing dangers of human life. So going to the theatre and watching tragedies is like going to school. These artistic activities educate men to life. Burke's tragic view was that theatre is an even better school of moral sentiments than church. In particular, for him, watching tragedy in the theatre relies upon intuitive feelings rather than political computation.

Unlike Plato's negative view of tragedy, Aristotle sees the positive role of tragedy in man's education to virtue. The Platonic view is that art is synonymous with deception and that the art of drama is that of manipulating the truth. For Plato, tragedy is just fictitious reality. Keynes accepts Aristotle's view of art and drama as positive. Aristotle conceives tragic art as a positive moment in the education of men to knowledge and virtue, because in tragedy human reality is represented 'as it could be' (*Poetics* 9, 1451b, 1 ff.) according to ideal structures which often get mixed up and lost in the actual reality of history. Tragic poetry is able to represent the intrinsic structures of human reality. This capability is also connected with the power that this kind of poetry has to produce a catharsis, a purification from passions. Thus tragedy performs an important social function of moral education, both didactically, by improving the minds of the spectators, and cathartically, by supplying an outlet for their natural aggression. Catharsis is another important notion of tragedy. Tragic scenes purged the passions of the audience who watched them.

In human education the role of theatre, drama and tragedy is therefore important. In Greek poetry the role assigned to tragedy is to teach how to behave in life in the face of difficult situations by conveying the complexity of human life and experience. It educates men to form their decisions in situations of dilemma, that is, in situations we now call of radical uncertainty.

Thus watching tragedy at the theatre teaches men how to face uncertainty, tragic choices and dilemmas: tragedy helps educate men to form their decisions. Education provides reasons and permits the acquisition of real knowledge. And knowledge is not just getting information but critical reflection. Further, going to the theatre and watching tragedies allows one to enjoy and admire noble feelings *without* the evil happenings which generally accompany them in real life. Now, by watching tragedy we come into contact with noble feelings and escape the bad practical consequences. We get the best of both worlds: heroism without pain and happiness without tragedy. Going to the theatre and watching tragedy is a way of experiencing life without paying the full consequences. This is what Keynes stressed in his letter to F. L. Lucas on 19 April 1928:

> If, on the other hand, it were possible to sympathise with, enjoy at second hand, or admire, the noble feelings *without* the evil happenings which generally accompany them in real life, we would get the best of both worlds. Now, as it seems to me, the object of tragedy is precisely to secure for us a conjecture in which this comes about. . . . We come into contact with noble feelings and escape the bad practical consequences.
>
> (Keynes MSS 1928 *General Correspondence*, letter to F. L. Lucas, 19 April 1928)

In his 'Keynes's philosophy of practice and economic policy' Skidelsky writes that in Keynes:

> the cost of heroism, or pity . . . can be reduced to the price of a theatre-ticket: a good bargain for the social reformer, but hardly likely to convince the sceptic that the states of mind of the spectator hero and the real hero are of equal value.
>
> (Skidelsky 1991: 108–9)

But, as we have seen, for Keynes tragedy at the theatre – not real tragedy – plays a fundamental role in man's education towards the good life. In his early paper on *Beauty* he had already distinguished these two aspects:

> Tragedy has a beauty of its own, but it is for the outside observer not for its living actors: save perhaps whose, as with Hecuba in the Troads, the victims

> of fate. . . . It is good for us to read or see the tragedy of Lear, but it would not be good . . . for the history of the king to be enacted in reality.
>
> (Keynes MSS, *Beauty*: 30)

Aesthetics: 'tragic beauty'

We have seen so far Keynes's ethical pluralism and variety and the role tragedy has in his view on ethics. In aesthetics, too, Keynes believed that there are 'as many different kinds of beauty as of virtue' (Keynes MSS, *On Beauty and Art. On Art Criticism and the Appreciation of Beauty*: 5) and there are many 'instances of the different kinds of aesthetics fitness' (Keynes MSS, *Beauty*: 30).[15] Tragedy also plays a role in his views on aesthetics.

Pluralism in aesthetics: the beautiful and sublime

Keynes believes that there is a plurality of concepts of beauty as there is of goodness. In his essay *Beauty* he first distinguished between moral excellence and moral beauty:

> I distinguish moral excellence and moral beauty. . . . The ordinary practice of mankind is both explained and justified if the most beautiful minds are not necessarily those that are most valuable in themselves. Such a theory is in undoubted accordance with human practice but there is a strong argument against identifying it with the ideal. I cannot decide between the conflicting arguments; probably no general decision is possible. Sometimes the one and sometimes the other is true. The widest rule of guidance is this: where there is only a low or moderate degree of excellence or beauty, there is no great tendency of the two to coincide; amongst the moderately good the orders in beauty and excellence of spirit widely differ. But as the value increases, so also does the coincidence of goodness and beauty; until finally the most excellent mind we can know is also the most beautiful.
>
> (Ibid.: 24–5)

Then he adds 'tragic beauty' to moral excellence and moral beauty:

> tragic beauty. I am taking these as instances of the different kinds of aesthetic fitness. Tragedy has a beauty of its own.
>
> (Ibid.: 30)

In his *Virtue and Happiness*, as we have seen, he also refers to Hecuba's situation as 'the splendour of her own tragedy':

> When at the end of the *Troads*, despite and through the overwhelming horror of her situation Hecuba suddenly realises the splendour of her own tragedy, she is happy.
>
> (Keynes MSS, *Virtue and Happiness*: 8)

From these passages it is clear that Keynes was influenced by the concept of the 'sublime' in his view on aesthetics. The theory of the sublime represents the evolution of English aesthetic taste from the classicism of the first part of the eighteenth century to the romanticism of the end of that century. In aesthetics, the sublime represents the praise of the genius and hero over and above any rules. In art, the sublime represents a re-evaluation of irrational and fantastic elements and an appeal to sentiment rather than to cold reason: we speak of Michelangelo's 'terribleness'; the picturesqueness of Gothic buildings; and Blake's prophetic visions.

There is a substantial difference between the concepts of the beautiful and sublime. A tragic element is present in the latter. One of the most powerful elements of the sublime is the existence of two opposite ideas; their conflicting nature is brought together and concurs to produce the sublime: for example, horror and beauty, splendour and tragedy. In the sublime the idea of the attraction of opposites exists. In his early papers, as we have seen above, Keynes writes of the 'tragic beauty', the 'splendour of her own tragedy' and the 'overwhelming horror' when referring to Hecuba's situation.

Keynes may have been directly influenced by Burke himself on this aspect: his aesthetic theory is based on the sublime. In his *Enquiry into the Sublime and Beautiful* (1968) [1757], which deals with the origin of our ideas of the sublime and beautiful, Burke maintains that the sublime is an aesthetic category independent of the beautiful and connected with the ideas of infinite and terror. In Burke's concept of sublime there is something which is bad, ugly, not perfect. In his view, the sentiment of the sublime is of universal character and arises in us from what is indeterminate, obscure and even dramatic. In the sublime there is a sense of infinity, inexpressible in terms of clarity and distinction. In line with his view of the sublime, Burke maintained that the object of the writer is to provoke thought rather than to encompass it. A point which Keynes endorsed in his economic writings.[16]

Moral conflicts and dilemmas: tragic choices

The existence of a plurality and variety of goodness (as well as of beauty) implies the possibility of a clash between opposite and irreconcilable claims, hence the possibility that the character of our value structure is indeterminate.[17] Ends, goals and concerns that the agent brings to a situation may be diverse and incommensurable and may not in themselves dictate any determinate decision and choice. As Aristotle notes, we face an indefinite or infinite range of contingencies with only finite powers of prediction and imagination (*Nicomachean Ethics* 1137b).

For there to be a moral dilemma, first there must be a situation in which a plurality of moral ends and values exist.[18] Plurality of values means that what is good necessarily lies in a large number of incompatible directions and it is intrinsically impossible that all of them should be followed through into realisations. For example, one cannot achieve pure simplicity and variegated richness in the same thing or on the same occasion. Yet both make claims upon us. In practice we often sacrifice one good to another or we reach a compromise and an accommodation. Practical compromises and accommodations override the claims of certain values. In tragic situations, however, we cannot easily sacrifice one good for another or override the claims of certain values. Both make a claim upon us and we have to choose anyway. A moral dilemma is a situation in which, through no prior moral fault of his own, an individual finds it impossible to avoid wrongdoing and objective guilt. An agent finds it impossible to make a moral choice between two or more alternatives. This means that the good and happy human life may sometimes include tragic choices, for the circumstances of life do not always promote the harmonious realisation of all our distinct ends. A good human life is associated with tragic choices and dilemmas.

Plural values imply that they may be incommensurable and eventually clash. The plurality of heterogeneous and multidimensional claims means that they may be in conflict among themselves. Conflicting claims may generate dilemmas in choice. Conflicts originate because there is no common unit of measure or a common scale on which to weigh the opposite claims.

Tragedy represents the typical situation of moral conflict in which whatever one does something will be regretted. According to Antonin Artaud, tragedy and drama originated as an expression of man's great fears, as a response to the dangers of human life and as a reflection of conflict. Conflict was the thread of all ancient drama. The basic human action that created drama is the conflict between the forces of good and the forces of evil. The conflictual nature of drama developed from the religious theme of good versus evil and from the permanent contrast between God and evil. Drama represents the means of resisting evil and promoting good. This is the concept of the struggle and conflict of human life. Anxiety and fear were important elements of the tragic outlook because this meant that man was constantly in a dilemma as to the necessary course of human action. History is the story of the fragility of human civilisation (see Artaud 1958).

In literature, tragedy has been read either as rational sublimate contemplation or as a participate immersion. Hence, on the one hand, as an overcoming of conflicts in a static manner or, on the other, as a disclosure of contradictions and conflicts. The typical characteristic of tragedy is pathos, i.e. suffering which brings about awareness. The fabric of tragedy is myth which, as the anthropologist Lévi-Strauss noted, is the act of becoming aware of certain oppositions and the tendency to their progressive mediation.

In the most frequently discussed putative case of moral dilemma, Aeschylus's *Oresteia*, Agamemnon has to choose between violating his duty as a parent and violating his duty as the leader of a military expedition. The conflicting claims are family love and love of one's country. Agamemnon's situation is indeed morally tragic: each of these duties urges with undiminished force despite the existence and applicability of the other. That is, neither duty overrides the other, thus making it right not to fulfil the other; rather, both have their full force as duties. For that reason Agamemnon must incur guilt whatever he decides to do. Each of the conflicting obligations, duties or claims has a moral force of its own. The superiority of commonsense morality over consequentialism lies in the fact that it allows for such varying sources of moral obligation and thus can accommodate the complexity of moral life. The existence of dilemmas is but one illustration of the richness, subtlety and difficulty of moral life.

Keynes's moral conflicts

Keynes referred to moral conflicts and dilemmas in many places and also paid attention to various types of conflicts in his early writings: the conflicts of duties, moral claims, values, interests and desires. In particular he referred to:

1 The conflict between rational egoism and rational benevolence (Keynes MSS, *Modern Civilisation* and *Egoism*).[19]

2 The conflict between 'being good' and 'doing good'. In his paper *Egoism*:

> But is the obligation to do good? Is it not rather to be good? . . . Suppose they conflict: which is then paramount? The long train of English ethical philosophers have either accepted the paramount authority of Egoism or have expressly reconciled the conflict and harmonised the moral consciousness by invoking the Justice of God or the essentially just order of the Universe. For my goodness and the goodness of the Universe both seem to have a claim upon me and claims which I cannot easily reduce to common terms and weigh against one another upon a common balance.
>
> But why on earth should I sacrifice my peace and comfort in order to produce this quality in remote parts of the globe or in future time, where and when I shall have no opportunity of perceiving or appreciating it? Where is the motive? Where is the obligation?
>
> (Keynes MSS, *Egoism*)

And in his paper *Obligation*:

> I think I know now – at any rate in some cases – what states of mind are good, but I still waver as to what ought to exist. And my attempt to identify the two has constantly led to difficulties.
>
> (Keynes MSS, *Obligation*)

3 The conflict between public and private life. In his *Modern Civilisation* (1905) Keynes already considers public life as equally important as private life and a possible source of conflict (Keynes MSS, *Modern Civilisation*).

4 The conflict between moral duties: between particular and general good; between the interest of the individual and the interest of the community. In his essay on Burke, Keynes comments on Burke's remarks on duties admitting the possibility of a clash between them:

> Duties will sometimes cross one another. Then questions will arise, which of them is to be placed in subordination? . . . the possibility of a clash between the achievement of the greatest amount of good experienced by an individual and that of the greatest amount experienced by the community.
>
> (Keynes MSS, *The Political Doctrines of Edmund Burke*: 10–11)

Here Keynes explicitly refers to Agamemnon's tragic dilemma (either to save his daughter or to save his kingdom). In his view, Burke could not appreciate Agamemnon's tragic situation as he did not believe in a clash between the two interests:

> Agamemnon's behaviour to his daughter would not have met with approval in Burke's eyes, whether it were certainly conducive to general utility or not. He was aided in the maintenance of this position by the belief that there can be no clash between particular and general goods, that the real interest of individual always coincides with the interest of the community.
>
> (Ibid.: 12)

In his view, Burke did not stress the conflict between particular and general good also because he was not really interested in distinguishing between the *real* interest of the individual and the interest of the community:

> he [Burke] is very careful to insert the word 'real' and it is possible that thus he hid from himself the latent difficulty . . . he cannot be distinguishing *real* from *apparent* interest, for the maintenance of property is clearly of the latter type. I think he means that it is to the *real* interest of an individual that the greatest amount of good should exist, and if this is the case it plainly coincides with the general interest.
>
> (Ibid.)

Keynes stresses that Burke's lack of perception of Agamemnon's tragic situations is to be linked with 'his disbelief in the value to morality of a true analysis into moral judgements, prejudices, and motives – if not his belief in the active perniciousness of such analysis' (ibid.: 21).

5 The conflicts of desires: in particular, the conflict between the desire for pleasure and for goodness. Keynes devoted special attention to this last type of conflict in his paper *Virtue and Happiness*. Desires being multiple and heterogeneous, they may clash.[20] In Keynes's case the specific conflict is between the desire for pleasure and the desire for goodness. Both of these desires are ultimate, so they cannot be ordered on a univocal scale. Pleasure and goodness are both worthy in themselves, not only as a means for something else: he writes, 'both are alike in this respect'. He considers the desire for pleasure and the desire for goodness as irreconcilable. Why are they irreconcilable? Because the two units of measure are incommensurable: 'In the attempt to reconcile these two incommensurable units . . .'. In *Egoism* the same point is restressed: 'claims which I cannot easily reduce to common terms and weigh against one another upon a common balance' (Keynes MSS, *Egoism*). It means that there is no common unit of measure, no common balance on which to weigh the two heterogeneous desires. The two units of measure are heterogeneous; pleasure and goodness are qualitatively and dimensionally different:

> We seem to have these two conflicting kinds of judgement, a hedonistic judgement and an ethical judgement – both ultimate and both alike in this respect. . . . We desire pleasure, and we desire the good; it is as little worth while to ask why in the one case as in the other; and the first is as much or as little of a purely psychological statement as is the second. It is – obviously enough – in the attempt to reconcile these two incommensurable units that a score or so of religions and philosophies have begun.
>
> (Keynes MSS, *Virtue and Happiness*: 4)

In *Virtue and Happiness* Keynes criticises all the methods of reconciling this conflict adopted in history both by religion and philosophy. Four main methods are identified by him:

(a) the good is only the pleasurable; this solution has been adopted by utilitarians,
(b) the good is always associated with the pleasurable,
(c) to deny the authenticity either of the goodness or of the pleasure (the second is Moore's method),
(d) it is a mystery.[21]

Keynes holds that all these four attempts to solve the conflict between these opposite claims can actually be reduced to two: either by reducing the two terms to one or by denying the existence of one of the two terms. The latter method is particularly interesting, as it is Moore's method of solving conflict, a method which Keynes opposes. On this point Keynes's criticism of Moore is again typically Aristotelian. Let us recall that Aristotle, unlike Plato, stresses the plurality and the variety of goodness and the fact that good is not reducible to a univocal scale. In Keynes's view, Moore abolishes conflict by denying the existence of pleasure. In this way Moore avoids the problems of the incommensurability and non-comparability of magnitudes. In this way he reduces his notion of goodness to a univocal scale and to a common unit in a way similar to that of both Plato with his concept of good and the utilitarians with their concept of pleasure or utility. Thus, in Keynes's view, Plato, the Utilitarians and Moore too, although in different ways, abolish conflict between the different kinds of goodness, by reducing goodness, pleasure or utility to a unidimensional magnitude. Keynes considers this unacceptable.

Rational conflicts and dilemmas: conflicting arguments, judgements, evidence and reasons

The theme of rational conflicts is obviously connected with that of moral conflicts. In moral dilemmas a conflict exists between moral claims, while in rational dilemmas a conflict exists between reasons, grounds, arguments or evidence (conflicting reasons). Conflicting arguments as too conflicting moral claims lead equally to indecision, vacillation of judgement, indeterminate action and uncertainty: no general rule of decision to solve the dilemma is possible in either case:

> I cannot decide between the conflicting arguments; probably no general decision is possible. Sometimes the one and sometimes the other is true.
>
> (Keynes MSS, *Beauty*: 25)

In logic, rational dilemmas have been carefully considered by theorists. One of them is the dilemma of Buridan's ass, which represents a typical situation of indecision. Keynes refers to this dilemma both in his early 1907–8 versions of the *Principles of Probability* and in his 1938 letter to Townshend (Keynes 1971–89, XXIX: 289, 294):

> when there is no reason for preferring any one to any others, when there is nothing, as with Buridan's ass, to determine the mind in any one of the several possible directions.
>
> (Keynes MSS, 1907 version of *The Principles of Probability*: 75)

The dilemma is well known: the ass faces two equal heaps, one of straw and one of hay, but, being unable to choose between the two, dies of hunger. Truly, this dilemma is not a real situation of tragic conflict and dilemma, as in this case the alternatives are equally *right* and there is a general rule of decision to overcome it: just eat one of the heaps. In real tragic conflicts and dilemmas, on the contrary, the alternatives are truly conflicting. In Agamemnon's moral conflict, for example, the two alternatives are ethically equally unacceptable and regrettable: the death of his daughter Iphigenia and the death of his soldiers. In true rational conflict, both alternatives should be compelling reasons. Neither is more reasonable but the decision has to be taken anyway and with regret. In true rational conflict, further, the compelling reasons which back our judgement may not only conflict one with the other but move in opposite multidimensional directions and we have to reach an overall judgement anyway.

Similarly to the case of moral dilemmas, to give rise to irresolvable rational conflict, the reasons have first to be plural. Secondly, they are to be dimensionally non-homogeneous. Thus there should not be a common unit of measure, a common balance to weigh or order reasons. This raises the general problem of the incommensurability and non-comparability of magnitudes.

In the beginning Keynes was interested in rational dilemmas mainly as concern probability: the conflict is between *some* reasons within probable judgement. But the theme of incommensurability and non-comparability of magnitudes spread out from his theory of probability almost immediately to enter the heart of his economics: in his *Essay on Index Numbers* (1909); at the beginning of *A Treatise on Money*; in chapter 4 of the *General Theory*.

As to probability, Keynes dealt with the incommensurability and non-comparability of reasons in probable judgements in his early 1907 and 1908 versions of *The Principles of Probability* and in the final 1921 version, *A Treatise on Probability*.[22]

Situations of rational dilemmas arise when there is conflict between incommensurable or opposite heterogeneous reasons (evidence or grounds) within a single judgement of probability so that these reasons cannot be weighed one against the others. As a result, the probabilities of the different alternatives cannot be ordered in terms of equal, more or less. In *A Treatise on Probability* the best known example is the so-called dilemma of the umbrella. High barometer and black clouds represent opposite and conflicting reasons:

> Is our expectation of rain, when we start out for a walk, always more likely than not, or less likely than not, or as likely as not? I am prepared to argue that on some occasions none of these alternatives hold, and that it will be an arbitrary matter to decide for or against the umbrella. If the barometer is high, but the clouds are black, it is not always rational that one should prevail over the other in our minds, or even that we should balance them – though it would be rational to allow caprice to determine us and to waste no time on the debate.
>
> (Keynes 1971–89, VIII: 32)

In probability, situations of rational dilemmas can also arise when there is conflict between the different orders of probability – that is, note, even when probabilities are rankable. In that case, orders of probability are heterogeneous and move in different incommensurable directions and dimensions. Other situations can arise when there is conflict between orders of probability and orders of goodness, or between orders of probability and orders of the weight of argument respectively.

> It has been argued that in these cases the probabilities are, in fact, not comparable. As in the example of similarities, where there are different orders of increasing and diminishing similarity, but where it is not possible to say of every pair of objects which of them is on the whole the more like a third object, so there are different orders of probability, and probabilities, which are not of the same order, cannot be compared.
>
> (Ibid.: 122)

In Keynes's economics we find it already emerges in the papers he wrote for Marshall in 1905. In his 9 November essay on the comparison between the railway services of different countries he stressed the difficulty of using incommensurable reasons of 'different kinds' which move in different directions to reach a judgement as a whole. It is difficult to compare the railway services of Prussia and the United States if the passenger and freight services in the two countries move in opposite, incommensurable directions:

> the matter will be argued under several different heads, and there is no method of making these different considerations altogether *commensurable*. There is no practical rule for adding and subtracting advantages and disadvantages of different kinds. When we have as many considerations before us as is possible, the best we can do is to summarise them in some general statement based rather on common sense than on any scientific principle.
>
> Any weighing of the two [the passenger services and the freight services of Prussia and the United States] against one another is almost impossible . . . if, as is probable, the passenger service of Prussia is superior to that of USA and the freight service inferior, it is difficult to see on what principles we are to decide as to which country has the superior service on the whole.
>
> (Keynes MSS, *Economic Essays*, 9 November 1905)[23]

His early interest in incommensurability and non-comparability in ethics and in probability may have been reinforced by his discussions with Marshall, as Raffaelli (1996) suggests. But it should be noted that the economic essays which Keynes wrote for Marshall are posterior to his ethical paper *Virtue and Happiness*, which was written after the Easter vacation 1905 and in which, as we saw on p. 271, he points out the negative 'attempt to reconcile these two incommensurable units' (Keynes MSS, *Virtue and Happiness*: 4). These essays are also posterior to his *A Scheme for an Essay on the Principles of Probability* of 5 September 1905 (Keynes MSS, *A Scheme for an Essay on the Principles of Probability*, 5 September 1905).

In Keynes's economics, incommensurability and non-comparability are connected with his notion of complex magnitudes, such as real income, real capital and the general price level.[24] In the *General Theory* Keynes likens the difficulty of comparing complex economic magnitudes with that of comparing the two queens, Queen Elizabeth and Queen Victoria, when orders of happiness and goodness move in opposite directions. The 1936 comparison recalls the 1905 comparison of the different kinds of railway services in Prussia and the United States. The passage ends, in an Aristotelian way, with a reference to 'mock precision':

> To say that net output today is greater, but the price level lower, than ten years ago or one year ago, is a proposition of a similar character to the statement that Queen Victoria was a better queen but not a happier woman than Queen Elizabeth – a proposition not without meaning and not without interest, but unsuitable as material for differential calculus. Our precision will be a mock precision if we try to use such partly vague and non-quantitative concepts as the basis of a quantitative analysis.
>
> (Keynes 1971–89, VII: 40)

The dilemmas of the umbrella in *A Treatise on Probability*, of Queens Victoria and Elizabeth in *The General Theory*, of Buridan's ass in the letter to Townshend in 1939 (Keynes 1971–89, XXIX) are some of the examples to which Keynes refers in his later writings. Certainly in comparison with the great moral dilemmas of Agamemnon in Greek tragedy (the dilemma of whether to save his daughter or to save his kingdom) the rational dilemma of the umbrella described by Keynes in particular is not very heroic. It is typically bourgeois, and slightly English as well. Keynes's solution is just to take the umbrella and waste no time (Keynes 1971–89, VIII: 32).[25] However, it does represent a situation of non-comparability of reasons in human decision making and it can be applied to economic decisions too. Rational dilemmas characterise situations of indecision, of irreducible conflict where reasons (*some* reasons, to be precise) cannot be weighed. These situations are similar to tragic situations. They are the domain of radical uncertainty.[26]

Conclusion

We have seen how tragedy influenced Keynes from the very beginning of his intellectual career. I have suggested that his constant attention to the incommensurability and incomparability of magnitudes (probability and economic magnitudes such as real income and general price level) may derive from his early interest in dilemmas and that his concept of uncertainty could be connected with rational dilemmas and tragic choices. So, in brief, I have suggested that, in Keynes, incommensurability, incomparability and uncertainty are somehow loosely connected with Greek tragedy.

Notes

I thank the Keynes Trustees for permission to quote from Keynes's manuscripts, held in King's College, Cambridge.

1 Keynes writes: 'But we cannot, for that reason, ignore the outside world, real life – London and New York and Paris and Vienna, where fortunes are made and tragedies enacted, where men really bugger one another and go to prison for it' (Keynes MSS, *Modern Civilisation*; see also Moggridge 1992: 128).

2 As to the condition of Europe after the First World War, an explicit reference to Aeschylus's *Oresteia* can be found in Keynes's letter to H. de Peyster on 25 February 1921: 'I will be no party to a continuation of a European blood feud, however great the past guilt. In Cambridge here, this term, we are performing the Aeschylean trilogy and the theme of that great drama is in our minds. I want to see the Furies turned into Eumenides, clothed in red robes, and pacifically housed under the Acropolis' (Keynes 1971–89, XVII: 219–20).

3 His interest in the 'heroic' mixture of sentiment and reason can be seen also from the books he read. Among them we find Jane Austen's *Sense and Sensibility*, a book on the mingling of reason and sentiment (Keynes MSS, *Books Read* in 1905–6).

4 In his theory of probability another example of Keynes's attention to the interplay between reason and passion is his comment on Locke's passage in the *Essay concerning Human Understanding*: 'Tell a man, passionately in love, that he is jilted; bring a score of witnesses of the falsehood of his mistress, it is ten to one but these kind words of hers shall invalidate all their testimonies' (p. 333). In this passage Locke points out that passion clouds reason. Keynes's comment is that Locke considers this 'as a case where passions overbear probabilities', that is, where passion clouds limited reason. In his view, on the contrary, this is 'a case when action – rightly – depends not merely on probability, but on probability multiplied by importance' (Keynes MSS, *Notes on Locke*).

5 On the role of intuition in the *General Theory* (Keynes 1971–89, VII: 249): 'If we examine any actual problem along the lines of the above schematism, we shall find it more manageable; and our practical intuition (which can take account of more detailed complex of facts than can be treated on general principles) will be offered a less intractable material upon which to work'. On animal spirits see Keynes 1971–89, VII: chapter 12.

6 See also: 'Let this be agreed on from the start, that every statement concerning matters of practice ought to be said in outline and not with precision, as we said in the beginning that statements should be demanded in a way appropriate to the matter at hand. And matters of practice and questions of what is advantageous never stand fixed, any more than do matters of health. If the universal definition is like this, the definition concerning particulars is even more lacking in precision. For such cases do not fall under any science (*techne*) nor under any precept, but the agents themselves must in each case look for what suits the occasion, as is also the case in medicine and navigation' (Aristotle, *Nicomachean Ethics* 1103b 34–1104a 10). Martha Nussbaum (1986: especially chapter 10 on 'Non-scientific deliberation' and p. 258) points out that the demands of Platonic *techne* for generality, commensurability and precision were not accepted by Aristotle as to ethics.

7 See Anagnostopoulos (1994: 55–60, 91, 269–70) and especially chapter 8 on 'Variation, indefiniteness and exactness'.

8 On this, it could be noted that Hayek held the exactly opposite view. Hayek held that we can never know what other people think (see Carabelli and De Vecchi 1999; see also Skidelsky 1996: 4).

9 Plurality, incommensurability and non-comparability of values imply difficulties as to the *intra*-personal comparison of values. Difficulties may also arise in the *inter*-personal comparison of values, that is, in the comparison between different subjects' values. Difficulties in comparing one man's virtues with those of another are equally stressed by Keynes: 'For granting . . . that there is a sense in which probability is capable of more or less, is it the case that *all* probabilities are comparable with one another in respect of magnitude? I think I can show that it is as impossible strictly to compare the magnitude of the probabilities of some pairs of statements, each relative to given evidence, as to compare the magnitude of one man's virtue with that of another man's talent' (Keynes MSS, *Draft of the Chapter on the Measurement of Probability*).

10 The existence of a contrast between Keynes and Moore on ethics already in 1905 is shown by a comment that Moore made to Russell on 23 October 1905 while discussing a paper on ethics by the latter. Moore's comment concerning Keynes's own interpretation of ethics is quoted in P. Levi's biography of Moore: 'After insisting that 'right conduct' depends so much on good results, I think it would be absurd not to try to indicate what results are good. I don't know what Keynes's view about goods and organic unities is. But it seems to me plain that, in the form you mention it, it must be wrong' (P. Levi 1979: 258; Moore's letter to Russell is in the Russell papers at McMaster University).

11 Keynes did not accept Moore's Platonic contemplation as early as 1905. In contrast to what he wrote in his *My Early Beliefs* (1938), in that year Keynes had already 'reached' Plato's later dialogues, the *Republic*, the *Laws* and, I would add, Aristotle's writings on ethics and politics. He read Plato's *Republic*, the *Symposium* and Aristotle's *Politics* during the Easter vacation 1905 (Keynes MSS, *Books Read* on Easter vacation 1905). He read Plato's *Laws* on 1 December 1905, the *Philebus* on 19 January 1906, Aristotle's *Ethics* (*Eudimian Ethics* and *Nicomachean Ethics*) on 20–23 January (Keynes MSS, *Diary* 1905–6).

12 In the 1960s attention was paid to plurality and the mutual irreducibility of goodness by many authors. In 1963 Von Wright stressed the plurality of goodness in his book on 'the variety of goodness'. In 1966 B. A. O. Williams did the same in his article 'Consistency and realism'. After that Bernard Williams was very critical of both the Utilitarian and Kantian theories and revived ancient Greek thought in ethics. He was

also sceptical of all systematic theorising in ethics. In 1969 Isaiah Berlin pointed this theme out in his introduction (p. xlix) to his book *Four Essays on Liberty*. In the 1970s the theme was revived by David Wiggins in 'Truth invention and the meaning of life' (1976), now reprinted in his *Needs, Values, Truth, Essays in the Philosophy of Value* (1987). In 1988 Shelly Kagan denied that different sorts of good and the factors that go into moral calculation are generally separable. From ethics the theme entered into economics, where attention was paid to plurality and the mutual irreducibility of goodness, in particular by Amartya Sen in his article 'Plural utility' (1981). From Sen's early contribution the theme has now fully entered economic literature (see Broome 1991). It is to be noted, however, that none of these authors has noticed that this same point lies right at the beginning of Keynes's own reflections on ethics and probability and is also at the root of his notion of radical uncertainty.

13 Keynes writes: '[Practical ethics] would concern itself with conduct; it would investigate the difficult questions of the probable grounds of actions, and the curious connection between 'probable' and 'ought'; and it would endeavour to formulate or rather to investigate existing general maxims, bearing in mind their strict relativity to particular circumstances' (Keynes MSS, *Miscellanea Ethica*).

14 For Keynes, virtue, education and politics belong to practical ethics: 'Practical Ethics: (i) The nature and value of virtue; (ii) The theory and methods of Education; (iii) The theory and methods of Politics' (Keynes MSS, *Miscellanea Ethica*, 31 July 1905).

15 In his undated paper *On Beauty and Art. On Art Criticism and the Appreciation of Beauty* Keynes writes: 'But it is my opinion that the larger number of errors and quarrels concerning aesthetic theory are due to a neglect to notice that there are many and as different kinds of beauty as of virtue and that those differing classes which are just entitled to the general name of beautiful are with difficulty distinguished from yet wider class and further the usurpation of the title for one particular but varying division of the general class' (Keynes MSS, *On Beauty and Art. On Art Criticism and the Appreciation of Beauty*: 5).

16 Another influence may also have been Kant. In his *Observations on the Sentiment of the Beautiful and Sublime* (1764) and in his *Critique of Judgement* (1790) Kant maintains that the sublime is what is absolutely great, that is, great beyond any possible comparison.

17 The literature on moral dilemmas has been growing (Gowans 1987; Sinnot-Amstrong 1988). A persuasive example of modern tragic dilemma is Sophie's choice from William Styron's book of that name: the choice between saving her son or saving her daughter from extermination by the Nazis. (In order to save one child she must offer the other for extermination, and if she does nothing, both will be taken.) Another is Sartre's example: the young partisan whose choice was between caring for his infirm mother and joining the Free French army.

18 On the plurality and incommensurability of moral considerations and on the complex whole of disparate and incommensurable elements see Stocker (1990: especially chapter 5, 'Plurality and choice', and chapter 8, 'Monism, pluralism and conflict').

19 It should be noted – as Moggridge (1992: 112–13; see also 128–30) points out – that in *Principia Ethica*, Moore had argued that 'rational egoism was self-contradictory' and that 'Sidgwick's method of resolving the conflict between rational egoism and rational benevolence which had required him to bring divine omnipotence into play had resulted from a false antithesis'.

20 On internal conflicts in desires and morals see Jackson (1985).

21 The whole passage reads: 'Some have solved the difficulty by denying the distinction – the good is the pleasurable. We know the arguments against that. The next method is to admit the distinction but to assert that the two are always found together, either in this life, which experience contradicts, or ultimately in the life to come, which you may believe or not as you choose. The third method is to deny altogether the claims or authenticity of one of the two, either the good – which is not considered respectable –, or of pleasure – which is the method of Moore. The last method is to regard the entire business as a holy mystery, and to hope for a higher synthesis

out of time – not that this really lessens the mystery' (Keynes MSS, *Virtue and Happiness*: 4).

22 As to probability, Keynes maintains that probability relations are of different kinds and are characterised by a multiplicity of units of measure: 'The magnitudes of probability relations must be measured in various units according to the particular case in question, these units being incommensurable among themselves' (Keynes MSS, 1907 version of *The Principles of Probability*: 67). And in the 1921 final version: 'A degree of probability is not composed of some homogeneous material, and is not apparently divisible into parts of like character with one another' (Keynes 1971–89, VIII: 32).

23 See also a passage from his essay on index numbers of 31 October 1905 which he wrote for Marshall: 'In [question] (a) we are treating a vague question (for general purchasing power is a vague expression) with perfectly definite data . . . difficulties . . . arise from the inexplicit character of our object and we require practical judgement' (Keynes MSS, *Essay on Index Numbers*).

24 See Carabelli (1992, 1994).

25 To face dilemmas Keynes suggests having recourse to direct judgements on the situation as a whole and to intuition. Recourse to these solutions is not judged by him as irrational. On the rationality of decision in situations of dilemmas see Polock (1984).

26 Situations of radical uncertainty different from those of rational dilemmas here analysed are: probability with low weight of argument; total lack of reasons or evidence.

19 Was Keynes a truly heretic economist?

Marcello De Cecco

Many attempts have been made to place Keynes in the camp of the heretic economists. Caravale (1997b), on the contrary, tried to emphasise the similarities between Keynes and the classical tradition especially as regards the notion of equilibrium. Some of Caravale's reasoning concerning equilibrium was motivated in part by an article by Giorgio Lunghini (1997), in which the underemployment equilibrium was grouped with what Lunghini called 'heretical' equilibria. These included Marx, Schumpeter and Keynes, who considered crisis as equilibrium and equilibrium in the orthodox sense as so rare a case as to be insignificant. Caravale makes a very noble and very serious attempt to move Keynes back within the bounds of the classical tradition. But, as Caravale himself admits, this attempt faces the difficulty of coming to terms with the very first page of the *General Theory*, where Keynes offers a different reading of the classical school – that school whose 'modes of thought and expression' Keynes had such a struggle to escape from.

Actually, Keynes's position is far from free of contradictions and ambiguities. And this is why any attempt at boxing him within a definitive interpretation is bound to be unsuccessful. Most of Keynes's positions can be considered a sort of compromise between the opposite forces of the new ideas he was elaborating and the need he felt to communicate authoritatively with the establishment of his day. It is this latter aspect of Keynes's thought that I want to focus on here.

Goodwin (1992) maintains that Keynes's *General Theory* challenges the hypothesis that the economy can be thought of in terms of a constrained maximisation approach, with the constraint imposed by non-produced resources, most notably labour. The consequence of this challenge is that cleared markets everywhere will not be found, particularly as regards the labour market. This is why, as Goodwin often said, Keynes adopted the aggressive concept of underemployment equilibrium, which the prevailing orthodoxy held could not exist. Goodwin pointed out that it could not exist in an instantaneous sense, and the same criticism was reiterated by Tinbergen and others. Goodwin's article magisterially summarises this debate in the space of a few lines.

Keynes's work, particularly the *General Theory*, contains a series of contradictions that are one reason why it is so fascinating. However, this same factor has also offered everyone a leg up in the never-ending discussion about what Keynes really wanted to say. And the things he wanted to say were legion, as are the echoes transmitted by this most learned of men, who had few peers in practising the very Italian art of speaking authoritatively and convincingly even on matters of which he had rather limited knowledge. There is a great affinity between Keynes and Italian culture. He is a reviewer of little-read books. Keynes must be taken for what he actually was: a man who often changed his mind, taking up the latest and most interesting ideas suggested to him by his readings and associations in every field, and always apparently genuinely convinced of the truth of what he was saying. That at least is what Sraffa was fond of telling me and, I believe, many others who questioned him about the ambiguities of the *General Theory*.

The attempt, therefore, is to move Keynes from the camp of the heretics to that of the theorists of orthodox equilibrium, the classical school. If you examine Keynes's work closely, you will find that even in the *General Theory* his reference model is that of his teachers, including Marshall. The error arises because Keynes wanted to polarise Marshall, but in this he could not succeed by willpower alone. Those who have read both Marshall and Keynes find the differences between them less striking than the similarities. I am surely not the first to have found Marshall in Keynes and Keynes *in statu nascenti* in Marshall. Keynes took a further step – a giant step, to be sure, but along the path of continuity with the Cambridge school.

The problem is that Keynes also wanted to adhere to the developments that had followed Marshall. And this in an era, after the First World War, when more than one science had turned back from the determinism of the 1800s to the uncertainty of the 1600s, a century in which we find plagues striking with even greater virulence than in the past and men no longer resigned to their destiny but not yet able to challenge it, as they would later thanks to the quantum leap of the applied sciences. In the 1600s gambling was rampant, perhaps as a reaction to the prevalent uncertainty, and there appeared a spate of theoretical analyses of the supposed principles underlying games of chance, most notably probability theory. It is no coincidence that probability theory enjoyed a great revival after the First World War, which destroyed the certainty of Victorians everywhere. Victorianism was a category of the spirit, and Keynes quite rightly made it the target of his fiercest and most convincing criticism. But he directed his fire above all at Victorians-after-the-fact, at those who dreamt of resurrecting what was in fact a largely illusory pre-war world, a world that Keynes knew was gone for good. None the less, in his theory Keynes wished, as it were, to combine Queen Victoria and gambling – he would have been better advised to have done without the Queen – and one is never quite sure which of the theory's elements are essential and which superfluous. This is because Keynes himself wanted to keep both components as fundamental.

One of the phrases cited by Victoria Chick (see p. 172, this volume), and which can be appropriately invoked against Anna Carabelli's idea that Keynes renounced tradition, concerns the 'real wage, which is no greater than the marginal disutility of that amount of employment'. Such expressions carry weight, and Keynes used them intentionally in order to create a frame of reference, a language that would allow him to be taken seriously by his fellow economists and to avoid being lumped in with the heretics, as in Lunghini's classification. To be taken for a heretic meant having to make tragic decisions, which Keynes always wanted to avoid; being relegated among the 'cranks', a universe taken seriously only by the tabloid press and by a few extremist politicians such as Mosley; leading a shadow existence outside the gilded halls of the great colleges and London clubs, of the country houses, where the decisions were made that would determine the future of Britain and the rest of the world, where admission depended on wearing the mantle of authority of an official science, a status that orthodox economics had attained only a few decades earlier. Keynes wanted to be taken seriously and he was in fact taken seriously, but he had to pay the price of using a language that was still tied to tradition. If he had turned his back on the world from which he came, he would have passed beyond the 'wormhole' that Rotheim has spoken of. This he absolutely did not want to do. He knew that his ability to influence Britain's economy, his overriding concern, depended on his being part of the establishment; forsaking the language of economic orthodoxy would inevitably have placed him too far to the right or left, outside the establishment. He would have become 'irrelevant', a fate he feared more than death itself. The sentiment is easily understood by those who ply Keynes's trade.

Gianni Caravale attempted to combine the Keynesian short-term equilibrium with the classical long-term equilibrium, the equilibrium of equal profitability across all sectors. And he did so even while recognising, as Chick correctly points out, that it makes little sense to imagine a Keynesian long run: Keynes truly thought of the world as ever changing, as Hemingway's movable feast, where today exists and yesterday is dead but for some peripheral lingering features and the future concerns us only for the small bit that we can decide within the sphere of the horrible, total uncertainty in which, at bottom, Keynes believed more strongly than anything else. Thus, even with the aid of Robinson's 'logical time' – I personally think that the cause of clarity would be advanced if it were called 'thought experiment', because the word 'time' for us truly means time and is associated with a dimension known to all, precise and unambiguous – I believe that the only message to be drawn is that the Keynesian approach is totally opposed to the sequential approach. Keynes himself considered this certain, ridiculing those who were declared to be Keynesian but adopted the sequential approach. And he was correct, because the Keynesian method consists in 'telescoping' the analysis into a thought experiment. Everything is thought in this moment of time, which lasts only as long as we think and the decisions are made, and no more. At this point that is all we can do.

All that is revolutionary. Whether it belongs to a revolution that can be carried on is the question, however, for Keynes's is a very English revolution, one conducted by following Ricardo's method of saying 'Suppose not': let us suppose the contrary of what is ordinarily supposed, maintain the preceding model but turn it upside down, reverse the relationship of causality between the variables but not seek to create new ones. For this it was possible to develop the Keynesian synthesis, including Keynes within the fold of orthodoxy. If the variables had changed, if Keynes had invented other ones in the fashion of a true heretic, Hicks would not have been able to construct a model that embraces both the classical case and the Keynesian case as alternatives. They are alternatives, but the world is the same world, or at least so it seems to many who read Keynes through the lens of orthodoxy. They are wrong, but it was Keynes himself who wanted to be read through that lens; it was he who sent his book to Hicks for review and showed he was content with the review. Kahn and Robinson openly disapproved of this ambiguity on the part of the master, and for this they were clamorously passed over for the Nobel prize for economics, whereas I would bet any amount that had Keynes lived to be ninety he would have won the prize and been immensely proud of it.

This difference between the master and his disciples may make the master seem less consistent, but it also makes him far more human. And that was really what Keynes himself wanted as a theoretical economist, so as not to forsake any part of reality, including economic orthodoxy. To endeavour to resolve the Keynesian ambiguity, which is what Gianni Caravale and Victoria Chick appear to wish to do, means boxing poor Keynes into a corner, forcing him to abandon the gilded world that he loved being part of and to frequent the austere, no-frills (but certainly not uncomfortable) environment of those who, like the old man with the beard who is now out of favour, spent their days seated on the benches of the Reading Room in the British Museum.

20 Keynes, disequilibrium theory and New Keynesian economics

Bruno Jossa

As our current understanding of the working of the economy is far better than Keynes's, 'if New Keynesian economics is not a true representation of Keynes's view, then so much the worse for Keynes' (Mankiw 1992: 561). While this much-quoted statement of Mankiw's can barely be called into question, it remains that establishing whether New Keynesian economics (from here on NKE) will reflect fresh credit on *a non-neoclassical view* of economic activity (despite its departures from Keynes's thought) is a not unimportant undertaking. For this reason, following a cursory analysis of Keynes's place within economic theory we wish to point out if and how NKE can provide fresh scope for *a Keynesian view* of macroeconomics. However, as Keynes's services to economic theory are many and 'New Keynesian economists are an extremely heterogeneous group' (see Snowdon *et al.* 1994: 289; also Nisticò and D'Orlando 1995, 1998), before we can deny or endorse the Keynesian nature of NKE we will have to single out Keynes's main contribution to economic thought and the characteristics that writings by NKE theorists have in common.

This study is laid out as follows. The next section discusses the core contribution of the *General Theory*, which in our opinion is the theory of the multiplier in a situation with fixed prices. The following section (pp. 286–7) points out how NKE writings are reinforcing a Keynesian view of economic activity. Pages 287–8 address the issue of the neutrality of money and cancel from the list of 'Keynesian' theories those that accept the separation of the real sector from the monetary sector or the theory of the neutrality of money. Pages 289–90 investigate the reasons why Keynes's thinking may appear all the more consistent today provided it is referred to a system with fixed prices and wages. Pages 290–2 discuss the assumption that the Phillips curve is decreasing in the long run and the implications of this assumption in terms of assessing the Keynesian nature of NKE. Pages 292–4 highlight the points where Meltzer's approach to the *General Theory* differs from ours and analyse other aspects that may endorse the Keynesian nature of NKE. Pages 294–6 pose the question whether, and if so to what extent, NKE fits within a new paradigm of economic theory alternative to the neoclassical one.

Keynes's main legacy

In August 1939 Keynes was in a position to state: 'I have yet to discover anyone, who has really understood what I have said, who has disputed it' (see Keynes 1971–89, XIV: 276); years later Patinkin still maintained that 'the *General Theory* stood up most successfully under the criticisms that followed its appearance' and that its basic structure 'not only remained intact, but also defined the framework of both theoretical and empirical research in macroeconomics for decades to come' (Patinkin 1975: 268). Today thorough changes under way in the scenario of economic science may justify the doubt that there is still such a thing as a valid and widely accepted 'basic structure' of Keynesian theory.

The view that 'the crucial point of the *General Theory*' is 'the theory of effective demand as a theory which equilibrates aggregate demand with supply by means of automatic changes in the level of output' (Patinkin 1977: 11) has been widely shared up to the present; and in our opinion the most rigorous statement of the principle of effective demand is owed to the 'disequilibrium' or 'rationing models' theorists who hold that this principle is most clearly borne out in a situation with fixed prices.[1] Setting out from the differences between the actual decision-making process and the one theorised by Walras, they argue that Keynesian theory, by explaining how the economy works in the absence of an auctioneer, throws light on the real mechanisms governing a market economy where full-employment equilibrium is impeded by price viscosity.[2]

As a rule, demands and supplies will not balance out as long as prices are fixed. But, however strange this idea may at first appear, even the analysis of a situation in which demand does not equate with supply can be termed a general economic *equilibrium* study.[3] Indeed, the findings of the rationing models theorists generated a consistent theoretical framework about 'equilibrium with unemployment' which 'at last', forty years following the *General Theory*, stated intuitions that Keynes doubtless had although he failed to express them in clear terms.[4]

The adoption of a situation with fixed prices obviously entailed dropping the perfect competition assumption. As is well known, Keynes himself never took the trouble to criticise the perfect competition assumption or to incorporate into his analysis the theory of imperfect competition that Mrs Robinson had worked out while he was writing the *General Theory*. Nowhere in his book did he even mention imperfect competition, preferring to spell out that his thinking was entirely independent of the 'degree of competition' (Kregel 1998: 40);[5] hence the well known conclusion of Kregel and Casarosa, according to whom the Keynesian model is no more easily understood if the perfect competition hypothesis is dropped (see Kregel 1976: 218 n. 1; Casarosa 1981; Kregel 1987; Lawlor *et al.* 1987; Kregel and Nardozzi 1996: 174–5, 184).

In point of fact the opposite is true. According to Mrs Robinson, Keynes 'proposed a micro–macro theory in which the prices of commodities are primarily governed by the cost of production',[6] and Kahn repeatedly stressed that in Keynes 'the price level under conditions of equilibrium is determined by money costs of production per unit of product'.[7] These views endorse the argument that

Keynes's model is better understood in the light of imperfect competition or full-cost theory and may also explain why full-cost theory is often assumed to be the microeconomic basis of 'Post-Keynesian' theory (see, for example, Eichner and Kregel 1975: 1305–6; Kenyon 1978: 43 ff.; Jossa 1979). In the opinion of Tobin, 'Keynes certainly would have done better to assume imperfect or monopolistic competition throughout the economy' (Tobin 1993: 48; see also Brothwell 1997; Harcourt and Riach 1997b: xviii) and in the closing section of his exhaustive analysis of this subject Marris (1997) reached much the same conclusion.

According to Arrow, perfect competition is incompatible with Keynesian theory (see Arrow 1959: 41 ff.). As perfect competition entails unlimited outlets for individual firms, it is barely (or rather, merely formally but not substantially) reconcilable with Keynes's core assumption that firms reduce their output levels in consequence of insufficient effective demand (see Kahn 1977: 379, 386; Lindbeck 1998: 172–3). Also Weitzman (1982) went so far as to argue that unemployment can be explained only in terms of a situation of imperfect competition with increasing returns.[8]

The Keynesian nature of New Keynesian economics

The foregoing may help explain the Keynesian nature of NKE. As is well known, one crucial aspect common to the analyses we categorise as 'New Keynesian' is the assumption that firms and consumers have available an insufficient amount of information. As the rejection of the perfect information assumption necessarily entails dropping the perfect competition assumption as well, this is tantamount to arguing that NKE is trying to reconcile microeconomics with Keynesian macroeconomics by rejecting traditional microeconomic assumptions.

Accordingly it is fair to say that while new classical macroeconomics is adopting a modern perfect competition approach with *market clearing* (even when information is assumed to be imperfect), NKE never makes the perfect-competition assumption for all markets. Compared with neoclassical equilibrium models where firms act as *price takers*, NKE reverses the roles of prices and output levels by assuming that firms freely determine prices, but not output levels. 'Thus price-setting behavior is the essence of Keynesian economics', old and new (see Gordon 1990: 1136).[9] The behaviour of firms with limited outlets – in other words, imperfect competition – results in a gap between private and social costs which in turn creates both 'externalities of aggregate demand' and multiplier effects of changes in demand (see Mankiw and Romer 1991b: 7–8).[10]

A major merit of macroeconomic theories based on the imperfect competition assumption is the light they shed on pro-cyclical trends in real wages. According to some, 'it is a matter for regret that Keynes's summary of his arguments in chapter 18 of the *General Theory* and the formal modelling of Keynes's thinking by many later writers relied so much upon the neoclassical and Marshallian tools which then, as now, were the style of the day' (Greenwald and Stiglitz 1987: 127; see also Brothwell 1997; Darity and Young 1997). In line with the arguments set forth in the *General Theory*, but not with practical observation, the aim of these tools is to determine a decline of wages in periods of diminishing unemployment, while the imperfect competition assumption enables firms to increase output in proportion to demand even if wages do not decrease. And the latter argument is one with which many NKE authors concur (see, above all, Hart 1982; Hall 1986; Ball *et al.* 1991: 158).

Another theoretical insight owed to the imperfect-competition (versus perfect-competition) assumption is that increases in demand may boost employment even when prices are stable (see Ball *et al.* 1991: 156–7).[11] On closer analysis, this is just a way to reword our previous conclusion that perfect competition is incompatible with the principle of effective demand and one of the reasons why New Keynesians (departing from Keynes) prefer to lay stress on price stickiness rather than money-wage rigidity (Lindbeck 1998: 174). We shall come back to this point on pp. 289–90.

This concern with rigidity may explain why NKE is often taken for a theory which explains rigidities. And there is little doubt that the most important writings of NKE theorists are those in which real and monetary rigidities are shown to be determined by rational behaviour.[12]

Actually, nothing is further from the true spirit of these new theoretical approaches than the rigidity *assumption*. New Keynesian theorists usually share the view that macroeconomics cannot do without firm microeconomic foundations and that economic agents must necessarily be assumed to behave according to private profit calculations. 'Any attempt to build a model based on irrational behavior or sub-maximizing behavior is viewed as cheating' by New Keynesian economists (see Gordon 1990: 1137).[13] Hence the need to emphasise that NKE studies have provided demonstrations that prices and wages are rigid[14] or slow to adjust to market-clearing levels.[15]

According to many authors, one point to be emphasised when addressing the issue of imperfect markets is the distinction between product markets and the labour market. While it is true that all NKE theorists emphasise the imperfections of markets for industrial products and services, the Europeans among them lay greater stress on imperfect competition in the labour market – a fact which is usually associated with higher unionisation rates in Europe versus the United States (where only one in five workers is a union member).[16] The markedly conflictual thrust noted in papers by European writers, such as Carlin and Soskice (1990) and Layard *et al.* (1991), is usually traced back to the same reason.

Concerning the relative weight of rigidity in the commodities versus the labour market, orthodox theorists tend to assume a higher degree of rigidity in the labour market, while New Keynesians are either prepared to admit that the opposite may be true or, at least, that price viscosity has a major role in explaining nominal rigidity in general (see, among others, Ball and Romer 1990; Layard *et al.* 1991).

Rigidity, the neutrality of money and hysteresis[17]

Thus the New Keynesian macroeconomic research programme revolves mainly around the idea that any economic system is affected by pervading uncertainties, imperfect competition and rigidities of various kinds – characteristics which lead us to term NKE a non-Walrasian research programme. As has rightly been pointed out, in some non-Walrasian research programmes prices and wages fail to balance out demand and supply because they perform additional functions that often go to explain price and wage rigidity. In implicit contract theory, for example, wages are the means by which firms provide insurance to their workers; in many bargaining models they are the tools whereby profits from exchanges of goods are allocated between the firm and its workers; in efficiency wage theory they are a lever to increase worker productivity (see Romer 1993: 7).

A fundamental distinction is that between *monetary* and *real* rigidities. As rational individuals are concerned with real magnitudes, in models with rational expectations – i.e. purged of any 'monetary illusion' – the emphasis is mainly on real rigidities. In actual fact, however, prices and wages are expressed in monetary terms and (unless they are assumed to be infinitely flexible) are always characterised, by definition, by a certain degree of nominal rigidity; contracts, too, are mostly entered into on monetary terms and their amendment or prior termination necessarily entails paying a price. In a comparatively free market economy these monetary rigidities are generally found to play a negligible role, for prices can promptly be renegotiated at fairly low cost and contracts are usually entered into for a limited duration; all the same, the main NKE finding is that nominal rigidities, though small at the microeconomic level, may produce significant macroeconomic effects (see Mankiw 1985; Akerlof and Yellen 1985b).

Whereas the foregoing may explain the above-mentioned emphasis of NKE theorists on real and monetary rigidities alike, one argument may induce us to prioritise nominal versus real rigidity. Major merits to Keynes's credit are his stress on the indissoluble links between the real and monetary sectors and his criticism of the quantitative theory of money, which assumed a dichotomy between the real and monetary sectors or, at least, a neutral role of money. But real rigidities do not contradict the neutrality of money. NKE models accounting for real imperfections do explain unemployment, but not the way these two sectors interact with each other. As a result, they assume each increase in money supply to cause proportional increases in all prices without any impact on relative prices. Conversely, models accounting for monetary rigidities are essentially in conflict with the neutrality of money and will thus appear much more Keynesian (see Lindbeck 1998: 171–3).

A proper awareness of the weightiness of this issue will lead us to categorise as non-Keynesian any approaches which accept the quantitative theory of money. If we distinguish four schools of economics, traditional Keynesianism, new classical macroeconomics, New Keynesian economics and coordination failure theories, only the non-Walrasian current denying the neutral role of money falls within the scope of New Keynesian economics. This distinction determines that major approaches generally passed off as New Keynesian should actually be excluded from this group because (by admitting real rigidities only) they fail to confute the neutrality of money assumption. According to those who accept this classification, non-Walrasian approaches that do not reject the neutrality of money must be categorised as coordination failure theories (see Romer 1993: 20–2; also Mankiw and Romer 1991b: 2).

Disequilibrium theory, the Phillips curve and New Keynesian economics

At this point we may ask ourselves why the rigidity issue should carry such a great weight when it comes to assessing the Keynesian nature of a theory. In our opinion this can be explained by the particular turn the debate on the Phillips curve took in the 1970s and by the crisis that Keynesian theory experienced when many Keynesians accepted the verticality of the long-run Phillips curve.[18] A vertical long-run Phillips curve, even in its NAIRU version, entails the assumption that there is only one income equilibrium value. When even those endorsing a conflictual view of the Phillips curve accepted this idea, most economists concluded that Keynesian theory was valid only in a short-term time horizon. In other words, price rigidity was associated with a short-term view and price flexibility with a long-term view, and Keynesian theory itself was linked with price rigidity in consequence of the assumption that price flexibility leads to the NRU or NAIRU – an equilibrium income level (even with involuntary unemployment, as is the NAIRU) not accounted for in Keynesian theory.[19]

This problem requires further discussion. As has often been argued, the debate on Keynesian theory has been so thorough and divisive that the term 'Keynesian' means widely differing things to different theorists (see, for example, Mankiw and Romer 1991b: 2–3); as mentioned before, that is why the correct identification of the main legacy of the *General Theory* within economic science is an essential prerequisite for assessing the Keynesian nature of NKE or its place within Keynesian theory. If the multiplier theorem is actually the core of the *General Theory*, the most rigorous statement of Keynesian theory is owed to disequilibrium theorists, and this may explain why we are trying to establish a link between disequilibrium theory and NKE. Yet, as New Keynesian macroeconomic theorists have never shown any interest in disequilibrium theory, to avoid the charge of distorting historical truth we shall have to back up our conclusion with further evidence.

Let us start with the idea that NKE theorists have greatly diverging ideas concerning economic policy. They are little concerned with the monetarism/fiscalism option; and there is no doubt that NKE theorists may be categorised as monetarists when they assume that economic fluctuations are determined mainly by money supply. In other words, as traditional monetarists have always failed to explain price rigidity while holding monetary variables to produce real effects as long as prices are rigid, many of the theories here under review may even be said to make up a sort of 'new monetarist economy' (see Mankiw and Romer 1991b: 3). For this reason, the scant concern of NKE with economic policy can be traced to its lack of clear political economy implications. NKE's main concern is to emphasise that imperfect markets are the rule and that the product combinations devised in the world in which we live are consequently inefficient; but from this NKE fails to derive major suggestions for government action both because its approach to market imperfections differs from that of traditional welfare theory and because it does not confute the criticisms of state intervention in the economy voiced by economic liberalists (ibid.).

As for us, these are not the main reasons of the scant attention of NKE for economic policy. We rather think that the main reason behind NKE's scant concern with economic policy is that New Keynesians, while firmly grounded in microeconomics, are still sensitive to the criticisms of Keynesian interventionism from advocates of the verticality (of the NAIRU version)[20] of the Phillips curve in the long run.[21] And our conclusion is confirmed by the fact that most opponents of the vertical Phillips curve, including hysteresis theorists, endorse Keynesian-type stabilising policies.

The main reason why the multiplier theorem – considered as a means of determining short-term income levels – ranks as Keynes's main legacy within economic theory seems thus to be the awareness that the Phillips curve becomes vertical in the long run. Many Keynesians are currently inclined to think that long-term income cannot be determined in a Keynesian manner in a situation with flexible prices (because it is determined by the NRU or NAIRU), but that disequilibrium theorists have been able to work out a rigorous multiplier theory applicable to a situation with fixed prices. And this goes to explain why, of Keynes's major contributions, the one associated with fixed prices is now generally classed as his *main* contribution to economic theory.[22]

Based on the reflections developed so far we are now in a position to address the criticisms of those who deny the Keynesian nature of NKE because of its scant concern with effective demand (see, for example, Gordon 1990; Kregel and Nardozzi 1996; Darity and Young 1997; McCombie 1998: 149; Sawyer 1998: 129–32; Davidson 1999). If grounded, these criticisms would greatly attenuate, if not altogether cancel, the Keynesian nature of NKE. But if it is true that NKE's main contribution to Keynesianism may be associated with disequilibrium theory – by general agreement the most consistent statement of the principle of effective demand in a situation with fixed prices – by accounting for price rigidity NKE provides valuable insights into the theory of effective demand.[23] In a situation with perfect competition and a given money wage level, employment can increase only if prices also increase and real wages decrease. Conversely, in the situation with imperfect competition assumed by NKE theorists any increase in aggregate demand will directly impact the employment level and produce shifts in the demand curves of individual firms without any changes in real wages.

The argument that 'ever since John Maynard Keynes, the standard explanation for why movements in aggregate demand affect output in the short run has relied on the presence of nominal rigidities' (Blanchard 1997: 245) seems to be the main reason for categorising as Keynesian all those NKE studies which try to account for the rigidity of prices and wages in a short-term perspective.[24]

Nonetheless the fact remains that some NKE models are not compatible with Keynes's theory of effective demand.[25]

The verticality of the Phillips curve and different interpretations of Keynesian theory

At this point we should try to identify the main reason why our evaluation of NKE differs thoroughly provided we accept the idea of a decreasing long-run Phillips curve.[26] Let us write the short-run Phillips curve in the following form:

$$\dot{w}_t = a - b(u_t - u_F) + c\dot{p}^e_t + \dot{\pi}^* \tag{1}$$

where $\dot{w}$ is the rate of change in money wages, $\dot{p}^e$ the expected rate of change in the price level, u the unemployment rate, u_F the unemployment rate at which demand for labour exactly matches supply, $\dot{\pi}^*$ the rate of change in labour productivity over the past years and a, b and c are constant. Let the rate of change in the price level be:

$$\dot{p}_t = \dot{w}_t - \dot{\pi}_t \tag{2}$$

where $\dot{\pi}_t$ is the rate of change in labour productivity over the period of time considered. Substituting (2) into (1), we obtain:

$$\dot{p}_t = a - b(u_t - u_F) + c\dot{p}^e_t + (\dot{\pi}^* - \dot{\pi}_t) \tag{3}$$

We may assume expectations to be as follows:

$$\dot{p}^e_t - \dot{p}^e_{t-1} = d(\dot{p}_{t-1} - \dot{p}^e_{t-1})$$

i.e. of the adaptive type; if the constant $d = 1$, we obtain:

$$\dot{p}^e_t = \dot{p}_{t-1} \tag{4}$$

Substituting (4) into (3), we obtain:

$$\dot{p}_t = a - b(u_t - u_F) + c\dot{p}_{t-1} + (\dot{\pi}^* - \dot{\pi}_t) \tag{5}$$

In long-run equilibrium when $\dot{p} = \dot{p}_{t-1} = \dot{p}_E$ and $\dot{\pi}^* - \dot{\pi}_t$ we consequently obtain:

$$\dot{p}_E = \frac{a - b(u_t - u_F)}{1 - c} \tag{6}$$

Substituting (6) into (1), the equilibrium rate of growth in money wages will be:

$$\dot{w}_E = a - b(u_t - u_F) + c(\dot{w}_E - \dot{\pi}) + \dot{\pi}$$

and therefore:

$$\dot{w}_E = \frac{a - b(u_t - u_F)}{1 - c} + \dot{\pi} = \dot{p}_E + \dot{\pi} \tag{7}$$

Equation (7) shows that a value of c less than 1 will determine a decreasing slope in the Phillips curve even in the long run.[27]

As argued before, a decreasing long-run Phillips curve is consistent with Keynesian theory because it offers the possibility of tackling demand in such a way as to reduce unemployment and use economic policy to stabilise the economy. But is a short-run Phillips curve like that in (1), with a value of c less than 1, at all reasonable?

The objection generally raised against the Phillips curve in (1), i.e. the fact that it refers to a situation with money-wage bargaining instead of real-wage bargaining, can be countered by arguing that in a real-case scenario bargaining is actually conducted by reference to the money wage and that the wage claims put in by unions are not always expected to recover the full extent of the expected inflation rate. A Phillips curve like that in (1), where wages are also linked with increases in labour productivity, is thus compatible with the assumption that the actions of workers and their union representatives are governed by rationality (see Cornwall and Cornwall 1997). The fact that bargaining is actually based on the money wage may even lead us to reverse the above-mentioned critique, i.e. to counter the arguments of those who assume the Phillips curve to be vertical in the long run with the argument that the real wage is determined in the commodities market (the place where the general price level is determined) and not in the labour market (where the money wage is determined) (see Galbraith 1997: 95).[28]

Money-wage bargaining may even justify the thesis that there is actually no such thing as a labour supply curve (see Tuchscherer 1979: 97–9, 1984: 528–30; Jossa 1997: 180–2; Chick 1998 [1996]: 42–4; Galbraith 1997: 95) – an argument which obviously reflects great credit on Keynesian-style interpretations.[29]

Far from corroborating the Keynesian nature of NKE, a decreasing long-run Phillips curve would reinforce the criticisms of those who emphasise that NKE (1) disregards aggregate demand, (2) has nothing to say on the monetarism/fiscalism opposition, and (3) lacks clear economic policy implications.

New Keynesian economics and Meltzer's interpretation of the *General Theory*

A core issue in Keynesian theory that NKE fails to address is the repercussions of fluctuations in investment on the economy. Many writers have argued that while uncertainty is doubtless a central theme of NKE theory, it is not 'the Keynes–Knight uncertainty', i.e. the non-insurable risk caused by the lack of reliable information concerning the future. According to Keynes, the peculiarity of investment is also 'double counting of the premium for bearing uncertainty' (see Meltzer 1996: 37): borrowers try to secure risk-adjusted returns equal to the marginal efficiency of the capital they are investing in the undertaking, while lenders increase lending costs to make good the price of such uncertainty. In Keynes's view these peculiarities of investment produce two far-reaching effects that are not rightly valued in NKE: from a social point of view, the volume of investment remains short of the optimal level and, methodologically speaking, it is impossible to accommodate demand for consumption goods and demand for capital goods within one and the same function.

Far from diverting attention to minor aspects of Keynesian theory, the foregoing sheds light on the bearing that Meltzer's famous interpretation of the *General Theory* (see Meltzer 1988, 1996) has certainly had on our train of thought (in terms of suggesting the reflections developed above), but proves of little help when it comes to assessing the true nature of NKE.

As is well known, Meltzer holds that the true merits of Keynesian theory become apparent when it is viewed against the background of the information issue. If the *General Theory* is still rated an excellent book whose teachings are relevant even today, he argues, this is due to the fact that it 'takes seriously that information is costly, that the future is difficult to know, and that the model of an almost fully informed representative agent is not useful as the basis for short-run analysis' (see Meltzer 1996: 44).

The moment Keynes's contribution is viewed as a set of ideas revolving around the uncertainty issue there emerges a prominent line of continuity between Keynes's thought and the stances of New Keynesian theorists. Nevertheless Keynes addresses the issue with specific focus on uncertainties that NKE fails to address (as mentioned) and with implications it tends to underrate. Furthermore, the main point for the purposes of this chapter is that Meltzer's remaining reflections proceed in a direction opposite to our own line of reasoning.

According to Meltzer, the *General Theory* is not primarily concerned with economic policy. To interpret Keynesianism as a theory of unemployment or as one concerned with short-term fluctuations and policies to counter them would thus be tantamount to underrating, or altogether missing, the most innovative point of Keynes's thought. Contending that Keynes never succeeded in fully stating a theory of employment, in support of his opinion that Keynes had a clear view of the multiplier principle even before he wrote the *Treatise*, Meltzer quotes a Keynesian passage dating from 1928:

> Generally speaking, the indirect employment which schemes of capital expenditure would entail is far larger than the direct employment . . . the greater part of employment they would provide would be spread far and wide over the industries of the country.
>
> (Keynes 1971–89, IX: 106)[30]

However, the point we mean to address here is not 'what Keynes actually said' but, as mentioned at the beginning, whether or not any part of Keynes's legacy can still be viewed as relevant in our day. And in our opinion there is no doubt that the theory of effective demand whereby he determines income in situations with fixed prices is not only a formidable contribution to economic analysis, but also (as argued by disequilibrium theorists) one still relevant today. From this it follows that those who maintain that Keynes's endeavours to state an unemployment theory (though, admittedly, only a short-period theory, provided the notion of a vertical long-run Phillips curve is accepted) have proved unsuccessful can be said to miss the point.

Be that as it may, for the purposes of our own analysis an interpretation of Keynesianism such as Meltzer's is unquestionably relevant because of its concurrent focus on the issues of uncertainty and information. And this will be the subject of the next section.

New Keynesian economics and the 'uncertainty paradigm'

Until lately, the scenario of economic science was dominated by the so-called *competition paradigm*, namely the neoclassical and Walrasian model with perfect competition. The most rigorous approach to this paradigm so far has certainly been that of Arrow and Debreu (1954; see also Debreu 1959), who analysed the behaviour of a large number of maximising agents demanding and offering goods in a complete set of present and future markets characterised by perfect competition. The ability of this model to account for the world in which we live has quite rightly been called into question because its findings are no longer acceptable as soon as its highly restrictive assumptions (such as the existence of a whole set of future markets) are removed.

In the opinion of Stiglitz (1994), the main shortcoming of the neoclassical paradigm is its failure to account for a variety of problems linked with uncertainty and the costs associated with collecting information. As is well known, in today's economic theory the concern with information issues is such as to justify the conclusion that the recently developed 'information paradigm' seems better able to account for a number of basic aspects of the world in which we live. In addition to such traditional issues as 'what should be produced, how and for whom', this new paradigm has raised a fourth major problem previously not addressed in economic science, namely the problem of how decisions should be made, who should make them and how to guarantee that the right decisions are made. And the importance of these issues in economic theory is borne out by the fact that the core issue of today's economic theory, namely the incentive problem, would altogether be solved provided optimal decisions were guaranteed throughout.

More specifically, in Stiglitz's view the perfect competition paradigm is marred by three main errors. First, it assumes that employers are able to appraise their employees' true commitment to work without paying a price, thus taking it for granted that major variables can be correctly monitored at no cost. Secondly, it fails to focus on the problem of how decisions are actually made. Thirdly, the Walrasian paradigm ignores the costs incurred in enforcing contracts and fails to point out that managers may try to act in their own, in lieu of their employers' interests, that borrowers may prove unable to repay their loans, that supplies may not be delivered within the agreed time limits, etc.

Besides underrating the importance of incentives, the competition paradigm also overrates the role of prices while failing to lay stress on the drawbacks that hamper the proper working of markets. Yet 'prices do not function in the manner assumed by the standard model, *nor could they*' (Stiglitz 1994: 83). Very often the requisite information is drawn, not from the price mechanism, but from direct dealings between the partners to an exchange. Contracts and reputation play a crucial role in business relationships and the terms negotiated for details other than price are often as important as price stipulations.

On closer analysis, the idea that market relations are mainly governed by prices is just myth, for a number of reasons. First of all, it fails to realise that business activity is mainly conducted within firms (and governed by prices only in part). Secondly, it fails to draw attention to the wide spectrum of non-price-related information firms use, e.g. information on their own or other firms' inventories. Thirdly, it ignores several aspects of business transactions that have nothing to do with price (see Stiglitz 1994: 249–50).

To recognise that the paramount role of prices in business relations is just myth is tantamount to realising that so, too, is the impersonal essence of such relations. The Post-Walrasian paradigm conceives of exchange as a strategic, though far from anonymous, relation: from the perspective of this new paradigm, to maximise profit the partners to an exchange often renounce price flexibility in order to secure long-term contracts, i.e. agreements based on interpersonal relationships in which the partners' human characteristics are all-important. In the Post-Walrasian paradigm market relations do not generate impersonal links between inanimate objects but bilateral exchanges between individuals acting in strict accordance with the response their actions elicit from the other party, and business activity itself is the result, not of the actions of single agents upon an external context viewed as given (as happens in a perfect competition context), but of the interactions between two or more individuals (see Bowles and Gintis 1993: 7).

The foregoing has far from negligible implications. The importance attached to information as such and the fact that often it is not conveyed through the price mechanism lead to the abandonment of the idea that markets generally tend to be in equilibrium.

And that is not all. The new information paradigm also highlights the notion that 'market failures' are the rule within the business community: lack of information and market fragmentation are shown to generate inefficiencies which, though negligible in each individual transaction between private individuals, acquire great weight when such transactions are considered in bulk (see Stiglitz 1989: 57–8). Moreover the market failures on which this new paradigm throws light differ from those generally addressed in conventional welfare theory and can be corrected by means of specific economic policy actions (e.g. air pollution). Owing to their very nature and frequency, the market failures emphasised by this new paradigm undermine not only confidence in market efficiency, but also the belief that the state is in a position to correct the failures of the market and, consequently, the idea that centralisation is a better solution than decentralisation.

Further implications of the Post-Walrasian paradigm are a critique of neoclassical economic methodology and the rehabilitation of 'path dependence', 'a method more characteristic of biology and geology than of physics, to which economists of the Walrasian persuasion have turned for a model of their intellectual pursuits' (see Bowles and Gintis 1993: 10). Actually this method goes back to Marx and has rightly been considered to be part of the most valuable legacy of that great revolutionary (see Sylos Labini 1993: 203).

The reflections developed so far are clear evidence that NKE is very firmly grounded in the information paradigm. The paramount role of information and the rejection of perfect competition are as fundamental in NKE as they are in Stiglitz's paradigm; and the path-dependence method is known to be the central point of hysteresis theory, which in turn is a crucial part of NKE. Moreover the imperfections of many markets – in particular, financial markets – can to a large extent be explained by reference to insufficient information.

Consequently the main insight provided by our chapter is that today, side by side with the older neoclassical model with perfect competition and rational expectations ('the quite irrelevant paradigm of perfect competition' (Stiglitz 1994: 267)), there is again a major Keynesian paradigm with imperfect competition and great emphasis on the information issue.

Conclusion

According to orthodox Keynesians, very little of Keynes's analytical thought and overall legacy survives in NKE;[31] the monetarist Meltzer has stressed time and again that sixty and more years of ceaseless debate have led to the awareness that there is no way of stating a correct Keynesian theory of employment and that viewing Keynesianism as a theory of employment would mean misinterpreting its essence (see Meltzer 1988, 1996: 39–42). As for us, who strongly object to these conclusions, the main legacy of Keynesianism is disequilibrium theory, which ranks as a consistent statement of the theory of levels of activity and employment founded on the fixed-price assumption. In Keynesian theory, fixed prices are more than a gratuitous assumption; this assumption is suggested by the relative rigidity of money wages in real-case scenarios and the reasons why wages and prices are rigid have been variously and convincingly accounted for in traditional Keynesian theory. The fact that price and wage rigidity (or a certain degree of stickiness) is not only a reasonable hypothesis but also a crucial aspect of capitalism gives interpretative vigour to disequilibrium theory. Thus the reflections developed so far may prompt the conclusion that the genuinely Keynesian parts of NKE are the numerous models in which prices and wages are shown to be sticky or rigid for a variety of reasons although the business agents concerned are seen to behave rationally.

This does not mean we are prepared to subscribe to the argument that 'macroeconomics may be in the process of returning to a state similar to that of the 1960s' (see Mankiw and Romer 1991b: 15), when Keynesian theory was dominant. As is suggested by the foregoing reflections, while we are ready to admit that NKE has helped breathe fresh life into Keynesian thought, we basically agree with those who argue that the 'New Keynesian economics' label has been happily attached to a variety of models which generate 'Keynesian results' although they do not depart from the basic canons of neoclassical microeconomics. More precisely, although much NKE thinking is barely in agreement with Keynes's original thought, we doubt that NKE and Post-Keynesian thought (as summarised, for example, in Nell 1998: 89–90) are as incompatible with each other as many Keynesians hold them to be (in addition to authors already mentioned above, see also Darity and Young 1997; Howitt 1997). The aim of our chapter was to provide evidence that NKE significantly corroborates the finding that equilibrium is reached through changes in output levels, which in our opinion is Keynes's main legacy within economic theory.

Notes

I wish to thank Andrea Boitani, Roberto Cagliozzi, Salvatore D'Acunto, Marco Musella and Carlo Panico for their useful comments, but I am obviously prepared to bear exclusive responsibility for the contents of this chapter.

1 Pasinetti does not share this view. According to him it is essential to distinguish between two distinct levels of investigation, behavioural and fundamental, and make it clear that the principle of effective demand, being independent of the institutional context, pertains to the deeper level (see Pasinetti 1974b, 1997).

2 Many authors have emphasised that the shorter response times of output volumes versus prices observed in Keynes's model are mainly due to price rigidity (see, in addition to others, Leijonhufvud 1968: 52; Hines 1971: 70 ff.; Pasinetti 1974b: 33; Patinkin 1976: 118). For a different view see Hahn (1977) and Davidson (1996: 56–8). According to Malinvaud, 'the classical teaching according to which prices quickly react to excess supplies or demands is more and more inadequate for short-run macroeconomic analysis as we move into ever higher degrees of organization of society' (Malinvaud 1977, 1985: 8).

3 A brilliant discussion of the core idea behind disequilibrium theory is to be found in Dixon (1997: 165–7).

4 Quoting Malinvaud: 'after more than two decades during which the formal model derived from the *General Theory* remained substantially unchanged, a number of research workers have undertaken a reconsideration that, bearing on the basic foundations, would now lead us to a better understanding of the unemployment phenomenon itself'. At that time Malinvaud had already realised that disequilibrium theory is 'an important step forward in the development of our science', because 'it tends to have the characteristics of a major theoretical contribution: clear foundations, consistency with many observed facts, unification of theories which previously appeared to be fundamentally distinct' (Malinvaud 1977, 1985: xii). Tobin's view is much less favourable. In his opinion, although disequilibrium theorists 'were giving the general theory a formal logical structure it previously lacked, they added little macroeconomic content to Keynesian multiplier theory' (see Tobin 1997: 19).

5 Although the term 'perfect competition' is nowhere mentioned in the *General Theory*, from several passages we can clearly infer that it was the situation Keynes was thinking of (see Marris 1997: 52–3). As for the scant weight Keynes attributed to market form, when Ohlin pointed out that what mainly prevented Keynes from discarding obsolete ideas was his idea of perfect competition in the labour market (see Keynes 1971–89, XIV: 196), Keynes himself replied, 'the reference to perfect competition is highly perplexing. I cannot see what bearing it may have. Let me mention that Mrs Robinson read my draft manuscript without discovering any connection' (ibid.: 190). On the subject see also Marris (1991) and Dixon (1997: 197–8).

6 See Robinson (1977: 1327).

7 See Kahn (1978: 548).

8 'Microeconomists have long recognised that sticky prices and perfect competition are incompatible' (see Ball *et al.* 1991: 156); and it is right to state that 'a demand-curve is very similar to quantity constraint' (see Bliss 1997: 207).

9 Similarly Dixon wrote: 'the fundamental "new" idea behind New Keynesian models is that of *imperfect competition*' (Dixon 1997: 159).

10 As for us, we disagree with those who hold that basing a theory on the imperfect competition assumption in periods when markets appear to become ever more competitive will result in major interpretative problems (see Kregel and Nardozzi 1996: 185).

11 'Under imperfect competition firms are always eager to sell an additional unit of output, since price exceeds marginal costs. This profit margin creates the potential for the multiplier' (see Mankiw 1991: 377). As is well known, when demand is on the increase in an imperfect competition market, prices will remain stable only when marginal costs are constant and in the presence of isoelastic demand function transpositions: otherwise, they will either increase or decrease (as Mrs Robinson first showed in Robinson 1933: chapter 4).

12 To say that NKE explains rigidity is one thing; to contend that it provides the microeconomic foundations of Keynesian macroeconomics is another. As Davidson (1999) has argued in opposition to Lindbeck (1998), the *General Theory* is not devoid of microeconomic foundations; nor does it make the rigidity *assumption*. What is sure is that NKE variously and convincingly explains why wages and prices are rigid or sticky.

13 According to Solow, a Keynesian model with sticky wages and prices 'is made more respectable when its premise is shown to be compatible with optimisation or near optimisation' (Solow 1998: 14).

14 In private conversation A. Boitani has pointed out that in this context the terms 'rigid' or 'rigidity' are totally inappropriate, since NKE authors never assume that price or wage flexibility is affected by institutional or other constraints. All the same, these terms are commonly used in the literature on this subject.

15 Arguing that rational expectations are not in line with practical observation, numerous Keynesian economists (among them Greenwald and Stiglitz 1987: 324; Blinder 1987, 1997; Phelps 1992; Solow 1997) and a handful of monetarists (see Laidler 1992) have denied any theoretical validity to the rational expectations hypothesis. However, the idea that rational expectations are by no means in conflict with Keynesian theory has been making headway ever since Fischer (1977) and Phelps and Taylor (1977) showed that monetary disturbances may have real effects even in rational expectation models provided the market equilibrium assumption is dropped. Rosser refers to the rational expectation models of NKE theorists as 'Strong New Keynesian Models' (see Rosser 1998).

16 According to some, the insights contributed by NKE to economic science arise in connection with two new analysis procedures: the introduction of imperfect competition and greater emphasis on price rigidity versus wage rigidity (see Ball *et al.* 1991: 156).

17 This section is a slightly modified version of Jossa and Musella (1995).

18 Concerning the verticality of the long-run Phillips curve, Taylor has argued: 'although controversial at one time, this does not appear to be controversial any more; empirical and theoretical research provides strong support' (Taylor 1997: 233).

19 According to others, it was the unsatisfactory results they were obtaining through the use of Keynesian wage/price adjustment equations founded on a stable Phillips curve that induced Keynesians to adapt their models in ways that would account for the effects of inflationary expectations and supply shocks (see Snowdon *et al.* 1994: 286).

20 For an analysis of the distinction between NRU and NAIRU see Jossa (1997: 177–8); Galbraith (1997: 94–5); Balzano and Musella (1999).

21 Among critics of the NAIRU see Arestis and Sawyer (1997: chapter 10); Galbraith (1997).

22 It is a well known fact that the desire to state his theory in the most general terms possible led Keynes to contend that it was applicable irrespective of whether prices and wages were rigid or flexible (see Kregel and Nardozzi 1996: 184–5). However, the debate which subsequently developed in connection with the verticality of the long-run Phillips curve led to the conclusion that in situations with flexible prices equilibrium is not determined according to Keynesian theory.

23 As argued in Nisticò *et al.* (1998), NKE models include 'labour market' models and 'commodity market' models and it is the latter that are specifically intended to account for lack of effective demand (see also Nisticò and D'Orlando 1995: 54–7).

24 In NKE 'prices are envisioned as possibly not clearing in the *short run* (there seems to be this underlying belief that sticky prices are not persistent)' (see Rotheim 1998b: 52; emphasis in the original).

25 According to Sawyer, some NKE models in which equilibrium is identified on the basis of supply-side considerations fail to explain why aggregate demand should be sufficient to buy the quantity of commodities produced (Sawyer 1998: 129). Models not compatible with Keynesian effective demand theory include, in particular, those where the labour market is assumed to be a self-contained subset because the aggregate demand level does not appear in the labour demand and supply functions (Lindbeck 1998: 171).

26 See Tarantelli (1986: 539–49); Cornwall (1994: 152–69); Palley (1996: 166–81); Akerlof *et al.* (1996); Cornwall and Cornwall (1997).

27 There is general agreement that the values of *c* for the United States can be assumed to lie very close to 1 (see, *inter alia*, Gordon 1997: 24–7). A decreasing long-run Phillips curve may be assumed for Europe, where few countries have a generally accepted Phillips curve.

28 According to some, the main implication of the NAIRU hypothesis is that most of the changes in the rate of inflation originate in the labour market and that their magnitudes are commensurate with tensions in the labour market, i.e. with the rate of unemployment (see Stiglitz 1997: 4; for a different view see Staiger *et al.* 1997). The reason why this argument is far from convincing is that a decreasing long-run Phillips curve offers much the same explanation to account for changes in the rate of inflation. To trace changes in the inflation rate to tensions in the labour market is tantamount to accepting the Keynesian interpretation of inflation suggested by Kahn and Joan Robinson as mentioned above – an approach which becomes even more distinctively Keynesian as soon as we assume that *money* wages are determined in the labour market while real wages are determined in the commodities market.

29 See, also, Rotheim (1998b: 57 ff.). For a different view see Davidson (1999: 573–6).

30 Mrs Robinson rightly argued that this passage contains a clear statement of multiplier theory (see Robinson and Wilkinson 1985: 86).

31 This is an opinion to which both Davidson (1992, 1995, 1999) and most of the contributors to Rotheim (1998a) subscribed.

21 Keynesian economics from a non-price theoretic framework

Roy J. Rotheim

> [T]he core contribution of the *General Theory* . . . in our opinion is the theory of the multiplier in a situation with fixed prices.
>
> (Jossa, this volume: 284)

> The classical [read New Keynesian] theorists resemble Euclidean geometers in a non-Euclidean world who, discovering that in experience straight lines apparently parallel often meet, rebuke the lines for not keeping straight – as the only remedy for the unfortunate collisions which are occurring.
>
> (Keynes 1936: 16)

We begin with an analogy from the science-fiction television programme *Star Trek.* The story focuses on the USSS *Enterprise,* a star ship that travels through space spreading and maintaining peace among the galaxies of the universe. No matter how far away from the Earth the *Enterprise* travelled, it would always return periodically – which sometimes was defined as years or decades – to Earth just to 'touch base' if you like, to reaffirm its ties with the place that gave it its sense of purpose, which then safely allowed it to move throughout the universe without ever jeopardising its fundamental sense of who it was or what was its mission. If the *Enterprise* travelled too far from the Earth, there would always be the remote chance that it could travel through what is called a 'wormhole', i.e. a fold in the universe where, once through, the hole would close up behind and it could never return from where it came.

Now, with that science-fiction picture in your minds, consider the state of New Keynesian and Post-Walrasian economics. For what should be considered is that these perspectives are just one thread away from losing their grip and slipping into a macroeconomic wormhole, causing them to lose contact completely with the last remaining vestige of neoclassicism, i.e. the heuristical device of thinking about macroeconomics in terms of *market* phenomena: about fictitious conceptualisations such as *the* labour market, *the* capital market and *the* goods market. Will they make it to the other side of this macroeconomic wormhole? And if so, what may they find there?

Consider, for example, the compelling chapter by Bruno Jossa which precedes this one. Professor Jossa takes us through a well written narrative depicting the path of macroeconomic thought in the sixty years since Keynes: from neo-Keynesian wage rigidity interpretations of unemployment equilibrium; to disequilibrium price rigidity theories of speeds of adjustment of output relative to price; to weak New Keynesian models (the designation is Barkley Rosser's, see 1998) which purport to provide rational bases for wage, interest rate and price rigidity; to Strong New Keynesian models (again the designation is Rosser's) where questions of coordination failure, leading to spill-over and multiplier effects and strategic complementarities take on a more profound role; to what David Colander calls 'Stiglitzian economics' where questions of stickiness in markets take a back seat to the asymmetries in information flows that cause multiple equilibria emanating from strategies put forth in the face of uncertainty; and finally to considerations of what Colander has coined Post-Walrasian economic theory (Colander 1998).

Observing the development of the history of macroeconomics after Keynes (with the exclusion of Post-Keynesian macroeconomics), one is struck by the observation that the discourse, itself, becomes ever more discursive and tentative as it reaches the very frontiers of the discipline. Moreover I would contend (see Rotheim 1998b) that, as the frontier is approached, contemporary theorists will find themselves treading on thinner and thinner ice: they know they are moving in the right direction, but they also realise where they are going and what will have to be left behind and discarded as their line of thought is pursued. Their form becomes more tentative, discursive, descriptive and less analytical and rigorous than has come to be expected of macroeconomic discourse (see, for example, Van Ees and Garretsen 1992; Colander 1996b, 1998; Stiglitz 1993). Each of these economists is pushing the boundaries, or in my framework pushing beyond the boundaries, where analysis and rigour give way to outright storytelling, of a reversion to an earlier form where practitioners find themselves groping for a firm footing that clearly, to them, is becoming more and more elusive.

Where do we find the ice finally cracking? Certainly not in the discussions of 'wage-rigidity Keynesianism' nor in 'price-rigidity Keynesianism', nor even in weak New Keynesianism. For in each of these instances the common thread is the utilisation of a market metaphor for understanding purported economic fluctuations: unemployment equilibrium occurs, we are told, because real wages in an aggregate labour market are sticky downward, because prices are reluctant to fall in goods markets, and because real interest rates are sticky downward in aggregate capital markets. For as Murray Milgate has stated so aptly:

> I contend that the overwhelming majority of modern controversies in the theory of employment are about whether the existence of imperfections are out to temper the application of our most basic vision of the market mechanism to everyday situations. If this is correct, then there is no ultimate theoretical principle at stake in most of the debates which have occupied the pages of our professional journals and the columns of our newspapers over the past decade or so. It all becomes a matter of degree. I further contend that among those who feel that it is impossible to ignore imperfections, controversy in the theory of employment is exclusively over the question of

> exactly which of the many possible imperfections is, practically speaking, the most important.
>
> (Milgate 1988: 80)

Like the Star Ship *Enterprise*, such imperfectionist interpretations cause macroeconomic thought to move all about the theoretical universe. However, the lifeline to their planet Earth, i.e. the heuristical device of thinking in terms of market metaphors, is never broken, and therefore, in Milgate's words: 'no ultimate theoretical principle is at stake'. The fear of being sucked into a theoretical wormhole compels them to revert to the neoclassical *terra firma*.

Orthodox Keynesians, on the other hand, pay no heed to such imperfectionist interpretations of fluctuations in economic activity. The reason for this lack of interest and concern comes from an understanding of Keynes's criticism of all attempts at macroeconomic reasoning that rely on market metaphors to describe fluctuations in employment and output as a whole. From an operational perspective, one cannot think in terms of an aggregate labour market in which a real wage mediates independent supply and demand functions for labour except at the point of full employment. At any other point the conditions underlying the construction of the aggregate demand and supply curves for labour are not independent; the real wage becomes a compound phrase – numerator and denominator are not independent, while nothing can be said about the effect of changes in the real wage on the level of employment as a whole (Rotheim 1998b). Keynes identified such a mechanism as being useful only to explain relative movements in employment between and among sectors, but having nothing whatsoever to say about movements in employment and output as a whole. In fact, he showed clearly that the laws of logic mandated that output and employment as a whole must be fixed if we are to construct aggregate demand and supply curves for labour. It is for this reason that Keynes lamented to Harrod that 'the most extraordinary thing from an historical point of view', in the works of his predecessors, was 'the complete disappearance of the theory of demand and supply for output as a whole', and observed that 'the sudden realisation of this fact' was decisive for him. It was for this reason that Keynes rejected Harrod's and Hicks's versions of the IS–LM framework (see Rotheim 1995).

As such, efficiency wage stories – and they are just stories – may be interesting, and possibly true at the level of individual firms. However, they hold no credible theoretical merit as explanations of unemployment in the aggregate. Thinking in terms of sticky money or real wages in terms of rational responses by employers to possible shirking behaviour has no plausibility, as there is no theoretical framework for understanding its effect in terms of movements in labour demand and supply as a whole. Keynes showed clearly that such thinking suffered from an *ignoratio elenchi*, the inappropriate use of one logical structure (micro-theoretic labour market theory) for another (the conceptualisation of an aggregate labour market mediated by fluctuations in a real wage rate). The reader is directed to the quotation from Keynes at the head of this chapter.

Keynes had the same to say about the conceptualisation of an aggregate capital market, i.e. one by which the supply of savings in an economy interfaces with a demand for savings function (based on declining marginal product of capital in the aggregate), mediated by fluctuations in some real rate of interest. Here, however, he considered this metaphor to be simply a 'nonsense' theory, because he could imagine no level of saving in the aggregate that was ever independent of a level of investment, regardless of the money rate of interest or some measure of the aggregate level of prices. Here again, the interdependence of savings and investment functions, just like the interdependence of aggregate labour demand and supply functions, occurs as soon as output and employment are permitted to fluctuate in the economy as a whole.

The dilemma, Keynes observed, was that thinking in terms of aggregate labour and capital markets made no sense unless it were assumed that employment and output as a whole were fixed in the economy. But if that were true, why would we have any interest in stories that purported to explain relative movements in employment and output in the economy based on such fictitious markets not clearing? And if these conclusions are true, then, likewise, it makes no sense to think about an aggregate goods market clearing with fluctuations in prices (are we talking about absolute or relative prices here?), especially when logic demands that output as a whole can never change if we are to think in the terms that the model expects us to.

Trouble does begin for the discipline of macroeconomics, however, when we proceed from the safety of weak fix-price New Keynesian models to the dangerous realm of strong New Keynesianism. For in these instances, questions of fluctuations in relative prices to clear markets fall to the background, or out of sight entirely. The frame of reference changes from market and market-clearing behaviour to behaviours between and among individual actors. Thinking in terms of what Jossa calls the Stiglitzian 'information paradigm', we hear him say: 'Besides underrating the importance of incentives, the competition paradigm also overrates the role of prices while failing to lay stress on the drawbacks that hamper the proper working of markets' (Jossa, p. 294 above). Now the ice is beginning to crack and we get closer to being sucked into our macroeconomic wormhole.

But matters get worse as we begin to think about the coordination failure literature, another aspect of strong New Keynesianism, especially the work of Cooper and John (1988) where spill-over effects (the effect that one person's strategy has on another's pay-offs) and strategic complementarities (the effect that one person's strategy has on another person's pay-offs and *plans*) prevail. For in these cases, such organic interdependences result clearly in traditional Keynesian multiplier effects, i.e. fluctuations in output, spending and therefore employment *as a whole*. In other words, the literature which has us thinking in terms of spill-overs and strategic complementarities allows for cumulatively causative mechanisms which do not require a reduction in employment and output in one sector of the economy (as was true of the weak New Keynesian models) in order for employment and output to increase in another. These are profound conclusions, because we are now barely holding on to the last thread of orthodoxy where market metaphors assist us in understanding economic fluctuations. The conditions underlying the supply and demand curves from which such heuristical utterances emanate are themselves fundamentally altered. Consequently, questions concerning the relative speeds of adjustment of prices and quantities lose all relevance (see Davidson 1998; Kregel 1998).

This historical post-Keynesian (not Post Keynesian) exegesis through macroeconomics brings us ultimately to what David Colander has defined as Post-Walrasian economics. As Colander has stated:

> 1 Not only does the economy exhibit multiple equilibrium, it also exhibits complex dynamics. An economy with complex dynamics cannot meaningfully be analysed within a comparative static model that assumes the aggregate equilibria are unaffected by the dynamic adjustment process.
> 2 I further conjecture that the aggregate economy is so complex that general equilibrium rational decision making is impossible. I do not give up rationality – I simply give up global rationality as being beyond the capabilities of individuals. For Post Walrasians rationality is bounded rationality.
> 3 The above two conjectures would likely mean that the economy would exhibit chaotic results. What prevents those chaotic results is a third conjecture – that the reason the aggregate economy is relatively stable is the existence of multi-layered institutions – conventions, legal and social, that impose restrictions in individual actions – which limit individual actions within ranges. These institutions impose the stability that exists in the system and reduce the complexity of decision making for individuals. Thus, institutions play a central role in Post Walrasian macroeconomics; one cannot analyse an institutionless world. Markets coordinate individual actions within institutions; to understand that coordination, one must understand how institutions work.
>
> (Colander 1998: 282–3)

But what of this perspective? Colin Rogers has observed the following:

> [Post-Walrasian economics] has merit subject to the proviso that the Arrow–Debreu framework is abandoned [because the Arrow–Debreu framework is decisively a non-monetary conceptualisation]. . . . [Moreover] the importance of strategic behaviour undermines the view that the behaviour of the aggregate economy can be understood from an individualistic perspective.
>
> (Rogers 1998: 319)

Ah, but we have just pushed right through the wormhole – for now we have allowed ourselves to think of an economic mechanism whereby individuals (no longer atomistic, but rather socially contextual and organic individuals) make decisions in light of an uncertain future, that organically affect others' abilities to act and make plans in a cumulative fashion. Here there is no separation of real and nominal sectors. Moreover, market metaphors lose their relevance at the aggregate level. To the extent that so much of what needs to be explained occurs at the level of the firm, the institutional imperatives of contracts and their enforcement leads us into a *monetary* theory of production, where money enters directly into the decision making of individuals.

Now, my guess is that even the most 'open-minded' macroeconomists will turn back at the last minute, finding comfort in the more traditional weaker New Keynesian models. However, for those few brave souls who push so far as to be sucked into the wormhole of a Post-Walrasian nature, my prediction is that they'll find an old friend on the other side: namely Keynes's economics from a non-price theoretic framework.

Note

The author wishes to thank, without implicating them, Sergio Nisticò and Giorgia Tortora for commenting on earlier versions of this chapter.

22 The controversies in contemporary macroeconomics

Giorgio Rodano

1. Macroeconomics is a relatively new field in economic theory. Its history starts actually with the twentieth century. In the words of Michael Woodford, '[t]he rise of macroeconomics . . . is a novelty of the twentieth century, the result both of intellectual developments (notably the rise of Keynesian theory) and of a new importance attached to management of the economy in twentieth-century ideas about the role of government' (Woodford 1999: 2). Another important characteristic is that the development of new ideas in macroeconomics has been characterised by controversies, lively debates and serious clashes, typically between Keynesian and neoclassical economists. To take the words of Woodford once more, '[d]iscussions of twentieth-century developments in macroeconomics make frequent references to "revolutions" and "counter-revolutions", and the question of whether there has been progress at all (or which broad developments should count as progress) is a more lively topic of debate among economists' (ibid.).[1]

It may be worth, then, investigating the link between such controversies and the effective progress of the discipline. For instance, in his paper on the history of macroeconomics in the twentieth century Olivier Blanchard maintains that it would be inappropriate to regard macroeconomic history 'as a series of battles, revolutions and counterrevolutions, from the Keynesian revolution of the 1930s and 1940s, to the battles between Monetarists and Keynesians of the 1950s and 1960s, to the Rational Expectations revolution of the 1970s, and the battles between New Keynesians and New Classicals of the 1980s'. Such a description appears in fact to be realistic 'on the surface', but provides 'the wrong image' of a discipline which, squeezed under the pressure of the events, starts again from zero every twenty years, thus failing to achieve a solid and common body of knowledge. On the contrary, according to Blanchard the 'right image' should be that 'of a surprisingly steady accumulation of knowledge'.[2]

In my opinion, the label 'steady' sounds a bit exaggerated. Nevertheless, I do agree with most of Blanchard's claim that macroeconomics should not simply be considered a battlefield on a front line of armed economists. Instead, through the course of the century, macroeconomics has witnessed noticeable and consolidated progress. Macroeconomics deals 'with fluctuations in the overall level of business activity, with the determinants of inflation, interest rates, and exchange rates, and with the effects of government policies – such as fiscal policy, monetary policy, and exchange rate policy – that are considered mainly with regard to their effects upon the economy as a whole' (Woodford 1999: 1). Today we know much more about these issues than we did in the past: not just with respect to what we knew at the beginning of the twentieth century, but also with respect to what was achieved by Keynes, or even to what we knew fifty or thirty years ago.

Within the narrow bounds of this chapter I would like to argue how the disputes, debates, skirmishes and head-on battles between scholars played a constructive role in the progress of the discipline. The issue I want to put forward here is that discussion in macroeconomics, far from being sterile, has actually favoured a real improvement of the discipline, thus enriching the ability of the theory to explain economic reality; I also want to point out that, in past years, debates in economics, as well as fierce controversies, represented, and still represent, a sound and effective means of selecting and gradually expanding the core of economic knowledge.

To corroborate such a statement, I will go through two steps. First (sections 2–3), I will focus on some features of macroeconomics which have brought about a favourable environment for discussion, debates and even vigorous fights. I also want to stress how such controversies themselves have often resulted in fruitful outcomes, in a new consensus and a new synthesis. Eventually these achievements will be brought into question by new debates and controversies, which sooner or later will converge on a richer synthesis, although a temporary one.

Second (sections 4–7), I will try to highlight the interpretative capacity of such an approach, by illustrating some essential events of macroeconomic history in the second half of the twentieth century. At the beginning of the 1950s macroeconomics went through a period of general consensus. Later, during the 1970s and 1980s, it encountered some phases of turbulence. Now it is perhaps going to end up with a new (temporary) synthesis, much richer and more advanced than the previous one.

2. The epistemological statute of economics (and within it, of macroeconomics) is extremely complex and cannot be fully examined in this chapter. However, scholars maintain an overall consensus on one point: economics is, of all the social sciences, the one which is closest to physics – the supreme 'hard' science. And this is because quite often economics is written in a highly formal and axiomatic language.[3] Of course, the distance between economics and physics remains very large indeed. For our purpose, it is important to highlight at least two crucial differences which are typical of economics but are particularly important for macroeconomics as well.

First of all, it is almost impossible for economics to implement experiments. In fact, unlike most of the natural sciences, economics cannot possibly isolate a 'piece' of the world, where all the relevant variables are under control, in order to check what happens when the value of one variable changes.[4] With this in mind, if one really wanted to compare economics to a hard science, one should think of astrophysics rather than physics. Economists, as well as astrophysicists, only have observable information to check whether real events strengthen or weaken their theories.

I will soon get back to this issue, but first I want to highlight the second peculiar feature characterising economics. Unlike astrophysics, economics is a 'dual' science: on the one hand, it studies how its own world works (and that is economic *theory*). On the other hand, it provides indications of how the results of this world can be influenced or changed through the adoption of more or less appropriate interventions (and that is economic *policy*). In this sense economics is more similar to medicine and, like medicine, has similar branches: anatomy, physiology, pathology, surgery, etc.

Nevertheless, even such a comparison with medicine may be misleading. It is true that economists, just like doctors, can learn from experiments *in corpore vili*, or from past experience of economic policy. It must still be stressed that the relationship between the policy maker and the economic environment is quite different from the one between a doctor and a patient. This is because agents, in their economic behaviour, do not passively endure the economic policies, but actively react to them. In fact, they do evaluate the intentions, the announcements and the actions of the policy makers in order to define their strategies and take their decisions.

The reason for such interdependence is very well known. It has to do with the basic methodological assumption through which economists investigate their topics – that is, the assumption of rationality: every agent takes decisions as if maximising the objective function's value, given the constraints imposed by the relevant economic environment. Therefore the various strategies and interventions of economic policy, through the definition of the environment in which decisions are taken, determine the set of possible choices available to the agent, and hence the agent's decisions themselves. That is why macroeconomic policy implies a strategic interdependence between the agent and the policy maker, which is more and more often investigated by means of the tools of game theory.[5]

The peculiar epistemological statute of economics can be further specified by quickly examining the (involved and problematic) relationship between economics (including macroeconomics) and the facts. What follows cannot possibly claim to be complete. I will only mention three statements which are in my opinion helpful to clarify the point I want to make here.

First, economic theory has to cope with empirical facts that do not remain constant, but rather change through time. These changes make macroeconomics close to historical sciences and are very familiar to researchers. On the one hand, there are autonomous ('exogenous') changes, that have to do with economic growth, with technological change and with institutional change. On the other hand, there are 'endogenous' changes, induced by economic policies, such as those mentioned above. At the outset of this chapter I argued that macroeconomics can be regarded as an autonomous discipline in that it deals with the effects on the economic system of government policies (and of its agencies, mainly the central bank). What these effects are is definitely a vexed question, the polar positions being that of neoclassical economists on one hand, who see the economic system as 'a self-regulating mechanism leading spontaneously to an efficient allocation of resources'; and that of Keynesian economists on the other, who believe that the system is 'subject to arbitrary forces and in need of constant management through government policy to keep it on track' (Woodford 1999: 9).

The second remark on the relationship between facts and economic theory is the following: notwithstanding the 'historical' (and therefore slippery) feature of the environment that it investigates, economics aims at producing a 'meta-historical' body of knowledge, whose general statements remain valid for every period or institutional environment. This represents a peculiar feature of micro-economics, but it is also typical in macroeconomic research, especially in the neoclassical case.

The third remark is largely connected with the previous two and, as a matter of fact, derives in large part from them: economics cannot rely on a too narrow relationship with the facts, even if, especially in macroeconomics, it must deal with them. The solution is, as we know, constituted by 'stylised facts'. The notion and expression date back to Kaldor (1961) and convey the idea that economic theories must conform to rough empirical regularities, the only ones which can be extracted from a continuously changing environment. Some examples of stylised facts concerning macroeconomics may give a clearer idea: (1) the national product of various economic systems, in *real* terms, tends to grow at an approximately constant percentage rate; (2) the national product, in *nominal* terms, has a direct relation with the nominal amount of money; (3) the pace of economic growth in various economies exhibits periods of expansion and periods of recession, giving rise to economic fluctuations (once labelled 'business cycles').[6]

Of course, there are stylised facts concerning more detailed issues, which are more specific in terms of space and time. The following are some examples: (1) until the mid-1970s the rate of unemployment in Europe was clearly lower than that of the United States, whereas afterwards the situation was reversed; (2) in the 1970s inflation was significantly higher, practically everywhere, than in the two preceding and following decades.

The rough and changing nature of stylised facts, along with the impossibility of implementing experiments, has a very strong theoretical implication: economic theory can match empirical facts in a *qualitative*, rather than *quantitative*, way. In other words, we cannot expect economic theories to cope with all the detailed features of reality; what is reasonable to expect is that economic theories should not contradict the fundamental stylised facts. This in turn means that more rival theories can coexist – and this is not a peculiarity of economics – without our having at our disposal a filter to choose among them in an efficient and not too controversial way. The absence of such a filter is decisively more specific of economics.[7]

3. The coexistence, in many fields of economics, and especially in macro-economics, of rival theories, along with the lack of an 'objective' selection criterion, has a straightforward consequence. The comparison among different theories cannot be made only by means of empirical testing, because often rival theories are corroborated by the same stylised facts. Therefore, there is room for discussion of the benefits and drawbacks of alternative explanations. Economists in fact debate quite a lot. And they do it in quite a passionate way. They are divided

among schools of thought. In other words, they 'quarrel'. I do not think they are the only scientists who quarrel, but they definitely quarrel more than others do. However the interesting thing is that, more often than we would expect, discussion in macroeconomics, rather than being sterile, has ended up provoking real advances, enriching the discipline's ability to explain economic reality.

In this perspective the comparison between microeconomics and macroeconomics is particularly interesting. As we know, the first is older than the latter: its earliest important insights were developed in the second half of the nineteenth century, when the so-called 'marginalist revolution'[8] turned the existing understandings of the theory of value upside down. At that time the debate in microeconomics was quite animated and economists were divided in different schools of thought.[9] A mainstream school of thought emerged, in terms of substantial agreement on the basic propositions of the theory, which were shared by the majority of scholars through the course of the twentieth century.[10] As Woodford maintains, the history of microeconomics of the twentieth century 'would be one with little suspense. For it would not be too much of an oversimplification to present the field as having progressed smoothly and steadily, developing theories of ever greater power and broader scope within an essentially unchanged explanatory framework, based on the concepts of optimizing individual behavior and market equilibrium, that were already central to economic thought in the previous century' (Woodford 1999: 2).

Instead, macroeconomics has not yet reached the stage of an 'essentially unchanged explanatory framework'. It is still going through a period characterised by controversies paving the way to the progress of knowledge; even if – as we shall see – at moments in the last half-century some kind of established consensus seems to have been achieved. However such a consensus has always been questioned, ending up in a crisis. Anyway, it must be added that debate is unavoidable, once the discipline moves along the 'frontier' of economic research. This is true of all the scientific disciplines. After a while, in the natural sciences, controversies usually cease, as only one stance wins the confrontation of the predictions with facts. In economic sciences, rather, the confrontation with facts is *important* (below we will see some examples), but not *conclusive*.

The success (or failure) of a theory or approach in economics arises in a different way, through a progressive accumulation of *consensus* within the community of economists. The consensus usually consolidates around a particular theory (or approach) when it exhibits two essential features: first, such a theory must be capable 'of organising in a single framework many disparate phenomena and many disparate ideas' (Aumann 1985: 35); second, it has to prove apt to suggest new insights, which nurture new research. These features – comprehensiveness and fertility – can be considered a criterion to appraise the scientific quality of a particular theory. To Aumann, in fact, it makes no sense to wonder whether a theory is *true*.[11] The question we have to ask instead is 'What does it tie together, where does it lead?' (ibid.).

To support his argument, Aumann refers to an example which lies at the heart of modern economic theory: 'the fundamental notion of utility maximisation'. Everybody knows that 'individuals do not *really* maximise utility';

alternative approaches such as the bounded rationality and the satisficing approach, 'which sometimes seem more appropriate as descriptions of true individual behaviour', are also very well known. This, however, is not the point. Aumann argues that the real point is that:

> the validity of utility maximisation does not depend on its being an accurate description of individuals' behaviour. Rather it derives from its being the underlying postulate that pulls together most economic theory; it is the major component of a certain way of thinking, with many important and familiar implications, which have been part of economics for decades and even centuries. Alternatives such as satisficing have proven to be next to useless in this respect. While attractive as hypotheses, there is little theory built on them.
>
> (Ibid.)

In my opinion, and with the qualifications made further in this chapter, the criterion suggested by Aumann to assess the validity of an economic theory appears convincing.[12] Incidentally, it would explain the rationale behind most Nobel prize awards for economics. Some of the acknowledgements were obtained by scholars who were already pretty late in their career. Moreover, most of the works eligible for the Nobel prize were often not capable of establishing a *definite* result; rather they were those which could bring about a new perspective, a new line of research, new debates, even if, at the end, they did not hold true. Two illustrative examples demonstrate this clearly. The first is the Modigliani–Miller theorem in 1958. Such a theorem paved the way to the modern theory of finance, thus turning out to be extremely fertile. However, the theory of finance regarded that theorem being valid only under very restrictive hypotheses, which rarely occur in reality. The second example refers to the article by Lucas in 1972, which revolutionised research in macroeconomics, even if its basic hypothesis has now been abandoned by almost everyone.[13]

Of course, from the epistemological viewpoint, the fertility criterion is very 'delicate', if not dangerous. It opens the way to a risk of path dependence in the evolution of a theory that, like the evolution in biology, may abandon a promising perspective just because the environment is not receptive enough. In other words, I am not sure that the present 'main stream' represents the discipline's best possible frontier. Rather, I think that it represents the best among the available alternatives, given the tracks undertaken by researchers. It goes without saying that these were not the only possible tracks (recall the example of satisficing mentioned by Aumann, but many others exist as well). In addition, the criterion we are discussing here does not exclude that a theory, or a research approach, which was previously abandoned because it led nowhere, may be reborn because new facts or ideas re-establish its fertility. A well known case, extensively discussed in this volume, is the reproposal by Piero Sraffa, of the classical approach. In the following pages we will come upon other cases dealing with the evolution of ideas in macroeconomics which are less striking but equally significant.

Before I start dealing with the evolution of ideas in macroeconomics in the second half of the twentieth century, I want to reply to one possible objection that can be put forward against those who think of controversies as an efficient means of selection among rival theories. It goes as follows: 'economists do not quarrel because of scientific reasons, but rather because of ideological ones. Behind their stances, obviously, there lie political conflicts (when not academic envy or jealousy)'. This is undoubtedly true. But the point is that these aspects, even if important, remain in the background; they matter only on a pre-analytical level, which is not under discussion. Debate *is* scientific. And that is exactly what makes the progress of the theory possible and able to push forward the frontier of knowledge in this discipline.

4. Unlike microeconomics, as we previously stated, the evolution of ideas in macroeconomics did not occur within a consolidated paradigm. Its past has been, on the contrary, so turbulent that the terms 'revolution', 'counter-revolution' and 'crisis', used to describe some of its phases, appear to be rather appropriate (as seen from their frequent use by researchers).

The Keynesian revolution was obviously the first and most famous one. Begun in the early 1930s and booming in 1936, with the publication of the *General Theory*, the revolution witnessed considerable developments over the ten years to follow and reached its first synthesis in the 1950s. In those years, Keynes's ideas, disclosed in the works of Hicks (1937b), Modigliani (1944) and Klein (1947), were already widespread as the new orthodoxy, overcoming previous doubts and opposition. There were still 'some traditionalists' – with Milton Friedman immediately coming to mind – who 'maintained that Keynesian theory was fundamentally wrong' (Woodford 1999: 9); but they were a small minority, whose influence held very little weight within the profession. At that time the labels 'macroeconomics' and 'Keynesian economics' almost overlapped, and were used synonymously. The leading framework was given by a combination of a demand side, based on the IS–LM model, and a supply side, based on an aggregate production function exhibiting decreasing returns to scale and a labour market characterised by rigid nominal wages. This was the macroeconomics taught in universities all round the world. This was 'the' reference paradigm for the majority of the scholars engaged on the frontiers of the discipline.

One of the problematic questions which attracted widespread attention was that of the relationship between Keynesian and neoclassical economics. In the *General Theory* Keynes had already emphasised the profound difference between his approach and that of the neoclassical orthodoxy.[14] This explains the already mentioned attitude of the 'traditionalists' who criticised Keynesians' ideas, reclaiming the value of the neoclassical approach. However, it must be said that in the 1950s and 1960s there were a few scholars, particularly those from Cambridge (UK), who embraced a symmetrical logic and 'hoped that the insights of the *General Theory* would provide the foundation for an entirely new economics' (Woodford 1999: 9). A few of these radical Keynesians thought it was possible to free Keynes's new ideas from their neoclassical substrate and to integrate them with those proposed by Sraffa in those years.

The majority of scholars, however, were exploring the opposite hypothesis. They wanted to match Keynes's macroeconomics with neoclassical microeconomics. To accomplish this goal, two types of problems had to be overcome. The first one was the micro foundations of the aggregate behavioural functions. The second was that of the seeming incompatibility between the results stemming from the Keynesian models and the general equilibrium theory.

Let us deal with the first problem. Notwithstanding the general consensus for the Keynesian standard model, many scholars focused their attention on the aggregate functions that describe the demand for goods and money by households and firms in the IS–LM model. Even if these functions passed the empirical testing, they had very weak theoretical foundations as to their coherence with the assumption of individuals' behaviour. In the 1950s and 1960s much work was done to fill this gap. The results were brilliant, and often those scholars responsible were awarded the Nobel prize. We refer obviously to the work of Modigliani and Friedman on the consumption function, that of Baumol and Tobin on the demand for money, and of Jorgenson and Tobin again on the investment function.[15] All their works have a common characteristic: the behaviour of both households and firms is derived from a constrained maximisation procedure on the part of the representative agents, and thus coherently with the general principle of rationality of (micro) economic theory.

Let us now deal with the second issue, that is, the consistency of the standard macroeconomic model with the general principles of economic theory. In other words, let us come to the relationship between Keynesian economics and the outcomes of general equilibrium theory (namely the standard *microeconomic* model). As is well known, this latter theory portrays the functioning of the economic system in terms of interaction between rational individuals who take their decisions by observing market-clearing prices determined within perfectly competitive markets (one for each product). An important aspect of the general equilibrium theory is that individual choices depend only on *relative* prices. The agents taken into consideration by this theory are exempted from money illusion. That is, within general equilibrium, money is neutral; its changes do not have any real effects, only nominal ones.

In the 1950s Patinkin (1957) studied the problem of compatibility between Keynesian economics and general equilibrium theory. His solution was to consider the first as a description of how the macroeconomic system works in the short run, where prices and (especially) wages have not had time to adjust and can therefore be considered rigid. While the second can be considered as a description of how the system works

> in the long run, once wages and prices had had sufficient time to adjust to clear markets; thus the self-regulating property of the market system was not denied, but simply argued to sometimes be slow enough to profitably allow for interventions intended to speed the sort of adjustment that markets would ideally arrange on their own.
>
> (Woodford 1999: 10)

The standard macroeconomic model at the end of the 1950s had therefore a twofold characteristic: it was Keynesian in the short term with an equilibrium characterised by involuntary unemployment, by money not being neutral, and by effective economic policies (capable of driving the economy in the desired direction). It was neoclassical instead in the long term, with equilibrium determined only by the fundamentals (endowments, preferences and technology), and characterised by the full utilisation of resources, and by money being neutral. For this reason it is referred to as the 'neoclassical synthesis' model.[16]

Such a model was a static one in that it pinned down the *level* of production and prices, while it was not able to account for inflation. For this reason, an attempt was made in the 1960s to integrate this model with a decreasing relation between the change of wage rates and the rate of unemployment or, better yet, with the Phillips curve, from which it was easy to derive a direct relation between the product level and the inflation rate, referred to as the aggregate supply function.[17] At that time, the statistical regularity (the stylised fact) described by the Phillips curve was explained with reference to the functioning of the labour market (cf. Lipsey 1960). Two relevant propositions were made: (1) nominal wages react with finite velocity according to the excess demand in the labour market; (2) when the labour market is in equilibrium the nominal wages do not vary even if the equilibrium is generally characterised by a positive unemployment rate, because of the inevitable presence of voluntary or frictional unemployment.

The Phillips curve allowed the possibility to outweigh the first versions of the standard model (where wages were assumed to be perfectly rigid in the short run and completely flexible in the long run). The novelty was that nominal wages are *sticky* – that is, they react slowly to the imbalance between the supply of and demand for labour. The combination of the IS–LM model with a supply side based on the Phillips curve gave way to a version of the standard model capable of keeping together, in the same framework, both the Keynesian (short-term) and the neoclassical (long-term) results. This model, given its aptitude to explain also the inflation phenomena, became the analytical reference in macroeconomics for most scholars. At the same time, it was believed that macroeconomics, as well as microeconomics, had reached a general consensus around the unifying principles of the agents' rationality and market equilibrium – principles which were best expressed within the general equilibrium theory.

In the 1960s it was believed that the phase of 'scientific revolution' was over, and that the task of providing macroeconomics with a 'paradigm' (characterised by a rigorous statute coherent with the general principles of economic theory) was already accomplished. From this point onwards, the progress of the discipline would have been that of a 'normal science', and the research work able to accumulate knowledge smoothly and steadily. Throughout the decade scholars mainly focused on the extension of the model to open economies, to long-run analysis (growth theory) and, above all, to the econometric estimation of quantitative models with increasing dimensions, to be used in forecasts and for evaluating alternative economic policies.

5. Obviously, the illustration just described provides a simplified sketch of the reality of that time. With hindsight the situation appears much less homogenous and consolidated. An attentive eye would have been able to see some problematic areas and unresolved issues as well as phases of friction and doubt. The following are just a few examples and we will see that all of them had an important role in determining, in the next decade, the profound crisis of the neoclassical synthesis paradigm.

First, a gradual but increasing disjunction was taking place between the research which explored the theoretical foundations of the aggregate behavioural functions (consumption, investment and money demand) and the econometric analysis based on extended scale models whose theoretical content appeared definitely much poorer in comparison with that research. To a great extent, these two lines of research developed 'along separate tracks', but the fact did not give rise to much concern because 'as long as both programs seemed to be making good progress there was ample ground for faith that eventually the theory and the quantitative models would be shown to be consistent with one another' (Woodford 1999: 11).

Secondly, problems related to the different degree of theoretical investigation were between the model's supply and demand sides. As Blanchard observes, 'most macro models developed in the 1960s . . . had a schizophrenic feeling: a careful modelling of consumption, investment and asset demand decisions on the one hand, and an a-theoretical specification of price and wage setting on the other' (Blanchard 2000: 15).

It is easily explained why scholars focused on the demand side. The main novelty of the Keynesian revolution was that demand *matters*. The neoclassical synthesis had specified this 'message' by showing that things are just so in the presence of nominal rigidities, particularly in the labour market. However, an analytical treatment of these imperfections was only hinted at. We have seen that within the first generation of models, money wages were simply assumed to be fixed (in the short run), and that, in the second generation, wages were sticky and specified through the introduction of the Phillips curve. 'But there was surprisingly little work on what exactly lay behind the Phillips curve, why and how wages were set this way, why there was little apparent relation between real wages and the level of employment' (ibid.).

Thirdly, the aspect of macroeconomic research in the 1960s which deserves to be mentioned is related to a result obtained by macroeconomic growth theory. I refer to what used to be known as optimal growth models (Koopmans 1965; Cass 1965) which enriched the standard growth model (Solow 1956) through the endogenous determination of the propensity to save. This task was accomplished by incorporating in the model a well known and consolidated result of microeconomic theory: the intertemporal choice theory, the first formulations of which dated back to the work of Irving Fisher in the early years of the twentieth century.[18]

These latter results, contrary to the first two mentioned above, refer to an area which is seemingly very distant from the neoclassical synthesis paradigm. The reason why I decided to consider these three elements as all contributing to delineate the same problematic picture is the following. Optimal growth models provide a base which will soon be developed into a macroeconomic framework *alternative* to that of the neoclassical synthesis. On the one hand, this framework is firmly grounded in the general principles of economic theory, namely those of agents' rationality and market clearing. On the other hand, it constitutes an explicitly dynamic framework in which the objective functions, and therefore the agents' decisions, have an intertemporal dimension. In short, it constitutes the extension to macroeconomics of the typical approach of modern general equilibrium theory.[19]

All these elements served to play an important role in determining the crisis of the Keynesian paradigm at the end of the 1960s. The first signal emerged on theoretical grounds when, independently of each other, Milton Friedman (1968) and Edmund Phelps (1968) criticised the Keynesian rationale for the Phillips's curve and introduced into the model an endogenous correction of inflation expectations. The second crisis signal came instead from the reality of the economic systems at the beginning of the 1970s.

> The appearance of chronic inflation as an economic problem, following a couple of decades of relatively stable prices, and not long after Keynesian ideas about demand management began to be put into practice, highlighted a critical weakness of the somewhat oversimplified Keynesian model that was used in practical policy analyses. This was its relative neglect of the effects of demand stimulus upon the general level of prices.
>
> (Woodford 1999: 12)

The third signal came with the failure of the extended macroeconometrical models to forecast correctly the effects of alternative economic policies within a context characterised by the presence of both rising inflation and economic stagnation.

In the early 1970s Keynesian economics was criticised, above all, for its weak microeconomic foundations. In the very first year of that decade a very important book was published (Phelps *et al.* 1970) dedicated entirely to the study of micro-foundations in unemployment and inflation theories. The essays in this book became an essential point of reference for anyone interested in macroeconomics. From these works a set of rules emerged on how to pursue macroeconomic research: (1) describe the aggregate behavioural functions of *all* agents (not only on the demand side) explicitly on the basis of the assumption of *rationality*, keeping in mind the fact that choices are taken within an intertemporal setting; (2) devote your closest attention to the role played by markets in determining agents' behaviour, and in particular to the *reactions* of the latter in response to the *signals* coming from the markets; (3) model the economic environment, taking explicitly into account the presence of uncertainty (that is, to build stochastic models). Under all these profiles, the Keynesian orthodoxy of the 1960s proved not to have reached the same level; and this was a big blow.

Another area in which Keynesian economics got into trouble was with economic policy. In reference to the standard Keynesian model (with the only, inevitable integration of correcting the Phillips curve with the expectations of inflation), neoclassical economists showed that, 'if one assumed rational expectations of inflation, the effects of money on output lasted only for a brief moment, until the relevant information about money was released. So, even on its own terms, once rational expectations were introduced, the standard model seemed unable to deliver its traditional conclusions' (Blanchard 2000: 17). In other words, monetary policies have real effects (temporary) only if they are unexpected (if they surprise the agents); but when the agents have rational expectations, the policies turn out to be unexpected only if they are unforeseeable, that is, they are not systematic. This is what makes up the famous policy ineffectiveness proposition (Sargent 1973).

Another attack, maybe a bit more direct and effective, on the Keynesian theory of economic policy came with an influential and rightly famous article by Lucas (1976). He explained why the macroeconometric models had started to fail from early on in the decade. The reason had to do, in this case also, with inattention to the fundamentals. The fact was that the reduced form of those models did not take into account that optimal responses of agents are not invariant in respect to changes in the environment, and therefore in the policies as well. But when Lucas expressed his evaluation policy proposition the crisis of Keynesian economics was already well under way.

6. After ten years of (almost) general consensus on the Keynesian paradigm, macroeconomics in the 1970s entered a turbulent phase again. Economists have been divided between schools and have held heated debates among themselves. There is not enough space here to go into the details of the long, complex, and troubled history of this debate, which lasted for most of the next two decades. Those interested in that history can read Rodano (1996, 1997) or the two short, updated and interesting profiles contained in Woodford (1999) and Blanchard (2000) which have often been quoted above; the first, as we have already seen, places more emphasis on the evolution of the debate among different schools whereas the second emphasises the expansion of knowledge.[20]

Here I will focus on only a few episodes of this debate. I will try to show that these episodes confirm the thesis put forward on pp. 309–10 to explain why there were so many debates in macroeconomics and their role in increasing the amount of knowledge in this field.

The first episode is of assistance in illustrating the important but not decisive relationship between macroeconomic theory and empirical observations. We can start by noticing that the first steps forward in the neoclassical counter-revolution, and the opening of hostilities against the dominant Keynesian orthodoxy, were not at first based on the confrontation between theories and facts, even if the latter would end up maintaining an important role at a later date.

I refer to Friedman's criticism of the Keynesian interpretation of the Phillips curve, which is unanimously considered today to be the most decisive blow to the standard model of the 1960s. This criticism is not in fact based on the argument that the (Keynesian) theory is not in line with the observations, since it complies satisfactorily with them. Actually, Friedman's criticism is founded on a specific point relevant to the theory's coherence with the general principles of economic theory, namely on the circumstance that *real* but not *nominal* wages respond to excess demand. This is a relevant point for Friedman, even if the observations seem to contradict his thesis, given that, at least on the surface, they do not show any significant relation between real wages and the business cycle.

Where do the empirical observations become relevant? Starting from his criticism, Friedman pushes as far as making the following forecast, even if it is conditioned by the implementation of an economic policy: if governments try to take advantage of the trade-off implicit in the Phillips curve between inflation and unemployment, to bring the system below the natural rate of unemployment, the result will be but temporary because the Phillips curve will move up.[21] Governments actually tried to take advantage of this trade-off, and after a few years statistical data showed a significant indication that a movement like the one forecasted by Friedman had actually taken place.

This result undoubtedly contributed to make the shares of New Classical Macroeconomics rise and those of Keynesian Macroeconomics fall. However, it was anything but conclusive. In the first half of the 1970s, rather, the issue of whether the data effectively highlighted a movement of the Phillips curve and whether this movement had to be explained in the terms suggested by Friedman became the subject of a long and heated debate that engaged the energies of many theorists and econometricians. In the end, the neoclassical position on this point won and, in giving it more weight on the scales, the consensus it gained at the theoretical level was at least as important as the empirical evidence.

Moreover, the inconclusive nature of the theory's compliance (or conflict) with stylised facts is endorsed by another two episodes from the debate. The first attempt by Keynesian economists to react to the crisis of the standard model of the 1970s was to explore the implications of nominal rigidity through the 'equilibrium with fixed prices' approach (Barro and Grossman 1976; Malinvaud 1984). Such models exhibited exemplary compliance with stylised facts, but nevertheless they 'turned out to be a dead end' (Blanchard 2000: 15).[22]

A symmetrical situation came about when Lucas (1972, 1973) launched the New Classical Macroeconomics research programme among scholars. The main tenet of the approach was that agents, up against price changes, cannot distinguish, owing to lack of information, between changes in relative prices and changes in the general price level induced by monetary policies. The models which Lucas used to formalise his ideas were deficient in the face of empirical evidence; however, they acquired scholars' consensus and imposed on the academic world the New Classical Macroeconomics as the most successful approach of the 1970s.

It was not coincidental but largely 'a result of its empirical shortcomings and, more specifically, the difficulties of the "nominal confusion" mechanism to generate fluctuations of sufficient magnitude and persistence' that the Lucas approach 'was soon abandoned' (Galí 2000: 3); but this circumstance did not imply the crisis of the New Classical Macroeconomics. On the contrary, the neoclassical approach continued to gain consensus among scholars against the Keynesian one throughout the 1970s and at the end of that period proved to be the most successful paradigm in macroeconomics.

Let us now take into consideration an event that shows how the debate among different schools does not start from zero each time but rather generates a continuous, still laborious progress of knowledge. It should be noted that, almost always, the new positions that emerge as in conflict with those which were previously the centre of attention assume as their starting point a position on territory already occupied by the adversary. Let us consider, for example, the theses through which Keynesian economists confronted the neoclassical positions in the second half of the 1970s. Their models are microfounded (that is, coherent with the rules of the microfoundation of macroeconomics programme as designed in Phelps *et al.* 1970) and expectations are assumed to be rational. In this sense they are very different from the Keynesian models of the 1960s. The New Keynesians (cf. Fischer 1980; Taylor 1985) show that, assuming imperfect competition, where prices are fixed through menus and/or wages through contracts, a macroeconomic model comes out equivalent to a neoclassical one though yielding different results: even with rational expectations, the announced changes in the quantity of money have real effects in the short term. That is, the Keynesians have accepted to compete on the ground chosen by the neoclassicals, thus showing that their conclusions do not hold in general but only under relatively restrictive hypotheses.

Even the second wave of New Keynesian economics builds its own theses in an analogous way. In this instance the objective is not to study the effects of rigidities (nominal or real) within a macroeconomic model of aggregate supply and aggregate demand – a task, as we have seen before, already accomplished during the first wave – but rather to explain the presence of such rigidities not as an empirical fact but as a result of the agents' rational choices. Thus the consequences of the rational behaviour hypothesis are studied when the goods, labour and financial activities markets are characterised by imperfect competition and/or asymmetrical information.[23] As is the case here again, this research programme undoubtedly set itself against the one implemented in those same years by neoclassical economists, but it is achieved using the same research instruments, in order to explore a different territory. Consequently, its relevant polemic intent did not turn into sterile opposition. Throughout the 1980s, behind the (seeming and actual) dispute, a continuous exchange took place, that is, a substantial cross-fertilisation concerning not only the premises but also the results of the theory. However, at that time the convergence process was still not mature enough for a new synthesis.

7. Notwithstanding the undoubted recovery of consensus by New Keynesian economics, the neoclassical one was still the overall dominant approach in macroeconomics in the 1980s. It was also known as the Real Business Cycle (RBC) approach. It constitutes the third wave following both that of Milton Friedman's monetarists and that which, under the leadership of Robert Lucas, had taken up the ground in the 1970s. These three waves are characterised by the increasing importance attached to the general equilibrium approach. For Friedman, the general equilibrium theory was no more than an ideal point of reference, an effective source of information and suggestions. For Lucas, however, it was more than that. It indicated the work methodology, the pattern to follow and imitate

when trying to develop macroeconomic theory.[24] The RBC approach takes a further decisive step forward in the sense that, from then on, the use of dynamic stochastic general equilibrium models became systematic.

The RBC theories are grounded in the following methodological stance. In order to investigate the nature and the effects of the business cycle, it is necessary to begin with the consideration of a perfectly functioning dynamic system. Only from there on can an analysis be developed of what fluctuations emerge as a consequence of a change either in technology or in any of the other fundamentals. The procedure described above, that is, that of analysing the movement of the system through time, as it is driven by agents' rational responses to technological shocks, is the only legitimate one. In particular, it is the only adequate procedure for trying to find out whether business cycles are the result of market failures or just of the optimal functioning of the economic system, thus implying no welfare loss.

There are now numerous versions of RBC theories in existence.[25] Though many of them assume an overlapping generations model as a base, the majority use as a framework the standard intertemporal optimisation model with an infinite horizon, enriched by the essential addition of a stochastic shock on technology. The results obtained with this approach show – not surprisingly – that, at least in the basic model, the evolution of product, employment and consumption as well as investment choices is optimal: 'there are no market failures in this economy' (Plosser 1989: 56). The other relevant theoretical result, which was, like the former, largely foreseeable, is the possibility of 'explaining economic fluctuations without reference to any monetary variables' (Galí 2000: 3). The conclusion therefore is that money is neutral.

The RBC approach represented a relevant novelty even as regards the empirical analyses. These are based on the 'adjustment' technique of 'calibration', that is, the comparison (after a homogenous dimension has been established) between the statistical data generated by the model and those emerging from actual time series. 'In fact, much of the success and popularity of the RBC program can arguably be explained by the ability of calibrated versions of the model to reproduce, at least qualitatively, the sign and patterns of some key second moments of US time series' (Galí 2000: 3).

Kydland and Prescott (1996) maintain that the combination of RBC models (specified for answering very precise questions) and econometric techniques based on calibration allow the construction of 'computational experiments' articulated in 'five major steps: pose a question; use a well-tested theory; construct a model economy; calibrate the model economy; and run the experiment' on computer (ibid.: 70). According to the authors, the computational experiments 'have become invaluable tools in quantitative aggregate theory' (ibid.: 69) and constitute the solution to the problems which arise in economic science from the 'unfeasibility of controlled experiments' (ibid.: 84). In this sense, they offer themselves as the new reference framework for applied macroeconomic research.

Obviously, not everything is that smooth in the RBC approach. For example, there are still problems of harmonisation with stylised facts (a non-decisive comparison, as we know, but not to be underestimated). The first difficulty has to do with the role of technological shocks. In the RBC models, such shocks are taken to be an approximation of the data emerging from the series of Solow's residuals. But, as Mankiw (1989) has shown, the circumstance that they are undoubtedly pro-cyclical does not justify considering them 'as a measure of year-to-year changes in the available production technology' (Mankiw 1989: 85); on the contrary, their characteristic of being pro-cyclical would instead be the consequence of a statistical error (Galí 2000). The use of other technological shock indicators did not give similarly satisfying results. Another relevant empirical problem with the RBC paradigm is represented by the consolidated evidence that money is not neutral in the short run, a stylised fact which makes up an unresolved and troublesome contradiction with the RBC model, notwithstanding the various attempts (all unsuccessful) to solve it.

What could be considered the most promising of these attempts is outlined in the last part of this short survey of macroeconomics in the last fifty years. We are now in the 1990s. A new research programme finds favour amongst scholars by contaminating the general equilibrium dynamic models in a stochastic environment with Keynesian elements. Up to then, only neoclassical versions of those models were available. But now this research programme makes use, without any scruples or hesitation, of the methodology established in the RBC approach. This methodology is now applied in an economic environment exhibiting two clearly Keynesian characteristics: the presence of imperfect competition within goods and labour markets and the presence of nominal rigidities.

This match between the neoclassical apparatus of general equilibrium (dynamic and stochastic) and the typical assumptions which in the past decade were made by New Keynesian economics is referred to by Goodfriend and King (1997) as the New Neoclassical Synthesis. It is at the base of the recently matured research work (cf. Rotemberg and Woodford 1997; Clarida *et al.* 1999) on the effects of monetary policies and on the other links between money and the performance of economic systems. Those links, in the preceding decades, were submerged and forgotten as a consequence of the dominance of the RBC approach.

One of the most interesting aspects of this research programme is that the introduction of the above-mentioned Keynesian elements (imperfect competition and microfounded nominal rigidities) in the framework used by the RBC approach leads to the development of a model which is surprisingly simple and familiar. It consists of three equations: an IS schedule, an LM schedule and a Phillips curve.[26] In the end, our story concludes at the point where it started – the IS–LM model, as David Romer remarks, 'has been a central tool of macroeconomic teaching and practice for over half a century' (Romer 2000: 149).

This circumstance, however, does not imply that the past half-century did not leave its mark on macroeconomics. The new version of the IS–LM–Phillips curve framework is not at all identical to that of the 1960s. And it is not only because the tendency today is to replace the LM schedule with other monetary policy rules (such as Taylor's rule – cf. Taylor 1993) based on the idea that the variable controlled by the central bank is the interest rate. The most important reason is that the new versions of the IS schedule and the Phillips curve differ on one essential element from the old versions: in both cases, the expectations of the *future* values of product and inflation play a relevant role. Basically, the new versions of the model are not only explicitly microfounded but also explicitly dynamic. The great debate among macroeconomists did not bring our knowledge back to square one but to a much richer and more mature equilibrium.

The outline of macroeconomic research seems again therefore to have reached a phase of synthesis, analogous to that of the 1960s in which the reference model for all scholars was basically the same. We can then conclude, with Blanchard, that the distinction between New Keynesian and New Classical scholars does not make sense any more and that 'these two labels will soon join others in the trash bin of history of thought' (Blanchard 2000: 18). This statement seems, actually, a bit premature.[27] The history of macroeconomics in the past half-century has taught us to be suspicious about the actual end of the controversies and above all of the division in schools of thought. Forty years ago the neoclassicals seemed to have almost disappeared (only Milton Friedman insisted on swimming against the tide). Twenty years later, the same fate seemed to have overtaken the Keynesians.[28] What is certain is that when sooner or later the next controversies manifest themselves, the battleground will be much more advanced territory.[29]

Notes

1 The words 'revolution' and 'counter-revolution' appear in the titles of many important works in the field of macroeconomics. The following are just a few examples: *The Keynesian Revolution*, the well known book by Lawrence Klein (1947), and Harry Johnson's 'The Keynesian revolution and the monetarist counter-revolution' (*American Economic Review*, 1971); a third notable example is a popular book by David Begg (1982) on macroeconomics and rational expectations entitled *The Rational Expectations Revolution in Macroeconomics*. These terms still appear in the titles of macroeconomic works today, e.g. a book by Laidler (1999) entitled *Fabricating the Keynesian Revolution*, a title which in this case is more justified, given that the book deals with the history of macroeconomic thought.

2 All quotations are from Blanchard (2000: 2). Blanchard's claim is clearly synthesised in the title of his paper – 'What do we know about macroeconomics that Fisher and Wicksell did not?' – and in the opening words of the abstract, 'The answer to the question in the title is: A lot.'

3 For a cross-border comparison between economics and other scientific disciplines see Boitani and Rodano (1995b) and Boitani and Rodano (1995a).

4 What was said is not invalidated by recent rapid developments in 'experimental economics'. At least, not for now. In fact, the experiments in economics (and particularly in macroeconomics) are extremely limited by nature in comparison with those implemented in the natural sciences. For more on this theme refer to, for example, Loomes (1991) and Hey (1994).

5 The game-theory approach to economic policy is still a very lively research field. On this argument see Persson and Tabellini (1994) and the survey by the same authors for the *Handbook of Macroeconomics* (Persson and Tabellini 1997). These new developments constitute a typical example of the progress of knowledge in macroeconomics.

6 Also, the stylised facts which the theories must confront are subject to changes through time. Such changes, for example, can be attributed to the evolution of the environment. They can also be attributed to the availability of statistical observations which

did not exist before. Finally, it is not unusual for the changes in stylised facts to depend on the evolution of theories. The large mass of stylised facts which emerge from national accounting statistics (for example: the variance in consumption throughout a cycle is lower than that of the national product which in turn is less than that of investment) is obviously related to the same discipline's development, which was in turn born as a consequence of the development of macroeconomics. Sometimes the link between stylised facts and theory becomes more narrow and intricate. Again, an example is useful here: fifty years ago, a theory of economic fluctuations had to be able to explain and describe broad fluctuations of substantially regular length and amplitude, that is, the business *cycles*; later on, the expression 'business cycle' remained a tribute to tradition, while the regularities scholars try to explain have less to do with duration and size than with the variance of fluctuations and their 'co-movements'.

7 In a paper which I will consider in more detail below Aumann writes, 'the existence of parallel scientific theories side by side . . . occurs even in the natural sciences; but in our disciplines [economics and game theory] is ubiquitous' (Aumann 1985: 34).

8 Notice the recurrence once again of the word 'revolution' in this context.

9 The main schools were the school of Lausanne, with Walras and later Pareto, and then the Austrian school, with Menger. The British economists who made reference to Alfred Marshall represented an intermediate position. Seen 'close up' through the eyes of a late nineteenth-century economist (or in terms of the history of thought), the differences between these schools were numerous, relevant and strongly felt. Seen from 'afar' through the eyes of a late twentieth-century economist (or in the optic of economic theory), the same differences fade away, giving rise to a homogenous and unified framework.

10 We know that there was an important exception, represented by those scholars who were inspired by the work of Piero Sraffa (1960). The contrast between the Sraffian school and the mainstream has been thoroughly analysed. Most chapters of this volume are dedicated to this theme and here we can only suggest reading them. We can observe though that the acute phase of debate lasted the entire decade of the 1960s. The discussion clarified the nature of the differences and, at least from the quantitative viewpoint (the number of scholars adhering to either side), concluded with the supremacy of the neoclassical mainstream.

11 'The concept of truth applies to *observations*; one can say that such and such were truly the observations. It also applies to all kinds of everyday events, like whether or not one had hamburger for dinner yesterday. It does not apply to *theories*' (Aumann 1985: 34).

12 Applying Aumann's criterion to the criterion itself, one can say that it draws together many points and seems fertile.

13 The article by Lucas introduced the rational expectations hypothesis in macroeconomics (originally proposed by John Muth 1961) and is considered the seminal paper of the New Classical Macroeconomics research. We will focus on this issue below.

14 It is perhaps worth recalling that Keynes used the expression 'classical economics' for orthodoxy.

15 Bibliographical references: on the consumption function, Modigliani and Brunberg (1954) and Friedman (1957); on the demand for money, Baumol (1952) and Tobin (1956, 1958); on the investment function, Jorgenson (1963) and Tobin (1969).

16 For an authoritative summary of this model elaborated during that time period, we still recommend reading the work of one of the leading protagonists, Modigliani (1963).

17 The Phillips curve is an *empirical* relation between the rates of unemployment and inflation. In correspondence to very high unemployment rates, the rate of change of prices can be negative. The Phillips curve was observed and estimated for the first time at the end of the 1950s using statistical data from the United Kingdom (cf. Phillips 1958). Later, it was estimated also for other major countries. In the first studies, the relations observed and estimated were those between the rate of unemployment and the rate of change of money wage rates. Subsequently, relations between the

unemployment rate and the rate of change of prices were also observed and estimated. The relation between prices and the national product can obviously be derived taking into consideration the direct relation between the national product and employment and the inverse relation between the latter and unemployment.

18 The appearance in macroeconomics of the Fisherian approach as the intertemporal choice theory is one of the many examples of the way in which old ideas suddenly become fashionable again in economics and succeed in nourishing areas diverse and distant from that in which they have been developed. Today the intertemporal choice approach has become an essential ingredient in standard macroeconomic models and therefore appears in the textbooks (cf. Blanchard and Fischer 1989; Romer 1996; Obstfeld and Rogoff 1996). Another example of an idea which became fashionable in macroeconomics after a relatively long latent period is the rational expectations hypothesis; ten years elapsed between an article by Muth which appeared in 1961 and its introduction into macroeconomics by Lucas in 1972. A third example is the 'learning by doing' idea of Arrow (1962): another twenty years go by before the theme becomes one of the fundamental structures of the new endogenous growth theories (see Aghion and Howitt 1998).

19 In the literature on optimal growth it is assumed that the agents' temporal horizon is infinite. The economic models which incorporate this characteristic are also known, in macroeconomic textbooks, as Ramsey-type models, in recognition of the first formalisation proposed at the end of the 1920s by Frank Ramsey, a mathematical genius and friend of Keynes, who died prematurely in 1930 when he was only twenty-six years old. Quite widespread also are the models with finite temporal horizon and *overlapping generations* introduced in the macroeconomic literature by Samuelson (1958) and Diamond (1965).

20 For a more extensive work on New Classical Macroeconomics, the ample work by Hoover (1988) is also useful, while for an introduction to the various themes of New Keynesian economics Ardeni *et al.* (1999) is recommended.

21 Given its problematic relationship with the *facts*, it is clear that economics has an equally problematic relationship with *forecasts* (and this explains the pitiless definition of economists as those 'who will explain to you tomorrow why what they forecast yesterday hasn't happened today'). Simplifying a bit, it can be said that the 'forecasting ability' of a theory can have three principal meanings: (1) the theory suggests that a specific event must be observed in reality, without necessarily implicating a temporal dimension (for example, central bankers are more 'conservative' than the governments which appoint them); (2) the theory suggests that one specific event will take place in the future (for example, in 2001 the average price of petrol will be lower than it was in 2000); (3) the theory suggests that, if a certain event takes place, another one will follow (which is the case under consideration in the text). For further details of this theme see Stewart (1991) and Boland (1991).

22 For an interesting discussion of why this research programme ended up being abandoned see Blanchard (2000: 15–17). In terms of 'Aumann's criterion' one could agree that this approach failed to establish a 'critical mass' of consensus among scholars and has therefore been shown to be scarcely fertile (at least for the time being).

23 The principal essays on New Keynesian economics can be found in Mankiw and Romer (1991a). For a critical appraisal see also Rotheim (1998a).

24 It can be said that Lucas's idea was to make macroeconomics flow together with microeconomics or, better, with the *tout court* economic theory. Of course there are typical macro *problems* such as unemployment, business cycles, the role of economic policies, etc., but only one serious *method* is available to scholars who face these problems, namely the method refined over a century by microeconomics on the basis of the postulates of agents' rationality and market clearing. In the words of Lucas, '[t]he private jargon that macroeconomics developed during the period when it was cut off from mainstream economic theory – multipliers and gaps and Phillips curves and so on – has largely passed out of use. Macroeconomists today are expected to be able to

discuss their ideas in the language of Arrow, Debreu, and McKenzie. This is progress' (Lucas 1993: 184).

25 The work of Kydland and Prescott (1982) paves the way to the real business cycle models. The basic version of this model can be found in Prescott (1986). A good survey, updated at the end of the 1980s, is Plosser (1989).

26 One of the youngest representatives of this new research programme, Jordi Galí, is therefore justified in having entitled one of his works 'The return of the Phillips curve' (Galí 2000); and this all in spite of Lucas, who, as we have seen, considered the Phillips curve as a notion whose destiny was to disappear from the language of macroeconomists (see the quotation in note 24). One of the most significant works of this new research programme is the excellent survey by Clarida *et al.* in the *Journal of Economic Literature* (1999). Interestingly enough, its subtitle is 'A New Keynesian perspective'.

27 The wise Robert Solow observes that the convergence process affects only the 'moderates of both sides', and a 'stridency' that 'comes from the extremes' still exists (Solow 2000: 154). He himself remains sceptical in his 'more pessimistic moments' about the microfoundation project. He writes, for instance, 'I think that the only reason to insist on optimising behaviour is to get welfare conclusions that no one believes anyway, the most spectacularly implausible one being that the observed business cycle is really an optimal adjustment to unexpected shocks to technology' (ibid.: 152).

28 In reference to those years, Robert Eisner recalls having been introduced at a conference as an 'eminent Keynesian, or better yet, the only Keynesian survivor' (Eisner 1986).

29 What ground exactly is this? For further suggestions as to which are potentially the most important themes of macroeconomic research in the twenty-first century refer to Blanchard (2000: 36–41) and Solow (2000).

23 On the relevance of the distinction between Keynesian and neoclassical macroeconomics

Ignazio Musu

The recent development of macroeconomics is generally described in terms of the evolution of the relationship between two competing theoretical approaches to macroeconomic analysis and policy, the Keynesian approach and the neoclassical one. While some macroeconomists could be tempted to regard the two tracks as progressively converging on the same consolidated body of scientific knowledge, others see the distinction between the two approaches continuing to maintain its original significance. My attempt in this chapter is to lend further support to the claim that the distinction between a Keynesian and a neoclassical macroeconomics is still meaningful and to argue that the long period of controversy and debate which occupied the past decades has produced the relevant outcome in making the nature of the distinction more precise.

The traditional distinction had to do with the ability of markets to spontaneously achieve an efficient general equilibrium for the economy and with the role of economic policy: the neoclassical vision gave much credit to the potentialities of markets, assumed to be competitive and perfectly functioning, and considered that economic policy should essentially have a passive role; the Keynesian vision was more sceptical about the automatic market adjustments and more confident about the positive role of economic policy.

Taking everything into account, it turns out that the basic reason for a distinction lies in the fact that neoclassical macroeconomics refers to a world of perfect and complete markets, whilst Keynesian macroeconomics refers to a world where markets are imperfect and incomplete and where strategic interaction plays a crucial role.

Contributions from recent debates and specifically from the New Classical side, such as for instance the idea of rational expectations and the idea that private reaction functions to policy actions should be taken into account, can be easily embodied in the Keynesian framework, so they cannot be considered the fundamental distinguishing factor of the New Classical theory. The main result of the New Classical macroeconomics (that macroeconomic equilibrium is market-clearing without involuntary unemployment) cannot be explained by referring to rational expectations *alone*: basically it depends on the assumption of perfect and complete markets where market clearing is ensured by complete price flexibility.

If markets are imperfect, with strategic interaction and asymmetric information, rational expectations can still be used, but the 'true' model of the economy changes and the rational expectations have to be formed in a way consistent with the new model.

Traditional interpretations of the *General Theory*, such as the famous 'neoclassical synthesis', have been built accepting the assumption of perfect and complete goods markets, the only imperfection being in the labour market, where fixed money wages were assumed, but without a convincing microeconomic explanation. Within this institutional market framework, the monetarist critique and the New Classical critique of the Phillips curve would be quite natural on purely theoretical grounds, and it turned out to be even more successful because of its strong empirical counterpart.

However, the message of the *General Theory* becomes much easier to understand in a world of imperfect and incomplete markets. For instance, within a framework of intertemporal market incompleteness, the typical Keynesian result that an act of saving, which entails the reduction of current consumption, does not automatically imply an act of substitution of future for present consumption comes out as a very natural one.

The most promising results in what we still have good reason to call 'Keynesian macroeconomics' come precisely from the analytical work with imperfect and incomplete markets, asymmetric information, strategic interaction, transaction and search costs. This work has produced convincing explanations for inefficient (subgame perfect non-cooperative) macroeconomic equilibria (with involuntary unemployment) deriving from coordination failures; this work has also evolved firmer microeconomic bases of a positive role for economic policy.

The coordination failure approach is the most interesting and promising feature in the revival of Keynesian macroeconomics. Keynes's central message was very much concerned with the way markets operate as a coordination mechanism among economic agents. In the Walrasian model and in its macroeconomic prototype, the New Classical macroeconomic model, the only source of coordination among agents is the price mechanism. In his *General Theory* Keynes questioned the success of price flexibility precisely as a coordination mechanism. He was convinced that deflation produced by a negative aggregate demand shock would generate instability and a compensating aggregate demand policy would allow quicker adjustment to a full employment equilibrium.

This issue raised by Keynes, to which Keynesian macroeconomics has paid insufficient attention, is important today at a time where a new positive attitude to the benefits of a dynamic free competition process is gaining ground. Keynes warns us that this process can entail destabilising consequences which may be costly in terms of welfare. These undesired consequences may be compensated for by an aggregate demand policy sustaining the positive supply effects of increased competition.

Keynesian macroeconomics accepts the market as a successful mechanism for ensuring coordination, but does not consider it the unique and perfect one. Because of the organisational and institutional complexity of markets, adjustments of quantities operate together with adjustments of prices. In the Keynesian world we do not have the dichotomy of the Walrasian world, where agents only send quantity signals and receive only price signals from an auctioneer. This artificial simplicity of the Walrasian world, which persists in the New Classical macroeconomic model, has precluded New Classical macroeconomics from interacting with the recent interesting results of microeconomic research in industrial organisation. This is not the case with Keynesian macroeconomics, which is based upon precisely the same features of the economic reality studied by the modern microeconomics of strategic interaction and asymmetric information.

In this framework economic policy has two tasks. The first is to help improve coordination by smoothing fluctuations produced by coordination failures: this task is accomplished by using active aggregate demand policies. The second task is to help overcome coordination failures. This requires credible strategies to improve the efficiency of market institutions, their competition and transparency, and at the same time induce agents to assume optimistic coordinated beliefs from which coordinated behaviour will follow. This strategy requires a combination of demand and supply policies and a set of microeconomic policies affecting economic institutions and sending agents the appropriate incentives.

I conclude that modern Keynesian macroeconomics implies a complex vision of economic policy which cannot be reduced to the traditional aggregate demand policy, but which does not discard it. This complex vision cannot accept the minimalist approach to economic policy entailed by the New Classical macroeconomics and deriving from theoretical premises too remote from the features of market economies in the real world.

Part V

Economic theorising and institutions

> I stick to a notion of Economics – or rather, to use the older and more appropriate term, *Political Economy* – which . . . participates of the nature of both the classics' and Keynes's views of the question. In fact, I view Political Economy as the social science whose principal task is that of spelling out the *laws* that govern the phenomena of value, production and distribution in given social and institutional contexts, with a view to supplying insights and points of reference for those who are responsible for the policy choices to be made; that is of supplying those 'ideas' about the functioning of the economic system which, 'for good or evil' are stronger than 'vested interests' in 'ruling' the world. (Keynes 1971–89, VII: 383–4) The central logical moment of the above process is the identification of a 'model', that is, a simplified representation of the 'world' (or that portion of it which is the object of the analysis) capable of capturing the essential features, the fundamental traits of the reality that surrounds the political economist – like the drawing of a landscape or of a portrait, where the artist makes no attempt at a faithful reproduction of *every single* aspect of the real world, but tries only to fix on paper what appears to him/her the most important elements of the things he/she is looking at.
>
> (Caravale 1993: 138)

24 Economic theory and institutions

Luigi L. Pasinetti

The parallel foundation and growth of an Association for Evolutionary Political Economy in Europe and of an Association for Evolutionary Economics with strong institutionalist background in the United States (with the more recent addition of a Joseph A. Schumpeter Society and a *Journal of Evolutionary Economics*) are hopefully going to represent major events in the development of fruitful and innovative economic thinking. I thought it might be useful, to help towards a convergence of endeavours, to devote some attention to the relations between economic theory and the analysis of economic institutions.

Institutional economists have become more and more worried, recently, about the lack of connection, or of communication, between theory and institutional analysis. Let me give only two quotations, which seem to me to synthesise these preoccupations. The first is from Robert Langlois:

> The problem with the Historical School and many of the early Institutionalists is that they wanted an economics with institutions but without theory; the problem with many neoclassicists is that they want economic theory without institutions; what we should really want is both institutions and theory.
>
> (Langlois 1986: 5)

The second quotation is from Douglass North, himself more an economic historian than an economist. He claims that:

> What has been missing is the development of an analytical framework to integrate institutional analysis into economics and economic history.
>
> (North 1993: 243)

This sounds like a research programme aimed at marrying economic theory and economic institutional analysis. But a research programme, to be successful, must be feasible. It is not enough to try to marry the two sides: one must ensure that they are compatible with each other, otherwise one simply sets the preconditions for early divorce.

In the present chapter I shall develop three contentions.

1 The stated task, or research programme, is impossible, as long as by economic theory we mean (as, alas, too widely it is taken to mean) neoclassical economic theory.
2 Neoclassical economics is not the only source of economic theory. There exist other alternative sources. In particular there is a brand of economic theory that is based on the idea of production, and more generally of economic activity as a process, which goes back to the glorious tradition of classical economics and is continued by Keynesian and Post-Keynesian economics. This alternative is at least as powerful as neoclassical economics.
3 This line of (classical/Keynesian) thought, if appropriately developed, is not only compatible but actually affords exceptionally favourable features for a unified theoretical framework in which to place the economic analysis of social institutions.

The relevance of institutional analysis

Before starting, one must posit a crucial preliminary question. Is the task worth while? Is institutional economic analysis really important? I think one can safely affirm that economists are becoming more and more convinced of its importance.

Some colleagues are actually arguing that the failure of development in the Third World is not so much a failure to mobilise aid or loans or to make machinery available or anything else of the sort, but essentially a failure to provide clear ideas on how to set up the appropriate economic institutions and to shape the appropriate international economic institutions.

There is even more ground for saying that the collapse of the whole Eastern European bloc and of 'real socialism' itself is not due to lack of technological advances, or ability to set aside savings, or to make investments, but is essentially a failure to shape the appropriate economic institutions and indeed a failure on the part of economists and social scientists in general to carry out appropriate investigations and put forward suitable proposals for them. I shall not take issue with these claims. I mention them to highlight the widespread conviction that the study and analysis of institutions has become, for practical purposes, very important.

Of this some scholars, namely all the early institutionalists – particularly Thorstein Veblen, Wesley Clair Mitchell and John Roger Commons in the United States at the end of the nineteenth century and the beginning of the twentieth – were of course deeply convinced already, though pursuing different lines of thought, as Mark Perlman (1992) has so clearly indicated (see also Samuels 1987). Equally deeply convinced of it were the members of the German historical school in Europe, even earlier than in America.

Yet we must not forget that they lost the battle. They insisted on pointing out the sterility of the dominant economics of their times (which has since become the neoclassical economics of our day). They proposed institutional and historical investigation as an *alternative*. And they lost.

Ever since, the representatives of the economic theory that has become dominant in our universities have been looking at them with a sort of contempt. I have been struck, for example, by reading what Ronald Coase (one of the latest Nobel prize laureates) has written about early American institutionalism: 'American institutionalists,' he says, 'were not theoretical but anti-theoretical. . . . Without a theory they had nothing to pass on, except a mass of descriptive material waiting for a theory, or a fire' (Coase 1984: 230). This is a severe evaluation; it is worth pondering.

Neoclassical economic theory

We may look at the problem, for a moment, from the side of neoclassical economic theory. My claim here is that it is not correct to say – as Robert Langlois asserts – that neoclassical theory is 'theory without institutions'. Neoclassical economic theory presupposes, in fact, a very specific set of institutions, namely the institutions of a free-market competitive economy in their purest form. In fact it is *only* compatible with such a set of institutions.

I have devoted some space elsewhere (especially in Pasinetti 1986) to singling out the basic features of what is dominant neoclassical economics, and I have claimed that, stripped to essentials, they are reducible to a basic model that is known as the Walrasian pure exchange model. In it there are: a set of resources that are taken as given and are supposed to be scarce: a set of individuals with well defined and perfectly known sets of logically consistent preferences; and the postulate is that they maximise their utilities subject to their budget constraints. In the most sophisticated version of Arrow and Debreu (1954), in which intertemporal maximisation, contingent markets and various states of the world are introduced, this model has become a powerful intellectual analytical tool that can reduce all economic problems to one single problem, to which it can offer a solution: the problem of optimum allocation of scarce resources. The point to be stressed here is that all this presupposes a social framework in which there is private property in the resources and in which utility-maximising individuals can freely exchange their scarce resources in perfectly competitive markets.

For years, in the stream of dominant neoclassical economics, no one has felt it necessary to consider institutions, simply because it was thought that neoclassical economics does not need to go into a study of institutions. A set of institutions, though of a very idealised and pure type, are already included – or, rather, implied – in the basic model of neoclassical economics. They are the institutions of a perfectly functioning free-market economy.

We may in fact go one step further: no other type of institutional set-up can be introduced into such a model. The model is – with regard to institutions – very demanding; or, we may say, from another point of view, very constraining and exclusive.

Institutionalism in the neoclassical mould

A rather dramatic change, however, has taken place recently. In different ways, from different sources, from different points of view, various scholars have begun to talk of and to analyse institutions explicitly *without* rejecting neoclassical economic theory – in fact applying neoclassical analytical tools to explain institutions, and making it a point of strength that they maintain basic neoclassical theory, though relaxing slightly some of its stricter assumptions. This has happened in the direction of property-rights analysis (e.g. Coase), of game-theory analytical tools (e.g. Schotter, Solow) and, above all, of transaction-cost economics (e.g. Williamson, Matthews). A few hints will be made about at least two of these developments (those of Solow and of Williamson).

In a brilliant little book Bob Solow makes the point that, with respect to the demand and supply apparatus of dominant economics, 'the labour market really *is* different' (Solow 1990: 3). He elaborates a series of arguments based on concepts such as 'equity', 'fairness', 'social norms', even 'just price', i.e. concepts that have nothing to do with the standard textbook neoclassical treatment of the subject. His final explanation (without going into detail here) is in terms of the labour-market outcome 'considered as a single episode in a repeated game involving firms and workers' (ibid.: 44). This is very far indeed from standard neoclassical economics. But Solow takes great pains to claim explicitly that 'none of this is radically subversive of mainstream economic theory' (ibid.: 23). He actually claims that he wants to save mainstream economic theory, in the same way as 'Franklin Roosevelt's New Deal legislation . . . was trying . . . to save capitalism from its worst excesses' (ibid.: 23).

Even more ambitious is Oliver Williamson, who explicitly calls his analysis 'new institutionalism'. He relaxes slightly the neoclassical assumption of supposedly perfect rational behaviour by individuals and adopts a type of behaviour dominated by 'bounded' rationality and opportunism. He too openly indicates as a merit that he is building fundamentally on the bases of dominant neoclassical economics (Williamson 1981, 1985).

This institutional economics in a neoclassical mould must be taken very seriously. As far as Solow's contribution is concerned, one may feel that his paying tribute to neoclassical economics is simply an expedient of convenience. But it may not be so. He seems to me to be falling into the trap of his own loyalty to tradition. His explanation of the behaviour of the labour market looks to me to share all those 'partial equilibrium' characteristics of the Marshallian analysis. In the *General Theory* Keynes showed these to be no longer applicable when considering overall employment, which inevitably concerns the economic system as a whole. Solow's analysis could in fact become much more fruitful if inserted into a more appropriate 'Keynesian' framework.

As far as Williamson is concerned, I shall simply mention that in a paper presented to the annual meeting of the (American) 'Association for Evolutionary Economics' William Dugger singled out six 'unifying characteristics' of institutionalism. He carefully examined Williamson's work and concluded that it shares none of these unifying characteristics. The reason is that 'Central to institutionalism is the concept of process, while central to Williamson's "new institutionalism" is the concept of optimum' (Dugger 1990: 424). Dugger's conclusion is that Williamson's would-be 'institutionalism' is no doubt something new; but it is *not* institutionalism.

Yet this is an awkward position to maintain. How can we legitimately assert that an analysis concerning the workings of institutions and dealing with economic institutions is *not* institutional analysis? On whose authority are we going to say whether any work dealing with institutions is or is not 'true' institutional economic analysis?

It seems to me much better to contend explicitly that Williamson's analysis is very restricted. Though timidly relaxing some neoclassical assumptions, it does not depart from, and still remains a prisoner of, the narrow horizon neoclassical economics can offer. In fact, it should be said explicitly that neoclassical economic analysis itself is mainly responsible for the insufficiencies of 'new institutionalism', on which it acts as a sort of constraining straitjacket.

The upshot is paradoxical. The theoretical framework of neoclassical economics allows little room for institutional economic analysis. In fact, it prevents a satisfactory development of it. At the same time, those institutional investigations claiming reliance on the neoclassical model derive prestige and legitimation from its theoretical strength.

We may well be at a turning point for institutional economic analysis. Those institutionalists (the great majority) who, claiming freedom from preconceived ideas, do not rely on neoclassical theory risk ending up as the earlier institutionalists did, that is, with what is going to be considered as no more than 'a mass of descriptive material'.

The search for an alternative theoretical scheme seems therefore to have become vital. If present-day institutionalists do not find it, not only do they cede the field to neoclassical economic theorists (as the early institutionalists did), but – worse still – they even risk losing the right to exist; for the appellation 'institutionalists' is claimed by the 'new' institutionalists, the institutionalists in the neoclassical mould.

The need for an alternative theoretical framework

If the arguments developed so far are correct, it has really become urgent for, let us say, the 'true' institutionalists to find a theoretical framework on which to rely. Here is where the connection with 'evolutionary economics' comes to the fore. Ideas from the biological and especially from the evolutionary field of enquiry were strongly invoked by Thorstein Veblen (1898) at the very beginning of institutional economic analysis. Many institutionalists today find in the idea of evolutionary relations (rather than in that of mechanical relations) a more congenial and friendly intellectual milieu in which to pursue their own investigations.

I am sure the direction is correct. But I should like to claim that this is not enough. Let us not forget that a century ago Veblen's ideas on evolutionary economics failed to take off. What do we have today that Veblen did not have a century ago? No doubt we have a lot more. The resumption and the development of evolutionary ideas in economic analysis have been massive and extraordinarily fruitful over the past two decades. Yet I am sure few would object if I say that a general unifying theoretical framework is still badly lacking.

Evolutionary political economy can offer today a series of remarkable yet *ad hoc* elaborations and hints. For the purposes of institutional economic investigation each of them may well become useful for some particular task. But it would become awkward to refer to different types of institutionalism according to the particular brand of evolutionary theory it relies on. I do not even think that, in the end, it would be workable to aim at an evolutionary institutional analysis as opposed to a neoclassical institutional analysis.

If we really want a theoretical framework able to integrate institutional and economic analysis, this theoretical framework must be solid and comprehensive enough to be used as an *alternative* to the neoclassical one and to be able to support *all* institutional investigations: those of the old or, if you like, 'true' institutionalism as well as those of the so-called 'new' institutionalism.

Pure economic theory at a pre-institutional analytical level: a proposal

Now I come to my proposal. My contention is that economic theory (I mean *strict*, or if you like *pure*, economic theory, not all economic analysis in the broadest sense) has invaded, and thus constrained unduly, social science investigations in general and institutional investigations in particular. It has done so by imposing its own set of assumptions concerning individuals' behaviour in a way which appears exclusive and sometimes even arrogant.

Strict economic theory (as distinct – I repeat – from economic analysis in a broad sense) should be pushed a little bit back, or rather a little bit deeper, to a more fundamental, *pre-institutional* level. In this way it could open up – without undue interference – the whole field of institutional analysis, while at the same time providing sturdy and rocklike theoretical foundations for such analysis.

This cannot be done with the Walras–Arrow–Debreu theoretical framework, which is crucially based on the maximisation principle and thus on a specific rule of individuals' behaviour leading straight away to specific social institutions. But it can be done with a theoretical framework whose basic lines can be traced as far back as to the classics – a theoretical framework that has in fact emerged in the development of economic thought as an alternative to the one which is at the basis of neoclassical analysis.

Here, for lack of time and space, I shall simply refer to an earlier work (1981) and to a more recent work (1993) of mine, where I have claimed that, in the historical development of economic theory, parallel to the aforementioned pure exchange model at the basis of the neoclassical paradigm, one can detect another basic model (which I have called the 'model of pure production'), which is at the basis of a whole series of economic theories that belong to what may be called the classical/Keynesian paradigm.

The pure production model has symmetrical features (with respect to the pure exchange model): it refers to a certain type of goods (the reproducible goods, as against the scarce goods of the pure exchange model), is aimed at the solution of a specific economic problem (the ever improving production of goods and services, as against the optimum allocation of existing goods), and is dominated by a general principle (*learning*, as against maximisation).

Now I can put my contention more clearly. It is possible, within this theoretical framework (although it has been done fully neither by the classical economists, nor by Keynes, nor by the Post-Keynesians, nor by dynamic process analysts, so far), to confine strict economic theory to a really fundamental framework of relations that can be dealt with at a level of investigations that is *pre-institutional*.

The problems of economic theory that emerge at this stage are either in terms of necessary relations, if certain goals are to be achieved (e.g. full employment, price stability, etc.), or in terms of logically consistent relations, or in terms of normative rules, or in terms of those problems which are generated by the basic forces at work in a dynamic context. None of these relations requires that any specific stand is taken on the economic institutions that have to be set up to bring the economic magnitudes considered into existence.

I have called this stage of investigation the 'natural' stage of economic investigation, a term that itself has a distinctly classical flavour. Actually, the classical economists did have the remarkable intuition of the existence of, and the necessity of investigating, relations that are so fundamental as to be definable on some objective standards which are independent of, and precede, what market forces will then cause to emerge. But the analysis I am proposing at the 'natural' level does not exactly coincide with that of the classical economists. The classical economists did have the intuition that they had to go deeper than the relations that may be observed superficially as the outcome of market forces. But they were too ambitious. They thought they could also detect 'natural' institutions. But, on that they have been proved wrong. The approach I am proposing is less ambitious but more fundamental.

I have actually shown that it is possible to construct a solid, strong skeleton of basic economic relations which refer to a production economy expanding through time with structural change. A series of 'natural' relations is defined and investigated, concerning the determination of a complete set of 'natural' economic magnitudes (prices, wage rate, rate of profit, sectoral productions, sectoral employment, rate of interest). Their evolution through time is traced, at a stage of analysis at which behavioural and organisational devices – and therefore institutions – are indeed *not* considered. The 'natural' magnitudes possess a series of remarkable normative properties, but are singled out in a way that is independent of *how* they may actually be achieved. At the same time, they bring to the surface a series of problems that have then to be solved at the institutional level, i.e. by setting up the appropriate institutions.

Here then we come to a second stage of investigation for which economic analysis can no longer claim exclusiveness. Here economic analysis is no longer autonomous. The whole field of enquiry is thus thrown open for the investigation of institutions. It is at this stage that hypotheses on individuals' and social behaviour become relevant. This does not exclude the application of economic analysis in its broad sense or even of the more traditional utility-maximising analytical tools, but in this way the explicative value of strictly economic hypotheses – far from being imposed in an exclusive way – has to be openly confronted with, and set against, or complemented by, those offered by other hypotheses and by other approaches. It is precisely at this stage, it seems to me, that the evolutionary approach to individual and social behaviour is given the full possibility of displaying its enormous potential.

Institutional and evolutionary analysis, and economic theory

One way of looking at what has been presented in the previous sections is to say that a drastic reorientation is proposed of both economic theory and institutional economic research. What is proposed is the introduction of a separation between two quite distinct fields of investigation. There is a field of investigation that refers to relations that are so fundamental as to be independent of economic and social institutions. This is a field of investigation for pure economic theory. Then another field of investigation opens up (that logically follows the first one and comes to complement and integrate it) which refers to the institutions that have to be set up, and that have to be assessed as to whether they are appropriate or not, to bring the fundamental features (which have normative properties, such as 'efficiency') into existence.

The consequences of this separation for a satisfactory development of institutional economic analysis should be clear.

The first field of investigation, the one at the 'natural' level, offers many advantages of non-interference with institutional analysis:

1 It brings out where, and for which problems, institutions are necessary.
2 It does not predetermine the types of institutions that may be developed, or may be analysed.
3 It leaves the field of institutional economic analysis entirely open.

And yet it provides a solid theoretical background for all purposes of institutional investigation.

Looking at it from a point of view closer to institutional analysis, one can further say:

1 No constraint or preconception is imposed on the hypotheses or on the analysis of economic or social behaviour or on the type of institutions to be considered.
2 The field of institutional analysis remains entirely autonomous.
3 At the same time, investigations of a historical, sociological or anthropological character are thrown entirely open, and thereby become not only possible and compatible with economic and institutional analysis, but actually able to bring complementary and enriching fruitful developments.

A few final remarks may be added for an audience particularly keen on evolutionary political economy and receptive to the ideas that inspired institutional economists.

A century ago, Thorstein Veblen (1898) looked with apprehension at the obstacles that prevented economics from becoming an 'evolutionary science'. It is time we reconsidered his attempts with care not only to find new inspiration for fruitful research but also to evaluate critically the reasons why his extraordinarily brilliant insights failed to take off or why scholars found so many difficulties in picking them up, so that the results of his enquiries still appear to traditionalists as no more than 'a mass of descriptive material'.

Perhaps his rejection of prevailing economic theory *en bloc*, with the aim of building up an alternative which borrowed its major concepts from evolutionary biology, was unnecessarily radical. The claim I am venturing here is that he could, and should, have been more selective. A great deal of economic investigation of classical origin not only does not interfere with, but actually provides strong support for, his ideas. At the same time, it should be noted that the economic field, in which evolutionary concepts seem most appropriate, is precisely that of individual and social behaviour. This is the field which ever since has been invaded, rather arrogantly and overwhelmingly, by the utility-maximising approach, an invasion which has pre-empted other approaches and lines of research.

At the same time, it has been insufficiently appreciated that the alternative economic paradigm (coming through classical analysis and based on a production approach to economic problems) leaves the whole field of economic and social behaviour free for original investigation, without any necessary interference, as I have tried to indicate above. In this context, it should be no surprise that evolutionary economists share so many affinities with classical/Keynesian and Post-Keynesian economic theory.

It is in this direction that institutionalists can recover a solid theoretical background. It is in this direction, I should like to claim, that they can find the supporting 'economic theory' which they have been seeking for a century.

Note

Most of the work connected with the present chapter was carried out while I was holding a Distinguished Scholar's Research Fellowship at WIDER (the UN University World Institute for Development Economics Research), Helsinki, July–August 1992. Secretarial help and hospitality are gratefully acknowledged.

25 Economic theory and institutions

An introductory note

Giovanni Caravale

The purpose of this chapter is threefold. First, it emphasises that reference to the institutional framework represents an integral part of economic theory if the latter is to be conceived as a tool mainly directed to the comprehension of the functioning of actual economic systems. Thus conceived, economic theory emerges as basically evolutionary in nature.

Second, it underscores that the integration of the institutional framework in the theoretical construct cannot be achieved with reference to the neoclassical scheme of analysis, either in its traditional or in its more recent versions. An alternative theoretical approach, of classical and Keynesian flavour, seems to offer – it is maintained – a far better chance.

Third, the chapter supplies a critique of Pasinetti's recent position on the relationship between economic theory and institutions: though placed in the correct 'alternative' (i.e. non-neoclassical) perspective, Pasinetti's distinction between two phases in the construction of economic theory (the 'pre-institutional' one of 'pure' theory and that in which institutions are introduced in the argument) should give way – it is concluded – to the direct consideration of the institutional framework in the theoretical context.

Institutions and economic theory

It has been recently maintained, by Langlois (1986: 5) and Coase (1984: 230) respectively, that 'neoclassical theory is a theory without institutions', while '[early] American institutionalists . . . had nothing to pass on, except a mass of descriptive material waiting for a theory, or fire'.

I shall comment later in a little more detail on the former statement. I feel it is important to emphasise at once, however, that the substance of the point emerging from the compound sentence can be shared with no reservation whatsoever. Neither a theoretical scheme without appropriate institutional foundation nor an institutional framework without a theory can be of any use from an economic viewpoint; and therefore the two aspects, or the two 'sides', as Pasinetti calls them (in the previous chapter), must be put together in the construction of an adequate interpretative tool.

The problem is connected with the very conception of our discipline, Economics, or – to use the old and perhaps more appropriate term – Political Economy. As I have emphasised elsewhere (Caravale 1992c, 1997b), this is to be thought of as the social science whose principal aim is that of spelling out the regularities that characterise the phenomena of value, production and distribution in given social and institutional contexts, with a view to supplying points of reference for those responsible for the policy choices to be made.

The central logical moment of the process of theorising is the identification of the model, i.e. a simplified representation of the world (or that portion of it which is the object of the analysis) capable of capturing the essential features, the fundamental traits of the reality that surrounds the political economist, like the depiction of a landscape or a portrait where the artist makes no attempt at a faithful reproduction of every single aspect of the real world but tries only to fix on paper or canvas what appear to him the most important elements of what he is looking at. In order to be relevant, the representation of economic reality must show a series of essential, and strictly interconnected, properties.

1 The description should be *significant* in that it should capture the essential features of the world; in other words it should depict, on the one hand, the dominant, or systematic, forces at work in the economic system (as the classics put it) and, on the other hand, the context – *the institutional context* – in which those forces operate.
2 The description should also be *significant* in another sense, in that the position so described should represent a (potential) point of attraction for actual values.[1] Should this attraction not exist, or not be proved, the description – however accurate – would in a way remain *separate* from the actual working of the economic system, and would thus be meaningless for the comprehension of the latter.
3 The position described by theory should represent the 'outcome' of the rational choices made by economic agents in the institutional framework which has been assumed.

It is clear that this way of conceiving Political Economy implies an essentially evolutionary vision of its nature. Differences in the institutional framework of different economic systems in the same period, or changes in the institutional context of one country through time, imply – in this perspective – different behaviour patterns on the part of the agents, or different outcomes of their decisions; hence a different theoretical explanation of the functioning of the economy, and a different position of equilibrium for the system. In turn this implies the need for a much more *humble* approach to economic theorising: the Lucifer-like ambition to identify 'eternal' economic laws can no longer be cultivated, thus giving way to the more down-to-earth attempt to identify specific 'regularities', or 'uniformity rules' in specific institutional frameworks.

Neoclassical analysis and the 'alternative' approach

The recognition of the need to integrate economic theory and institutions does not in itself solve the question concerning the choice of the theoretical approach upon which the integration should be based.

The first candidate is of course the theory which has been dominant for over a century: what is generally termed neoclassical economics. The point allows me to go back to the statement by Langlois cited above, according to which 'neoclassical theory is a theory without institutions'. Is that true? Is neoclassical economics a theory without institutions? According to Pasinetti (Chapter 24) the question calls for a negative answer. 'Neoclassical economic theory presupposes,' he writes, 'a very specific set of institutions; namely the institutions of a free-market competitive economy in their purest form', that is, a social framework characterised by private ownership of resources and by the assumption that utility-maximising individuals freely exchange their resources in perfectly competitive markets. 'Stripped to essentials', writes Pasinetti, 'the basic features of neoclassical economics

> are reducible to a . . . model that is known as the Walrasian pure exchange model. In it there are a set of resources that are taken as given and are supposed to be scarce; a set of individuals with well defined and perfectly known sets of logically consistent preferences; and the postulate is that they maximise their utilities subject to their budget constraints.
>
> (Ibid.: 333, this volume)

The same is true also of the more recent, and highly sophisticated, version of the theory supplied by Arrow and Debreu (1954), the basic problem posed being the optimum allocation of scarce resources.

Contrary to what Pasinetti maintains, Langlois's thesis that neoclassical economic theory is a theory 'without institutions' appears substantially correct, in the sense that it refers to an institutional framework which has no counterpart in historically experienced economic systems. The delicate issue is made no easier by the fact that neoclassical economists, while denying that their theoretical edifice plays an apologetic role with regard to existing 'market' systems, claim that the theory only intends to show how a fully decentralised economic system is capable of reaching an equilibrium which is optimal both from the viewpoint of the utilisation of available resources and from that of social equity. This contention raises in effect a number of problems.

1 First of all, in order to attain its objective – whatever this may be (the abstract representation of an allegedly decentralised system, or the representation of the 'core' of the functioning of actual market economies), the theory should be free from ambiguities and logical inconsistencies. As the long and intense debate of the 1960s has shown, this is certainly not the case with neoclassical theory.
2 Second, the claim regarding the 'remoteness' of the theory from the actual reality of contemporary capitalist systems appears difficult to accept: neoclassical economics cannot be thought simply to represent a refined intellectual game with no connection whatsoever with reality, but must be seen as the result of the ingenious and generous lifelong efforts made in order to construct a representation, a 'mirror' of that same reality, or at least of its relevant aspects.

3 Last, but certainly not least, the idea of a 'fully decentralised' system – or, to put it differently, the idea of a market economy 'in [its] purest form' (Pasinetti, p. 333, this volume) – is falsified by the theory's need to have recourse to the role of the so-called 'auctioneer' in order to determine prices. In the words of Nicola, it 'clearly means that for Walras general equilibrium is not the prototype of a fully decentralized economy; on the contrary, the Lausanne economist describes a totally centralized economy especially in the crucial area for a nonprimitive economic system of price determination' (Nicola 1994: 6).

The point appears particularly relevant from the perspective of the present chapter – the search for an appropriate combination of theoretical framework and institutional context. The neoclassical scheme refers to an institutional framework which in no way resembles that of present-day economic systems. In fact the atomistic, freely competitive structure of property-owning and utility-maximising agents, who are, however, centrally coordinated by a sort of 'social planner' (the auctioneer)[2] who performs the crucial role of determining equilibrium prices does not coincide either with a 'pure' competitive market economy (that is, with a totally decentralised economic system) or with the diametrically opposed scheme of a centrally planned economic system in which the economic plan identifies the objectives of the system and assigns productive tasks to all state-owned firms. The 'neoclassical' institutional framework cannot, therefore, be employed in the construction of an institutionally oriented theoretical scheme. Nowhere, except perhaps on the Paris stock exchange in the time of Walras, are transactions allowed only at 'equilibrium' market-clearing prices; nowhere are economic agents placed on an exactly identical footing with respect to the role they play in the economic system, to their behaviour, to their objectives, to their 'power'; nowhere do perfect information and perfect foresight characterise the choices made by individual agents. The list could continue.

The problem cannot be solved with the introduction of modifications of the basic assumptions of the theory, for the simple reason that no other type of institutional framework is compatible with the model. We must turn elsewhere for a solution of our problem.

Fortunately, the traditional neoclassical approach is not all there is in the history of economic thought. Early classical and Keynesian economic theory supply a promising alternative in which a number of crucial features of actual economic systems can be conveniently placed (such as the different role played by different social groups, or the presence of uncertainty and the crucial importance of the expectations held by agents) and in which a sufficient degree of flexibility regarding the institutional set-up can be found. But before proceeding along this 'alternative' path, a preliminary question of method must be raised.

Pasinetti's 'two phases' distinction

This question – extremely relevant from a methodological viewpoint – bears on the way in which institutions should be taken account of in the construction of the theory. Pasinetti's contribution in Chapter 24 to the analysis of the relation between institutions and economic theory offers the occasion for a reflection on this crucial theme. Pasinetti writes that, in his view, 'economic theory' is an expression by which he means

> *strict* or . . . *pure* economic theory, not all economic analysis in the broadest sense, has invaded, and thus constrained unduly, social science investigations in general and institutional investigations in particular. It has done so by imposing its own set of assumptions concerning individuals' behaviour in a way which appears exclusive and sometimes even arrogant.
>
> Strict economic theory [Pasinetti continues] should be pushed a little bit back, or rather a little bit deeper, to a more fundamental, *pre-institutional* level. In this way it could open up – without undue interference – the whole field of institutional analysis, while at the same time providing sturdy and rocklike theoretical foundations for such analysis.
>
> (p. 336, this volume)

The objective of a fruitful integration of economic theory and institutions cannot be reached, according to Pasinetti:

> with the Walras–Arrow–Debreu theoretical framework, which is crucially based on the maximisation principle and thus on a specific rule of individuals' behaviour leading straight away to specific social institutions. But it can be done with a theoretical framework whose basic lines can be traced as far back as to the classics. . . . [In fact], in the historical development of economic theory, parallel to the aforementioned pure exchange model . . . one can detect another basic model (. . . the 'model of pure production'), which is at the basis of a whole series of economic theories that belong to what may be called the classical/Keynesian paradigm.
>
> (Ibid.)

According to Pasinetti it is possible

> within this theoretical framework . . . to confine strict economic theory to a really fundamental framework of relations that can be dealt with at a level of investigation that is *pre-institutional*.
>
> The problems of economic theory that emerge at this stage are either in terms of necessary relations, if certain goals are to be achieved (e.g. full employment, price stability, etc.), or in terms of logically consistent relations, or in terms of normative rules, or in terms of those problems which are generated by the basic forces at work in a dynamic context. None of these relations requires that any specific stand is taken on the economic institutions that have to be set up to bring the economic magnitudes considered into existence.
>
> (Ibid.: 336–7)

Referring to his previous work (Pasinetti 1981), the author claims to have shown 'that it is possible to construct a solid, strong skeleton of basic economic relations which refer to a production economy expanding through time with structural change'. The evolution of the 'natural' economic magnitudes is, according to Pasinetti,

> traced, at a stage of analysis at which behavioural and organisational devices – and therefore institutions – are indeed *not* considered. The 'natural' magnitudes possess a series of remarkable normative properties, but are singled out in a way that is independent of *how* they may actually be achieved. At the same time, they bring to the surface a series of problems that have then to be solved at the institutional level, i.e. by setting up the appropriate institutions.
>
> Here then we come to a second stage of investigation for which economic analysis can no longer claim exclusiveness. . . . The whole field of enquiry is . . . open for the investigation of institutions. It is at this stage that hypotheses on individuals' and social behaviour become relevant. . . . It is precisely at this stage . . . that the evolutionary approach to individual and social behaviour is given the full possibility of displaying its enormous potential.
>
> (p. 337, this volume)

Conclusion

Pasinetti's conception, though far-reaching and extremely stimulating, seems to be open to two interconnected criticisms: the first relates to the compatibility between his two-phase distinction and his 'preliminary' choice of a theoretical perspective (in his case, the classical/Keynesian approach); the second refers to the possibility of identifying a *distinct* pre-institutional stage of the theoretical process if an essential part of this latter process is represented precisely by the systematic consideration of the institutional features (social framework and individual agent's behaviour within this framework). Both points are complex and can be discussed only briefly in very general terms.

1 As has been just recalled, Pasinetti 'proposes' to identify two distinct phases in the process of economic theorising: (a) the pre-institutional phase in which '[a] series of "natural" relations is defined and investigated, concerning the determination of a complete set of "natural" economic magnitudes (prices, wage rate, rate of profit, sectoral productions, sectoral employment, rate of interest)' without making any reference to behavioural and organisational devices – and therefore to institutions; (b) a second stage in which institutions are introduced in the theoretical framework, in order to assess their appropriateness, and 'to bring [their] fundamental features (which have normative properties, such as "efficiency") into existence' (pp. 337–8 above). In Pasinetti's view, this perspective cannot be analysed within the neoclassical Walras–Arrow–Debreu theoretical framework, but it can be done with a

theoretical framework reconducible to what may be called the 'classical/ Keynesian paradigm'. In other words the choice of the theoretical framework in which the two-phase analysis is to be carried out appears to be preliminary with respect to the identification of the first of the two phases of which the analysis should consist (the pre-institutional one). But this preliminary choice is made precisely on the basis of the evaluation of arguments relating to institutions: in fact the rejection of the neoclassical framework of analysis is explicitly linked with the circumstance that this framework 'is crucially based on the maximisation principle and thus on a specific rule of individuals' behaviour leading straight away to specific social institutions' (p. 336, this volume).

2 As regards the second aspect, the problem is to clarify what conception of economic theorising underlies Pasinetti's proposal of the above-mentioned distinction in two phases. Apart from the fact that the ambition to identify a pre-institutional stage may be seen as dangerously close to the neoclassical aspiration to identify the 'eternal economic laws', what is the nature and what is the scope of economic theory implicit in the 'proposal'? For if Economics, or Political Economy, is conceived as the social science whose principal aim is that of spelling out the regularities that characterise the phenomena of value, production and distribution in given social and institutional contexts, Pasinetti's 'proposal' seems to be based on a rather weak foundation. In other words, if the systematic consideration of the institutional framework, of the types of agents operating in it, of their behavioural patterns, represents an integral part of the process of economic theorising, how is it possible to conceive of one phase of this same process of economic theorising which should be explicitly pre-institutional in nature? How can the basic 'natural' relations be identified and investigated, abstracting from the framework in which economic agents make their decisions and carry on their activities? Clearly, in spite of apparent similarities, in different contexts the same activity (e.g. the entrepreneurial function) can be carried on in totally different ways, in totally different perspectives; moreover, the same type of decision would be bound to have radically different types of outcomes in different institutional contexts.

In order to ignore all this, and to maintain the idea of a process of economic theorising based on the distinction in two phases proposed by Pasinetti, it would be necessary to reject the classical-type notion of Political Economy indicated above. But in that case the only alternative would be the neoclassical idea of Economics as the study of rational choices in the face of scarce resources – the negation of which represents the starting point of Pasinetti's proposal.

Research must then be addressed to the direct integration of the basic features of the institutional context in an adequately 'opened' theoretical framework – for the construction of a tool capable of helping us interpret the economic dimension of historical reality. This task, obviously, cannot be carried out here, but certainly represents an ambitious and exciting research programme.

Notes

1 This expression should be taken to mean a situation which would be reached if the basic conditions contributing to identify the equilibrium position were to remain unchanged through time (at least until the adjustment process was complete). The fact that this condition is never met, since there is continuous change in the above-mentioned conditions, implies that the point of attraction for the actual system moves through time (and may in fact never be actually reached), but does not deprive the 'description' of its significance. The process of gravitation can in fact be thought of as the movement of the actual system in the direction of the relevant equilibrium position: a direction which is bound to change continually as a consequence of the change in the 'basic conditions'.

2 The institutional nature of this crucial 'meta-agent' remains a mystery to be solved.

26 Economics and institutions from a central bank perspective

Pierluigi Ciocca

Three brief thoughts on economics and public institutions, dedicated to the memory of Gianni Caravale, a fine economist, a gentleman and a respected friend. Three brief considerations that are not epistemological but pragmatic, relating to the practical problems involved at the intersection between the economic and institutional spheres: one global, one European, one Italian. I enjoyed the privilege, to my delight and personal enrichment, of discussing these themes with Gianni Caravale.

The borderline between economics and institutions is the locus of one of the most acute contradictions in modern society. At the national level, representative democracy, electoral systems, methods of producing an executive are being developed to heighten the efficiency of the decision-making process (presidential republics, 'strong' governments, majoritarian election systems). Governing is less and less guided by politico-ideologico-social choices and increasingly attentive to the demands of sound day-to-day administration, the ordinary conduct of economic policy. This primacy of economic things is confirmed by the qualities now demanded of politicians and administrators. They are chosen and reconfirmed more for their ability (real or apparent) to manage public affairs than for the general ideas and values they stand for. This is accompanied by a blurring of the differences between the political and economic models advocated by the contending political forces. The model based on the primacy of private markets – interpreted, to be sure, in various ways – is virtually never questioned. And at the international level we are witnessing intensive integration. The growth in trade and especially in financial transactions is extremely rapid, driven by the liberalisation of capital movements, the computer revolution and the ease of communication.

The financial interrelations ratio (the ratio of the stock of financial instruments to that of real wealth) has risen considerably everywhere. In the G-7 countries it has reached values ranging from 1.3 in Germany to 2.9 in the United Kingdom. Gross portfolio flows in these countries surged from US$5 billion in 1970 to more than US$1 trillion in 1997, and from 0.2 per cent to 6 per cent of GDP. Between 1990 and 1999 in the same seven countries the value of financial assets – deposits, bonds and shares – held by households and firms rose from 210 per cent to 360 per cent of GDP, the stock of bonds – government, corporate and international – from 100 per cent to 160 per cent, the capitalisation of the stock markets from 40 per cent to 125 per cent and the value of listed and unlisted derivative instruments from 40 per cent to 340 per cent.

The effects of the dominion exercised by global, 'stateless' finance are controversial. On the one hand, it is argued that freedom of capital movement generates efficiency, fosters trade and spurs a more vigorous search for profit opportunities on a global scale. On the other hand, warnings are issued against the high level of risk. Information asymmetries are typical of financial markets, even efficient ones. They are inherent in the fact that participants have only incomplete information on their counterparts. These asymmetries generate distortions. They reduce allocational efficiency. Through perverse selection, irresponsibility, herd behaviour and emulation they can give rise to major crises. Above all, many observers criticise as over-constrictive, suffocating, the constraints financial globalisation imposes on the sovereign power of the nation state in two fundamental respects: money and taxes. It is argued that this jeopardises the ability of individual states, both large and small, to make economic policy choices – political choices – independently. Some talk of the 'end of politics' at the national level, of the 'dethroning of politics by the market'.

The *conventions* – what Keynes called changeable beliefs – of global finance do effectively constrain the economic policy choices of national governments. The market – as it should – excludes countries that do not observe internationally agreed or even merely customary norms and standards of conduct. A government or a policy that the markets do not 'like' may be saddled with astronomical risk premia and swept away, even if the government is democratically elected or the policy excellent. For the emerging countries, the conflict between national sovereignty and economic and financial globalisation is dramatic. In the developed countries, the losers are less numerous. They are compensated by a system of social shock absorbers, which makes the renunciation of national sovereignty in economic affairs less painful. In the emerging economies the conditions for this to happen are rarely found.

Globalisation and economic integration are not an unprecedented phenomenon. Under the gold standard in force before the First World War (1870–1914) the world economy experienced a degree of integration comparable and in some respects superior to today's. What are the differences between that system and the present one? What lessons can we learn from that historical period? Essentially, there are three fundamental differences.

1 Under the gold standard net payment balances were comparable to today's, but gross movements of capital were much smaller.
2 There was a single 'brain' for the system: Britain, which the market regarded as wise and cosmopolitan. Flows of information were heavily asymmetrical. Britain had significant knowledge of the rest of the world, but the converse was not the case. The higher level of information and the authority deriving from being the centre of the system enabled British institutions to intervene to manage crises in defence of the foundations of the gold standard when needed, mustering also the support of foreign institutions, especially the Bank of France. All this was upheld in theory, accepted. An example is the

power of coercion exercised by the Bank of England in the Baring crisis of 1890.

3 Suffrage was limited. The main political systems were based on monarchical institutions. They had an oligarchic structure. International politics and the world economy were dominated by agreements among the few. The five Rothschilds could, with fair prospects of success, agree to avoid wars by refusing to finance them.

In relation to GDP the volume of long-term capital movements was probably greater during the period before the First World War. But foreign debt was restricted to a small number of countries. It served to finance a narrow range of sectors – railways, mining, public services – and the subscription of government bonds. The United Kingdom was the leading exporter of capital, with foreign lending accounting for about half the world total. The remainder came from France and Germany. The United States began to export capital to a significant extent only at the very end of the period. Today financial flows are much more highly diversified by sector and region. Direct investment is considerably greater. There were few multinational corporations. Their activity was circumscribed. Such companies play a key role in the globalised economy. Their business is diversified by product and geographical area. Recent estimates put their share of world exports at a third of the total.

Just as today, social and economic tensions were not lacking in the pre-1914 era; globalisation was accompanied by an enormous increase in international migration (30 million people emigrated to the United States between 1860 and 1920). Drastic changes in the distribution of income followed, in the countries of both destination and origin. The strains generated played a part, beginning in the 1920s, in the rise of restrictive measures on trade and immigration.

In short, the most significant result in social and institutional terms of economic and financial globalisation threatens to be the primacy of finance, of the financial market, over politics; even of a politics reduced to economic policy, practically to mere ordinary administration. The contradiction is pronounced. It is potentially explosive, especially considering that no law of nature, no superior wisdom, no guarantee of efficiency and equity is intrinsic to the policy guidelines dictated by the financial market.

The question is inseparably both economic and institutional. What are the possible responses, the likely scenarios?

1 *The 'enlightened' scenario.* Utopian reformers – an increasingly rare, hence precious, breed – imagine a single government for the world economy, restoring supranationally the powers lost at the national level. They think, for instance, of exporting to the rest of the world the type of economic and monetary union that Europe, with difficulty, is working on. Robert Mundell has recently relaunched the idea of a global currency, which would eradicate the perils and the instability connected with currency fluctuations.
2 *The 'interventionist' scenario.* Like Keynes in 1944 at Bretton Woods, since the early 1970s James Tobin has invoked limitations on short-term capital

movements. In contrast with Keynes, his calls have been made in a context of flexible exchange rates. A flat-rate tax on international financial transactions would encourage investors to channel their resources into longer-term and more stable investments. The implications of the Tobin tax have recently received renewed attention. There have been practical applications: in Chile in 1991, in Colombia in 1993 and in Thailand in 1996. In fact, requiring unremunerated reserves to be deposited with the central bank against foreign currency liabilities arising from firms' direct borrowing can be considered as a sort of experiment with a Tobin-type tax. There remains the problem of how to apply the tax generally.

3 *The 'autarchic' scenario.* The extreme hypothesis is that of a major crisis, with a reaction by the political sphere, claiming back its primacy over the economy, and counter-reactions in the world of finance. Such a situation could lead to the rise of national movements that, by winning demagogic support, might succeed in imposing authoritarian forms of government, ultimately in 'closing' the economy. Financial markets would react by accentuating their typically 'clubbish' behaviour. As a result, international economic integration might be undermined, to the detriment of the development process and economic growth worldwide.

Faced with such widely divergent scenarios, the only certainty is the presence of deep contradictions in the current configuration of the world economy. The crises of national banking and financial systems in the 1930s called for the creation of institutions able to regulate and supervise the behaviour of economic agents within national borders. Analogously, today's globalised finance requires the international community to show it has the will and the muscle to formulate a common response. Close international cooperation appears to be the least original, but also the only realistic, way to achieve a new world economic order.

The fact that the financial system is driven by market forces does not necessarily make the economy less governable. It requires that action should be directed to guiding the expectations, conventions and needs created by the operation of the market, to changing their course and pointing them in the desired direction. The drafting of uniform international rules and standards that can be applied to the generality of countries – in the monetary and fiscal fields and as regards the supervision and prudential organisation of the various sectors of finance – appears consistent with this approach. But above all it is by making the market think what policy makers want – turning it into a member of the team, a means and not an end in itself – that economic policy is implemented in a monetary economy in which production has been globalised by international finance. This is feasible. The necessary condition, as easy to perceive as it is difficult to fulfil, is for the policy makers of the leading countries to show the way by coordinating, through reinvigorated cooperation, their actions.

The conflict between the political and economic spheres is most acute in Europe. There is absolutely no precedent, in institutional terms, for a central bank unaccompanied by a parliament and an executive having appropriate powers, with which to interact. The ECB is the only European institution with complete autonomy and a precisely defined mission: the management of monetary policy with the aim of ensuring price stability. But monetary policy cannot make good the lack of an economic policy and a true political programme.

If it remains set within a political vacuum, the autonomy rightly granted to the ECB in the field of price stability risks appearing excessive and arbitrary in the long run and thus of being opposed, negated, by national governments and parliaments. Without an institutional and political partner to legitimate the dialectical process of formulating economic policy, the ECB is in danger of seeing the effectiveness of its action undermined, of being held solely responsible in the event of a crisis, even if responsibility really lay elsewhere.

Europe needs to be completed at the political and institutional level. The markets themselves are discounting this outcome. Monetary union cannot remain an isolated achievement for long. With the introduction of the euro, the interaction between economy, money and institutions has only just begun. Financial integration must be increased, economic policy coordinated and the anti-inflationary reputation of the ECB consolidated. Europe must implement the theoretical model of an optimal currency area, something from which it diverges considerably today. Only in this way can the gain in efficiency deriving from the introduction of the euro exceed the costs.

In Italy, participation in EMU has deprived the country of the two main instruments traditionally used to govern the economy: the exchange rate and the money supply. Reducing wages in Italy in order to compete appears difficult, since earnings are lower than the European average and productivity is higher. Decreasing the tax burden, in order not to lose out in the fiscal competition that has begun among member states, will inevitably be slower than in countries with ratios of public debt to GDP half that of Italy.

Another, complementary, path that needs to be followed in Italy in order to increase the competitiveness of the economy is institutional reform – particularly as regards the legal framework within which the economy operates and the institutions charged with its application.

Rapid and coordinated measures are necessary, especially as regards company and bankruptcy law, but also to improve labour laws and those governing dispute procedures and competition. Extensive streamlining of primary and secondary legislation is necessary and feasible. If such reforms are not enacted, Italy's economy is unlikely to grow as fast as it could. This is what happened in the 1990s, when the trend growth in potential output declined from an annual rate of 2.7 per cent to just 2 per cent. Rather than copying (to little advantage) the solutions adopted elsewhere, or pursuing the mirage of a perfect legal system, it is necessary to create one that suits the Italian economy as it actually is, different in so many ways from those of the other European countries.

The bulk of the Italian economy consists of small independent businesses in which the individual entrepreneur plays a key role; sometimes, but by no means always, they are clustered together in industrial districts. Not only does this structure make taxation difficult and call for a larger endowment of public infrastructure but it also requires a company law that is made to measure. This is especially true for unlisted companies. The revision of the rules of corporate governance enacted in the Consolidated Law on Financial Intermediation had to take account of principles originating in other legal traditions and adapt them to Italian reality while still creating a model that would be familiar and acceptable to international finance. For unlisted companies there are more degrees of freedom. At the same time there is a greater need to match the specific features of the Italian productive system. The objective must be to devise the company law that is most likely to foster the growth of small enterprises. It is necessary to overcome the present situation, where firms are born small and remain small, partly because the legal and institutional framework lacks the features that would facilitate their growth.

The current company law, even though it is rooted in a time-honoured, otherwise commendable legal tradition, is the expression of an economic reality that no longer exists. It has ceased to be appropriate. It limits the scope for company contracts other than the traditional ones. It is too narrowly focused on joint-stock companies. It fails to foster firms' entrepreneurial nature. The top priority is therefore to broaden the range of corporate models for businessmen to choose from according to their requirements. There is also a need for greater freedom as regards company by-laws and shareholder agreements, a clearer distinction between the roles of administrative and decision-making bodies, access to a greater variety of financing and a large reduction in red tape.

A radical revision of bankruptcy law is no less desirable with a view to encouraging entrepreneurship. Unless there is fraud, bankruptcy must be considered a normal event. It is inherent in the nature of enterprise, it is part and parcel of risk taking. The regulation of business failures cannot be limited to punishing the unsuccessful entrepreneur. Conserving the value of the business must take priority even over the protection of creditors, who are often much more powerful than the companies they finance. Bankruptcy law must ensure – with the necessary precautions – that failed entrepreneurs can be rehabilitated, given a second chance, at both the personal and the professional levels.

The need for reform of the law in these two fields is especially urgent. But, looking at the larger picture, which is harder to draw in just a few lines, it is the whole relationship between the legal system and the economy that needs to be reversed. The traditional approach, in which the economy has to adapt to a legal system based on general and unchanging principles, conflicts stridently with today's market reality. The law must be put at the service of the economy. This is the only lesson to be drawn from the common-law tradition, whose philosophy – regardless of its specific content and forms – lay at the root of the first industrial revolution and is now shaping the emerging world financial market.

27 Economics and institutions

Some reflections on Pasinetti and Caravale

Luigi Spaventa

I remember Gianni first of all as a friend – intelligent, learned and wise, gifted with a gentle irony about himself as well as others and a dry sense of humour. And I remember him as a valorous colleague whose academic career began with mine at the same university (though I was the older of the two). Our intellectual interests initially coincided, then diverged. My interest gravitated downward to the level of facts, not least because, rightly or wrongly, I thought that the theories and critical analyses on which both of us had worked had little more to give and could not take us very far. Gianni's interests remained at a higher level, but he also incorporated them in contributions to policy making.

Gianni Caravale dealt with the debate between economic theory and institutions, and in the process I believe he displayed a comprehensible unease. It is a debate that, like the neo-communists after the fall of the Berlin Wall, seeks a third way: between a theory devoid of institutions and a prevalently descriptive analysis of institutions devoid of theory. With the eclipse of Marxist economics, whose kit contained quite a few tools for the theoretical analysis of institutions, this debate is developing mainly at the level of methodology and is marked by not a few inflated or at least sterile claims; the grand programme has never been followed with a specific application. Gianni Caravale is an exception. In one of his last works Caravale (1997d) brought theory to bear, in terms with which I do not necessarily agree, on an examination of the labour market institutions introduced with the incomes policy agreement of 1993.

Strangely enough, one finds that the aims of those arrayed on opposing sides of the debate paradoxically coincide. Consider Pasinetti's quest for 'relations that are so fundamental as to be independent of economic and social institutions [research that paves the way to] another field of investigation . . . (that logically follows the first one and comes to complement and integrate it) which refers to the institutions that have to be set up' (p. 338 above). How does this differ methodologically from the programme of the New Classical macroeconomics of Thomas Sargent and Robert Lucas, a programme Sargent describes as 'the quest for the primitive object', for a theory so pure that it needs no 'free' parameters?

Gianni Caravale wisely held that 'the Lucifer-like ambition to identify "eternal" economic laws can no longer be cultivated', and he called for a 'more down-to-earth attempt to identify specific "regularities", or "uniformity rules" in specific institutional frameworks' (p. 341 above). I do not think that this wise suggestion can be embodied in a two-phase approach: first, acquisition of a pure and uncontaminated theoretical base; second, historical and institutional analysis to verify if, how and why the actual movements of the economic variables in a specific institutional context diverge from their equilibrium (some would say natural) configuration. Every reality is an institution. And so what happy Ricardian or Crusoean island will allow us to identify and verify the natural values? And even supposing we succeeded, what would come of it? Would we have indications to offer on institution building? The programme is reductive. It leaves analysis of the institutions to institutionalism, albeit an institutionalism steeped in the pure theory (of natural values or primitive objects). It involves the risk of drawing a map on a scale of one to one, as Joan Robinson said. And in any case it rules out the possibility of a positive, normative economic and political–economic analysis of the institutions that frame economic developments.

However, reassuring signs have been emerging of late from the renewal of interest in institutional studies. Let me offer a haphazard list of some of the questions addressed by recent studies. How does production take place and how is it organised in a natural, classical or neoclassical system? In a firm. But who owns the firm? And what are the boundaries of the firm? Why doesn't a firm actually, and not just as a theoretical expedient, integrate vertically? Where, when and how does integration end? Why does a firm have suppliers and customers that are not consumers? What is the structure of property rights in a firm and what is the structure of control? What decides the choice between equity capital and debt capital in a firm? We are not in a Modigliani and Miller world, are we? What is the best protection for the rights of owners and those of creditors? Do different systems of protection produce different arrangements? Oliver Hart, for one, offers interesting answers to these problems in terms of incomplete contracts. In the theorisations that Gianni Caravale called 'Lucifer-like', contracts are implicitly complete or else they do not exist; the problem is not even posed, in a quasi-engineering approach.

To continue my list. Why do banks exist? Why do the supply of and demand for savings have to be intermediated? What are the consequences of the degree of intermediation on the structure of control? In this case there arises a problem of informational asymmetries, which can be larger or smaller depending on the presence and effectiveness of public intervention to create and regulate markets, of public intervention to define the right to information and more generally to protect savings. Those who object to the notions of incomplete contracts and informational asymmetries as too mainstream, too closely associated with the dominant theory, ought to propose and apply different tools of analysis. We must guard against being completely disarmed and avert the normative sterility that would result from the implicit suggestion that in an initial phase economic analysis should not be involved with studying institutions.

Some further examples, again with apologies for the lack of order. Passing over a somewhat musty dispute on the relative merits of Rhenish capitalism and Anglo-Saxon capitalism, I shall quote from an interview (4 June 1998) with Igor Gaidar, the Russian reformer: 'What has to be understood is that when socialism collapses under the weight of its own contradictions, the capitalism that rushes in does not resemble Venus, risen from the waves in all her beauty; at birth it is covered with sores and wounds.' Where in today's Russia can one find a tradition of contract or, more generally, a tradition of the circulation of goods and respect for private property? With the demise of socialism the Mafia and the black market have appeared on the scene owing to the lack of institutions.

To conclude, I shall cite a few more questions on which economic theory and institutional analysis are fruitfully intertwined: the consequence of the institutional position of the central bank; the effects of labour-market institutions (centralised or decentralised negotiation or both, the problems of the differing interests of the actors involved, trade unions as a contractual actor or economic policy actor); the need for and limits of regulation in the financial markets; the effects of governance systems on growth; and, lastly, the south of Italy. An interesting strand of literature on the economic theory of corruption evaluates the incentive compatibility of individual laws and measures. Before drafting a law we should see what incentives it offers to behaviour that we consider deviant but that in fact is not, taking into account that such behaviour derives from maximisation under an incorrectly posed constraint.

I could continue this jumbled list but I shall stop here. It is a list of institutional issues in respect of which economic analysis has an important task: to explain the motivations of a certain institutional arrangement, its consequences for the system's configuration and efficiency, and the different arrangements that could be suggested. Analysis of these questions is not an optional or a subsequent point on the agenda. The attitude must not be 'Let's deal with serious matters first and then see about the rest.' This attitude prevails when it is argued that the various institutional arrangements are merely specifics of a given time and place that should not divert the scholar's attention from the inevitable path leading towards natural or equilibrium values. As I said at the beginning, this view inevitably reproduces dichotomy between economic theory and institutions and constitutes a relapse into that institutionalism that is neither the fish of serious historiography nor the fowl of decent economic theory and is unable to explain how and why certain situations have come into being. To respond or attempt to respond to the problems that I have indicated, I am convinced it is necessary to fly relatively low, to be open-minded, eclectic and flexible in the choice of instruments, without undue concern about the particular vision to which they may be traced in the great history of thought. To be sure, the representative agent is a character who must be killed off without mercy; on this, and on the need to reject any conclusion deriving from that assumption, I think a consensus can be easily reached. But why should we do without a hypothesis of more or less bounded rationality, with all its complications, for the financial markets? Or the notion of moral hazard in regulating and protecting savings and investment? Or principal–agent theory? Or the problem of leads and lags for monetary policy and the central bank? Or the effects of an incentive system on maximising behaviour?

In the great visions of economic thought, too often one finds only a *pars destruens*. A reluctance to be open-minded and to use all the available instruments has prevented the criticism of economic theory from making a constructive contribution.

28 Economics and institutions

The constraints of history

Paolo Sylos Labini

Let me start with an anecdote. It came to my mind the moment Luigi Spaventa mentioned Gianni Caravale's comment on the evil ambition to discover the eternal laws of economics. Many years ago I graduated from the University of Rome. I decided on my own the topic of my dissertation, which was about the relationship between economic development and innovation. A topic foreign to the traditional neoclassical theory, to the so-called 'pure' economics. It was an 'impure' dissertation by nature. The concept of 'eternal laws' was made clear to me by a senior government official who, as many older officials do when meeting a young student, enquired into my work. I explained I was assistant professor of economics, and he replied, 'Ah, economics, the eternal laws of economics.' He spoke as still a student who read textbooks. But then he spoke as a man of the world and said, 'Ah, what times are these, no one respects them!' I think it was involuntary irony.

In what follows I will shortly focus on the three following issues: (1) the business cycle and growth; (2) prices and wages; (3) the institution of failure.

The business cycle and growth

I knew Giovanni Caravale for several years, though, for a long time, we seldom met. We started to meet more often and our relationship grew closer. Caravale, as President of the Atlantic Economic Society, asked me to deliver the invited speech for the annual European meeting of the society, held in Rome in 1991. Caravale warmly welcomed a topic I suggested: the changing nature of the so-called business cycle.

During the preparation of my Laurea thesis I realised that the questions of growth and innovation had been tackled only incidentally in economic theory. At that time – but the situation is to a large extent still the same – economic theory was fundamentally static; it dealt with market equilibrium and neglected the question of growth. Basically, save for the odd article or chapter of a book, the economic literature did not deal with these topics. Apart from Marx, I could find only one exception, and that was Schumpeter. So I decided to apply for a scholarship to study with him at Harvard. I won the scholarship and in 1948 – that was the Bronze Age – I went to America, where I stayed for a year.

According to Schumpeter, and Marx before him, the business cycle goes together with growth. The cycle is the shape under which growth is disguised in the evolution of industrial capitalism. Schumpeter maintained that the business cycle starts in the mists of time because the growth process started long ago, though slowly and irregularly as innovations were also irregular. On this point I part company with Schumpeter and I agree with Marx: the modern growth process, and with it the cycle, makes its appearance when the investment sector of the manufacturing industry becomes socially relevant. In England, when the industrial revolution was well advanced, that sector became important during the Napoleonic Wars, which, like all wars, stimulated innovations above all because of the navy's needs.

Since then, and until World War I, the evolution of industrial economies becomes cyclical. As clearly emerges from Schumpeter's monumental work, the business cycle exhibits extraordinary regularity both as regards its length – ranging from seven to ten years – and its features – I refer especially to the variations of income and unemployment. That regularity is really surprising if we consider the great variety of economic and non-economic forces affecting economic development. After World War I, starting from 1929, the Great Depression represented an earthquake with its epicentre in the United States and contributed to determine relevant political changes. I think that the positive heritage of the Great Depression, from an economic viewpoint, was the reorganisation of banking institutions in the United States, which served as a model for other countries as well. In the inter-war period the economic fluctuations became quite irregular, not least because of the growing importance of economic policy measures, and the business cycles are difficult to identify. After World War II the growth process starts again but with much less regular features compared with the period preceding World War I. If we want to build a meaningful theory of business cycles we must start from an analysis of their empirical characteristics, otherwise we run the risk of entering the world of metaphysics.

Prices and wages

In the course of time the behaviour of prices and wages has significantly changed. During the nineteenth century prices fell almost steadily. If we take the price index as 100 in 1801, by 1897 it had become 22, incredible as it may seem. In the following period the situation changed radically, especially after World War II, when inflation became the rule throughout the world: the differences concern only the rates of change among different countries and in different times. Here I will not enter any analytical argument; I want just to raise two points for further reflection. I limit myself to observing that at the heart of the differences among the various rates there are structural changes both in the commodities market and in the labour market. Two processes affecting both markets deserve special attention: the concentration of production and the differentiation of both products and labour services. The former leads to companies of ever increasing size whereas the latter, in the last decades, has offered new opportunities to dynamic small firms.

The second point relates to wages. Since World War II there has been much debate about the Phillips curve, which identifies a relation between the rate of change of wages and the unemployment rate. This relation has since been proposed by Solow with reference to the rates of change of wages and prices. I do not agree with the use that has been made of the Phillips curve, which has been unacceptably oversimplified. Phillips himself, and more systematically Lipsey afterwards, had emphasised that the rate of change of wages does not depend primarily on the unemployment rate but also on changes in the cost of living – and this amendment clearly depends on those structural changes mentioned above. The implication is that according to the various phases of history there are at least two wage equations: the historical and the mathematical interpretations of observable economic phenomena are perfectly compatible with one another; or better: there is no divide between mathematics and history, as there is none between theory and history. In the dispute, which started at the beginning of the twentieth century, over economic method, between the advocates of pure economics and the historical school, both were wrong. The essence of economic analysis lies precisely in the harmonious integration of theory and history. The latter provides the factual premises which, when transformed into hypotheses, allow the elaboration – if necessary also with the benefit of mathematics – of historically restricted theoretical models. It is not that their logical coherence is historically restricted; that coherence is on the contrary timeless. It is rather their interpretative capacity which is historically contingent.

Bankruptcy as an institution

Development needs innovation, and innovation, by necessity, implies risk. Laws intended to reduce risk, favour innovation. The laws which have introduced and later modified the institution of bankruptcy in the capitalist countries have mostly contributed to reducing risk. Some laws relating to credit institutions and companies, in particular share companies, have contributed to the same end – I especially have in mind those laws which have imposed some kind of separation between the company and the entrepreneurs' own private property. All these laws varied over time in order to increase entrepreneurs' propensity to risk and have therefore enhanced the growth process. The institution of failure and the other laws which I have mentioned above pertain typically to market economies. In centrally planned economies, managers were required to follow the orders emanating from the office of central planning; they could not take any personal initiative and they could not fail. It is not paradoxical to maintain that socialist economies collapsed because production units could not go bankrupt. Capitalism, on the other hand, prevailed because its production units were allowed to fail.

Let me point out in conclusion that the transition from socialism to capitalism in the ex-Soviet Union is going on with very great difficulties because as a rule economists limit their advice to the quantitative aspects of the problem, traditionally accounted by mainstream economists – abolition of price controls, annulment of public deficit, currency devaluation etc. – while neglecting the need for an organic reform of the legislation shaping the functioning of the market. In fact, the market does not mean the absence of any rules; it is, on the contrary, a system of laws that, if well devised, can enhance development, but can hamper it if faulty. The fundamental problem of the formerly centrally planned economies is precisely that of building up a system of rules – a market – capable of enhancing development.

29 A summing up

Luigi L. Pasinetti

I am pleased and honoured to have been asked to preside over the final round table of the conference organised in memory of Giovanni Caravale, an eminent economist and a great friend. My original intention was to preside over the discussions and not to interfere; or to intervene as little as possible. But some polemic has broken out over how Caravale considered institutional economic analysis. This makes it difficult for me to say absolutely nothing on the problem. I shall try to be very brief.

The polemics stem from the fact that Giovanni Caravale in his paper of 1996 'Economic theory and institutions: an introductory note', reproduced as Chapter 25 of the present volume, expresses a partial (and I should like to stress the word *partial*) disagreement with some proposals made in a previous paper of mine (Pasinetti 1994), also reproduced in the present volume (Chapter 24). In order to be constructive, I think it may be useful to state, first of all, the points on which both Giovanni Caravale and I are in agreement.

The discussion sprang from the following three quotations which both Caravale and I have taken as a starting point:

> American institutionalists were not theoretical but anti-theoretical. . . . Without a theory they had nothing to pass on, except a mass of descriptive material waiting for a theory, or a fire.
>
> (Coase 1984: 230)

> The problem with the Historical School and many of the early Institutionalists is that they wanted an economics with institutions but without theory; the problem with many neoclassicists is that they want economic theory without institutions; what we should really want is both institutions and theory.
>
> (Langlois 1986: 5)

> What has been missing is the development of an analytical framework to integrate institutional analysis into economics and economic history.
>
> (North 1993: 243)

Indeed, the working out of an analytical framework in which we may integrate both economic theory and institutional analysis was the major common aim of both my own original paper and of Caravale's note.

It is easier for me to start from the three contentions I made in my paper, namely that:

1 'A research programme aimed at marrying economic theory and economic institutional analysis . . . is impossible, as long as by economic theory we mean neoclassical economic theory.'
2 In any case, 'neoclassical economics is not the only source of economic theory'.
3 But fortunately 'classical/Keynesian thought, if appropriately developed, is not only compatible, but actually affords exceptionally favourable features for a unified theoretical framework in which to place the economic analysis of social institutions' (pp. 331–2 above).

It is important to stress that Caravale is in agreement with me on *all* three contentions. His disagreement is only on the question of how to achieve contention No. 3. I am proposing a two-stage approach: stage one consisting of the elaboration of a self-contained analytical scheme expressing the classical fundamental, or 'natural' economic relations); and stage number two consisting of integrating into it the actual *behavioural* relations deriving from the specific institutional systems that are investigated, so as to achieve a final unified framework. This approach has been presented, in detail, in Pasinetti (1981, 1986, 1993) and there is no need or space to present it here again. The interested reader is referred to the original sources.

Caravale has raised objections to the two-stage distinction because the first stage would appear to him as 'dangerously close to the neoclassical aspiration to identify the "eternal economic laws"' (p. 346 above) – a neoclassical pretence which, earlier in his paper, he had rejected as a 'Lucifer-like ambition' (p. 341 above).

I can only say that such an 'ambition' remains very far indeed from my purpose as well. In an economists' world dominated by neoclassical economics I can only share Caravale's humble intention of stressing the point that neoclassical economics is not the only source of economic theory. In any case, Caravale's note is an 'introductory note'. As such, it is short and simply ends up with the admission that 'the task' of carrying out a 'direct integration of the basic features of the institutional context in an adequately "opened" theoretical framework . . . cannot be carried out here, but certainly represents an ambitious and exciting research programme' (p. 346 above).

It is unfortunate that Giovanni and I never succeeded in getting together for a discussion of this issue, in spite of our positive intentions. His entry into active politics as Minister of Transport and then, sadly, his premature death have nullified the possibility of interaction. As far as I am concerned, my position is extensively presented in the references I have given. As to Caravale I hope his pupils will take up his lead. In any case, the point to stress is that the difference between Giovanni Caravale and me only concerns the problem of how to carry out the third contention specified above. It is a point of methodology, not a point of substance.

I feel therefore that, while Pierluigi Ciocca (Chapter 26 in this volume) and Paolo Sylos Labini (Chapter 28 of this volume) have concentrated admirably on putting substantial stress on the importance of the economic analysis of institutions, Luigi Spaventa on the other hand has missed the point of the exchanges between Giovanni Caravale and me. He does not seem to realise that the whole set of problems and of fields of analysis which he lists are *all* compatible both with Caravale's and with my own two-stage analytical approach. Perhaps Spaventa has failed to read carefully the sources of the discussion (especially my own). Perhaps the unfortunate image of a 'Lucifer-like ambition to identify "eternal" economic laws', presented by Caravale as a neoclassical pretence (pp. 341 and 346 above), and his fear that the first stage of my approach may get 'dangerously close to [it]' (ibid.: 346) have suggested to Spaventa too easy a way of caricaturing my position. I can only hope that the conscientious scholar will be amused by Spaventa's caricature but at the same time, on referring to the original sources, will see clearly the inconsistency of his claims.

References

Aghion, P. and Howitt, P. (1998) *Endogenous Growth Theory*, Cambridge MA: MIT Press.

Akerlof, G. A. and Yellen, J. L. (1985a) 'Can small deviations from rationality make significant differences to economic equilibria?', *American Economic Review* 75, 4: 708–20.

Akerlof, G. A. and Yellen, J. L. (1985b) 'A near rational model of the business cycle, with wages and price inertia', *Quarterly Journal of Economics* 100, 5: 823–38.

Akerlof, G. A., Dickens, W. T. and Perry, G. L. (1996) 'The macroeconomics of low inflation', *Brookings Papers on Economic Activity* 1: 1–59.

Aksoy, E. G. (1991) *The Problem of Multiple Interpretations of Ricardo*, Greenwich CT: JAI Press.

Alvi, E. (1993) 'Near-rationality/menu costs, strategic complementarity, and real rigidity: an integration', *Journal of Macroeconomics* 15, 4: 619–25.

Amendola, A. (ed.) (1995) *Disoccupazione. Analisi macroeconomica e mercato del lavoro*, Naples: ESI.

Amendola, M. and Gaffard, J. L. (1998) *Out of Equilibrium*, Oxford: Clarendon Press.

Anagnostopoulos, G. (1994) *Aristotle on the Goals and Exactness of Ethics*, Berkeley CA: University of California Press.

Ardeni, P. G., Boitani, A., Delli Gatti, D. and Gallegati, M. (1999) 'The New Keynesian economics', in M. Messori (ed.) *Financial Constraints and Market Failure*, Aldershot: Elgar.

Arestis, P. and Sawyer, M. (eds) (1997) *The Relevance of Keynesian Policies Today*, London: Macmillan.

Arestis, P., Palma, G. and Sawyer, M. (eds) (1997) *Essays in Honour of G. C. Harcourt*, I *Capital Controversy, Post-Keynesian Economics and the History of Economic*, II *Markets, Thought employment and Economic Policy*, London and New York: Routledge.

Arrow, K. J. (1950) 'A difficulty in the concept of social welfare', *Journal of Political Economy* 58: 328–46.

Arrow, K. J. (1959) 'Towards a theory of price adjustment', in A. Abramovitz (ed.) *The Allocation of Economic Resources. Essays in Honor of Bernard Francis Haley*, Stanford CA: Stanford University Press.

Arrow, K. J. (1962) 'The economic implications of learning by doing', *Review of Economic Studies* 29: 155–73.

Arrow, K. J. (1971) 'The firm in general equilibrium theory', in R. Marris and A. Wood (eds) *The Corporate Economy. Growth Competition and Innovative Potential*, London: Macmillan.

Arrow, K. J. (1986) 'Rationality of self and others in an economic system', in R. M. Hogarth and M. W. Reder (eds) *Rational Choice. The Contrast Between Economics and Psycology*, Chicago: University of Chicago Press.

Arrow, K. J. (1991) 'Ricardo's work as viewed by later economists', *Journal of the History of Economic Thought* 13, 1: 70–7.

Arrow, K. J. and Debreu, G. (1954), 'Existence of an equilibrium for a competitive economy', *Econometrica* 22, 3: 265–90.

Arrow, K. J. and Hahn, F. H. (1971) *General Competitive Analysis*, San Francisco: Holden-Day and Edinburgh: Oliver & Boyd.

Arrow, K. J. and Honkapohja, S. (eds) (1985) *Frontiers of Economics*. Oxford and New York: Blackwell.

Artaud, A. (1958) *The Theatre and its Double*, New York: Grove Press.

Aspromourgos, T. (1996) *On the Origins of Classical Economics. Distribution and Value Theory from William Petty to Adam Smith*, London: Routledge.

Aumann, R. J. (1985) 'What is Game Theory trying to accomplish?', in K. J. Arrow and S. Honkapohja (eds) *Frontiers of Economics*, Oxford: Blackwell.

Aumann, R. J. (1987) 'Correlated equilibrium as an expression of Bayesian rationality', *Econometrica* 55, 1: 1–18.

Bacharach, M. and Hurley, S. (eds) (1991) *Foundations of Decision Theory. Issues and Advances*, Oxford: Blackwell.

Backhouse, R. E. (1990) 'Competition', in J. Creedy (ed.) *Foundations of Economic Thought*, Oxford: Blackwell.

Bailey, S. (1821) *An Inquiry into those Principles respecting the Nature of Demand and the Necessity of Consumption*, London: Hunter.

Bailey, S. (1825) *A Critical Dissertation on the Nature, Measure and Causes of Value*, London: Hunter.

Balasko, Y. (1988) *Foundations of the Theory of General Equilibrium*, Orlando FL: Academic Press.

Ball, L. and Romer, D. (1990) 'Real rigidities and the non-neutrality of money', *Review of Economic Studies* 57, 2: 183–203.

Ball, L. and Romer, D. (1991) 'Sticky prices as coordination failures', *American Economic Review* 81, 32: 539–52.

Ball, L., Mankiw, N. G. and Romer, D. (1991) 'The New Keynesian economics and the output–inflation trade-off', in N. G. Mankiw and D. Romer (eds) *New Keynesian Economics*, I *Imperfect Competition and Sticky Prices*, Cambridge MA: MIT Press. First published in *Brookings Papers on Economic Activity* 1: 1–65, 1988.

Balzano, B. and Musella, M. (1999) 'Ascesa e declino del concetto di "natural rate of unemployment"', *Studi e note di economia* 2: 31–51.

Barkai, H. (1965) 'Ricardo's static equilibrium', *Economica* 32, 125: 15–31.

Barkai, H. (1967) 'A note on Ricardo's notions of demand', *Economica* 34, 133: 75–9.

Barnett, W. A. (ed.) (1977) *Macroeconomic Dynamics* I, Cambridge: Cambridge University Press.

Barro, R. and Grossman, H. (1976) *Money, Employment and Inflation*, Cambridge: Cambridge University Press.

Barry, B. (1984) 'Tragic choices', *Ethics* 94: 303–18.

Baumol, W. J. (1952) 'The transactions demand for cash: an inventory theoretic approach', *Quarterly Journal of Economics* 66, 4: 545–56.

Baumol, W. J. (1970) *Economic Dynamics*, 3rd edn, New York: Macmillan.

Becattini, G. (ed.) (1990) *Il pensiero economico. Temi, problemi e scuole*, Biblioteca dell'economista, series VIII, sec. iii, vol. 3, Turin: UTET.

Begg, D. K. H. (1982) *The Rational Expectations Revolution in Macroeconomics*, Oxford: Allan.

Benassy, J. P. (1976) 'The disequilibrium approach to monopolistic price setting and general monopolistic equilibrium', *Review of Economic Studies* 43, 1: 69–81.

Benassy, J. P. (1982) *The Economics of Market Disequilibrium*, New York: Academic Press.

Benassy, J. P. (1988) 'The objective demand curve in general equilibrium with price makers', *Economic Journal* 98, 390 (supplement): 37–49.

Berlin, I. (1969) *Four Essays on Liberty*, Oxford: Oxford University Press.

Berlin, I. (1978) *Concepts and Categories*, New York: Harper.

Bharadwaj, K. (1985) 'Sraffa's return to classical theory', in K. Bharadwaj and B. Schefold (eds) *Essays on Piero Sraffa. Critical Perspectives on the Revival of Classical Theory*, London: Unwin Hyman.

Bharadwaj, K. (1989) *Themes in Value and Distribution*, London: Unwin Hyman.

Bharadwaj, K. and Schefold, B. (eds) (1990) *Essays on Piero Sraffa. Critical Perspectives on the Revival of Classical Theory*, London: Unwin Hyman.

Bhaskar, V. (1990) 'Wage relativities and the natural range of unemployment', *Economic Journal* 100, 400 (supplement): 60–6.

Bidard, C. (1991) *Prix, réproduction, rareté*, Paris: Dunod.

Blanchard, O. J. (1997) 'Is there a core of usable macroeconomics?', *American Economic Review* 87, 23: 244–6.

Blanchard, O. J. (2000) 'What do we know about macroeconomics that Fisher and Wicksell did not?', NBER Working Paper Series 7550, Washington DC: NBER.

Blanchard, O. J. and Fischer, S. (1989) *Lectures on Macroeconomics*, Cambridge MA and London: MIT Press.

Blanchard, O. J. and Kiyotaki, N. (1987) 'Monopolistic competition and the effects of aggregate demand', *American Economic Review* 77, 4: 647–66.

Blaug, M. (1958) *Ricardian Economics. A Historical Study*, New Haven CT: Yale University Press.

Blaug, M. (1982) 'Another look at the labour reduction problem in Marx', in I. Bradley and M. Howard (eds) *Classical and Marxian Political Economy*, London: Macmillan.

Blaug, M. (1985) 'What Ricardo said and what Ricardo meant', in G. Caravale (ed.) *The Legacy of Ricardo*, Oxford: Blackwell.

Blaug, M. (1987) 'Classical economics', in *The New Palgrave. A Dictionary of Economics* I, London: Macmillan.

Blaug, M. (1990) 'On the historiography of economics', *Journal of the History of Economic Thought* 12, 1: 27–37.

Blaug, M. (1993) 'Education and the employment contract', *Education Economics* 1, 1: 21–33.

Blaug, M. (1997a) 'Competition as an end-state and competition as a process', in B. C. Eaton and R. O. Harris (eds) *Trade, Technology and Economics. Essays in Honour of Richard G. Lipsey*, Cheltenham: Elgar.

Blaug, M. (1997b) *Not only an Economist. Recent Essays*, Cheltenham: Elgar.

Blaug, M. (1997c) [1962] *Economic Theory in Retrospect*, 5th edn, Cambridge: Cambridge University Press.

Blinder, A. S. (1987) 'Keynes, Lucas and scientific progress', *American Economic Review* 77, 2: 130–6; reprinted in A. S. Blinder (ed.) *Macroeconomics under Debate*, New York: Harvester Wheatsheaf (1989).

Blinder, A. S. (1997) 'Is there a core of practical macroeconomics that we should all believe?', *American Economic Review* 87, 2: 240–3.

Blinder, A. S., Canetti, E. R. D., Lebow, D. E. and Rudd, J. B. (1998) *Asking about Prices. A New Approach to Understanding Price Stickiness*, New York: Russell Sage Foundation.

Bliss, C. (1997) 'Mr Keynes and the anti-neoclassics', in P. C. Arestis, G. Palma and M. Sawyer (eds) *Essays in Honour of G. C. Harcourt*, I *Capital Controversy, Post-Keynesian Economics and the History of Economic Thought*, London and New York: Routledge.

Boggio, L. (1998) 'Gravitation', in H. D. Kurz and N. Salvadori (eds) *The Elgar Companion to Classical Economics*, Cheltenham: Elgar.

Böhm, V. (1994) 'The foundation of the theory of monopolistic competition revisited', *Journal of Economic Theory* 63, 2: 208–18.

Böhm-Bawerk, E. von. (1884) *Capital and Interest*, I *History and Critique of Interest Theories*, transtated by G. D. Huncke and H. F. Sennholz, South Holland IL: Libertarian Press (1959).

Boitani, A. and Damiani, M. (1999) 'Heterogeneous agents, indexation and the non-neutrality of money', *Quaderni dell'Istituto di Economia e Finanza* 23: 1–28, Catholic University of Milan.

Boitani, A. and Damiani, M. (2000) 'Strategic complementarity, near rationality and coordination', *Quaderni dell'Istituto di Economia e Finanza* 31: 1–33, Catholic University of Milan.

Boitani, A. and Delli Gatti, D. (2001) 'Effective demand and coordination failures', *Journal of Post Keynesian Economics* 23, 3: 411–40.

Boitani, A. and Rodano, G. (eds) (1995a) *Relazioni pericolose. Le avventure dell'economia nella cultura contemporanea*, Bari and Rome: Laterza.

Boitani, A. and Rodano, G. (1995b) 'Economia e . . .', in A. Boitani and G. Rodano (eds) *Relazioni pericolose. Le avventure dell'economia nella cultura contemporanea*, Bari and Rome: Laterza.

Boland, L. A. (1991) 'Current views on current positivism', in D. Greenaway, M. Bleaney and I. Stewart (eds) *Companion to Contemporary Economic Thought*, London and New York: Routledge.

Bonanno, G. (1988) 'Oligopoly equilibria when firms have local knowledge of demand', *International Economic Review* 29, 1: 45–55.

Bonanno, G. (1990) 'General equilibrium with imperfect competition', *Journal of Economic Surveys* 4, 4: 297–328.

Bonanno, G. and Zeeman, E. C. (1985) 'Limited knowledge of demand and oligopoly equilibria', *Journal of Economic Theory* 35, 2: 276–83.

Bortkiewicz, L. von (1906–7) 'Wertrechnung und Preisrechnung in Marxschen System', *Archiv für Sozialwissenschaft und Sozialpolitik*, 23, 1: 1–50; 25, 1: 10–51; 25, 2: 445–88. Translated into English (1952) as 'Value and prices in the Marxian system', *International Economic Papers*, 2.

Bowles, S. and Gintis, H. (1993) 'Post-Walrasian political economy', in S. Bowles, H. Gintis and B. Gustafsson (eds) *Markets and Democracy. Participation, Accountability and Efficiency*, Cambridge: Cambridge University Press.

Bowles, S., Gintis, H. and Gustafsson, B. (eds) (1993) *Markets and Democracy. Participation, Accountability and Efficiency*, Cambridge, New York and Melbourne: Cambridge University Press.

Brewer, A. A. (1988) 'Edward West and the classical theory of distribution and growth', *Economica* 55, 220: 505–15.

Bronfenbrenner, M. (1989) 'A rehabilitation of classical economics', *Aoyama Kokusai Seikei Ronshu* (*Aoyama University Journal of International Political Economy*) 13: 35–41.

Broome, J. (1991) *Weighing Goods. Equality, Uncertainty and Time*, Oxford: Blackwell.

Brothwell, J. F. (1997) 'The relation of *The General Theory* to the classical theory', in G. C. Harcourt and P. A. Riach (eds) *A 'Second Edition' of The General Theory*, London and New York: Routledge.

Burke, E. (1968) [1757] *A Philosophical Enquiry into the Origin of our Ideas of the Sublime and Beautiful*, edited by J. I. Boulton, London: Notre Dame University Press.

Burke, E. (1969) *Reflections on the Revolution in France*, edited by C. C. O'Brien, London: Penguin.

Burnyeat, M. (1980) 'Aristotle on learning to be good', in A. O. Rorty (ed.) *Essays on Aristotle's Ethics*, Berkeley CA: University of California Press.

Cairnes, J. E. (1874) *Some Leading Principles of Political Economy*, London: Macmillan.

Caldwell, B. (1997) 'Hayek and socialism', *Journal of Economic Literature* 35, 4: 1856–90.

Cannan, E. (1929) *A Review of Economic Theory*, London: King.

Cannan, E. (1967) [1897] *A History of the Theories of Production and Distribution*, reprinted New York: Kelley.

Carabelli, A. (1988) *On Keynes's Method*, London: Macmillan.

Carabelli, A. (1992) 'Organic interdependence and the choice of units in the *General Theory*', in B. Gerrard and J. V. Hillard (eds) *The Philosophy and Economics of J. M. Keynes*, Aldershot: Elgar.

Carabelli, A. (1994), 'Keynes on mensuration and comparison', in K. Vaugh (ed.) *Perspectives on the History of Economic Thought*, Aldershot: Elgar.

Carabelli, A. (1995) 'Uncertainty and measurement in Keynes: probability and organicness', in S. Dow and J. Hillard (eds) *Keynes, Knowledge and Uncertainty*, Aldershot: Elgar.

Carabelli, A. and De Vecchi, N. (1999) '"Where to draw the line?" Hayek and Keynes on knowledge, ethics and economics', *European Journal of the History of Economic Thought* 6, 2: 271–96.

Caravale, G. (1961) *Cicli economici e trend*, Milan: Giuffre.

Caravale, G. (1967) *Fluttuazioni e sviluppo nella dinamica di squilibrio di un sistema economico*, Rome: ISCONA.

Caravale, G. (1973) *Oligopolio differenziato e processo di svillupo*, Rome: Bulzoni.

Caravale, G. (ed.) (1985a) *The Legacy of Ricardo*, Oxford and New York: Blackwell.

Caravale, G. (1985b) 'Diminishing returns and accumulation in Ricardo', in G. Caravale (ed.) *The Legacy of Ricardo*, Oxford: Blackwell.

Caravale, G. (1991a) 'On the role of demand in Ricardo and Marshall', *Journal of the History of Economic Thought* 13, 2: 175–83.

Caravale, G. (ed.) (1991b) *Marx and Modern Economic Analysis*, 2 vols, Aldershot: Elgar.

Caravale, G. (1992a) 'The notion of equilibrium in economic theorizing', *Atlantic Economic Journal* 20, 1: 32–9.

Caravale, G. (1992b) 'Keynes and the concept of equilibrium', in M. Sebastiani (ed.) *The Notion of Equilibrium in the Keynesian Theory*, London: Macmillan.

Caravale, G. (1992c) 'Alcune considerazioni sulla nozione di equilibrio nella teoria economica', *Studi economici* 47, 47: 5–44.

Caravale, G. (1992d) Comment on Margaret Schabas, *Breaking Away. History of Economics as History of Science*, *History of Political Economy* 24, 1: 204–7.

Caravale, G. (1993) 'Keynes, equilibrium and modern economic systems' in R. F. Hébert (ed.) *Perspectives on the History of Economic Thought*, IX *Themes on Economic Discourse, Method, Money and Trade*, Aldershot: Elgar for the History of Economics Society.

Caravale, G. (1994a) 'Demand conditions and the interpretation of Ricardo', *Journal of the History of Economic Thought* 16, 2: 229–47.

Caravale, G. (1994b) 'Prices and quantities: Walras, Sraffa and beyond', *Studi economici* 49, 52: 43–64.

Caravale, G. (ed.) (1997a) *Equilibrium and Economic Theory*, London: Routledge; first published as *Equilibrio e teoria economica*, Bologna: Il Mulino (1994).

Caravale, G. (1997b) 'The notion of equilibrium in economic theory', in G. Caravale (ed.) *Equilibrium and Economic Theory*, London: Routledge.

Caravale, G. (1997c) 'Convergence to equilibrium: chronological or logical?', paper delivered to the EEA conference, Washington DC, April, mimeo.

Caravale, G. (1997d) 'Some notes on inflation and employment: incomes policy and the perspective of the European Monetary Union', *International Advances in Economic Research* 3, 3: 231–9.

Caravale, G. (1998a) 'On a recent change in the notion of incomes policy', in R. J. Rotheim (ed.) *New Keynesian Economics/Post-Keynesian Alternatives*, London: Routledge.

Caravale, G. (1998b) 'Supply and demand', in H. Kurz and N. Salvadori (eds) *The Elgar Companion to Classical Economics*, Cheltenham: Elgar.

Caravale, G. and Tosato, D. (1978) 'Saggio di proffito e merce tipo nella teoria di Ricardo', *Rivista di politica economica* 68: 3–70.

Caravale, G. and Tosato, D. (1980) *Ricardo and the Theory of Value, Distribution and Growth*, London: Routledge.

Carlin, W. and Soskice, D. (1990) *Macroeconomics and Wage Bargaining*, Oxford: Oxford University Press.

Carlsson, H. and Ganslandt, M. (1998) 'Noisy equilibrium selection in coordination games', *Economics Letters* 60, 1: 23–34.

Carvalho, F. J. C. (1990) 'Keynes and the long period', *Cambridge Journal of Economics* 14, 3: 277–90.

Casarosa, C. (1981) 'The microfoundations of Keynes's aggregate supply and expected demand analysis', *Economic Journal* 91, 361: 188–94.

Casarosa, C. (1985) 'The "new view" of the Ricardian theory of distribution and economic growth', in G. Caravale (ed.) *The Legacy of Ricardo*, Oxford: Blackwell.

Caserta, M. and Chick, V. (1997) 'Provisional equilibrium and macroeconomic theory', in P. Arestis, G. Palma and M. Sawyer (eds) *Essays in Honour of G. C. Harcourt*, II *Markets, Unemployment and Economic Policy*, London and New York: Routledge.

Cass, D. (1965) 'Optimum growth in an aggregative model of capital accumulation', *Review of Economic Studies* 32, 91: 233–40.

Cassels, J. M. (1935) 'A reinterpretation of Ricardo on value', *Quarterly Journal of Economics* 49, 3: 518–32.

Cesarano, F. (1983) 'On the role of the history of economic analysis', *History of Political Economy* 15, 1: 63–82.

Cesaratto, S. (1996) 'Long-period positions and economic change: a rejoinder', *Review of Political Economy* 8, 4: 409–25.

Chalmers, T. (1832) *On Political Economy*, Glasgow: Collins.

Chamberlin, E. H. (1933) *The Theory of Monopolistic Competition*, Cambridge MA: Harvard University Press.

Chamberlin, E. H. (1953) 'The product as an economic variable', *Quarterly Journal of Economics* 67, 1: 1–29.

Champernowne, D. (1945) 'A note on J. v. Neumann's article on "A model of economic equilibrium"', *Review of Economic Studies* 13: 10–18.

Chick, V. (1983a) *Macroeconomics after Keynes. A Reconsideration of the General Theory*, Cambridge MA: MIT Press.

Chick, V. (1983b) 'A question of relevance: *The General Theory* in Keynes's time and ours', *South African Journal of Economics* 51, 3: 388–406.

Chick, V. (1985) 'Time and the wage-unit in Keynes's method: history and equilibrium', in T. Lawson and H. Pesaran (eds) *Keynes's Economics. Methodological Issues*, Armonk NY: Sharpe.

Chick, V. (1992) 'The small firm under uncertainty: a puzzle of *The General Theory*', in B. Gerrard and J. Hillard (eds) *The Philosophy and Economics of J. M. Keynes*, Aldershot: Elgar.

Chick, V. (1996) 'Equilibrium and determination in open systems', *History of Economics Review* 25: 172–83.

Chick, V. (1997) 'The multiplier and finance', in G. C. Harcourt and P. A. Riach (eds) *A 'Second Edition' of The General Theory*, London and New York: Routledge.

Chick, V. (1998) [1996] 'A struggle to escape: equilibrium in *The General Theory*', in S. Sharma (ed.) *John Maynard Keynes. Keynesianism into the Twenty-first Century*, Cheltenham: Elgar; first printed in *Ekonomska misao i praksa* (Dubrovnic) 5: 345–62.

Clarida, R., Galí, J. and Gertler, M. (1999) 'The science of monetary policy: a New Keynesian perspective', *Journal of Economic Literature* 37, 4: 1661–707.

Clower, R. W. (1965) 'The Keynesian counterrevolution: a theoretical appraisal', in F. H. Hahn and F. P. R. Brechling (eds) *The Theory of Interest Rates*, London: Macmillan.

Clower, R. W. and Howitt, P. (1996) 'Taking markets seriously: groundwork for a post-Walrasian macroeconomics', in D. Colander (ed.) *Beyond Microfoundations. Post-Walrasian Macroeconomics*, Cambridge: Cambridge University Press.

Coase, R. H. (1984) 'The new institutional economics', *Zeitschrift für die gesamte Staatswissenschaft* (*Journal of Institutional and Theoretical Economics*) 140, 1: 229–31.

Codognato, G. and Gabszewicz, J. J. (1991) 'Equilibres de Cournot–Walras dans une économie d'échange', *Revue économique* 42, 6: 1013–26.

Colander, D. (ed.) (1996a) *Beyond Microfoundations. Post-Walrasian Macroeconomics*, Cambridge, New York and Melbourne: Cambridge University Press.

Colander, D. (1996b) 'The macrofoundations of micro', in D. Colander (ed.) *Beyond Microfoundations. Post-Walrasian Macroeconomics*, Cambridge: Cambridge University Press.

Colander, D. (1998) 'Beyond New Keynesian economics: towards a post-Walrasian macroeconomics', in R. J. Rotheim (ed.) *New Keynesian Economics/Post-Keynesian Alternatives*, London: Routledge.

Cooper, R. (1994) 'Equilibrium selection in imperfectly competitive economies with multiple equilibria', *Economic Journal* 104, 426: 1106–22.

Cooper, R. (1999) *Coordination Games. Complementarities and Macroeconomics*, Cambridge: Cambridge University Press.

Cooper, R. and John, A. (1988) 'Coordinating coordination failures in Keynesian models', *Quarterly Journal of Economics* 103, 3: 441–63.

Cooper, R., DeJong, D. V., Forsythe, R. and Ross, T. W. (1994) 'Alternative institutions for resolving coordination problems', in J. W. Friedman (ed.) *Problems of Coordination in Economic Activity*, Boston MA and Dordrecht: Kluwer.

Cornwall, J. (1994) *Economic Breakdown and Recovery. Theory and Policy*, New York: Sharpe.

Cornwall, J. and Cornwall, W. (1997) 'The unemployment problem and the legacy of Keynes', *Journal of Post-Keynesian Economics* 19, 4: 525–42.

Cornwall, R. R. (1977) 'The concept of general equilibrium in a market economy with imperfectly competitive producers', *Metroeconomica* 29: 55–72.

Cournot, A. A. (1838) *Recherches sur les principes mathématiques de la théorie des richesses*, Paris: Hachette.

Darity, W. A. and Young, W. (1997) 'On rewriting chapter 2 of *The General Theory*', in G. C. Harcourt and P. A. Riach (eds) *A 'Second Edition' of The General Theory*, London and New York: Routledge.

Dasgupta, P. and Maskin, E. (1986) 'The existence of equilibrium in discontinuous economic games', *Review of Economic Studies* 53, 1: 1–26.

d'Aspremont, C., Dos Santos Ferreira, R. and Gérard-Varet, L.-A. (1991) 'Pricing schemes and Cournotian equilibria', *American Economic Review* 81, 3: 666–73.

d'Aspremont, C., Dos Santos Ferreira, R. and Gérard-Varet, L.-A. (1997) 'General equilibrium concepts under imperfect competition: a Cournotian approach', *Journal of Economic Theory* 73, 1: 199–230.

d'Aspremont, C., Dos Santos Ferreira, R. and Gérard-Varet, L.-A. (1999) 'Imperfect competition and general equilibrium: elements for a new approach', in A. Kirman and L.-A. Gérard-Varet (eds) *Economics beyond the Millennium*, Oxford: Oxford University Press.

Davidson, P. (1972) *Money and the Real World*, London: Macmillan.

Davidson, P. (1992) 'Would Keynes be a New Keynesian?', *Eastern Economic Journal* 18, 4: 449–63.

Davidson, P. (1995) 'Reality and economic theory', *Journal of Post-Keynesian Economics* 18, 4: 479–508.

Davidson, P. (1996) 'What revolution? The legacy of Keynes', *Journal of Post-Keynesian Economics* 19, 1: 47–60.

Davidson, P. (1998) 'Setting the record straight', in R. J. Rotheim (ed.) *New Keynesian Economics/Post-Keynesian Alternatives*, London: Routledge.

Davidson, P. (1999) 'Keynes's principle of effective demand versus the bedlam of the New Keynesians', *Journal of Post-Keynesian Economics* 21, 4: 571–88.

De Marchi, N. and Sturges, R. P. (1973) 'Malthus and Ricardo's inductivist critics', *Economica* 40, 160: 379–93.

De Quincey, T. (1897) [1844]. *The Logic of Political Economy*, in D. Masson (ed.) *Political Economy and Politics*, London: Black.

de Vivo, G. (1996) 'Piero Sraffa and the Mill–Ricardo Papers: a comment', *Cambridge Journal of Economics* 20, 5: 637–39.

Debreu, G. (1959) *Theory of Value*, New York: Wiley.

Debreu, G. (1970) 'Economies with a finite set of equilibria', *Econometrica* 38, 3: 387–92.

Debreu, G. (1982) 'Existence of competitive equilibrium', in K. J. Arrow and M. D. Intrilligator (eds) *Handbook of Mathematical Economics* II, Amsterdam: North Holland.

Diamond, P. A. (1965) 'National debt in a neoclassical growth model', *American Economic Review* 55, 5: 1126–50.

Dierker, E. and Grodal, B. (1986) 'Non-existence of Cournot–Walras equilibrium in a general equilibrium model with two oligopolists', in W. Hildenbrand and A. Mas-Colell (eds) *Contributions to Mathematical Economics in Honor of Gerard Debreu*, Amsterdam: North Holland.

Dierker, E. and Grodal, B. (1998) 'Modelling policy issues in a world of imperfect competition', *Scandinavian Journal of Economics* 100, 1: 153–79.

Dierker, E. and Grodal, B. (1999) 'The price normalization problem in imperfect competition and the objective of the firm', *Economic Theory* 14, 2: 257–84.

Dimand, R. (1998) 'The fall and rise of Irving Fisher's macroeconomics', *Journal of the History of Economic Thought* 20, 2: 191–201.

Dixon, H. D. (1990) 'Imperfect competition, unemployment benefit and the non-neutrality of money: an example', *Oxford Economic Papers* 42, 2: 402–13.

Dixon, H. D. (1997) 'The role of imperfect competition in New Keynesian economics', in B. Snowdon and H. Vane (eds) *Reflections on the Development of Modern Macroeconomics*, Cheltenham: Elgar.

Dmitriev, V. K. (1974) [1904] *Economic Essays*, edited by D. M. Nuti, Cambridge: Cambridge University Press.

Dobb, M. H. (1973) *Theories of Value and Distribution Since Adam Smith. Ideology and Economic Theory*, Cambridge: Cambridge University Press.

D'Orlando, F. and Nisticò, S. (2000) 'Prices and quantities: possible solutions within a post-classical research program', *Economie appliquée* 53, 3: 9–29.

Drazen, A. (1987) 'Reciprocal externality models of low employment', *European Economic Review* 37, 1: 436–43.

Dugger, W. (1990) 'The new institutionalism: new but not institutionalist', *Journal of Economic Issues* 24, 2: 423–31.

Duménil, G. and Lévy, D. (1987) 'The dynamics of competition: a restoration of classical analysis', *Cambridge Journal of Economics* 11, 2: 133–64.

Duménil, G. and Lévy, D. (1998) 'Dynamics', in H. D. Kurz and N. Salvadori (eds) *The Elgar Companion to Classical Economics*, Cheltenham: Elgar.

Eatwell, J. and Panico, C. (1987) 'Sraffa Piero', in *The New Palgrave. A Dictionary of Economics* IV, London: Macmillan.

Edgeworth, F. Y. (1891) 'The objects and methods of political economy', reprinted in *Papers Relating to Political Economy* I, New York: Franklin.

Edwards, M. (1977) 'Agamemnon's decision: freedom and folly in Aeschylus' Agamemnon', *California Studies in Classical Antiquity* 10: 17–38.

Eichenbaum, M. (1997) 'Some thoughts on practical stabilization policy', *American Economic Review* 87, 2: 236–9.

Eichner, A. S. and Kregel, J. A. (1975) 'An essay on Post-Keynesian theory: a new paradigm in economics', *Journal of Economic Literature* 13, 4: 1293–314.

Einaudi, L. (1951) 'Dalla leggenda al monumento', *Giornale degli economisti e Annali di economia*, n.s.; also in *Saggi bibliografici e storici intorno alle dottrine economiche*, Rome: Edizioni di storia e letteratura (1953).

Eisner, R. (1986) 'The revolution restored: Keynesian unemployment, inflation and budget deficits', *Eastern Economic Journal* 12, 3: 217–21.

Elster, J. (1979) *Ulysses and the Sirens*, Cambridge: Cambridge University Press.

Elster, J. (1991) *Interpersonal Comparisons of Well-being*, Cambridge: Cambridge University Press.

Eltis, W. (1984) *The Classical Theory of Economic Growth*, London: Macmillan.

Fenn, R. A. (1991) *Textbook for Utilitarians. James Mill's Articles in the Encyclopaedia Britannica*, Toronto: Fenn.

Fetter, F. W. (1965) 'The relation of the history of economic thought to economic history', *American Economic Review. Papers and Proceedings* 55, 2: 137–42.

Fetter, F. W. (1980) *The Economist in Parliament*, Durham NC: Duke University Press.

Fischer, S. (1977) 'Long-term contracts, rational expectations and the optimal money supply rule', *Journal of Political Economy* 85, 1: 191–206.

Fischer, S. (ed.) (1980) *Rational Expectations and Economic Policy*, Chicago: University of Chicago Press.

Fisher, F. (1983) *Disequilibrium Foundations of Equilibrium Economics*, Cambridge: Cambridge University Press.

Fisher, I. (1932) *Booms and Depressions*, New York: Adelphi.

Fisher, I. (1936) 'The depression, its causes and cures', *Abstracts of Papers presented at the Research Conference on Economics and Statistics held by the Cowles Commission Research in Economics*, Colorado College Publication, General Series 28, Study Series 21, Colorado Springs CO, Colorado College: 104–20.

Flaschel, P. and Semmler, W. (1987) 'Classical and neoclassical competitive adjustment processes', *Manchester School* 55, 1: 13–37.

Foot, P. (1978) *Virtues and Vices*, Oxford: Oxford University Press.

Foot, P. (1983) 'Moral realism and moral dilemmas', *Journal of Philosophy* 80: 379–98.

Friedman, M. (1957) *A Theory of the Consumption Function*, Princeton NJ: Princeton University Press.

Friedman, M. (1968) 'The role of monetary policy', *American Economic Review* 58, 1: 1–17.

Gabszewicz, J. J. (1985) 'Imperfect competition in general equilibrium: an overview of recent work: comment', in K. J. Arrow and S. Honkapohja (eds) *Frontiers of Economics*, Oxford: Blackwell.

Gabszewicz, J. J. (1999) 'GeneRal EQuilibrium Economics: allowing for imperfect competition', in A. Kirman and L.-A. Gérard-Varet (eds) *Economics beyond the Millennium*, Oxford: Oxford University Press.

Gabszewicz, J. J. and Michel, P. (1997) 'Oligopoly equilibrium in exchange economies', in B. C. Eaton and R. G. Harris (eds) *Trade, Technology and Economics. Essays in Honour of Richard G. Lipsey*, Cheltenham and Lyme NH: Elgar.

Gabszewicz, J. J. and Vial, J. P. (1972) 'Oligopoly "*à la* Cournot" in a general equilibrium analysis', *Journal of Economic Theory* 4, 3: 381–400.

Galbraith, J. K. (1997) 'Time to ditch the NAIRU', *Journal of Economic Perspectives* 11, 1: 93–108.

Galí, J. (2000) 'The return of the Phillips curve and other recent developments in business cycle theory', *Spanish Economic Review* 2, 1: 1–10.

Garegnani, P. (1958) 'A Problem in the Theory of Distribution from Ricardo to Wicksell', Cambridge Ph.D. dissertation.

Garegnani, P. (1960) *Il capitale nelle teorie della distribuzione*; Milan: Giuffrè.

Garegnani, P. (1970) 'Heterogeneous capital, the production function and the theory of distribution', *Review of Economic Studies* 37, 3: 407–36.

Garegnani, P. (1976) 'On a change in the notion of equilibrium in recent work on value and distribution: a comment on Samuelson', in M. Brown, K. Sato and P. Zarembka (eds) *Essays in Modern Capital Theory*, Amsterdam: North Holland.

Garegnani, P. (1981) *Marx e gli economisti classici*, Turin: Einaudi.

Garegnani, P. (1983) 'The classical theory of wages and the role of demand schedules in the determination of relative prices', *American Economic Review* 73, 2: 309–13.

Garegnani, P. (1984) 'Value and distribution in the classical economists and Marx', *Oxford Economic Papers* 36, 2: 291–325.

Garegnani, P. (1987) 'Surplus approach to distribution', in *The New Palgrave. A Dictionary of Economics* IV. London: Macmillan.

Garegnani, P. (1990) 'Sraffa: classical versus marginalist analysis', in K. Bharadwaj and B. Schefold (eds) *Essays on Piero Sraffa. Critical Perspectives on the Revival of Classical Theory*, London: Unwin Hyman.

Garegnani, P. (1997) [1990] 'On some supposed obstacles to the tendency of market prices towards natural prices', in G. Caravale (ed.) *Equilibrium and Economic Theory*, London: Routledge; first printed in *Political Economy. Studies in the Surplus Approach* 6, 1–2: 329–59.

Garegnani, P. (2000a) 'Savings, investment and capital in a system of general intertemporal equilibrium', in H. D. Kurz (ed.) *Critical Essays on Piero Sraffa's Legacy in Economics*, Cambridge: Cambridge University Press.

Garegnani, P. (2000b) 'Samuelson on Sraffa's "hits and misses" ', unpublished.

Garegnani, P. (2002) 'Misunderstanding Classical Economics', *History of Political Economy*, forthcoming.

Garretsen, H. (1992) *Keynes, Coordination and Beyond*, Aldershot: Elgar.

Gary-Bobo, R. (1987) 'Locally consistent equilibria are Cournot–Walras equilibria', *Economic Letters* 23: 217–21.

Gary-Bobo, R. (1988) 'Equilibre général et concurrence imparfaite: un tour d'horizon', *Recherches économiques de Louvain* 54, 1: 53–84.

Gary-Bobo, R. (1989) 'Cournot–Walras and locally consistent equilibria', *Journal of Economic Theory* 49, 1: 10–32.

Gerrard, B. and Hillard, J. (eds) (1992) *The Philosophy and Economics of J. M. Keynes*, Aldershot: Elgar.

Gnesutta, C. (ed.) (1996) *Incertezza, moneta, aspettative, equilibrio*, Bologna: Il Mulino.

Goodfriend, M. and King, R. G. (1997) 'The new neoclassical synthesis and the role of monetary policy', in B. S. Bernanke and J. J. Rotemberg (eds) *NBER Macroeconomics Annual 1997*, Cambridge MA and London: MIT Press.

Goodwin, R. (1992) 'The *General Theory*: critical and constructive', in M. Sebastiani (ed.) *The Notion of Equilibrium in the Keynesian Theory*, London: Macmillan.

Gordon, D. F. (1965) 'The role of the history of economic thought in the understanding of modern economic theory', *American Economic Review. Papers and Proceedings* 55, 2: 119–27.

Gordon, R. J. (1990) 'What is New Keynesian economics?', *Journal of Economic Literature* 28, 3: 1115–71.

Gordon, R. J. (1997) 'The time-varying NAIRU and its implications for economic policy?', *Journal of Economic Perspectives* 11, 1: 11–32.

Gowans, C. (ed.) (1987) *Moral Dilemmas*, Oxford: Oxford University Press.

Grandmont, J.-M. (1992) 'Transformations of the commodity space, behavioral heterogeneity, and the aggregation problem', *Journal of Economic Theory* 57, 1: 1–35.

Grandmont, J.-M. (1993) 'Behavioural heterogeneity and Cournot oligopoly equilibrium', *Ricerche economiche* 47, 2: 167–87.

Greenaway, D., Bleaney, M. and Stewart, I. (eds) (1991) *Companion to Contemporary Economic Thought*, London and New York: Routledge.

Greenwald, B. C. and Stiglitz, J. E. (1987) 'Keynesian, New Keynesian and new classical economics', *Oxford Economic Papers* 39, 1: 119–33.

Grodal, B. (1996) 'Profit maximization and imperfect competition', in B. Allen (ed.) *Economics in a Changing World* II, London: Macmillan.

Groenewegen, P. (1997) 'Economics does have a useful past and yes, history is important', in A. Heertje (ed.) *The Makers of Modern Economics*, Cheltenham: Elgar.

Haberler, G. (1937) *Prosperity and Depression. A Theoretical Analysis of Cyclical Movements*, 3d edn, Lake Success NY: United Nations (1946).

Hahn, F. H. (1977) 'Keynesian economics and general equilibrium theory', in G. C. Harcourt (ed.) *The Microfoundations of Macroeconomics*, London: Macmillan.

Hahn, F. H. and Negishi T. (1962) 'A theorem on non-*tâtonnement* stability', *Econometrica* 30, 3: 463–9.

Halévy, E. (1955) [1928]. *The Growth of Philosophical Radicalism*, translated by M. Morris, Boston MA: Beacon Press.

Hall, R. E. (1986) 'Market structure and macroeconomic fluctuations', *Brookings Papers on Economic Activity* 2: 285–322; reprinted in N. G. Mankiw and D. Romer (eds) *New Keynesian Economics*, I *Imperfect Competition and Sticky Prices*, Cambridge MA: MIT Press.

Haltiwanger, J. and Waldman, M. (1985) 'Rational expectations and the limits of rationality: an analysis of heterogeneity', *American Economic Review* 75, 3: 326–40.

Haltiwanger, J. and Waldman, M. (1989) 'Limited rationality and strategic complementarity: the implications for macroeconomics', *Quarterly Journal of Economics* 104, 3: 463–83.

Haltiwanger, J. and Waldman, M. (1991) 'Responders versus non-responders: a new perspective on heterogeneity', *Economic Journal* 101, 408: 1085–102.

Harcourt, G. C. and Riach, P. A. (eds) (1997a) *A 'Second Edition' of The General Theory*, London and New York: Routledge.

Harcourt, G. C. and Riach, P. A. (eds) (1997b) 'Introduction' to G. C. Harcourt and P. A. Riach (eds) *A 'Second Edition' of The General Theory*, London and New York: Routledge.

Harrod, R. (1951) *The Life of J. M. Keynes*, London: Macmillan.

Harrod, R. (1961) Review of Piero Sraffa's *Production of Commodities by Means of Commodities*, *Economic Journal* 71, 284: 783–7.

Harsanyi, J. (1973) 'Games with randomly disturbed payoffs: a new rationale for mixed strategies', *International Journal of Game Theory* 2: 1–23.

Harsanyi, J. and Selten, R. (1988) *A General Theory of Equilibrium Selection in Games*, Cambridge MA and London: MIT Press.

Hart, O. D. (1982) 'A model of imperfect competition with Keynesian features', *Quarterly Journal of Economics* 97, 1: 109–38.

Hart, O. D. (1985) 'Imperfect competition in general equilibrium: an overview of recent work', in K. J. Arrow and S. Honkapohja (eds) *Frontiers of Economics*, Oxford: Blackwell.

Hey, J. D. (1994) *Experimental Economics*, Berlin: Springer.

Hicks, J. R. (1937a) 'Letter to J. M. Keynes' (9 April), in J. M. Keynes *The Collected Writings of J. M. Keynes*, edited by D. E. Moggridge, London: Macmillan (1971–89), XIV: 81–3.

Hicks, J. R. (1937b) 'Mr Keynes and the "classics": a suggested interpretation', *Econometrica* 5: 147–59.

Hicks, J. R. (1939) *Value and Capital*, London: Oxford University Press.

Hicks, J. R. (1969) *A Theory of Economic History*, Oxford: Clarendon Press.

Hicks, J. R. (1976) '"Revolutions" in economics', in S. Latsis (ed.) *Method and Appraisal in Economics*, Cambridge: Cambridge University Press.

Hicks, J. R. (1985) 'Sraffa and Ricardo: a critical view', in G. Caravale (ed.) *The Legacy of Ricardo*, Oxford: Blackwell.

Hicks, J. R. (1990) 'Ricardo and Sraffa', in K. Bharadwaj and B. Schefold (eds) *Essays on Piero Sraffa. Critical Perspectives on the Revival of Classical Theory*, London Unwin Hyman.

Hildenbrand, W. and Kirman, A. P. (1988) *Equilibrium Analysis. Variations on Themes by Edgeworth and Walras*, Amsterdam: North Holland.

Hindson, P. and Gray, T. (1988) *Burke's Dramatic Theory of Politics*, Aldershot: Avebury.

Hines, A. G. (1971) *On the Reappraisal of Keynesian Economics*, London: Robertson.

Hollander, J. H. (1910) *David Ricardo: A Centenary Estimate*, Baltimore MD.

Hollander, S. (1973a) *The Economics of Adam Smith*, Toronto: University of Toronto Press.

Hollander, S. (1973b) 'Ricardo's analysis of the profit rate, 1813–15', *Economica* 40, 159: 260–82.

Hollander, S. (1979) *The Economics of David Ricardo*, Toronto: University of Toronto Press.

Hollander, S. (1987) *Classical Economics*, Oxford and New York: Blackwell.

Hollander, S. (1995) *Ricardo: The New View. Collected Essays* I, London: Routledge.

Hollander, S. (1997) *The Economics of Thomas Robert Malthus*, Toronto: University of Toronto Press.

Hollander, S. (1998) 'Sraffa in historiographical perspective: a provisional statement', *European Journal of the History of Economic Thought* 5, 3: 430–6.

Hollander, S. (2000) 'Sraffa and the interpretation of Ricardo: the Marxian dimension', *History of Political Economy* 32, 2: 187–232.

Hoover, K. D. (1988) *The New Classical Macroeconomics*, Oxford: Blackwell.

Howitt, P. (1997) 'Expectations and uncertainty in contemporary Keynesian models', in G. C. Harcourt and P. A. Riach (eds) *A 'Second Edition' of The General Theory*, London and New York: Routledge.

Hume, D. (1938) *An Abstract of a Treatise on Human Nature*, edited and introduced by J. M. Keynes and P. Sraffa, Cambridge: Cambridge University Press.

Hutchison, T. W. (1953) *A Review of Economic Doctrines*, Oxford: Clarendon Press.

Hynes, J. A. (1998) 'The emergence of the neoclassical consumption function: the formative years, 1940–1952', *Journal of the History of Economic Thought* 20, 1: 25–49.

Jackson, F. (1985) 'Internal conflict in desires and morals', *American Philosophical Quarterly* 22: 105–14.

Jevons, W. S. (1862) 'Brief account of a general mathematical theory of political economy', *Journal of the Royal Statistical Society* 29, 2: 282–7.

Jevons, W. S. (1879) *The Theory of Political Economy*, 2nd edn, London: Macmillan.

Jevons, W. S. (1977) *Papers and Correspondence*, VI *Lectures on Political Economy 1875–1876*, edited by R. D. C. Black, London: Macmillan.

Johnson, H. G. (1971) 'The Keynesian revolution and the monetarist counter-revolution', *American Economic Review* 61, 2: 91–106.

Jones, J. (1962) *On Aristotle and Greek Tragedy*, London: Macmillan.

Jones, R. (1831) *An Essay on the Distribution of Wealth*, London: John Murray.

Jorgenson, D. W. (1963) 'Capital theory and investment behavior', *American Economic Review. Papers and Proceedings* 53, 2: 247–59.

Jossa, B. (1979) 'Equilibri keynesiani e teoria del costo pieno', *Giornale degli economisti e Annali di economia* 38, 5–6: 329–56.

Jossa, B. (1997) 'The concept of equilibrium and the reality of unemployment', in G. Caravale (ed.) *Equilibrium and Economic Theory*, London: Routledge.

Jossa, B. and Musella, M. (1995) 'Curva di Phillips, isteresi e teoria keynesiana', in A. Amendola (ed.) *Disoccupazione. Analisi macroeconomica e mercato del lavoro*, Naples: ESI.

Kagan, S. (1988) 'The additive fallacy', *Ethics* 99: 5–31.

Kahn, R. F. (1977) 'Malinvaud on Keynes', *Cambridge Journal of Economics* 1, 4: 375–88.

Kahn, R. F. (1978) 'Some aspects of the development of Keynes's thought', *Journal of Economic Literature* 16, 2: 545–59.

Kahn, R. F. (1989) *The Economics of the Short Period*, London: Macmillan.

Kaldor, N. (1956) 'Alternative theories of distribution', *Review of Economic Studies* 23, 2: 83–100.

Kaldor, N. (1961) 'Capital accumulation and economic growth', in F. A. Lutz and D. C. Hague (eds) *The Theory of Capital*, New York: St Martin's Press.

Kaldor, N. (1972) 'The irrelevance of equilibrium economics', *Economic Journal* 82, 328: 1237–55.

Kenyon, P. (1978) 'Pricing in Post-Keynesian economics', *Challenge* 21, 3: 43–8.

Keynes, J. M. (1922/33) 'Robert Malthus, 1766–1835, the first of the Cambridge economists', in Keynes, *Essays in Biography*; and with the title 'Thomas Robert Malthus' in Keynes *The Collected Writings of J. M. Keynes*, edited by D. E. Moggridge, London: Macmillan (1971–89), X: 71–103.

Keynes, J. M. (1930) *A Treatise on Money*, I *The Pure Theory of Money*, London: Macmillan.

Keynes, J. M. (1933) *Essays in Biography*, reprinted with additional biographies in 1951; in J. M. Keynes (1971–89) *The Collected Writings of J. M. Keynes*, edited by D. E. Moggridge, London: Macmillan, X.

Keynes, J. M. (1936) *The General Theory of Employment, Interest and Money*, London: Macmillan.

Keynes, J. M. (1937) 'The general theory of employment', *Quarterly Journal of Economics* 51: 209–23.

Keynes, J. M. (1971–89) *The Collected Writings of J. M. Keynes*, edited by D. E. Moggridge, 30 vols, London and Basingstoke: Macmillan, St Martin's Press for the Royal Economic Society.

Keynes, J. M. MSS (held at King's College, Cambridge)

A Scheme for an Essay on the Principles of Probability, 5 September 1905.

A Theory of Beauty, 6 November 1905.

Beauty, 3 October 1905.

Books read on 1905–6.

Diary, 1905–6.

Draft of the Chapter on the Measurement of Probability.

Economic Essays marked by Marshall, 18 October–23 November 1905.
Egoism, 24 February 1906.
Essay on Index Numbers marked by Marshall, 31 October 1905.
General Correspondence.
Miscellanea Ethica, July–September 1905.
Modern Civilisation, 28 October 1905.
Notes on Locke.
Obligation.
On Beauty and Art. On Art Criticism and the Appreciation of Beauty, undated.
On the Principle of Organic Unity, undated but read again on 22 January 1921.
Science and Art, 20 February 1909.
The 1907 version of *The Principles of Probability.*
The Political Doctrines of Edmund Burke, 1904.
Virtue and Happiness, written after the Easter vacation 1905.

Klamer, A. (1989) 'A conversation with Amartya Sen', *Journal of Economic Perspectives* 3, 1: 135–50.

Klein, L. R. (1947) *The Keynesian Revolution*, New York: Macmillan.

Knight, F. H. (1937) 'Unemployment and Mr Keynes's revolution in economic theory', *Canadian Journal of Economics and Political Science* 3: 100–23.

Knight, F. H. (1956) [1935] 'The Ricardian theory of production and distribution', *Canadian Journal of Economic and Political Science*, February and May, as reprinted (1956) in *On the History and Method of Economics*, Chicago: University of Chicago Press.

Koopmans, T. C. (1965) 'On the concept of optimal economic growth', in T. C. Koopmans, *The Economic Approach to Development Planning*, Amsterdam: North Holland.

Kregel, J. A. (1976) 'Economic methodology in the face of uncertainty: the modelling methods of Keynes and the Post-Keynesians', *Economic Journal* 86, 342: 209–25.

Kregel, J. A. (1987) 'Keynes's given degree of competition: comment on MacKenna and Zannoni', *Journal of Post-Keynesian Economics* 9, 4: 490–5.

Kregel, J. A. (1998) 'Keynes and the New Keynesians on market competition', in R. J. Rotheim (ed.) *New Keynesian Economics/Post-Keynesian Alternatives*, London: Routledge.

Kregel, J. A. and Nardozzi, G. (1996) 'Una valutazione critica', in C. Gnesutta (ed.) *Incertezza, moneta, aspettative, equilibrio*, Bologna: Il Mulino.

Kurz, H. D. (1998a) 'Against the current: Sraffa's unpublished manuscripts and the history of economic thought', *European Journal of the History of Economic Thought* 5, 3: 437–51.

Kurz, H. D. (1998b) 'Le fonds Sraffa à Cambridge: aperçu sur les écrits non-publiés', *Revue d'économie politique* 108, 6: 813–37.

Kurz, H. D. (ed.) (2000) *Critical Essays on Piero Sraffa's Legacy in Economics*, Cambridge, Melbourne and New York: Cambridge University Press.

Kurz, H. D. and Salvadori, N. (1993a) 'The "Standard commodity" and Ricardo's search for an "invariable measure of value"', in M. Baranzini and G. C. Harcourt (eds) *The Dynamics of the Wealth of Nations. Growth, Distribution and Structural Change. Essays in Honour of Luigi Pasinetti*, New York: St Martin's Press.

Kurz, H. D. and Salvadori, N. (1993b) 'Von Neumann's growth model and the "classical" tradition', *European Journal of the History of Economic Thought* 1, 1: 129–60.

Kurz, H. D. and Salvadori, N. (1995) *Theory of Production. A Long-period Analysis*, Cambridge, Melbourne and New York: Cambridge University Press.

Kurz, H. D. and Salvadori, N. (eds) (1998a) *The Elgar Companion to Classical Economics*, 2 vols, Cheltenham: Elgar.

Kurz, H. D. and Salvadori, N. (1998b) *Understanding 'Classical' Economics. Studies in Long-period Theory*, London: Routledge.

Kurz, H. D. and Salvadori, N. (2000a) 'Sraffa and the mathematicians: Frank Ramsey and Alister Watson', in T. Cozzi and R. Marchionatti (eds) *Piero Sraffa's Political Economy: A Centenary Estimate*, London and New York: Routledge.

Kurz, H. D. and Salvadori, N. (2000b) 'Sraffa e von Neumann', in M. Pivetti (ed.) *Piero Sraffa. contributi per una biografia intellettuale*, Rome: Carocci.

Kydland, F. E. and Prescott, E. C. (1982) 'Time to build and aggregate fluctuations', *Econometrica* 50, 6: 1345–70.

Kydland, F. E. and Prescott, E. C. (1996) 'The computational experiment: an econometric tool', *Journal of Economic Perspectives* 10, 1: 69–85.

Laffont, J. J. and Laroque, G. (1976) 'Existence d'un équilibre de concurrence imparfaite: une introduction', *Econometrica* 44, 2: 283–94.

Laidler, D. E. W. (1992) 'Issues in contemporary macroeconomics', in A. Vercelli and N. Dimitri (eds) *Macroeconomics. A Survey of Research Strategies*, Oxford: Oxford University Press.

Laidler, D. E. W. (1999) *Fabricating the Keynesian Revolution. Studies in the Inter-war Literature on Money, the Cycle, and Unemployment*, Cambridge: Cambridge University Press.

Lange, O. (1944) *Price Flexibility and Employment*, San Antonio TX: Trinity University Press.

Langlois, R. (ed.) (1986) *Economics as a Process. Essays in the New Institutional Economics*, Cambridge: Cambridge University Press.

Lawlor, M. S., Darity, W. A. and Horn, B. L. (1987) 'Was Keynes a chapter two Keynesian?', *Journal of Post-Keynesian Economics* 9, 4: 516–28.

Layard, R., Nickell, S. and Jackman, R. (1991) *Unemployment. Macroeconomic Performance and Labour Market*, Oxford: Oxford University Press.

Leijonhufvud, A. (1968) *On Keynesian Economics and the Economics of Keynes. A Study in Monetary Theory*, Oxford: Oxford University Press.

Leijonhufvud, A. (1981) *Information and Coordination. Essays in Macroeconomic Theory*, London: Oxford University Press.

Leijonhufvud, A. (1997) 'The Wicksellian heritage', *Economic Notes* 26, 1: 1–9.

Leith, J. C. and Patinkin, D. (eds) (1977) *Keynes, Cambridge and the General Theory*, London: Macmillan.

Leontief, W. (1941) *The Structure of the American Economy*, Cambridge MA: Harvard University Press.

Lerner, A. (1940) 'Some Swedish stepping stones in economic theory', *Canadian Journal of Economics and Political Science* 6: 574–91.

Levi, I. (1986) *Hard Choices*, Cambridge: Cambridge University Press.

Levi, P. (1979) *G. E. Moore and the Cambridge Apostles*, London: Weidenfeld & Nicolson.

Lewin, S. B. (1996) 'Economics and psychology: lessons for our own day from the early twentieth century', *Journal of Economic Literature* 34, 3: 1293–323.

Lindbeck, A. (1998) 'New Keynesianism and aggregate economic activity', *Economic Journal* 108, 446: 167–80.

Lipsey, R. G. (1960) 'The relation between unemployment and the rate of change of money wage rates in the United Kingdom 1862–1957: a further analysis', *Economica* 27, 105: 1–31.

Longfield, M. (1834) *Lectures on Political Economy*, London: Milliken.

Loomes, G. (1991) 'Experimental methods in economics', in D. Greenaway, M. Bleaney and I. Stewart (eds) *Companion to Contemporary Economic Thought*, London and New York: Routledge.

Lucas, R. E., Jr (1972) 'Expectations and the neutrality of money', *Journal of Economic Theory* 4, 2: 103–24.

Lucas, R. E., Jr (1973) 'Some international evidence on output–inflation trade-offs', *American Economic Review* 63, 3: 326–34.

Lucas, R. E., Jr (1976) 'Econometric policy evaluation: a critique', *Journal of Monetary Economics* 1, 2: 19–46.

Lucas, R. E., Jr (1993) 'General equilibrium conference: money and macroeconomics', CORE discussion paper 9482, Louvain: Université Catholique de Louvain, 184–7.

Lunghini, G. (1997) 'Equilibrium, reproduction and crisis', in G. Caravale (ed.) *Equilibrium and Economic Theory*, London and New York: Routledge.

McCloskey, D. (1985) *The Rhetoric of Economics*, Madison WI: University of Wisconsin Press.

McCombie, J. S. L. (1998) 'Keynes, involuntary unemployment and wage and price inflexibility', in S. Sharma (ed.) *John Maynard Keynes. Keynesianism into the Twenty-first Century*, Cheltenham: Elgar.

McCulloch, J. R. (1823) 'Political economy', *Supplement to the Encyclopaedia Britannica*, April, VI, I: 2–64.

McCulloch, J. R. (1825) *The Principles of Political Economy*, Edinburgh: Tait.

McCulloch, J. R. (1845) *The Literature of Political Economy. A Classified Catalogue of Select Publications in the Different Departments of that Science*, London: Longman.

McDowell, J. (1980) 'The role of *Eidaimonia* in Aristotle's ethics', in A. O. Rorty (ed.) *Essays on Aristotle's Ethics*, Berkeley CA: University of California Press.

MacIntyre, A. (1981) *After Virtue*, London: Notre Dame University Press.

Magnusson, L. (ed.) (1993) *Mercantilist Economics*, Boston MA: Kluwer.

Malinvaud, E. (1977 and 1985) *The Theory of Unemployment Reconsidered*, 2nd edn, Oxford: Blackwell.

Malinvaud, E. (1984) *Mass Unemployment*, Oxford: Blackwell.

Malinvaud, E. (1999) 'The theory of prices and resource allocation', in A. Kirman and L.-A. Gérard-Varet (eds) *Economics beyond the Millennium*, Oxford: Oxford University Press.

Malthus, T. R. (1815) *An Inquiry into the Nature and Progress of Rent and the Principles by which it is Regulated*, London: John Murray.

Malthus, T. R. (1817) *Essay on Population*, 5th edn, 3 vols, London: John Murray.

Malthus, T. R. (1820) *Principles of Political Economy*, London: John Murray.

Malthus, T. R. (1823) *The Measure of Value Stated and Illustrated*, London: John Murray.

Malthus, T. R. (1836) *Principles of Political Economy*, 2nd edn, London: Pickering.

Mankiw, N. G. (1985) 'Small menu costs and large business cycles: a macroeconomic model of monopoly', *Quarterly Journal of Economics* 100, 2: 529–38.

Mankiw, N. G. (1989) 'Real business cycles: a New Keynesian perspective', *Journal of Economic Perspectives* 3, 3: 79–90.

Mankiw, N. G. (1991) 'Imperfect competition and the Keynesian cross', in N. G. Mankiw and D. Romer (eds) *New Keynesian Economics*, I *Imperfect Competition and Sticky Prices*, Cambridge MA: MIT Press. First published in *Economic Letters* (1988), 26, 1: 7–13.

Mankiw, N. G. (1992) 'The reincarnation of Keynesian economics', *European Economic Review* 36, 2–3: 559–65.

Mankiw, N. G. and Romer, D. (eds) (1991a) *New Keynesian Economics*, I *Imperfect Competition and Sticky Prices*, II *Coordination Failures and Real Rigidities*, Cambridge MA: MIT Press.

Mankiw, N. G. and Romer, D. (1991b) 'Introduction', in N. G. Mankiw and D. Romer (eds) *New Keynesian Economics*, I *Imperfect Competition and Sticky Prices*, Cambridge MA: MIT Press.

Marcus, R. B. (1980) 'Moral dilemmas and ethical consistency', *Journal of Philosophy* 77: 121–36.

Marget, A. W. (1938–42) *The Theory of Prices. A Re-examination of the Central Problems of Monetary Theory*, 2 vols, reprinted, New York: Kelley (1966).

Marris, R. (1991) *Reconstructing Keynesian Economics with Imperfect Competition. A Desk-top Simulation*, Aldershot: Elgar.

Marris, R. (1997) 'Yes, Mrs Robinson!', in G. C. Harcourt and P. A. Riach (eds) *A 'Second Edition' of The General Theory*, London and New York: Routledge.

Marschak, T. and Selten, R. (1974) *General Equilibrium with Price-making Firms*, Lecture Notes in Economics and Mathematical Systems, Berlin: Springer.

Marshall, A. (1890) *Principles of Economics*, London and New York: Macmillan.

Marshall, A. (1920) *Principles of Economics*, 8th edn, London and New York: Macmillan.

Marshall, A. (1961) *Principles of Economics* I, 9th (variorum) edn, edited by C. W. Guillebaud, London: Macmillan.

Marx, K. (1862–63) *Theorien über den Mehrwert* (*Vierter Band des 'Kapitals'*), in *Marx-Engels Werke* XXVI, Berlin: Dietz (1965–68).

Marx, K. (1963) [1862–63] *Theories of Surplus Value* I, New York: International Publishers.

Marx, K. (1967) [1867] *Capital* I, New York: International Publishers.

Marx, K. (1967) [1894] *Capital* III, New York: International Publishers.

Marx, K. (1969) [1862–63] *Theories of Surplus Value*, London: Lawrence & Wishart.

Marx, K. (1976) [1867] *Capital*, vol. I of *A Critique of Political Economy*, translated by B. Fowkes, Harmondsworth: Penguin Books.

Mas-Colell, A. (1982) 'The Cournotian foundations of Walrasian equilibrium: an exposition of recent theory', in W. Hildenbrand (ed.) *Advances in Economic Theory*, New York: Cambridge University Press.

Matthews, R. C. O. (1986) 'The economics of institutions and the sources of growth', *Economic Journal* 96: 903–18.

Meek, R. (1967) *Economics and Ideology and other Essays*, London: Chapman & Hall.

Meltzer, A. H. (1988) *Keynes's Monetary Theory. A Different Interpretation*, Cambridge: Cambridge University Press.

Meltzer, A. H. (1996) 'The *General Theory* after sixty years', *Journal of Post-Keynesian Economics* 19, 1: 35–45.

Messori, M. (1991) 'Keynes's *General Theory* and the endogenous money supply', *Economie appliquée* 44, 1: 125–52.

Milgate, M. (1988) 'Controversies in the theory of employment', *Contributions to Political Economy* 7: 65–82.

Mill, J. (1818) 'Colony', in R. A. Fenn (ed.) *Textbook for Utilitarians. James Mill's Articles in the Encyclopaedia Britannica*, Toronto: Fenn.

Mill, J. (1821) *Elements of Political Economy*, London: Baldwin Cradock & Joy.

Mill, J. (1824) *Elements of Political Economy*, 2nd edn, London: Baldwin Cradock & Joy.

Mill, J. (1826) *Elements of Political Economy*, 3rd edn, London: Baldwin.

Mill, J. S. (1961) [1871] *Principles of Political Economy*, edited by W. J. Ashley, reprinted New York: Kelley.

Mill, J. S. (1965) [1848] *Principles of Political Economy*, last (7th) edn by J. S. Mill 1871, in J. M. Robson (ed.), *Collected Works of John Stuart Mill* II–III, Toronto: University of Toronto Press.

Modigliani, F. (1944) 'Liquidity preference and the theory of interest and money', *Econometrica* 12: 45–88.

Modigliani, F. (1963) 'The monetary mechanism and its interaction with real phenomena', *Review of Economics and Statistics* 45: 79–107.

Modigliani, F. and Brunberg, R. (1954) 'Utility analysis and the consumption function: an interpretation of cross-section data', in K. Kurihara (ed.) *Post-Keynesian Economics*, New Brunswick NJ: Rutgers University Press.

Modigliani, F. and Miller, M. (1958) 'The cost of capital, corporate finance and the theory of investment', *American Economic Review* 48, 3: 261–97.

Moggridge, D. E. (1992) *Maynard Keynes. An Economist's Biography*, London: Routledge.

Mongiovi, G. (1996) 'Sraffa's critique of Marshall: a reassessment', *Cambridge Journal of Economics* 20, 2: 207–24.

Mongiovi, G. (2000) 'Note sull'interpretazione Sraffiana di Ricardo', in M. Pivetti and (ed.) *Piero Sraffa. Contributi per una biografia intellettuale*, Rome: Carocci.

Moore, G. E. (1903) *Principia Ethica,* Cambridge: Cambridge University Press.

Morishima, M. (1989) *Ricardo's Economics*, Cambridge: Cambridge University Press.

Morishima, M. (1996) 'Morishima on Ricardo: two replies', *Cambridge Journal of Economics* 20, 2: 91–109.

Morton, A. (1985) 'The variety of rationality', *Proceedings of the Aristotelian Society* 59 (supplement): 139–62.

Morton, A. (1991) *Disasters and Dilemmas. Strategies for Real-life Decision Making*, Oxford: Blackwell.

Muth, J. F. (1961) 'Rational expectations and the theory of price movements', *Econometrica* 29, 3: 315–35.

Negishi, T. (1961) 'Monopolistic competition and general equilibrium', *Review of Economic Studies* 28: 196–201.

Negishi, T. (1972) *General Equilibrium Theory and International Trade*, Amsterdam: North-Holland.

Negishi, T. (1989) 'Monopolistic competition and general equilibrium', in J. Eatwell, M. Milgate and P. Newman (eds) *The New Palgrave. General Equilibrium*, London: Macmillan.

Nell, E. J. (1998) 'Price theory and macroeconomics: stylized facts and New Keynesian fantasies', in R. J. Rotheim (ed.) *New Keynesian Economics/Post-Keynesian Alternatives*, London: Routledge.

Neumann, J. von (1945) [1937] 'A model of general economic equilibrium', *Review of Economic Studies* 13, 1: 1–9. English translation of J. von Neumann, 'Über ein ökonomisches Gleichungssystem und eine Verallgemeinerung des Brouwerschen Fixpunktsatzes', *Ergebnisse eines mathematischen Kolloquiums* 8 (1937): 73–83.

Nicola, P. C. (1994) *Imperfect General Equilibrium. The Economy as an Evolutionary Process: Individualistic, Discrete, Deterministic*, Berlin: Springer.

Nikaido, H. (1975) *Monopolistic Competition and Effective Demand*, Princeton NJ: Princeton University Press.

Nisticò, S. (1991a) 'On Marx's critical reading of Adam Smith's theory of price', in G. Caravale (ed.) *Marx and Modern Economic Analysis*, II *The Future of Capitalism and the History of Thought*, Aldershot: Elgar.

Nisticò, S. (1991b) 'Prices and distributive antagonism in the work of Smith and Kalecki', *Journal of the History of Economic Thought*, 13, 1: 54–69.

Nisticò, S. and D'Orlando, F. (1995) 'Alcune perplessità sulla nuova economia keynesiana', *Studi economici* 50, 57: 53–78.

Nisticò, S., D'Orlando, F. and Scoppola, B. (1998) 'Some questions for New Keynesians', in R. J. Rotheim (ed.) *New Keynesian Economics/Post-Keynesian Alternatives*, London: Routledge.

North, D. C. (1993) 'Institutions and economic performance', in U. Mäki, B. Gustafsson and C. Knudsen (eds) *Rationality, Institutions, and Economic Methodology*, London: Routledge.

Nussbaum, M. C. (1984) 'Plato on commensurability and desire', *Proceedings of the Aristotelian Society*, supplement to vol. 58: 55–80.

Nussbaum, M. C. (1986) *The Fragility of Goodness. Luck and Ethics in Greek Tragedy and Philosophy*, Cambridge: Cambridge University Press.

O'Brien, D. P. (1975) *The Classical Economists*, Oxford: Clarendon Press.

O'Brien, D. P. and Darnell, A. C. (1982) *Authorship Puzzles in the History of Economics*, London: Macmillan.

Obstfeld, M. and Rogoff, K. (1996) *Foundations of International Macroeconomics*, Cambridge MA: MIT Press.

O'Donnell, R. (1990) *Adam Smith's Theory of Value and Distribution*, New York: St Martin's Press.

O'Donnell, R. M. (ed.) (1991) *Keynes as Philosopher-Economist*, London: Macmillan.

O'Donnell, R. M. (1995) 'Keynes on aesthetics', in A. F. Cottrell and M. S. Lawlor (eds) *New Perspectives on Keynes*, Durham NC: Duke University Press.

Pack, S. J. (1997) 'Adam Smith on the virtues: a partial resolution of the Adam Smith problem', *Journal of the History of Economic Thought* 19, 1: 127–40.

Palley, T. (1996) *Post-Keynesian Economics. Debt, Distribution and the Macro-economy*, London: Macmillan.

Pareto, V. (1896–97) *Cours d'économie politique*, 2 vols, Lausanne: Rouge; edited by G.-H. Bousquet and G. Busino, Geneva: Droz (1964).

Pareto, V. (1909) *Manuel d'économie politique*, Paris: Giard & Brière.

Pasinetti, L. L. (1974a) *Growth and Income Distribution. Essays in Economic Theory*, London: Cambridge University Press.

Pasinetti, L. L. (1974b) 'The economics of effective demand', in L. Pasinetti (ed.) *Growth and Income Distribution. Essays in Economic Theory*, London: Cambridge University Press.

Pasinetti, L. L. (1981) *Structural Change and Economic Growth. A Theoretical Essay on the Dynamics of the Wealth of Nations*, Cambridge: Cambridge University Press.

Pasinetti, L. L. (1986) 'Theory of value: a source of alternative paradigms in economic analysis', in M. Baranzini and R. Scazzieri (eds) *Foundations of Economics. Structure of Inquiry and Economic Theory*, Oxford: Blackwell.

Pasinetti, L. L. (1993) *Structural Economic Dynamics. A Theory of the Economic Consequences of Human Learning*, Cambridge: Cambridge University Press.

Pasinetti, L. L. (1997) 'The principle of effective demand', in G. C. Harcourt and P. A. Riach (eds) *A 'Second Edition' of The General Theory*, London and New York: Routledge.

Pasinetti, L. L. (ed.) (1998a) *Italian Economic Papers* III, Bologna: Il Mulino and Oxford: Oxford University Press.

Pasinetti, L. L. (1998b) 'Piero Sraffa: from youth to maturity. Some notes on the evolution of his attitudes and thought', paper presented at the centenary conference on Piero Sraffa, Turin: Fondazione Luigi Einaudi, 15 October 1998.

Patinkin, D. (1957) *Money, Interest and Prices. An Integration of Monetary and Value Theory*, New York: Harper & Row; 2nd edn (1965).

Patinkin, D. (1975) 'The collected writings of John Maynard Keynes from the *Tract* to the *General Theory*', *Economic Journal* 85, 338: 249–71.

Patinkin, D. (1976) *Keynes's Monetary Thought. A Study of its Development*, Durham NC: Duke University Press.

Patinkin, D. (1977) 'The process of writing *The General Theory*: a critical survey', in J. C. Leith and D. Patinkin (eds) *Keynes, Cambridge and the General Theory*, London: Macmillan.

Peach, T. (1993) *Interpreting Ricardo*, Cambridge: Cambridge University Press.

Peach, T. (1998) 'On "interpreting Ricardo": a reply to Sraffians', *Cambridge Journal of Economics* 22, 5: 597–616.

Peart, S. (1990) 'The population mechanism in W. S. Jevons' applied economics', *Manchester School* 58, 1: 32–53.

Perlman, M. (1992) 'Understanding the "old" American institutionalism', *Revue d'économie politique* 102, 2: 281–95.

Persson, T. and Tabellini, G. (eds) (1994) *Monetary and Fiscal Policy*, I *Credibility*, II *Politics*, Cambridge MA and London: MIT Press.

Persson, T. and Tabellini, G. (1997) 'Political economics and macroeconomic policy', in J. Taylor and M. Woodford (eds) *Handbook of Macroeconomics* III, Amsterdam: North-Holland.

Phelps, E. S. (1968) 'Money-wage dynamics and labor-market equilibrium', *Journal of Political Economy* 76, 4: 678–711.

Phelps, E. S. (1992) 'Expectations in macroeconomics and the rational expectations debate', in A. Vercelli and N. Dimitri (eds) *Macroeconomics. A Survey of Research Strategies*, Oxford: Oxford University Press.

Phelps, E. S. and Taylor, J. B. (1977) 'Stabilizing power of monetary policy under rational expectations', *Journal of Political Economy* 85, 1: 163–90.

Phelps, E. S., *et al.* (1970) *Microeconomic Foundations of Employment and Inflation Theory*, New York: Norton.

Phillips, A. W. (1958) 'The relationship between the unemployment rate and the rate of change of money wage rates in the United Kingdom 1861–1957', *Economica* 25, 100: 283–99.

Pigou, A. C. (1950) [1932] *The Economics of Welfare*, 4th edn, London: Macmillan.

Plosser, C. I. (1989) 'Understanding real business cycles', *Journal of Economic Perspectives* 3, 3: 51–77.

Polock, J. (1984) 'How do you maximise expectation value?', *Nous* 17: 409–21.

Porta, P. L. (1982) 'I fondamenti ricardiani del marxismo', *Giornale degli economisti e annali di economia* 41, 11–12: 721–39.

Porta, P. L. (1985) 'The debate on Ricardo: old results in new frameworks', in G. Caravale (ed.) *The Legacy of Ricardo*, Oxford: Blackwell.

Porta, P. L. (1986) 'Understanding the significance of Piero Sraffa's standard commodity: a note on the Marxian notion of surplus', *History of Political Economy* 18, 3: 443–54.

Porta, P. L. (1988) 'The classical theory of price: a note on the Sraffian interpretation', *Economies et sociétés* 22, 10: 53–74.

Porta, P. L. (1990) 'David Ricardo: la sistemazione teorica della concorrenza e del mercato', in G. Becattini (ed.) *Il pensiero economico. Temi, problemi e scuole*, Turin: UTET.

Porta, P. L. (1991) 'Sundry observations on the concept of exploitation', in G. Caravale (ed.) *Marx and Modern Economic Analysis*, I *Values, Prices and Exploitation*, Aldershot: Elgar.

Porta, P. L. (1992) 'Piero Sraffa, "superb editor"', *Revue européenne des sciences sociales* 30, 92: 25–34.

Porta, P. L. (1996) 'Piero Sraffa and the Mill–Ricardo papers: a rejoinder', *Cambridge Journal of Economics* 20, 5: 641–3.

Potestio, P. (1986) 'Equilibrium and employment in *The General Theory*', *Giornale degli economisti e annali di economia* 45, 7–8: 363–88.

Potestio, P. (1989) 'Alternative aspects of monetary theory in the *General Theory*: significance and implications', *Recherches économiques de Louvain* 55, 1989: 257–72.

Potier, J. P. (1991) *Piero Sraffa. Unorthodox Economist 1898–1983. A Biographical Essay*, London: Routledge.

Prescott, E. C. (1986) 'Theory ahead of business cycle measurement', *Carnegie Rochester Conference Series on Public Policy* 25: 11–44.

Preti, G. (1986) *Il problema dei valori: l'Etica di G. E. Moore*, Milan: Angeli.

Prychitko, D. L. (ed.) (1977) *Why Economists Disagree. An Introduction to the Alternative Schools of Thought*, Ithaca NY: State University of New York Press.

Raffaelli, T. (1996) 'La formazione di Keynes nel laboratorio marshalliano', *Rivista italiana degli economisti* 1, 1: 125–46.

Ricardo, D. (1817) *The Principles of Political Economy, and Taxation*, London: Murray.

Ricardo, D. (1821) *On the Principles of Political Economy, and Taxation*, 3rd edn, London: Murray; reprinted in *The Works and Correspondence of David Ricardo*, edited by P. Sraffa with M. H. Dobb, Cambridge: Cambridge University Press (1951–73), vol. I.

Ricardo, D. (1823) 'Absolute value and exchangeable value', in *The Works and Correspondence of David Ricardo*, edited by P. Sraffa with M. H. Dobb, Cambridge: Cambridge University Press (1951–73), vol. IV.

Ricardo, D. (1951–73) *The Works and Correspondence of David Ricardo*, edited by P. Sraffa with the collaboration of M. H. Dobb, 11 vols, Cambridge: Cambridge University Press.

Ricardo, D. (1992) *Notes on Mr. Malthus's 'Measure of Value'*, edited by P. L. Porta, Cambridge: Cambridge University Press.

Roberts, J. and Sonnenschein, H. (1977) 'On the foundations of the theory of monopolistic competition', *Econometrica* 45, 1: 101–13.

Roberts, K. (1980) 'The limit points of monopolistic competition', *Journal of Economic Theory* 22, 2: 256–78.

Robertson, D. H. (1926) *Banking Policy and the Price Level*, London: King.

Robertson, D. H. (1935) 'Letter to J. M. Keynes' (3 February), in J. M. Keynes, *The Collected Writings of J. M. Keynes*, edited by D. E. Moggridge, London: Macmillan (1971–89), XIII: 496–7.

Robinson, A. (1951) Review of *The Works and Correspondence of David Ricardo, Economic Journal* 61, 3: 849–51.

Robinson, J. (1933) *The Economics of Imperfect Competition*, London: Macmillan.

Robinson, J. (1956) *The Accumulation of Capital*, London: Macmillan.

Robinson, J. (1966) 'Marx and Keynes', in *Collected Economic Papers* I, Oxford: Blackwell.

Robinson, J. (1977) 'What are the questions?', *Journal of Economic Literature* 15, 4: 1318–39.

Robinson, J. and Wilkinson, F. (1985) 'Ideology and logic', in F. Vicarelli (ed.) *Keynes's Relevance Today*, Philadelphia PA: University of Pennsylvania Press.

Rodano, G. (1996) 'Tendenze del pensiero economico contemporaneo', in L. Geymonat, *Storia del pensiero filosofico e scientifico* IX, 4: *Il Novecento*, edited by E. Bellone and C. Mangione, Milan: Garzanti.

Rodano, G. (1997) 'La scuola neoclassica nella macroeconomia contemporanea', *Rivista italiana degli economisti* 2, 3: 383–424.

Rogers, C. (1998) 'Post-Keynesian and strong New Keynesian macroeconomics: compatible bedfellows?', in R. J. Rotheim (ed.) *New Keynesian Economics/Post-Keynesian Alternatives*, London: Routledge.

Romer, D. (1993) 'The New Keynesian synthesis', *Journal of Economic Perspectives* 7, 1: 5–22.

Romer, D. (1996) *Advanced Macroeconomics*, New York: McGraw-Hill.

Romer, D. (2000) 'Keynesian macroeconomics without the LM curve', *Journal of Economic Perspectives* 14: 149–69.

Roncaglia, A. (1990) 'Comment on P. Garegnani', in K. Bharadwaj and B. Schefold (eds) *Essays on Piero Sraffa. Critical Perspectives on the Revival of Classical Theory*, London: Unwin Hyman.

Roncaglia, A. (1996a) 'The classical approach and long-period positions: a comment on Cesaratto', *Review of Political Economy* 8, 4: 403–8.

Roncaglia, A. (1996b) 'Why should economists study the history of economic thought?', *European Journal of the History of Economic Thought* 3, 2: 296–309.

Rosen, S. (1997) 'Austrian and neoclassical economics: any gains from trade?', *Journal of Economic Perspectives* 11, 4: 139–52.

Ross, W. D. (1963) *The Right and the Good*, Oxford: Oxford University Press.

Rosselli, R. (2001) 'Sraffa's edition of Ricardo's *Work*: reconstruction of a reconstruction', in T. Cozzi and R. Marchionatti (eds) *Piero Sraffa's Political Economy. A Centenary Estimate*, London: Routledge.

Rosser, J. B. (1998) 'Complex dynamics in New Keynesian and Post-Keynesian models', in R. J. Rotheim (ed.) *New Keynesian Economics/Post-Keynesian Alternatives*, London: Routledge.

Rotemberg, J. J. and Woodford, M. (1997) 'An optimization-based econometric framework for the evaluation of monetary policy', in B. S. Bernanke and J. J. Rotemberg (eds) *NBER Macroeconomics Annual 1997*, Cambridge MA and London: MIT Press.

Rotheim, R. J. (1995) 'Keynes on uncertainty and individual behaviour within a theory of effective demand', in S. Dow and J. Hillard (eds) *Keynes, Knowledge and Uncertainty*, Aldershot: Elgar.

Rotheim, R. J. (ed.) (1998a) *New Keynesian Economics/Post-Keyensian Alternatives*, London: Routledge.

Rotheim, R. J. (1998b) 'New Keynesian macroeconomics and markets', in R. J. Rotheim (ed.) *New Keynesian Economics/Post-Keynesian Alternatives*, London: Routledge.

Rowthorn, B. (1974) 'Neo-classicism, neo-Ricardianism and Marxism', *New Left Review* 29: 34–69.

Sabooglu, M. (1996) 'Hayek and spontaneous orders', *Journal of the History of Economic Thought* 18, 2: 347–64.

Sacco, P. L. (1996) 'Coordinating coordination failures: does risk-dominance help?', *Economic Notes* 25, 2: 369–91.

Salop, S. C. (1985) 'Practices that (credibly) facilitate oligopoly coordination', in J. E. Stiglitz and C. F. Mathewson (eds) *New Developments in Market Structure*, Cambridge: Cambridge University Press.

Samuels, W. J. (1987) 'Institutional economics', in *The New Palgrave. A Dictionary of Economics* II. London: Macmillan.

Samuels, W. J. (1988) 'Schumpeter's treatment of Samuelson', *History of Economic Society Bulletin* 10: 25–31.

Samuelson, P. A. (1958) 'An exact consumption–loan model of interest with or without the social contrivance of money', *Journal of Political Economy* 66, 6: 467–82.

Samuelson, P. A. (1962), 'Parable and realism in capital theory: the surrogate production function', *Review of Economic Studies* 29: 193–206.

Samuelson, P. A. (1978) 'The canonical classical model of political economy', *Journal of Economic Literature* 16, 4: 1415–34.

Samuelson, P. A. (1987a) 'Out of the closet: a program for the Whig history of economic science', *History of Economic Society Bulletin* 9: 51–60.

Samuelson, P. A. (1987b) 'Sraffian economics', in *The New Palgrave. A Dictionary of Economics* IV, London: Macmillan.

Samuelson, P. A. (1991) 'Sraffa's other leg', *Economic Journal* 101, 406: 570–4.

Samuelson, P. A. (2000) 'Sraffa's hits and misses', in H. D. Kurz (ed.) *Critical Essays on Piero Sraffa's Legacy in Economics*, Cambridge: Cambridge University Press.

Samuelson, P. A. and Nordhaus, W. D. (1992) [1981] *Economics*, 14th edn, New York: McGraw-Hill.

Sargent, T. (1973) 'Rational expectations, the real rate of interest, and the natural rate of unemployment', *Brookings Papers on Economic Activity* 2: 429–72.

Sawyer, M. (1998) 'New Keynesian macroeconomics and the determination of employment and wages', in R. J. Rotheim (ed.) *New Keynesian Economics/Post-Keynesian Alternatives*, London: Routledge.

Scheffler, S. (1982) *The Rejection of Consequentialism*, Oxford: Oxford University Press.

Schefold, B. (1985) 'Sraffa and applied economics: joint production', *Political Economy. Studies in the Surplus Approach* 1, 1: 17–40.

Schefold, B. (1989) *Mr Sraffa on Joint Production and other Essays*, London: Macmillan.

Schefold, B. (1996) 'Piero Sraffa 1898–1983', *Economic Journal* 106, 438: 1314–25.

Schefold, B. (1998) 'Reading Sraffa's indices: a note', *European Journal of the History of Economic Thought* 5, 3: 468–79.

Schefold, B. (2000) 'Paradoxes of capital and counterintuitive changes of distribution in an intertemporal equilibrium model', in H. D. Kurz (ed.) *Critical Essays on Piero Sraffa's Legacy in Economics*, Cambridge: Cambridge University Press.

Schotter, A. (1981) *The Economic Theory of Social Institutions*, Cambridge: Cambridge University Press.

Schulz, N. (1983) 'On the global uniqueness of fix-price equilibria', *Econometrica* 51, 1: 47–68.

Schumpeter, J. A. (1954) *A History of Economic Analysis*, New York and Oxford: Oxford University Press.

Sebastiani, M. (ed.) (1992) *The Notion of Equilibrium in the Keynesian Theory*, London: Macmillan.

Semmler, W. (1987) 'Competition: Marxian conceptions', in *The New Palgrave. A Dictionary of Economics* I, London: Macmillan.

Sen, A. (1974) 'On some debates in capital theory', *Economica* 41(163): 328–35.

Sen, A. (1981) 'Plural utility', *Proceedings of the Aristotelian Society* 81: 193–215.

Sen, A. and Williams, B. A. O. (eds) (1982) *Utilitarianism and Beyond*, Cambridge: Cambridge University Press.

Senior, N. (1830) *Three Lectures on the Cost of Obtaining Money*, London: Murray.

Senior, N. (1836) *Outline of the Science of Political Economy*, London: Clowes.

Senior, N. (1852) *Four Introductory Lectures on Political Economy*, London: Longman.

Seton, F. (1957) 'The transformation problem', *Review of Economic Studies* 24: 149–60.

Sharma, S. (ed.) (1998) *John Maynard Keynes. Keynesianism into the Twenty-first Century*, Cheltenham and Northampton MA: Elgar.

Silvestre, J. (1977) 'A model of general equilibrium with monopolistic behavior', *Journal of Economic Theory* 16, 2: 425–42.

Silvestre, J. (1993) 'The market power foundations of macroeconomic policy', *Journal of Economic Literature* 31, 1: 105–41.

Sinnot-Amstrong, W. (1985) 'Moral dilemmas and incomparability', *American Philosophical Quarterly* 20: 321–9.

Sinnot-Amstrong, W. (1987) 'Moral dilemmas and moral realism', *Journal of Philosophy* 84: 263–76.

Sinnot-Amstrong, W. (1988) *Moral Dilemmas*, Oxford: Blackwell.

Skidelsky, R. (1983) *J. M. Keynes. Hopes Betrayed 1883–1920*, London: Macmillan.

Skidelsky, R. (1991) 'Keynes's philosophy of practice and economic politics', in R. M. O'Donnell (ed.) *Keynes as Philosopher-Economist*, London: Macmillan.

Skidelsky, R. (1996) 'After serfdom: Hayek and the death of collectivism', *Times Literary Supplement*, 20 September.

Slote, M. (1983) *Goods and Virtues*, Oxford: Clarendon Press.

Slote, M. (1985a) *Commonsense Morality and Consequentialism*, London: Routledge & Kegan Paul.

Slote, M. (1985b) 'Utilitarianism, moral dilemmas, and moral cost', *American Philosophical Quarterly* 22: 161–8.

Slote, M. (1986) 'Rational dilemmas and rational supererogation', *Philosophical Topics* 14, 2; reprinted in M. Slote (ed.) *Beyond Optimizing. A Study of Rational Choice*, Cambridge MA: Harvard University Press.

Slote, M. (1989) *Beyond Optimizing. A Study of Rational Choice*, Cambridge MA: Harvard University Press.

Smart, J. J. C. and Williams, B. A. O. (eds) (1973) *Utilitarianism. For and Against*, Cambridge: Cambridge University Press.

Smith, A. (1950) [1776] *The Wealth of Nations* I, London: Dent.

Smith, A. (1976) [1776] *An Inquiry into the Nature and Causes of the Wealth of Nations*, edited by E. Cannan, Chicago: University of Chicago Press.

Smith, A. (1983) [1762–63] *Lectures on Rhetoric and Belles Lettres*, Oxford: Clarendon Press.

Snowdon, B. and Vane, H. (eds) (1997) *Reflections on the Development of Modern Macroeconomics*, Cheltenham and Lyme NH: Elgar.

Snowdon, B., Vane, H. and Wynarczyk, P. (1994) *A Modern Guide to Macroeconomics. An Introduction to Competing Schools of Thought*, Aldershot: Elgar.

Solow, R. M. (1956) 'A contribution to the theory of economic growth', *Quarterly Journal of Economics* 70, 1: 65–94.

Solow, R. M. (1990) *The Labour Market as a Social Institution*, Oxford: Blackwell.

Solow, R. M. (1997) 'Is there a core of usable macroeconomics we should all believe in?', *American Economic Review* 87, 2: 230–2.

Solow, R. M. (1998) *Monopolistic Competition and Macroeconomic Theory*, Cambridge: Cambridge University Press.

Solow, R. M. (2000) 'Toward a macroeconomics of the medium run', *Journal of Economic Perspectives* 14: 151–8.

Sonnenschein, H. (1985) 'Imperfect competition in general equilibrium: an overview of recent work: comment', in K. J. Arrow and S. Honkapohja (eds) *Frontiers of Economics*, Oxford: Blackwell.

Spray, D. E. (ed.) (1964) *The Principal Stock Exchanges of the World. Their Operation, Structure and Development*, Washington DC: International Economic Publishers.

Sraffa, P. (1922) 'The bank crisis in Italy', *Economic Journal* 32: 178–97.

Sraffa, P. (1925) 'Sulle relazioni fra costo e quantità prodotta', *Annali di Economia* 2, 1: 277–328. Translated into English in L. L. Pasinetti (ed.) *Italian Economic Papers* III, Bologna: Il Mulino and Oxford: Oxford University Press.

Sraffa, P. (1926) 'The laws of returns under competitive conditions', *Economic Journal* 36, 144: 535–50.

Sraffa, P. (1930) 'A criticism' and 'Rejoinder', contributions to the symposium on Increasing Returns and the Representative Firm, *Economic Journal* 40: 89–93.

Sraffa, P. (1932a) 'Dr Hayek on money and capital', *Economic Journal* 42: 42–53.

Sraffa, P. (1932b) 'Rejoinder', *Economic Journal* 42: 249–51.

Sraffa, P. (1951) Introduction to *The Works and Correspondence of David Ricardo*, in *The Works and Correspondence of David Ricardo*, edited by P. Sraffa with the collaboration of M. H. Dobb, Cambridge: Cambridge University Press (1951–73), I: xiii–lxii.

Sraffa, P. (1960) *Production of Commodities by Means of Commodities. Prelude to a Critique of Economic Theory*, Cambridge: Cambridge University Press.

Stahn, H. (1993) 'A remark on the uniqueness of fix-price equilibria in an economy with production', *Journal of Mathematical Economics* 22, 5: 421–30.

Stahn, H. (1996) 'Un modèle de concurrence monopolistique: une approche en équilibre général', *Annales d'économie et de statistique* 43: 29–56.

Staiger, D., Stock, J. H. and Watson, M. W. (1997) 'The NAIRU, unemployment and monetary policy', *Journal of Economic Perspectives* 11, 1: 33–49.

Steedman, I. (1984) 'Natural prices, differential profit rates and the classical competitive process', *Manchester School* 52, 2: 123–40.

Steedman, I. (ed.) (1988) *Sraffian Economics*, 2 vols, Aldershot: Elgar.

Stern, S. (1997) 'Simulation-based estimation', *Journal of Economic Literature* 35, 4: 2006–39.
Stewart, I. M. T. (1991) 'The role of the methodologist', in D. Greenaway, M. Bleaney and I. Stewart (eds) *Companion to Contemporary Economic Thought*, London and New York: Routledge.
Stigler, G. J. (1953) 'Sraffa's Ricardo', *American Economic Review* 43, 4: 586–99; also in *Essays in the History of Economics*, Chicago: University of Chicago Press (1965).
Stigler, G. J. (1981) Review of S. Hollander, *The Economics of David Ricardo*, *Journal of Economic Literature* 19, 1: 100–2.
Stigler, G. J. (1982) *The Economist as Preacher and other Essays*, Chicago: University of Chicago Press.
Stigler, G. J. (1990) 'Ricardo or Hollander?', *Oxford Economic Papers* 42, 4: 765–8.
Stiglitz, J. E. (1989) *The Economic Role of the State*, Oxford: Blackwell.
Stiglitz, J. E. (1993) 'Post-Walrasian and post-Marxian economics', *Journal of Economic Perspectives* 7, 1: 109–14.
Stiglitz, J. E. (1994) *Whither Socialism?*, Cambridge MA and London: MIT Press.
Stiglitz, J. E. (1997) 'Reflections on the natural rate hypothesis', *Journal of Economic Perspectives* 11, 1: 3–10.
Stocker, M. (1990) *Plural and Conflicting Values*, Oxford: Oxford University Press.
Summers, L. H. (1988) 'Relative wages, efficiency wages, and Keynesian unemployment', *American Economic Review* 78, 2: 383–8.
Swartz, T. R. and Bonello, F. J. (1997) *Taking Sides. Clashing Views on Controversial Economic Issues*, 8th edn, Guilford CT: Dushkin/McGraw-Hill.
Sylos Labini, P. (1993) *Carlo Marx: e' tempo di bilancio*, Bari: Laterza.
Tamborini, R. (1995) 'Price determination in polypolistic markets and exchange rate changes', *Metroeconomica* 46, 1: 63–89.
Tarantelli, E. (1986) *Economia politica del lavoro*, Turin: UTET.
Taylor, C. (1982) 'The diversity of goods', in A. Sen and B. Williams (eds) *Utilitarianism and Beyond*, Cambridge: Cambridge University Press.
Taylor, J. B. (1985) 'Rational expectations models in macroeconomics', in K. J. Arrow and S. Honkapohja (eds) *Frontiers of Economics*, Oxford: Blackwell.
Taylor, J. B. (1993) 'Discretion versus policy rules in practice', *Carnegie Rochester Conference Series on Public Policy* 39: 195–214.
Taylor, J. B. (1997) 'A core of practical macroeconomics', *American Economic Review* 87, 2: 233–5.
The New Palgrave. A Dictionary of Economics (1987) edited by J. Eatwell, M. Milgate and P. Newman, 4 vols, London: Macmillan.
Tobin, J. (1956) 'The interest-elasticity of transactions demand for cash', *Review of Economics and Statistics* 38, 3: 241–7.
Tobin, J. (1958) 'Liquidity preference as a behavior towards risk', *Review of Economic Studies* 25: 65–86.
Tobin, J. (1969) 'A general equilibrium approach to monetary theory', *Journal of Money, Credit and Banking* 1, 1: 15–29.
Tobin, J. (1993) 'Price flexibility and output stability: an old Keynesian view', *Journal of Economic Perspectives* 7, 1: 45–65.
Tobin, J. (1997) 'An overview of *The General Theory*', in G. C. Harcourt and P. A. Riach (eds) *A 'Second Edition' of The General Theory*, London and New York: Routledge.
Tonveronachi, M. (1992) 'Keynes and equilibrium: a note', in M. Sebastiani (ed.) *The Notion of Equilibrium in the Keynesian Theory*, London: Macmillan.
Torrens, R. (1815) *An Essay on the External Corn Trade*, London: Hatchard.
Torrens, R. (1820) *An Essay on the External Corn Trade*, 2nd edn, London: Hatchard.

Torrens, R. (1821) *An Essay on the Production of Wealth*, London: Longman.

Torrens, R. (1826) *An Essay on the External Corn Trade*, 3rd edn, London: Longman.

Torrens, R. (1829) *An Essay on the External Corn Trade*, a new edition, London: Longman.

Torrens, R. (1834) *On Wages and Combination*, London: Longman.

Tuchscherer, T. (1979) 'Keynes's model and the Keynesians: a synthesis', *Journal of Post Keynesian Economics* 1, 4: 96–109.

Tuchscherer, T. (1984) 'Meltzer on Keynes's labor market theory: a review of *The General Theory*'s second chapter', *Journal of Post Keynesian Economics* 6, 4: 523–31.

Turgot, A. R. J. (1844) [1767] 'Observations sur le mémoire de M. de Saint-Peravy', in E. Daire and H. Dussard (eds) *Oeuvres de Turgot* I, Paris: Guillaumin.

Van Ees, H. and Garretsen, H. (1992) 'On the contributions of New Keynesian economics', *Eastern Economic Journal* 18, 4: 465–77.

Van Huyck, J. B., Battalio, R. C. and Beil, R. O. (1990) 'Tacit coordination games, strategic uncertainty and coordination failure', *American Economic Review* 80, 1: 234–48.

Veblen, T. (1898) 'Why is economics not an evolutionary science?', *Quarterly Journal of Economics* 12: 373–97.

Vercelli, A. (1991) *Methodological Foundations of Macroeconomics: Keynes and Lucas*, Cambridge: Cambridge University Press.

Vercelli, A. (1997) 'Equilibrium, disequilibrium and macroeconomic theory', in G. Caravale (ed.) *Equilibrium and Economic Theory*, London: Routledge.

Vercelli, A. and Dimitri, N. (eds) (1992) *Macroeconomics. A Survey of Research Strategies*, Oxford: Oxford University Press.

Vicarelli, F. (ed.) (1985) *Keynes's Relevance Today*, Philadelphia PA: University of Pennsylvania Press.

Walker, D. A. (1986) 'Keynes as a historian of economic thought: the perspectives of the *General Theory*', *Research in the History of Economic Thought and Methodology* 4: 1–36.

Walker, D. A. (1988) 'Ten major problems in the study of the history of economic thought', *History of Economics Society Bulletin* 10, 2: 99–115.

Walker, D. A. (1997) *Advances in General Equilibrium Theory*, Cheltenham and Lyme NH: Elgar.

Walras, A. (1849) *Théorie de la richesse sociale*, in Auguste and Léon Walras, *Œuvres économiques complètes* II, Paris: Economica.

Walras, L. (1874) *Eléments d'économie politique pure ou théorie de la richesse sociale*, Lausanne: Corbaz; Paris: Guillaumin; Basel: Georg.

Walras, L. (1881) 'Théorie mathématique du bimétallisme', *Journal des économistes, revue de la science économique et de la statistique*, 4th series, 14, 41: 189–99.

Walras, L. (1889) *Eléments d'économie politique pure ou Théorie de la richesse sociale*, 2nd edn, Lausanne: Rouge; Paris: Guillaumin; Leipzig: Duncker & Humblot.

Walras, L. (1900) *Eléments d'économie politique pure ou théorie de la richesse sociale*, 4th edn, Lausanne: Rouge; Paris: Pichon.

Walras, L. (1905) 'Cournot et l'économie mathématique', *Gazette de Lausanne*, 13 July; and in *Mélanges d'économie politique et sociale*, edited by C. Hébert and J.-P. Potier, in the *Œuvres économiques complètes* VII, Paris: Economica.

Walras, L. (1954) [1874] *Elements of Pure Economics*, translated by W. Jaffé, London: Allen & Unwin.

Walras, L. (1965) *Correspondence of Léon Walras and Related Papers*, 3 vols, edited by W. Jaffé, Amsterdam: North-Holland.

Walras, L. (1987) *Mélanges d'économie politique et sociale*, edited by C. Hébert and J.-P. Potier, in Auguste and Léon Walras, *Œuvres économiques complètes* VII, Paris: Economica.

Walras, L. (1988) *Eléments d'économie politique pure ou théorie de la richesse sociale*, comparative edition by C. Mouchot, in Auguste and Léon Walras, *Œuvres économiques complètes* VIII, Paris: Economica.

Walsh, V. and Gram, H. (1980) *Classical and Neoclassical Theories of General Equilibrium*, New York: Oxford University Press.

Waterman, A. M. C. (1998) 'Reappraisal of "Malthus the Economist, 1933–97"', *History of Political Economy* 30, 2: 293–334.

Weitzman, M. L. (1982) 'Increasing returns and the foundation of unemployment theory', *Economic Journal* 92, 368: 787–804.

West, E. (1815) *Essay on the Application of Capital to Land*, London: Underwood.

West, E. (1826) *Price of Corn and Wages of Labour*, London: Hatchard.

Whewell, W. (1831) *Mathematical Exposition of Some of the Leading Doctrines in Mr. Ricardo's 'Principles of Political Economy and Taxation'*, Cambridge: Smith.

Wicksell, K. (1898) *Geldzins und Güterpreise. Eine Studie über die den Tauschwert des Geldes Bestimmenden Urasachen*, Jena: Fischer.

Wiggins, D. (1976) 'Truth invention and the meaning of life', *Proceedings of the British Academy* LXII; reprinted in D. Wiggins, *Needs, Values, Truth. Essays in the Philosophy of Value*, Oxford: Blackwell (1987).

Wiggins, D. (1979) 'Weakness of will, commensurability, and the objects of deliberation and desire', *Proceedings of the Aristotelian Society* 79: 251–77.

Williams, B. A. O. (1965) 'Ethical consistency?', *Proceedings of the Aristotelian Society* 39: 103–24; also in B. A. O. Williams, *Problems of the Self*, Cambridge: Cambridge University Press (1973).

Williams, B. A. O. (1966) 'Consistency and realism', *Proceedings of the Aristotelian Society*, supplementary volume.

Williams, B. A. O. (1979) 'Conflicts of values', in A. Ryan (ed.) *The Idea of Freedom: Essays in Honour of Isaiah Berlin*, Oxford: Oxford University Press; reprinted in B. A. O. Williams, *Moral Luck. Philosophical Papers 1973–80*, Cambridge: Cambridge University Press.

Williams, B. A. O. (1981) *Moral Luck. Philosophical Papers 1973–80*, Cambridge: Cambridge University Press.

Williams, B. A. O. (1985) *Ethics and the Limits of Philosophy*, Cambridge MA: Harvard University Press.

Williamson, O. E. (1981) 'The modern corporation: origins, evolution, attributes', *Journal of Economic Literature* 19, 4: 1537–68.

Williamson, O. E. (1985) *The Economic Institutions of Capitalism. Firms, Markets, Relational Contracting*, New York: Free Press.

Winch, D. (1997) 'Adam Smith's problems and ours', *Scottish Journal of Political Economy* 44, 4: 384–402.

Woodford, M. (1999) 'Revolution and evolution in twentieth-century macroeconomics', paper presented at the conference on Frontiers of the Mind in the Twenty-first Century, Washington DC: Library of Congress, 14–18 June 1999; in P. Gifford (ed.) *Frontiers of the Mind in the Twenty-first Century*, Cambridge MA: Harvard University Press (forthcoming).

Wright, G. H. von (1963) *The Varieties of Goodness*, London: Macmillan.

Zaghini, E. (1990) 'Quale equilibrio?', *Economia Politica* 7, 1: 3–12.

Zaghini, E. (1993) 'Equilibrio istantaneo ed equilibrio dinamico nella teoria walrasiana', in E. Zaghini (ed.) *Economia matematica. Equilibri e dinamica*, Turin: UTET.

Zamagni, S. (1990) 'On changes in the composition of output: comment', in K. Bharadwaj and B. Schefold (eds) *Essays on Piero Sraffa. Critical Perspectives on the Revival of Classical Theory*, London: Unwin Hyman.

Index

adding up 3; determination of prices by A. Smith 118, 120; English term coined by Sraffa 136–7; notion derived from Marx 149, 153
Aeschylus 251, 269, 276
Aghion, P. 324
Akerlof, G. A. 243, 288, 299
Aksoy, E. G. 95
Alvi, E. 244
Amendola, M. 4–5, 236, 241
Anagnostopoulos, G. 277
Ardeni, P. G. 324
Arestis, P. 298
Aristotle 254–5, 257, 260–5, 268, 272, 277
Arrow, K. J. 5, 29, 91, 115, 131–2, 198–9, 201–3, 209, 211, 213–14, 231–3, 286, 294, 304, 324–5, 333, 336, 342, 344–5
Arrow–Debreu model 5, 91, 304
Artaud, A. 269
Ashley, W. J. 132, 147
Aspromourgos, T. 82
Aumann, R. J. 216, 310–11, 323
Aumann's criterion 310–11, 323
Austrian: school 18, 20, 323; theory 182; view 91

Backhouse, R. E. 91, 94
Bailey, S. 41, 43, 49–50, 55–6, 95
Balasko, Y. 212
Ball, L. 244–6, 287, 297–8
Balzano, B. 298
bankruptcy 7, 352–3, 359
Barkai, H. 95
Barnett, W. A. 20
Barro, R. 318
Bastiat, F. 92
Baumol, W. J. 9, 64, 313, 323
Begg, D. K. H. 322
Benassy, J. P. 226–7, 232
Berlin, I. 278
Bertrand, J. 198, 206, 222–6, 229, 232
Besicovitch, A. S. 184
Bharadwaj, K. 77, 81, 86, 90–1, 139, 180, 196
Bhaskar, V. 245
Bidard, C. 196
Blake, W. 268
Blanchard, O. J. 1–2, 6, 243, 290, 306, 315, 317–18, 322, 324–5
Blaug, M. 2–3, 9, 76–8, 80, 83–6, 88–92, 94–5, 97–100, 115, 129, 133, 164, 186, 196
Blinder, A. S. 246, 298
Bliss, C. 297
Boggio, L. 92
Böhm, V. 218, 221
Böhm-Bawerk, E. von 23, 182, 191
Boitani, A. 4–5, 243–5, 297–8, 322
Boland, L. A. 324
Bonanno, G. 198, 209–10, 223
Bonello, F. J. 19
Bortkiewicz, L. von 10, 75, 99, 118, 196
Bowles, S. 295
Brentano, F. 261
Brewer, A. A. 60–1, 64–5
Bronfenbrenner, M. 151, 160
Broome, J. 278
Brothwell, J. F. 286
Brunberg, R. 323
Buridan, G. 273, 275
Burke, E. 249–50, 253, 260, 265, 268, 270–1
Burnyeat, M. 264
Butterfield, H. 80

Cairnes, J. E. 41, 43, 51, 57–8, 63, 65, 144–5
Caldwell, B. 18
Cambridge 'Circus' 193
Cambridge controversies 177
Cannan, E. 78, 132, 137, 143–4, 153
canonical classical growth model 3, 41–66 *passim*; its consistency with the natural equilibrium interpretation of Ricardo's theory 116, 123; the limits of 102–4, 122
Cantillon, R. 82

capital 16, 41, 84, 93, 101–2, 147, 164, 176, 236, 292–3; accumulation of 41–66 *passim*, 72, 77–8, 82–3, 94, 103, 122, 125, 164, 174, 184, 189, 242; circulating 126; fixed 75, 149, 184, 189, 191, 195; liberalisation of 348–50; marginal efficiency of 194–5, 292; the marginalist theory and the problem of 75–6, 157, 177, 182, 189–90; 'quantity' of 190–1; real 249, 275; stock of 170, 173–5, 192
capital critique 156
capital market: as a fictitious conceptualisation 6, 300–3
capital–labour ratio 191–2
Carabelli, A. 5, 249, 264, 277, 279, 281
Caravale, G. 1–2, 4, 6–13, 27, 33, 39, 94–5, 97, 106, 113, 120–1, 129–30, 153, 163–5, 167–70, 173–6, 196–8, 203, 231, 233, 247, 280, 282–3, 329, 340, 348, 354–5, 357, 361–3
Carey, H. C. 145
Carlin, W. 287
Carlsson, H. 246
Carvalho, F. J. C. 175
Casarosa, C. 129, 285
Caserta, M. 167–8, 174
Cass, D. 315
Cassell, K. G. 145
Cassels, J. M. 89
Cesarano, F. 16
Cesaratto, S. 92
Chalmers, T. 43, 50, 65
Chamberlin, E. H. 26–7, 200, 203
Champernowne, D. 192
Chick, V. 4, 167–71, 173–4, 176, 231, 281–3, 292
choice of technique 84, 86, 184, 189
Ciocca, P. 6, 348, 362
circular flow 189
Clarida, R. 321, 325
Clark, J. B. 143
classical theory 2–4, 97, 104, 115, 118, 174; absence of a labour demand function in 73; 'core' of 71–3, 90; discussion of Garegnani's interpretation of 105–14 *passim*, 119; and distributive antagonism 128; of an evolutionary process 94; getting again hold of 143, 163; modern revival of 156; peculiarities of 68–78 *passim*; portrayed in terms of a sequence of temporary natural equilibrium positions 116, 120–1; as a robust alternative to the marginalist approach 157, 160; role of demand functions in 107; role of the Malthusian theory of population in 90; of value and distribution in Sraffa's reconstruction 178, 182, 186–7, 189
Clower, R. W. 20, 108, 245
Coase, R. H. 332–4, 340, 361
Codognato, G. 231
Colander, D. 301, 304
commodity rate of interest 177, 194
Commons, J. R. 332
competition 45, 53–4, 110, 124, 129, 191, 328; of capitals 56, 163; degree of in Keynes's model 285–90, 296–8, 319–21, 327; 'end-state' and a 'process' conception of 91–2; fiscal 352; free 71, 73–4, 78, 92, 185, 189; imperfect 67, 92, 285; invisible hand of 91; monopolistic (imperfect) 28, 197–234; perfect 5, 29, 35, 199–200, 218, 230–1, 285, 294–6; Smith's theory of 89
composition of output 11, 86
continental banking 183
controversies 24, 75, 152; Cambridge- *see* Capital, the marginalist theory and the problem of; caused by Sraffa's work 134; in macroeconomics 306–12, 322, 326; originated from Ricardo 140; Ricardo's own 132; in the theory of employment 301
conventions: of global finance 349–51; imposing restrictions on individual actions 304; preventing any threatening movement in wages 74
convergence 8, 10–11, 170, 175–6; of market prices towards natural prices 3, 112–13; taking place in logical time 168–9, 175; through chronological time 169
Cooper, R. 243, 245, 303
cooperation failure 243
coordination failure 243–5, 288, 301–3, 327–8
core–periphery distinction: a critique of 80–96 *passim*
corn law pamphlets 42
corn model 101, 135, 152; indirect evidence of 99; where it comes from 149, 160–3
Cornwall, J. 292, 299
Cornwall, R. R. 203, 220
Cornwall, W. 292, 299
corporative state 183
Cournot, A. A. 25, 91–2, 144, 198, 205–6, 209, 211–13, 215–18, 220, 224, 228–9, 234
critique of marginalist theory 177

Damiani, M. 243–4
Darity, W. A. 286, 290, 297
Darnell, A. C. 65
Dasgupta, P. 216
d'Aspremont, C. 222, 225, 228, 232
data 77, 83, 91, 99–100, 108–14, 120–2, 185, 188–9, 247, 253; persistence of 10–11, 121, 129

Davenport, H. J. 145
Davidson, P. 176, 290, 297–9, 304
De Cecco, M. 5, 280
De Marchi, N. 55
de Peyster, H. 276
De Quincey, T. 43, 53, 63
De Vecchi, N. 264, 277
de Vivo, G. 81, 91, 131
Debreu, G. 5, 29, 91, 199, 212–13, 217, 233, 294, 304, 325, 333, 336, 342, 344–5
Delli Gatti, D. 245
demand function 34, 70, 78, 83, 199–200, 298; in Cournot's model 234; effective 108; not necessarily deriving from utility maximisation 3, 108; not to be found in classical theory 20, 71–3, 75, 95, 107–8, 113–14, 186, 189; objective (direct or inverse) of the monopolistic firm 198, 203–6, 212–32 *passim*, 234–5; subjective (direct or inverse) of the monopolistic firm 206, 234; wage-elastic 73–4, 77, 302
Descartes, R. 142
Diamond, P. A. 324
Dierker, E. 216, 220–1, 231
Dimand, R. 25
diminishing agricultural returns 41–66 *passim*
Dini, L. 8
disequilibrium 8, 20, 91, 165, 172, 194, 203, 229, 240; approach 232; theory 284–5, 289–90, 293, 296–7, 301; as treated by classical economists 106, 114
Dixon, H. D. 243, 297–8
Dmitriev, V. K. 75, 118
Dobb, M. H. 8, 81, 91, 94, 117, 145, 155, 177
D'Orlando, F. 129, 284, 299
Drazen, A. 243
Dugger, W. 334
Duménil, G. 92
Dupuit, J. 144

Eatwell, J. 91, 139, 154, 180
economic policy 10, 235, 266, 308, 317–18, 356, 358; constrained by global finance 7, 348–52; diverging New Keynesian ideas concerning 289–95; game theoretical approach to 322; minimalist approach to 6, 37, 326–8; Pareto-improving 245; Russian 17
economic theories: diversity of schools of 19–21; invalidity of many past 21–2; judging the validity of 34–5
Edgeworth, F. Y. 24, 27, 92, 181
effectual demand: market- 106–7, 111–12; 112; normal- 106–14; as opposed to demand schedule 68–70, 105–6, 108, 113–14, 165
efficiency wages 238, 302
Eichner, A. S. 286
Einaudi, L. 132, 163–4
Eisner, R. 325
Eltis, W. 85
equations of production 182, 186
equilibrium 1, 3–4, 8, 11, 27, 113, 140, 165, 194, 200, 236–42, 295, 341, 355–6; agents' knowledge outside of 106, 114; apologetic 168, 342; based on supply-side considerations 299; Bertrandian approach to 204; Bertrand–Nash–Walras- 222–6, 229; Caravale's notion of 4, 10–11, 27, 167–9, 173–6, 197, 231, 233, 280, 347; competitive general 4, 23, 213–18, 233; conjectural (Negishi) 207–8, 213; contingent on the constraints imposed by other frameworks 174; Cournot–Nash–Walras 204, 209, 211–18, 220–9 *passim*, 233–5, 243; as a desirable state 10; different models of general- 20, 29; dynamic 41, 47, 49–50, 60, 64, 112; existence of 10, 23, 91, 171, 175; fixprice non-Walrasian- 226; general, supposedly existing in classical theory 116–18; heretical 168, 170, 172–3, 280; history and 169; imperfect (non competitive) general 5, 233–4; instantaneous 113; intertemporal general 75, 91; its alleged independence of demand conditions in classical theory 110; Keynesian models and general- 313–22 *passim*, 326; Keynesian notion of 169–72; in the labour market 314; long-period (term)- 4, 92–3, 99, 169, 174, 194, 247, 282, 314; long-run- 81, 174, 291; macroeconomic 5, 36–7, 286, 289, 297, 304, 310, 314, 326–7; monopolistic general 4, 198–232 *passim*; moving 87, 94; multiple- 304; natural 3, 9, 39 116, 121, 126, 129, 247; neutral or hypothetical 168, 170, 173; Nikaido's *objective approach* to the determination of 199, 222–6; out-of- 1, 3, 5, 165, 197, 233–42 *passim*; Pareto dominant (Nash)- 243, 245; as a part of the data of the classical competitive process 110; partial 5, 67, 91, 177, 198–204, 217–21, 228–32, 334; as a persistent position of rest 105, 113; in the presence of nominal rigidities 244; sequential 214; short-period (term)- 174, 282; Sraffa's notes on Pareto's theory of general 182; stability of 113; static 87, 89, 357; systematic change in one of the basic conditions of 120; as a temporary centre of gravity in classical theory 116; temporary natural 120, 123, 128; the price level under conditions of 285;

vacuous outside a dynamic framework 170; virtual 175; Walrasian general 36, 90, 92, 214, 343; with fixed prices 318
equilibrium selection: in coordination games 245–6; in Cournot–Nash–Walras models 212, 214–15
ethics: Keynes on 249–79 *passim*
Euripides 249, 261
evolutionary analysis 338–41, 345
exogenous variables: in classical theory 82–3

factor substitution 75, 77, 88, 157
Fenn, R. A. 48
Ferrara, F. 132, 145
Fetter, F. W. 25, 64, 147
Fischer, S. 298, 319, 324
Fisher, F. M. 29
Fisher, I. 23, 25, 195, 315, 322
fixed point 232; theorem 200
Flaschel, P. 92
forward prices 195
Friedman, M. 312–13, 316–19, 322–3

Gabszewicz, J. J. 200, 202, 211, 214, 217–18, 220, 229, 231, 234
Gaffard, J. L. 241
Gaidar, I. 355
Galbraith, J. K. 292, 298
Galí, J. 318, 320–1, 325
game theory 201, 213, 230, 308, 322–3
Ganslandt, M. 246
Garegnani, P. 2–3, 9, 11, 20, 39, 67, 77–9, 81–3, 86, 90–3, 95, 105–15, 118–19, 120–1, 128–9, 139, 152–3, 156, 178, 180, 196
Garretsen, H. 245, 301
Gary-Bobo, R. 198, 209–10
General Theory 4, 30, 68, 167–76 *passim*, 193–4, 249, 263, 273–7, 285–6, 298–300, 312, 334; containing a series of contradictions and ambiguities 280–1; different interpretations of 327; Meltzer's interpretation of 284, 292–3; the multiplier theorem as the core of 289; notion of long-period employment in 169; statics and dynamics in 170
Gintis, H. 295
given quantities: in classical theory 86–7, 184–6
Goethe, J. W. 187
Goodfriend, M. 321
Goodwin, R. 280
Gordon, D. F. 18, 28
Gordon, R. J. 286–7, 290, 299
Gowans, C. 278
Gram, H. 82, 91
Grandmont, J.-M. 217
Gray, T. 250–1
Graziani, A. 2, 33, 151
Greenwald, B. C. 286, 298
Grodal, B. 216, 218, 220–1, 231–2
Groenewegen, P. 82
Grossman, H. 318

Haberler, G. 23
Hahn, F. H. 29, 203, 209, 211, 214, 232
Halévy, E. 65
Hall, R. E. 287
Haltiwanger, J. 243, 245
Harcourt, G. C. 92, 175, 286
Harrod, R. 77, 302
Harsanyi, J. 216, 245
Hart, O. D. 198, 208–9, 224, 227–9, 232, 234, 287, 355
Hayek, F. A. von 17–18, 177, 183, 194, 277
Hébert, R. F. 12
Heckscher, E. 182
Heckscher–Ohlin–Samuelson trade theory 182
Hegel, G. W. F. 142
Hemingway, E. M. 282
Henderson, H. D. 145, 172
heretic(s) 5, 173, 280–2
Hey, J. D. 322
Hicks, J. R. 9, 21, 27, 29, 30, 85, 129, 196, 240, 282–3, 302, 312
Hildenbrand, W. 27
Hindson, P. 250–1
Hines, A. G. 297
historical reconstruction(s): the impossibility of faithful 93; necessarily influenced by what the interpreter knows and feels 98; as opposed to rational reconstruction(s) 3, 80–1, 84, 87, 97, 115; by Sraffa, which leads to the central role of the notion of cost 147
history of economic thought: alleged irrelevance for current theorising 18–19; distinguished from current theorising 15; how it should be taught 31; necessary to understand current theory 28; reasons for the present-day neglect of 37; relevance for current theorising 23–30; used to evaluate current theory 32
Hobbes, T. 142
Hodgskin, T. 141, 143, 145
Hollander, J. H. 132, 146, 153
Hollander, S. 2–4, 9, 21, 25–6, 39, 41–2, 62, 64, 78, 80–1, 93, 95, 97, 102–4, 115–17, 120–3, 128–9, 135, 151–3, 155, 157, 160
Hoover, K. D. 324
Howitt, P. 20, 297, 324
Huck, E. 64–5
Hume, D. 142, 177, 265
Hutcheson, F. 142

Hutchison, T. W. 23
Hynes, J. A. 30
hysteresis 287, 290, 296

increasing returns 209, 230; in Marshall's and classical theories according to Sraffa 159–60, 177; as a necessary condition for unemployment 286; Smith's insistence on 85; Smith's, Young's and Kaldor's theories of 99
industrial organisation 86, 94, 183, 228, 328
institutional analysis 335, 338, 344, 355–6, 362; evolutionary as opposed to neoclassical 336; lack of communication between theory and 331, 361; relevance of 332
institutionalists/institutionalism 20, 336, 339, 355–6; early 331–3, 335, 340, 361; new 333–5; unifying characteristics of 334
interdependence: of aggregate labour demand and supply functions 303; between prices and distribution 10, 115–18, 161; between prices and outputs in neoclassical theory 4, 78, 197; between private agents and government 244, 308; of savings and investment functions 303; strategic among firms 198, 201, 209, 213, 216, 230–1
interest, compound 191; determination of 69, 75–6, 192; Hayek's theory of 194; in the Keynesian theory 170–1, 176, 193–5; rate of 62, 64, 181, 306, 321, 337, 345; in Smith's theory 124–5; own 194–5; rigidity of 301
intermediate data: in classical theory 70–3, 77; doubts that these are true data 108–9
invariable measure (standard) of value 83, 118, 137, 158; its relation with Sraffa's standard commodity 89, 151, 160–1; Ricardo's search for 87, 138, 163, 188
inverse wage–profit relation 43, 63–4; its alleged incompatibility with Smith's theory of value 118–20
Italian fascism 183

Jackson, F. 278
Jevons, W. S. 22–3, 42–3, 62–3, 65, 82, 97, 132, 140–1, 144, 148, 150, 153, 155
John, A. 243, 303
Johnson, B. 250
Johnson, H. G. 322
joint production 75, 184, 187, 189, 192–3, 196
Jones, R. 55
Jorgenson, D. W. 313, 323
Jossa, B. 5, 284, 286, 292, 298, 300, 303

Kagan, S. 278
Kahn, R. F. 170, 183, 283, 285–6, 297, 299
Kaldor, N. 8, 67, 94, 99, 191–2, 309
Kant, I. 142, 262, 278
Kautsky, K. 154
Kenyon, P. 286
Keynes, J. M. 1, 4–6, 11–13, 23, 25–6, 30, 34, 68, 95, 131, 133, 142, 159, 167, 169–70, 172–4, 176–9, 183, 187, 193–5, 247, 249–68, 270–88, 290, 292–3, 296–8, 300–3, 305, 307, 312–13, 323–4, 327, 329, 334, 337, 349–51
Keynesian: and classical theories 6, 10, 283, 336, 339, 343–5, 362; interpretation of inflation 299; interventionism 290; long run 282; macroeconomics 5–6, 28, 284–6, 298, 316–18, 324, 326–8, 332; (standard) model(s) 26, 285, 288, 298, 313–14, 319; and neoclassical economics 6, 306–8, 312–13, 318–19, 326; paradigm 296, 316–17; revolution 36, 306, 312, 315, 322; school 108; and sequential approaches 282; short period 76, 282; synthesis 282; theory 1, 284–6, 289–93, 296–9, 306, 312, 317
King, R. G. 321
Kirman, A. P. 27
Kiyotaki, N. 243
Klamer, A. 179
Klein, L. R. 26, 30, 312, 322
Knight, F. H. 20, 78, 95, 292
Koopmans, T. C. 315
Kregel, J. A. 285–6, 290, 298–9, 304
Kuhn, T. 62
Kurz, H. D. 4, 77, 81, 83–4, 86, 88–92, 94–6, 98–9, 101, 118, 148, 151, 153, 164, 177, 184, 186, 192, 196
Kydland, F. E. 320, 325

labour commanded 118–20, 126
labour theory of value 23, 75, 83, 115, 148; as an attempt to escape from the interdependency problem 118; and the marginalist theory 190; as part of the 'core' of classical economics 94; its relationship with Sraffa's work 184–6; its role in Marx's theory 85–6, 150; its role in Ricardo's theory 9–10, 87, 101, 128, 134, 138; as opposed to the Smithian theory of the component parts 119
Laffont, J. J. 229
Laidler, D. E. W. 298, 322
Lange, O. 203, 232
Langlois, R. 331, 333, 340, 342, 361
Laroque, G. 229
Lawlor, M. S. 285
Layard, R. 287
Leijonhufvud, A. 27, 245, 297

Leontief, W. 77, 222–5, 234
Lerner, A. 26, 30
Levi, P. 277
Lévi-Strauss, C. 269
Lévy, D. 92
Lewin, S. B. 29
Lindbeck, A. 286–8, 298–9
Lipsey, R. G. 314, 359
liquidity preference 171, 187, 193–4
Locke, J. 142, 276
logical (and chronological) time 168–76, 282
long period (term) 76, 96; in Marshall's sense 175
long run 314; for a competitive firm 27; as distinct from the long period 175
Longfield, M. 43, 59, 60, 63
long-period employment 169, 174
long-period equilibrium: and expectations 174; in a logical sense 4, 11, 175, 197, 247; of marginal theory 75, 182
long-period positions 3–4, 11, 92, 99–100, 105–14, 121, 129, 167, 282
long-period prices 11, 69–73, 90, 93
long-run equilibrium 81, 291
Loomes, G. 322
Lucas, F. L. 261, 266
Lucas, R. E., Jr 228, 311, 317–19, 323–5, 354
Lunghini, G. 280, 282

machinery: Ricardo's analysis of 64; 77, 84, 88, 184, 240
McCloskey, D. 17
McCombie, J. S. L. 290
McCulloch, J. R. 23, 41, 43, 50, 57, 60, 63, 65, 82, 102, 146–7, 149
McKenzie, L. 233, 325
macroeconomics: after Keynes 301; as an autonomous discipline 308; the coexistence of rival theories in 309–10; contemporary 306; distinction between Keynesian and neoclassical 326; distinction between micro and 35, 310; and empirical facts 308–9, 322; evolution of ideas in 311–22, 326; and the Fisherian approach to intertemporal choice theory 324; its distance from physics 307; and general equilibrium theory 316; Keynesian *see* Keynesian macroeconomics; new-classical *see* new-classical macroeconomics; microfoundations of 287, 298, 319; new-Keynesian *see* new-Keynesian (macro)economics; its relation with individual behaviour 37; scientific progress in 1, 6, 306–7, 322; teaching a course in 30; in terms of *market* phenomena 300; various approaches to 35–7
Magnusson, L. 25
Malinvaud, E. 203, 231, 297, 318
Malthus, T. R. 23, 25, 36, 41–7, 53–5, 58, 60–6, 90, 95, 100, 102–3, 123–4, 135–8, 147, 152, 164
Malthusian theory of population 44, 64, 65, 88, 90, 94
Mankiw, N. G. 243, 284, 286, 288–9, 296, 298, 321, 324
Marget, A. W. 20
marginalist economics 157, 178
market-clearing 286–7, 316, 324; absence of 235, 303; in new Keynesian economics 299; state of general 10; and stationarity 109–14; temporary 77, 109; unemployment 172; without unvoluntary unemployment 326
market-clearing prices (or quantities) 204–32 *passim*, 313, 346
Marris, R. 286, 297
Marschak, T. 202–3, 222, 227–9
Marshall, A. 4, 11, 13, 25, 27, 30, 34, 41, 67, 70, 77–8, 82–3, 91–2, 95, 97, 100–1, 112, 140–4, 147–9, 152–6, 159–60, 169, 175, 177–8, 181–2, 247, 253, 274–5, 279, 281, 323
Marx, K. 3–4, 9–10, 13, 31, 56, 67, 75, 81–90, 92–3, 95, 97, 102, 115–17, 122, 126–7, 139–51, 153–4, 156–64, 184–5, 196, 280, 295, 357–8
Mas-Colell, A. 214, 217
Maskin, E. 216
Matthews, R. C. O. 334
Meek, R. 94
Meltzer, A. H. 284, 292–3, 296
Menger, C. 140, 144, 155, 182, 323
Messori, M. 171
Michel, P. 200, 231
Michelangelo Buonarroti 268
Milgate, M. 301–2
Mill, J. 43, 48–9, 58–9, 63–5, 94, 137–8, 153, 161
Mill, J. S. 3, 41, 43, 51–2, 55–7, 63, 76–7, 81–2, 84–5, 90, 92–4, 97, 115–17, 122, 126–7, 141, 144–5
Miller, M. 311, 355
Mitchell, W. C. 95, 332
Modigliani, F. 30, 311–13, 323, 355
Moggridge, D. E. 276, 278
monetary overinvestment theory 177
Mongiovi, G. 2, 4, 76, 81, 91, 128, 151, 155, 163–4
Moore, G. E. 255–6, 258, 260, 272, 277–8
Morishima, M. 80–1, 93, 95, 155
Mosley, O. 282
Mundell, R. A. 350
Musella, M. 297, 298

Musu, I. 5–6, 326
Muth, J. F. 323–4

NAIRU 289–90, 298–9
Nardozzi, G. 285, 290, 298–9
Nash, J. F., Jr 204, 209, 211–13, 215–18, 220, 222–6, 229, 243, 245
natural rate of unemployment (NRU) 237–8, 289–90, 298, 318
natural resources 75, 184–5, 187, 189, 198
near-rationality 243–5
negative labour values 192–3
Negishi, T. 29, 200, 207–11, 213, 222, 229–30, 232, 234
Nell, E. J. 297
neo-Austrian approach 5, 238–9
neoclassical: analysis of individual behaviour 37; and classical theories 97–8, 111–12, 115–17, 123; competitive theory of distribution 74; concern for analytical rigour 12; counter-revolution 317–18; demand functions 70, 108; determination of goods and factors prices 4, 9, 71–2; economic methodology 295; economics 81–4, 93; foundations in *Value and Capital* 27; general equilibrium models and Sraffa-type solutions 118; interpretation of Ricardo 39, 150; and Keynesian economics 312–14, 319–21, 326; macroeconomics 6, 286, 309, 322–3; 326; metaphor 6; paradigm of utility maximisation 3, 30, 294; synthesis 314–16, 327; *terra firma* 302; theory 3, 10–11, 69, 134, 156–7, 197; timelessness 169, 175; toolbox 5, 286; tradition 35; treatment of economic institutions 6; 332–47 *passim*, 357, 362–3
Neumann, J. von 29, 77, 187, 192
neutrality of money 284, 287–8
new classical macroeconomics 6, 286, 288, 318, 323–8 *passim*, 354
new neoclassical synthesis 321
new-Keynesian: economics 5–6, 12, 20, 76, 284–99 *passim*, 300, 319–24 *passim*; models 5, 243, 301–6 *passim*
Nicola, P. C. 4–5, 208, 233–4, 343
Nikaido, H. 199, 204, 206, 209, 222, 224–7, 231–2, 234
Nisticò, S. 2–3, 115, 124, 129, 284, 299, 305
non-constant returns 157, 159–60
non-substitution theorem 69, 110
Nordhaus, W. D. 85
normalisation rule 5, 203, 218–21, 230, 232
North, D. C. 331, 361
Nussbaum, M. C. 257, 264, 277

O'Brien, D. P. 65, 82, 95
Obstfeld, M. 324
O'Donnell, R. 129
Ohlin, B. 182, 297
old classical economists: on Garegnani's interpretation of 105, 110, 117; Sraffa's interpretation of 67–79 *passim*, 88, 178
ordering of techniques 191
organic interdependency 6, 303
orthodox equilibrium 281
Owen, R. 141

Pack, S. J. 17
Palley, T. 299
Panico, C. 2–3, 97, 154, 297
Pantaleoni, M. 177
parable and realism 190, 196
Pareto, V. 13, 27, 92, 182, 243, 245, 323
Pasinetti, L. L. 1, 6–7, 81, 151–3, 297, 331, 333, 340, 342–6, 354, 361–2
Pasinetti's two phases 340, 343, 345–6, 362
path dependency 169–73, 295–6, 311
Patinkin, D. 285, 297, 313
Peach, T. 89, 94–5, 97, 99, 164
Peart, S. 63, 65
Perlman, M. 332
Persson, T. 322
Petty, W. 19, 31, 67, 82, 141, 145, 148, 153, 182, 187
Phelps, E. S. 228, 298, 316, 319
Phillips curve 284, 289, 314–18, 321, 323–5, 327, 359; verticality of 290–3, 298–9
Phillips, A. W. 284, 289–93, 298–9, 314–18, 321, 323–5, 327, 359
physical real cost 140, 185, 187
physician's outlook 187
physiocrats 67, 141, 145, 148–9, 154, 162, 182, 188
Pigou, A. C. 78
Plato 251–2, 257–8, 260–2, 265, 272, 277
Plosser, C. I. 320, 325
Polock, J. 279
Porta, P. L. 2, 4, 130, 139, 151–3, 156–64
post-Keynesian economics 12, 20, 99–100, 168, 286, 297, 301, 304, 332, 337, 339
post-Walrasian economics 295, 300–5
Potestio, P. 174
Potier, J. P. 196
Prescott, E. C. 320, 325
price correspondence 212, 215, 224, 229
price rigidity 289–90, 296–8, 301
prices: anticipated by firms 170; classical determination of relative 68–78 *passim*, 83–4, 87, 89–96 *passim*, 99–100; 115–18, 121–9 *passim*, 156–62 *passim*, 165; and constant returns to scale 71–3, 75, 78; as determined by physical labour costs 88; disequilibrium 11, 165; the extent to

which depend on demand 182–3; false 6, 245; fixed 244, 284–90, 300–2, 313, 318–19; flexible 237, 290, 299; fluctuations in 303; general level of 249, 303, 314–16; laws of variation of 62; market and natural- in classical economics 3, 11, 68–75 *passim*, 105–14 *passim*; under monopolistic competition 201–32 *passim*, 234; in new Keynesian economics 286–99 *passim*; normal 68, 167; under perfect competition 199–200, 313; and quantities 165, 304, 327; rate of change of 323–4; Smithian theory of 118–20, 126–7, 153; Sraffa's theory of 185–9, 191; steered towards an equilibrium state by the auctioneer 233, 343; their relation with wages in Ricardo's theory 136–7; and wages 358–9

price-setting approach 199, 204, 222, 224, 226, 229

probability: Keynes on 5, 249, 253–4, 262, 273–9, 281

production equations: Sraffa's work on 182, 186

profit(s) 16, 71, 82, 108, 189, 214, 219–32, 288, 349; being zero 185–6; feedback effect on market demand of 199; in the Malthusian system 36, 152; increasing at a compound rate 188; in the nature of 'surplus value' in Marx's theory 84–6; marginal 219; 'of the farmer' which 'regulate the profits of all other trades' 164; not independent of the choice of the normalisation rule 203, 220–1; possibly regulated by interest rates 76; Sraffa's critique of their explanation in terms of the marginal product of 'capital' 182, 191; the residual distributive share according to the later classicists 124; and wages *see* wages; as a component of prices according to Smith 118–19, 137, 149, 153; as a part of the consumers' endowment 199, 204–5, 214; as the *difference* between corn output and corn capital in Ricardo's theory 75, 136, 138, 152, 162; as the payoff functions 204; as the potential for the multiplier 298; as the surplus of the product over wages in classical theory 78, 120; bad effects on prices of 127

profit function 4, 209–29 *passim*

profit maximisation 6, 199–205, 218–30 *passim*, 295

profit, rate of 31, 121, 164–5, 189–93, 337, 345; competition of capitals theory of 163; expected 109, 168, 170, 174; natural 107; taken as given within Smith's theory of prices 3, 116, 120, 124–7; classicists' and Sraffa's determination of 39, 75, 82–3, 99–101, 122–3, 127–8, 136, 156–7, 189; declining together with the real wage in classical theory 41–66 *passim*, 102–3; equalisation of 168, 170, 173–5, 177, 188; fully determined when the wages are at the subsistence 188; independent of the productive conditions of the 'luxury' sector 127; in each industry compared with the natural rate 92, 109, 113, 129; in material terms 163; irrelevance of constant returns for Sraffa's determination of 71–3; its relationship with agricultural diminishing returns in Ricardo's theory 9–10, 39, 89, 93, 121–3, 161; falling in Marx's theory 87, 184; not determined simultaneously with relative prices in Ricardo's theory 93

Proudhon, P.-J. 143, 145

Prychitko, D. L. 20

psychic: cost 144

pure economic theory 336, 338, 344

quantity-setting approach 198, 207, 210–11, 223–4

Quesnay, F. 63, 82

Rae, J. 145

Raffaelli, T. 275

Ramsey, F. P. 184, 324

rational expectations 20, 27, 288, 296, 298, 306, 317, 319, 322–7

rational reconstruction(s) 2, 88, 90, 93, 115, 247; as opposed to historical reconstruction(s) 3, 80–1, 84, 97–8

real business cycle 20, 319–21, 325

rent(s) 9–10, 16, 39, 44, 54–5, 60–2, 65, 77, 82–9 *passim*, 93, 101, 118–19, 122, 137, 153, 159, 175, 183, 188–9

Riach, P. A. 286

Ricardo debates 155–6, 158

Ricardo, D. 1–4, 9–10, 12–13, 19, 23, 25, 27, 31, 36, 39, 41–3, 45–8, 53–8, 60–7, 69, 72–3, 75–7, 80–90, 92–3, 95, 97–100, 102–3, 105, 115–19, 121–4, 126–41, 143–53, 155–65, 167, 177–8, 183–4, 186, 188–9, 196, 240, 282

Robbins, L. 97

Roberts, J. 216–17, 221

Roberts, K. 216

Robertson, D. H. 30

Robinson, A. 132–3

Robinson, J. 4, 26–7, 67, 169, 175, 190, 210, 247, 282–3, 285, 297–9, 355

Rodano, G. 5–6, 148, 306, 317, 322

Rogers, C. 304

Rogoff, K. 324

Romer, D. 243–6, 286–9, 296, 321, 324

Roncaglia, A. 81, 86, 91–2, 129, 139, 180
Roosevelt, F. D. 334
Rorty, R. 94
Rosen, S. 91
Rosselli, R. 101
Rosser, J. B. 298, 301
Rotemberg, J. J. 321
Rotheim, R. J. 5–6, 12, 282, 299–302, 324
Rowthorn, B. 86
Russell, B. 179, 277

Sabooglu, M. 17
Sacco, P. L. 245
Salop, S. C. 228
Salvadori, N. 77, 81, 83–4, 86, 88–92, 94–6, 98–9, 101, 128, 151, 184, 186, 192, 196
Samuels, W. J. 15, 332
Samuelson, P. A. 9, 13, 15, 28, 41, 43, 62–4, 77, 85, 88, 102–3, 133–4, 152, 182, 196, 324
Sargent, T. 317, 354
Sartre, J.-P. 278
Sawyer, M. 290, 298–9
Say, J. B. 36, 82, 94
Schefold, B. 79, 91, 130–1, 134, 152, 158, 163, 196
Schleiermacher, F. D. 95
Schotter, A. 334
Schulz, N. 226
Schumpeter, J. A. 13, 15, 17–18, 24, 26, 29, 32, 85, 94–5, 112, 117, 161–2, 280, 331, 357–8
Sebastiani, M. 175
Selten, R. 202–3, 222, 227–9, 245
Semmler, W. 92
Sen, A. 29, 35, 179, 278
Senior, N. 31, 36, 41, 43, 50–1, 57, 63, 94, 144–5, 181–2
sequential determination of prices and quantities 240
Seton, F. 75
Shakespeare, W. 250–2
shared incidence principle 41–3, 63–4; its consistency with the natural equilibrium interpretation of Ricardo's theory 121–4
Shaw, G. B. 17
short period 171, 173–5, 293
Sidgwick, H. 278
Sieber, N. 162
Silvestre, J. 209–10, 245
Sinnot-Amstrong, W. 278
Skidelsky, R. 250, 262, 266, 277
Skinner, Q. 94
Smith, A. 3, 16, 17, 19, 36, 41–2, 54, 60, 63, 65, 67–9, 71–2, 74, 76–8, 80–2, 85, 87–90, 92–5, 97, 99–100, 102–3, 105–6, 108, 110, 113–20, 122, 124–9, 132, 136–9, 141–6, 149, 152–3, 162, 165, 178, 180, 196
Snowdon, B. 284, 298
Socrates 258
Solow, R. M. 298, 315, 321, 325, 334, 359
Sonnenschein, H. 216–17, 221, 234
Soskice, D. 287
Spaventa, L. 6–7, 354, 357, 363
Spinoza, B. 142
Spray, D. E. 28
Sraffa, P. 3–4, 8–10, 12–13, 34, 67–8, 71–2, 74–9, 81, 83–4, 86–95, 97–101, 105, 115–18, 121, 124, 128–64, 177–96, 281, 311–12, 323
Sraffa papers 140, 154
Sraffa's Lectures on Value 146, 182
Stahn, H. 222, 224, 226–7
Staiger, D. 299
standard commodity 9, 75, 95, 118, 184–8 *passim*; its relation with Ricardo's invariable measure of value 89, 151, 160–1
Steedman, I. 92, 94, 196
Stern, S. 19
Steuart, J. 31
Stewart, I. M. T. 324
Stigler, G. J. 42, 48, 50, 64, 95, 99, 135
Stiglitz, J. E. 286, 294–6, 298–9, 301
Stocker, M. 278
Strachey, G. L. 262
strategic complementarity 5, 243–5
strategic interdependence: a non cooperative approach to 198
Sturges, R. P. 55
Styron, W. 278
surplus: its disposition in the form of investment or consumption 82, 103, 162; its distribution between wages and profits 75–7; as a peculiarity of the classical theory of distribution 39, 70, 77–8, 81–3, 86, 94, 101, 124, 134, 145, 149–50, 154–5, 161–2, 182, 185, 187–9
surplus value 84–5, 140, 154, 162
Swartz, T. R. 19
Swithinbank, B. W. 252
Sylos Labini, P. 6–7, 295, 357, 362

Tabellini, G. 322
Tamborini, R. 170
Tarantelli, E. 299
Taylor, J. B. 210, 298, 319, 321
technology: effects on unemployment of a change in 240–2; and employment within an equilibrium context 236–8
temporary natural positions 120
theoretical progress: definition of 33; examples of 34

Thompson, W. 145
Tinbergen, J. 280
Tobin tax 7, 351
Tobin, J. 7, 286, 297, 313, 323, 350–1
Tonveronachi, M. 174
Torrens, R. 42–3, 47–8, 58, 64–6, 99, 147
Tosato, D. 4–5, 9–10, 95, 121, 130, 197, 234
Townshend, H. 273, 275
trade (business) cycles 8, 22, 320, 324, 358
tragic choices: Keynes on 5, 249, 251, 266, 268–9, 276
transformation problem 83, 93, 160–1, 196
Trower, H. 164
Tuchscherer, T. 292
Turgot, A. R. J. 64

uncertainty 5, 12, 35, 172, 174, 197, 281–2, 292, 316, 343; in new Keynesian theory 292–4, 301 radical 249–79 *passim*; strategical 244
unemployment: as a disequilibrium phenomenon 240; involuntary 289, 314, 326–7; voluntary (or frictional) 314
unemployment equilibrium 5–6, 12, 172, 238, 247, 280, 285, 296, 301, 314

value theory of labour 185
Van Ees, H. 301
Van Huyck, J. B. 245
Veblen, T. 332, 335, 338
Vercelli, A. 170
Vial, J. P. 202, 211, 214, 218, 220, 229
von Neumann model 187, 192

wage(s) 36, 75–7, 82, 100–1, 357–9; and population 90; determined by broad social forces 69–71, 99, 105, 156, 189; effect on prices of an increase of 116, 127, 136–8, 149; fixed 5, 238, 284, 315, 319, 327; growth rate of 7, 291, 323, 359; as intermediate datum 70, 77–8, 108; in Italy 352; market- 45, 90, 123; natural 9, 36, 45, 90, 123; money- 46, 88–9, 95, 120, 126–7; and profits 10, 42–3, 68–9, 76–8, 86, 88, 102–3, 115, 118–21, 127, 161, 182, 192; proportionate 43, 49, 63; shares of product other than 70, 77–8, 118; subsistence- 76, 188
wage bargain 170, 238, 292
wage differentials 88–9
wage earner(s) 36, 185
wage rigidity 287–90, 296–9, 301, 312–13
wage, real 100, 121, 188, 192; alternative levels of 9; given in classical theory 3, 39, 45, 69, 70, 83, 88, 90, 110, 112–16, 122, 127; declining in classical theory 4, 41–66 *passim*, 95; demand and supply determination of 73, 112, 117; determining the profit rate 163–4; its exogenous treatment compatible with its decline during accumulation 123; minimum level of 74, 78, 90, 127; but not *nominal* wages respond to excess demands 318; pro-cyclic trends in 286; Smith's endogenous determination of 124–6; transforming into a compound phrase 302; and unemployment 73–4, 76–7, 237–40, 247, 290, 296, 314; 'which is not greater than the marginal disutility of that amount of employment' 172, 281
wage-fund 23
Wald, A. 29
Waldman, M. 243, 245
Walker, D. A. 2, 15–16, 20, 25, 128
Walras, A. 65
Walras, L. 12, 22, 25, 27–8, 43, 62, 82, 91–2, 140, 144, 155, 209, 211–13, 215–18, 220–6, 229, 233, 285, 323, 336, 343–5
Walsh, V. 82, 91
Waterman, A. M. C. 94
Watson, A. 184
Weitzman, M. 286
West, E. G. 42–3, 46–7, 50, 55, 60–1, 64–5
Whewell, W. 55, 65
Wicksell, K. 27, 101, 112, 191, 322
Wicksteed, P. H. 181
Wieser, F. von 182
Wiggins, D. 278
Wilkinson, F. 299
Williams, B. A. O. 277
Williamson, O. E. 334–5
Winch, D. 85
Wittgenstein, L. 178–9
Woodford, M. 1–2, 6, 306–7, 309–10, 312–13, 315–17, 321
Wright, G. H. von 277

Yellen, J. L. 243, 288
Young, A. 99
Young, W. 286, 290, 297

Zagari, E. 2–3, 102
Zaghini, E. 2–3, 105, 113–14
Zamagni, S. 94
Zeeman, E. C. 210